fifth edition

ETHICAL ISSUES IN BUSINESS

a philosophical approach

 769-2352

Edited by

Thomas Donaldson
Georgetown University

Patricia H. Werhane
University of Virginia

PRENTICE HALL
Upper Saddle River, New Jersey   07458

Library of Congress Cataloging-in-Publication Data

Ethical issues in business : a philosophical approach / edited by
  Thomas Donaldson, Patricia H. Werhane.—5th ed.
      p.   cm.
  Includes bibliographical references.
  ISBN 0-13-504440-5
    1. Business ethics—Case studies.   2. Social responsibility of
  business—Case studies.   I. Donaldson, Thomas (date).
  II. Werhane, Patricia Hogue.
  HF5387.E8   1996
  174'.4—dc20   95–42123
                                                          CIP

Acquisitions editor: Charlyce Jones Owen
Editorial production/supervision
  and interior design: F. Hubert
Manufacturing buyer: Lynn Pearlman

 © 1996, 1993, 1988, 1983, 1979 by Prentice-Hall, Inc.
Simon & Schuster / A Viacom Company
Upper Saddle River, New Jersey 07458

Printed in the United States of America

10   9   8   7   6   5   4   3   2   1

ISBN 0-13-504440-5

PRENTICE-HALL INTERNATIONAL (UK) LIMITED, *London*
PRENTICE-HALL OF AUSTRALIA PTY. LIMITED, *Sydney*
PRENTICE-HALL CANADA INC., *Toronto*
PRENTICE-HALL HISPANOAMERICANA, S.A., *Mexico*
PRENTICE HALL OF INDIA PRIVATE LIMITED, *New Delhi*
PRENTICE-HALL OF JAPAN, INC., *Tokyo*
SIMON & SCHUSTER PTE. LTD., *Singapore*
EDITORA PRENTICE-HALL DO BRASIL, LTDA., *Rio de Janeiro*

Contents

Truth Telling 129

• PART TWO •
Property, Profit, and Justice
Introduction 178

Traditional Theories of Property and Profit 186

Property and Profit: Modern Discussions 215

• **PART THREE** •
Corporations, Persons, and Morality
Introduction   **286**

The Moral Responsibility of Corporations   **295**

Employee Rights and Responsibilities   **345**

Diversity 377

Sexual Harassment 402

• PART FOUR •
Contemporary Business Issues
Introduction 420

Environment 424

Marketing 459

Corporations in the Twenty-First Century   482

Biographical Information   510

Preface

Since we first published *Ethical Issues in Business* in 1979, the field of business ethics has developed into a mature academic discipline bristling with practical implications for managerial practice. Happily, the development of business ethics and the continuing challenges in business have been accompanied by a rapidly growing body of literature. When the first edition was published in 1979, *Ethical Issues in Business* was one of only three texts in the field; by 1996 at least fifty texts are available. Along with the growth of course offerings and college teaching materials has been an explosion of new articles, cases, and journals. Hundreds of companies have corporate ethics officers, and thousands have instituted ethics training programs as part of managerial education. The fifth edition is a product of these new developments and changes.

Some theoretical perspectives maintain importance as foundational materials for the study of business ethics. The insights of Adam Smith and John Locke and the challenges of Karl Marx are no less relevant today than in the eighteenth and nineteenth centuries. Yet some issues are clearly time-bound. When the last edition appeared, Bhopal was still on the minds of many managers, the Exxon Valdez incident had just occurred, the proliferation of mergers and acquisitions was being questioned, and the Dalkon Shield was still an important news item. Since the publication of the fourth edition, the AIDS crisis has become exacerbated, the glass ceiling has been recognized by Wall Street, companies and governments have tumbled on derivatives, and environmental concerns have become critical. In the increasingly competitive commercial environment, corporate leaders are faced with new challenges in employment, in corporate structure, and in training. Readings that focus on ethical issues raised by these new kinds of challenges are included in this new edition.

The Idea of Business Ethics

Ethical problems in business are as old as business itself. Just as we are acutely aware of the problems surrounding the Orange County derivatives mess or the Barings Bank scandal, earlier generations were aware of other ethical problems in business. Names such as the "Teapot Dome scandal" or the "Mississippi Bubble" are not familiar today, but they once were as well known as "Drexel Burnham" and "Bhopal" are now. The issues about which there has been public concern include trusts and monopolies, child labor, working hours and conditions, meat packing standards, the distribution of salaries, and the liability of producers for dangerous products. Not only complaints but attempts at reform have a long and interesting history. The Code of Hammurabi, written nearly two thousand years before Christ, records the fact that Mesopotamian rulers attempted to legislate honest prices from local merchants by instituting wage and price controls.

To explain the special relationship between business and ethics, it is necessary to see how focusing merely on problems of business efficiency and profit making may overlook important issues. For example, when the manufacture of a certain product can eventually be linked to human disease or a decrease in the quality of human life, then the issues surrounding it are no longer simply traditional "business" issues. No amount of expertise in marketing, accounting, or management can deal adequately with such problems, and yet they are clearly connected to the activities of the business world. Nor can situations like these be reduced simply to legal problems, understandable only to the lawyer. When Ralph Nader claimed in the late 1960s that General Motors was producing automobiles which, despite their many consumer advantages, were contributing to thousands of highway deaths each year, he was not arguing that GM's practices were against the law—because at that time they were not illegal at all. Rather, Nader was arguing that General Motors had special obligations to its consumers that were not simply of a traditional business nature. Those obligations were *ethical* or *moral* ones.

It appears, then, that confronting questions like those implied by the Nader case—such as, "Does business have an obligation to its consumers (or to others) that extends beyond its obligation to make a profit and satisfy its investors?"—means confronting ethical and moral issues. The words *ethical* and *moral* in this book are not simply used as they might be in a modern newspaper, for example, "That movie is thoroughly immoral" (meaning, "That movie is pornographic."). Instead, they are used as philosophers have traditionally used them, as words that arise from the study of what is good or right. Although there is dispute even among philosophers over how to define the subject matter of ethics, most would agree that it includes the study of what people ought to pursue (i.e., what the *good* is for people) and, alternatively, the determination of which actions are the *right* actions for people to perform. Such general definitions may leave one with the feeling that studying ethics must be a hopelessly vague task; yet interestingly, ethical philosophers have succeeded in presenting a great many detailed ethical theses and in conducting a number of successful investigations into specific ethical topics.

The word *ethics,* then, refers generally to the study of whatever is right and good for humans. The study of *business* ethics, in turn, seeks to understand business practices, institutions, and actions in light of some concept of human value. Traditional business ends (e.g., profit making, growth, or technical advance) are certainly relevant to the subject of business ethics insofar as they can be related to the achievement of some more fundamental good. In other words, business ethics looks at corporate profits not for their own sake but with respect to the achievement of some basic human good, perhaps increased investor satisfaction, higher levels of employment, or increased capacity to improve working conditions.

Because business ethics involves relating business activities to some concept of human good, it is a study that has as one of its aspects the *evaluation* of business practices. Indeed, most of the fundamental criticisms and commendations of contemporary business practices are cast in terms of how modern business either contributes to, or fails to contribute to, the general human good. For example, when modern corporations are criticized for their failure to respond to environmental needs by limiting the amount of pollutants they discharge, they are being evaluated on ethical grounds; the charge is that they are neglecting the public good. Alternatively, when businesses are praised for achieving high levels of efficiency and satisfying consumer needs, it is implied that efficiency and consumer satisfaction contribute directly to the sum total of human good. Even traditional economic theory justifies economic practices in the light of their contribution to human good.

Another aspect of the evaluative dimension in business ethics is seen in the contrast between evaluation and simple description. There is an important difference between answering a moral question and answering a question in the areas of, say, marketing and economics. In the latter, it is often sufficient to establish the immediate facts that pertain to the subject. For example, if one hopes to determine the best advertising strategy for the introduction of a new product, one would only need to determine that a certain advertising strategy will have, as a matter of fact, the desired effect (i.e., that it will sell the product). It is usually possible in such cases to utilize indicators which more or less establish whether or not a given strategy will be effective: consumer polls, trends in sales, etc. These indicators are then used as factual information upon which one's strategy is based.

However, answering an ethical question may demand very different methods. Determining the immediate and specific facts may only be the first step in a long process. For example, if one wants to determine whether discriminatory hiring practices by corporations ought to be corrected by instituting affirmative action programs that favor women and minorities, there may be no question at all about the immediate facts. Two people could thoroughly agree that discrimination of a certain type has taken place and that women and African Americans need equal job opportunities to reach relevant levels of social equality. Yet, after agreeing on all these facts, the two people may still disagree vehemently over whether affirmative action programs should be imposed in the wake of past discriminatory practices. Thus, solving an ethical problem may require making evaluative judgments about issues that seem far removed from the facts at hand.

Even though business ethics focuses primarily on evaluative issues, its scope is surprising large. Insofar as it is concerned with relating business practices to some concept of human good, almost any business issue that relates to human values may become part of its subject matter. Thus, the scope of business ethics includes such issues as:

1. advertising practice (e.g., false or misleading advertising);
2. product safety;
3. monopolistic price schemes;
4. the acceptability of the pursuit of profits;
5. employee rights, including rights to free speech and due process;
6. child labor and the treatment of children;
7. economic and environmental effects of pollution;
8. use of natural resources;
9. multinational corporate responsibilities, including the manufacturing and selling of products in other countries;
10. "sensitive payments" to foreign governments, foreign agents, or local politicians;
11. the status of corporate stakeholders who are not shareholders;
12. derivatives and other sophisticated financial instruments;
13. discriminatory hiring policies, working conditions, and policies of advancement;

14. drugs and AIDS in the workplace;
15. hazardous technology abroad;
16. product liability;
17. mergers and acquisitions;
18. insider trading;
19. the limits of free enterprise.

The analysis of such issues requires a systematic investigation of both general ethical theory and specific business practices. To accomplish this goal, we have selected a series of writings which includes not only theoretical and philosophical material relevant to business practices but case descriptions of ethical problems found in the business world. The advantage of investigating ethical problems from a philosophical point of view should be apparent. One cannot successfully examine a case involving payments made by U.S. corporations to foreign governments, for example, until one has considered the more general issue of how differing ethical attitudes in the United States and in foreign countries affect the morality of such actions.

This edition, like earlier ones, has not been simply the product of its editors, but owes greatly to those whose suggestions, criticism, and editorial assistance made it a better book. These include Thomas Carson, John Dienhart, Thomas Dunfee, R. Edward Freeman, A. R. Gini, Thomas McMahon, c.s.v., Mark Schneider, David P. Schmidt, Tom Mitchell, and Neil Florek. Most important, we want to thank Cynthia Rudolph for her excellent organizational and editorial skills without which there would not have been a second, a third, a fourth, and now a fifth edition.

T. D. and P. H. W.

General Introduction

Introduction to Ethical Reasoning

THOMAS DONALDSON • PATRICIA H. WERHANE

What is the basis for making ethical decisions? Should Joan challenge Fred the next time he cracks a sexist joke? Should John refrain from lying on his job application despite his temptation to do so? What, if anything, should make Hillary decide that eating meat is corrupting, whereas vegetarianism is uplifting? It is obvious that the kind of evidence required for an ethical decision is different from that needed to make a nonethical one; but what is the nature of the difference? These questions give rise to a search for a *method* of ethical justification and decision making, a method that will specify the conditions that any good ethical decision should meet.

To see how such questions arise concretely, consider the following case.[1]

Some years ago, a large German chemical firm, BASF, decided to follow the lead of many other European firms and build a factory in the United States. BASF needed land, lots of it (1,800 acres), an inexpensive labor pool, almost 5 million gallons of fresh water every day, a surrounding area free of import taxes, and a nearby railroad and ocean port. Obviously, only a handful of locations could meet all these requirements. The spot the company finally picked seemed perfect, an area near the coast of South Carolina called Beaufort County. It purchased 1,800 acres.

South Carolina and Beaufort County were pleased with BASF's decision. The surrounding area, from which the company would pick its workers, was economically depressed and per capita income stood well below the national average. Jobs of any kind were desperately needed. Even the Governor of South Carolina and his staff were eager for BASF to build in South Carolina, and although BASF had not yet finalized its exact production plans, the State Pollution Central Authority saw no problems with meeting the State pollution laws. BASF itself said that although it would dump chemical byproducts into the local Colleton River, it planned not to lower the river's quality.

But trouble started immediately. To see why, one needs to know that Beaufort County is the home of the internationally famous resort area called "Hilton Head." Hilton Head attracts thousands of vacationers every year—most of them with plenty of money—and its developers worried that the scenic splendor of the area might be marred by the air and water pollution. Especially concerned about water pollution, resort developers charged that the proposed chemical plant would pollute the Colleton River. They argued that BASF plants in Germany had polluted the Rhine and, in Belgium, the Schelde River. Further, they noted that on BASF's list of proposed expenditures, pollution control was allocated only one million dollars.

The citizens of Beaufort County, in contrast to the Hilton Head Developers, welcomed BASF. They presented the company with a petition bearing over 7,000 signatures endorsing the new plant. As one local businessman commented, "I would say 80 percent of the people in Beaufort County are in favor of BASF. Those who aren't rich." (William D. McDonald, "Youth Corps Looking for Jobs," *The State*, February 23, 1970.)

The manager of BASF's U.S. operations was clearly confronted by an economic and moral dilemma. He knew that preventing massive pollution was virtually impossible and, in any case, outrageously expensive. The eagerness of South Carolina officials for new industry suggested that pollution standards might be "relaxed" for BASF. If it decided to go ahead and build, was the company to push for the minimum pollution control it could get away with under the law? Such a policy might maximize corporate profits and the financial interests of the shareholders, while at the same time it would lower the aesthetic quality of the environment. It might make jobs available to Beaufort County while ignoring the resort industry and the enjoyment of vacationers. Moreover, the long-term effects of dumping chemicals was hard to predict, but past experience did not give the manager a feeling of optimism. Pollution seemed to be not only a business issue but a *moral* one. But how should the manager sort out, and eventually decide upon, such a moral issue?

To solve his moral problem, BASF's manager might try a variety of strategies. He might, for example, begin by assuming that he has three basic options: (1) Build with minimal pollution control; (2) build with maximal pollution control; or (3) do not build.

Then, he might reason

The consequences of option 1 will be significant but tolerable water pollution, hostility from the Hilton Head Developers, high short-term corporate profits, and satisfied shareholders.

The consequences of option 2 will be unnoticeable pollution, no complaints from the Hilton Head Developers, high pollution-control costs, low profits, and unsatisfied stockholders.

The consequences of option 3 will be approval from the Hilton Head Developers, low short-term profits (while a search for a new location is underway), and strong disapproval from the local townspeople.

My job from a *moral* perspective is to weigh these consequences and consider which of the alternatives constitutes a maximization of good. Who will benefit from each decision? How many people will be adversely affected and in what ways?

Or the manager might reason

Both BASF Corporation and I are confronted with a variety of *duties, rights,* and *obligations.* First there is the company's obligation to its stockholders, and my duty as manager is to protect the economic interests and rights of our stockholders. Next there are the rights of those Beaufort residents and visitors in the area to clean air and water. Finally there are the rights of other property owners in the area, including the Hilton Head Developers, not to be harmed unreasonably by other industries. There is an implied obligation to future generations to protect the river. And finally, there are broader considerations: Is this an act I would want others to do? What kind of moral example will I be setting?

My job from a *moral* perspective is to balance and assess these duties, rights, and obligations, and determine which have priority.

Finally, the manager might reason

I cannot confront a moral problem from either the abstract perspective of "consequences," or of "duties, rights, and obligations." Instead, I must use a concrete con-

cept of *human nature* to guide my deliberations. Acts that aid persons to develop their potential human nature are morally good; ones that do the opposite are bad.
I believe that crucial potentialities of human nature include such things as health, knowledge, moral maturity, meaningful employment, political freedom, and self-respect.
My job from a *moral* perspective is to assess the situation in terms of its harmony or disharmony with these basic concepts of human potential.

Notice how different each of these approaches is. The first focuses on the concept of *consequences;* the second on *duties, rights* and *obligations;* and the third on *human nature.* Of course, the three methods may overlap; for example, applying the concept of "human nature" in the third approach may necessitate referring to concepts drawn from the first and second, such as "consequences" and "rights," and vice versa. Even so, the approaches reflect three classical types of ethical theory in the history of philosophy. Each has been championed by a well-known traditional philosopher, and most ethical theories can be categorized under one of the three headings. The first may be called *consequentialism,* the second, *deontology,* and the third, *human nature ethics.*

CONSEQUENTIALISM

As its name implies, a consequentialist theory of ethical reasoning concentrates on the consequences of human actions, and all actions are evaluated in terms of the extent to which they achieve desirable results. Such theories are also frequently labeled *teleological,* a term derived from the Greek word *telos,* which means "end" or "purpose." According to consequential theories, the concepts of right, wrong, and duty are subordinated to the concept of the end or purpose of an action.

There are at least two types of consequential theory. The first—advocated by only a few consequentialists—is a version of what philosophers call ethical egoism. It construes right action as action whose consequences, considered among all the alternatives, maximizes *my* good—that is, action that benefits *me* the most or harms *me* the least. The second type—advocated by most consequentialists—denies that right action concerns only *me.* Rather, right action must maximize *overall* good; that is, it must maximize good (or minimize bad) from the standpoint of the entire human community. The best-accepted label for this type of consequentialism is *utilitarianism.* This term was coined by the eighteenth-century philosopher Jeremy Bentham, although its best-known proponent was the nineteenth-century English philosopher John Stuart Mill. As Bentham formulated it, the principle of utility states that an action is right if it produces the greatest balance of pleasure or happiness and unhappiness in light of alternative actions. Mill supported a similar principle, using what he called the "proof" of the principle of utility—namely, the recognition that the only proof for something's being desirable is that someone actually desires it. Since everybody desires pleasure or happiness, it follows, according to Mill, that happiness is the most desirable thing. The purpose of moral action is to achieve greatest overall happiness, and actions are evaluated in terms of the extent to which they contribute to this end. The most desirable state of affairs, the greatest good and the goal of morality, said Mill, is the "greatest happiness for the greatest number."

While later utilitarians accept the general framework of Mill's argument, not all utilitarians are hedonists. That is, not all utilitarians equate "the good" with pleasure or happiness. Some utilitarians have argued that in maximizing the "good," one must be concerned not only with maximizing pleasure, but with maximizing other things, such as knowledge, moral maturity, and friendship. Although it could be claimed that such goods also bring pleasure and happiness to their possessor, it is arguable whether their goodness is ultimately *reducible* to whatever pleasure they bring. These philosophers are sometimes called pluralistic utilitarians. Still other philosphers have adapted utilitarianism to modern methods of economic theory by championing what is known as preference utilitarianism. Instead of referring to the maximization of specific goods, such as pleasure or knowledge, preference utilitarians understand the ultimate foundation of goodness to be the set of preferences people actually possess. One person prefers oysters to strawberries; another prefers rock music to Mozart. Each person has a set of preferences, and so long as the set is internally consistent, it makes no sense to label one set morally superior to another. Preference utilitarianism thus interprets right action as that which is optimal among alternatives in terms of everyone's preferences. Disputes, however, rage among preference utilitarians and their critics over how to specify the meaning of *optimal*.

Bentham and Mill thought that utilitarianism was a revolutionary theory, both because it accurately reflected human motivation and because it had clear application to the political and social problems of their day. If one could measure the benefit or harm of any action, rule or law, they believed, one could sort out good and bad social and political legislation as well as good and bad individual actions.

But how, specifically, does one apply the traditional principle of utility? To begin with, one's race, religion, intelligence, or condition of birth is acknowledged to be irrelevant in calculating one's ultimate worth. Each person counts for "one," and no more than "one." Second, in evaluating happiness, one must take into account not only present generations, but ones in the future. In calculating the effects of pollution, for instance, one must measure the possible effects pollution might have on health, genetics, and the supply of natural resources for future generations. Third, pleasure or happiness is measured *en toto* so that the thesis does not reduce to the idea that "one ought to do what makes the most persons happy." Utilitarianism does not reduce to a dictatorship of majority interests. One person's considerable unhappiness might outweigh the minor pleasures of many other persons added together. Utilitarians also consider the long-term consequences for single individuals. For instance, it might be pleasurable to drink a full bottle of wine every evening, but the long-term drawbacks of such a habit might well outweigh its temporary pleasures.

Finally, according to many utilitarians (such as Mill), some pleasures are *qualitatively* better than others. Intellectual pleasure, for example, is said to be higher than physical pleasure. "Better to be Socrates unsatisfied," writes Mill, "than a pig satisfied." The reasons that drove Mill to formulate this qualitative distinction among pleasures are worth noting. Since Mill believed that the optimal situation was one of "greatest happiness for the greatest number," then what was he to say about a world of people living at the zenith of merely *physical* happiness? If science could invent a wonder drug, like the "soma" in Aldous Huxley's *Brave New World,* that provided a permanent state of drugged happiness (without even a hangover), would the consequence be a perfect world? Mill believed not, and to remedy this difficulty in his theory, he introduced *qualitative levels* of happiness. For example, he said that the happiness of understanding Plato is "higher" than that of drinking three martinis. But how was Mill to say *which* pleasures were higher? Here he retreated to an ingenious proposal: When deciding which of two pleasures is higher, one should poll the group of persons who are experienced—that is, who know *both* pleasures. Their decision will indicate which is the higher pleasure. Ah, but might the majority decision not be wrong? Here Mill provides no clear answer.

Modern-day utilitarians divide themselves roughly into two groups: *act utilitarians* and *rule utilitarians.* An *act* utilitarian believes that the principle of utility should be applied to individual acts. Thus one measures the consequences of each *individual action* according to whether it maximizes good. For example, suppose a certain community were offered the opportunity to receive a great deal of wealth in the form of a gift. The only stipulation was that the community force some of its citizens with ugly, deteriorated homes to repair and beautify them. Next, suppose the community held an election to decide whether to accept the gift. An act utilitarian would analyze the problem of whether to vote for or against the proposal from the standpoint of the *individual voter.* Would an individual's vote to accept the gift be more likely to maximize the community's overall good than would a vote to the contrary?

A *rule* utilitarian, on the other hand, believes that instead of considering the results of specific actions, one must weigh the consequences of adopting a *general rule* exemplified by that action. According to the rule utilitarian, one should act according to a general rule which, if adopted, would maximize good. For example, in the hypothetical case of the community deciding whether to accept a gift, a rule utilitarian might adopt the rule "Never vote in a way that lowers the self-respect of a given class of citizens." She might accept this rule because of the general unhappiness that would ensue if society systematically treated some persons as second-class citizens. Here the focus is on the general rule and not on the individual act.

Critics raise objections to utilitarianism. Perhaps the most serious objection is that it is unable to account for justice. Because the utilitarian concentrates on the consequences of an action for a majority, the employment of the principle of utility can be argued to allow injustice for a small minority. For example, if overall goodness were maximized in the long run by making slaves of 2 percent of the population, utilitarianism seemingly is forced to condone slavery. But clearly this is unjust. Utilitarianism's obvious response is that such slavery will not, as a matter of empirical fact, maximize goodness. Rule utilitarians, as we have seen, can argue that society should embrace the rule "Never enslave others," because following such a principle will, in the long run, maximize goodness. Even so, the battle continues between utilitarians and their critics. Can utilitarianism account for the widely held moral conviction that injustice to a minority is wrong *regardless* of the consequences? The answer is hotly contested.

Another criticism concerns the determination of the good to be maximized. Any consequentialist has the problem of identifying and ranking whatever is to be maximized. For a utilitarian such as Mill, as we have seen, the problem involves distinguishing between higher and lower pleasures. But for pluralistic utilitarians, a similar problem exists: What is the basis for selecting, for example, friendship and happiness as goods to be maximized and not, say, aesthetic sensitivity? And even granted that this problem can be solved, there is the future problem of arbitrating trade-offs between goods such as happiness and friendship when they *conflict*. When one is forced to choose between enhancing happiness and enhancing friendship, which gets priority? And under what conditions?

An interesting fact about consequentialist reasoning is that most of us employ it to some degree in ordinary decisions. We weigh the consequences of alternatives in choosing colleges, in deciding on a career, in hiring and promoting others, and in many other judgments. We frequently weigh good consequences over bad ones and predict the long- and short-term effects of our choices. We often even cite consequentialist-style principles—for example, "No one should choose a college where he or she will be unhappy," or, "No one should pollute the environment when his or her action harms others."

However, for a variety of reasons, including the objections to utilitarianism mentioned earlier, some philosophers refuse to acknowledge consequentialism as an adequate theory of ethics. They argue that the proper focus for ethical judgments should not be consequences, but moral *precepts*—that is, the rules, norms, and principles we use to guide our actions. Such philosophers are known as deontologists, and the next section will examine their views.

DEONTOLOGY

The term *deontological* comes from the Greek word for "duty," and what is crucial according to the deontologist are the rules and principles that guide actions. We shall discuss here two approaches to deontological ethical reasoning that have profoundly influenced ethics. The first is that of the eighteenth-century philosopher Immanuel Kant and his followers. This approach focuses on duty and universal rules to determine right actions. The second—actually a subspecies of deontological reasoning—is known as the "social contract" approach. It focuses not on individual decision making, but on the general social principles that rational persons in certain ideal situations would agree upon and adopt.

Kantian Deontology

Kant believed that ethical reasoning should concern activities that are rationally motivated and should utilize precepts that apply universally to all human actions. To this end, he opens his treatise on ethics by declaring

It is impossible to conceive anything at all in the world, . . . which can be taken as good without qualification except a *good* will.[2]

This statement sums up much of what Kant wants to say about ethics and is worth unraveling. What Kant means is that the only thing that can be good or worthwhile without any provisos or stipulations is an action of the will freely motivated for the right reasons. Other goods such as wealth, beauty, and intelligence are certainly valuable, but they are not good *without qualification* because they have the potential to create both good and bad effects. Wealth, beauty, and intelligence can be bad when they are used for purely selfish ends. Even human happiness—which Mill held as the highest good—can, according to Kant, create complacency, disinterest, and excessive self-assurance under certain conditions.

According to Kant, reason is the faculty that can aid in the discovery of correct moral principles; thus it is *reason, not inclination, that should guide the will.* When reason guides the will, Kant calls the resulting actions ones done from "duty." Kant's use of the term *duty* turns out to be less formidable than it first appears. Kant is simply saying that a purely good and free act of the will is one done not merely because you have an *inclination* to do it, but because you have the right reasons for doing it. For example, suppose you discover a wallet belonging to a stranger. Kant would say that despite one's inclination to keep the money (which the stranger may not even need), one should return it. This is an act you know is right despite your inclinations. Kant also believes you should return the wallet even when you believe the *consequences* of not returning it are better. Here his views are at sharp odds with consequentialism. Suppose that the stranger is known for her stinginess, and you plan to donate the money to a children's hospital. No matter. For Kant, you must return the wallet. Thus the moral worth lies in the act itself and not in either your happiness or the consequences brought about by the act. Acts are good because they are done for the sake of what is right and not because of the consequences they might produce.

But how do I know what my duty is? While it may be clear that one should return a wallet, there are other circumstances in which one's duty is less evident. Suppose you are in a six-person lifeboat at sea with five others and a seventh person swims up? What is one's duty here? And how does one even know that what one *thinks* is right *is* right? To settle such problems, Kant claims that duty is more than doing merely what you "feel" is right. Duty is acting with *respect for other rational beings.* It almost goes without saying, then, that "acting from duty" is not to be interpreted as action done in obedience to local, state, or national laws, since these can be good or bad. Instead, "duty" is linked to the idea of universal principles that should govern all our actions.

But is there any principle that can govern *all* human beings? Kant believes the answer is yes, and he calls the highest such principle the "categorical imperative." He formulates the categorical imperative in three ways (although we shall only consider two formulations here). The first formulation, roughly translated, is

One ought only to act such that the principle of one's act could become a universal law of human action in a world in which one would hope to live.

For example, one would want to live in a world where people followed the principle "Return property that belongs to others." Therefore one should return the stranger's wallet. We do not, however, want to live in a world where everyone lies. Therefore, one should not adopt the principle "Lie whenever it seems helpful."

The second formulation of the categorical imperative is

One ought to treat others as having intrinsic value in themselves, and *not* merely as means to achieve one's ends.

In other words, one should respect every person as a rational and free being. Hitler treated one group of persons as nonpersons in order to achieve his own ends, and thus he acted contrary to the categorical imperative. Another instance of treating persons as means would occur if a teacher looked up the grade records of new students to determine how to assign grades in her own class. She would be treating students as if they had no control over their destinies. Such actions are immoral according to Kant because they fail to respect the inherent dignity of rational beings.

Ethical reasoning for Kant implies adopting principles of action and evaluating one's actions in terms of those principles. Even Kant grants that the evaluation is sometimes difficult. For example, there is the problem of striking the proper level of generality in choosing a principle. A principle that read, "If one is named John Doe and attends Big State University and has two sisters, then he should borrow fifty dollars without intending to repay it" is far too specific. On the other hand, the principle "You should always pay your debts" might be too general, since it would require that a starving man repay the only money he possesses to buy a loaf of bread. Because of the problem of striking the proper degree of generality, many modern deontologists have reformulated Kant's basic question to read: "Could I wish that everyone in the world would follow this principle *under relevantly similar conditions?*"

As with utilitarianism, critics challenge deontological reasoning. Some assert that fanatics such as Hitler could at least *believe* that the rule "Persecute Jews whenever possible" is one that the world should live by. Similarly, a thief might universalize the principle "Steal whenever you have a good opportunity." Moreover, a strict interpretation of deontological ethical reasoning is said to allow no exceptions to a universal principle. Such strict adherence to universal principles might encourage moral rigidity and might fail to reflect the diversity of responses required by complex moral situations. Finally, critics argue that, in a given case, two principles may conflict without there being a clear way to decide which principle or rule should take precedence. Jean-Paul Sartre tells of his dilemma during World War II when he was forced to choose between staying to comfort his ill and aging mother, and fighting for the freedom of France. Two principles seemed valid: "Give aid to your father and mother," and "Contribute to the cause of freedom." But with conflicting principles, how is one to choose? Nevertheless, deontological ethical reasoning represents a well-respected and fundamentally distinctive mode of ethical reasoning, one which, like consequentalism, appears in the deliberations of ordinary persons as well as philosophers. We have all heard actions condemned by the comment, "what would it be like if everyone did that?"

The Contractarian Alternative

Kant assumes that the categorical imperative is something all rational individuals can discover and agree upon. A different version of deontology is offered by many philosophers who focus less on the actions of individuals, and more on the principles that govern society at large. These include two philosophers whose writings appear in our book: the seventeenth-century political philosopher John Locke and the twentieth-century American philosopher John Rawls. They and others try to establish universal principles of a just society through what might be called "social contract thought experiments." They ask us to imagine what it would be like to live in a situation where there are no laws, no social conventions, and no political state. In this so-called state of nature, we imagine that rational persons gather to formulate principles or rules to govern political and social communities. Such rules would resemble principles derived through the categorical imperative in that they are presumably principles to which every rational person would agree and which would hold universally.

Locke and Rawls differ in their approach to establishing rules or principles of justice, and the difference illustrates two distinct forms of contractarian reasoning. Locke argues from a "natural rights" position, while Rawls argues from a "reasonable person" position. Locke claims that every person is born with, and possesses, certain basic rights that are "natural." These rights are inherent to a person's nature, and they are possessed by every one equally. Like other inherent traits, they cannot be taken away. They are, in the words of the Declaration of Independence, "inalienable." When rational persons meet to formulate principles to govern the formation of social and political communities, they construct a social contract that is the basis for an agreement between themselves and their government, and whose rules protect natural rights. Rights, then, become deontological precepts by which one forms and evaluates rules, constitutions, government, and socioeconomic systems. While many philosophers disagree with Locke's view that each of us has inherent or *natural* rights, many do utilize a theory of human rights as the basis for justifying and evaluating political institutions.

Rawls adopts a different perspective. He does not begin from a natural rights position. Instead, he asks which principles of justice rational persons would formulate if they were behind a "veil of ignorance"—that is, if each person knew nothing about who he or she was. That is, one would not know whether one were old or young, male or female, rich or poor, highly motivated or lazy, or anything about one's personal status in society. Unable to predict which principles, if picked, will favor them personally, Rawls argues, persons will be forced to choose principles that are fair to all.

Rawls and Locke are not in perfect agreement about which principles would be adopted in such hypothetical situations, and more will be said about their views later in the book. For now it is important to remember that the social contract approach maintains a deontological character. It is used to formulate principles of justice that apply universally. Some philosophers note, however, that from an original position in a "state of nature" or behind a "veil of ignorance," rational persons *could* adopt consequentialist principles as rules for a just society. Thus, while the social contract approach is deontological in style, the principles it generates are not necessarily ones that are incompatible with consequentialism.

In the moral evaluations of business, all deontologists—contractarians included—would ask questions such as the following:

1. Are the rules fair to everyone?
2. Do the rules hold universally even with the passage of time?
3. Is every person treated with equal respect?

What may be missing from a deontological approach to ethical reasoning is a satisfactory means of coping with valid exceptions to general rules. Under what circumstances, if any, are exceptions allowed? Deontologists believe that they can answer this question, but their solutions vary. Suffice it to say that deontologists, just as utilitarians, have not convinced everyone.

HUMAN NATURE ETHICS

According to some contemporary philosophers, the preceding two modes of ethical reasoning exhaust all possible modes. That is to say, all theories can be classified as either teleological or deontological. Whether this is true cannot be settled here, but it will be helpful to introduce briefly what some philosophers consider to be a third category, namely the *human nature* approach.

A *human nature* approach assumes that all humans have inherent capacities that constitute the ultimate basis for all ethical claims. Actions are evaluated in terms of whether they promote or hinder, coincide with, or conflict with these capacities. One of the most famous proponents of this theory was the Greek philosopher Aristotle. In Aristotle's opinion, human beings have inherent *potentialities,* and thus human development turns out to be the struggle for self-actualization, or in other words, the perfection of inherent human nature. Consider the acorn. It has the natural potential to become a sturdy oak tree. Its natural drive is not to become an elm or a cedar or even a stunted oak, but to become the most robust oak tree possible. Diseased or stunted oak trees are simply deficient; they are instances of things in nature whose potential has not been fully developed. Similarly, according to Aristotle, persons are born with inherent potentialities. Persons, like acorns, naturally are oriented to actualize their potentialities, and for them this means more than merely developing their physical potential. It also means developing their mental, moral, and social potential. Thus, human beings in this view are seen as basically good; evil is understood as a deficiency that occurs when one is unable to fulfill one's natural capacities.

It is important to understand that the concept of human nature need not be an individualistic one. According to Aristotle, persons are "social" by nature and cannot be understood apart from the larger community in which they participate. "Man," Aristotle wrote, is a "social animal." For Aristotle, then, fulfilling one's natural constitution implies developing wisdom, generosity, and self-restraint, all of which help to make one a good member of the community.

The criterion for judging the goodness of any action is whether or not the action is compatible with one's inherent human capacities. Actions that enhance human capacities are good; those that deter them are bad unless they are the best among generally negative alternatives. For example, eating nothing but starches is unhealthy, but it is clearly preferable to starving.

Because this theory puts great emphasis on the nature of persons, how one undersands that "nature" will obviously be the key to determining both what counts as a right action and how one defines the proper end of human action in general. Aristotle argued that intelligence and wisdom are uniquely human potentialities and consequently that intellectual virtue is the highest virtue. The life of contemplation, he believed, is the best sort of life, in part because it represents the highest fulfillment of human nature. Moral virtue, also crucial in Aristotle's theory, involves the rational control of one's desires. In action where a choice is possible, one exercises moral virtue by restraining harmful desires and cultivating beneficial ones. The development of virtue requires the cultivation of good habits, and this in turn leads Aristotle to emphasize the importance of good upbringing and education.

One problem said to affect human nature theories is that they have difficulty justifying the supposition that human beings *do* have specific inherent capacities and that these capacities are the same for all humans. Further, critics claim that it is difficult to warrant the assumption that humans are basically good. Perhaps the famous psychoanalyst Sigmund Freud is correct in his assertion that at bottom we are all naturally aggressive and selfish. Finally, critics complain that it is difficult to employ this theory in ethical reasoning, since it appears to lack clear-cut rules and principles for use in moral decision making. Obviously, any well-argued human nature ethic will take pains to spell out the aspects of human nature which, when actualized, constitute the ultimate ground for moral judgments.

CONCLUSION

The three approaches to ethical reasoning we have discussed—consequentialism, deontology, and human nature ethics—all present theories of ethical reasoning distinguished in terms of their basic methodological elements. Each represents a type or model of moral reasoning that is applicable to practical decisions in concrete situations. Consider, for example, the case study with which we began our discussion, involving BASF and its proposed new plant. As it happened, BASF chose option 3 and decided to build elsewhere. In making his decision, did the BASF manager actually use any or all of the methods described above? Although we cannot know the answer to this question, it is clear, as we saw earlier, that each method was applicable to his problem. Indeed, the three methods of moral reasoning are sufficiently broad that each is applicable to the full range of problems confronting human moral experience. The question of which method, if any, is superior to the others must be left for another time. The intention of this essay is not to substitute for a thorough study of traditional ethical theories—something for which there is no substitute—but to introduce the reader to basic modes of ethical reasoning that will help to analyze the ethical problems in business that arise in the remainder of the book.

Notes

1. "BASF Corporation vs. The Hilton Head Island Developers," in *Business and Society,* Robert D. Hay, et al., eds. (Cincinnati: South-Western Publishing Co., 1984). pp. 100–12.

2. Immanuel Kant, *Groundwork of the Metaphysic of Morals,* trans. H. J. Paton (New York: Harper & Row, 1948, 1956), p. 61.

Does Business Ethics Make Economic Sense?

AMARTYA SEN[1]

Abstract: The importance of business ethics is not contradicted in any way by Adam Smith's pointer to the fact that our "regards to our own interests" provide adequate *motivation for exchange*. There are many important economic relationships other than exchange, such as the institution of production and arrangements of distribution. Here business ethics can play a major part. Even as far as exchange is concerned, business ethics can be crucially important in terms of organization and behavior, going well beyond basic motivation.

1. Introduction

I begin not with the need for business ethics, but at the other end—the idea that many people have that there is no need for such ethics. That conviction is quite widespread among practitioners of economics, though it is more often taken for granted implicitly rather than asserted explicitly. We have to understand better what the conviction rests on, to be able to see its inadequacies. Here, as in many other areas of knowledge, the importance of a claim depends to a great extent on what it denies.

How did this idea of the redundancy of ethics get launched in economics? The early authors on economic matters, from Aristotle and Kautilya (in ancient Greece and ancient India respectively—the two were contemporaries, as it happens) to medieval practitioners (including Aquinas, Ockham, Maimonides, and others), to the economists of the early modern age (William Petty, Gregory King, François Quesnay, and others) were all much concerned, in varying degrees, with ethical analysis. In one way or another, they saw economics as a branch of "practical reason," in which concepts of the good, the right and the obligatory were quite central.

What happened then? As the "official" story goes, all this changed with Adam Smith, who can certainly be described—rightly—as the father of modern economics. He made, so it is said, economics scientific and hardheaded, and the new economics that emerged in the 19th and 20th centuries was all ready to do business, with no ethics to keep it tied to "morals and moralizing." That view of what happened—with Smith doing the decisive shooting of busi-

A paper presented at the International Conference on the Ethics of Business in a Global Economy, held in Columbus, Ohio, in March 1992. Reprinted by permission of the author, Amartya Sen, Harvard University, and *Business Ethics Quarterly,* January 1993, Vol. 3, Issue 1.

ness and economic ethics—is not only reflected in volumes of professional economic writings, but has even reached the status of getting into the English literature via a limerick by Stephen Leacock, who was both a literary writer and an economist:

Adam, Adam, Adam Smith
Listen what I charge you with!
Didn't you say
In a class one day
That selfishness was bound to pay?
Of all doctrines that was the Pith.
Wasn't it, wasn't it, wasn't it, Smith?[2]

The interest in going over this bit of history—or alleged history—does not lie, at least for this conference, in scholastic curiosity. I believe it is important to see how that ethics-less view of economics and business emerged in order to understand what it is that is being missed out. As it happens, that bit of potted history of "who killed business ethics" is altogether wrong, and it is particularly instructive to understand how that erroneous identification has come about.

2. Exchange, Production and Distribution

I get back, then, to Adam Smith. Indeed, he did try to make economics scientific, and to a great extent was successful in this task, within the limits of what was possible then. While that part of the alleged history is right (Smith certainly did much to enhance the scientific status of economics), what is altogether mistaken is the idea that Smith demonstrated—or believed that he had demonstrated—the redundancy of ethics in economic and business affairs. Indeed, quite the contrary. The Professor of Moral Philosophy at the University of Glasgow—for that is what Smith was—was as interested in the importance of ethics in behavior as anyone could have been. It is instructive to see how the odd reading of Smith—as a "no-nonsense" sceptic of economic and business ethics—has come about.

Perhaps the most widely quoted remark of Adam Smith is the one about the butcher, the brewer and the baker in *The Wealth of Nations:* "It is not from the benevolence of the butcher, the brewer, or the baker that we expect our dinner, but from their regard to their own interest. We address ourselves, not to their humanity but to their self-love. . . ."[3] The butcher, the brewer and the baker want our money, and we want their products, and the exchange benefits us all. There would seem to be no need for any ethics—business or otherwise—in bringing about this betterment of all the parties involved. All that is needed is regard for our own respective interests, and the market is meant to do the rest in bringing about the mutually gainful exchanges.

In modern economics this Smithian tribute to self-interest is cited again and again—indeed with such exclusivity that one is inclined to wonder whether this is the only passage of Smith that is read these days. What did Smith really suggest? Smith did argue in this passage that the pursuit of self-interest would do fine to motivate the exchange of commodities. But that is a very limited claim, even though it is full of wonderful insights in explaining why it is that we seek exchange and how come exchange can be such a beneficial thing for all. But to understand the limits of what is being claimed here, we have to ask, first: Did Smith think that economic operations and business activities consist only of exchanges of this kind? Second, even in the context of exchange, we have to question: Did Smith think that the result would be just as good if the businesses involved, driven by self-interest, were to try to defraud the consumers, or the consumers in question were to attempt to swindle the sellers?

The answers to both these questions are clearly in the negative. The butcher-brewer-baker simplicity does not carry over to problems of production and distribution (and Smith never said that it did), nor to the problem as to how a system of exchange can flourish institutionally. This is exactly where we begin to see why Smith could have been right in his claim about *the motivation for exchange* without establishing or trying to establish *the redundancy of business or ethics* in general (or even in exchange). And this is central to the subject of this conference.

The importance of self-interest pursuit is a helpful part of understanding many practical problems, for example, the supply problems in the Soviet Union and East Europe. But it is quite unhelpful in explaining the success of, say, Japanese economic performance *vis-à-vis* West Europe or North America (since behavior modes in Japan are often deeply influenced by other conventions and pressures). Elsewhere in *The Wealth of Nations,* Adam Smith considers other problems which call for a more complex motivational structure. And in his *The Theory of Moral Sentiments,* Smith goes extensively into the need to go beyond profit maximization, arguing that "humanity, justice, generosity, and public spirit, are the qualities most useful to others."[4] Adam Smith was very far from trying to deny the importance of ethics in behavior in general and business behavior in particular.[5]

Overlooking everything else that Smith said in his wide-ranging writings and concentrating only on this one butcher-brewer-baker passage, the father of modern economics is too often made to look like an ideologue. He is transformed into a partisan exponent of an ethics-free view of life which would have horrified Smith. To adapt a Shakespearian aphorism, while some men are born small and some achieve smallness, the unfortunate Adam Smith has had much smallness thrust upon him.

It is important to see how Smith's whole tribute to self-interest as a motivation for exchange (best illustrated in the butcher-brewer-baker passage) can co-exist peacefully with Smith's advocacy of ethical behavior elsewhere. Smith's concern with ethics was, of course, extremely extensive and by no means confined to economic and business matters. But since this is not the occasion to review Smith's ethical beliefs, but only to get insights from his combination of economic and ethical expertise to understand better the exact role of business ethics, we have to point our inquiries in that particular direction.

The butcher-brewer-baker discussion is all about *motivation for exchange,* but Smith was—as any good economist should be—deeply concerned also with *production* as well as *distribution.* And to understand how exchange might itself actually work in practice, it is not adequate to concentrate only on the motivation that makes people *seek* exchange. It is necessary to look at the behavior patterns that could sustain a flourishing system of mutually profitable exchanges. The positive role of intelligent self-seeking in motivating exchange has to be supplemented by the motivational demands of production and distribution, and the systemic demands on the organization of the economy.

These issues are taken up now, linking the general discussion with practical problems faced in the contemporary world. In the next three sections I discuss in turn (1) the problem of organization (especially that of exchange), (2) the arrangement and performance of production, and (3) the challenge of distribution.

3. Organization and Exchange: Rules and Trust

I come back to the butcher-brewer-baker example. The concern of the different parties with their own interests certainly can adequately *motivate* all of them to take part in the exchange from which each benefits. But whether the exchange would operate well would depend also on organizational conditions. This requires institutional development which can take quite some time to work—a lesson that is currently being learned rather painfully in East Europe and the former Soviet Union. That point is now being recognized, even though it was comprehensively ignored in the first flush of enthusiasm in seeking the magic of allegedly automatic market processes.

But what must also be considered now is the extent to which the economic institutions operate on the basis of common behavior patterns, shared trusts, and a mutual confidence in the ethics of the different parties. When Adam Smith pointed to the motivational importance of "regard to their own interest," he did not suggest that this motivation is all that is needed to have a flourishing system of exchange. If he cannot trust the householder, the baker may have difficulty in proceeding to produce bread to meet orders, or in delivering bread without prepayment. And the householder may not be certain whether he would be sensible in relying on the delivery of the ordered bread if the baker is not always altogether reliable. These problems of mutual confidence—discussed in a very simple form here—can be incomparably more complex and more critical in extended and multifarious business arrangements.

Mutual confidence in certain rules of behavior is typically implicit rather than explicit—indeed so implicit that its importance can be easily overlooked in situations in which confidence is unproblematic. But in the context of economic development across the Third World, and also of institutional reform now sweeping across what used to be the Second World, these issues of behavioral norms and ethics can be altogether central.

In the Third World there is often also a deep-rooted scepticism of the reliability and moral quality of business behavior. This can be directed both at local businessmen and the commercial people from abroad. The latter may sometimes be particularly galling to well-established business firms including well-known multinationals. But the record of some multinationals and their unequal power in dealing with the more vulnerable countries have left grounds for much suspicion, even though such suspicion may be quite misplaced in many cases. Establishing high standards of business ethics is certainly one way of tackling this problem.

There is also, in many Third World countries, a traditional lack of confidence in the moral behavior of particular groups of traders, for example merchants of food grains. This is a subject on which—in the context of the then-Europe—Adam Smith himself commented substantially in *The Wealth of Nations,* though he thought these suspicions were by and large unjustified. In fact, the empirical record on this is quite diverse, and particular experiences of grain trade in conditions of scarcity and famine have left many questions to be answered.

This is an issue of extreme seriousness, since it is now becoming increasingly clear that typically the best way of organizing famine prevention and relief is to create additional incomes for the destitute (possibly through employment schemes) and then to rely on normal trade to meet (through standard arrangements of transport and sales) the resulting food demand.[6] The alternative of bureaucratic distribution of food in hastily organized relief camps is often much slower, more wasteful, seriously disruptive of family life and normal economic operations, and more conducive to the spread of epidemic diseases. However, giving a crucial role to the grain traders at times of famine threats (as a complement to state-organized employment schemes to generate income) raises difficult issues of trust and trustworthiness, in particular, that the traders will not manipulate the precarious situation in search of unusual profit. The issue of business ethics, thus, becomes an altogether vital part of the arrangement of famine prevention and relief.

The problem can be, to some extent, dealt with by skillful use of the threat of government intervention in the market. But the credibility of that threat depends greatly on the size of grain reserves the government itself has. It can work well in some cases (generally it has in India), but not always. Ultimately, much depends on the extent to which the relevant business people can establish exacting standards of behavior, rather than fly off in search of unusual profits to be rapidly extracted from manipulated situations.

I have been discussing problems of organization in exchange, and it would seem to be right to conclude this particular discussion by noting that the need for business ethics is quite strong even in the field of exchange (despite the near-universal presence of the butcher-brewer-baker motivation of "regard to their own interest"). If we now move on from exchange to production and distribution, the need for business ethics becomes even more forceful and perspicuous. The issue of trust is central to all economic operations. But we now have to consider other problems of interrelation in the process of production and distribution.

4. Organization of Production: Firms and Public Goods

Capitalism has been successful enough in generating output and raising productivity. But the experiences of different countries are quite diverse. The recent experiences of Eastern Asian economies—most notably Japan—raise deep questions about the modeling of capitalism on traditional economic theory. Japan is often seen—rightly in a particular sense—as a great example of successful capitalism, but it is clear that the motivation patterns that dominate Japanese business have much more content than would be provided by pure profit maximization.

Different commentators have emphasized distinct aspects of Japanese motivational features. Michio Morishima has outlined the special characteristics of "Japanese ethos" as emerging from its particular history of rule-based behavior pattern.[7] Ronald Dore has seen the influence of "Confucian ethics."[8] Recently, Eiko Ikegami has pointed to the importance of the traditional concern with "honor"—a kind of generalization of the Samurai code—as a crucial modifier of business and economic motivation.[9]

Indeed, there is some truth, oddly enough, even in the puzzlingly witty claim made by *The Wall Street Journal* that Japan is "the only communist nation that works" (30 January 1989, p. 1). It is, as one would expect, mainly a remark about the non-profit motivations underlying many economic and business activities in Japan. We have to understand and interpret the peculiar fact that the most successful capitalist nation in the world flourishes economically with a motivation structure that departs firmly—and often explicitly—from the pursuit of self-interest, which is meant to be the bedrock of capitalism.

In fact, Japan does not, by any means, provide the only example of a powerful role of business ethics in promoting capitalist success. The productive merits of selfless work and devotion to enterprise have been given much credit for economic achievements in many countries in the world. Indeed, the need of capitalism for a motivational structure more complex than pure profit maximization has been acknowledged in various forms, over a long time, by various social scientists (though typically not by any "mainstream" economists): I have in mind Marx, Weber, Tawney, and others.[10] The basic point about the observed success of non-profit motives is neither unusual nor new, even though that wealth of historical and conceptual insights is often thoroughly ignored in professional economics today.

It is useful to try to bring the discussion in line with Adam Smith's concerns, and also with the general analytical approaches successfully developed in modern microeconomic theory. In order to understand how motives other than self-seeking can have an important role, we have to see the limited reach of the butcher-brewer-baker argument, especially in dealing with what modern economists call "public good." This becomes particularly relevant because the overall success of a modern enterprise is, in a very real sense, a public good.

But what *is* a public good? That idea can be best understood by contrasting it with a "private good," such as a toothbrush or a shirt or an apple, which either you can use or I, but not both. Our respective uses would compete and be exclusive. This is not so with public goods, such as a livable environment or the absence of epidemics. All of us may benefit from breathing fresh air, living in an epidemic-free environment, and so on. When uses of commodities are non-competitive, as in the case of public goods, the rationale of the self-interest-based market mechanism comes under severe strain. The market system works by putting a price on a commodity and the allocation between consumers is done by the intensities of the respective willingness to buy it at the prevailing price. When "equilibrium prices" emerge, they balance demand with supply for each commodity. In contrast, in the case of public goods, the uses are—largely or entirely—non-competitive, and the system of giving a good to the highest bidder does not have much merit, since one person's consumption does not exclude that of another. Instead, optimum resource allocation would require that the *combined* benefits be compared with the costs of production, and here the market mechanism, based on profit maximization, functions badly.[11]

A related problem concerns the allocation of private goods involving strong "externalities," with interpersonal interdependencies working outside the markets. If the smoke from a factory makes a neighbor's home dirty and unpleasant, without the neighbor being able to charge the factory owner for the loss she suffers, then that is an "external" relation. The market does not help in this case, since it is not there to allocate the effects—good or bad—that work outside the market.[12] Public goods and externalities are related phenomena, and they are both quite common in such fields as public health care, basic education, environmental protection, and so on.

There are two important issues to be addressed in this context, in analysing the organization and performance of production. First, there would tend to be some failure in resource allocation when the commodities produced are public goods or involve strong externalities. This can be taken either (1) as an argument for having *publicly owned enterprises,* which would be governed by principles other than profit maximization, or (2) as a case for *public regulations* governing private enterprise, or (3) as establishing a need for the use of non-profit values—particularly of *social concern*—in private decisions (perhaps because of the goodwill that it might generate). Since public enterprises have not exactly covered themselves with glory in the recent years, and public regulations—while useful—are sometimes quite hard to implement, the third option has become more important in public discussions. It is difficult, in this context, to escape the argument for encouraging business ethics, going well beyond the traditional values of honesty and reliability, and taking on social responsibility as well (for example, in matters of environmental degradation and pollution).

The second issue is more complex and less recognized in the literature, but also more interesting. Even in the production of private commodities, there can be an important "public good" aspect in the production process itself. This is because production itself is typically a joint activity, supervisions are costly and often unfeasible, and each participant contributes to the over-all success of the firm in a way that cannot be fully reflected in the private rewards that he or she gets.

The over-all success of the firm, thus, is really a public good, from which all benefit, to which all contribute, and which is not parcelled out in little boxes of person-specific rewards strictly linked with each person's *respective contribution.* And this is precisely where the motives other than narrow self-seeking become productively important. Even though I do not have the opportunity to pursue the point further here, I do believe that the successes of "Japanese ethos," "Confucian ethics," "Samurai codes of honor," etc., can be fruitfully linked to this aspect of the organization of production.

5. The Challenge of Distribution: Values and Incentives

I turn now to distribution. It is not hard to see that non-self-seeking motivations can be extremely important for *distributional* problems in general. In dividing a cake, one person's gain is another's loss. At a very obvious level, the contributions that can be made by ethics—business ethics and others—include the amelioration of misery through policies explicitly aimed at such a result. There is an extensive literature on donations, charity, and philanthropy in general, and also on the willingness to join in communal activities geared to social improvement. The connection with ethics is obvious enough in these cases.

What is perhaps more interesting to discuss is the fact that distributional and productional problems very often come mixed together, so that how the cake is divided influences the size of the cake itself. The so-called "incentive problem" is a part of this relationship. This too is a much discussed problem,[13] but it is important to clarify in the present context that the extent of the conflict between size and distribution depends crucially on the motivational and behavioral assumptions. The incentive problem is not an immutable feature of production technology. For example, the more narrowly profit-oriented an enterprise is, the more it would, in general, tend to resist looking after the interests of others—workers, associates, consumers. This is an area in which ethics can make a big difference.

The relevance of all this to the question we have been asked to address ("Does business ethics make economic sense?") does, of course, depend on how "economic sense" is defined. If economic sense includes the achievement of a good society in which one lives, then the distributional improvements can be counted in as parts of sensible outcomes even for business. Visionary industrialists and businesspersons have tended to encourage this line of reasoning.

On the other hand, if "economic sense" is interpreted to mean nothing other than achievement of profits and business rewards, then the concerns for others and for distributional equity have to be judged entirely instrumentally—in terms of how they indirectly help to promote profits. That connection is not to be scoffed at, since firms that treat its workers well are often very richly rewarded for it. For one thing, the workers are then more reluctant to lose their jobs, since more would be sacrificed if dismissed from this (more lucrative) employment, compared with alternative opportunities. The contribution of goodwill to team spirit and thus to productivity can also be quite plentiful.

We have then an important contrast between two different ways in which good business behavior could make economic sense. One way is to see the improvement of the society in which one lives as a reward in itself; this works directly. The other is to use ultimately a business criterion for improvement, but to take note of the extent to which good business behavior could in its turn lead to favorable business performance; this enlightened self-interest involves an indirect reasoning.

It is often hard to disentangle the two features, but in understanding whether or how business ethics make economic sense, we have to take note of each feature. If, for example, a business firm pays inadequate attention to the safety of its workers, and this results accidentally in a disastrous tragedy, like the one that happened in Bhopal in India some years ago (though I am not commenting at present on the extent to which Union Carbide was in fact negligent there), that event would be harmful both for the firm's profits and for the general objectives of social well-being in which the firm may be expected to take an interest. The two effects are distinct and separable and should act cumulatively in an overall consequential analysis. Business ethics has to relate to both.

6. A Concluding Remark

I end with a brief recapitulation of some of the points discussed, even though I shall not attempt a real summary. First, the importance of business ethics is not contradicted in any way by Adam Smith's pointer to the fact that our "regards to our own interest" provide adequate motivation for exchange (section 2). Smith's butcher-brewer-baker argument is concerned (1) directly with *exchanges* only (not production or distribution), and (2) only with the *motivational aspect* of exchange (not its organizational and behavioral aspects).

Second, business ethics can be crucially important in economic organization in general and in exchange operations in particular. This relationship is extensive and fairly ubiquitous, but it is particularly important, at this time, for the development efforts of the Third World and the reorganizational attempts in what used to be the Second World (section 3).

Third, the importance of business ethics in the arrangement and performance of production can be illustrated by the contrasting experiences of different economies, e.g., Japan's unusual success. The advantages of going beyond the pure pursuit of profit can be understood in different ways. To some extent, this question relates to the failure of profit-based market allocation in dealing with "public goods." This is relevant in two different ways: (1) the presence of public goods (and of the related phenomenon of externalities) in the commodities produced (e.g., environmental connections), and (2) the fact that the success of the firm can itself be fruitfully seen as a public good (section 4).

Finally, distributional problems—broadly defined—are particularly related to behavioral ethics. The connections can be both direct and valuational, and also indirect and instrumental. The interrelations between the size of the cake and its distribution increase the reach and relevance of ethical behavior, e.g., through the incentive problem (section 5).

Notes

1. Lamont University Professor, and Professor of Economics and Philosophy, at Harvard University.

2. Stephen Leacock, *Hellements of Hickonomics* (New York: Dodd, Mead & Co., 1936), p. 75.

3. Adam Smith, *An Inquiry into the Nature and Causes of the Wealth of Nations* (1776; republished, London: Dent, 1910), vol. I, p. 13.

4. Adam Smith, *The Theory of Moral Sentiments* (revised edition, 1790; reprinted, Oxford: Clarendon Press, 1976), p. 189.

5. On this and related manners, see my *On Ethics and Economics* (Oxford: Blackwell, 1987); Patricia H. Werhane, *Adam Smith and His Legacy for Modern Capitalism* (New York: Oxford University Press, 1991); Emma Rothschild, "Adam Smith and Conservative Economics," *Economic History Review,* 45 (1992).

6. On this see Jean Drèze and Amartya Sen, *Hunger and Public Action* (Oxford: Clarendon Press, 1989).

7. Michio Morishima, *Why Has Japan 'Succeeded'? Western Technology and Japanese Ethos* (Cambridge: Cambridge University Press, 1982).

8. Ronald Dore, "Goodwill and the Spirit of Market Capitalism," *British Journal of Sociology,* 34 (1983), and *Taking Japan Seriously: A Confucian Perspective on Leading Economic Issues* (Stanford: Stanford University Press, 1987).

9. Eiko Ikegami, "The Logic of Cultural Change: Honor, State-Making, and the Samurai," mimeographed, Department of Sociology, Yale University, 1991.

10. Karl Marx (with F. Engels), *The German Ideology* (1845–46, English translation, New York: International Publishers, 1947); Richard Henry Tawney, *Religion and the Rise of Capitalism* (London: Murray, 1926); Max Weber, *The Protestant Ethic and the Spirit of Capitalism* (London: Allen & Unwin, 1930).

11. The classic treatment of public goods was provided by Paul A. Samuelson, "The Pure Theory of Public Expenditure," *Review of Economics and Statistics,* 35 (1954).

12. For a classic treatment of external effects, see A. C. Pigou, *The Economics of Welfare* (London: Macmillan, 1920). There are many different ways of defining "externalities," with rather disparate bearings on policy issues; on this see the wide-ranging critical work of Andreas Papandreou (*Jr.,* I should add to avoid an ambiguity, though I don't believe he uses that clarification), *Ideas of Externality,* to be published by Clarendon Press, Oxford, and Oxford University Press, New York.

13. A good general review of the literature can be found in A. B. Atkinson and J. E. Stiglitz, *Lectures on Public Economics* (New York: McGraw-Hill, 1980). On the conceptual and practical importance of the incentive problem and other sources of potential conflict between efficiency and equity, see my *Inequality Reexamined* (Cambridge, MA: Harvard University Press, 1992), Chapter 9.

• PART ONE •

General Issues in Ethics
Introduction

At a time when the reputation of business in general is low . . . one would expect corporate executives to be especially sensitive even to appearances of conflict of interest. . . . Yet this seems not, on the whole, to be the case. . . .

IRVING KRISTOL

- If you were a manager of a large corporation doing business in a country where bribery was an accepted practice in getting business contracts, would you participate in this activity?
- Suppose as manager of a foreign division of a multinational corporation you discover that an allegedly benign product you manufacture is being used as a drug by a substantial population of children in that culture. Would you withdraw your product from that market or close your plant in that country?
- If you were operating a branch of a U.S. company in a foreign country, would you follow that country's tax procedures if they conflicted with procedures in the United States and even required falsifying earnings reports?
- As an account executive, you feel that one of the advertisements for which you are responsible presents misleading information about the product. Would you request a change in the advertisement?

Each of these vignettes is drawn from an actual business situation illustrated in this section, and, in fact, such incidents occur more frequently than one might expect. Understanding their ethical implications requires not only an awareness of concrete situations but also the ability to subsume business problems under categories of more general ethical concern. The philosophical material in Part One introduces three traditional ethical concerns: virtue, ethical relativism, and truth telling. Stated as questions these concerns are:

Virtue: What role does personal character play in commercial activity? Is personal "virtue" an outmoded concept?

Ethical relativism: Are values simply relative to the groups of people who espouse them such that value differences between cultures cannot be resolved? Or is it possible to identify universal values which resolve ethical differences and apply to all people? How *does* one resolve conflicts of values between cultures, between individuals and organizations, or even between individuals?

Truth telling: What obligations, if any, exist for individuals and organizations to communicate honestly? When, if ever, is not telling the truth justified?

Virtues and the Virtuous Manager

In an age in which technological systems and complex organizational structures dominate business activity, what role can the integrity of the individual manager play? Mega corporations and world-wide trading systems mask the importance of the single business person, the final focal point of all business decision making.

Finding inspiration in the philosophy of the ancient thinker Aristotle, Robert Solomon argues in "Corporate Roles, Personal Virtues: An Aristotelean Approach to Business Ethics" that virtue does matter in business. He asserts that the personal and community aspects of business are no less relevant today than they were centuries ago. To neglect personal virtues, in turn, is to condemn business ethics to sterile irrelevance. In so doing, he reflects the late twentieth century trend toward what has been called "virtue ethics."

Still a different aspect of the virtue issue is treated by Robert Jackall, who decries the hypocrisy of modern management culture. Jackall's research suggests that the connection between work and reward has become more capricious. Instead, the role of loyalties and alliances, of patrons, of luck, and of outrunning one's mistakes in achieving corporate success has increased. The problem is serious, writes Jackall, in that many men and women no longer see success as necessarily connected to hard work. The Protestant ethic, self-reliance, and devotion to work, have been replaced by adminstrative hierarchies, standardized work procedures, regularized timetables, uniform policies, and centralized control. It all adds up, believes Jackall, to a bureaucratic phenomenon.

Ethical Relativism

The issue of honesty is difficult in practice because it must be faced every day. The issue of the relativity of value judgments is less commonplace but no less difficult. It asks whether some moral principles apply universally to all persons or whether, instead, all values and ethical judgments are relative to particular contexts. As Norman Bowie notes in "Relativism, Cultural and Moral," this question is particularly acute in contemporary business because most major corporations today are "transnational" or "multinational" corporations that conduct business in many countries. How should businesses operate in foreign countries? For example, should an American multinational company adopt the practices of the host country even when those practices conflict with an American way of doing business and are morally questionable at least according to United States standards? In general, should one lie, bribe, or submit to extortion in a foreign country if that activity is common practice in that culture? According to some views of ethical relativism, one cannot say that bribery, for example, is wrong in a particular culture if it is an acceptable practice in the value system of that culture. The ethical relativist, says Bowie, is defined as someone who believes that what is really right or wrong is what the culture says is right or wrong. In turn, there are no universal standards or objective values by which one can judge the moral principles of all cultures. Nor are there any general standards by which one can adjudicate between two clashing principles.

Ethical relativism frequently uses evidence provided by a closely related point of view known as cultural relativism. Cultural relativism is a descriptive view that emphasizes how the ways in which people reason about morality vary in different cultures because of different customs, religious traditions, and methods of education. But it requires an additional step from cultural relativism to reach the position of ethical relativism. After noting the fact of cultural relativism and moral diversity, ethical relativism holds that no ethical assertion or set of assertions has any greater claim to objectivity or universality than any other. From the obvious empirical evidence of differences between cultures, an ethical relativist may go further to argue that there are no ultimate, universal ethical principles and that all value judgments are relative to particular contexts. Therefore, the truth of an ethical statement such as "Bribery is wrong" is determined solely by the beliefs of the culture espousing that claim. Although Americans typically think bribery is wrong, in some other cultures it seems to be an accepted part of business and political practice. According to a relativist, this value conflict cannot be resolved. Value conflicts within a particular society, too, may for the same reason not be resolvable. For at least some ethical disagreements, there is no single correct view to which even an ideal rational observer can appeal in solving conflicts of values, particularly those of a more serious nature.

The relativity of value judgments can be an issue within a culture as well. One can argue that values are not merely relative to particular cultures but also relative to particular spheres of activity. For example, although tackling in football is part of that game, it is not an accepted practice in other social interactions. If business itself is a game, as Albert Carr argues, then that sphere of activity has certain conventions and values that might not be acceptable in other spheres. According to this line of argument, the values of the medical community might differ from, say, those of certain religious groups, or the values espoused by corporations might differ from, and sometimes even conflict with, ideals espoused by individuals. Because values affect expectations, what is expected of a person as an employee, for example, might be different from the values she espouses away from the workplace.

An obvious way to challenge ethical relativism is to argue that there are some values that are universal, that is, which apply without exception. Both Norman Bowie and Richard De George find relativism implausible, but nonetheless have difficulty isolating universal ethical truths. Richard De George rejects relativism even while recognizing that there are practical difficulties in specifying particular ethical principles that apply universally. Different background institutions such as socialism and capitalism, he asserts, can confound cross-cultural ethical pronouncements. "Some actions," he writes, "are wrong no matter which system of background institutions are in place." He goes on to say that present circumstances in Russia mean that some actions will appropriately be judged unethical when viewed from the assumption that *socialist* background conditions are operative, and will appropriately be viewed as ethically justifiable when viewed from the assumption that *free market* conditions are operative. Business ethics is always embedded in socioeconomic and political conditions which form and engulf business.

The conduct of multinational corporations has been under severe scrutiny in recent years. As a result of incidents involving sensitive payments, in 1977 the U.S. Congress passed the Foreign Corrupt Practices Act (FCPA). The FCPA is an attempt to legislate standards of conduct for multinational corporations by making it a crime for U.S.-based multinationals to offer or to acquiesce to sensitive payments to officials of foreign governments. The Act implies that what U.S. citizens in this country think is morally right should apply to their dealings in other countries. This position would be criticized by ethical relativists, since according to them, value differences between cultures preclude the justification of exporting the laws or moral principles of one country to another.

In his article "Moral Minimums for Multinationals," Thomas Donaldson considers the vexing problems that arise when moral and legal standards vary between countries, especially between a multinational corporation's home and host countries. How, he asks, should highly placed multinational managers, typically schooled in home-country moral traditions, reconcile conflicts between their values and the practices of the host country? If host-country standards appear lower than home-country ones, should the multinational manager always take the "high road" and implement home-country standards? Or does the "high road" sometimes signal a failure to respect cultural diversity and national integrity? The answer may be fairly obvious in the instance of South Africa (where acquiescing to racism and discrimination would surely be immoral), but how about other instances involving differences in wage rates, pollution standards, or "sensitive payments?"

To deal with these complex issues, Donaldson appeals to the notion of a human right to establish minimum requirements for morally acceptable behavior in multinational settings. Respecting very basic rights, it turns out, entails a number of duties, duties not merely not to harm others, but positive duties to assist in protecting workers, customers, and the public from harm. Donaldson carries his arguments further. In order to settle conflicts of norms without resolving all cultural disputes in terms of one's own cultural norms, or acquiescing to practices one ordinarily finds morally questionable, Donaldson develops what he calls a two-step moral algorithm that takes into account basic rights, economic development of the country in which one is operating, and an analysis of the norms of the host and home countries. Such an algorithm rejects relativism in multinational decision making while respecting cultural and national differences.

The case study "H. B. Fuller" raises a complex set of issues. Fuller is a well-managed company with the highest ethical standards. Indeed, in 1995 the company won the *Forbes Magazine* prize for corporate ethics. But when what Fuller thought was an innocent product, glue, was sniffed as a drug by Honduran children, they were faced with a number of ethical dilemmas. Should the company continue to manufacture a product in a country where children have easy access to the product and misuse it? Do multinationals have social responsibilities to the country in which they operate, responsibilities that go beyond merely manufacturing safe products and include such matters as alleviating poverty, improving educational standards, and the like?

Truth Telling

The concept of truth telling can be used to investigate a wide variety of issues, including those relating to non-deceptive advertising, the accuracy of consumer information, and the responsibilities a business has to communicate honestly with its employees and stockholders. A philosopher well-known for his vigorous defense of truth telling is the eighteenth-century German philosopher Immanuel Kant. In this section, selections from his *Lectures on Ethics* are presented in which Kant claims that truth telling is an essential feature of morally right communication. Kant equates honesty both with frankness and reserve, and supports the principle of never telling a lie on three grounds. First, the principle of truth telling is one which each of us would like everyone else to follow. In other words, it is a principle that philosophers call "universalizable," meaning that each of us would like to see it universally followed by all human beings. Second, truth telling is a necessary element for society because all societies depend upon mutual bonds of honesty and truthfulness to enforce their unity and orderly continuation. Finally, lying destroys the major sources of human development—that is, knowledge—since it thwarts the discovery of new truths.

In contrast with Kant, Albert Carr, in his lively article, "Is Business Bluffing Ethical?" suggests that the moral requirement of truth telling depends on the context in which the activity takes place. For example, in advertising, although few advertisers actually lie about their products, many advertisements "puff" their products or make unfair comparisons between their product and the competition. This is all right, according to Carr, because everyone understands the "game" of advertising and no one is really fooled by the puffery.

Because perfect market information, or in Kant's terms, the "whole truth," is never obtainable, it is usually impossible to determine whether an advertiser or person is bluffing or lying. So it is not always to the economic advantage of business to reveal the "whole truth" about a product or service, nor is it unprofitable to engage in competitive bluffing when other businesses are doing so. Despite Carr's persuasive arguments, many advertisers as well as other business persons and philosophers are worried about the impact of the "game" of advertising on the public. Is bluffing or puffery justified when some persons affected by them do not understand the game and are deceived or misled?

If Carr's game analogy is questionable in advertising, the reader might want to consider its application to other aspects of business. Does the analogy ever justify making an exception to Kant's dictum that one should never lie? The case study "Italian Tax Mores" presents a situation in which truth telling, as well as relativism, are major issues. The case concerns an American executive managing a branch of a U.S. bank in Italy, who finds that typical Italian practices encourage actions that he believes constitute both bribery and lying. Is it morally acceptable to misrepresent the bank's income tax figures if it appears that most other companies in Italy do the same thing, and if truth telling will do harm to the bank? As a matter of self-defense, should the executive "play the game" and adopt the practices of the Italian tax system when those practices involve outright lying? Or can the manager justify providing the truth to the Italian tax authorities even when this might threaten the well-being of his bank?

Virtues
and
the Virtuous Manager

• *Case Study* •

RUN, Inc.

AMERICAN INSTITUTE OF CERTIFIED PUBLIC ACCOUNTANTS

The work of preparing the 1991 financial statements for RUN, Inc., was largely complete and the company's Controller, Martin Field, recognized that this final reading of the draft statements was a critical time. Once the statements were released to the printer and distribution was begun there would be no chance for second thoughts. He had been on the job at RUN, Inc. for only five months, but they had been the most tumultuous months of his career. Now all of that tumult was coming down to this single February afternoon. He was proud of the work he had done in cleaning up the Company's balance sheet, and he had satisfied himself that there would be no more unpleasant surprises in that area. He had also pretty well convinced himself that the compromise which had been developed by the CEO for the presentation of the Income Statement was acceptable, but compromises had always made him uncomfortable. It was soon going to be time to accept that compromise or do something else—although what the something else might be was not really clear.

The Company

RUN, Inc. manufactured and marketed a variety of products and parts for automobiles, from starters, alternators and brakes to complete replacement interiors. The Company had originally been known as Rebuilt and Used Auto Parts, Inc. but the acronym RUN had been adopted as the Company's name when the product line was expanded to include new replacement parts and other auto accessories. Sales had been good during the early 1980's as interest rates and credit problems discouraged people from buying new cars and encouraged them to repair and rehabilitate their existing cars. As consumer confidence waned in the later eighties and early nineties, even the upgrading process came under pressure and the company's spectacular sales curve began to flatten out. Still, the company had been well received by the financial markets and the stock traded (on NASDAQ) at an attractive multiple. (Earnings data and stock price activity for the period 1987–91 is detailed in Exhibit I.)

The company sold its products primarily to independent and chain auto parts retailers in the Southeast. Most of the products in the Company's line were either rebuilt from parts which had been scrapped or were manufactured by RUN to meet original equipment specifications. The Company also sold parts and accessories manufactured by offshore suppliers. There were several other companies in the field about the same size as RUN and there was very little to distinguish one firm's rebuilt starter (for example) from another. RUN stressed its distribution system and its prompt delivery as its competitive advantage. The company's primary facilities were in Montgomery, Alabama, but 12 warehouses had been established at strategic locations throughout the Southeast.

RUN's management team included The Chairman (and founder) Harry White; the Chief Executive Officer, John Harvey; the Sales VP, Joanne Jones; the Operations VP, Tex Armor; and the Secretary/Treasurer (and Harry's wife), Mary White. All of those people were members of the Board of Directors, together with a partner in the company's law firm, and a vice-president from the company's bank. Both of those men were long time friends of the Whites, and had been associated with the company since its earliest days. The management team was a close knit group and met frequently for working lunches. Because of the strength of that working relationship, and the strength of the White's personalities, the Board was not significant to the structure of the firm. Board meetings tended to be formalities, where the results of the previous period and plans for the next period were reviewed and approved.

The company's accounting functions were Mary White's responsibility but the day-to-day accounting activities had been the primary responsibility of Lester Foote, until his retirement in the summer of 1991. Martin Field assumed those day-to-day responsibilities in October, 1991, with the title of Controller. He had taken the job with the understanding that he would become CFO and Treasurer in two years when the Whites were planning to step out of active involvement in the firm.

Earlier, Martin Field had been able to land a job with the the Atlanta office of a major CPA firm as a junior auditor. He easily passed the CPA exam on the first try and moved through the ranks of his firm. As he moved up in the firm he found that he was measured against different and more intangible standards: he was expected to resolve accounting problems with client managements at higher and higher levels, and he was asked to look aggressively for opportunities where the firm's tax and consulting services might be brought to bear on clients' business problems. He didn't really like the new marketing-type responsibility he was being asked to undertake, and because he was uncomfortable in that role he did not do it very well. When one of the firm's partners pointed him to an assistant controller's job with one of Atlanta's most prestigious companies, Martin jumped at the chance.

In that new job, Martin was responsible for the preparation of the company's annual and quarterly filings with the SEC, and was the company's primary liaison with the external auditors. It was easy for him to learn the annual reporting process from the other side of the desk and after several years he was bored. He decided that he wanted to get into the financing aspect of business and to move toward a CFO position.

Martin first heard about RUN when a headhunter, looking for a replacement for Lester Foote, called in early 1991. After some initial interviews, the

Company expressed real interest in Martin and he was sorely tempted. The Company's suggestion, that he start as controller and then in two years move up to CFO, seemed to be exactly what he had in mind. Still, he wavered because he was uncomfortable with what he took to be a very unstructured management environment. He reasoned that that nonchalant environment was partly a reflection of the family-style management the company had experienced in its early years, and partly the shirt sleeve nature of the industry. John Harvey assured him that the company's management style was evolving and would continue to become more business-like as the Whites phased out into retirement and played a decreasing role in the firm. Martin understood that the industry would always be a little rough and tumble, but those concerns were somewhat offset by the company's very attractive salary offer. He was finally convinced to take the job when the Whites offered him a five year option to buy 5,000 shares of stock in the firm at $1.50 a share.

Earlier, when Martin had first left public practice, he had carefully weighed the cost of maintaining his membership in the AICPA and his state society. Ultimately he decided to retain those memberships because he was proud of his CPA status, and because those memberships gave him a network of professional associates and brought him journal subscriptions. He also complied with the Continuing Professional Education requirements imposed by his state society and the AICPA, because he felt it was important that he keep his skills up to date. He had joined the Institute of Management Accountants when he first took the assistant controller's job and he found their publications to be of interest as well. When he decided to take the job with RUN, he checked into the membership requirements for the Financial Executives Institute, but found that they would not consider him until he achieved the CFO position.

Problems With the Prior Financials

During Martin's first week on the job, in early October 1991, he studied the firm's systems and began to get into the details of the accounts. In one sense he was pleased that the year-end was fast approaching; he understood that the effort of pulling together the financial statements for the first time would force him to understand the numbers in depth, in a hurry. For example, he was concerned that the inventories seemed to be very high—even for a firm which prided itself on prompt service—and the receivables had been growing much faster than sales. The audit process would surely flush out any problems which might be lurking in those slow turn-over numbers.

After he had been on the job for about three weeks, Martin was invited to a working lunch staff meeting which included all of the other senior executives. He was asked for his impressions after his short time on board. He expressed his concern about the levels of inventory and receivables, and said that in preparation for the year-end audit he planned to visit the warehouses and study the receivables files. Mr. White broke in and told him that it would be better for him to stay around home for a while and be sure he had the lay of the land. He said, "We each take care of our own areas of expertise around here—that's what has gotten us to where we are today. Tex will worry about operations and the inventory, Joanne will worry about the customers and receivables, and you just worry about accounting. We'll all get along fine."

Martin decided to go along for a while but on his own began to do some analysis of the company's operating and balance sheet numbers, comparing them to industry data he was able to get from Dun and Bradstreet. What he saw heightened his concerns (See Exhibit II). He went to see John Harvey and showed him the ratio data he had developed. John expressed surprise at the company's performance against the industry, but said, "We have always been a customer-oriented firm, and we have not let financial details get in the way of service. It may be that we will have to exercise a little more control than we have in the past. And you can help us do that—we're glad you are here." Martin reminded him that the auditors would be in soon and that they would be looking at both receivables and inventory. Martin mused, "Maybe I'll ask them to really get into the details this year, to help us get a good understanding of where we are." John simply waved Martin on.

The next day, John Harvey called Martin into his office. All of the officers of RUN were there, even Mr. and Mrs. White. Mr. White led off, saying, "Martin, we think you are entitled to know what has been going on here. We have all been concerned about the slow-down in the economy caused by those idiots in Washington. Sales have been harder and harder to get, and we have been concerned that the stock price would be badly hurt by any drop-off in our results. I don't have to tell you that this is an important time for the firm, what with Mary and me planning to phase out and sell off some of our holdings. After all we have done to build this firm over the last 25 years we could not let the stock price slip at this critical juncture—I'm not sure you understand that. To keep the price where it belongs, we have been forced to work the books a bit. I'm not sure of the numbers, but some of those receivables you have been so concerned about are the result of sales that we are sure will happen, and some of that inventory is stuff that we have shipped but not yet recorded as cost of goods sold. We knew that eventually things would have to turn around—and they are beginning to do so now. In the next several years, as operations pick back up, we will work those borrowed profits out of receivables and inventories. We decided that you would figure it all out yourself soon enough, and so we thought we had better tell you what you will find."

Martin felt a little weak in the knees. His anger cleared his head however and he said, "Borrowed profits, indeed! You have to face up to those misstatements now. If you can't agree to clean up all of that stuff, I'm going to have to resign. Decide now!" There was an awkward silence, but John Harvey eventually spoke up; he told Martin to work with Tex and Joanne and figure out the dollar effect of the problems and prepare the 1991 financial statements on the assumption that all of those past misstatements would be resolved this year.

Over the next several weeks, Martin picked up worksheets from Tex and Joanne which suggested that the preliminary December 31, 1991 balance sheet included $10 million in receivables and inventory which would have to be written off. Neither of them was exactly sure as to when the results-inflating entries had been recorded but, based on some sketchy notes they had in their files, Tex and Joanne estimated that $5 million of the errors had been booked in the prior quarters of 1991; $3.5 million had been booked in 1990; and $1.5 million had been booked in 1989. Using the data Tex and Joanne provided,

Martin prepared the three year income statements required for the 10-K showing these adjustments as "Corrections of Errors." (See Exhibit III.)

When he showed those results to John Harvey, John blanched. He said, "Martin we can't do that. No one is really sure which years are affected, in what amounts. Besides, if we report that we are adjusting the earnings we reported in prior years, we will lose all credibility with our stockholders. Because of the economy, the results we have been forced to report have been depressing anyway, and if we add a new insult to the existing injury, we will probably get sued. I can't let the Whites wrap up their careers here with that hanging over their heads. If we can't work out another way of putting that $10 million behind us, we'll have to find a way to bleed it in over the next several years. The economy *is* picking up you know." When Martin started to protest, John went on, "Why don't we just charge all of that stuff off this year as a restructuring charge and say that we are taking a belt-tightening approach to the business. If we do that right, the stock price might even go up—I've seen that happen to other companies."

John Harvey had Martin's draft re-typed, pulling the $10 million into 1991 as an unusual item. John also drafted a note which described that charge as a result of a fresh look at inventory and receivables (See the revised statements and the draft note in Exhibit IV), and took the package to show to Mr. and Mrs. White. Later, Mrs. White came to see Martin and told him how pleased she was that he had forced the company to clean house. She said that she was glad that these problems would be resolved now because she had always worried about what people would say if the company had been forced to take a big write-off the year after she retired. She commented that this was one year she would be happy to sign the 10-K, saying "Next year you can sign off as the person responsible for the statements, but please let me have this satisfaction this year." The income statement with the special charge in 1991 was presented to the CPA firm for their audit.

As the audit progressed, the partner and manager asked about the special charge, and Martin explained that because he was going to be responsible for the December 31, 1991 balance sheet as the starting point for 1992, he had insisted that that balance sheet be as clean as possible. He referred the auditors to John Harvey's draft footnote as a further explanation for the big write-off. However, he also took the CPAs to lunch at an out-of-the-way place and suggested that they look very carefully at the receivables and inventory items that were written off in that special charge. He reminded the auditors that he was new on the job and didn't have all of the details, but that "some of those things in that write-off don't pass the smell test." In a subsequent meeting with Martin and John Harvey, the CPAs challenged the special-item treatment for the write-offs. John explained his belt-tightening philosophy, and when the CPAs nodded sympathetically, Martin sat quietly, saying nothing.

That had been two weeks ago. The external audit team had completed their work and had reported that the balance sheet was as clean as Martin had said. They accepted the income statement presentation for the $10 million, treating it as a special charge—one of the staff people referred to it as a "change in estimate." All of the documentation for the audit was completed: the attorneys' letters were in, the important confirmations had all been returned and Mr. and Mrs. White and John Harvey had signed the usual representation letter for the CPA firm. The typed financial statement package was on Martin's desk ready for one final reading before being delivered to the printer. The statements were scheduled to be mailed to the shareholders the next day, and would be reviewed at the shareholders' meeting two weeks from today. Martin poured himself another cup of coffee and sat down to read the statements carefully one more time.

EXHIBIT I. RUN, Inc.: Five Year Income and Stock Price Data (000)

	1991*	1990	1989	1988	1987
SALES	$75,000	$68,000	$58,000	$45,000	$35,000
growth rate, ty/ly	10.3%	17.2%	28.9%	28.6%	
COST OF SALES	$39,500	$35,500	$30,000	$22,500	$17,000
% of sales	52.7%	52.2%	51.7%	50.0%	48.6%
EXPENSES	$18,500	$17,500	$16,250	$13,500	$11,000
EARNINGS PRE TAX	$17,000	$15,000	$11,750	$9,000	$7,000
% of sales	22.7%	22.1%	20.3%	20.0%	20.0%
growth rate, ty/ly	13.3%	27.7%	30.6%	28.6%	
EARNINGS AFTER TAX	$11,050	$9,300	$7,050	$5,220	$4,060
% of sales	14.7%	13.7%	12.2%	11.6%	11.6%
growth rate, ty/ly	18.8%	31.9%	35.1%	28.6%	
EARNINGS PER SHARE	$0.111	$0.095	$0.074	$0.055	$0.051
MIDDLE OF STOCK PRICE RANGE	$1.44	$1.33	$1.11	$0.77	$0.61
multiple	13	14	15	14	12

*The estimated results for 1991 are the numbers expected by the market, based on the results reported through the first nine months, and trends in the industry. The company's book numbers, before consideration of any adjustments discussed in the case, were very cose to these estimates.

ty/ly means that the ratio is the growth rate from last year to this.

EXHIBIT II. RUN Inc.: Comparative Ratio Analysis

	RUN data		Industry data	
	1991	1990	1991	1990
Return on sales, %	14.7%	13.7%	11.8%	10.7%
Asset turnover	.58	.54	.66	.58
Days sales outstanding	161	166	141	155
Inventory turn	.70	.65	.82	.74

EXHIBIT III. RUN, Inc.: Five Year Income Statement (000)

	1991	1990	1989	1988	1987
SALES	$75,000	$68,000	$58,000	$45,000	$35,000
growth rate, ty/ly	10.3%	17.2%	28.9%	28.6%	
COST OF SALES	$39,500	$35,500	$30,000	$22,500	$17,000
% of sales	52.7%	52.2%	51.7%	50.0%	48.6%
EXPENSES	$18,500	$17,500	$16,250	$13,500	$11,000
EARNINGS PRE TAX	$17,000	$15,000	$11,750	$9,000	$7,000
% of sales	22.7%	22.1%	20.3%	20.0%	20.0%
growth rate, ty/ly	13.3%	27.7%	30.6%	28.6%	
EARNINGS AFTER TAX	$11,050	$9,300	$7,050	$5,220	$4,060
% of sales	14.7%	13.7%	12.2%	11.6%	11.6%
growth rate, ty/ly	18.8%	31.9%	35.1%	28.6%	
CORRECTION OF ERROR (after tax)	$3,250	$2,170	900		
NET EARNINGS	$7,800	$7,130	$6,150	$5,220	$4,060
EARNINGS PER SHARE:					
Before error correction	$0.110	$0.094	$0.074	$0.055	$0.051
After error correction	$0.078	$0.073	$0.065	$0.055	$0.051

EXHIBIT IV. RUN, Inc.: Five Year Income Statement (000)

	1991		1990		1989		1988		1987	
SALES	$75,000		$68,000		$58,000		$45,000		$35,000	
growth rate, ty/ly		10.3%		17.2%		28.9%		28.6%		48.6%
COST OF SALES	$39,500		$35,500		$30,000		$22,500		$17,000	
% of sales		52.7%		52.2%		51.7%		50.0%		
EXPENSES	$18,500		$17,500		$16,250		$13,500		$11,000	
SPECIAL CHARGE	$10,000		0		0		0			
EARNINGS PRE TAX	$ 7,000		$15,000		$11,750		$ 9,000		$ 7,000	
% of sales		9.3%		22.1%		20.3%		20.0%		20.0%
growth rate, ty/ly		−53.3%		27.7%		30.6%		28.6%		
EARNINGS AFTER TAX	$ 4,550		$ 9,300		$ 7,050		$ 5,220		$ 4,060	
% of sales		6.1%		13.7%		12.2%		11.6%		11.6%
growth rate, ty/ly		−51.1%		31.9%		35.1%		28.6%		
EARNINGS PER SHARE	$0.046		$0.095		$0.074		$0.055		$0.051	

Financial Statement Footnote

SPECIAL CHARGE
Because of the continued decline in the economy, the company determined to challenge the levels of the assets it would carry forward into the next year, and in fourth quarter of 1991 took an objective look at receivables and inventories. That fresh look, together with an understanding that business operations in the future will be more rigorous than they have been in the past years, resulted in a writedown of excess inventory and slow paying receivables. The company believes that the writedown was necessary to account for those assets at the lower of cost or market, as market conditions are perceived today.

**EXHIBIT IV. RUN, Inc.: Extracts from the AICPA Code,
Applicable to the Case**

ARTICLE II—THE PUBLIC INTEREST

Members should accept the obligation to act in a way that will serve the public interest, honor the public trust, and demonstrate commitment to professionalism.

.01 A distinguishing mark of a profession is acceptance of its responsibility to the public. The accounting profession's public consists of clients, credit grantors, governments, employers, investors, the business and financial community, and others who rely on the objectivity and integrity of certified public accountants to maintain the orderly functioning of commerce. This reliance imposes a public interest responsibility on certified public accountants. The public interest is defined as the collective well-being of the community of people and institutions the profession serves.

.02 In discharging their professional responsibilities, members may encounter conflicting pressures from among each of those groups. In resolving those conflicts, members should act with integrity, guided by the precept that when members fulfill their responsibility to the public, clients' and employers' interests are best served.

.03 Those who rely on certified public accountants expect them to discharge their responsibilities with integrity, objectivity, due professional care, and a genuine interest in serving the public. They are expected to provide quality services, enter into fee arrangements, and offer a range of services—all in a manner that demonstrates a level of professionalism consistent with these Principles of the Code of Professional Conduct.

.04 All who accept membership in the American Institute of Certified Public Accountants commit themselves to honor the public trust. In return for the faith that the public reposes in them, members should seek continually to demonstrate their dedication to professional excellence.

ARTICLE III—INTEGRITY

To maintain and broaden public confidence, members should perform all professional responsibilities with the highest sense of integrity.

.01 Integrity is an element of character fundamental to professional recognition. It is the quality from which the public trust derives and the benchmark against which a member must ultimately test all decisions.

.02 Integrity requires a member to be, among other things, honest and candid within the constraints of client confidentiality. Service and the public trust should not be subordinated to personal gain and advantage. Integrity can accommodate the inadvertent error and the honest difference of opinion; it cannot accommodate deceit or subordination of principle.

.03 Integrity is measured in terms of what is right and just. In the absence of specific rules, standards, or guidance, or in the face of conflicting opinions, a member should test decisions and deeds by asking: "Am I doing what a person of integrity would do? Have I retained my integrity?" Integrity requires a member to observe both the form and the spirit of technical and ethical standards; circumvention of those standards constitutes subordination of judgment.

.04 Integrity also requires a member to observe the principles of objectivity and independence and of due care.

ARTICLE IV—OBJECTIVITY AND INDEPENDENCE

A member should maintain objectivity and be free of conflicts of interest in discharging professional responsibilities. A member in public practice should be independent in fact and appearance when providing auditing and other attestation services.

.01 Objectivity is a state of mind, a quality that lends value to a member's services. It is a distinguishing feature of the profession. The principle of objectivity imposes the obligation to be impartial, intellectually honest, and free of conflicts of interest. Independence precludes relationships that may appear to impair a member's objectivity in rendering attestation services.

.02 Members often serve multiple interests in many different capacities and must demonstrate their objectivity in varying circumstances. Members in public practice render attest, tax, and management advisory services. Other members prepare financial statements in the employment of others, perform internal auditing services, and serve in financial and management capacities in industry, education, and government. They also educate and train those who aspire to admission into the profession. Regardless of service or capacity, members should protect the integrity of their work, maintain objectivity, and avoid any subordination of their judgment.

.03 For a member in public practice, the maintenance of objectivity and independence requires a continuing assessment of client relationships and public responsibility. Such a member who provides auditing and other attestation sevices should be independent in fact and appearance. In providing all other services, a member should maintain objectivity and avoid conflicts of interest.

.04 Although members not in public practice cannot maintain the appearance of independence, they nevertheless have the responsibility to maintain objectivity in rendering professional services. Members employed by others to prepare financial statements or to perform auditing, tax, or consulting services are charged with the same responsibility for objectivity as members in public practice and must be scrupulous in their application of generally accepted accounting principles and candid in all their dealings with members in public practice.

**EXHIBIT IVA. RUN, Inc.: Extracts from the AICPA Ethics
Rules and Interpretations—Section 102**

INTEGRITY AND OBJECTIVITY

.01 Rule 102—Integrity and objectivity. In the performance of any professional service, a member shall maintain objectivity and integrity, shall be free of conflicts of interest, and shall not knowingly misrepresent facts or subordinate his or her judgment to others. [As adopted January 12, 1988.]

Interpretations under Rule 102—Integrity and Objectivity

Interpretations and Ethics Rulings which existed before the adoption of the Code of Professional Conduct on January 12, 1988, will remain in effect until further action is deemed necessary by the appropriate senior technical committee.

.02 102-1—Knowing misrepresentations in the preparation of financial statements or records. A member who knowingly makes, or permits or directs another to make, false and misleading entries in an entity's financial statements or records shall be considered to have knowingly misrepresented facts in violation of rule 102 [ET section 102.01].

.03 102-2—Conflicts of interest. A conflict of interest may occur if a member performs a professional service for a client or employer and the member or his or her firm has a significant relationship with another person, entity, product, or service that could be viewed as impairing the member's objectivity. If this significant relationship is disclosed to and consent is obtained from such client, employer, or other appropriate parties, the rule shall not operate to prohibit the performance of the professional service. When making the disclosure, the member should consider rule 301, "Confidential Client Information" [ET section 301.01].

Certain professional engagements require independence. Independence impairments under rule 101 [ET section 101.01] and its interpretations cannot be eliminated by such disclosure and consent.
[Effective August 31, 1989.]

.04 102-3—Obligations of member to his or her employer's external accountant. Under rule 102 [ET section 102.01], a member must maintain objectivity and integrity in the performance of a professional service. In dealing with his or her employer's external accountant, a member must be candid and not knowingly misrepresent facts or knowingly fail to disclose material facts. This would include, for example, responding to specific inquiries for which his or her employer's external accountant requests written representation.
[Effective November 30, 1993.]

.05 102-4—Subordination of judgment by a member. Rule 102 [ET section 102.01] prohibits a member from knowingly misrepresenting

facts or subordinating his or her judgment when performing professional services. Under this rule, if a member and his or her supervisor have a
disagreement or dispute relating to the preparation of financial statements or the recording of transactions, the member should take the following steps to ensure that the situation does not constitute a subordination of judgment:[1]

1. The member should consider whether (a) the entry or the failure to record
   a transaction in the records, or (b) the financial statement presentation or
   the nature or omission of disclosure in the financial statements, as proposed
   by the supervisor, represents the use of an acceptable alternative and does
   not materially misrepresent the facts. If, after appropriate research or consultation, the member concludes that the matter has authoritative support
   and/or does not result in a material misrepresentation, the member need
   do nothing further.

2. If the member concludes that the financial statements or records could be
   materially misstated, the member should make his or her concerns known
   to the appropriate higher level(s) of management within the organization
   (for example, the supervisor's immediate superior, senior management, the
   audit committee or equivalent, the board of directors, the company's owners). The member should consider documenting his or her undertanding of
   the facts, the accounting principles involved, the application of those principles to the facts, and the parties with whom these matters were discussed.

3. If, after discussing his or her concerns with the appropriate person(s) in the
   organization, the member concludes that appropriate action was not taken,
   he or she should consider his or her continuing relationship with the employer. The member also should consider any responsibility that may exist to
   communicate to third parties, such as regulatory authorities or the employer's (former employer's) external accountant. In this connection, the member may wish to consult with his or her legal counsel.

4. The member should at all times be cognizant of his or her obligations under
   interpretation 102-3 [ET section 101.04].

[Effective November 30, 1993.]

ACCOUNTING PRINCIPLES

.01 Rule 203—Accounting principles. A member shall not (1) express an opinion or state affirmatively that the financial statements or
other financial data of any entity are presented in conformity with generally accepted accounting principles or (2) state that he or she is not
aware of any material modifications that should be made to such statements or data in order for them to be in conformity with generally accepted accounting principles, if such statements or data contain any departure from an accounting principle promulgated by bodies designated
by Council to establish such principles that has a material effect on the
statements or data taken as a whole. If, however, the statements or data
contain such a departure and the member can demonstrate that due to
unusual circumstances the financial statements or data would otherwise
have been misleading, the member can comply with the rule by describ-

ing the departure, its approximate effects, if practicable, and the reasons why compliance with the principle would result in a misleading statement.

[As adopted January 12, 1988.]

Interpretations under Rule 203—Accounting Principles

Interpretations and Ethics Rulings which existed before the adoption of the Code of Professional Conduct on January 12, 1988, will remain in effect until further action is deemed necessary by the appropriate senior technical committee.

.02 203-1—Departures from established accounting principles. Rule 203 [ET section 203.01] was adopted to require compliance with accounting principles promulgated by the body designated by Council to establish such principles. There is a strong presumption that adherence to officially established accounting principles would in nearly all instances result in financial statements that are not misleading.

However, in the establishment of accounting principles it is difficult to anticipate all of the circumstances to which such principles might be applied. This rule therefore recognizes that upon occasion there may be unusual circumstances where the literal application of pronouncements on accounting principles would have the effect of rendering financial statements misleading. In such cases, the proper accounting treatment is that which will render the financial statements not misleading.

The question of what constitutes unusual circumstances as referred to in rule 203 [ET section 203.01] is a matter of professional judgment involving the ability to support the position that adherence to a promulgated principle would be regarded generally by reasonable men as producing a misleading result.

Examples of events which may justifiy departures from a principle are new legislation or the evolution of a new form of business transaction. An unusual degree of materiality or the existence of conflicting industry practices are examples of circumstances which would not ordinarily be regarded as unusual in the context of rule 203 [ET section 203.01].

.03 203-2—Status of FASB interpretations. Council is authorized under rule 203 [ET section 203.01] to designate a body to establish accounting principles and has designated the Financial Accounting Standards Board as such body. Council also has resolved that FASB Statements of Financial Accounting Standards, together with those Accounting Research Bulletins and APB Opinions which are not superseded by action of the FASB, constitute accounting principles as contemplated in rule 203 [ET section 203.01].

In determining the existence of a departure from an accounting principle established by a Statement of Financial Accounting Standards, Accounting Research Bulletin or APB Opinion encompassed by rule 203 [ET section 203.01], the division of professional ethics will construe such Statement, Bulletin or Opinion in the light of any interpretations thereof issued by the FASB.

[.04] [203-3] [Deleted]

.05 203-4—Responsibility of employees for the preparation of financial statements in conformity with GAAP, Rule 203 [ET section 203.01] provides, in part, that a member shall not state affirmatively that financial statements or other financial data of an entity are presented in conformity with generally accepted accounting principles (GAAP) if such statements or data contain any departure from an accounting principle promulgated by a body designated by Council to establish such principles that has a material effect on the statements or data taken as a whole.

Rule 203 [ET section 203.01] applies to all members with respect to any affirmation that financial statements or other financial data are presented in conformity with GAAP. Representation regarding GAAP conformity included in a letter or other communication from a client entity to its auditor or others related to that entity's financial statements is subject to rule 203 [ET section 203.01] and may be considered an affirmative statement within the meaning of the rule with respect to members who signed the letter or other communication; for example, signing reports to regulatory authorities, creditors and auditors.

[Effective November 30, 1993.]

Note

1. A member in the practice of public accounting should refer to the Statements on Auditing Standards. For example, see SAS No. 22, *Planning and Supervision* [AU section 311], which discusses what the auditor should do when there are differences of opinion concerning accounting and auditing standards.

EXHIBIT V. RUN, Inc.: Standards of Ethical Conduct for Management Accountants

STANDARDS OF ETHICAL CONDUCT FOR MANAGEMENT ACCOUNTANTS

Management accountants have an obligation to the organizations they serve, their profession, the public, and themselves to maintain the highest standards of ethical conduct. In recognition of this obligation, the National Association of Accountants has promulgated the following standards of ethical conduct for management accountants. Adherence to these standards is integral to achieving the *Objectives of Management Accounting.*[1] Management accountants shall not commit acts contrary to these standards nor shall they condone the commission of such acts by others within their organizations.

Competence

Management accountants have a responsibility to:

- Maintain an appropriate level of professional competence by ongoing development of their knowledge and skills.
- Perform their professional duties in accordance with relevant laws, regulations, and technical standards.
- Prepare complete and clear reports and recommendations after appropriate analyses of relevant and reliable information.

Confidentiality

Management accountants have a responsibility to:

- Refrain from disclosing confidential information acquired in the course of their work except when authorized, unless legally obligated to do so.
- Inform subordinates as appropriate regarding the confidentiality of information acquired in the course of their work and monitor their activities to assure the maintenance of that confidentiality.
- Refrain from using or appearing to use confidential information acquired in the course of their work for unethical or illegal advantage either personally or through third parties.

Integrity

Management accountants have a responsibility to:

- Avoid actual or apparent conflicts of interest and advise all appropriate parties of any potential conflict.
- Refrain from engaging in any activity that would prejudice their ability to carry out their duties ethically.
- Refuse any gift, favor, or hospitality that would influence or would appear to influence their actions.
- Refrain from either actively or passively subverting the attainment of the organization's legitimate and ethical objectives.
- Recognize and communicate professional limitations or other constraints that would preclude responsible judgment or successful performance of an activity.
- Communicate unfavorable as well as favorable information and professional judgments or opinions.
- Refrain from engaging in or supporting any activity that would discredit the profession.

Objectivity

Management accountants have a responsibility to:

- Communicate information fairly and objectively.
- Disclose fully all relevant information that could reasonably be expected to influence an intended user's understanding of the reports, comments, and recommendations presented.

Resolution of Ethical Conflict

In applying the standards of ethical conduct, management accountants may encounter problems in identifying unethical behavior or in resolving an ethical conflict. When faced with significant ethical issues, management accountants should follow the established policies of the organization bearing on the resolution of such conflict. If these policies do not resolve the ethical conflict, management accountants should consider the following course of action:

- Discuss such problems with the immediate superior except when it appears that the superior is involved, in which case the problem should be presented initially to the next higher managerial level. If satisfactory resolution cannot be achieved when the problem is initially presented, submit the issues to the next higher managerial level.

    If the immediate superior is the chief executive officer, or equivalent, the acceptable reviewing authority may be a group such as the audit committee, board of directors, board of trustees, or owners. Contact with levels above the immediate superior should be initiated only with the superior's knowledge, assuming the superior is not involved.

- Clarify relevant concepts by confidential discussion with an objective advisor to obtain an understanding of possible courses of action.

- If the ethical conflict still exists after exhausting all levels of internal review, the management accountant may have no other recourse on significant matters than to resign from the organization and to submit an informative memorandum to an appropriate representative of the organization.

Except where legally prescribed, communication of such problems to authorities or individuals not employed or engaged by the organization is not considered appropriate.

Note

1. National Association of Accountants. *Statements on Management Accounting: Objectives of Management Accounting.* Statement No. 1B, New York, N.Y., June 17, 1982.

EXHIBIT VI. RUN, Inc.: Code of Ethics for the Membership of the Financial Executives Institute

CODE OF ETHICS

To be eligible for active membership in Financial Executives Institute, applicants must possess those personal attributes such as character, personal integrity and business ability that will be an asset to the Institute. They must also meet pre-established criteria indicating a high degree of participation in the formulation of policies for the operation of the enterprises they represent and in the administration of the financial functions. Members of the Institute are expected to follow this Code of Ethics.

As a member of Financial Executives Institute, I will:

Conduct my business and personal affairs at all times with honesty and integrity.

Provide complete, appropriate and relevant information in an objective manner when reporting to management, stockholders, employees, government agencies, other institutions and the public.

Comply with rules and regulations of federal, state, provincial, and local governments, and other appropriate private and public regulatory agencies.

Discharge duties and responsibilities to my employer to the best of my ability, including complete communication on all matters within my jurisdiction.

Maintain the confidentiality of information acquired in the course of my work except when authorized or otherwise legally obligated to disclose. Confidential information acquired in the course of my work will not be used for my personal advantage.

Maintain an appropriate level of professional competence through continuing development of my knowledge and skills.

Refrain from committing acts discreditable to myself, my employer, FEI or fellow members of the Institute.

Corporate Roles, Personal Virtues:
An Aristotelean Approach to Business Ethics

ROBERT C. SOLOMON

Each of us is ultimately lonely. In the end, it's up to each of us and each of us alone to figure out who we are and who we are not, and to act more or less consistently on those conclusions.

—TOM PETERS "The Ethical Debate"
Ethics Digest Dec 1989, p. 2.

We are gratefully past that embarrassing period when the very title of a lecture on "business ethics" invited—no, required—those malapert responses, "sounds like an oxymoron" or "must be a very short lecture." Today, business ethics is well-established not only in the standard curriculum in philosophy in most departments but, more impressively, it is recommended or required in most of the leading business schools in North America, and it is even catching

Reprinted by permission of the author, Robert C. Solomon, University of Texas at Austin, and *Business Ethics Quarterly*, October 1993, Vol. 2, Issue 3, the Journal of the Society for Business Ethics.

on in Europe (one of the too rare instances of intellectual commerce in that direction). Studies in business ethics have now reached what Tom Donaldson has called "the third wave," beyond the hurried-together and overly-philosophical introductory textbooks and collections of too-obvious concrete case studies, to serious engagement in the business world. Conferences filled half-and-half with business executives and academics are common, and in-depth studies based on immersion in the corporate world, e.g. Robert Jackall's powerful *Moral Mazes,* have replaced more simple-minded and detached glosses on "capitalism" and "social responsibility." Business ethics has moved beyond vulgar "business as poker" arguments to an arena where serious ethical theory is no longer out-of-place but seriously sought out and much in demand.

The problem with business ethics now is not vulgar ignorance but a far more sophisticated confusion concerning exactly what the subject is supposed to do and how (to employ a much overworked contrast) the theory applies to the practice of business. Indeed, a large part of the problem is that it is by no means clear what a theory in business ethics is supposed to look like or whether there is, as such, any such theoretical enterprise. It has been standard practice in many business ethics courses and—whether cause or effect—in most standard textbooks, to begin with a survey of ethical theory. This means, inevitably, a brief summary of Kant and deontological ethics, a brief survey of utilitarianism with a note or two about John Stuart Mill and a distinction or two between act and rule, pleasure versus preference utilitarianism and some replay of the much-rehearsed contest between the two sorts of theories. Given the business context, liberatarianism or some form of contractualism is often included as a third contender. "Justice" is a natural introductory section, and John Locke on natural property rights is an appropriate inclusion too. But is this the theory of business ethics? Not only is the application to concrete business situations in question—and then the message to students is too often an unabashed relativism ("if you are a utilitarian, you'll do this, if you're a Kantian, you'll do that")—but it is not even clear whether there is, then, anything distinctive about *business* ethics. There is just ethics, or rather ethical theory, whatever that may be. Indeed, one is almost tempted to retreat to the tongue-in-cheek advice of Robert Townsend, former CEO of Avis and author of *Up the Organization,* that if a company needs a corporate code of ethics, it should tack up the Ten Commandments. And so with its success assured, at least for the time being, business ethics faces both a crisis of theory and a pragmatic challenge, that is, what is to count as a theory in business ethics and how that theory applies and can be used by flesh-and-blood managers in concrete, real life, ethically charged situations. . . .

THE ARISTOTELEAN APPROACH TO BUSINESS ETHICS

Economists and economic theorists naturally tend to look at systems and theories about systems, while ethicists tend to look at individual behavior, its motives and consequences. Neither of these approaches is suitable for business ethics. One of the problems in business ethics, accordingly, is the *scope* and *focus* of the disciplines and the proper *unit* of study and discourse. Much of the work in business ethics courses and seminars centers around "case studies," which almost always involve one or several particular people within the realm of a particular corporation in a particular industry facing some particular crisis or dilemma. Individual ethical values are, of course, relevant here, but they are rarely the focus of attention. Economics, of course, is essential to the discussion—since the realm of the corporation is, after all, a business, but the desire to show a profit is virtually taken for granted while our attention is drawn to other values. Insofar as business ethics theories tend to be drawn from either individualistic ethics or economics they remain remote from the case study method which often seems so inadequate with regard to more general implications and conclusions in business and why business ethics theory lags so far behind theory in both ethics and economics. In this paper, I want to begin to develop a more appropriate focus for business ethics theory, one that centers on *the individual within the corporation*. For reasons that should be evident to anyone who has had the standard Philosophy 102 History of Ethics course, I call this the Aristotelean Approach to Business Ethics.

In a book *It's Good Business,* I once distingushed between macro-, micro-, and molar ethics, and within this limited dichotomy it should be evident that I am going to argue for the neglected importance of micro-business-ethics—the concepts and values that define individual responsibilities and role behavior as opposed to the already well-developed theories of macro-business ethics—the principles and policies that govern or should govern our overall system of (re-)distribution and reward. (In ethics as such, one might argue, the neglect has taken the opposite twist, ignoring the larger social anthropological setting in favor of individual autonomy, rights and well-being.) The distinction between micro and macro is borrowed from and intended to be parallel to a similar dichotomy in economics. (I have elsewhere argued that economics is a branch of ethics, but that is another story.)[1] That distinction, however, is left over from the ancient days of Lord Keynes and is also inadequate. The integral or "molar" unit of commerce today is neither the individual entrepreneur or consumer nor the all-embracing system that still goes by the antiquated nineteenth century name "capitalism." It is the *corporation,* a type of entity barely mentioned by Adam Smith in a few dismissive sentences (and of minimal interest even to Keynes). While I will continue to hold that the existential unit of responsibility and concern is and remains the individual, the individual in today's business world does not operate in a social vacuum. He or she is more likely than not an employee—whether in the stockroom or as Chief Financial Officer—and our basic unit of understanding has to be the company whose perceived primary purpose is "to make money." Theory in business ethics thus becomes the theory—that is, description and contemplation about—individuals in (and out) of business roles as well as the role of business and businesses in society. People in business are ultimately responsible as individuals in a corporate setting where their responsibilities are at least in part defined by their roles and duties in the company and, of course, by "the bottom line," businesses in turn are defined by their role(s) and responsibilities in the larger community, where the bottom line is only an internal concern (if the business is to stay in business and the shareholders are to hold onto their shares) but for everyone else may be a minimal consideration. . . .

Aristotle is the philosopher who is best known for this emphasis on the cultivation of the virtues. But isn't it inappropriate if not perverse to couple

Aristotle and business ethics? True, he was the first economist. He had much to say about the ethics of exchange and so might well be called the first (known) business ethicist as well. But Aristotle distinguished two different senses of what I call economics, one of them *"oecinomicus"* or household trading, which he approved of and thought essential to the working of any even modestly complex society, and *"chrematisike,"* which is trade for profit. Aritstotle declared that latter activity wholly devoid of virtue and called those who engaged in such purely selfish practices "parasites." All trade, he believed, was a kind of exploitation. Such was his view of what I call "business." Indeed, Aristotle's attack on the unsavory and unproductive practice of "usury" and the personal vice of avarice held force virtually until the seventeenth century. Only outsiders at the fringe of society, not respectable citizens, engaged in such practices. (Shakespeare's Shylock, in *The Merchant of Venice,* was such an outsider and a usurer, though his idea of a forfeit was a bit unusual.) It can be argued that Aristotle had too little sense of the importance of production and based his views wholly on the aristocratically proper urge for acquisition, thus introducing an unwarranted zero-sum thinking into his economics.[2] And, of course, it can be charged that Aristotle, like his teacher Plato, was too much the spokesman for the aristocratic class and quite unfair to the commerce and livelihoods of foreigners and commoners.[3] It is Aristotle who initiates so much of the history of business ethics as the wholesale attack on business and its practices. Aristotelean prejudices underlie much of business criticism and the contempt for finance that preoccupies so much of Christian ethics even to this day, avaricious evangelicals notwithstanding. Even defenders of business often end up presupposing Aristotelean prejudices in such Pyrrhonian arguments as "business is akin to poker and apart from the ethics of everyday life"[4] (Albert Carr) and "the [only] social responsibility of business is to increase its profits" (Milton Friedman).[5] But if it is just this schism between business and the rest of life that so infuriated Aristotle, for whom life was supposed to fit together, in a coherent whole, it is the same holistic idea—that business people and corporations are first of all part of a larger community—that drives business ethics today. I can no longer accept the amoral idea that "business is business" (not a tautology but an excuse for insensitivity). According to Aristotle, one has to think of oneself as a member of the larger community, the *Polis,* and strive to excel, to bring out what was best in ourselves and our shared enterprise. What is best in us—our virtues—are in turn defined by that larger community, and there is therefore no ultimate split of antagonism between individual self-interest and the greater public good. Of course, there were no corporations in those days, but Aristotle would certainly know what I mean when I say that most people in business now identify themselves—if tenuously—in terms of their companies, and corporate policies, much less corporate codes of ethics, are not by themselves enough to constitute an ethics. But corporations are not isolated city-states, not even the biggest and most powerful of the multinationals (contrast the image of "the sovereign state of ITT"). They are part and parcel of a larger global community. The people that work for them are thus citizens of two communities at once, and one might think of business ethics as getting straight about the dual citizenship. What I need to cultivate is a certain way of thinking about ourselves in and out of the corporate context, and this is the aim of ethical theory in business, as I understand it. It is not, I insist, anti-individualistic in any sense of "individualism" that is worth defending. The Aristotelean approach to business ethics rather begins with the idea that it is individual virtue and integrity that counts: good corporate and social policy will follow: good corporate and social policy are both the preconditions and the result of careful cultivation and encouragement.

With what is this Aristotelean approach to be contrasted? . . .

It is to be contrasted with that two hundred or so year old obsession in ethics that takes everything of significance to be a matter of *rational principles,* "morality" as the strict Kantian sense of duty to the moral law. This is not to say, of course, that Aristotelean ethics dispenses with rationality, or for that matter with principles or the notion of duty. But Aristotle is quite clear about the fact that it is cultivation of character that counts, long before we begin to "rational-ize" our actions, and the formulation of general principles (in what he fa-mously but confusingly calls his "practical syllogism") is not an explicit step in correct and virtuous behavior as such but rather a philosopher's formulation about what it means to act rationally.[6] And, most important for our purposes here, duties too are defined by our roles in a community, e.g. a corporation, and not by means of any abstract ratiocination, principle of contradiction or *a priori* formulations of the categorical imperative. Kant, magnificent as he was a thinker, has proved to be a kind of disease in ethics. It's all very elegant, even brilliant, until one walks into the seminar room with a dozen or so bright, rest-less corporate managers, waiting to hear what's new and what's relevant to them on the business ethics scene. And then we tell them: don't lie, don't steal, don't cheat—elaborated and supported by the most gothic non-econometric construction ever allowed in a company training center. But it's not just its impracticality and the fact that we don't actually do ethics that way; the problem is that the Kantian approach shifts our attention away from just what I would call the "inspirational" matters of business ethics (its "incen-tives") and the emphasis on "excellence" (a buzz-word for Aristotle as well as Tom Peters and his millions of readers). It shifts the critical focus from oneself as a full-blooded person occupying a significant role in a productive organiza-tion to an abstract role-transcendent morality that necessarily finds itself empty-handed when it comes to most of the matters and many of the motives that we hear so much about in any corporate setting.

The Aristotelean approach is also to be contrasted with that rival ethical theory that goes by the name of "utilitarianism." I have considerably more to say about utilitarianism, its continued vulgarization and its forgotten humanis-tic focus in John Stuart Mill, but not here. For now, I just want to point out that utilitarianism shares with Kant that special appeal to anal compulsives in its doting over principles and rationalization (in crass calculation) and its neglect of individual responsibility and the cultivation of character. (John Stuart Mill exempted himself from much of this charge in the last chapter of *Utilitarian-ism,* but I promised not to talk about that here.) But I can imagine a good exis- · tentialist complaining quite rightly that the point of all such "decision proce-dures" in ethics is precisely to neutralize the annoyance of personal responsi-bility altogether, appealing every decision to "the procedure" rather than taking responsibility oneself. Of course, I am not denying the importance of concern for the public good or the centrality of worrying, in any major policy decision, about the number of people helped and hurt. But I take very seriously the problems of measurement and incommensurability that have been standard criticisms of utilitarianism ever since Bentham, and there are considerations that often are more basic than public utility—if only because, in most of our actions, the impact on public utility is so small in contrast to the significance for our personal sense of integrity and "doing the right thing" that it becomes a negligible factor in our deliberations.

I would also distinguish the Aristotelean approach to business ethics from all of those approaches that primarily emphasize rights, whether the rights of free enterprise as such, the rights of the employee, the customer or the community and even civil rights. Again, I have no wish to deny the relevance of rights to ethics or the centrality of civil rights, but I think that we should remind ourselves that talk about rights was never intended to eclipse talk about responsibilities and I think the emphasis in business ethics should move from *having* rights oneself to *recognizing* the rights of others, but then, I'm not at all sure that all of this couldn't just as well or better be expressed by saying that there are all sorts of things that a virtuous person should or shouldn't ever do to others.[7] Of course, Aristotle's defense of slavery in his *Politics* should be more than enough to convince us that we would still need the language of rights even with a fully developed language of the virtues. The problem with virtue ethics is that it tends to be provincial and ethnocentric. It thereby requires the language of rights and some general sense of utility as a corrective.

It will be evident to most of you that I am arguing—or about to argue—for a version of what has recently been called "virtue ethics," but I do want to distance myself from much of what has been defended recently under that title. . . .

I want to distance myself from some of the now-familiar features of what is being defended as virtue ethics, in particular the rather dangerous nostalgia for "tradition" and "community" that is expressed by Alasdair MacIntyre and Charles Taylor among others.[8] Of course, the Aristotelean approach does presuppose something of sense of community that I particularly want to emphasize. But there is a difference between the more or less singular, seemingly homogeneous, autonomous (and very elite) community that Aristotle simply took for granted and the nostalgic (I think purely imaginary) communities described or alluded to by recent virtue ethicists, often defined by a naive religous solidarity and unrealistic expectation of communal consensus. No adequate theory of ethics today can ignore or wish away the pluralistic and culturally diverse populations that make up almost every actual community. Even the smallest corporation will be rent by professional and role-related differences as well as divided by cultural and personal distinctions. Corporate cultures like the larger culture(s) are defined by their differences and disagreements as well as by any shared purpose or outside antagonist or competition, and no defense of the concept of corporate culture can or should forget that corporations are always part of a larger culture and not whole cultures themselves. And yet, in place of the abstract nostalgia that defines much of the current fascination with "communities," many modern corporations would seem to represent just such community. They enjoy a shared sense of *telos* as many communities do not. They invoke an extraordinary, almost military emphasis on loyalty and, despite the competitive rhetoric, they first of all inspire and require teamwork and cooperation. Corporations are real communities, neither ideal nor idealized, and therefore the perfect place to start understanding the nature of the virtues. . . .

THE SIX DIMENSIONS OF VIRTUE ETHICS

So what defines the Aristotelean approach to business ethics? What are its primary dimensions? There is a great deal of ground to be covered, from the general philosophical questions "what is a virtue?" and "what is the role of the virtues in ethics and the good life?" to quite specific questions about virtues and supposed virtues in business, such as loyalty, dependability, integrity, shrewdness and "toughness." But I can only begin to answer these general questions or speak much of these particular virtues here, but what I want to do first is to very briefly circumscribe the discussion of the virtues in business ethics with a half dozen considerations not usually so highlighted in the more abstract and principle-bound discussions of ethics nor so personalized in the policy discussions that so dominate the field. Those six considerations make up the framework of virtue ethics in business, and for the sake of brevity I simply call them: *community, excellence, role identity, holism, integrity, judgment.*

Community

The Aristotelean approach and, I would argue, the leading question for business in the nineties begins with the idea that the corporation is first of all a community. We are all individuals, to be sure, but we find our identities and our meanings only within communities, and for most of us that means—at work in a company or an institution. The philosophical myth that has grown almost cancerous in many business circles, the neo-Hobbesian view that "it's every man[sic] for himself" and the newer Darwinian view that "it's all a jungle out there" are direct denials of the Aristotelean view that we are all *first of all* members of a community and our self-interest is for the most part identical to the larger interests of the group. Our individuality is socially constituted and socially situated. Furthermore, our seemingly all-important concept of competition presumes, it does not replace, an underlying assumption of mutual interest and cooperation. Whether we do well, whether we like ourselves, whether we lead happy productive lives, depends to a large extent on the companies we choose. As the Greeks used to say, "to live the good life one must live in a great city." To my business students today, who are all too prone to choose a job on the basis of salary and start-up bonus alone, I always say, "to live a decent life choose the right company." In business ethics the corporation is one's community, which is not to deny, of course, that there is always a larger community—as diverse as it may be—that counts even more.

Excellence

The Greek *"arete"* is often translated either "virtue" or "excellence," as opposed to the rather modest and self-effacing notion of "virtue" that we inherited from our Victorian ancestors (indeed, even Kant used the term). The dual translation by itself makes a striking point. It is not enough to do no wrong.

"Knowingly do no harm" *(Primus non nocere)* is *not* the end of business ethics (as Peter Drucker suggests[9]). The hardly original slogan I sometimes use to sell what I do, "ethics and excellence" (the title of the book in which this essay finds its home) is not just a tag-along with Peters and Waterman. Virtue is doing one's best, excelling, and not merely "toeing the line" and "keeping one's nose clean." The virtues that constitute business ethics should not be conceived as purely ethical or moral virtues, as if (to come again) business ethics were nothing other than the general application of moral principles to one specific context (among others). Being a "tough negotiator" is a virtue in business but not in babysitting. It does not follow, however, that the virtues of business are therefore opposed to the ordinary virtues of civilized life—as Albert Carr famously argued in his *Harvard Business Review* polemic of several years ago. The virtues of business ethics are business virtues but they are nonetheless virtues, and the exercise of these virtues is aimed at both "the bottom line" and ethics.

Role Identity

Much has been written, for example, by Norman Bowie in his good little book *Business Ethics,* on the importance of "role morality" and "My Position and its Duties."[10] It is the situatedness of corporate roles that lends them their particular ethical poignancy, the fact that an employee or an executive is not just a person who happens to be in a place and is constrained by no more than the usual ethical prohibitions. To work for a company is to accept a set of particular obligations, to assume a *prima facie* loyalty to one's employer, to adopt a certain standard of excellence and conscientiousness that is largely defined by the job itself. There may be general ethical rules and guidelines that cut across most positions but as these get more general and more broadly applicable they also become all but useless in concrete ethical dilemmas. Robert Townsend's cute comment that "if a company needs an ethical code, use the Ten Commandments" is thus not only irreverent but irrelevant too.[11] The Aristotelean approach to business ethics presumes concrete situations and particular people and their place in organizations. There is little point to an ethics that tries to transcend all such particularities and embrace the chairman of the board as well as a middle manager, a secretary and a factory worker. All ethics is contextual, and one of the problems with all of those grand theories is that they try to transcend context and end up with vacuity. The problem, of course, is that people in business inevitably play several roles ("wear several hats") at once, and these roles may clash with one another as they may clash with more personal roles based on family, friendship and personal obligation. This, I will argue, is the pervasive problem in micro-business ethics, and it is the legitimacy of roles and their responsibilties, and the structures of the corporation that defines those roles and their responsibilities, that ought to occupy a good deal more of our time and attention.

Integrity

Integrity, accordingly, in the key to Aristotelean ethics, not, perhaps, as a virtue as such but rather as the linchpin of all of the virtues, the key to their unity or, in conlict and disunity, an anchor against personal disintegration. "Integrity" is a word, like "honor"—its close kin—that sometimes seems all but archaic in the modern business world. To all too many business executives, it suggests stubbornness and inflexibility, a refusal to be a "team player." But integrity seems to have at least two divergent meanings, one of them encouraging conformity, the other urging a belligerent independence.[12] Both of these are extreme and potentially dangerous. The very word suggests "wholeness," but insofar as one's identity is not that of an isolated atom but rather the product of a larger social molecule, that wholeness includes—rather than excludes—other people and one's social roles. A person's integrity on the job typically requires him or her to follow the rules and practices that define that job, rather than allow oneself to be swayed by distractions and contrary temptations. And yet, critical encounters sometimes require a show of integrity that is indeed antithetical to one's assigned role and duties. At that point some virtues, notably moral courage, become definitive and others, e.g. loyalty, may be jettisoned. (In other cases, of course, it is loyalty that might require moral courage.) But in harmony or in conflict, integrity represents the integration of one's roles and responsibilitites and the virtues defined by them.

Judgment *(phronesis)*

The fact that our roles conflict and there are often no singular principles to help us decide on an ethical course of action shifts the emphasis away from our calculative and ratiocinative faculties and back towards an older, often ignored faculty called "judgment." Against the view that ethics consists primarily of general principles that get applied to particular situations, Aristotle thought that it was "good judgment" or *phronesis* that was of the greatest importance in ethics. Good judgment (which centered on "perception" rather than the abstract formulation and interpretation of general principles) was the product of a good up-bringing, a proper education. It was always situated, perhaps something like Joseph Fletcher's still much referred-to notion of a "situation ethics," and took into careful account the particularity of the persons and circumstances involved. But I think the real importance of *phronesis* is not just its priority to ethical deliberation and ratiocination; it has rather to do with the inevitable conflicts of both concerns and principles that define almost every ethical dilemma. Justice, for example, may sound (especially in some philosophers) as if it were a monolithic or hierarchically layered and almost mechanical process. But, as I have argued elsewhere, there are a dozen or more different considerations that enter into most deliberations about justice, including not only rights and prior obligations and the public good but questions of merit (which themselves break down into a variety of sometimes conflicting categories) and responsibility and risk.[13] I won't go into this here but the point is that there is *no* (non-arbitrary) mechanical decision procedure for resolving most disputes about justice, and what is required, in each and every particular case, is the ability to balance and weigh competing concerns and come to a "fair" conclusion. But what's fair is not the outcome of one or several pre-ordained principles of justice; it is (as they say) a "judgment call," always disputable but nevertheless well or badly made. I have often thought that encouraging abstract ethical theory actually discourages and distracts us from the need to make judgments. I have actually heard one of my colleagues say (without qualms) that, since he's been studying ethical theory, he no longer has any sense of ethics. And if this sounds implausible, I urge you to remember your last department or faculty senate meeting, and the inverse relationship between high moral tone of the conversation and ridiculousness of the proposals and decisions that followed.

Holism

It more or less follows from what I've said above that one of the problems of traditional business thinking is our tendency to isolate our business or professional roles from the rest of our lives, a process that Marx, following Schiller, described as "alienation." The good life may have many facets, but they are facets and not mere components, much less isolated aspects despite the tiresome emphasis on tasks, techniques and "objectives," that a manager's primary and ultimate concern is *people*. It's gotten trite, but as I watch our more ambitious students and talk with more and more semi-successful but "trapped" middle managers and executives, I become more and more convinced that the tunnel-vision of business life encouraged by the too narrow business curriculum and the daily rhetoric of the corporate community is damaging and counter-productive. Good employees are good people, and to pretend that the virtues of business stand isolated from the virtues of the rest of our lives—and this is not for a moment to deny the particularity of either our business roles or our lives—is to set up that familiar tragedy in which a pressured employee violates his or her "personal values" because, from a purely business point of view, he or she "didn't really have any choice." It is the integration of our roles—or at least their harmonization—that is our ideal here, and that integration should not be construed as either the personal yielding to the corporate or the corporate giving in to the personal. The name of that integration is *ethics,* construed in an Aristotelean way.

BUSINESS AND THE VIRTUES

Business ethics is too often conceived as a set of impositions and constraints, obstacles to business behavior rather than the motivating force of that behavior. So conceived, it is no surprise that many people in business look upon ethics and ethicists with suspicion, as antagonistic if not antithetical to their enterprise. But properly understood, ethics does not and should not consist of a set of prohibitive principles or rules, and it is the virtue of an ethics of virtue to be rather an intrinsic part and the driving force of a successful life well lived. Its motivation need not depend on elaborate soul searching and deliberation but in the best companies moves along with the easy flow of interpersonal relations and a mutual sense of mission and accomplishment.

"The virtues" is a short-hand way of summarizing the ideals that define good character. There are a great many virtues that are relevant to business life; in fact, it would be a daunting task to try to even list them all. Just for a start, we have honesty, loyalty, sincerity, courage, reliability, trustworthiness, benevolence, sensitivity, helpfulness, cooperativeness, civility, decency, modesty, openness, cheerfulness, amiability, tolerance, reasonableness, tactfulness, wittiness, gracefulness, liveliness, magnanimity, persistence, prudence, resourcefulness, cool-headedness, warmth and hospitality.[14] Each of these has subtle sub-traits and related virtues, and there are a great many virtues of strength, energy and skill as well as attractiveness, charm and aesthetic appeal that I have not yet mentioned. There are "negative" virtues, that is, virtues that specify the absence of some annoying, inefficient or anti-social trait, such as non-negligence, non-vengefulness, non-vindictiveness and non-pretentiousness, and there are virtues of excess and superiority, such as super-conscientiousness and super-reliability. Then there are those virtues that seem peculiar (though not unique) to business, such as being shrewd and ruthless and "tough," which may well be vices in other aspects of life.

From the variety of virtues, one of the most important conclusions to be drawn immediately is the impoverished nature of ethical language when it limits itself to such terms as "good" and "bad," "right" and "wrong." To be sure, most of the virtues are "good" and lead to "right" action, and most of the contrary vices are "bad" and lead to "wrong"-doing. But not only does such ethical language lead us to ignore most of what is significant and subtle in our ordinary ethical judgments, it tends to lead us away from just that focus on personal character that is most essential to most of our interpersonal decisions, whether it is to trust a colleague, make a new friend, hire or fire a new assistant, respect a superior or invite the boss over to the house for dinner. Ethics is not the study of right and wrong, anymore than art and aesthetics are the study of beauty and ugliness.[15] Ethics (like art and aesthetics) is a colorful, multifaceted appreciation and engagement with other people in the world. In business ethics, it is only the extreme and sinister misdeed that we label simply "wrong"; more often, we invoke an artist's palette of imaginative descriptions such as "sleazy" and "slimy." Even the phrase "good character" (or "good person") strikes us as uninteresting and vacuous; it is the details that count, not the gloss. And there are many, many details, any of which might become more or less significant in some particular situation.

A virtue, according to Aristotle, is an excellence. It is not, however, a very specialized skill or talent (like being good with numbers or a brilliant researcher) but an exemplary way of getting along with other people, a way of manifesting in one's own thoughts, feelings and actions the ideals and aims of the entire community. Thus honesty is a virtue not because it is a skill necessary for any particular endeavor or because it represents the ideal of straight dealing, fair play, common knowledge and open inquiry. What is public is probably approved of and what is hidden is probably dangerous. So, too, courage is a virtue not just because it requires a special talent or because "somebody's got to do it" but because we all believe (with varying degrees of commitment) that a person should stand up for what he or she cares about and what he or she believes in. But not all virtues need to be so serious or so central to our idea of integrity. Aristotle listed charm, wit and a good sense of humor as virtues, and with corporate life in particular I think that we would probably agree. To be sure, the circumstances in which congeniality is a central virtue and in which courage becomes cardinal will be very different, but it is a troubled organization that requires the more heroic virtues all the time and does not have the relative security and leisure to enjoy those virtues that make life worthwhile rather than those that are necessary for mere survival. Indeed, part of the folly of the familiar military, machine and jungle metaphors in business is that they all make business life out to be something threatening and relentless. But the truth (even in the military and in the jungle) is that there are long and sometimes relaxed respites and a need for play and playfulness as well as diligence. There is welcome camaraderie and the virtues of "getting along" are just as important to group survival as the coordination needed for fighting together. There are reasons why we want to survive—apart from sheer Darwinian obstinacy—and the fact that we relish and enjoy the social harmony of our life and our jobs is one of them. One of the most powerful but most ignored arguments against hostile takeovers and unfriendly mergers is the desire on the part of the members of a corporate community to maintain that community, and this is not the same as executives "fighting to keep their jobs." . . .

If business life was like the brutal and heroic world of Homer's *Iliad*, corporations in mortal conflict with one another, we would expect the business virtues to be those warrior virtues most closely associated with combat, not only strength and prowess but courage, imperviousness to pain or pity, frightfulness (that is, causing fright in others, not being frightened oneself). We would expect the warrior to have an appropriately insensitive personality, rather clumsy social habits, and an enormous ego. Not surprising, these are precisely the virtues often praised and attributed to top business executives, summarized (badly) in the single word, "toughness." But, of course, warrior metaphors depend on a war-like situation, but business ethicists have taken considerable pains to dismiss that picture of corporate business life as pathological and misleading. Most CEOs, however "tough," do not fit this picture at all. Consider, instead, a very different and usually more representative picture of the corporation, the corporation as a wealthy and prosperous "polis," a free and sophisticated city-state with considerable pride in its products, philosophy, and corporate culture. There will still be external threats and an occasional battle, but this is not the day-to-day concern of the community. Courage might still be an important virtue, but most of the other warrior virtues and the typical characteristics of the warrior personality will seem boorish and bullish, inappropriate in most social settings and downright embarrassing in some. The virtues, in such a society, will tend to be the genteel, congenial virtues, those which lubricate a rich, pleasant social life. And these will be just as applicable to the CEO as to the boy at the loading dock or the teller at the check-out window. . . .

One might insist, just to waylay the argument I seem to be developing here, that warrior virtues, congeniality (Aristotelean) virtues and moral virtues are in fact quite compatible, and there is no reason why a James Burke or a Warren Buffett, for example, can't display warrior toughness, Aristotelean gentility and Christian righteousnes. And indeed, this is the case. But my argument is not that three sets of virtues are incompatible as such, but rather that they present us with three quite distinct contexts and three different ethical frameworks, and to understand business ethics is to understand the confluence, the priorities and the potential conflicts between these. Excessive attention paid to a corporation may become a screaming alliance of desperation and one's personal sense of integrity can be threatened or fatally damaged.

Excessive attention to the congenial virtues may in fact "soften" a company so that it becomes less competitive, and an exaggerated sense of righteousness to the detriment of congeniality and competitiveness may well cause a company to shatter into a thousand rigid little moralists, incapable of working together. But the Aristotelean framework tells us that it is cooperation and not an isolated individual sense of self-worth that defines the most important virtues, in which the warrior virtues play an essential but diminished role, in which the well-being of the community goes hand in hand with individual excellence, not by virtue of any "invisible hand" but precisely because of the social consciousness and public spirit of each and every individual.

Almost all of Aristotle's virtues are recognizable as business virtues, and this is, of course, not surprising. Business is, above all, a social activity, involving dealing with other people in both stressful and friendly situations (and trying to make the former into the latter). Despite our emphasis on hardheadedness and the bottom line, we do not praise and often despise tightfistedness and we do praise great-souled generosity ("magnificence"). But such virtues may be misleading for us. We would not praise an executive who "gave away the store"; we would rather think that executive mentally unhinged. But the virtues for Aristotle do not involve radical demands on our behavior, and the sort of fanaticism praised if not preached in many religions ("give away all of your worldly goods") is completely foreign to Aristotle's insistence on "moderation." Thus the generous or "magnificent" person gives away only as much of wealth as will increase his or her status in the community. Here we would encounter the familiar charge that such giving is not true generosity, for it involves no personal sacrifice and includes a "selfish" motive, the quest for self-aggrandizement. But Aristotle would refuse to recognize this oppositon between enlightened self-interest and virtue, and we continue to enforce it at our peril. The argument here, of course, is exactly the skeptical argument leveled against generous corporations when they give to the arts, to education, to social welfare programs: "They're only doing it for the P. R." But here executives (and everyone else) would be wise to follow Aristotle and reject the notion that "true" generosity is self-sacrifice and self-benefiting generosity is only "P. R." There are occasions that call for self-sacrifice, but to insist that such extreme action is essential to the virtues is to deny the virtues their relevance to business (and most of) life.

This brings us to the perhaps most misunderstood virtue in business life, the virtue of *toughness*. The word "tough" is typically used by way of admiration, though often coupled with a shake of the head and an expression of frustration. Sometimes, it is used as a euphemism, in place of or in conjunction with various synonyms for a nasty or odious human being. Not infrequently, it simply means stubborn, impossible or mean-spirited. But toughness is generally and genuinely perceived as virtue, albeit a virtue that is often misplaced and misconceived. Insofar as business consists of bargaining and dealing with other people, toughness is essential, and its opposite is not so much weakness as incompetence. But much of what is called toughness is neither a virtue nor a vice. It is not a character trait so much as it is a skill, whether cultivated or "natural." In certain central business practices, notably negotiating, toughness is not so much a personal virtue as it is a technique or set of techniques, an acquired manner and an accomplished strategy, "knowing when to hold 'em, knowing when to fold 'em." Toughness includes knowing how to bluff and when to keep silent, when to be cooperative and when not to be. But such a skill is not, contra Carr, unethical or divorced from ordinary morals; it is a legitimate part of a certain kind of obviously legitimate activity. Yet, as a specific skill or set of skills, being a tough negotiator is not sufficiently personal or general to count as a virtue, which is not to say, of course, that it is not therefore admirable or necessary. . . .

Toughness in an executive also has an ethically painful element. Sometimes it is necessary to do something wrong in order to do what is right. Powerful politicians, of course, face such dilemmas all of the time, giving rise to a substantial literature on the controversial virtues of toughness and "ruthlessness" and the allegedly opposed domains of public and private morality.[16] Sometimes, to reach a higher goal, one must do what one otherwise would not and should not even consider. For example, in the face of debts or deficiencies that will very likely capsize the company, a chairman may need to let go perfectly qualified, hard-working loyal employees. Viewed as an action isolated from the circumstances, letting people go for no reason whatever, that is, for no fault of their own, would be the height of injustice. But if it is a matter of saving the company, then this otherwise unjust act may nevertheless be necessary. Toughness is being able and willing to undertake such measures. This is not to say, however—and this cannot be emphasized enough—that such decisions can or should be made without guilt or pain or bad feelings. It does not mean that what one has done is not, despite its necessity, wrong. The chief executive of a large corporation once told me that "down-sizing" his company was the most painful thing he had ever had to do. His toughness lay not in callousness or indifference but in his willingness to do what was necessary and in his insistence on doing it as humanely as possible. Indeed, callousness and indifference are not themselves signs of toughness but the very opposite, indications of that form of weakness that can face moral issues only by denying them. Toughness is a virtue, but callousness and indifference are not, and the two should never be confused. . . .

THE BOTTOM LINE (Conclusion)

The bottom line of the Aristotelean approach to business ethics is that we have to get away from both traditional individualistic ethics and "bottom line" thinking. This does not in any way imply that the individual "checks his or her values at the office door" nor does it suggest that, except in the unusual and unfortunate case, there will be any thoroughgoing disharmony or incompatability between one's personal and professional values. Quite to the contrary, the point of what I am arguing is that we are, as Aristotle famously insisted, social creatures who get our identity from our communities and measure our worth accordingly. And as much as many employees may feel the need to divorce themselves from their work and pretend that what they "do" is not indicative of their true selves, the truth is that most adults spend literally half of their waking adult life on the job, in the office, in the role or position that defines them as a citizen of the corporation. The Aristotelean approach to business ethics ultimately comes down to the idea that, while business life has its specific goals and distinctive practices and people in business have their particular concerns, loyalties, roles and responsibilities, there is no "business world" apart from the people who work in business and the integrity of those people determines the integrity of the organization as well as vice versa. The Aristotelean approach to business ethics is, perhaps, just another way of saying that people come before profits.

Notes

Earlier versions of this essay were presented at a number of conferences, the Ruffin conference at the University of Virginia, the Applied Ethics conference at the University of British Columbia and (with Nick Imparato) the International Association of Business and Society conference in Sundance, Utah, the Center of Ethics conference at the University of Melbourne. Some parts of this essay have been published in some of the proceedings of those conferences and I have benefited from comments and criticism from my colleagues there, most notably, from Patricia Werhane, Peter French, Ed Freeman and Tony Coady. Parts of this essay also appear in my book, *Ethics and Excellence* (Oxford: Oxford University Press, 1992).

1. *Business and Society Review* (1984) Solomon and Hanson, *It's Good Business* (New York: Atheneum, 1985).

2. Anthony Flew, "The Profit Motive," in *Ethics,* vol 86 (July 1976), pp. 312–22.

3. Manuel Velasquez, comment on Joanne Ciulla, Ruffin lectures, 1989.

4. Albert Carr, "Is Business Bluffing Ethical?" *Harvard Business Review* (Jan.–Feb. 1968).

5. Milton Friedman, "The Social Responsibility of Business is to Increase its Profits" *The New York Times Magazine* (1971).

6. This has been the topic of considerable debate. See, notably, G. E. M. Anscombe, *Intentionality,* and John Cooper, *Reason and Human Good in Aristotle* (Cambridge, 1975).

7. Elizabeth Wolgast, *A Grammar of Justice* (Cornell, 1989).

8. Alasdair MacIntyre, *After Virtue,* 2nd ed. (Notre Dame, 1981).

9. Peter Drucker, *Management* (Harper and Row, 1973), pp. 366f.

10. Norman Bowie, *Business Ethics* (NJ: Prentice-Hall, 1982), pp. 1–16.

11. Peter Townsend, *Up the Organization.*

12. Lynne McFall, "Integrity," in *Ethics* (October 1987).

13. Robert C. Solomon, *A Passion for Justice* (New York: Addison-Wesley, 1989), Chapter 2.

14. A complex taxonomy of the virtues is in Edmund Pincoffs, *Quandries and Virtues* (Kansas, 1986), p. 84.

15. See Frithjof Bergmann, "The Experience of Values," in Hauerwas and MacIntyre, eds., *Revisions* (Notre Dame 1983), pp. 127–59.

16. See, for example, Stuart Hampshire, ed., *Public and Private Morality* (Cambridge: Cambridge University Press, 1978) and his own *Innocence and Experience* (Cambridge: Harvard University Press, 1989). See also Bernard Williams, "Politics and Moral Character" in his moral *Luck* (Cambridge University Press, 1981) and Thomas Nagel, "Ruthlessness in Public Life" in the Hampshire Collection.

Moral Mazes: Bureaucracy and Managerial Work

ROBERT JACKALL

Generations of Americans have been taught that the way to move up in corporate management is to work hard and make sound decisions. Has the bureaucratic world changed all that? Has the connection between work and reward become more capricious? The author of this study believes that the answer to both questions is yes. Interviewing more than 100 managers, he sought answers to such questions as: What kind of ethic does bureaucracy produce in middle and upper middle managers? Why does one person rise to the top while another doesn't? The managers interviewed offer many provocative answers to questions like these. They describe the experiences of themselves and their acquaintances. They speak freely—and sometimes humorously—of how they see credit for accomplishments being awarded, the role of loyalties and alliances, the meaning of team play, the significance of patrons, the ambiguities of "hitting your numbers," the part played by luck, "blame time," outrunning one's mistakes, the subtleties of bureaucratic language, and other elements of their work. While the impressions reported are unlikely to gratify top management, they may lead the HBR reader to rethink the unintended consequences of working for large-scale enterprises and to see the problems of executive development in a new light.

Corporate leaders often tell their charges that hard work will lead to success. Indeed, this theory of reward being commensurate with effort has been an enduring belief in our society, one central to our self-image as a people where the "main chance" is available to anyone of ability who has the gumption and the persistence to seize it. Hard work, it is also frequently asserted, builds character. This notion carries less conviction because businessmen, and our society as a whole, have little patience with those who make a habit of finishing out of the money. In the end, it is success that matters, that legitimates striving, and that makes work worthwhile.

What if, however, men and women in the big corporation no longer see success as necessarily connected to hard work? What becomes of the social morality of the corporation—I mean the everyday rules in use that people play by—when there is thought to be no "objective" standard of excellence to explain how and why winners are separated from also-rans, how and why some people succeed and others fail?

This is the puzzle that confronted me while doing a great many extensive interviews with managers and executives in several large corporations, particularly in a large chemical company and a large textile firm. I went into these corporations to study how bureaucracy—the prevailing organizational form of our society and economy—shapes moral consciousness. I came to see that managers' rules for success are at the heart of what may be called the bureaucratic ethic.

This article suggests no changes and offers no programs for reform. It is, rather, simply an interpretive sociological analysis of the moral dimensions of managers' work. Some readers may find the essay sharp-edged, others familiar. For both groups, it is important to note at the outset that my materials are managers' own descriptions of their experiences.[1] In listening to managers, I have had the decided advantages of being unencumbered with business responsibilities and also of being free from the taken-for-granted views and vocabularies of the business world. As it happens, my own research in a variety of other settings suggests that managers' experiences are by no means unique; indeed they have a deep resonance with those of other occupational groups.

WHAT HAPPENED TO THE PROTESTANT ETHIC?

To grasp managers' experiences and the more general implications they contain, one must see them against the background of the great historical transformations, both social and cultural, that produced managers as an occupational group. Since the concern here is with the moral significance of work in business, it is important to begin with an understanding of the original Protestant Ethic, the world view of the rising bourgeois class that spearheaded the emergence of capitalism.

The Protestant Ethic was a set of beliefs that counseled "secular asceticism"—the methodical, rational subjection of human impulse and desire to God's will through "restless, continuous, systematic work in a worldly calling."[2] This ethic of ceaseless work and ceaseless renunciation of the fruits of one's toil provided both the economic and the moral foundations for modern capitalism.

On one hand, secular asceticism was a ready-made prescription for building economic capital; on the other, it became for the upward-moving bourgeois class—self-made industrialists, farmers, and enterprising artisans—the ideology that justified their attention to this world, their accumulation of wealth, and indeed the social inequities that inevitably followed such accumulation. This bourgeois ethic, with its imperatives for self-reliance, hard work, frugality, and rational planning, and its clear definition of success and failure, came to dominate a whole historical epoch in the West.

But the ethic came under assault from two directions. First, the very accumulation of wealth that the old Protestant Ethic made possible gradually stripped away the religious basis of the ethic, especially among the rising middle class that benefited from it. There were, of course, periodic reassertions of the religious context of the ethic, as in the case of John D. Rockefeller and his turn toward Baptism. But on the whole, by the late 1800s the religious roots of the ethic survived principally among the independent farmers and proprietors of small businesses in rural areas and towns across America.

In the mainstream of an emerging urban America, the ethic had become secularized into the "work ethic," "rugged individualism," and especially the "success ethic." By the beginning of this century, among most of the economically successful, frugality had become an aberration, conspicuous consumption the norm. And with the shaping of the mass consumer society later in this century, the sanctification of consumption became widespread, indeed crucial to the maintenance of the economic order.

Affluence and the emergence of the consumer society were responsible, however, for the demise of only aspects of the old ethic—namely, the imperatives for saving and investment. The core of the ethic, even in its later, secularized form—self-reliance, unremitting devotion to work, and a morality that postulated just rewards for work well done—was undermined by the complete transformation of the organizational form of work itself. The hallmarks of the emerging modern production and distribution systems were administrative hierarchies, standardized work procedures, regularized timetables, uniform policies, and centralized control—in a word, the bureaucratization of the economy.

This bureaucratization was heralded at first by a very small class of salaried managers, who were later joined by legions of clerks and still later by technicians and professionals of every stripe. In this century, the process spilled over from the private to the public sector and government bureaucracies came to rival those of industry. This great transformation produced the decline of the old middle class of entrepreneurs, free professionals, independent farmers, and small independent businessmen—the traditional carriers of the old Protestant Ethic—and the ascendance of a new middle class of salaried employees whose chief common characteristic was and is their dependence on the big organization.

Any understanding of what happened to the original Protestant Ethic and to the old morality and social character it embodied—and therefore any understanding of the moral significance of work today—is inextricably tied to an analysis of bureaucracy. More specifically, it is, in my view, tied to an analysis of the work and occupational cultures of managerial groups within bureaucracies. Managers are the quintessential bureaucratic work group; they not only fashion bureaucratic rules, but they are also bound by them. Typically, they are not just *in* the organization; they are *of* the organization. As such, managers represent the prototype of the white-collar salaried employee. By analyzing the kind of ethic bureaucracy produces in managers, one can begin to understand how bureaucracy shapes morality in our society as a whole.

PYRAMIDAL POLITICS

American businesses typically both centralize and decentralize authority. Power is concentrated at the top in the person of the chief executive officer and is simultaneously decentralized; that is, responsibility for decisions and profits is pushed as far down the organizational line as possible. For example, the chemical company that I studied—and its structure is typical of other organizations I examined—is one of several operating companies of a large and growing conglomerate. Like the other operating companies, the chemical concern has its own president, executive vice presidents, vice presidents, other executive officers, business area managers, entire staff divisions, and operating plants. Each company is, in effect, a self-sufficient organization, though they are all coordinated by the corporation, and each president reports directly to the corporate CEO.

Now, the key interlocking mechanism of this structure is its reporting system. Each manager gathers up the profit targets or other objectives of his or her subordinates, and with these formulates his commitments to his boss; this boss takes these commitments, and those of his subordinates, and in turn makes a commitment to *his* boss. (Note: henceforth only "he" or "his" will be used to allow for easier reading.) At the top of the line, the president of each company makes his commitment to the CEO of the corporation, based on the stated objectives given to him by his vice presidents. There is always pressure from the top to set higher goals.

This management-by-objectives system, as it is usually called, creates a chain of commitments from the CEO down to the lowliest product manager. In practice, it also shapes a patrimonial authority arrangement which is crucial to defining both the immediate experiences and the long-run career chances of individual managers. In this world, a subordinate owes fealty principally to his immediate boss. A subordinate must not overcommit his boss; he must keep the boss from making mistakes, particularly public ones; he must not circumvent the boss. On a social level, even though an easy, breezy informality is the prevalent style of American business, the subordinate must extend to the boss a certain ritual deference: for instance, he must follow the boss's lead in conversation, must not speak out of turn at meetings, and must laugh at the boss's jokes while not making jokes of his own.

In short, the subordinate must not exhibit any behavior which symbolizes parity. In return, he can hope to be elevated when and if the boss is elevated, although other important criteria also intervene here. He can also expect protection for mistakes made up to a point. However, that point is never exactly defined and always depends on the complicated politics of each situation.

Who Gets Credit?

It is characteristic of this authority system that details are pushed down and credit is pushed up. Superiors do not like to give detailed instructions to subordinates. The official reason for this is to maximize subordinates' autonomy; the underlying reason seems to be to get rid of tedious details and to protect the privilege of authority to declare that a mistake has been made.

It is not at all uncommon for very bald and extremely general edicts to emerge from on high. For example, "Sell the plant in St. Louis. Let me know when you've struck a deal." This pushing down of details has important consequences:

1. Because they are unfamiliar with entangling details, corporate higher echelons tend to expect highly successful results without complications. This is central to top executives' well-known aversion to bad news and to the resulting tendency to "kill the messenger" who bears that news.
2. The pushing down of detail creates great pressure on middle managers not only to transmit good news but to protect their corporations, their bosses, and themselves in the process. They become the "point men" of a given strategy and the potential "fall guys" when things go wrong.

Credit flows up in this structure and usually is appropriated by the highest ranking officer involved in a decision. This person redistributes credit as he chooses, bound essentially by a sensitivity to public perceptions of his fairness. At the middle level, credit for a particular success is always a type of refracted social honor; one cannot claim credit even if it is earned. Credit has to be given, and acceptance of the gift implicitly involves a reaffirmation and strengthening of fealty. A superior may share some credit with subordinates in order to deepen fealty relationships and induce greater future efforts on his behalf. Of course, a different system is involved in the allocation of blame, a point I shall discuss later.

Fealty to the 'King'

Because of the interlocking character of the commitment system, a CEO carries enormous influence in his corporation. If, for a moment, one thinks of the presidents of individual operating companies as barons, then the CEO of the parent company is the king. His word is law; even the CEO's wishes and whims are taken as commands by close subordinates on the corporate staff, who zealously turn them into policies and directives.

A typical example occurred in the textile company last year when the CEO, new at the time, expressed mild concern about the rising operating costs of the company's fleet of rented cars. The following day, a stringent system for monitoring mileage replaced the previous casual practice.

Great efforts are made to please the CEO. For example, when the CEO of the large conglomerate that includes the chemical company visits a plant, the most important order of business for local management is a fresh paint job, even when, as in several cases last year the cost of paint alone exceeds $100,000. I am told that similar anecdotes from other organizations have been in circulation since 1910; this suggests a certain historical continuity of behavior toward top bosses.

The second order of business for the plant management is to produce a complete book describing the plant and its operations, replete with photographs and illustrations, for presentation to the CEO; such a book costs about $10,000 for the single copy. By any standards of budgetary stringency, such expenditures are irrational. But by the social standards of the corporation, they make perfect sense. It is far more important to please the king today than to worry about the future economic state of one's fief, since if one does not please the king, there may not be a fief to worry about or indeed any vassals to do the worrying.

By the same token, all of this leads to an intense interest in everything the CEO does and says. In both the chemical and the textile companies, the most common topic of conversation among managers up and down the line is speculation about their respective CEOs' plans, intentions, strategies, actions, styles, and public images.

Such speculation is more than idle gossip. Because he stands at the apex of the corporation's bureaucratic and patrimonial structures and locks the intricate system of commitments between bosses and subordinates into place, it is the CEO who ultimately decides whether those commitments have been satisfactorily met. Moreover, the CEO and his trusted associates determine the fate of whole business areas of a corporation.

Shake-Ups & Contingency

One must appreciate the simultaneously monocratic and patrimonial character of business bureaucracies in order to grasp what we might call their contingency. One has only to read the *Wall Street Journal* or the *New York Times* to realize that, despite their carefully constructed "eternal" public image, corporations are quite unstable organizations. Mergers, buy-outs, divestitures, and especially "organizational restructuring" are commonplace aspects of business life. I shall discuss only organizational shake-ups here.

Usually, shake-ups occur because of the appointment of a new CEO and/or division president, or because of some failure that is adjudged to demand retribution; sometimes these occurrences work together. The first action of most new CEOs is some form of organizational change. On the one hand, this prevents the inheritance of blame for past mistakes; on the other, it projects an image of bareknuckled aggressiveness much appreciated on Wall Street. Perhaps most important, a shake-up rearranges the fealty structure of the corporation, placing in power those barons whose style and public image mesh closely with that of the new CEO.

A shake-up has reverberations throughout an organization. Shortly after the new CEO of the conglomerate was named, he reorganized the whole business and selected new presidents to head each of the five newly formed companies of the corporation. He mandated that the presidents carry out a thorough reorganization of their separate companies complete with extensive "census reduction"—that is, firing as many people as possible.

The new president of the chemical company, one of these five, had risen from a small but important specialty chemicals division in the former company. Upon promotion to president, he reached back into his former division, indeed back to his own past work in a particular product line, and systematically elevated many of his former colleagues, friends, and allies. Powerful managers in other divisions, particularly in a rival process chemicals division, were: (1) forced to take big demotions in the new power structure; (2) put on "special assignment"—the corporate euphemism for Siberia (the saying is: "No one ever comes back from special assignment"); (3) fired; or (4) given "early retirement," a graceful way of doing the same thing.

Up and down the chemical company, former associates of the president now hold virtually every important position. Managers in the company view all of this as an inevitable fact of life. In their view, the whole reorganization could easily have gone in a completely different direction had another CEO been named or had the one selected picked a different president for the chemical company, or had the president come from a different work group in the old organization. Similarly, there is the abiding feeling that another significant change in top management could trigger yet another sweeping reorganization.

Fealty is the mortar of the corporate hierarchy, but the removal of one well-placed stone loosens the mortar throughout the pyramid and can cause things to fall apart. And no one is ever quite sure, until after the fact, just how the pyramid will be put back together.

SUCCESS & FAILURE

It is within this complicated and ambiguous authority structure, always subject to upheaval, that success and failure are meted out to those in the middle and upper middle managerial ranks. Managers rarely spoke to me of objective criteria for achieving success because once certain crucial points in one's career are passed, success and failure seem to have little to do with one's accomplishments. Rather, success is socially defined and distributed. Corporations do demand, of course, a basic competence and sometimes specified training and experience; hiring patterns usually ensure these. A weeding-out process takes place, however, among the lower ranks of managers during the first several years of their experience. By the time a manager reaches a certain numbered grade in the ordered hierarchy—in the chemical company this is Grade 13 out of 25, defining the top 8 1/2% of management in the company—managerial competence as such is taken for granted and assumed not to differ greatly from one manager to the next. The focus then switches to social factors, which are determined by authority and political alignments—the fealty structure—and by the ethos and style of the corporation.

Moving to the Top

In the chemical and textile companies as well as the other concerns I studied, five criteria seem to control a person's ability to rise in middle and upper middle management. In ascending order they are:

1. Appearance and dress. This criterion is so familiar that I shall mention it only briefly. Managers have to look the part, and it is sufficient to say that corporations are filled with attractive, well-groomed, and conventionally well-dressed men and women.

2. Self-control. Managers stress the need to exercise iron self-control and to have the ability to mask all emotion and intention behind bland, smiling, and agreeable public faces. They believe it is a fatal weakness to lose control of oneself, in any way, in a public forum. Similarly, to betray valuable secret knowledge (for instance, a confidential reorganization plan) or intentions through some relaxation of self-control—for example, an indiscreet comment or a lack of adroitness in turning aside a query—can not only jeopardize a manager's immediate position but can undermine others' trust in him.

3. Perception as a team player. While being a team player has many meanings, one of the most important is to appear to be interchangeable with other managers near one's level. Corporations discourage narrow specialization more strongly as one goes higher. They also discourage the expression of moral or political qualms. One might object, for example, to working with chemicals used in nuclear power, and most corporations today would honor that objection. The public statement of such objections, however, would end any realistic aspirations for higher posts because one's usefulness to the organization depends on versatility. As one manager in the chemical company commented: "Well, we'd go along with his request but we'd always wonder about the guy. And in the back of our minds, we'd be thinking that he'll soon object to working in the soda ash division because he doesn't like glass."

Another important meaning of team play is putting in long hours at the office. This requires a certain amount of sheer physical energy, even though a great deal of this time is spent not in actual work but in social rituals—like reading and discussing newspaper articles, taking coffee breaks, or having informal conversations. These rituals, readily observable in every corporation that I studied, forge the social bonds that make real managerial work—that is, group work of various sorts—possible. One must participate in the rituals to be considered effective in the work.

4. Style. Managers emphasize the importance of "being fast on your feet"; always being well organized; giving slick presentations complete with color slides; giving the appearance of knowledge even in its absence; and possessing a subtle, almost indefinable sophistication, marked especially by an urbane, witty, graceful, engaging, and friendly demeanor.

I want to pause for a moment to note that some observers have interpreted such conformity, team playing, affability, and urbanity as evidence of the decline of the individualism of the old Protestant Ethic.[3] To the extent that commentators take the public images that managers project at face value, I think they miss the main point. Managers up and down the corporate ladder adopt the public faces that they wear quite consciously; they are, in fact, the masks behind which the real struggles and moral issues of the corporation can be found.

Karl Mannheim's conception of self-rationalization or self-streamlining is useful in understanding what is one of the central social psychological processes of organizational life.[4] In a world where appearances—in the broadest sense—mean everything, the wise and ambitious person learns to cultivate assiduously the proper, prescribed modes of appearing. He dispassionately takes stock of himself, treating himself as an object. He analyzes his strengths and weaknesses, and decides what he needs to change in order to survive and flourish in his organization. And then he systematically undertakes a program to reconstruct his image. Self-rationalization curiously parallels the methodical subjection of self to God's will that the old Protestant Ethic counseled; the difference, of course, is that one acquires not moral virtues but a masterful ability to manipulate personae.

5. Patron power. To advance, a manager must have a patron, also called a mentor, a sponsor, a rabbi, or a godfather. Without a powerful patron in the higher echelons of management, one's prospects are poor in most corporations. The patron might be the manager's immediate boss or someone several levels higher in the chain of command. In either case the manager is still bound by the immediate, formal authority and fealty patterns of his position; the new—although more ambiguous—fealty relationships with the patron are added.

A patron provides his "client" with opportunities to get visibility, to showcase his abilities, to make connections with those of high status. A patron cues his client to crucial political developments in the corporation, helps arrange lateral moves if the client's upward progress is thwarted by a particular job or a particular boss, applauds his presentations or suggestions at meetings, and promotes the client during an organizational shake-up. One must, of course, be lucky in one's patron. If the patron gets caught in a political crossfire, the arrows are likely to find his clients as well.

Social Definitions of Performance

Surely, one might argue, there must be more to success in the corporation than style, personality, team play, chameleonic adaptability, and fortunate connections. What about the bottom line—profits, performance?

Unquestionably, "hitting your numbers"—that is, meeting the profit commitments already discussed—is important, but only within the social context I have described. There are several rules here. First, no one in a line position—that is, with responsibility for profit and loss—who regularly "misses his numbers" will survive, let alone rise. Second, a person who always hits his numbers but who lacks some or all of the required social skills will not rise. Third, a person who sometimes misses his numbers but who has all the desirable social traits will rise.

Performance is thus always subject to a myriad of interpretations. Profits matter, but it is much more important in the long run to be perceived as "promotable" by belonging to central political networks. Patrons protect those already selected as rising stars from the negative judgments of others; and only the foolhardy point out even egregious errors of those in power or those destined for it.

Failure is also socially defined. The most damaging failure is, as one middle manager in the chemical company puts it, "when your boss or someone who has the power to determine your fate says: 'You failed.'" Such a godlike pronouncement means, of course, out-and-out personal ruin; one must, at any cost, arrange matters to prevent such an occurrence.

As it happens, things rarely come to such a dramatic point even in the midst of an organizational crisis. The same judgment may be made but it is usually called "nonpromotability." The difference is that those who are publicly labeled as failures normally have no choice but to leave the organization; those adjudged nonpromotable can remain, provided they are willing to accept being shelved or, more colorfully, "mushroomed"—that is, kept in a dark place, fed manure, and left to do nothing but grow fat. Usually, seniors do not tell juniors they are nonpromotable (though the verdict may be common knowledge among senior peer groups). Rather, subordinates are expected to get the message after they have been repeatedly overlooked for promotions. In fact, middle managers interpret staying in the same job for more than two or three years as evidence of a negative judgment. This leads to a mobility panic at the middle levels which, in turn, has crucial consequences for pinpointing responsibility in the organization.

Capriciousness of Success

Finally, managers think that there is a tremendous amount of plain luck involved in advancement. It is striking how often managers who pride themselves on being hardheaded rationalists explain their own career patterns and those of others in terms of luck. Various uncertainties shape this perception. One is the sense of organizational contingency. One change at the top can create profound upheaval throughout the entire corporate structure, producing startling reversals of fortune, good or bad, depending on one's connections. Another is the uncertainty of the markets that often makes managerial planning simply elaborate guesswork, causing real economic outcome to depend on factors totally beyond organizational and personal control.

It is interesting to note in this context that a line manager's credibility suffers just as much from missing his numbers on the up side (that is, achieving profits higher than predicted) as from missing them on the down side. Both outcomes undercut the ideology of managerial planning and control, perhaps the only bulwark managers have against market irrationality.

Even managers in staff positions, often quite removed from the market, face uncertainty. Occupational safety specialists, for instance, know that the bad publicity from one serious accident in the workplace can jeopardize years of work and scores of safety awards. As one high-ranking executive in the chemical company says, "In the corporate world, 1,000 'Attaboys!' are wiped away by one 'Oh, shit!'"

Because of such uncertainties, managers in all the companies I studied speak continually of the great importance of being in the right place at the right time and of the catastrope of being in the wrong place at the wrong time. My interview materials are filled with stories of people who were transferred immediately before a big shake-up and, as a result, found themselves riding the crest of a wave to power; of people in a promising business area who were terminated because top management suddenly decided that the area no longer fit the corporate image desired; of others caught in an unpredictable and fatal political battle among their patrons; of a product manager whose plant accidentally produced an odd color batch of chemicals, who sold them as a premium version of the old product, and who is now thought to be a marketing genius.

The point is that managers have a sharply defined sense of the *capriciousness* of organizational life. Luck seems as good an explanation as any of why, after a certain point, some people succeed and others fail. The upshot is that many managers decide that they can do little to influence external events in their favor. One can, however, shamelessly streamline oneself, learn to wear all the right masks, and get to know all the right people. And then sit tight and wait for things to happen.

'GUT DECISIONS'

Authority and advancement patterns come together in the decision-making process. The core of the managerial mystique is decision-making prowess, and the real test of such prowess is what managers call "gut decisions," that is, important decisions involving big money, public exposure, or significant effect on the organization. At all but the highest levels of the chemical and textile companies, the rules for making gut decisions are, in the words of one upper middle manager: "(1) Avoid making any decisions if at all possible; and (2) if a decision has to be made, involve as many people as you can so that, if things go south, you're able to point in as many directions as possible."

Consider the case of a large coking plant of the chemical company. Coke making requires a gigantic battery to cook the coke slowly and evenly for long periods; the battery is the most important piece of capital equipment in a coking plant. In 1975, the plant's battery showed signs of weakening and certain managers at corporate headquarters had to decide whether to invest $6 million to restore the battery to top form. Clearly, because of the amount of money involved, this was a gut decision.

No decision was made. The CEO had sent the word out to defer all unnecessary capital expenditures to give the corporation cash reserves for other investments. So the managers allocated small amounts of money to patch the battery up until 1979, when it collapsed entirely. This brought the company into a breach of contract with a steel producer and into violation of various Environmental Protection Agency pollution regulations. The total bill, including lawsuits and now federally mandated repairs to the battery, exceeded $10 million. I have heard figures as high as $150 million, but because of "creative accounting," no one is sure of the exact amount.

This simple but very typical example gets to the heart of how decision making is intertwined with a company's authority structure and advancement patterns. As the chemical company managers see it, the decisions facing them in 1975 and 1979 were crucially different. Had they acted decisively in 1975—in hindsight, the only rational course—they would have salvaged the battery and saved their corporation millions of dollars in the long run.

In the short run, however, since even seemingly rational decisions are subject to widely varying interpretations, particularly decisions which run counter to a CEO's stated objectives, they would have been taking a serious risk in restoring the battery. What is more, their political networks might have unraveled, leaving them vulnerable to attack. They chose short-term safety over long-term gain because they felt they were judged, both by higher authority and by their peers, on their short-term performances. Managers feel that if they do not survive the short run, the long run hardly matters. Even correct decisions can shorten promising careers.

By contrast, in 1979 the decision was simple and posed little risk. The corporation had to meet its legal obligations; also it had to either repair the battery the way the EPA demanded or shut down the plant and lose several hundred million dollars. Since there were no real choices, everyone could agree on a course of action because everyone could appeal to inevitability. Diffusion of responsibility, in this case by procrastinating until total crisis, is intrinsic to organizational life because the real issue in most gut decisions is: Who is going to get blamed if things go wrong?

'Blame Time'

There is no more feared hour in the corporate world than "blame time." Blame is quite different from responsibility. There is a cartoon of Richard Nixon declaring: "I accept all of the responsibility, but none of the blame." To blame someone is to injure him verbally in public; in large organizations, where one's image is crucial, this poses the most serious sort of threat. For managers, blame—like failure—has nothing to do with the merits of a case; it is a matter of social definition. As a general rule, it is those who are or who become politically vulnerable or expendable who get "set up" and become blamable. The most feared situation of all is to end up inadvertently in the wrong place at the wrong time and get blamed.

Yet this is exactly what often happens in a structure that systematically diffuses responsibility. It is because managers fear blame time that they diffuse responsibility; however, such diffusion inevitably means that someone, somewhere is going to become a scapegoat when things go wrong. Big corporations encourage this process by their complete lack of any tracking system. Whoever is currently in charge of an area is responsible—that is, potentially blamable—for whatever goes wrong in the area, even if he has inherited others' mistakes. An example from the chemical company illustrates this process.

When the CEO of the large conglomerate took office, he wanted to rid his capital accounts of all serious financial drags. The corporation had been operating a storage depot for natural gas which it bought, stored, and then resold. Some years before the energy crisis, the company had entered into a long-term contract to supply gas to a buyer—call him Jones. At the time, this was a sound deal because it provided a steady market for a stably priced commodity.

When gas prices soared, the corporation was still bound to deliver gas to Jones at 20¢ per unit instead of the going market price of $2. The CEO ordered one of his subordinates to get rid of this albatross as expeditiously as possible. This was done by selling the operation to another party—call him Brown—with the agreement that Brown would continue to meet the contractual obligations to Jones. In return for Brown's assumption of these costly contracts, the corporation agreed to buy gas from Brown at grossly inflated prices to meet some of its own energy needs.

In effect, the CEO transferred the drag on his capital accounts to the company's operating expenses. This enabled him to project an aggressive, asset-reducing image to Wall Street. Several levels down the ladder, however, a new vice president for a particular business found himself saddled with exorbitant operating costs when, during a reorganization, those plants purchasing gas from Brown at inflated prices came under his purview. The high costs helped to undercut the vice president's division earnings and thus to erode his position in the hierarchy. The origin of the situation did not matter. All that counted was that the vice president's division was steadily losing big money. In the end, he resigned to "pursue new opportunities."

One might ask why top management does not institute codes or systems for tracking responsibility. This example provides the clue. An explicit system of accountability for subordinates would probably have to apply to top executives as well and would restrict their freedom. Bureaucracy expands the freedom of those on top by giving them the power to restrict the freedom of those beneath.

On the Fast Track

Managers see what happened to the vice president as completely capricious, but completely understandable. They take for granted the absence of any tracking of responsibility. If anything, they blame the vice president for not recognizing soon enough the dangers of the situation into which he was being drawn and for not preparing a defense—even perhaps finding a substitute scapegoat. At the same time, they realize that this sort of thing could easily happen to them. They see few defenses against being caught in the wrong place at the wrong time except constant wariness, the diffusion of responsibility, and perhaps being shrewd enough to declare the ineptitude of one's predecessor on first taking a job.

What about avoiding the consequences of their own errors? Here they enjoy more control. They can "outrun" their mistakes so that when blame time arrives, the burden will fall on someone else. The ideal situation, of course, is to be in a position to fire one's successors for one's own previous mistakes.

Some managers, in fact, argue that outrunning mistakes is the real key to managerial success. One way to do this is by manipulating the numbers. Both the chemical and the textile companies place a great premium on a division's or a subsidiary's return on assets. A good way for business managers to increase their ROA is to reduce their assets while maintaining sales. Usually they will do everything they can to hold down expenditures in order to decrease the asset base, particularly at the end of the fiscal year. The most common way of doing this is by deferring capital expenditures, from maintenance to innovative investments, as long as possible. Done for a short time, this is called "starving" a plant; done over a longer period, it is called "milking" a plant.

Some managers become very adept at milking businesses and showing a consistent record of high returns. They move from one job to another in a company, always upward, rarely staying more than two years in any post. They may leave behind them deteriorating plants and unsafe working conditions, but they know that if they move quickly enough, the blame will fall on others. In this sense, bureaucracies may be thought of as vast systems of organized irresponsibility.

FLEXIBLITY & DEXTERITY WITH SYMBOLS

The intense competition among managers takes place not only behind the agreeable public faces I have described but within an extraordinarily indirect and ambiguous linguistic framework. Except at blame time, managers do not publicly criticize or disagree with one another or with company policy. The sanction against such criticism or disagreement is so strong that it constitutes, in managers' view, a suppression of professional debate. The sanction seems to be rooted principally in their acute sense of organizational contingency; the person one criticizes or argues with today could be one's boss tomorrow.

This leads to the use of an elaborate linguistic code marked by emotional neutrality, especially in group settings. The code communicates the meaning one might wish to convey to other managers, but since it is devoid of any significant emotional sentiment, it can be reinterpreted should social relationships or attitudes change. Here, for example, are some typical phrases describing performance appraisals followed by their probable intended meanings:

Stock Phrase	Probable Intended Meaning
Exceptionally well qualified	Has commited no major blunders to date
Tactful in dealing with superiors	Knows when to keep his mouth shut
Quick thinking	Offers plausible excuses for errors
Meticulous attention to detail	A nitpicker

| Slightly below average | Stupid |
| Unusually loyal | Wanted by no one else |

For the most part, such neutered language is not used with the intent to deceive; rather, its purpose is to communicate certain meanings within specific contexts with the implicit understanding that, should the context change, a new, more appropriate meaning can be attached to the language already used. In effect, the corporation is a setting where people are not held to their word because it is generally understood that their word is always provisional.

The higher one gets in the corporate world, the more this seems to be the case; in fact, advancement beyond the upper middle level depends greatly on one's ability to manipulate a variety of symbols without becoming tied to or identified with any of them. For example, an amazing variety of organizational improvement programs marks practically every corporation. I am referring here to the myriad ideas generated by corporate staff, business consultants, academics, and a host of others to improve corporate structure; sharpen decision making; raise morale; create a more humanistic workplace; adopt Theory X, Theory Y, or, more recently, Theory Z of management; and so on. These programs become important when they are pushed from the top.

The watchword in the large conglomerate at the moment is productivity and, since this is a pet project of the CEO himself, it is said that no one goes into his presence without wearing a blue *Productivity!* button and talking about "quality circles" and "feedback sessions." The president of another company pushes a series of managerial seminars that endlessly repeats the basic functions of management: (1) planning, (2) organizing, (3) motivating, and (4) controlling. Aspiring young managers attend these sessions and with a seemingly dutiful eagerness learn to repeat the formulas under the watchful eyes of senior officials.

Privately, managers characterize such programs as the "CEO's incantations over the assembled multitude," as "elaborate rituals with no practical effect," or as "waving a magic wand to make things wonderful again." Publicly, of course, managers on the way up adopt the programs with great enthusiasm, participate in or run them very effectively, and then quietly drop them when the time is right.

Playing the Game

Such flexibility, as it is called, can be confusing even to those in the inner circles. I was told the following by a highly placed staff member whose work requires him to interact daily with the top figures of his company:

"I get faked out all the time and I'm part of the system. I come from a very different culture. Where I come from, if you give someone your *word,* no one ever questions it. It's the old hard-work-will-lead-to-success ideology. Small community, Protestant, agrarian, small business, merchant-type values. I'm disadvantaged in a system like this."

He goes on to characterize the system more fully and what it takes to succeed within it:

"It's the ability to play this system that determines whether you will rise. . . . And part of the adeptness [required] is determined by how much it bothers people. One thing you have to be able to do is to play the game, but you can't be disturbed by the game. What's the game? It's bringing troops home from Vietnam and declaring peace with honor. It's saying one thing and meaning another.

"It's characterizing the reality of a situation with *any* description that is necessary to make that situation more palatable to some group that matters. It means that you have to come up with a culturally accepted verbalization to explain why you are *not* doing what you are doing. . . . [Or] you say that we had to do what we did because it was inevitable; or because the guys at the [regulatory] agencies were dumb; [you] say we won when we really lost; [you] say we saved money when we squandered it; [you] say something's safe when it's potentially or actually dangerous. . . . Everyone knows that it's bullshit, but it's *accepted*. This is the game."

In addition, then, to the other characteristics that I have described, it seems that a prerequisite for big success in the corporation is a certain adeptness at inconsistency. This premium on inconsistency is particularly evident in the many areas of public controversy that face top-ranking managers. Two things come together to produce this situation. The first is managers' sense of beleaguerment from a wide array of adversaries who, it is thought, want to disrupt or impede management's attempts to further the economic interests of their companies. In every company that I studied, managers see themselves and their traditional prerogatives as being under siege, and they respond with a set of caricatures of their perceived principal adversaries.

For example, government regulators are brash, young, unkempt hippies in blue jeans who know nothing about the business for which they make rules; environmental activists—the bird and bunny people—are softheaded idealists who want everybody to live in tents, burn candles, ride horses, and eat berries; workers' compensation lawyers are out-and-out crooks who prey on corporations to appropriate exorbitant fees from unwary clients; labor activists are radical troublemakers who want to disrupt harmonious industrial communities; and the news media consist of rabble-rousers who propagate sensational antibusiness stories to sell papers or advertising time on shows like "60 Minutes."

Second, within this context of perceived harassment, managers must address a multiplicity of audiences, some of whom are considered adversaries. These audiences are the internal corporate hierarchy with its intricate and shifting power and status cliques, key regulators, key local and federal legislators, special publics that vary according to the issues, and the public at large, whose goodwill and favorable opinion are considered essential for a company's free operation.

Managerial adeptness at inconsistency becomes evident in the widely discrepant perspectives, reasons for action, and presentations of fact that explain, excuse, or justify corporate behavior to these diverse audiences.

Adeptness at Inconsistency

The cotton dust issue in the textile industry provides a fine illustration of what I mean. Prolonged exposure to cotton dust produces in many textile workers a chronic and eventually disabling pulmonary disease called byssinosis or, colloquially, brown lung. In the early 1970s, the Occupational Safety and Health Adminstration proposed a ruling to cut workers' exposure to cotton dust sharply by requiring textile companies to invest large amounts of money in cleaning up their plants. The industry fought the regulation fiercely but a final OSHA ruling was made in 1978 requiring full compliance by 1984.

The industry took the case to court. Despite an attempt by Reagan appointees in OSHA to have the case removed from judicial consideration and remanded to the agency they controlled for further cost/benefit analysis, the Supreme Court ruled in 1981 that the 1978 OSHA ruling was fully within the agency's mandate, namely, to protect workers' health and safety as the primary benefit exceeding all cost considerations.

During these proceedings, the textile company was engaged on a variety of fronts and was pursuing a number of actions. For instance, it intensively lobbied regulators and legislators and it prepared court materials for the industry's defense, arguing that the proposed standard would crush the industry and that the problem, if it existed, should be met by increasing workers' use of respirators.

The company also aimed a public relations barrage at special-interest groups as well as at the general public. It argued that there is probably no such thing as byssinosis; workers suffering from pulmonary problems are all heavy smokers and the real culprit is the government-subsidized tobacco industry. How can cotton cause brown lung when cotton is white? Further, if there is a problem, only some workers are afflicted, and therefore the solution is more careful screening of the work force to detect susceptible people and prevent them from ever reaching the workplace. Finally, the company claimed that if the regulation were imposed, most of the textile industry would move overseas where regulations are less harsh.[5]

In the meantime, the company was actually addressing the problem but in a characteristically indirect way. It invested $20 million in a few plants where it knew such an investment would make money; this investment automated the early stages of handling cotton, traditionally a very slow procedure, and greatly increased productivity. The investment had the side benefit of reducing cotton dust levels to the new standard in precisely those areas of the work process where the dust problem is greatest. Publicly, of course, the company claims that the money was spent entirely to eliminate dust, evidence of its corporate good citizenship. (Privately, executives admit that, without the productive return, they would not have spent the money and they have not done so in several other plants.)

Indeed, the productive return is the only rationale that carries weight within the corporate hierarchy. Executives also admit, somewhat ruefully and only when their office doors are closed, that OSHA's regulation on cotton dust has been the main factor in forcing technological innovation in a centuries-old and somewhat stagnant industry.

Such adeptness at inconsistency, without moral uneasiness, is essential for executive success. It means being able to say, as a very high-ranking official of the textile company said to me without batting an eye, that the industry has never caused the slightest problem in any worker's breathing capacity. It means, in the chemical company, propagating an elaborate hazard/benefit calculus for appraisal of dangerous chemicals while internally conceptualizing "hazards" as business risks. It means publicly extolling the carefulness of testing procedures on toxic chemicals while privately ridiculing animal tests as inapplicable to humans.

It means lobbying intensively in the present to shape government regulations to one's immediate advantage and, ten years later, in the event of a catastrophe, arguing that the company acted strictly in accordance with the standards of the time. It means claiming that the real problem of our society is its unwillingness to take risks, while in the thickets of one's bureaucracy avoiding risks at every turn; it means as well making every effort to socialize the risks of industrial activity while privatizing the benefits.

THE BUREAUCRATIC ETHIC

The bureaucratic ethic contrasts sharply with the original Protestant Ethic. The Protestant Ethic was the ideology of a self-confident and independent propertied social class. It was an ideology that extolled the virtues of accumulating wealth in a society organized around property and that accepted the stewardship responsibilities entailed by property. It was an ideology where a person's word was his bond and where the integrity of the handshake was seen as crucial to the maintenance of good business relationships. Perhaps most important, it was connected to a predictable economy of salvation—that is, hard work will lead to success, which is a sign of one's election by God—a notion also containing its own theodicy to explain the misery of those who do not make it in this world.

Bureaucracy, however, breaks apart substance from appearances, action from responsibility, and language from meaning. Most important, it breaks apart the older connection between the meaning of work and salvation. In the bureaucratic world, one's success, one's sign of election, no longer depends on one's own efforts and on an inscrutable God but on the capriciousness of one's superiors and the market; and one achieves economic salvation to the extent that one pleases and submits to one's employer and meets the exigencies of an impersonal market.

In this way, because moral choices are inextricably tied to personal fates, bureaucracy erodes internal and even external standards of morality, not only in matters of individual success and failure but also in all the issues that managers face in their daily work. Bureaucracy makes its own internal rules and social context the principal moral gauges for action. Men and women in bureaucracies turn to each other for moral cues for behavior and come to fashion specific situational moralities for specific significant people in their worlds.

As it happens, the guidance they receive from each other is profoundly ambiguous because what matters in the bureaucratic world is not what a person is but how closely his many personae mesh with the organizational ideal; not his willingness to stand by his actions but his agility in avoiding blame; not what he believes or says but how well he has mastered the ideologies that serve his corporation; not what he stands for but whom he stands with in the labyrinths of his organization.

In short, bureaucracy structures for managers an intricate series of moral mazes. Even the inviting paths out of the puzzle often turn out to be invitations to jeopardy.

Author's Note

I presented an earlier version of this paper in the Faculty Lecture Series at Williams College on March 18, 1982. The intensive field work done during 1980 and 1981 was made possible by a Fellowship for Independent Research from the National Endowment for the Humanities and by a Junior Faculty Leave and small research grant from Williams College.

References

1. There is a long sociological tradition of work on managers and I am, of course, indebted to that literature. I am particularly indebted to the work, both joint and separate, of Joseph Bensman and Arthur J. Vidich, two of the keenest observers of the new middle class. See especially their *The New American Society: The Revolution of the Middle Class* (Chicago: Quadrangle Books, 1971).

2. See Max Weber, *The Protestant Ethic and the Spirit of Capitalism,* translated by Talcott Parsons (New York: Charles Scribner's Sons, 1958), p. 172.

3. See William H. Whyte, *The Organization Man* (New York: Simon & Schuster, 1956), and David Riesman, in collaboration with Reuel Denney and Nathan Glazer, *The Lonely Crowd: A Study of the Changing American Character* (New Haven: Yale University Press, 1950).

4. Karl Mannheim, *Man and Society in an Age of Reconstruction* [London: Paul (Kegan), Trench, Trubner Ltd. 1940], p. 55.

5. On February 9, 1982, the Occupational Safety and Health Administration issued a notice that it was once again reviewing its 1978 standard on cotton dust for "cost-effectiveness." See *Federal Register,* vol. 47, p. 5906. As of this writing (May 1983), this review has still not been officially completed.

Ethical Relativism
and
International Business

• *Case Study* •

H. B. Fuller in Honduras:
Street Children and Substance Abuse

Norman Bowie • Stefanie Ann Lenway

In the summer of 1985 the following news story was brought to the attention of an official of the H. B. Fuller Company in St. Paul, Minnesota.

Glue Sniffing Among Honduran Street Children in Honduras: Children Sniffing Their Lives Away

An Inter Press Service Feature
By Peter Ford

Tegucigalpa July 16, 1985 (IPS)—They lie senseless on doorsteps and pavements, grimy and loose limbed, like discarded rag dolls.

Some are just five or six years old. Others are already young adults, and all are addicted to sniffing a commonly sold glue that is doing them irreversible brain damage.

Roger, 21, has been sniffing "Resistol" for eight years. Today, even when he is not high, Roger walks with a stagger, his motor control wrecked. His scarred face puckers with concentration, his right foot taps nervously, incessantly, as he talks.

Since he was 11, when he ran away from the aunt who raised him, Roger's home has been the streets of the capital of Honduras, the second poorest nation in the western hemisphere after Haiti.

Roger spends his time begging, shining shoes, washing car windows, scratching together a few pesos a day, and sleeping in doorways at night.

Sniffing glue, he says, "makes me feel happy, makes me feel big. What do I care if my family does not love me? I know it's doing me damage, but it's a habit I have got, and a habit's a habit. I can not give it up, even though I want to."

No one knows how many of Tegucigalpa's street urchins seek escape from the squalor and misery of their daily existence through the hallucinogenic

Norman Bowie and Stefanie Ann Lenway, University of Minnesota. All rights reserved by Graduate School of Business, Columbia University. The authors express their deep appreciation to the H. B. Fuller Company for providing access to company documents and personnel relevant to this case. Reprinted by permission.

fumes of "Resistol." No one has spent the time and money needed to study the question.

But one thing is clear, according to Dr. Rosalio Zavala, Head of the Health Ministry's Mental Health Department, "these children come from the poorest slums of the big cities. They have grown up as illegal squatters in very disturbed states of mental health, tense, depressed, aggressive.

"Some turn that aggression on society, and start stealing. Others turn it on themselves, and adopt self destructive behavior . . ."

But, he understands the attraction of the glue, whose solvent, toluene, produces feelings of elation. "It gives you delusions of grandeur, you feel powerful, and that compensates these kids for reality, where they feel completely worthless, like nobodies."

From the sketchy research he has conducted, Dr. Zavala believes that most boys discover Resistol for the first time when they are about 11, though some children as young as five are on their way to becoming addicts.

Of a small sample group of children interviewed in reform schools here, 56 percent told Zavala that friends introduced them to the glue, but it is easy to find on the streets for oneself:

Resistol is a contact cement glue, widely used by shoe repairers, and available at household goods stores everywhere . . .

In some states of the United States, glue containing addictive narcotics such as toluene must also contain oil of mustard—the chemical used to produce poisonous mustard gas—which makes sniffing the glue so painful it is impossible to tolerate. There is no federal U.S. law on the use of oil of mustard, however . . .

But even for Dr. Zavala, change is far more than a matter of just including a chemical compound, such as oil of mustard, in a contact cement.

"This is a social problem," he acknowledges. "What we need is a change in philosophy, a change in social organization."

Resistol is manufactured by H. B. Fuller S. A., a subsidiary of Kativo Chemical Industries, S. A. which in turn is a wholly owned subsidiary of the H. B. Fuller Company of St. Paul, Minnesota.[1] Kativo sells more than a dozen different adhesives under the Resistol brand name in several countries in Latin America for a variety of industrial and commercial applications. In Honduras the Resistol products have a strong market position.

Three of the Resistol products are solvent-based adhesives designed with certain properties that are not possible to attain with a water-based formula. These properties include rapid set, strong adhesion, and water resistance. These products are similar to airplane glue or rubber cement and are primarily intended for use in shoe manufacturing and repair, leatherwork, and carpentry.

Even though the street children of each Central American country may have a different choice of a drug for substance abuse, and even though Resistol is not the only glue that Honduran street children use as an inhalant, the term "Resistolero" stuck and has become synonymous with all street children, whether they use inhalants or not. In Honduras Resistol is identified as the abused substance.

Edward Sheehan writes in *Agony in the Garden:*

Resistol. I had heard about Resistol. It was a glue, the angel dust of Honduran orphans. . . . In Tegucigalpa, their addiction had become so common they were known as los Resistoleros. (p. 32)

Honduras[2]

The social problems that contribute to widespread inhalant abuse among street children can be attributed to the depth of poverty in Honduras. In 1989, 65 percent of all households and 40 percent of urban households in Honduras were living in poverty, making it one of the poorest countries in Latin America. Between 1950 and 1988, the increase in the Honduran gross domestic product (GDP) was 3.8 percent, only slightly greater than the average yearly increase in population growth. In 1986, the Honduran GDP was about U.S. $740 per capita and has only grown slightly since. Infant and child mortality rates are high, life expectancy for adults is 64 years, and the adult literacy rate is estimated to be about 60 percent.

Honduras has faced several economic obstacles in its efforts to industrialize. First, it lacks abundant natural resources. The mountainous terrain has restricted agricultural productivity and growth. In addition, the small domestic market and competition from more industrially advanced countries has prevented the manufacturing sector from progressing much beyond textiles, food processing, and assembly operations.

The key to the growth of the Honduran economy has been the production and export of two commodities—bananas and coffee. Both the vagaries in the weather and the volatility of commodity markets had made the foreign exchange earned from these products very unstable. Without consistently strong export sales, Honduras has not been able to buy sufficient fuel and other productive input to allow the growth of its manufacturing sector. It also had to import basic grains (corn and rice) because the country's traditional staples are produced inefficiently by small farmers using traditional technologies with poor soil.

In the 1970s the Honduran government relied on external financing to invest in physical and social infrastructures and to implement development programs intended to diversify the economy. Government spending increased 10.4 percent a year from 1973. By 1981, the failure of many of these development projects led the government to stop financing state-owned industrial projects. The public sector failures were attributed to wasteful administration, mismanagement, and corruption. Left with little increase in productivity to show for these investments, Honduras continues to face massive budgetary deficits and unprecedented levels of external borrowing.

The government deficit was further exacerbated in the early 1980s by increasing levels of unemployment. By 1983, unemployment reached 20–30 percent of the economically active population, with an additional 40 percent of the population underemployed, primarily in agriculture. The rising unemployment, falling real wages, and low level of existing social infrastructure in education and health care contributed to the low level of labor productivity. Unemployment benefits were very limited and only about 7.3 percent of the population was covered by social security.

Rural-to-urban migration has been a major contributor to urban growth in Honduras. In the 1970s the urban population grew at more than twice as fast a rate as the rural population. This migration has increased in part as a result of a high birth rate among the rural population, along with a move by large landholders to convert forest and fallow land, driving off subsistence farmers to use the land for big-scale cotton and beef farming. As more and more land was enclosed, an increasing number of landless sought the cities for a better life.

Tegucigalpa, the capital, has had one of the fastest population increases among Central American cities, growing by 178,000 between 1970 and 1980, with a projected population of 975,000 by the year 2000. Honduras' second largest city, San Pedro Sula, is projected to have a population of 650,000 by 2000.

The slow growth in the industrial and commercial sectors has not been adequate to provide jobs for those moving to the city. The migrants to the urban areas typically move first to cuarterias (rows) of connected rooms. The rooms are generally constructed of wood with dirt floors, and they are usually windowless. The average household contains about seven persons, who live together in a single room. For those living in the rooms facing an alley, the narrow passageway between buildings serves both as sewage and waste disposal area and as a courtyard for as many as 150 persons.

Although more than 70 percent of the families living in these cuarterias had one member with a permanent salaried job, few could survive on that income alone. For stable extended families, salaried income is supplemented by entrepreneurial activities, such as selling tortillas. Given migratory labor, high unemployment, and income insecurity many family relationships are unstable. Often the support of children is left to mothers. Children are frequently forced to leave school, helping support the family through shining shoes, selling newspapers, or guarding cars; such help often is essential income. If a lone mother has become sick or dies, her children may be abandoned to the streets.

Kativo Chemical Industries S.A.[3]

Kativo celebrated its 40th anniversary in 1989. It is now one of the 500 largest private corporations in Latin America. In 1989, improved sales in most of Central American were partially offset by a reduction of its sales in Honduras.

Walter Kissling, chairman of Kativo's board and senior vice president for H. B. Fuller's international operations, has the reputation of giving the company's local managers a high degree of autonomy. Local managers often have to respond quickly because of unexpected currency fluctuations. He comments that, "In Latin America, if you know what you are doing, you can make more money managing your balance sheet than by selling products." The emphasis on managing the balance sheet in countries with high rates of inflation has led Kativo managers to develop a distinctive competence in finance.

In spite of the competitive challenge of operating under unstable political and economic conditions Kativo managers emphasized in the annual report the importance of going beyond the bottom line:

Kativo is an organization with a profound philosophy and ethical conduct, worthy of the most advanced firms. It carries out business with the utmost respect for ethical and legal principles and its orientation is not solely directed to the customer, who has the highest priority, but also to the shareholders, and communities where it operates.

In the early 1980s the managers of Kativo, which was primarily a paint company, decided to enter the adhesive market in Latin America. Their strategy was to combine their marketing experience with H. B. Fuller's products. Kativo found the adhesive market potentially profitable in Latin America because it lacked strong competitors. Kativo's initial concern was to win market share. Resistol was the brand name for all adhesive products including the water-based school glue.

Kativo and the Street Children

In 1983, Honduran newspapers carried articles about police arrests of "Resistoleros"—street children drugging themselves by sniffing glue. In response to these newspaper articles, Kativo's Honduras advertising agency, Calderon Publicidad, informed the newspapers that Resistol was not the only substance abused by street children and that the image of the manufacturer was being damaged by using a prestigious trademark as a synonym for drug abusers. Moreover glue sniffing was not caused by something inherent in the product but was a social problem. For example, on one occasion the company complained to the editor, requesting that he "make the necessary effort to recommend to the editorial staff that they abstain from using the brand name Resistol as a synonym for the drug, and the adjective Resistolero as a synonym for the drug addict."

The man on the spot was Kativo's Vice President, Humberto Larach ("Beto"), a Honduran, who headed Kativo's North Adhesives Division. Managers in nine countries including all of Central America, Mexico, the Caribbean and two South American countries, Ecuador and Colombia, reported to him. He had became manager of the adhesive division after demonstrating his entrepreneurial talents managing Kativo's paint business in Honduras.

Beto had proven his courage and his business creativity when he was among 105 taken hostage in the Chamber of Commerce building in downtown San Pedro Sula by guerrillas from the Communist Popular Liberation Front. Despite fire fights between the guerrillas and government troops, threats of execution, and being used as a human shield, Beto had sold his product to two clients (fellow hostages) who had previously been buying products from Kativo's chief competitor! Beto also has a reputation for emphasizing the importance of "Making the bottom line," as a part of Kativo corporate culture.

By summer 1985, more than corporate image was at stake. As a solution to the glue sniffing problem social activists working with street children suggested that oil of mustard, allyl isothiocyanate, could be added to the product to prevent its abuse. They argued that a person attempting to sniff glue with oil of mustard added would find it too powerful to tolerate. Sniffing it has been described like getting an "overdose of horseradish." An attempt to legislate the addition of oil of mustard received a boost when Honduran Peace Corps volunteer, Timothy Bicknell, convinced a local group called the "Committee for the Prevention of Drugs at the National Level," of the necessity of adding oil of mustard to Resistol. All members of the committee were prominent members of Honduran society.

Beto, in response to the growing publicity about the "Resistoleros," requested staff members of H. B. Fuller's U.S. headquarters to look into the viability of oil of mustard as a solution with special attention to side effects and whether it was required or used in the U.S. H. B. Fuller's corporate industrial hygiene staff found 1983 toxicology reports that oil of mustard was a cancer-causing agent in tests run with rats. A 1986 toxicology report from the Aldrich Chemical Company described the health hazard data of allyl isothiocyanate as:

Acute Effects

May be fatal if inhaled, swallowed, or absorbed through skin.

Carcinogen.

Causes burns.

Material is extremely destructive to tissue of the mucous membranes and upper respiratory tract, eyes and skin.

Prolonged Contact Can Cause:

Nausea, dizziness and headache.

Severe irritation or burns.

Lung irritation, chest pain and edema which may be fatal.

Repeated exposure may cause asthma.

In addition the product had a maximum shelf-life of six months.

To the best of our knowledge, the chemical, physical and toxicological properties have not been thoroughly investigated.

In 1986, Beto contacted Hugh Young, president of Solvent Abuse Foundation for Education (SAFE), and gathered information on programs SAFE had developed in Mexico. Young, who believed that there was no effective deterrent, took the position that the only viable approach to substance abuse was education, not product modification. He argued that reformulating the product was an exercise in futility because "nothing is available in the solvent area that is not abusable." With these reports in hand, Beto attempted to persuade Resistol's critics, relief agencies, and government officials that adding oil of mustard to Resistol was not the solution to the glue sniffing problem.

During the summer of 1986 Beto had his first success in changing the mind of one journalist. Earlier in the year Mary Kawas, an independent writer, wrote an article sympathetic to the position of Timothy Bicknell and the Committee for the Prevention of Drugs in Honduras. In June, Beto met with her and explained how both SAFE and Kativo sought a solution that was not product-oriented but that was directed at changing human behavior. She was also informed of the research on the dangers of oil of mustard (about which additional information had been obtained). Kawas then wrote an article:

Education Is the Solution for Drug Addiction

LA CEIBA. (BY MARIE J. KAWAS).

A lot of people have been interested in combating drug addiction among youths and children, but few have sought solutions, and almost no one looks into the feasibility of the alternatives that are so desperately proposed . . .

Oil of mustard (allyl isothiocyanate) may well have been an irresponsible solution in the United States of America during the sixties and seventies, and the Hondurans want to adopt this as a panacea without realizing that their information sources are out of date. Through scientific progress, it has been found that the inclusion of oil of mustard in products which contain solvents, in order to prevent their perversion into use as an addictive drug, only causes greater harm to the consumers and workers involved in their manufacture . . .

Education is a primordial instrument for destroying a social cancer. An effort of this magnitude requires the cooperation of different individuals and organizations . . .

Future generations of Hondurans will be in danger of turning into human parasites, without a clear awareness of what is harmful to them. But if drugs and ignorance are to blame, it is even more harmful to sin by indifference before those very beings who are growing up in an environment without the basic advantages for a healthy physical and mental existence. Who will be the standard bearer in the philanthropic activities which will provide Honduras with the education necessary to combat drug addiction? Who will be remiss in their duty in the face of the nation's altruism?

At first, Beto did not have much success at the governmental level. In September 1986, Dr. Rosalio Zavala, Head of the Mental Health Division of the Honduran Ministry of Health, wrote an article attacking the improper use of Resistol by youth. Beto was unsuccessful in his attempt to contact Dr. Zavala. He had better luck with Mrs. Norma Castro, Governor of the State of Cortes, who after a conversation with Beto became convinced that oil of mustard had serious dangers and that glue sniffing was a social problem.

Beto's efforts continued into the new year. Early in 1987, Kativo began to establish Community Affairs Councils, as a planned expansion of the worldwide company's philosophy of community involvement. These employee committees had already been in place in the U.S. since 1978.

A company document gave the purpose of Community Affairs Councils:

To educate employees about community issues.

To develop understanding of, and be responsive to the communities near our facilities.

To contribute to Kativo/H. B. Fuller's corporate presence in the neighborhoods and communities we are a part of.

To encourage and support employee involvement in the community.

To spark a true interest in the concerns of the communities in which we live and work.

The document goes on to state, "We want to be more than just bricks, mortar, machines and people. We want to be a company with recognized values, demonstrating involvement, and commitment to the betterment of the communities we are a part of." Later that year, the Honduran community affairs committees went on to make contributions to several organizations working with street children.

In May 1987, Beto visited Jose Oqueli, Vice-Minister of Public Health, to explain the philosophy behind H. B. Fuller's Community Affairs program. He also informed him of the health hazards of oil of mustard; they discussed the cultural, family and economic roots of the problem of glue-sniffing among street children.

In June 1987, Parents Resource Institute for Drug Education (PRIDE) set up an office in San Pedro Sula. PRIDE's philosophy was that through adequate *parental* education on the drug problem, it would be possible to deal with the problems of inhalant use. PRIDE was a North American organization that had taken international Nancy Reagan's "just say no" approach to inhalant abuse. Like SAFE, PRIDE took the position that oil of mustard was not the solution to glue-sniffing.

Through PRIDE, Beto was introduced to Wilfredo Alvarado, the new Head of the Mental Health Division in the Ministry of Health. Dr. Alvarado, an advisor to the Congressional Committee on Health, was in charge of preparing draft legislation and evaluating legislation received by Congress. Together with Dr. Alvarado, the Kativo staff worked to prepare draft legislation addressing the problem of inhalant addicted children. At the same time, five Congressmen drafted a proposed law that required the use of oil of mustard in locally produced or imported solvent based adhesives.

In June 1988, Dr. Alvarado asked the Congressional Committee on Health to reject the legislation proposed by the five congressmen. Alvarado was given 60 days to present a complete draft of legislation. In August 1988, however, he retired from his position and Kativo lost its primary communication channel with the Committee. This was critical because Beto was relying on Alvarado to help insure that the legislation reflected the technical information that he had collected.

The company did not have an active lobbying or government monitoring function in Tegucigalpa, the capital, which tends to be isolated from the rest of the country. (In fact, the company's philosophy has generally been not to lobby on behalf of its own narrow self-interest.) Beto, located in San Pedro Sula, had no staff support to help him monitor political developments. Monitoring, unfortunately, was an addition to his regular, daily responsibilities. His ability to keep track of political developments were made more difficult by the fact that he traveled about 45 percent of the time outside of Honduras. It took over two months for Beto to learn of Alvarado's departure from government. When the legislation was passed in March, he was completely absorbed in reviewing strategic plans for the nine-country divisions which report to him.

On March 30, 1989, the Honduran Congress approved the legislation drafted by the five congressmen.

After the law's passage Beto spoke to the press about the problems with the legislation. He argued:

This type of cement is utilized in industry, in crafts, in the home, schools, and other places where it has become indispensable; thus by altering the product, he said, not only will the drug addiction problem not be solved, but rather, the country's development would be slowed.

In order to put an end to the inhalation of Resistol by dozens of people, various products which are daily necessities would have to be eliminated from the marketplace. This is impossible, he added, since it would mean a serious setback to industry at several levels . . .

There are studies that show that the problem is not the glue itself, but rather the individual. The mere removal of this substance would immediately be substituted by some other, to play the same hallucinogenic trip for the person who was sniffing it.

H. B. Fuller: The Corporate Response

In late April 1986, Elmer Andersen, H. B. Fuller Chairman of the Board, received the following letter:

4/21/86

Elmer L. Andersen
H. B. Fuller Co.

Dear Mr. Andersen

I heard part of your talk on public radio recently, and was favorably impressed with your philosophy that business should not be primarily for profit. This was consistent with my previous impression of H. B. Fuller Co. since I am a public health nurse and have been aware of your benevolence to the nursing profession.

However, on a recent trip to Honduras, I spent some time at a new home for chemically dependent "street boys" who are addicted to glue sniffing. It was estimated that there are 600 of these children still on the streets in San Pedro Sula alone. The glue is sold for repairing *tennis shoes* and I am told it is made by H. B. Fuller in *Costa Rica*. These children also suffer toxic effects of liver and brain damage from the glue . . .

Hearing you on the radio, I immediately wondered how this condemnation of H. B. Fuller Company could be consistent with the company as I knew it before and with your business philosophy.

Are you aware of this problem in Honduras, and, if so, how are you dealing with it?

That a stockholder should write the 76-year-old Chairman of the Board directly is significant. Elmer Andersen is a legendary figure in Minnesota. He is responsible for the financial success of H. B. Fuller from 1941–1971 and his values reflected in his actions as CEO are embodied in H. B. Fuller's mission statement.

H. B. Fuller Mission Statement

The H. B. Fuller corporate mission is to be a leading and profitable worldwide formulator, manufacturer, and marketer of quality specialty chemicals, emphasizing service to customers and managed in accordance with a strategic plan.

H. B. Fuller Company is committed to its responsibilities, in order of priority, to its customers, employees and shareholders. H. B. Fuller will conduct business legally and ethically, support the activities of its employees in their communities, and be a responsible corporate citizen.

It was also Elmer Andersen who, as President and CEO, made the decision that foreign acquisitions should be managed by locals. Concerning the 1967 acquisition of Kativo Chemical Industries Ltd. Elmer Andersen said:

> We had two objectives in mind. One was directly business related and one was altruistic. Just as we had expanded in America, our international business strategy was to pursue markets where our competitors were not active. We were convinced that we had something to offer Latin America that the region did not have locally. In our own small way, we also wanted to be of help to that part of the world. We believed that by producing adhesives in Latin America and by employing only local people, we would create new jobs and help elevate the standard of living. We were convinced that the way to aid world peace was to help Latin America become more prosperous.

Three years later a stockholder dramatically raised the Resistol issue for a second time directly by a stockholder. On June 7, 1989, Vice President for Corporate Relations, Dick Johnson, received a call from a stockholder whose daughter was in the Peace Corps in Honduras. She asked, "How can a company like H. B. Fuller claim to have a social conscience and continue to sell Resistol which is 'literally burning out the brains' of children in Latin America?"

Johnson was galvanized into action. This complaint was of special concern because he was about to meet with a national group of socially responsible investors who were considering including H. B. Fuller's stock in their portfolio. Fortunately Karen Muller, Director of Community Affairs, had been keeping a file on the glue sniffing problem. Within 24 hours of receiving the call, Dick had written a memo to CEO Tony Andersen.

In that memo he set forth the basic values to be considered as H. B. Fuller wrestled with the problem. Among them were the following:

1. H. B. Fuller's explicitly stated public concern about substance abuse
2. H. B. Fuller's "Concern for Youth" focus in its community affairs projects.
3. H. B. Fuller's reputation as a socially responsible company.
4. H. B. Fuller's history of ethical conduct.
5. H. B. Fuller's commitment to the intrinsic value of each individual.

Whatever "solution" was ultimately adopted would have to be consistent with these values. In addition, Dick suggested a number of options including the company's withdrawal from the market or perhaps altering the formula to make Resistol a water-based product, eliminating sniffing as an issue.

Tony responded by suggesting that Dick create a task force to find a solution and a plan to implement it. Dick decided to accept Beto's invitation to travel to Honduras to view the situation first hand. He understood that the problem crossed functional and divisional responsibilities. Given H. B. Fuller's high visibility as a socially responsible corporation, the glue sniffing problem had the potential for becoming a public relations nightmare. The brand name of one of H. B. Fuller's products had become synonymous with a serious social problem. Additionally, Dick understood that there was an issue larger than product misuse involved, and it had social and community ramifications. The issue was <u>substance abuse by children</u>, whether the substance is a H. B. Fuller product or not. As a part of the solution, a community relations response was required. Therefore, he invited Karen to join him on his trip to Honduras.

Karen recalled a memo she had written about a year earlier directed to Beto. In it she had suggested a community relations approach rather than Beto's government relations approach. In that memo Karen wrote:

> This community relations process involves developing a community-wide coalition from all those with a vested interest in solving the community issue—those providing services in dealing with the street children and drug users, other businesses, and the government. It does require leadership over the long-term both with a clear set of objectives and a commitment on the part of each group represented to share in the solution . . .

In support of the community relations approach Karen argued that:

1. It takes the focus and pressure off H. B. Fuller as one individual company.
2. It can educate the broader community and focus on the best solution, not just the easiest ones.
3. It holds everyone reponsible, the government, educators, H. B. Fuller's customers, legitimate consumers of our product, social service workers and agencies.
4. It provides H. B. Fuller with an expanded good image as a company that cares and will stay with the problem—that we are willing to go the second mile.
5. It can de-politicize the issue.
6. It offers the opportunity to counterbalance the negative impact of the use of our product named Resistol by re-identifying the problem.

Karen and Dick left on a four-day trip to Honduras September 18. Upon arriving they were joined by Beto, Oscar Sahuri, General Manager for Kativo's adhesives business in Honduras, and Jorge Walter Bolanos, Vice-President Director of Finance, Kativo. Karen had also asked Mark Connelly, a health consultant from an international agency working with street children, to join the group. They began the process of looking at all aspects of the situation. Visits to two different small shoe manufacturing shops and a shoe supply distributor helped to clarify the issues around pricing, sales, distribution, and the packaging of the product.

A visit to a well-run shelter for street children provided them with some insight into the dynamics of substance abuse among this vulnerable population in the streets of Tegucigalpa and San Pedro Sula. At a meeting with the officials at the Ministry of Health, they reviewed the issue of implementing the oil-of-mustard law, and the Kativo managers offered to assist the committee as it reviewed the details of the law. In both Tegucigalpa and San Pedro Sula, the National Commission for Technical Assistance to Children in Irregular Situations (CONATNSI), a county-wide association of private and public agencies working with street children, organized meetings of its members at which the

Kativo managers offered an explanation of the company's philosophy and the hazards involved in the use of oil of mustard.

As they returned from their trip to Honduras, Karen and Dick had the opportunity to reflect on what they had learned. They agreed that removing Resistol from the market would not resolve the problem. However, the problem was extremely complex. The use of inhalants by street children was a symptom of Honduras' underlying economic problems—problems with social, cultural, and political aspects as well as economic dimensions.

Honduran street children come from many different circumstances. Some are true orphans while others are abandoned. Some are runaways, while others are working the streets to help support their parents. Children working at street jobs or begging usually earn more than the minimum wage. Nevertheless, they are often punished if they bring home too little. This creates a vicious circle; they would rather be on the street than take punishment at home—a situation that increases the likelihood they will fall victim to drug addiction. The street children's problems are exacerbated by the general lack of opportunities and a lack of enforcement of school attendance laws. In addition, the police sometimes abuse street children.

Karen and Dick realized that Resistol appeared to be the drug of choice for young street children, and children were able to obtain it in a number of different ways. There was no clear pattern, and hence the solution could not be found in simply changing some features of the distribution system. Children might obtain the glue from legitimate customers, small shoe repair stalls, by theft, from "illegal" dealers or from third parties who purchased it from legitimate stores and then sold it to children. For some sellers the sale of Resistol to children could be profitable. The glue was available in small packages which made it more affordable, but the economic circumstances of the typical legitimate customer made packaging in small packages economically sensible.

The government had long been unstable. As a result there was a tendency for people working with the government to hope that new policy initiatives would fade away within a few months. Moreover there was a large continuing turnover of government, so that any knowledge of H. B. Fuller and its corporate philosophy soon disappeared. Government officials usually had to settle for a quick fix, for they were seldom around long enough to manage any other kind of policy. Although it was on the books for six months by the time of their trip, the oil-of-mustard law had not yet been implemented, and national elections were to be held in three months. During meetings with government officials, it appeared to Karen and Dick that no further actions would be taken as current officials waited for the election outcome.

Kativo company officers, Jorge Walter Bolanos and Humberto Larach, discussed continuing the government relations strategy hoping that the law might be repealed or modified. They were also concerned with the damage done to H. B. Fuller's image. Karen and Dick thought the focus should be on community relations. From their perspective, efforts directed toward changing the law seemed important but would do nothing to help with the long-term solution to the problems of the street children who abused glue.

Much of the concern for street children was found in private agencies. The chief coordinating association was CONATNSI, created as a result of a seminar sponsored by UNICEF in 1987. CONATNSI was under the direction of a general assembly and a Board of Directors elected by the General Assembly. It began its work in 1988; its objectives included a) improving the quality of services, b) promoting interchange of experiences, c) coordinating human and material resources, d) offering technical support, and e) promoting research. Karen and others believe that CONATNSI had a shortage of both financial and human resources, but it appeared to be well-organized and was a potential intermediary for the company.

As a result of their trip, they knew that a community relations strategy would be complex and risky. H. B. Fuller was committed to a community relations approach, but what would a community relations solution look like in Honduras? The mission statement did not provide a complete answer. It indicated the company had responsibilities to its Honduran customers and employees, but exactly what kind? Were there other responsibilities beyond that directly involving its product? What effect can a single company have in solving an intractable social problem? How should the differing emphases in perspective of Kativo and its parent, H. B. Fuller, be handled? What does corporate citizenship require in situations like this?

Notes

1. The Subsidiaries of the North Adhesives Division of Kativo Chemical Industries, S.A. go by the name "H. B. Fuller (Country of Operation)," e.g., H. B. Fuller S. A. Honduras. To prevent confusion with the parent company we will refer to H. B. Fuller S. A. Honduras by the name of its parent, "Kativo."

2. The following discussion is based on *Honduras: A Country Study*, 2nd ed., James D. Rudolph, ed. (Washington, D.C.: Department of the Army, 1984).

3. Unless otherwise indicated all references and quotations regarding H. B. Fuller and its subsidiary Kativo Chemical Industries S. A. are from company documents.

Sources

Acker, Alison, *The Making of a Banana Republic* (Boston: South End Press, 1988).

H. B. Fuller Company, *A Fuller Life: The Story of H. B. Fuller Company: 1887–1987* (St. Paul: H. B. Fuller Company, 1986).

Rudolph, James D., ed., *Honduras: A Country Study*, 2nd ed. (Washington, D.C.: Department of the Army, 1984).

Schine, Eric, "Preparing for Banana Republic U.S." *Corporate Finance* (December, 1987).

Sheehan, Edward, *Agony in the Garden: A Stranger in Central America* (Boston: Houghton Mifflin, 1989).

Relativism, Cultural and Moral

NORMAN BOWIE

Cultural relativism is a descriptive claim that ethical practices differ among cultures; that, as a matter of fact, what is considered right in one culture may be considered wrong in another. Thus truth or falsity of cultural relativism can be determined by examining the world. The work of anthropologists and sociologists is most relevant in determining the truth or falsity of cultural relativism, and there is widespread consensus among social scientists that cultural relativism is true.

Moral relativism is the claim that what is really right or wrong is what the culture says is right or wrong. Moral relativists accept cultural relativism as true, but they claim much more. If a culture sincerely and reflectively adopts a basic moral principle, then it is morally obligatory for members of that culture to act in accordance with that principle.

The implication of moral relativism for conduct is that one ought to abide by the ethical norms of the culture where one is located. This position is captured by the popular phrase "When in Rome, do as the Romans do." Relativists in ethics would say "One ought to follow the moral norms of the culture." In terms of business practice, consider the question, "Is it morally right to pay a bribe to gain business?" The moral relativist would answer the question by consulting the moral norms of the country where one is doing business. If those norms permit bribery in that country, then the practice of bribery is not wrong in that country. However, if the moral norms of the country do not permit bribery, then offering a bribe to gain business in that country is morally wrong. The justification for that position is the moral relativist's contention that what is really right or wrong is determined by the culture.

Is cultural relativism true? Is moral relativism correct? As noted, many social scientists believe that cultural relativism is true as a matter of fact. But is it?

First, many philosophers claim that the "facts" aren't really what they seem. Early twentieth-century anthropologists cited the fact that in some cultures, after a certain age, parents are put to death. In most cultures such behavior would be murder. Does this difference in behavior prove that the two cultures disagree about fundamental matters of ethics? No, it does not. Suppose the other culture believes that people exist in the afterlife in the same condition that they leave their present life. It would be very cruel to have one's parents exist eternally in an unhealthy state. By killing them when they are relatively active and vigorous, you insure their happiness for all eternity. The *underlying* ethical principle of this culture is that children have duties to their parents, including the duty to be concerned with their parents' happiness as they approach old age. This ethical principle is identical with our own. What looked like a difference in ethics between our culture and another turned out, upon close examination, to be a difference based on what each culture takes to be the facts of the matter. This example does, of course, support the claim that as a matter of fact ethical principles vary according to culture. However, it does not support the stronger conclusion that *underlying* ethical principles vary according to culture.

Cultures differ in physical setting, in economic development, in the state of their science and technology, in their literacy rate, and in many other ways. Even if there were universal moral principles, they would have to be applied in these different cultural contexts. Given the different situations in which cultures exist, it would come as no surprise to find universal principles applied in different ways. Hence we expect to find surface differences in ethical behavior among cultures even though the cultures agree on fundamental universal moral principles. For example, one commonly held universal principle appeals to the public good; it says that social institutions and individual behavior should be ordered so that they lead to the greatest good for the greatest number. Many different forms of social organization and individual behavior are consistent with this principle. The point of these two arguments is to show that differences among cultures on ethical behavior may not reflect genuine disagreement about underlying principles of ethics. Thus it is not so obvious that any strong form of cultural relativism is true.

But are there universal principles that are accepted by all cultures? It seems so; there does seem to be a whole range of behavior, such as torture and murder of the innocent, that every culture agrees is wrong. A nation-state accused of torture does not respond by saying that a condemnation of torture is just a matter of cultural choice. The state's leaders do not respond by saying, "We think torture is right, but you do not." Rather, the standard response is to deny that any torture took place. If the evidence of torture is too strong, a finger will be pointed either at the victim or at the morally outraged country: "They do it too." In this case the guilt is spread to all. Even the Nazis denied that genocide took place. What is important is that *no* state replies that there is nothing wrong with genocide or torture.

In addition, there are attempts to codify some universal moral principles. The United Nations Universal Declaration of Human Rights has been endorsed by the member states of the U.N., and the vast majority of countries in the world are members of the U.N. Even in business, there is a growing effort to adopt universal principles of business practice. In a recent study of international codes of ethics, Professors Catherine Langlois and Bodo B. Schlegelmich found that although there certainly were differences among codes, there was a considerable area of agreement (Langlois and Schlegelmich, 1990). William Frederick has documented the details of six international compacts on matters of international business ethics. These include the aforementioned U.N. Universal Declaration of Human Rights, the European Convention on Human Rights, the Helsinki Final Act, the OECD Guidelines for Multinational Enterprises and Social Policy, and the United Nations Conduct on Transnational Corporations (in progress) (Frederick 1991). The Caux Roundtable, a group of corporate executives from the United States, Europe, and Japan, are seeking worldwide endorsement of a set of principles of business ethics. Thus there are a number of reasons to think that cultural relativism, at least with respect to basic moral principles, is not true, that is, that it does not accurately describe the state of moral agreement that exists. This is consistent with maintaining that cultural relativism is true in the weak form, that is, when applied only to surface ethical principles.

But what if differences in fundamental moral practices among cultures are discovered and seem unreconcilable? That would lead to a discussion about the adequacy of moral relativism. The fact that moral practices do vary widely among countries is cited as evidence for the correctness of moral relativism. The discoveries, early in the century, by anthropologists, sociologists, and psychologists documented the diversity of moral beliefs. Philosophers, by and large, welcomed corrections of moral imperialist thinking, but recognized that the moral relativist's appeal to the alleged truth of cultural relativism was not enough to establish moral relativism. The mere fact that a culture considers a practice moral does not mean that it is moral. Cultures have sincerely practiced slavery, discrimination, and the torture of animals. Yet each of these practices can be independently criticized on ethical grounds. Thinking something is morally permissible does not make it so.

Another common strategy for criticizing moral relativism is to show that the consequences of taking the perspective of moral relativism are inconsistent with our use of moral language. It is often contended by moral relativists that if two cultures disagree regarding universal moral principles, there is no way for that disagreement to be resolved. Since moral relativism is the view that what is right or wrong is determined by culture, there is not higher appeal beyond the fact that culture endorses the moral principle. But we certainly do not talk that way. When China and the United States argue about the moral rights of human beings, the disputants use language that seems to appeal to universal moral principles. Moreover, the atrocities of the Nazis and the slaughter in Rwanda has met with universal condemnation that seemed based on universal moral principles. So moral relativism is not consistent with our use of moral language.

Relativism is also inconsistent with how we use the term "moral reformer." Suppose, for instance, that a person from one culture moves to another and tries to persuade the other culture to change its view. Suppose someone moves from a culture where slavery is immoral to one where slavery is morally permitted. Normally, if a person were to try to convince the culture where slavery was permitted that slavery was morally wrong, we would call such a person a moral reformer. Moreover, a moral reformer would almost certainly appeal to universal moral principles to make her argument; she almost certainly would not appeal to a competing cultural standard. But if moral relativism were true, there would be no place for the concept of a moral reformer. Slavery is really right in those cultures that say it is right and really wrong in the cultures that say it is wrong. If the reformer fails to persuade a slaveholding country to change its mind, the reformer's antislavery position was never right. If the reformer is successful in persuading a country to change its mind, the reformer's antislavery views would be wrong—until the country did, in fact, change its view. Then the reformer's antislavery view would be right. But that is not how we talk about moral reform.

The moral relativist might argue that our language should be reformed. We should talk differently. At one time people used to talk and act as if the world were flat. Now they don't. The relativist could suggest that we can change our ethical language in the same way. But consider how radical the relativists' response is. Since most, if not all, cultures speak and act as if there were universal moral principles, the relativist can be right only if almost everyone else is wrong. How plausible is that?

Although these arguments are powerful ones, they do not deliver a knockout blow to moral relativism. If there are no universal moral principles, moral relativists could argue that moral relativism is the only theory available to help make sense of moral phenomena.

An appropriate response to this relativist argument is to present the case for a set of universal moral principles, principles that are correct for all cultures independent of what a culture thinks about them. This is what adherents of the various ethical traditions try to do. The reader will have to examine these various traditions and determine how persuasive he finds them. In addition, there are several final independent considerations against moral relativism that can be mentioned here.

First, what constitutes a culture? There is a tendency to equate cultures with national boundaries, but that is naive, especially today. With respect to moral issues, what do U.S. cultural norms say regarding right and wrong? That question may be impossible to answer, because in a highly pluralistic country like the United States, there are many cultures. Furthermore, even if one can identify a culture's moral norms, it will have dissidents who do not subscribe to those moral norms. How many dissidents can a culture put up with and still maintain that some basic moral principle is the cultural norm? Moral relativists have had little to say regarding criteria for constituting a culture or how to account for dissidents. Unless moral relativists offer answers to questions like these, their theory is in danger of becoming inapplicable to the real world.

Second, any form of moral relativism must admit that there are some universal moral principles. Suppose a culture does not accept moral relativism, that is, it denies that if an entire culture sincerely and reflectively adopts a basic moral principle, it is obligatory for members of that culture to act in accord with that principle. Fundamentalist Muslim countries would reject moral relativism because it would require them to accept as morally permissible blasphemy in those countries where blasphemy was permitted. If the moral relativist insists that the truth of every moral principle depends on the culture, then she must admit that the truth of moral relativism depends on the culture. Therefore the moral relativist must admit that at least the principle of moral relativism is not relative.

Third, it seems that there is a set of basic moral principles that every culture must adopt. You would not have a culture unless the members of the group adopted these moral principles. Consider an anthropologist who arrives on a populated island: How many tribes are on the island? To answer that question, the anthropologist tries to determine if some people on some parts of the island are permitted to kill, commit acts of violence against, or steal from persons on other parts of the island. If such behavior is not permitted, that counts as a reason for saying that there is only one tribe. The underlying assumption here is that there is a set of moral principles that must be followed if there is to be a culture at all. With respect to those moral principles, adhering to them determines whether there is a culture or not.

But what justifies these principles? A moral relativist would say that a culture justifies them. But you cannot have a culture unless the members of the culture follow the principles. Thus it is reasonable to think that justification lies elsewhere. Many believe that the purpose of morality is to help make social cooperation possible. Moral principles are universally necessary for that endeavor.

Bibliography

Benedict, R. (1934). *Patterns of Culture*. New York: Penguin Books.
Bowie, N. (1988). The moral obligations of multinational corporations. In S. Luper-Foy (ed.), *Problems of International Justice*. (pp. 97–113). Boulder, CO: Westview Press.
Frederick, W.C. "The moral authority of transnational corporate codes," *Journal of Business Ethics*. 10 #3 (1991).
Harman, G. (1975). Moral relativism defended. *The Philosophical Review*. *84*. 3–22.
Hatch, E. (1983). *Culture and Morality*. New York: Columbia University Press.
Krausz, M., and Meiland, J. (1982). *Relativism: Cognitive and Moral*. Notre Dame, IN: University of Notre Dame Press.
Ladd, J. (1973). *Ethical Relativism*. Belmont, CA: Wadsworth.
Langlois, C., and Bodo B. Schlegelmich, "Do corporate codes of ethics reflect national character? Evidence from Europe and the United States," *Journal of International Studies*. 21 #9 (1990). pp. 519–39.
Mackie, J. (1977). *Ethics: Inventing Right and Wrong*. Harmondsworth: Penguin Books.
Rachels, J. (1993). *The Elements of Moral Philosophy*, second edition. New York: McGraw-Hill, Inc.
Sayre-McCord, G. (1991). Being a realist about relativism (in ethics). *Philosophical Studies*. *61*. pp. 155–76.
Wong, D. (1984). *Moral Relativity*. Berkeley: University of California Press.

Moral Minimums for Multinationals[1]

THOMAS DONALDSON

When exploring issues of international ethics, researchers frequently neglect multinational corporations. They are prone to forget that these commercial leviathans often rival nation-states in power and organizational skill, and that their remarkable powers imply nonlegal responsibilities. Critics and defenders agree on the enormity of corporate multinational power. Richard Barnet and Ronald Muller, well-known critics of multinationals, remark that the global corporation is the "most powerful human organization yet devised for colonizing the future."[2] The business analyst P. P. Gabriel, writing in the *Harvard Business Review,* characterizes the multinational as the "dominant institution" in a new era of world trade.[3] Indeed, with the exception of a handful of nation-states, multinationals are alone in possessing the size, technology, and economic reach necessary to influence human affairs on a global basis.

"Moral Minimums for Multinationals," by Thomas Donaldson, *Ethics and International Affairs,* Vol. 3 (1989). Reprinted with permission of the publisher and author.

Ethical issues stemming from multinational corporate activities often derive from a clash between the cultural attitudes in home and host countries. When standards for pollution, discrimination, and salary schedules appear lower in a multinational's host country than in the home country, should multinational managers always insist on home-country standards? Or does using home standards imply a failure to respect cultural diversity and national integrity? Is a factory worker in Mexico justified in complaining about being paid three dollars an hour for the same work a U.S. factory worker, employed by the same company, is paid ten dollars?[4] Is an asbestos worker in India justified in criticizing the lower standards for regulating in-plant asbestos pollution maintained by a British multinational relative to standards in Britain, when the standards in question fall within Indian government guidelines and, indeed, are stricter than the standards maintained by other Indian asbestos manufacturers? Furthermore, what obligations, if any, do multinationals have to the people they affect indirectly? If a company buys land from wealthy landowners and turns it to the production of a cash crop, should it ensure that displaced farmers will avoid malnutrition?

I

It is well to remember that multinational power is not a wholly new phenomenon. Hundreds of years ago, the East India Company deployed over 40 warships, possessed the largest standing army in the world, was lord and master of an entire subcontinent, had dominion over 250 million people, and even hired its own church bishops.[5] The modern multinational is a product of the post-World War II era, and its dramatic success has stemmed from, among other factors, spiraling labor costs in developed countries, increasing importance of economies of scale in manufacturing, better communication systems, improved transporation, and increasing worldwide consumer demand for new products.[6] Never far from the evolution of the multinational has been a host of ethical issues, including bribery and corrupt payments, employment and personnel issues, marketing practices, impact on the economy and development of host countries, effects on the natural environment, cultural impacts of multinational operations, relations with host governments, and relations with the home countries.[7]

The formal responsibilities of multinationals as defined in domestic and international law, as well as in codes of conduct, are expanding dramatically. While many codes are nonbinding in the sense that noncompliance will fail to trigger sanctions, these principles, taken as a group, are coming to exert significant influence on multinational conduct. A number of specific reasons lie behind the present surge in international codes and regulations. To begin with, some of the same forces propelling domestic attempts to bring difficult-to-control activities under stricter supervision are influencing multinationals.[8] Consider, for example, hazardous technology, a threat which by its nature recognizes no national boundaries yet must be regulated in both domestic and foreign contexts. The pesticide industry, which relies on such hazardous technology (of which Union Carbide's Bhopal plant is one instance), in 1987 grossed over $13 billion a year and has been experiencing mushrooming growth, especially in the developing countries.[9] It is little surprise that the rapid spread of hazardous technology has prompted the emergence of international codes on hazardous technology, such as the various U.N. resolutions on the transfer of technology and the use of pesticides.

Furthermore, just as a multiplicity of state regulations and laws generates confusion and inefficiency, and stimulates federal attempts to manage conduct, a multiplicity of national regulations stimulates international attempts at control. Precisely this push for uniformity lies behind, for example, many of the international codes of ethics, such as the WHO Code of Marketing Breast Milk Substitutes. Another well-known instance illustrating the need for uniformity involved the collision of French and U.S. law in the sale of equipment by Dresser Industries to the Soviets for the planned European pipeline. U.S. law forbade the sale of such technology to the Soviets for reasons of national security, while French law (which affected a Dresser subsidiary) encouraged it in order to stimulate commercial growth. It was neither to the advantage of Dresser Industries nor to the advantage of the French and U.S. governments to be forced to operate in an arena of conflict and inconsistency. For months the two governments engaged in a public standoff while Dresser, and Dresser's public image, were caught in the middle.

National laws, heretofore unchallenged in authority, are now being eclipsed by regulatory efforts falling into four categories: namely, inter-firm, inter-government, cooperative, and world-organizational efforts.[10] The first category of "inter-firm" standards is one which reflects initiatives from industries, firms, and consumer groups, and it includes the numerous inter-industry codes of conduct that are operative for international business, such as the World Health Organization's Code on Pharmaceuticals and Tobacco, and the World Intellectual Property Organization's Revision of the Paris Convention for the Protection of Industrial Patents and Trademarks. The second category of "inter-government" efforts includes specific-purpose arrangements between and among nation-states, such as the General Agreement on Tariffs and Trade (GATT), the International Monetary Fund (IMF), and the World Bank.[11] "Cooperative" efforts, which comprise the third category, involve governments and industries coordinating skills in mutual arrangements that regulate international commerce. The European Community (EC) and the Andean Common Market (ANCOM) are two notable examples of such cooperative efforts.[12]

Finally, the fourth or "world-organizational" category includes efforts from broad-based global institutions such as the World Court, the International Labor Organization (ILO), the Organization for Economic Cooperation and Development (OECD), and the various sub-entities of the United Nations.

II

The growing tradition of international business codes and policies suggests that the investigation of ethical issues in international business is pressing and proper. But what issues deserve attention?

One key set of issues relates to business practices that clearly conflict with the moral attitudes of most multinationals' home countries. Consider, for example, the practice of child labor, which continues to plague developing countries. While not the worst example, Central America offers a sobering lesson. In dozens of interviews with workers throughout Central America conducted in the fall of 1987, most respondents said they started working between the ages of 12 and 14.[13] The work week lasts six days, and the median salary (for all workers including adults) is scarcely over a dollar a day. The area is largely non-unionized, and strikes are almost always declared illegal. There is strong similarity between the pressures compelling child labor in Central America and those in early nineteenth-century England during the Industrial Revolution. With unemployment ranging from a low of 24 percent in Costa Rica to a high of 50 percent in Guatemala, and with families malnourished and older breadwinners unable to work, children are often forced to make growth-stunting sacrifices.[14]

Then, too, there are issues about which our moral intuitions seem confused, issues which pose difficult questions for researchers. Consider an unusual case involving the sale of banned goods abroad—one in which a developing country argued that being able to buy a banned product was important to meeting its needs. Banned pharmaceuticals, in contrast to other banned goods, have been subject to export restrictions for over 40 years. Yet, in defense of a recent Reagan initiative, drug manufacturers in the United States argued by appealing to differing cultural variables. For example, a spokesman for the American division of Ciba-Geigy Pharmaceuticals justified relaxing restrictions on the sale of its Entero-Vioform, a drug he agrees has been associated with blindness and paralysis, on the basis of culture-specific, cost-benefit analysis. "The government of India," he pointed out, "has requested Ciba-Geigy to continue producing the drug because it treats a dysentery problem that can be life threatening."[15]

III

The task for the international ethicist is to develop or discover concepts capable of specifying the obligations of multinational corporations in cases such as these. One such important concept is that of a human right.

Rights establish minimum levels of morally acceptable behavior. One well-known definition of a right construes it as a "trump" over a collective good, which is to say that the assertion of one's right to something, such as free speech, takes precedence over all but the most compelling collective goals, and overrides, for example, the state's interest in civil harmony or moral consensus.[16] Rights are at the rock bottom of modern moral deliberation. Maurice Cranston writes that the litmus test for whether something is a right or not is whether it protects something of "paramount importance."[17] Hence, it may help to define what minimal responsibilities should be assigned to multinational corporations by asking, "What specific rights ought multinationals to respect?"

The flip side of a right typically is a duty.[18] This, in part, is what gives aptness to Joel Feinberg's well-known definition of a right as a "justified entitlement *to* something *from* someone."[19] It is the "from someone" part of the definition which reflects the assumption of a duty, for without a correlative obligation that attaches to some moral agent or group of agents, a right is weakened—if not beyond the status of a right entirely, then significantly. If we cannot say that a multinational corporation has a duty to keep the levels of arsenic low in the work place, then the worker's right not to be poisoned means little.

Often, duties associated with rights fall upon more than one class of moral agent. Consider, for example, the furor over the dumping of toxic waste in West Africa by multinational corporations. During 1988, virtually every country from Morocco to the Congo on Africa's west coast received offers from companies seeking cheap sites for dumping waste.[20] In the years prior, dumping in the U.S. and Europe had become enormously expensive, in large part because of the costly safety measures mandated by U.S. and European governments. In February of 1988, officials in Guinea-Bissau, one of the world's poorest nations, agreed to bury 15 million tons of toxic wastes from European tanneries and pharmaceutical companies. The companies agreed to pay about $120 million, which is only slightly less than the country's entire gross national product. In Nigeria in 1987, five European ships unloaded toxic waste in Nigeria containing dangerous poisons such as polychlorinated biphenyls, or PCBs. Workers wearing thongs and shorts unloaded the barrels for $2.50 a day, and placed them in a dirt lot in a residential area in the town of Kiko.[21] They were not told about the contents of the barrels.[22]

Who bears responsibility for protecting the workers' and inhabitants' rights to safety in such instances? It would be wrong to place it entirely upon a single agent such as the government of a West African nation. As it happens, the toxic waste dumped in Nigeria entered under an import permit for "nonexplosive, nonradioactive and non-self-combusting chemicals." But the permit turned out to be a loophole; Nigeria had not meant to accept the waste and demanded its removal once word about its presence filtered into official channels. The example reveals the difficulty many developing countries have in creating the sophisticated language and regulatory procedures necessary to control high-technology hazards. It seems reasonable in such instances, then, to place the responsibility not upon a single class of agents, but upon a broad collection of them, including governments, corporate executives, host-country companies and officials, and international organizations.

One list receiving significant international attention is the Universal Declaration of Human Rights.[23] However, it and the subsequent International Covenant on Social, Economic and Cultural Rights have spawned controversy, despite the fact that the Declaration was endorsed by virtually all of the important post-World War II nations in 1948 as part of the affirmation of the U.N. Charter. What distinguishes these lists from their predecessors, and what serves also as the focus of controversy, is their inclusion of rights that have come to be called, alternatively, "social," "economic," "positive," or "welfare" rights.

Many have balked at such rights, arguing that no one can have a right to a specific supply of an economic good. Can anyone be said to have a "right," for example, to 128 hours of sleep and leisure each week? And, in the same spirit, some international documents have simply refused to adopt the welfare-affirming blueprint established in the Universal Declaration. For example, the European Convention of Human Rights omits mention of welfare rights, preferring instead to create an auxiliary document (The European Social Charter of 1961) which references many of what earlier had been treated as "rights," as "goals." Similar objections underlie the bifurcated covenants drawn up in an attempt to implement the Universal Declaration: one such covenant, entitled the Covenant on Civil and Political Rights, was drawn up for all signers, including those who objected to welfare rights, while a companion covenant, entitled the Covenant on Social, Economic, and Cultural Rights, was drawn up for welfare rights defenders. Of course, many countries signed both; but some signed only the former.[24]

Many who criticize welfare rights utilize a traditional philosophical distinction between so-called negative and positive rights. A positive right is said to be one that requires persons to act positively to *do* something, while a negative one requires only that people not directly deprive others. Hence, the right to liberty is said to be a negative right, whereas the right to enough food is said to be a positive one. With this distinction in hand, the point is commonly made that no one can be bound to improve the welfare of another (unless, say, that person has entered into an agreement to do so); rather, they can be bound at most to *refrain* from damaging the welfare of another.

Nonetheless, Henry Shue has argued persuasively against the very distinction between negative and positive rights. Consider the most celebrated and best accepted example of a negative right: namely, the right to freedom. The meaningful preservation of the right to freedom requires a variety of positive actions: for example, on the part of the government it requires the establishment and maintenance of a police force, courts, and the military, and on the part of the citizenry it requires ongoing cooperation and diligent (not merely passive) forbearance. The protection of another so-called negative right, the right to physical security, necessitates "police forces; criminal rights; penitentiaries; schools for training police, lawyers, and guards; and taxes to support an enormous system for the prevention, detention, and punishment of violations of personal security."[25]

This is compelling. The maintenance and preservation of many non-welfare rights (where, again, such maintenance and preservation is the key to a right's status as basic) require the support of certain basic welfare rights. Certain liberties depend upon the enjoyment of subsistence, just as subsistence sometimes depends upon the enjoyment of some liberties. One's freedom to speak freely is meaningless if one is weakened by hunger to the point of silence.

What list of rights, then, ought to be endorsed on the international level? Elsewhere I have argued that the rights appearing on such a list should pass the following three conditions:[26] 1) the right must protect something of very great importance; 2) the right must be subject to substantial and recurrent threats; and 3) the obligations or burdens imposed by the right must satisfy a fairness-affordability test.[27]

In turn, I have argued that the list of fundamental international rights generated from these conditions include: 1) the right to freedom of physical movement; 2) the right to ownership of property; 3) the right to freedom from torture; 4) the right to a fair trial; 5) the right to nondiscriminatory treatment (e.g., freedom from discrimination on the basis of such characteristics as race or sex); 6) the right to physical security; 7) the right to freedom of speech and association; 8) the right to minimal education; 9) the right to political participation; and 10) the right to subsistence.

This seems a minimal list. Some will wish to add entries such as the right to employment, to social security, or to a certain standard of living (say, as might be prescribed by Rawls's well-known "difference" principle). The list as presented aims to suggest, albeit incompletely, a description of a *minimal* set of rights and to serve as a point of beginning and consensus for evaluating international conduct. If I am correct, many would wish to add entries, but few would wish to subtract them.

As we look over the list, it is noteworthy that, except for a few isolated instances, multinational corporations have probably succeeded in fulfilling their duty not to actively deprive persons of their enjoyment of the rights at issue. But correlative duties involve more than failing to actively deprive people of the enjoyment of their rights. Shue, for example, notes that three types of correlative duties (i.e., duties corresponding to a particular right) are possible: 1) to avoid depriving, 2) to help protect from deprivation; and 3) to aid the deprived.[28]

While it is obvious that the honoring of rights clearly imposes duties of the first kind, i.e., to avoid depriving directly, it is less obvious, but frequently true, that honoring them involves acts or omissions that help prevent the deprivation of rights. If I receive a note from Murder, Incorporated, and it looks like business, my right to security is clearly threatened. Let's say that a third party (X) has relevant information which, if revealed to the police, would help protect my right to security. In this case, there is no excuse for X to remain silent, claiming that it is Murder, Incorporated, and not X, who wishes to murder me.

Similarly, the duties associated with rights often include ones from the third category, i.e., that of aiding the deprived, as when a government is bound to honor the right of its citizens to adequate nutrition by distributing food in the wake of famine or natural disaster, or when the same government, in the defense of political liberty, is required to demand that an employer reinstate or compensate an employee fired for voting for a particular candidate in a government election.

Which of these duties apply to corporations, and which apply only to governments? It would be unfair, not to mention unreasonable, to hold corporations to the same standards for enhancing and protecting social welfare to which we hold civil governments—since frequently governments are formally dedicated to enhancing the welfare of, and actively preserving the liberties of, their citizens. The profit-making corporation, in contrast, is designed to achieve an economic mission and as a moral actor possesses an exceedingly narrow personality. It is an undemocratic institution, furthermore, which is ill-suited to the broader task of distributing society's goods in accordance with a conception of general welfare. The corporation is an economic animal; although its responsibilities extend beyond maximizing return on investment for shareholders, they are informed directly by its economic mission. Hence, while it would be strikingly generous for multinationals to sacrifice some of their profits to buy milk, grain, and shelter for persons in poor countries, it seems difficult to consider this one of their minimal moral requirements. If anyone has such minimal obligations, it is the peoples' respective governments or, perhaps, better-off individuals.

The same, however, is not true of the second class of duties, i.e., to protect from deprivation. While these duties, like those in the third class, are also usually the province of government, it sometimes happens that the rights to which they correlate are ones whose protection is a direct outcome of ordinary corporate activities. For example, the duties associated with protecting a worker from the physical threats of other workers may fall not only upon the local police but also upon the employer. These duties, in turn, are properly viewed as correlative duties of the right—in this instance, the worker's right—to personal security. This will become clearer in a moment when we discuss the correlative duties of specific rights.

The following list of correlative duties reflects a second-stage application of the fairness-affordability condition to the earlier list of fundamental international rights, and indicates which rights do, and which do not, impose correlative duties upon multinational corporations of the three various kinds.[29]

Minimal Correlative Duties of Multinational Corporations

Fundamental Rights	To Avoid Depriving	To Help Protect From Deprivation	To Aid the Deprived
Freedom of physical movement	X		
Ownership of property	X		
Freedom from torture	X		
Fair trial	X		
Nondiscriminatory treatment	X	X	
Physical security	X	X	
Freedom of speech and association	X	X	
Minimal education	X	X	
Political participation	X	X	
Subsistence	X	X	

Let us illustrate the duty to protect from deprivation with specific examples. The right to physical security entails duties of protection. If a Japanese multinational corporation operating in Nigeria hires shop workers to run metal lathes in an assembly factory, but fails to provide them with protective goggles, then the corporation has failed to honor the workers' moral right to physical security (no matter what the local law might decree). Injuries from such a failure would be the moral responsibility of the Japanese multinational despite the fact that the company could not be said to have inflicted the injuries directly.

Another correlative duty, to protect the right of education, may be illustrated through the example mentioned earlier: namely, the prevalence of child labor in developing countries. A multinational in Central America is not entitled to hire an eight-year-old for full-time, ongoing work because, among other reasons, doing so blocks the child's ability to receive a minimally sufficient education. While what counts as a "minimally sufficient" education may be debated, and while it seems likely, moreover, that the specification of the right to a certain level of education will depend at least in part upon the level of economic resources available in a given country, it is reasonable to assume that any action by a corporation which has the effect of blocking the development of a child's ability to read or write will be proscribed on the basis of rights.

In some instances, corporations have failed to honor the correlative duty of protecting the right to political participation from deprivation. The most blatant examples of direct deprivation are fortunately becoming so rare as to be nonexistent, namely, cases in which companies directly aid in overthrowing democratic regimes, as when United Fruit, Inc., allegedly contributed to overthrowing a democratically elected regime in Guatemala during the 1950s. But a few corporations have continued indirectly to threaten this right by failing to protect it from deprivation. A few have persisted, for example, in supporting military dictatorships in countries with growing democratic sentiment, and others have blatantly bribed publicly elected officials with large sums of money. Perhaps the most celebrated example of the latter occurred when the prime minister of Japan was bribed with $7 million by the Lockheed Corporation to secure a lucrative Tri-Star Jet contract. The complaint from the perspective of this right is not against bribes or "sensitive payments" in general, but against bribes in contexts where they serve to undermine a democratic system in which publicly elected officials are in a position of public trust.

Even the buying and owning of major segments of a foreign country's land and industry have been criticized in this regard. As Brian Barry has remarked, "The paranoia created in Britain and the United States by land purchases by foreigners (especially the Arabs and the Japanese, it seems) should serve to make it understandable that the citizenry of a country might be unhappy with a state of affairs in which the most important natural resources are in foreign ownership."[30] At what point would Americans regard their democratic control threatened by foreign ownership of U.S. industry and resources? At 20 percent ownership? At 40 percent? At 60 percent? At 80 percent? The answer is debatable, yet there seems to be some point beyond which the right to national self-determination, and in turn national democratic control, is violated by foreign ownership of property.[31]

Corporations also have duties to protect the right to subsistence from deprivation. Consider the following scenario. A number of square miles of land in an underdeveloped country has been used for years to grow black beans. The bulk of the land is owned, as it has been for centuries, by two wealthy landowners. Poorer members of the community work the land and receive a portion of the crop, a portion barely sufficient to satisfy nutritional needs. Next, imagine that a multinational corporation offers the two wealthy owners a handsome sum for the land, and does so because it plans to grow coffee for export. Now if—and this, admittedly, is a crucial "if"—the corporation has reason to *know* that a significant number of people in the community will suffer malnutrition as a result—that is, if it has convincing reasons to believe either those persons will fail to be hired by the company and paid sufficiently or, if forced to migrate to the city, will receive wages insufficient to provide adequate food and shelter—then the multinational may be said to have failed in its correlative duty to protect persons from the deprivation of the right to subsistence. This despite the fact that the corporation would never have stooped to take food from workers' mouths, and despite the fact that the malnourished will, in Coleridge's words, "die so slowly that none call it murder."

In addition to articulating a list of rights and the correlative duties imposed upon multinational corporations, there is also a need to articulate a practical stratagem for use in applying the home-country norms of the multinational manager to the vexing problems arising in developing countries.

In particular, how should highly-placed multinational managers, typically schooled in home-country moral traditions, reconcile conflicts between those traditions and ones of the host country? When host-country standards for pollution, discrimination and salary schedules appear substandard from the perspective of the home country, should the manager take the high road and implement home-country standards? Or does the high road imply a failure to respect cultural diversity and national integrity?

What distinguishes these issues from standard ones about corporate practices is that they involve reference to a conflict of norms, either moral or legal, between home and host country. Consider two actual instances of the problem at issue.

Case #1: A new American bank in Italy was advised by its Italian attorneys to file a tax return that misstated income and expenses and consequently grossly underestimated actual taxes due. The bank learned, however, that most other Italian companies regarded the practice as standard operating procedure and merely the first move in a complex negotiating process with the Italian internal revenue service. The bank initially refused to file a fallacious return on moral grounds and submitted an "American-style" return instead. But because the resulting tax bill was many times higher than what comparable Italian companies were asked to pay, the bank changed policy in later years to agree with the "Italian style."[32]

Case #2: In 1966 Charles Pettis, employee of an American multinational, became resident engineer for one of the company's projects in Peru: a 146-mile, $46 million project to build a highway across the Andes. Pettis soon discovered the Peruvian safety standards were far below those in the United States. The highway design called for cutting through mountains in areas where rock formations were unstable. Unless special precautions were taken, slides could occur. Pettis blew the whistle, complaining first to Peruvian government officials and later to U.S. officials. No special precautions were taken, with the result that 31 men were killed by landslides during the construction of the road. Pettis was fired and had difficulty finding a job with another company.[33]

One may well decide that enforcing home-country standards was necessary in one of the above cases, but not in the other. One may decide that host-country precautions in Peru were unacceptable, while at the same time acknowledging that, however inequitable and inefficient Italian tax mores may be, a decision to file "Italian style" is permissible.

Thus, despite claims to the contrary, one must reject the simple dictum that whenever the practice violates a moral standard of the home country, it is impermissible for the multinational company. Arnold Berleant has argued that the principle of equal treatment endorsed by most U.S. citizens requires that U.S. corporations pay workers in less developed countries exactly the same wages paid to U.S. workers in comparable jobs (after appropriate adjustments are made for cost of living levels in the relevant areas).[34] But most observers, including those from the less developed countries, believe this stretches the doctrine of equality too far in a way that is detrimental to host countries. By arbitrarily establishing U.S. wage levels as the benchmark for fairness, one eliminates the role of the international market in establishing salary levels, and this in turn eliminates the incentive U.S. corporations have to hire foreign workers. Perhaps U.S. firms should exceed market rate for foreign labor as a matter of moral principle, but to pay strictly equal rates would freeze less developed countries out of the international labor market.[35] Lacking a simple formula such as "the practice is wrong when it violates the home country's norms," one seems driven to undertake a more complex analysis of the types and degrees of responsibilities multinationals possess.

What is needed is a more comprehensive test than a simple appeal to rights. Of course the earlier rights-based approach clarifies a moral bottom line regarding, say, extreme threats to workers' safety. But it leaves obscure not only the issue of less extreme threats, but of harms other than physical injury. Granted, the celebrated dangers of asbestos call for recognizing the right to workers' safety no matter how broadly the language of rights is framed. But what are we to say of a less toxic pollutant? Is the level of sulphur-dioxide air pollution we should tolerate in a struggling nation, one with only a few fertilizer plants working overtime to help feed its malnourished population, the same we should demand in Portland, Oregon?

In the end, nothing less than a general moral theory working in tandem with an analysis of the foundations of corporate existence is needed. But at the practical level a need exists for an interpretive mechanism or algorithm that multinational managers could use in determining the implications of their own moral views.

The first step in generating such an ethical algorithm is to isolate the distinct sense in which the norms of the home and host country conflict. If the practice is morally and/or legally permitted in the host country, but not in the home country, then either: 1) the moral reasons underlying the host country's view that the practice is permissible refer to the host country's relative level of economic development; or 2) the moral reasons underlying the host country's view that the practice is permissible are independent of the host country's relative level of economic development.

Let us call the conflict of norms described in (1) a type 1 conflict. In such a conflict, an African country that permits slightly higher levels of thermal pollution from electric power generating plants, or a lower minimum wage than that prescribed in European countries, would do so not because higher standards would be undesirable per se, but because its level of economic development requires an ordering of priorities. In the future, when it succeeds in matching European economic achievements, it may well implement the higher standards.

Let us call the conflict of norms described in (2) a type 2 conflict. In such cases, levels of economic development play no role. For example, low-level institutional nepotism, common in many developing countries, is justified not on economic grounds, but on the basis of clan and family loyalty. Presumably the same loyalties will be operative even after the country has risen to economic success—as the nepotism prevalent in Saudi Arabia would indicate. The Italian tax case also reflects an Italian cultural style with a penchant for personal negotiation and an unwillingness to formalize transactions, more than a strategy based on level of economical development.

The difference in norms between the home and host country, i.e., whether the conflict is of type 1 or 2, does not determine the correctness, or truth value, of the host country's claim that the practice is permissible. The practice may or may not be permissible, whether the conflict is of type 1 or 2. This is not to say that the truth value of the host country's claim is independent of the nature of the conflict. A different test will be required to determine whether the practice is permissible when the conflict is of type 1 as opposed to type 2. In a type 1 dispute, the following formula is appropriate:

> The practice is permissible if and only if the members of the home country would, under conditions of economic development similar to those of the host country, regard the practice as permissible.

Under this test, excessive levels of asbestos pollution would almost certainly not be tolerated by the members of the home country under similar economic conditions, whereas higher levels of thermal pollution would be tolerated. The test, happily, explains and confirms our initial moral intuitions.

Since in type 2 conflicts the dispute between the home and host country depends upon a fundamental difference of perspective, a different test is needed. In type 2 conflicts, the opposing evils of ethnocentricism and ethical relativism must be avoided. A multinational must forego the temptation to remake all societies in the image of its home society, while at the same time rejecting a relativism that conveniently forgets ethics when the payoff is sufficient. Thus, the ethical task is to tolerate cultural diversity while drawing the line at moral recklessness.

Since in type 2 cases the practice is in conflict with an embedded norm of the home country, one should first ask whether the practice is necessary to do business in the host country, for if it is not, the solution clearly is to adopt some other practice that is permissible from the standpoint of the home country. If petty bribery of public officials is unnecessary for the business of the Cummins Engine Company in India, then the company is obliged to abandon such bribery. If, on the other hand, the practice proves necessary for business, one must next ask whether the practice constitutes a direct violation of a basic human right. Here the notion of a fundamental international right outlined earlier, specifying a minimum below which corporate conduct should not fall, has special application. If Toyota, a Japanese company, confronts South African laws that mandate systematic discrimination against non-whites, then Toyota must refuse to comply with the laws. In type 2 cases, the evaluator must ask the following questions: 1) Is it possible to conduct business successfully in the host country without undertaking the practice? and 2) Is the practice a clear violation of a fundamental international right? The practice would be permissible if and only if the answer to both questions is "no."

What sorts of practice might satisfy both criteria? Consider the practice of low-level bribery of public officials in some developing nations. In some South American countries, for example, it is impossible for any company, foreign or national, to move goods through customs without paying low-level officials a few dollars. Indeed, the salaries of such officials are sufficiently low that one suspects they are set with the prevalence of the practice in mind. The payments are relatively small, uniformly assessed, and accepted as standard practice by the surrounding culture. Here, the practice of petty bribery would pass the type 2 test and, barring other moral factors, would be permissible.

The algorithm does not obviate the need for multinational managers to appeal to moral concepts both more general and specific than the algorithm itself. It is not intended as a substitute for a general theory of morality or even an interpretation of the basic responsibilities of multinationals. Its power lies in its ability to tease out implications of the moral presuppositions of a manager's acceptance of "home" morality, and in this sense to serve as a clarifying device for multinational decision-making. The algorithm makes no appeal to a universal concept of morality (as the appeal to fundamental rights does in type 2 cases), save for the purported universality of the ethics endorsed by the home-country culture. When the home country's morality is wrong or confused, the algorithm can reflect this ethnocentricity, leading either to a mild paternalism or to the imposition of parochial standards. For example, the home country's oversensitivity to aesthetic features of the environment may lead it to reject a certain level of thermal pollution, even under strained economic circumstances. This results in a paternalistic refusal to allow such levels in the host country, despite the host country's acceptance of the higher levels and its belief that tolerating such levels is necessary for stimulating economic development. It would be a mistake, however, to exaggerate this weakness of the algorithm; coming up with actual cases in which the force of the algorithm would be relativized is extremely difficult. Indeed, I have been unable to discover a single, non-hypothetical set of facts fitting this description.

IV

How might multinational corporations improve their moral performance and come to embody the normative concepts advanced in this article? Two classes of remedies suggest themselves: external remedies, i.e., those that rely on international associations or agreements on the one hand; and internal remedies, i.e., those that rely on internal, corporate initiative on the other.

Earlier we discussed the dramatic expansion of external remedies in the form of international laws, agreements, and codes of conduct. Again, while many of these are nonbinding in the sense that noncompliance will fail to trigger sanctions, they are as a group coming to exert significant influence on multinational conduct. One of the principal advantages of such global and industry-wide initiatives is that they distribute costs more fairly than initiatives undertaken by individual corporations. When, in line with the WHO Code of Marketing Breast Milk Substitutes, Nestlé curtails questionable marketing practices for the sale of infant formula, it does so with the confidence that the other signers of the WHO Code will not be taking unfair advantage by undertaking the same questionable practices, for they must adhere to its provisions. Still another advantage of external remedies stems from the fact that many nation-states, especially developing ones, are unable to gather sufficient information about, much less control, the multinational corporations that operate within their borders. Thus, the use of supranational entities, whether of an international or inter-industry form, will sometimes augment, or supplement, the power and information-gathering abilities of developing nations. It seems difficult to deny that the growth and maturation of such entities can enhance the ethical conduct of multinational corporations.

The most important change of an internal nature likely to enhance the ethical behavior of multinationals is for multinationals themselves to introduce ethical deliberation, i.e., to introduce factors of ethics into their decision-making mechanisms. That they should do so is a clear implication of the preceding discussion, yet it is a conclusion some will resist. Those who place great confidence in the efficacy of the market may, for example, believe that a corporate policy of moral disinterest and profit maximization will—*pace* Adam Smith's invisible hand—maximize overall global welfare.

This kind of ideological confidence in the international market may have been understandable decades ago. But persisting in the belief that market mechanisms will automatically ensure adequate moral conduct today seems recklessly idealistic. Forces such as Islamic fundamentalism, the global debt bomb, and massive unemployment in developing countries have drastically distorted the operation of the free market in international commerce, and even though a further selective freeing of market forces may enhance global productivity, it cannot solve automatically questions of fair treatment, hazardous technology, or discrimination.

Even adopting the minimal guidelines for corporate conduct advanced here would involve dramatic changes in the decision-making mechanisms of multinational corporations. Such firms would need to alter established patterns of information flow and collection in order to accommodate new forms of morally relevant information. The already complex parameters of corporate decision-making would become more so. Even scholarly research about international business would need to change. At present, research choices tend to be dictated by the goals of increased profits, long-term access to basic commodities needed for manufactured items, and increased global market share; but clearly these goals sometimes conflict with broader moral ends, such as refraining from violating human rights. Revised goals call for a revised program of research. And although we have rejected the view that multinational corporations must shoulder the world's problems of poverty, discrimination, and political injustice because, as economic entities, they have limited social missions, their goals nonetheless must include the aim of not impeding solutions to such problems.

Are such changes in the decision-making of multinational corporations likely or even possible? Resistance will be intense; clearly, there should be no delusions on this score. Yet, without minimizing the difficulties, I do not think the task impossible. At a minimum, corporations are capable of choosing the more ethical alternative in instances where alternative courses of action yield equal profits—and I believe they are capable of even more. Corporations are run by human beings, not beasts. As multinationals continue to mature in the context of an ever-expanding, more sophisticated global economy, we have reason to hope that they are capable of looking beyond their national borders and recognizing the same minimal claims made in the name of our shared humanity, that they accept at home.

Notes

1. Much of this article is extracted from Thomas Donaldson's book, *The Ethics of International Business* (Oxford: Oxford University Press, 1989). The book provides a framework for interpreting the ethics of global business. Excerpts reprinted by permission of Oxford University Press.

2. Richard Barnet and Ronald Muller, *Global Reach: The Power of Multinational Corporations* (New York: Simon and Schuster, 1974) p. 363.

3. P. P. Gabriel, "MNCs in the Third World: Is Conflict Unavoidable?" *Harvard Business Review*, Vol. 56 (March–April 1978) pp. 83–93.

4. An example of disparity in wages between Mexican and U.S. workers is documented in the case study by John H. Haddox, "Twin-Plants and Corporate Responsibilities," in *Profits and Responsibility*, eds. Patricia Werhane and Kendall D'Andrade (New York: Random House, 1985).

5. Barnet and Muller, *Global Reach*, p. 72.

6. J. R. Simpson, "Ethics and Multinational Corporations vis-à-vis Developing Nations," *Journal of Business Ethics*, Vol. 1 (1982) pp. 227–37.

7. I have borrowed this eight-fold scheme of categories from researchers Farr and Stening in Lisa Farr and Bruce W. Stening, "Ethics and the Multinational Corporation" (an unpublished paper) p. 4.

8. An analysis of such reasons, one which also contains many observations on the evolution of international public policy, is Lee E. Preston's "The Evolution of Multinational Public Policy Toward Business: Codes of Conduct," a paper read at the annual meeting of the American Academy of Management, New Orleans, August 1987.

9. Jon R. Luoma, "A Disaster That Didn't Wait," *The New York Times Book Review*, November 29, 1987, p. 16.

10. While I personally have coined the terms, "inter-industry," "inter-government," etc., the basic four-fold division of international initiatives is drawn from Preston, *op. cit.*

11. See, for example, Raymond J. Waldman, *Regulating International Business through Codes of Conduct* (Washington, D.C.: American Enterprise Institute, 1980).

12. See, for example, P. S. Tharp, Jr., "Transnational Enterprises and International Regulation: A Survey of Various Approaches to International Organizations," *International Organization*, Vol. 30 (Winter 1976) pp. 47–73.

13. James LeMoyne. "In Central America, the Workers Suffer Most," *The New York Times*, October 26, 1987, pp. 1 and 4.

14. *Ibid.*

15. Quoted in "Products Unsafe at Home are Still Unloaded Abroad," *The New York Times*, August 22, 1982, p. 22.

16. Ronald Dworkin, *Taking Rights Seriously* (Cambridge: Harvard University Press, 1977). For other standard definitions of rights, see: James W. Nickel, *Making Sense of Human Rights: Philosophical Reflections on the Universal Declaration of Human Rights* (Berkeley: University of California Press, 1987) especially chapter 2; Joel Feinberg, "Duties, Rights and Claims," *American Philosophical Quarterly*, Vol. 3 (1966) pp. 137–44. See also Feinberg, "The Nature and Value of Rights," *Journal of Value Inquiry*, Vol. 4 (1970) p. 243–57; Wesley N. Hohfeld, *Fundamental Legal Conceptions* (New Haven: Yale University Press, 1964); and H. J. McCloskey, "Rights—Some Conceptual Issues," *Australasian Journal of Philosophy*, Vol. 54 (1976) pp. 99–115.

17. Maurice Cranston, *What Are Human Rights?* (New York: Taplinger, 1973), p. 67.

18. H. J. McCloskey, for example, understands a right as a positive entitlement that need not specify who bears the responsibility for satisfying that entitlement. H. J. McCloskey, "Rights—Some Conceptual Issues," p. 99.

19. Joel Feinberg, "Duties, Rights and Claims," *American Philosophical Quarterly*, Vol. 3 (1966) pp. 137–44. See also Feinberg, "The Nature and Value of Rights," pp. 243–57.

20. James Brooke, "Waste Dumpers Turning to West Africa," *The New York Times*, July 17, 1988, pp. 1 and 7.

21. *Ibid.*

22. *Ibid.*, p. 7. Nigeria and other countries have struck back, often by imposing strict rules against the acceptance of toxic waste. For example, in Nigeria officials now warn that anyone caught importing toxic waste will face the firing squad.

23. See Ian Brownlie, *Basic Documents on Human Rights* (Oxford: Oxford University Press, 1975).

24. James W. Nickel, "The Feasibility of Welfare Rights in Less Developed Countries," in *Economic Justice: Private Rights and Public Responsibilities,* eds. Kenneth Kipnis and Diana T. Meyers (Totowa, N. J.: Rowman and Allenheld, 1985) pp. 217–26.

25. Henry Shue, *Basic Rights: Subsistence, Affluence, and U. S. Foreign Policy* (Princeton: Princeton University Press, 1980) pp. 37–38.

26. Donaldson, *The Ethics of International Business,* see especially chapter 5. My formulation of these three conditions is an adaptation from four conditions presented and defended by James Nickel in James W. Nickel, *Making Sense of Human Rights: Philosophical Reflections on the Universal Declaration of Human Rights* (Berkeley: University of California Press, 1987).

27. The fairness-affordability test implies that in order for a proposed right to qualify as a genuine right, all moral agents (including nation-states, individuals, and corporations) must be able under ordinary circumstances, both economically and otherwise, to assume the various burdens and duties that fall fairly upon them in honoring the right. "Affordable" here means literally capable of paying for; it does not mean "affordable" in the vernacular sense that something is not affordable because it would constitute an inefficient luxury, or would necessitate trading off other more valuable economic goods. This definition implies that— at least under unusual circumstances—honoring a right may be mandatory for a given multinational corporation, even when the result is bankrupting the firm. For example, it would be "affordable" under ordinary circumstances for multinational corporations to employ older workers and refuse to hire eight-year-old children for full-time, ongoing labor, and hence doing so would be mandatory even in the unusual situation where a particular firm's paying the higher salaries necessary to hire older laborers would probably bankrupt the firm. By the same logic, it would probably not be "affordable" for either multinational corporations or nation-states around the world to guarantee kidney dialysis for all citizens who need it. The definition also implies that any act of forbearance (of a kind involved in not violating a right directly) is "affordable" for all moral agents.

28. Shue, *Basic Rights,* p. 57.

29. It is possible to understand even the first four rights as imposing correlative duties to protect from deprivation under highly unusual or hypothetical circumstances.

30. Brian Barry, "The Case for a New International Economic Order," in *Ethics, Economics, and the Law: Nomos XXIV,* eds. J. Roland Pennock and John W. Chapman (New York: New York University Press, 1982).

31. Companies are also charged with undermining local governments, and hence infringing on basic rights, by sophisticated tax evasion schemes. Especially when companies buy from their own subsidiaries, they can establish prices that have little connection to existing market values. This, in turn, means that profits can be shifted from high-tax to low-tax countries, with the result that poor nations can be deprived of their rightful share.

32. Arthur Kelly, "Italian Tax Mores," in this volume, pp. 129–31.

33. Charles Peters and Taylor Branch, *Blowing the Whistle: Dissent in the Public Interest* (New York: Praeger, 1974) pp. 182–85.

34. Arnold Berleant, "Multinationals and the Problem of Ethical Consistency," *Journal of Business Ethics,* Vol. 3 (August 1982) pp. 182–95.

35. Some have argued that insulating the economies of the less developed countries would be advantageous to the less developed countries in the long run. But whether correct or not, such an argument is independent of the present issue, for it is independent of the claim that if a practice violates the norms of the home country, then it is impermissible.

International Business Ethics and Incipient Capitalism: A Double Standard?

RICHARD T. DE GEORGE

The term "international business ethics" is ambiguous, and this ambiguity leads to some confusion and to a number of disputes. It is ambiguous because its referent is not clear. It may refer to the ethical rules that govern all business everywhere in the world. But in that case it is arguably reducible to the general or basic ethical norms that govern human behavior, irrespective of society. For it is doubtful that there are special rules of business that are so general as to be applicable everywhere. International business ethics might refer to the ethical rules that ought to govern multinational corporations; or to the rules that apply to business as well as to nations in speaking of global problems, such as global warming and depletion of the ozone level; or to the different ethical norms applicable in different countries because of different social, economic, political, and historical conditions.

The term also leads to a number of debates, the chief of which is a debate about moral relativism. Moral relativism has a long tradition apart from international business ethics, and in the modern period stems from cultural relativism documented by anthropological studies. If mores and customs vary from society to society, what rules should one follow when one leaves one's own society and goes to another? Is one bound by the sexual moral rules of one's own monogamous society if one goes to another which allows polygamy or polyandry? If such relativism holds with respect to sex, does it also hold with respect to business?

In some ways the term "international business ethics"—like the term "business ethics"—is misleading, because both seem to refer to something that is modeled on general ethics. If general ethical theories of the standard kinds are correct, they are not dependent on particular circumstances, even though one must consider particular circumstances in applying them. But utilitarianism and Kantianism do not depend on particular circumstances for their defense.

Business ethics is an area of applied ethics. What distinguishes it from general ethics is its application to specific kinds of activity, namely business activity. As such it necessarily depends heavily for its content on the structures that define business and in which business operates. It gains its specificity by taking into account particular socio-economic circumstances; the political system and existing laws that are intertwined with these; the level of economic development and the standard of living of a country; the local traditions, beliefs, and expectations of the people in a given society; and a host of other similar considerations. These taken together form what can be called the background institutions or conditions within which business, and so business ethics, operate and make sense.

Presented to the Society for Business Ethics, May, 1994. © by Richard T. De George. Reprinted with the permission of the author.

Thus business ethics in a socio-economic-political system such as that found in the United States is very different from what might be called business ethics in a socialist system, to the extent that business is allowed in the latter.

What is allowed by legitimate legal structures varies from country to country and makes the practice of business vary accordingly. In a society in which social benefits for workers are mandated by law, the question of what ethics requires from employers with respect to the treatment of workers may be very different from a society in which such benefits are not mandated. If government provides health, old-age pension and other benefits to all its citizens, then the obligations of business in these regards are very different from a society in which these are not provided. If a country has a long tradition of business providing lifetime employment, the obligations of business are again different from a society which has no such tradition.

Business ethics as a movement and as an area of study had its birth in the United States. The issues that rose to the fore were those about which Americans were concerned. Business ethics in the United States developed within specifically American background institutions. As it was exported or as other countries followed America's lead in this area, business ethics texts written for America were often used as texts in other countries. It was not long before both business and those teaching business ethics saw the lack of fit in many areas. Because background institutions vary, so the issues of business ethics and specific applications vary. In a country such as Japan in the 1970s, when trading in the stock market was done almost exclusively by insiders, each of whom belonged to a system of interlocking companies, insider trading was not unethical, even though insider trading in the United States was both unethical and illegal. The same practice—or at least practices that went by the same name—was morally justifiable in the one case but not in the other. In Japan there was no unfairness, no one had advantages other traders did not equally enjoy, and the practice did not harm any of the participants. In the United States, however, insider trading did give insiders unfair advantage and did harm those who traded without access in principle to appropriate information. By the 1990s the situation had changed on the Tokyo exchange. Trading was done not only by insiders but significantly by small Japanese investors and by foreign investors. Hence the practice of insider trading came to be seen as unfair to non-insiders and the practice was eventually made illegal. Insider trading is neither ethical nor unethical in itself; it takes on a moral character only when considered in a specific social context.

Because background institutions vary to such a great extent, it is difficult to speak of international business ethics as if it were all of a piece. It cannot simply be American business ethics or German or Japanese or any other kind of business ethics, extended to an international level. But in one sense it is that. An American multinational must respect the ethical norms and values of the home company wherever the company is located. It must, of course, take into account local laws, traditions, and so on. But it cannot hire child labor, even if that is the local custom; nor can it discriminate against women, or follow apartheid laws, or buy goods made by slave labor, or fail to provide safe working conditions. The list goes on.

What might give one pause is my presenting these requirements as mandatory only for American companies, as if they were not required for all companies. After all, all companies must respect the human rights of workers, honor contracts, and not harm people by dumping toxic waste. Yet these are demanded not by any special ethics of business but by general moral norms, which apply in business as well as in every other realm in life.

As a test case for the thesis I have proposed, consider the differences, if any, between business in the United States on the one hand and in Russia at the present time on the other. The United States is the business leader of the world. It has a highly developed system of laws that control many of the socially negative tendencies of unrestrained capitalism. It has an educated citizenry conscious of its rights. It has critical and choosy consumers, who usually have the choice of which products to buy and which manufacturers to do business with. It has strong environmental protection groups. It has a tradition of business being expected to contribute to the welfare of the local community in which it operates. In sum, it has a host of well-defined background institutions, within which one can intelligently speak about business ethics and analyze practices from hostile buyouts to drug testing of employees to liability for dangerous products.

The background institutions in the United States did not come into place all at once. They developed slowly over time, often in response to abuses. The robber barons at the turn of the century are not a proud part of the history of American business, nor are the racketeers of the 1920s, or the sellers of snake oil, or the carpetbaggers in the South after the Civil War. Free enterprise is not as free as some of its early proponents would have wished. Government regulations aim to protect the public interest, promote health and safety, and keep competition fair. All of this developed within a democratic society with a free press. The history of capitalism in other countries with other background institutions is very different. Capitalism has been linked with dictatorships, with corrupt governments, with criminal elements, and with a variety of different background conditions and institutions. It is not all of a piece, and business ethics does not serve the same function or come up with the same evaluations of similar-sounding practices, often because the differing circumstances and legal backgrounds make the practices different in reality, despite the fact that they go by the same name.

What Americans consider just with respect to property transactions assumes the institution of private property, protected by law, and ethically justified within the system of free enterprise. In the former Soviet Union, in which private property was condemned as unethical and unjustifiable, there was no private ownership of the means of production and there was a very different notion of what justice with respect to property meant. A host of transactions that were legitimate and ethical in the United States were either not possible or were unethical in the former Soviet Union.

Because it is in transition between the state socialism under which it functioned for seventy years and some sort of still-to-be-defined free-market system, Russia at the present time makes for an interesting case study of the thesis that business ethics must take into account the existing background institutions in the societies in which business activities take place. Under existing conditions in Russia, which ethical rules can appropriately be applied to business?

In many instances the answer it not clear. But that does not mean that it is unclear in all instances. And I believe that with sufficiently careful analysis we can arrive at least at some tentative conclusions.

Russian Background

Since it is essential to keep the background conditions in mind, let me briefly sketch some of them. Under Soviet socialism there was no private ownership of the means of production. All productive resources were state owned. No individual was allowed to be in business for himself or to hire others, since that would constitute exploitation. The state employed all workers, and all able-bodied citizens were required to work. The state provided subsidized housing, free education and health care, old-age pensions, and a variety of other social benefits. Often these were provided by the factories at which people worked.

Bureaucracy was the rule, and centralized control dominated industry. Inefficiency was widespread. Without a market to determine supply and demand, the prices of goods, resources, and labor were more or less arbitrary.

The government sought to undermine traditional bourgeois morality and to replace it with a collectivist and state-oriented socialist morality. It succeeded in undermining traditional morality but failed in replacing it with an effective social morality. As a result, many Russians adopted a dualistic approach to morals.[1] Family, friends, and those with whom one was closely associated—often fellow workers—were treated according to standard rules of decency, concern, and respect. The system and those who represented it were seen as "them"—nameless and faceless and deserving no moral respect. Rules, which were too rigid and numerous to follow, were ignored or circumvented whenever possible. Since all property belonged in theory to everyone, one took what one could when and where one could. Invoices meant little. They were simply internal accounting procedures. There was little work discipline, since everyone was guaranteed employment by law, and there was no incentive for innovation or hard work. Reports were often falsified at all levels so as to meet paper production norms. The people felt that the government was a master of fabricating, slanting, distorting and suppressing the truth, and they followed suit in dealing with the government. The people were taught (and many people accepted) the claim that private property was exploitative and unethical, that large discrepancies in wealth were anti-social and represented the fruits of unethical activity, and that capitalism, despite the wealth it produced, was built on ethically unjustifiable principles.

It is from this background that Russia emerged in 1991. It moved from a communist type government to one that at least in theory was democratic. It moved from a socialist type economy to something else that at least in theory allowed free enterprise. It started privatizing its industry. But all its steps were tentative. Although background institutions must be developed in order to support the new way of life, these institutions have been slow in coming. Many of the large enterprises are still state owned, and of those that have been privatized, many still operate essentially the way they did before, including receiving subsidies from the government. The legal system is in disarray. A new constitution has only recently been adopted. But the legislature is divided and has not followed through with much of the legislation needed for a functioning market economy. The laws governing private enterprise are in a state of flux: they have been frequently rewritten during the past three years, and they are still not settled. Without laws, the judicial system cannot be expected to settle disputes. The enforcement apparatus of the government is also in disarray, and crime has burgeoned.

The Russians tend to distinguish business, which they consider is entrepreneurial activity on a relatively small level, from the running of factories and large enterprises. Laws have tended to favor large enterprises. Entrepreneurial activity, prohibited under socialism, has consisted of people opening small businesses, and to a large extent of importing and selling goods from abroad, acting as middlemen. Some have made quick fortunes. Those with money—and Russian TV now carries ads for Mercedes Benz and BMW, indicating there are quite a few such people—are looked at askance by the masses without much, who now live at a lower level than under socialism. The latter, given their own experience, feel that the nouveaux riches must be gangsters or members of the mafia, or exploiters, or former communist officials who were able to take advantage of their special position. The people were taught that capitalism is unethical, and those who take advantage of the market to amass wealth are unethical. Although the switch from socialism has made goods available in a quantity and of a quality not previously available, wages have not kept pace with costs, unemployment is rising, and the standard of living is falling.

Incipient Capitalism and Ethics

In such circumstances, what background institutions determine what is just, and how can one say what is fair or unfair, right or wrong, with respect to business? Failing to find any satisfactory answer, some claim that business ethics in this context is meaningless. Some characterize the situation as "wild" or primitive or incipient capitalism, reminiscent of conditions in the United States in the Wild West or under the robber barons. Many Russians, who were taught by their Marxist-Leninist teachers that capitalism is a rapacious system, think that the crime and corruption that has blossomed in Russia is a necessary price that goes together with the goods and higher standard of living that eventually capitalism will bring them. Is this so?

By way of response, I shall start with some broad generalizations. First, regardless of whether the characterization of wild or primitive or incipient capitalism is correct, the basic norms of morality apply to every society, whatever the background institutions. These norms are not dependent on particular background conditions. Murdering one's competitor, destroying the property of those who do not pay for protection, distributing poisoned food as pure— all such acts are unethical, no matter what the system. Hundreds of businessmen have been murdered by what has become known as the Russian mafia. This may resemble what took place as capitalism developed in 18th- and 19th-century Europe, but it is not a necessary stage on the way to a free-market economy today. Such behavior is clearly unethical. There are some acts that are wrong no matter what the background situation. Similarly, government officials who demand bribes to allow privileges that are legally restricted or who ignore violations of the law are unethical—no matter what the system. Such actions are generally and properly termed corrupt, no matter where practiced.

Second, although Russia will inevitably suffer the pangs of moving from a socialist economy to a free-market economy, it need not attempt to reinvent a market economy. Many rules necessary for its successful and efficient functioning have been developed elsewhere and need only be adopted. These include respect for private property and the honoring of contracts, among other norms. Without these, repeat business transactions will not take place or will be excessively costly. Efficient markets require rules, trust, enforcement mechanisms, and penalties for failure to perform.

Third, it is easier to control illegal and unethical behavior before it becomes a way of doing business, entrenched and powerful, than after it has become such. Hence there is no justification in terms of market development to allow unethical activity if it can be prevented.

Nonetheless, if we ask how Russia can move justly from a state-owned system to a privately owned system, the answer is anything but clear, and there may be no satisfactory answer. The reason is that what is just or fair depends in part on background institutions and assumptions, and these are systematically ambiguous in Russia with respect to privatization. Do the rules of socialism or of a free-market economy apply, for example, with respect to property rights? Under socialism, all property theoretically belonged to the people and was held and administered by the state. Property rights were not assigned to individuals. So if we ask who by right owns a particular factory or plant, the answer is not clear. Should the factory be turned over to the workers? But some factories were favored and are productive and worth a great deal, while others are for all intents and purposes worthless. Turning over a gold mine to the mine workers is different from turning over a university to its faculty. Should the rights to all state property be divided equally among all Russian citizens? An attempt to do just that consisted, in part, of giving each citizen vouchers worth 10,000 rubles ($40.00). But without a stock market to sell the vouchers and without information about how the system works, many quickly lost their share of Russian industry. Moreover neither approach brings in any new money, which is needed for many of the industries to function productively. To get new capital, some plants have been sold to non-Russian outside buyers. But such buyers are only interested in the more productive plants. No matter what method is chosen—and in Russia a variety of approaches to privatization have been used—each can be criticized as unjust to some group or portion of the population.[2]

Just as privatization cannot proceed justly because of different, changing and ambiguous background conditions, the difficulty spills over into other areas of economic life.

What then can we say about business ethics in Russia at the present time? As a start to answering this question I shall present and analyze four typical cases. I shall argue that these cases cannot be properly evaluated if we ignore the circumstances in which they are found, and that the evaluations that are justifiable may well be different from like-sounding cases in an American context. From the analyses I shall draw some tentative conclusions.

Four Cases

1.   Consider the case of Ivan Ivanovich, a Russian manager of a large formerly state-owned factory. Although he has the new responsibility of running his factory in order to make a profit for the shareholders, he takes upon himself the obligation of paying the company's workers all the benefits the workers received under the communist system. The factory supplies them with housing, health care, and old-age pensions. In order to do this and still stay in business, Ivan ignores a number of laws that are not strictly enforced, and falsifies the factory's records so as not to incur any taxes. This is similar to what he did under the communist regime.[3] For the factory to be at all efficient, he should fire at least ten percent of his employees. But because they would have to join the growing army of the unemployed, he refuses to do so.

Ivan does not run the company for his own profit or that of the shareholders. He breaks a number of Russian laws, which are not enforced anyway, in order to provide the kinds of benefits that the workers of the factory have traditionally received under communism, and which the state has not taken over. He chooses to keep people employed rather than make the company efficient. Are his actions ethically justifiable? In this case, what Ivan does is unethical if he has an ethical obligation to obey the law and an ethical obligation to run the factory efficiently and profitably. But arguably the ethical obligation to obey the law holds only when the law is itself ethically justifiable and equitably enforced. Since both are open to question in the given circumstances in Russia—the first because of the ambiguity and contradictory nature of many of the laws and the second because of the lack of any effective enforcement—the ethical obligation to obey such laws is questionable at best. Nonetheless, Ivan opens himself up to possible legal prosecution. What of his obligation to increase shareholder wealth, which he is not doing by continuing worker benefits that are no longer legally mandated? From a long-range perspective, is he not also delaying the transition of the society to a true market economy? From an ethical point of view, whether the obligations to shareholders and to develop the new system take precedence over former obligations of the firm to its employees depends on how one interprets the background assumptions. And it is these that are mixed. I would argue (although restrictions of space and time prevent my doing so here) that his actions are ethically justifiable, given the circumstances.

2.   Since I have implied that it may not be unethical to ignore the law in Russia, let us turn to Alexander Alexandrovich, a Russian manager of a large aluminum manufacturing company, *A,* who together with other managers of the firm forms an independent company, *B,* which they privately own.[4] Company *A* is state-owned and subsidized. It sells its aluminum to company *B* at subsidized prices, the same as it does to other Russian companies. The managers of company *B,* as is the custom, pay an official for an export permit. They then export the aluminum they buy at subsidized prices and receive much higher world prices for their product. They siphon off most of their earnings to private Swiss bank accounts, returning to Russia only enough funds to cover their next purchase.

In forming Company *B,* Alexander and his colleagues did nothing illegal, and were fostering the advent of a free-market economy. *B* pays *A* the government subsidized prices, legally exports the aluminum, sells it at world prices, banks the profit abroad, and brings back sufficient capital to make the next purchase. No laws are broken. Firm A continues in business, the workers receive the same pay they did previously, and the managers, in good entrepreneurial fashion, take advantage of a situation to become millionaires. Did they do anything for which they can be ethically faulted? If legality equaled ethical permissibility, the answer would be no. Yet some questions arise.

The workers of the aluminum firm feel that some injustice is being done them. The managers have used their position and experience to create an independent company that reaps great rewards for the managers, while the workers are no better off than they were before. Is this unethical? The workers are no worse off than they were, and unlike many of their fellow Russians they still have their jobs and their wages. Of course they would be better off if the managers of the firm did not create the trading company and shared their profits with the workers. The question is whether the managers were ethically required to do this or ethically precluded from doing what they did. Do the rules and expectations of socialism operate here, in which case we have a violation of socialist solidarity; or do we adopt the rules of capitalism, which ignore such claims? If we adopt the rules of capitalism, do we have a conflict of interest—a concept unfamiliar to many Russians—and a failure of Alexander in his capacity as the manager of A to manage it for the best interests of that company rather than of B? Would the situation be different if company A had been privatized and was owned by the workers? In a mixed situation must one choose which set of background assumptions apply or may one choose among them, more accurately reflecting the actual situation? More importantly, it is not outside observers but the Russians who decide what should apply. And there seems to be little consensus on this issue in the present state of flux.

The managers paid the government bureaucrat who issued the export license. Is this a bribe or a facilitating payment? In either case, is it justifiable? The managers did not pay the official to do anything that the official was not supposed to do or to break any Russian law. If the official required a payment to issue the export permit, the question is whether officials who require such payment are more to blame than those who pay them. Many Russians feel that the bureaucracy and many of the rules bureaucrats enforce exist solely for the benefit of those who enforce them. In this situation exactly who is unethical is not always clear. The government's purpose in permitting exports is to bring back hard currency into Russia for the benefit of the country. But the government has not been able to control companies that trade abroad, or to enforce any type of accountability. Is Alexander ethically required to follow the intent of export controls or may he take advantage of loopholes in the law?

Finally Alexander takes advantage of the fact that Company A is subsidized in various ways by the government. This provides the owners of B with a product that costs them relatively little, which they sell at a handsome profit. Clearly the state does not subsidize the aluminum industry so that managers can become wealthy. Yet what the managers do is not illegal. Rather than invoke ethics, both the market and the government are responding to the situation. The Russian aluminum firms over the past three years exported in such quantity that they created a glut on the international market. The price of aluminum dropped sharply, as did the profits of the Russian exporters. The government in the meantime stopped subsidizing the cost of electricity, thus forcing the producing firm to bear its real costs and raise its selling price to *B*, as well as to all other firms.

One might argue that Alexander exploits the workers, the country, and the legal loopholes that exist so that he can reap enormous profits. I am inclined to argue this position against those who claim that Alexander and his fellow managers are just acting as entrepreneurs do and so are justified in their actions. But making out the case that their actions are unethical is difficult in the given circumstances. The reason is that it is unclear which sets of rules—socialist or capitalist—form the background against which to evaluate the entrepreneurial actions.

3. An entrepreneur, Aleksey Alekseyevich, joins a private electricians' cooperative. They wire houses and provide all the services generally provided by electricians. Since copper wire is in short supply and electrical fixtures go first to large state-owned factories, Aleksey can operate only by getting wire and fixtures where and how he can. Sometimes Aleksey buys them from suppliers—no questions asked. Sometimes he can, for a fee, get a shipment of supplies rerouted from its intended destination to the cooperative. He pays the local protection agency (part of the Russian mafia) a monthly fee to be allowed to continue operating.

This case is typical of a considerable number of small firms in Russia. The transition from state-owned factories and shops to privately owned ones has taken place without the distribution and allocation system being effectively replaced by the market.[5] Large state-owned and formerly state-owned industries still have priority claims on many resources. Although small enterprises are allowed and sometimes verbally encouraged, it is often extremely difficult for them to get the supplies they need to function. To some extent this is not new and is similar to conditions under communism.

When everything is said to belong to everyone, as was the case under socialism, there is often little concern for exactly who gets what. If a shipment goes to one firm rather than another, the second firm in a sense owns it as appropriately as the first, since it is common property. Such an attitude is found in the U. S. military in which inventoried items that are lost or misplaced or stolen are frequently made up by trading among property officers and clerks from different units. With this sort of background, what the entrepreneurs are doing, as well as what those who supply the goods may be doing, fits in with the way of doing business under the former system. The allocation system has not caught up with the free-market thrust of the economy. From the point of view of a market economy, the allocation system is distorted, given a move to a partially developed private-ownership system. Under these circumstances a small entrepreneur like Aleksey must either operate as the situation describes or not operate at all. Let us suppose that this is an accurate characterization of the situation. In such a case, may the entrepreneur get the material he needs as he can, and may he pay extortion in order to be allowed to operate?

We can make several distinctions. First, it is unethical for the suppliers of protection to charge extortion. Extortion is unethical, no matter what the system. But paying extortion is less bad than charging it; and it may be justifiable, at least temporarily, under certain circumstances. It is an evil because it tends to perpetuate extortion, and helps it to escalate, to the detriment of society. Yet paying extortion is the lesser of two evils for Aleksey, if the alternative is for him and all small entrepreneurs to be driven out of business and for there either to be no such services available or for only those who have no ethical compunctions to operate businesses.

Similarly, if the goods sold to the small business are stolen, we can fault those who steal. If they are diverted from their intended receiver but the producer is paid, then the harm done to the system might be grounds for ethical complaint, except that the system is chaotic, and determining which recipient produces more good or harm may be difficult to determine. Even if we ethically fault the supplier (as we should), the fault of the receiver is certainly less, and operating in the same fashion as under the communist system may be preferable once again to leaving all enterprise to the criminal element.

Both of these justifications are justifications only insofar as they are truly necessary and temporary, given the current state of affairs, and only insofar as they are the lesser of two evils.

4. A U.S. multinational, represented by John Jones, purchases a portion of a formerly state-owned enterprise that has been privatized. Its Russian co-owners tell the U.S. company that if they are to succeed, they should be ready to pay bribes to a variety of government officials.

This case demands a different analysis from the other three. Although the American multinational operates in the Russian system in which the laws are ambiguous and often unenforced, in which bribery is rampant and extortion the norm for small businesses, none of this justifies American companies acting as Russian firms might justifiably act. The reason is that American companies are in a very different situation from the Russian companies.

First of all, no American company is forced to operate in Russia. It always has the option of not operating there, and many American firms, given the ambiguity of the laws, the ambiguous status of property claims, the uncertainty of adjudication of disputes and the prevalence of corruption on both the governmental and the criminal levels, have decided not to venture into those circumstances. Those who do venture, do so knowing that they take enormous risks in the hope of gaining equivalent returns. But unlike their Russian counterparts they operate from a position of power. They have hard currency, which is in great demand. They can successfully refuse to pay bribes that are prohibited by the Foreign Corrupt Practices Act, and they can successfully refuse to pay extortion. If in some instances the costs of protecting their property and employees from violence is too great, they have the option of leaving. Hence they are not in a position of either being forced to engage in corrupt practices, thereby helping to sustain and promote them, or of not operating at all—even though they will not operate in Russia.

To the extent that they do operate in Russia, because of their powerful position, they have the obligation to help bring ethical practices into the marketplace and to help make the market fair. They are potentially in a position to exploit the people and the country with relative impunity. But not only is that not in the long-term interest of the company or of the development of a market economy in Russia, it is exploitation of a gross kind.

Does this mean that there are two sets of ethical rules, one for Russian companies and one for American (and other) multinational corporations? The answer is no, but this must be properly understood. It is no because the actual circumstances of the Russian and of American firms operating in Russia are different, despite the fact that both operate in the same place at the same time.

Does this imply that because of their different circumstances less is expected of Russian companies, or more is tolerated from an ethical point of view than of American companies? The answer is a qualified yes. There is no special set of lesser ethical rules that applies to conditions of incipient capitalism. But ethics never demands more than can reasonably be expected of people, in business just as in other areas of life. Moreover, business itself embodies and presupposes certain ethical norms without which it cannot and does not function. The limits of corruption that it can tolerate are not great. Nor are the limits of intentional misinformation, deceit, and exploitation. As these increase, business tends to retreat, being replaced by barter and more primitive forms of exchange. We are presently seeing this phenomenon in Russia and in some of the other former Soviet and communist states.

Corruption is not justifiable simply because it is rampant. But operating amidst corruption is not easy. The actual alternatives that are open to one are frequently decisive in determining whether certain practices—such as paying extortion—are justifiable. The conditions are different for local and foreign firms. American and other multinationals can serve a positive function by being the exemplars and bearers of ethical business practices, and this is as important and perhaps more important to the developing system than the goods or services such firms might provide.

Generalizations From These Cases

What conclusions can we draw from this discussion?

1. Some actions are wrong no matter which system of background institutions are in place. Hence whether Russia's background institutions are socialist, free-market, mixed or chaotic, murder, extortion, violence and theft are unethical. The longer they are tolerated and become de facto part of the way of doing business, the more difficult it will be to achieve a reasonably efficient market.

2. The U.S. business ethics literature and a U.S. perspective on particular business issues reflects American background conditions and cannot be superimposed on Russia. In the present circumstances in Russia some actions will appropriately be judged unethical when viewed from the assumption that socialist background conditions are operative, and will appropriately be viewed as ethically justifiable when viewed from the assumption that free-market conditions are operative. Since both are partially operative—or inoperative—it is not only practically difficult but in principle impossible to decide from some outside perspective the morality of some business practices.

3. The discrepancies between aspects of the socialist system that are still in place—such as state subsidies—and the opportunities for profit by selling subsidized goods abroad under free-market rules is being exploited by some to their great advantage. Legislation and regulations that are rational, that are aimed at the common good, and that keep competition fair are essential. Russia can learn from the experience of developed countries what is required and need not learn only by trial and error.

4. The plight of the worker in Russia is worsening. Given the confusion about the role of the state in providing housing, health services, education, old-age benefits, and other social assistance, the obligations of industry and business to provide what was provided under the former socialist system are unclear. But business and industry cannot simply ignore the needs of their workers. How firms must treat employees, beyond respecting their basic human rights, is appropriately determined by considering the background conditions in which the firm operates. A pressing task is for Russia to determine and implement a clear policy. In the meantime Russian firms have some obligations to continue providing services that were formerly expected and considered entitlements.

5. American and other multinational corporations can serve an important function not only by economic joint ventures and economic activity, but also by adhering to the ethical standards that are expected at home and by helping guide the establishment of background institutions that are necessary for the long-run efficient and mutually beneficial development of business in Russia. Not only can they adhere to higher standards but they have the obligation to do so. This seemingly double set of ethical standards is justified by the fact that although operating in the same country, the circumstances of the foreign interest and of the local entrepreneur are different, and what is possible for each is different as well. Applying the principle of "ought implies can" yields different norms for foreign and for local businesses.[6]

Before closing, however, let me briefly extend the implications of my analysis to two other areas of international business ethics. I have discussed, first, business ethics within different countries (which one might call comparative international business ethics), and second, the possible difference between the obligations of multinationals and of indigenous businesses in a country like Russia. The third area is the area of mutual trade between or among countries.

If the thesis is correct that background institutions are necessary to the substantive norms of business ethics, then the background conditions of international trade and politics set the stage for international business and for international business ethics on this level. Here we frequently have negotiations not by multinationals but by the governments of countries. But in addition we have international codes, UN commissions, religious institutions, non-governmental organizations such as the Red Cross, and other similar groups and institutions that form part of the background. Expectations on the international level are also very different from on the national level. There is no effective redistribution mechanism among countries, no taxes for global redistribution, and so on. Issues of rich countries versus poor countries and of dependency versus independence form part of the background for trade negotiations, treaties, agreements, and the like for carrying on business. This area deserves more careful analysis and development for its ethical implications, problems, needs—especially the need for more effective background institutions—than it has received.

The fourth area is what I shall call the global area. There are some global issues—such as the depletion of the ozone level—that cannot be resolved and are not caused by individual companies or by companies from individual countries, but by countries and companies and people acting each in their own ways. With respect to the ozone level, to the extent that the problem is caused by chlorofluorocarbons, these are the results of modern chemistry, and are emitted by machines made by businesss—whether privately owned or government owned. No individual firm can solve the problem, nor can any individual country. The ethical responsibility falls collectively on all. Some contribute more to the problem than others. Some are able to do more to solve it than others. The background situation and conditions affect the obligations of different groups and different countries and different companies. The Rio Conference was a meeting of nations. Some American companies are ahead of the curve of the American government in their willingness to cut back on emissions; some poorer countries are unable to cut back as much as more affluent countries are. Are there two sets of norms here?

As in the case of Russia and incipient capitalism, it is possible to hold that some actions are simply wrong, no matter who does them; some actions are wrong, but may be tolerated in certain conditions as the lesser of two evils; and these same actions may be tolerated for some in certain conditions but not for others in other conditions. A greater burden falls on the industries in the developed countries than falls on the industries of developing countries both because the former are the greater cause of the degradation of the ozone level and because they have the financial and technological resources to do something to alleviate the problem. Similarly, affluent companies in developing countries have a greater responsibility to control their emissions than do struggling companies in such countries. The general rule to do no direct intentional harm plays out differently for different countries in different conditions. As we have seen, conditions may be different for two companies in the same country at the same time.

I started by noting the ambiguity of the term "international business ethics." It encompasses, I suggest, at least these four areas, although it is not exhausted by them. I also claimed at the start of this paper that even if general ethics had some claim to universality, business ethics, as an applied area, had much less, if any, such claim. As an applied area of ethics, it is always embedded in socio-economic-political conditions which form and engulf business. If this is correct, international business ethics is not more free from such constraints but equally tied to them, and is often more difficult because of the additional variables that one has to take into account.

Notes

1. See Richard T. De George, *Soviet Ethics and Morality*, Ann Arbor: Michigan University Press, 1969; Sheila M. Puffer, "Understanding the Bear: A Portrait of Russian Business Leaders," *The Academy of Management Executive*, Vol. 8, No. 1 (February 1994), pp. 41–54.

2. For a fuller discussion of privatization, see Richard T. De George, "International Business Ethics: Russia and Eastern Europe," *Social Responsibility: Business, Journalism, Law, Medicine,* Vol. XIX (1993), pp. 5–23.

3. Adi Ignatius, "Battling for Russia's Soul at the Factory," *The Wall Street Journal,* December 21, 1993, p. A6. In "Business Ethics of the Director of a Russian Industrial Enterprise," a paper presented at the 25th AAASS National Convention, Honolulu, November 12–22, 1993, Leonid Khotin describes such situations.

4. Ann Imse, "Russia's Wild Capitalists Take Aluminum for a Ride," *The New York Times,* February 13, 1994, p. F4.

5. See, among other sources, Alexander Filatov, "Unethical Business Behavior In Post-Communist Russia: Origins and Trends," *Business Ethics Quarterly,* Vol. 4, No. 1 (January 1994), pp. 11–15.

6. A somewhat similar analysis yields greater obligations to U.S. multinationals than to indigenous firms in less developed countries. See Richard T. De George, *Competing With Integrity in International Business,* New York: Oxford University Press, 1993.

The United Nations Declaration of Human Rights

Now, Therefore, The General Assembly *proclaims*

This universal declaration of human rights as a common standard of achievement for all peoples and all nations, to the end that every individual and every organ of society, keeping this Declaration constantly in mind, shall strive by teaching and education to promote respect for these rights and freedoms and by progressive measures, national and international, to secure their universal and effective recognition and observance, both among the peoples of Member States themselves and among the peoples of territories under their jurisdiction.

Article 1

All human beings are born free and equal in dignity and rights. They are endowed with reason and conscience and should act towards one another in a spirit of brotherhood.

Article 2

Everyone is entitled to all the rights and freedoms set forth in this Declaration without distinction of any kind, such as race, colour, sex, language, religion, political or other opinion, national or social origin, property, birth or other status.

Furthermore, no distinction shall be made on the basis of the political jurisdictional or international status of the country or territory to which a person belongs, whether it be independent, trust, non-self-governing or under any other limitation of sovereignty.

Article 3

Everyone has the right to life, liberty and security of person.

Article 4

No one shall be held in slavery or servitude; slavery and the slave trade shall be prohibited in all their forms.

Article 5

No one shall be subjected to torture or to cruel, inhuman or degrading treatment or punishment.

Article 6

Everyone has the right to recognition everywhere as a person before the law.

Article 7

All are equal before the law and are entitled without any discrimination to equal protection of the law. All are entitled to equal protection against any discrimination in violation of this Declaration and against any incitement to such discrimination.

Article 8

Everyone has the right to an effective remedy by the competent national tribunals for acts violating the fundamental rights granted him by the constitution or by law.

Article 9

No one shall be subjected to arbitrary arrest, detention or exile.

Article 10

Everyone is entitled in full equality to a fair and public hearing by an independent and impartial tribunal, in the determination of his rights and obligations and of any criminal charge against him.

Article 11

1. Everyone charged with a penal offence has the right to be presumed innocent until proved guilty according to law in a public trial at which he has had all the guarantees necessary for his defense.
2. No one shall be held guilty of any penal offence on account of any act or omission which did not constitute a penal offence, under national or international law, at the time when it was committed. Nor shall a heavier penalty be imposed than the one that was applicable at the time the penal offence was committed.

Article 12

No one shall be subjected to arbitrary interference with his privacy, family, home or correspondence, nor to attacks upon his honour and reputation. Everyone has the right to the protection of the law against such interference or attacks.

Article 13

1. Everyone has the right to freedom of movement and residence within the borders of each state.
2. Everyone has the right to leave any country, including his own, and to return to his country.

Article 14

1. Everyone has the right to seek and to enjoy in other countries asylum from persecution.
2. This right may not be invoked in the case of prosecutions genuinely arising from non-political crimes or from acts contrary to the purposes and principles of the United Nations.

Article 15

1. Everyone has the right to a nationality.
2. No one shall be arbitrarily deprived of his nationality nor denied the right to change his nationality.

Article 16

1. Men and women of full age, without any limitation due to race, nationality or religion, have the right to marry and to found a family. They are entitled to equal rights as to marriage, during marriage and at its dissolution.
2. Marriage shall be entered into only with the free and full consent of the intending spouses.
3. The family is the natural and fundamental group unit of society and is entitled to protection by society and the State.

Article 17

1. Everyone has the right to own property alone as well as in association with others.
2. No one shall be arbitrarily deprived of his property.

Article 18

Everyone has the right to freedom of thought, conscience and religion; this right includes freedom to change his religion or belief, and freedom, either alone or in community with others and in public or private, to manifest his religion or belief in teaching, practice, worship and observance.

Article 19

Everyone has the right to freedom of opinion and expression; this right includes freedom to hold opinions without interference and to seek, receive and impart information and ideas through any media and regardless of frontiers.

Article 20

1. Everyone has the right to freedom of peaceful assembly and association.
2. No one may be compelled to belong to an association.

Article 21

1. Everyone has the right to take part in the government of his country, directly or through freely chosen representatives.
2. Everyone has the right of equal access to public service in his country.
3. The will of the people shall be the basis of the authority of government; this will shall be expressed in periodic and genuine elections which shall be by universal and equal suffrage and shall be held by secret vote or by equivalent free voting procedures.

Article 22

Everyone, as a member of society, has the right to social security and is entitled to realization, through national effort and international cooperation and in accordance with the organization and resources of each State, of the economic, social and cultural rights indispensable for his dignity and the free development of his personality.

Article 23

1. Everyone has the right to work, to free choice of employment, to just and favourable conditions of work and to protection against unemployment.
2. Everyone, without any discrimination, has the right to equal pay for equal work.
3. Everyone who works has the right to just and favourable remuneration ensuring for himself and his family an existence worthy of human dignity, and supplemented, if necessary, by other means of social protection.
4. Everyone has the right to form and to join trade unions for the protection of his interests.

Article 24

Everyone has the right to rest and leisure, including reasonable limitation of working hours and periodic holidays with pay.

Article 25

1. Everyone has the right to a standard of living adequate for the health and well-being of himself and of his family, including food, clothing, housing and medical care and necessary social services, and the right to security in the event of unem-

ployment, sickness, disability, widowhood, old age or other lack of livelihood in circumstances beyond his control.

2. Motherhood and childhood are entitled to special care and assistance. All children, whether born in or out of wedlock, shall enjoy the same social protection.

Article 26

1. Everyone has the right to education. Education shall be free, at least in the elementary and fundamental stages. Elementary education shall be compulsory. Technical and professional education shall be made generally available and higher education shall be equally accessible to all on the basis of merit.
2. Education shall be directed to the full development of the human personality and to the strengthening of respect for human rights and fundamental freedoms. It shall promote understanding, tolerance and friendship among all nations, racial or religious groups, and shall further the activities of the United Nations for the maintenance of peace.
3. Parents have a prior right to choose the kind of education that shall be given to their children.

Article 27

1. Everyone has the right freely to participate in the cultural life of the community, to enjoy the arts and to share in scientific advancement and its benefits.
2. Everyone has the right to the protection of the moral and material interests resulting from any scientific, literary or artistic production of which he is the author.

Article 28

Everyone is entitled to a social and international order in which the rights and freedoms set forth in this Declaration can be fully realized.

Article 29

1. Everyone has duties to the community in which alone the free and full development of his personality is possible.
2. In the exercise of his rights and freedoms, everyone shall be subject only to such limitations as are determined by law solely for the purpose of securing due recognition and respect for the rights and freedoms of others and of meeting the just requirements of morality, public order and the general welfare in a democratic society.
3. These rights and freedoms may in no case be exercised contrary to the purposes and principles of the United Nations.

Article 30

Nothing in this Declaration may be interpreted as implying for any State, group or person any right to engage in any activity or to perform any act aimed at the destruction of any of the rights and freedoms set forth herein.

Truth Telling

• *Case Study* •

Italian Tax Mores

ARTHUR L. KELLY

The Italian federal corporate tax system has an official, legal tax structure and tax rates just as the U.S. system does. However, all similarity between the two systems ends there.

The Italian tax authorities assume that no Italian corporation would ever submit a tax return which shows its true profits but rather would submit a return which understates actual profits by anywhere between 30 percent and 70 percent; their assumption is essentially correct. Therefore, about six months after the annual deadline for filing corporate tax returns, the tax authorities issue to each corporation an "invitation to discuss" its tax return. The purpose of this notice is to arrange a personal meeting between them and representatives of the corporation. At this meeting, the Italian revenue service states the amount of corporate income tax which it believes is due. Its position is developed from both prior years' taxes actually paid and the current year's return; the amount which the tax authorities claim is due is generally several times that shown on the corporation's return for the current year. In short, the corporation's tax return and the revenue service's stated position are the opening offers for the several rounds of bargaining which will follow.

The Italian corporation is typically represented in such negotiations by its *commercialista,* a function which exists in Italian society for the primary purpose of negotiating corporate (and individual) tax payments with the Italian tax authorities; thus, the management of an Italian corporation seldom, if ever, has to meet directly with the Italian revenue service and probably has a minimum awareness of the details of the negotiation other than the final settlement.

Both the final settlement and the negotiation are extremely important to the corporation, the tax authorities, and the *commercialista.* Since the tax authorities assume that a corporation *always* earned more money this year than last year and *never* has a loss, the amount of the final settlement, i.e., corporate taxes which will actually be paid, becomes, for all practical purposes, the floor

This case was prepared by Arthur L. Kelly based on an actual occurrence and was first presented at Loyola University Chicago in April 1977 at a Mellon Foundation Symposium entitled "Foundations of Corporate Responsibility to Society." Mr. Kelly has served as Vice President-International of the management consulting firm, A.T. Kearney, Inc., President of LaSalle Steel Company, and is currently Managing Partner of KEL Enterprises Ltd., a Chicago holding and investment company. He serves as a member of the Board of Directors of corporations in the United States and Europe including Deere & Company and BMW A.G. Copyrighted 1977. All rights reserved.

for the start of next year's negotiations. The final settlement also represents the amount of revenue the Italian government will collect in taxes to help finance the cost of running the country. However, since large amounts of money are involved and two individuals having vested personal interests are conducting the negotiations, the amount of *bustarella*—typically a substantial cash payment "requested" by the Italian revenue agent from the *commercialista*—usually determines whether the final settlement is closer to the corporation's original tax return or to the fiscal authority's original negotiating position.

Whatever *bustarella* is paid during the negotiation is usually included by the *commercialista* in his lump-sum fee "for services rendered" to his corporate client. If the final settlement is favorable to the corporation, and it is the *commercialista's* job to see that it is, then the corporation is not likely to complain about the amount of its *commercialista's* fee, nor will it ever know how much of that fee was represented by *bustarella* and how much remained for the *commercialista* as payment for his negotiating services. In any case, the tax authorities will recognize the full amount of the fee as a tax deductible expense on the corporation's tax return for the following year.

About ten years ago, a leading American bank opened a banking subsidiary in a major Italian city. At the end of its first year of operation, the bank was advised by its local lawyers and tax accountants, both from branches of U.S. companies, to file its tax return "Italian-style," i.e., to understate its actual profits by a significant amount. The American general manager of the bank, who was on his first overseas assignment, refused to do so both because he considered it dishonest and because it was inconsistent with the practices of his parent company in the United States.

About six months after its "American-style" tax return, the bank received an "invitation to discuss" notice for the Italian tax authorities. The bank's general manager consulted with his lawyers and tax accountants who suggested he hire a *commercialista*. He rejected this advice and instead wrote a letter to the Italian revenue service not only stating that his firm's corporate return was correct as filed but also requesting that they inform him of any specific items about which they had questions. His letter was never answered.

About sixty days after receiving the initial "invitation to discuss" notice, the bank received a formal tax assessment notice calling for a tax of approximately three times that shown on the bank's corporate tax return; the tax authorities simply assumed the bank's original return had been based on generally accepted Italian practices, and they reacted accordingly. The bank's general manager again consulted with his lawyers and tax accountants who again suggested he hire a *commercialista* who knew how to handle these matters. Upon learning that the *commercialista* would probably have to pay *bustarella* to his revenue service counterpart in order to reach a settlement, the general manager again chose to ignore his advisors. Instead, he responded by sending the Italian revenue service a check for the full amount of taxes due according to the bank's American-style tax return even though the due date for the payment was almost six months hence; he made no reference to the amount of corporate taxes shown on the formal tax assessment notice.

Ninety days after paying its taxes, the bank received a third notice form the fiscal authorities. This one contained the statement, "We have reviewed your corporate tax return of 19__ and have determined that [the lira equivalent of] $6,000,000 of interest paid on deposits is not an allowable expense for federal tax purposes. Accordingly, the total tax due for 19__ is lira ____." Since interest paid on deposits is any bank's largest single expense item, the new tax assessment was for an amount many times larger than that shown in the initial tax assessment notice and almost fifteen times larger than the taxes which the bank had actually paid.

The bank's general manager was understandably very upset. He immediately arranged an appointment to meet personally with the manager of the Italian revenue service's local office. Shortly after the start of their meeting, the conversation went something like this:

General Manager: "You can't really be serious about disallowing interest paid on deposits as a tax deductible expense."

Italian Revenue Service: "Perhaps. However, we thought it would get your attention. Now that you're here, shall we begin our negotiations?"[1]

Note

1. For readers interested in what happened subsequently, the bank was forced to pay the taxes shown in the initial tax assessment, and the American manager was recalled to the United States and replaced.

Ethical Duties Towards Others: "Truthfulness"

IMMANUEL KANT

The exchange of our sentiments is the principal factor in social intercourse, and truth must be the guiding principle herein. Without truth social intercourse and conversation become valueless. We can only know what a man thinks if he tells us his thoughts, and when he undertakes to express them he must really do so, or else there can be no society of men. Fellowship is only the second condition of society, and a liar destroys fellowship. Lying makes it impossible to derive any benefit from conversation. Liars are, therefore, held in general contempt. Man is inclined to be reserved and to pretend. . . . Man is reserved in order to conceal his faults and shortcomings which he has; he pretends in order to make others attribute to him merits and virtues which he has not. Our proclivity to reserve and concealment is due to the will of Providence that the defects of which we are full should not be too obvious. Many of our propensities and peculiarities are objectionable to others, and if they became patent we should be foolish and hateful in their eyes. Moreover, the parading of these objectionable characteristics would so familiarize men with them that

From *Lectures on Ethics,* trans. Louis Infield (London: Routledge, 1930). Reprinted by permission of the publisher.

they would themselves acquire them. Therefore we arrange our conduct either to conceal our faults or to appear other than we are. We possess the art of simulation. In consequence, our inner weakness and error is revealed to the eyes of men only as an appearance of well-being, while we ourselves develop the habit of dispositions which are conducive to good conduct. No man in his true senses, therefore, is candid. Were man candid, were the request of Momus[1] to be complied with that Jupiter should place a mirror in each man's heart so that his disposition might be visible to all, man would have to be better constituted and possess good principles. If all men were good there would be no need for any of us to be reserved; but since they are not, we have to keep the shutters closed. Every house keeps its dustbin in a place of its own. We do not press our friends to come into our water-closet, although they know that we have one just like themselves. Familiarity in such things is the ruin of good taste. In the same way we make no exhibition of our defects, but try to conceal them. We try to conceal our mistrust by affecting a courteous demeanor and so accustom ourselves to courtesy that at last it becomes a reality and we set a good example by it. If that were not so, if there were none who were better than we, we should become neglectful. Accordingly, the endeavour to appear good ultimately makes us really good. If all men were good, they could be candid, but as things are they cannot be. To be reserved is to be restrained in expressing one's mind. We can, of course, keep absolute silence. This is the readiest and most absolute method of reserve, but it is unsociable, and a silent man is not only unwanted in social circles but is also suspected; every one thinks him deep and disparaging, for if when asked for his opinion he remains silent people think that he must be taking the worst view or he would not be averse from expressing it. Silence, in fact, is always a treacherous ally, and therefore it is not even prudent to be completely reserved. Yet there is such a thing as prudent reserve, which requires not silence but careful deliberation; a man who is wisely reserved weighs his words carefully and speaks his mind about everything excepting only those things in regard to which he deems it wise to be reserved.

We must distinguish between reserve and secretiveness, which is something entirely different. There are matters about which one has no desire to speak and in regard to which reserve is easy. We are, for instance, not naturally tempted to speak about and to betray our own misdemeanours. Everyone finds it easy to keep a reserve about some of his private affairs, but there are times about which it requires an effort to be silent. Secrets have a way of coming out, and strength is required to prevent ourselves betraying them. Secrets are always matters deposited with us by other people and they ought not to be placed at the disposal of third parties. But man has a great liking for conversation, and the telling of secrets adds much to the interest of conversation; a secret told is like a present given; how then are we to keep secrets? Men who are not very talkative as a rule keep secrets well, but good conversationalists, who are at the same time clever, keep them better. The former might be induced to betray something, but the latter's gift of repartee invariably enables them to invent on the spur of the moment something non-committal.

The person who is as silent as a mute goes to one extreme; the person who is loquacious goes to the opposite. Both tendencies are weaknesses. Men are liable to the first, women to the second. Someone has said that women are talkative because the training of infants is their special charge, and their talkativeness soon teaches a child to speak, because they can chatter to it all day long. If men had the care of the child, they would take much longer to learn to talk. However that may be, we dislike anyone who will not speak: he annoys us; his silence betrays his pride. On the other hand, loquaciousness in men is contemptible and contrary to the strength of the male. All this by the way; we shall now pass to more weighty matters.

If I announce my intention to tell what is in my mind, ought I knowingly to tell everything, or can I keep anything back? If I indicate that I mean to speak my mind, and instead of doing so make false declaration, what I say is an untruth, a *falsiloquium*. But there can be *falsiloquium* even when people have no right to assume that we are expressing our thoughts. It is possible to deceive without making any statement whatever. I can make believe, make a demonstration from which others will draw the conclusion I want, though they have no right to expect that my action will express my real mind. In that case I have not lied to them, because I had not undertaken to express my mind. I may, for instance, wish people to think that I am off on a journey, and so I pack my luggage; people draw the conclusion I want them to draw; but others have no right to demand a declaration of my will from me.

. . . Again, I may make a false statement (*falsiloquium*), when my purpose is to hide from another what is in my mind and when the latter can assume that such is my purpose, his own purpose being to make a wrong use of the truth. Thus, for instance, if my enemy takes me by the throat and asks where I keep my money, I need not tell him the truth, because he will abuse it; and my untruth is not a lie (*mendacium*) because the thief knows full well that I will not, if I can help it, tell him the truth and that he has no right to demand it of me. But let us assume that I really say to the fellow, who is fully aware that he has no right to demand it, because he is a swindler, that I will tell him the truth, and I do not, am I then a liar? He has deceived me and I deceive him in return; to him, as an individual, I have done no injustice and he cannot complain; but I am none the less a liar in that my conduct is an infringement of the rights of humanity. It follows that a *falsiloquium* can be a *mendacium*—a lie—especially when it contravenes the right of an individual. Although I do a man no injustice by lying to him when he has lied to me, yet I act against the right of mankind, since I set myself in opposition to the condition and means through which any human society is possible. If one country breaks the peace this does not justify the other in doing likewise in revenge, for if it did no peace would ever be secure. Even though a statement does not contravene any particular human right it is nevertheless a lie if it is contrary to the general right of mankind. If a man spreads false news, though he does no wrong to anyone in particular, he offends against mankind, because if such a practice were universal man's desire for knowledge would be frustrated. For, apart from speculation, there are only two ways in which I can increase my fund of knowledge, by experience or by what others tell me. My own experience must necessarily be limited, and if what others told me was false, I could not satisfy my craving for knowledge.

. . . Not every untruth is a lie; it is a lie only if I have expressly given the other to understand that I am willing to acquaint him with my thought. Every lie is objectionable and contemptible in that we purposely let people think that we are telling them our thoughts and do not do so. We have broken our pact and violated the right of mankind. But if we were to be at all times punctiliously truthful we might often become victims of the wickedness of others who were ready to abuse our truthfulness. If all men were well-intentioned it would not only be a duty not to lie, but no one would do so because there would be no point in it. But as men are malicious, it cannot be denied that to be punctiliously truthful is often dangerous. This has given rise to the conception of a white lie, the lie enforced upon us by necessity—a difficult point for moral philosophers. For if necessity is urged as an excuse it might be urged to justify stealing, cheating and killing, and the whole basis of morality goes by the board. Then, again, what is a case of necessity? Everyone will interpret it in his own way. And, as there is then no definite standard to judge by, the application of moral rules becomes uncertain. Consider, for example, the following case. A man who knows that I have money asks me: "Have you any money on you?" If I fail to reply, he will conclude that I have; if I reply in the affirmative he will take it from me; if I reply in the negative, I tell a lie. What am I to do? If force is used to extort a confession from me, if any confession is improperly used against me, and if I cannot save myself by maintaining silence, then my lie is a weapon of defence. The misuse of a declaration extorted by force justifies me in defending myself. For whether it is my money or a confession that is extorted makes no difference. The forcing of a statement from me under conditions which convince me that improper use would be made of it is the only case in which I can be justified in telling a white lie. But if a lie does no harm to anyone and no one's interests are affected by it, is it a lie? Certainly, I undertake to express my mind, and if I do not really do so, though my statement may not be to the prejudice of the particular individual to whom it was made, it is none the less in *praejudicium humanitatis*. Then, again, there are lies which cheat. To cheat is to make a lying promise, while a breach of faith is a true promise which is not kept. A lying promise is an insult to the person to whom it is made, and even if this is not always so, yet there is always something mean about it. If, for instance, I promise to send some one a bottle of wine, and afterwards make a joke of it, I really swindle him. It is true that he had no right to demand the present of me, but in Idea it is already a part of his own property.

. . . If a man tries to extort the truth from us and we cannot tell it [to] him and at the same time do not wish to lie, we are justified in resorting to equivocation in order to reduce him to silence and put a stop to his questionings. If he is wise, he will leave it at that. But if we let it be understood that we are expressing our sentiments and we proceed to equivocate we are in a different case; for our listeners might then draw wrong conclusions from our statements and we should have deceived them. . . . But a lie is a lie, and is in itself intrinsically base whether it be told with good or bad intent. For formally a lie is always evil; though if it is evil materially as well, it is a much meaner thing. There are no lies which may not be the source of evil. A liar is a coward; he is a man who has recourse to lying because he is unable to help himself and gain his ends by any other means. But a stout-hearted man will love truth and will not recognize a *casus necessitatis*. All expedients which take us off our guard are thoroughly mean. Such are lying, assassination, and poisoning. To attack a man on the highway is less vile than to attempt to poison him. In the former case he can at least defend himself, but, as he must eat, he is defenseless against the poisoner. A flatterer is not always a liar; he is merely lacking in self-esteem; he has no scruple in reducing his own worth and raising that of another in order to gain something by it. But there exists a form of flattery which springs from kindness of heart. Some kind souls flatter people whom they hold in high esteem. There are thus two kinds of flattery, kindly and treacherous; the first is weak, while the second is mean. People who are not given to flattery are apt to be fault-finders.

If a man is often the subject of conversation, he becomes a subject of criticism. If he is our friend, we ought not invariably to speak well of him or else we arouse jealousy and grudge against him; for people, knowing that he is only human, will not believe that he has only good qualities. We must, therefore, concede a little to the adverse criticism of our listeners and point out some of our friend's faults; if we allow him faults which are common and unessential, while extolling his merits, our friend cannot take it in ill part. Toadies are people who praise others in company in hope of gain. Men are meant to form opinions regarding their fellows and to judge them. Nature has made us judges of our neighbors so that things which are false but are outside the scope of the established legal authority should be arraigned before the court of social opinion. Thus, if a man dishonours some one, the authorities do not punish him, but his fellows judge and punish him, though only so far as it is within their right to punish him and without doing violence to him. People shun him, and that is punishment enough. If that were not so, conduct not punished by the authorities would go altogether unpunished. What then is meant by the enjoinder that we ought not to judge others? As we are ignorant of their dispositions we cannot tell whether they are punishable before God or not, and we cannot, therefore, pass an adequate moral judgment upon them. The moral dispositions of others are for God to judge, but we are competent judges of our own. We cannot judge the inner core of morality; no man can do that; but we are competent to judge its outer manifestations. In matters of morality we are not judges of our fellows, but nature has given us the right to form judgments about others and she also has ordained that we should judge ourselves in accordance with judgments that others form about us. The man who turns a deaf ear to other people's opinion of him is base and reprehensible. There is nothing that happens in this world about which we ought not to form an opinion, and we show considerable subtlety in judging conduct. Those who judge our conduct with exactness are our best friends. Only friends can be quite candid and open with each other. But in judging a man a further question arises. In what terms are we to judge him? Must we pronounce him either good or evil? We must proceed from the assumption that humanity is lovable, and, particularly in regard to wickedness, we ought never to pronounce a verdict either of condemnation or of acquittal. We pronounce such a verdict whenever we judge from his conduct that a man deserves to be condemned or acquitted. But though we are entitled to form opinions about our fellows, we have no right to spy upon them. Everyone has a right to prevent others from watching and scrutinizing his actions. The spy arrogates to himself the right to watch the doings of strangers; no one ought to presume to do such a thing. If I see two people whispering to each other so as to not be heard, my inclination ought to be to get farther away so that no sound may reach my ears. Or if I am left alone in a room and I see a letter lying open on the table, it would be contemptible to try to read it; a right-thinking man would not do so; in fact, in order to avoid suspicion and distrust he will endeavour not to be left alone in a room where money is left lying about, and he will be averse from learning other people's secrets in order to avoid the risk of the suspicion that he has betrayed them; other people's secrets trouble him, for even between the most intimate of friends suspicion might arise. A man who will let his inclination or appetite drive him to deprive his friend of anything, of his fiancée, for instance, is contemptible beyond a doubt. If he can cherish a passion for my sweetheart, he can equally well cherish a passion for my purse. It is very mean to lie in wait and spy upon a friend, or on anyone else, and to elicit information about him from menials by lowering ourselves to the level of our inferiors, who will thereafter not forget to regard themselves as our equals. Whatever militates against frankness lowers the dignity of man. Insidious, underhand conduct uses means which strike at the roots of society because they make frankness impossible; it is far viler than violence; for against violence we can defend ourselves, and a violent man who spurns meanness can be tamed to goodness, but the mean rogue, who has not the courage to come out into the open with his roguery, is devoid of every vestige of nobility of character. For that reason a wife who attempts to poison her husband in England is burnt at the stake, for if such conduct spread, no man would be safe from his wife.

As I am not entitled to spy upon my neighbour, I am equally not entitled to point out his faults to him; and even if he should ask me to do so he would feel hurt if I complied. He knows his faults better than I, he knows that he has them, but he likes to believe that I have not noticed them, and if I tell him of them he realizes that I have. To say, therefore, that friends ought to point out each other's faults, is not sound advice. My friend may know better than I whether my gait or deportment is proper or not, but if I will only examine myself, who can know me better than I can know myself? To point out his faults to a friend is sheer impertinence; and once fault finding begins between friends their friendship will not last long. We must turn a blind eye to the faults of others, lest they conclude that they have lost our respect and we lose theirs. Only if placed in positions of authority over others should we point out to them their defects. Thus a husband is entitled to teach and correct his wife, but his corrections must be well-intentioned and kindly and must be dominated by respect, for if they be prompted only by displeasure they result in mere blame and bitterness. If we must blame, we must temper the blame with a sweetening of love, good-will, and respect. Nothing else will avail to bring about improvement.

Note

1. CF. *Babrii fabulae Aesopeae*, ed. O. Cousins, 1897, Fable 59, p. 54.

Is Business Bluffing Ethical?

ALBERT CARR

A respected businessman with whom I discussed the theme of this article remarked with some heat, "You mean to say you're going to encourage men to bluff? Why, bluffing is nothing more than a form of lying! You're advising them to lie!"

I agreed that the basis of private morality is a respect for truth and that the closer a businessman comes to the truth, the more he deserves respect. At the same time, I suggested that most bluffing in business might be regarded simply as game strategy—much like bluffing in poker, which does not reflect on the morality of the bluffer.

I quoted Henry Taylor, the British statesman who pointed out that "falsehood ceases to be falsehood when it is understood on all sides that the truth is not expected to be spoken"—an exact description of bluffing in poker, diplomacy, and business. I cited the analogy of the criminal court, where the criminal is not expected to tell the truth when he pleads "not guilty." Everyone from the judge down takes it for granted that the job of the defendant's attorney is to get his client off, not to reveal the truth; and this is considered ethical practice. I mentioned Representative Omar Burleson, the Democrat from Texas, who was quoted as saying, in regard to the ethics of Congress, "Ethics is a barrel of worms"[1]—a pungent summing up of the problem of deciding who is ethical in politics.

I reminded my friend that millions of businessmen feel constrained every day to say *yes* to their bosses when they secretly believe *no* and that this is generally accepted as permissible strategy when the alternative might be the loss of a job. The essential point, I said, is that the ethics of business are game ethics, different from the ethics of religion.

He remained unconvinced. Referring to the company of which he is president, he declared: "Maybe that's good enough for some businessmen, but I can tell you that we pride ourselves on our ethics. In 30 years not one customer has ever questioned my word or asked to check our figures. We're loyal to our customers and fair to our suppliers. I regard my handshake on a deal as a contract. I've never entered into price-fixing schemes with my competitors. I've never allowed my salesmen to spread injurious rumors about other companies. Our union contract is the best in our industry. And, if I do say so myself, our ethical standards are of the highest!"

He really was saying, without realizing it, that he was living up to the ethical standards of the business game—which are a far cry from those of private life. Like a gentlemanly poker player, he did not play in cahoots with others at the table, try to smear their reputations, or hold back chips he owed them.

But this same fine man, at that very time, was allowing one of his products to be advertised in a way that made it sound a great deal better than it actually was. Another item in his product line was notorious among dealers for its "built-in-obsolescence." He was holding back from the market a much-improved product because he did not want to interfere with sales of the inferior item it would have replaced. He had joined with certain of his competitors in hiring a lobbyist to push a state legislature, by methods that he preferred not to know too much about, into amending a bill then being enacted.

In his view these things had nothing to do with ethics; they were merely normal business practice. He himself undoubtedly avoided outright falsehood—never lied in so many words. But the entire organization that he ruled was deeply involved in numerous strategies of deception.

Pressure to Deceive

Most executives from time to time are almost compelled, in the interests of their companies or themselves, to practice some form of deception when negotiating with customers, dealers, labor unions, government officials, or even other departments of their companies. By conscious misstatements, concealment of pertinent facts, or exaggeration—in short, by bluffing—they seek to persuade others to agree with them. I think it is fair to say that if the individual executive refuses to bluff from time to time—if he feels obligated to tell the truth, the whole truth, and nothing but the truth—he is ignoring opportunities permitted under the rules and is at a heavy disadvantage in his business dealings.

But here and there a businessman is unable to reconcile himself to the bluff in which he plays a part. His conscience, perhaps spurred by religious idealism, troubles him. He feels guilty; he may develop an ulcer or a nervous tic. Before any executive can make profitable use of the strategy of the bluff, he needs to make sure that in bluffing he will not lose self-respect or become emotionally disturbed. If he is to reconcile personal integrity and high standards of honesty with the practical requirements of business, he must feel that his bluffs are ethically justified. The justification rests on the fact that business, as practiced by individuals as well as by corporations, has the impersonal character of a game—a game that demands both special strategy and an understanding of its special ethics.

The game is played at all levels of corporate life, from the highest to the lowest. At the very instant that a man decides to enter business, he may be forced into a game situation, as is shown by the recent experience of a Cornell honor graduate who applied for a job with a large company:

- This applicant was given a psychological test which included the statement, "Of the following magazines, check any that you have read either regularly or from time to time, and double-check those which interest you most. *Reader's Digest, Time, Fortune, Saturday Evening Post, The New Republic, Life, Look, Ramparts, Newsweek, Business Week, U.S. News & World Report, The Nation, Playboy, Esquire, Harper's, Sports Illustrated.*"

His tastes in reading were broad, and at one time or another he had read almost all of these magazines. He was a subscriber to the *The New Republic,* an enthusiast for *Ramparts,* and an avid student of the pictures in *Playboy.* He was not sure whether his interest in *Playboy* would be held against him, but he had a shrewd suspicion that if he confessed to an interest in *Ramparts* and *The New Republic*, he would be thought a liberal, a radical, or at least an intellectual, and his chances of getting the job, which he needed, would greatly diminish. He therefore checked five of the more conservative magazines. Apparently it was a sound decision, for he got the job.

He had made a game player's decision, consistent with business ethics.

A similar case is that of a magazine space salesman who, owing to a merger, suddenly found himself out of a job:

- This man was 58, and, in spite of a good record, his chances of getting a job elsewhere in a business where youth is favored in hiring practice was not good. He was a vigorous, healthy man, and only a considerable amount of gray in his hair suggested his age. Before beginning his job search he touched up his hair with a black dye to confine the gray to his temples. He knew that the truth about his age might well come out in time, but he calculated that he could deal with that situation when it arose. He and his wife decided that he could easily pass for 45, and he so stated his age on his résumé.

This was a lie; yet within the accepted rules of the business game, no moral culpability attaches to it.

The Poker Analogy

We can learn a good deal about the nature of business by comparing it with poker. While both have a large element of chance, in the long run the winner is the man who plays with steady skill. In both games ultimate victory requires intimate knowledge of the rules, insight into the psychology of the other players, a bold front, a considerable amount of self-discipline and the ability to respond swiftly and effectively to opportunities provided by chance.

No one expects poker to be played on the ethical principles preached in churches. In poker it is right and proper to bluff a friend out of the rewards of being dealt a good hand. A player feels no more than a slight twinge of sympathy, if that, when—with nothing better than a single ace in his hand—he strips a heavy loser, who holds a pair, of the rest of his chips. It was up to the other fellow to protect himself. In the words of an excellent poker player, former President Harry Truman, "If you can't stand the heat, stay out of the kitchen." If one shows mercy to a loser in poker, it is a personal gesture, divorced from the rules of the game.

Poker has its special ethics, and here I am not referring to rules against cheating. The man who keeps an ace up his sleeve or who marks the cards is more than unethical; he is a crook, and can be punished as such—kicked out of the game or, in the Old West, shot.

In contrast to the cheat, the unethical poker player is one who, while abiding by the letter of the rules, finds ways to put the other players at an unfair disadvantage. Perhaps he unnerves them with loud talk. Or he tries to get them drunk. Or he plays in cahoots with someone else at the table. Ethical poker players frown on such tactics.

Poker's own brand of ethics is different from the ethical ideals of civilized human relationships. The game calls for distrust of the other fellow. It ignores the claim of friendship. Cunning deception and concealment of one's strength and intentions, not kindness and openheartedness, are vital in poker. No one thinks any the worse of poker on that account. And no one should think any the worse of the game of business because its standards of right and wrong differ from the prevailing traditions of morality in our society. . . .

We Don't Make the Laws

Wherever we turn in business, we can perceive the sharp distinction between its ethical standards and those of the churches. Newspapers abound with sensational stories growing out of this distinction:

- We read one day that Senator Philip A. Hart of Michigan has attacked food processors for deceptive packaging of numerous products.[2]
- The next day there is a Congressional to-do over Ralph Nader's book, *Unsafe At Any Speed,* which demonstrates that automobile companies for years have neglected the safety of car-owning families.[3]
- Then another Senator, Lee Metcalf of Montana, and journalist Vic Reinemer show in their book, *Overcharge,* the methods by which utility companies elude regulating government bodies to extract unduly large payments from users of electricity.[4]

These are merely dramatic instances of a prevailing condition; there is hardly a major industry at which a similar attack could not be aimed. Critics of business regard such behavior as unethical, but the companies concerned know that they are merely playing the business game.

Among the most respected of our business institutions are the insurance companies. A group of insurance executives meeting recently in New England was startled when their guest speaker, social critic Daniel Patrick Moynihan, roundly berated them for "unethical" practices. They had been guilty, Moynihan alleged, of using outdated actuarial tables to obtain unfairly high premiums. They habitually delayed the hearings of lawsuits against them in order to tire out the plaintiffs and win cheap settlements. In their employment policies they used ingenious devices to discriminate against certain minority groups.[5]

It was difficult for the audience to deny the validity of these charges. But these men were business game players. Their reaction to Moynihan's attack was much the same as that of the automobile manufacturers to Nader, of the utilities to Senator Metcalf, and of the food processors to Senator Hart. If the laws governing their business change, or if public opinion becomes clamorous, they will make the necessary adjustments. But morally they have in their view done nothing wrong. As long as they comply with the letter of the law, they are within their rights to operate their businesses as they see fit.

The small business is in the same position as the great corporation in this respect. For example:

- In 1967 a key manufacturer was accused of providing master keys for automobiles to mail-order customers, although it was obvious that some of the purchasers might be automobile thieves. His defense was plain and straightforward. If there was nothing in the law to prevent him from selling his keys to anyone who ordered them, it was not up to him to inquire as to his customers' motives. Why was it any worse, he insisted, for him to sell car keys by mail, than for mail-order houses to sell guns that might be used for murder? Until the law was changed, the key manufacturer could regard himself as being just as ethical as any other businessman by the rules of the business game.[6]

Violations of the ethical ideals of society are common in business, but they are not necessarily violations of business practices. Each year the Federal Trade Commission orders hundreds of companies, many of them of the first magnitude, to "cease and desist" from practices which, judged by ordinary standards, are of questionable morality but which are stoutly defended by the companies concerned.

In one case, a firm manufacturing a well-known mouthwash was accused of using a cheap form of alcohol possibly deleterious to health. The company's chief executive, after testifying in Washington, made this comment privately:

> We broke no law. We're in a highly competitive industry. If we're going to stay in business, we have to look for profit wherever the law permits. We don't make up the laws. We obey them. Then why do we have to put up with this 'holier than thou' talk about ethics? It's sheer hypocrisy. We're not in business to promote ethics. Look at the cigarette companies, for God's sake! If the ethics aren't embodied in the laws by the men who made them, you can't expect businessmen to fill the lack. Why, a sudden submission to Christian ethics by businessmen would bring about the greatest economic upheaval in history!

It may be noted that the government failed to prove its case against him.

Cast Illusions Aside

Talk about ethics by businessmen is often a thin decorative coating over the hard realities of the game:

- Once I listened to a speech by a young executive who pointed to a new industry code as proof that his company and its competitors were deeply aware of their responsibilities to society. It was a code of ethics, he said. The industry was going to police itself, to dissuade constituent companies from wrongdoing. His eyes shone with conviction and enthusiasm.

The same day there was a meeting in a hotel room where the industry's top executives met with the "czar" who was to administer the new code, a man of high repute. No one who was present could doubt their common attitude. In their eyes the code was designed primarily to forestall a move by the federal government to impose stern restrictions on the industry. They felt that the code would hamper them a good deal less than new federal laws would. It was, in other words, conceived as a protection for the industry, not for the public.

The young executive accepted the surface explanation of the code; these leaders, all experienced game players, did not deceive themselves for a moment about its purpose.

The illusion that business can afford to be guided by ethics as conceived in private life is often fostered by speeches and articles containing such phrases as, "It pays to be ethical," or, "Sound ethics is good business." Actually this is not an ethical question at all; it is a self-serving calculation in disguise. The speaker is really saying that in the long run a company can make more money if it does not antagonize competitors, suppliers, employees, and customers by squeezing them too hard. He is saying that oversharp policies reduce ultimate gains. That is true, but it has nothing to do with ethics. The underlying attitude is much like that in the familiar story of the shopkeeper who finds an extra $20 bill in the cash register, debates with himself the ethical problem—

should he tell his partner?—and finally decides to share the money because the gesture will give him an edge over the s.o.b. the next time they quarrel.

I think it is fair to sum up the prevailing attitude of businessmen on ethics as follows:

We live in what is probably the most competitive of the world's civilized societies. Our customs encourage a high degree of aggression in the individual's striving for success. Business is our main area of competition, and it has been ritualized into a game of strategy. The basic rules of the game have been set by the government, which attempts to detect and punish business frauds. But as long as a company does not transgress the rules of the game set by law, it has the legal right to shape its strategy without reference to anything but its profits. If it takes a long-term view of its profits, it will preserve amicable relations, so far as possible, with those with whom it deals. A wise businessman will not seek advantage to the point where he generates dangerous hostility among employees, competitors, customers, government, or the public at large. But decisions in this area are, in the final test, decisions of strategy, not of ethics.

Playing to Win

. . . If a man plans to make a seat in the business game, he owes it to himself to master the principles by which the game is played, including its special ethical outlook. He can then hardly fail to recognize that an occasional bluff may well be justified in terms of the game's ethics and warranted in terms of economic necessity. Once he clears his mind on this point, he is in a good position to match his strategy against that of the other players. He can then determine objectively whether a bluff in a given situation has a good chance of succeeding and can decide when and how to bluff, without a feeling of ethical transgression.

To be a winner, a man must play to win. This does not mean that he must be ruthless, cruel, harsh, or treacherous. On the contrary, the better his reputation for integrity, honesty, and decency, the better his chances of victory will be in the long run. But from time to time every businessman, like every poker player, is offered a choice between certain loss or bluffing within the legal rules of the game. If he is not resigned to losing, if he wants to rise in his company and industry, then in such a crisis he will bluff—and bluff hard.

Every now and then one meets a successful businessman who has conveniently forgotten the small or large deceptions that he practiced on his way to fortune. "God gave me my money," old John D. Rockefeller once piously told a Sunday school class. It would be a rare tycoon in our time who would risk the horse laugh with which such a remark would be greeted.

In the last third of the twentieth century even children are aware that if a man has become prosperous in business, he has sometimes departed from the strict truth in order to overcome obstacles or has practiced the more subtle deceptions of the half-truth or the misleading omission. Whatever the form of the bluff, it is an integral part of the game, and the executive who does not master its techniques is not likely to accumulate much money or power.

Notes

1. *The New York Times,* March 9, 1967.
2. *The New York Times,* November 21, 1966.
3. New York, Grossman Publishers, Inc., 1965.
4. New York, David McKay Company, Inc., 1967.
5. *The New York Times,* January 17, 1967.
6. Cited by Ralph Nader in "Business Crime," *The New Republic,* July 1, 1967, p. 7.

Promoting Honesty in Negotiation:
An Exercise in Practical Ethics

Peter C. Cramton • J. Gregory Dees

. . . There is such a gap between how one lives and how one ought to live that anyone who abandons what is done for what ought to be done learns his ruin rather than his preservation . . .

—Niccolo Machiavelli

We must make the world honest before we can honestly say to our children that honesty is the best policy.

—George Bernard Shaw

If business ethics is to have a significant impact on business practice, many of us working in the field will need to take a more pragmatic approach to our craft (Dees and Cramton, 1991). Our work should help ethically sensitive business people establish stable institutional arrangements that promote and protect ethically desirable conduct, and it should help individuals to develop strategies for effective ethical behavior in a competitive and morally imperfect world. This paper is offered as one model of more practical business ethics.

To illustrate the model, we have selected the topic of deception in negotiation. Negotiation is a pervasive feature of business life. Success in business typically requires successful negotiations. It is commonly believed that success in negotiation is enhanced by the skillful use of deceptive tactics, such as bluffing, exaggeration, posturing, stage-setting, and outright misrepresentation. As White (1980, p. 927) candidly states, "The critical difference between those who are successful negotiators and those who are not lies in this capacity both to mislead and not to be misled." Some shrewd practitioners have advanced

Reprinted by permission of the authors, Peter C. Cramton, University of Maryland, and J. Gregory Dees, Harvard University, *Business Ethics Quarterly,* October 1993, Vol. 3, Issue 4, the Journal of the Society for Business Ethics.

the art of deception beyond prudent concealment of preferences to more aggressive forms of strategic misrepresentation.[1]

Given the high value placed on honesty, the incentives for deception in negotiation create a serious moral tension for business people, as well as a public relations problem for business. The public relations problem is not new. In ancient Athens, Hermes, a trickster who stole his brother's (Apollo's) cattle on the day he was born and later lied about it, was the patron god of merchants. Anacharsis wrote in 600 B.C., "The market is the place set apart where men may deceive one another."

Not surprisingly, deception in negotiation is a widely discussed problem in business ethics. However, much of the attention has been devoted to the question of when (if ever) various deceptive tactics are ethically justified. Many writers have been highly critical of deception in business. Others, most notably Carr (1968) in his controversial piece on business bluffing, have argued that business has its own ethics, one that permits a wide range of deceptive practices that would not be acceptable outside of business.

We see little benefit from joining this debate. It is not our intent in this paper, nor was it our intent in Dees and Cramton (1991). Boatright's suggestion (1992) that our "mutual trust perspective" on practical ethics might best be understood as a two-tiered Hobbesian theory about the justification of deception misses our central point. We were not staking out a philosophical position, but rather attempting to articulate a deep-seated view reflected in the attitudes and behaviors of many negotiators with whom we have had experience. The point was to provide a backdrop for developing practical recommendations that negotiators might actually take up. Debating the possible philosophical justifications for different types of deception is intellectually engaging, but unlikely to have a direct impact on practice. How many negotiators would change their behavior when it is pointed out that their views are essentially Hobbesian and that Kant, who is regarded as a superior moral philosopher, would find them objectionable? Even if this claim were accompanied by a philosophical refutation of Hobbes and an explanation of Kant's categorical imperative, it seems doubtful that much negotiating behavior would change.

We also avoid the standard debate because it focuses too much attention on justification, obscuring the fact that behavior may be justified, but nonetheless regrettable. A dramatic example is the killing of civilians during a war, even a just war. In some instances, it may be justified, but even when justified, it is regrettable. Rather than engaging in (perhaps unresolvable) philosophical debates about the exact conditions under which the killing of civilians is justified, it seems that one who is concerned about the loss of civilian life in war would be better served by putting resources and intellectual energy into developing political, economic, diplomatic, and military strategies that reduce the risk to innocent civilians.

Our premise is that, outside of a few recreational contexts, deception is a regrettable feature of business negotiations, even when it is justified (or commonplace).[2] The Machiavellian gap between what is done and what (ideally) ought to be done is real when it comes to deception in business negotiations. A purely moralistic (or philosophical) response is likely to be ineffective. A Machiavellian response is likely to make things worse. In the spirit of Shaw, we prefer to explore means of constructively narrowing the gap, thereby making the world more honest.

ETHICS, OPPORTUNISM, AND TRUST

In an ideal world, people would do the right thing simply because it is right. In the world in which we live, morality is more complex. People often disagree about what is right. Even when a consensus on moral values is reached, many find that they do not consistently live up to moral standards. One reason for falling short is that most people place a high value on their own welfare. They may have moral ideals and commitments, but concern about personal well-being is a powerful motivating factor. It is more powerful for some than it is for others, but few can claim to be indifferent to it. Any significant gap between the demands of ethics and the urging of self-interest, narrowly defined,[3] creates incentive problems for individuals and for societies wishing to maintain high ethical standards. The problems arise on two levels.

At the first level are the direct incentive problems of opportunism and desperation. Problems of opportunism arise when individuals willingly violate ethical norms in order to pursue opportunities for private gain. They yield to temptation. Problems of desperation arise when individuals violate ethical norms to avoid personal loss or hardship. Even if we grant that most people place some intrinsic value on doing the right thing, as they see it, sometimes the risk or the temptation is just too great. Philosophers refer to this problem as "weakness of the will." Weakness of the will is not limited to moral deviants. Too often we are presented with evidence from our daily lives, from news stories, and from academic research,[4] that well-educated, apparently normal individuals can be tempted or pressured into compromising ethical standards.

The effects of opportunism and desperation are magnified by a second-level problem concerning trust and fair play. One of the reasons people are willing to behave ethically, even when their personal welfare is at risk, is that they expect others to behave likewise. It seems unfair for individuals with weaker ethical commitments to prosper materially, especially at the expense of individuals with stronger commitments. An atmosphere of mutual trust appears to play an important role in grounding ethical behavior for many people.[5] Suspicion that others are profiting from misconduct can destroy that atmosphere and spoil the sense of satisfaction that might be gained from principled behavior. A sense of fair play can motivate individuals with strong ethical commitments to engage in what they would otherwise consider unacceptable behavior.

Individual integrity and social stability are difficult to maintain in a social setting in which there is serious conflict between ethics and personal welfare. Traditionally, moral philosophers have responded to this conflict in one of two ways. Some, particularly Kantians, acknowledge the gap between ethics and self-interest, but assert on philosophical grounds the dominance of moral considerations over those of personal welfare. Others argue that the gap is only apparent. By refining the definition of self-interest, they attempt to reconcile ethics and self-interest (Kavka, 1984). As philosophically interesting as these views are, neither holds much promise of improving conduct. Practical, not conceptual, solutions are needed.

INCENTIVES FOR DECEPTION IN NEGOTIATION

To illustrate the practical approach to ethical incentive problems, we have chosen to concentrate on the phenomenon of deception in negotiation. Negotiation offers a familiar setting in which individuals often feel a tension between ethics and self-interest. In particular, individuals frequently face a temptation to deceive the other party, in hopes of bettering the outcome for themselves.

We adopt the following definitions:

A *negotiation* is any situation in which two or more parties are engaged in communications, the aim of which is agreement on terms affecting an exchange, or a distribution of benefits, burdens, roles, or responsibilities.

Deception is any deliberate act or omission by one party taken with the intention of creating or adding support to a false belief in another party.[6]

Honesty is the absence of deception.[7]

Notice that lying is only one tactic that may be used to deceive a negotiation partner. Lying, strictly interpreted, requires making a false statement (or at least a statement believed to be false by its maker). The clever manipulation of verbal and non-verbal signals to create or support a false impression, without making a false statement, also counts as deception. Likewise, concealing information is a deceptive tactic if and only if the concealment is intended to create or support a false belief. In some cases, there is a fine line between allowing the other party to continue to hold a false belief and adding support to the belief.

To understand the incentives for deception in negotiation, we use some basic game theory[8] and a fictional world called Metopia. The simplified world of Metopia allows us to put aside temporarily some of the complexity of the real world, in order to analyze the incentives for deception. Metopia is a world much like ours, but populated exclusively with rational, self-centered individuals. We adopt the standard definition of self-interest from economics.

An action is in a party's *self-interest* if, given the party's beliefs at the time of decision, the action yields greater expected utility for the party than any other available action.

Metopians always act in their self-interest. Their interests are even more self-centered and material, focused on their own personal welfare. Metopians' preferences are independent of the preferences of others. They have no specific preferences about the process of the negotiation. In particular, Metopians do not have an independent preference for honesty or dishonesty in the process of negotiation. They feel no guilt about deception, nor do they enjoy fooling others. Metopians have no interest in the opinions of others, except to the extent that such opinions are likely to inhibit or enhance their ability to satisfy their self-centered interests. Finally, Metopians do not have any religious belief system that provides moral rewards and punishments. These features characterize the narrow conception of self-interest in Metopia.

Opportunities for Deception in Metopia

The basis for deception in Metopia is the presence of (real or perceived)[9] informational differences among the parties. Negotiators often have private information about the item under discussion, about their ability and willingness to take future actions, and about their own settlement preferences. Private information, however, does not always present a profitable opportunity for deception. Often it is more prudent to be honest. In general, an opportunity for *A* to profitably deceive *B* arises only when *B* believes *A* has information that is of value to *B* in determining *B*'s negotiating position, *B* knows of no other cost-efficient way to get the information before making a commitment, and it is to *A*'s advantage if *B* acts on false beliefs about the matter. The opportunity will depend in part on the kind of information in question.

Deception About the Matter Under Negotiation. It is common for at least one of the parties to have privileged access to information about the subject matter under negotiation. In an exchange, often the seller has the information advantage. The classic example is the seller of a used car who knows more about the history and mechanical condition of the car than the buyer. Sometimes, however, the buyer has an advantage over an unsophisticated or uninformed seller. An example of this would be an art dealer buying a dusty old painting at a garage sale, or a real estate developer buying parcels of property for an unannounced development project. In a barter situation, both parties may have informational advantages about their side of the exchange. Information asymmetry is not limited to product exchanges. It is also common when the negotiation is about a service to be delivered, a benefit (or burden) to be distributed, or a right (or responsibility) to be assigned.

Even in Metopia, where negotiators recognize the other party's incentives to deceive, the possibility of deception can cause serious problems. For example, suppose a seller has private information about the quality, broadly interpreted, of the good being sold. The higher the quality, the more the good is worth to the buyer, and consequently the more the buyer is willing to pay. In a one-shot situation the seller has an interest in overstating the product's quality. If the seller is believed, she can get a higher profit by overstating, assuming it is more costly to produce high quality goods than low quality goods. A Metopian buyer, therefore, will not believe statements that the good is of high quality, even when it is. Thus, the incentive to deceive about quality leads to Akerlof's (1970) "market for lemons." The buyer, not believing statements of high quality, is only willing to pay a low quality price. The seller is only willing to produce low quality goods, even if both are better off with the exchange of high quality goods at a high quality price.

Deception About Future Actions. Statements about future actions play a key role in many business negotiations. Such statements fall into two categories: threats, and promises. Each of these presents an opportunity for deception about one's true intentions.

Threats are often used to place pressure on the other party to settle. They range from the simple threat of walking away from the negotiation to threats of causing harm to the other party. For instance, in a labor negotiation, management may threaten to close a plant if the union does not make concessions.

Threats can be bluffed, but for a bluffed threat to work, it must be credible. Suppose A threatens B. The threat is credible if B thinks that it is in A's interest to carry out the threat if B does not comply. The success of the threat, then, depends on how well B can assess A's true incentives. In the above example, if labor does not have information about plant-by-plant profitability, management may get concessions by threatening to close the plant. B may not be able to tell a bluffed threat from a real one. Legitimate threats and warnings may be robbed of their informational content. Even if management offered to present labor with the financial information, labor would recognize management's incentive to present deceptive information. Without a reliable source of information, B may have to discount all of A's threats, legitimate or bluffed.

Promises are an essential element in most negotiations. Often one party performs, or makes an investment before the other. Even if the central exchange appears to be simultaneous, there may be understandings and expectations about future actions. Sellers may promise to protect buyers in certain contingencies, for instance, allowing the buyer to return clothing that does not fit. On the other hand, buyers may ask for credit and promise to pay sellers at a later date. In any case, a party making a commitment is likely to know much more about the probability of compliance than the party to whom the commitment is made. For instance, a computer manufacturer who is planning to go out of business, but wants to sell as much of her remaining stock as possible, might continue to offer a warranty that she knows she will not be in a position to honor. Again, lack of information about the true incentives, abilities, and resources of A, the party making the commitment, makes B vulnerable to deception. When A has an incentive to deceive, even A's good faith promises are not believed. It is difficult for A to credibly reassure B of A's willingness and ability to fulfill the promise.

Deception About Settlement Preferences.   The third area of opportunity for deception in Metopia involves the settlement preferences of the negotiating parties. Settlement preferences include the negotiator's reservation price, time pressures, and the different values the negotiator places on specific terms of agreement. Sometimes it is useful to share these preferences, if the sharing does not make one vulnerable to exploitation by the other. Yet, often, negotiators find it in their interest to misrepresent their preferences. They may want to conceal a weak bargaining position, or to give the appearance of making a concession when they are getting what they want.[10] It is possible for the other party to gather indirect evidence about these matters. For instance, if house buyer, B, discovers that house seller, A, has accepted a job in another part of the country and has made a deposit on a house there, this points to A's eagerness to sell. If rug seller, A, sells many of the same rugs, rug buyer, B, may be able to get a history of the prices A has accepted in the past as an indicator of how low A is willing to go. Nonetheless, individual negotiators generally have privileged access to information about their own settlement preferences.

To see why uncertainty about settlement preferences may lead to deception, imagine the negotiation process between two traders, A and B, where each party is uncertain about the strength of the other's bargaining position. Neither trader knows the other's values or outside opportunities, or how these values and opportunities change as time passes. The negotiation consists of a sequence of offers and counteroffers until someone finally accepts the other's offer. Agreement occurs at a point where the further benefits of bargaining (improved terms of trade) do not seem worth the costs to secure them (delayed agreement or a risk of disagreement). The parties bargain until the marginal cost of continuing exceeds the marginal benefit. *B*'s net gain of continuing is based on her expectation about *A*'s future concessions, which, in turn, is based on *B*'s belief about the strength of *A*'s bargaining position. To do well, *A* would like to persuade *B* to accept *A*'s most recent offer by convincing *B* that only slight concessions will be made in the future. A natural justification for slight concessions in the future is a strong bargaining position—good outside opportunities and a lack of eagerness to reach agreement. Hence, *A* benefits from convincing *B* that her bargaining position is stronger than it truly is. *A* has an incentive to deceive *B* about any facts, beliefs, or values that might expose the weakness in *A*'s position.

For this reason, bargainers in Metopia are skeptical of information that the other party presents that bears on that party's settlement preferences. This has its costs. To convince *B* of the strength of her position, *B* must take actions that a weaker *A* would not want to imitate, such as delaying agreement or risking disagreement, both of which involve bargaining inefficiencies. Indeed, so long as there is some uncertainty about whether gains from trade exist, some bargaining inefficiencies must occur regardless of the bargaining process adopted, if the parties act in their own self-interest and have only costly means of signaling strength.[11]

Factors Inhibiting Deception in Metopia

One might think the Metopia would be riddled with attempted deception and bad faith, since Metopians exploit opportunities to misrepresent information in a negotiation. However, as Adam Smith observed, "The most notorious liar . . . tells the fair truth at least twenty times for once that he seriously and deliberately lies" (1759, p. 530). The same might be said of Metopians. Several mechanisms work to inhibit deception. Metopians would rationally invest in processes and mechanisms to protect themselves from deception and its untoward social consequences. Even potential deceivers recognize the effect that the possibility of deception has in undermining even their true statements. To create a climate of confidence that would facilitate negotiations, Metopians would investigate claims, construct contractual mechanisms to enforce honesty, and work to ease the availability of reputation information.

Ex Ante Verification. One remedy for the risk of deception is to verify claims and assumptions before making commitments that depend on those claims or assumptions. Negotiators could gather independent evidence themselves, or they might hire others to do it. Gathering it themselves is, generally, the most reliable method. However, an individual negotiator does not always have the expertise to verify claims efficiently. Accordingly, just as the use of house inspectors has become commonplace in residential real estate transactions, Metopians would employ auditors, testers, inspectors, and private detectives to verify the truth of claims made or implied in negotiations.[12]

One problem is that verification of every significant claim made in a negotiation would be quite costly. Often, it would not be justified. Metopians would be creative in reducing the costs of verification. Two mechanisms for doing so are the use of economies of scale and random verification. It would be highly inefficient, for instance, for everyone buying a refrigerator to hire a private inspector to evaluate different models. However, because refrigerators are standard products, we would expect to see information gathered by a third party who would sell it to those who need it. When economies of scale are not possible, Metopians could adopt random verification procedures to lower verification costs. This would work so long as the parties caught in a deceptive act could be punished harshly. For example, if the maximum penalty that A could apply to B is ten times B's individual net gain from deceiving A, then A's verifying information one out of ten times is sufficient to prevent deception by B. Verification is economical in this case, so long as the cost of verification is no more than ten times the net efficiency gain from honest behavior.

Contractual Mechanisms. Unfortunately, even with some creativity, ex ante verification is limited. Some claims are simply too difficult, or too costly to test ex ante with any confidence. Claims about the long-term reliability of a new product typically fall into this category, as do many claims about actions to be taken in the future and about settlement preferences. In such cases, Metopians would develop contractual mechanisms to add credibility to claims made or implied in a negotiation.

Ideally, the mechanisms would be self-enforcing. However, such mechanisms are limited in their applicability, and may be more costly than alternatives, even though the alternatives require third-party enforcement. Consequently, we would expect to find in Metopia systems of third-party enforcement and a high level of explicit contracting. The third-parties could play a variety of roles from holding collateral to adjudicating disputes and exacting settlements. Metopia would benefit from an analogue to our court system, with coercive authority. Although complete contracts in many negotiations would be impossible to write, because of unforeseen contingencies, Metopians vulnerable to deception would press for clarity on important matters. Explicit claims are more easily verified to third-parties. Ambiguity and vagueness make enforcement problematic.

1. Warranties are one type of contractual device that would be used in Metopia to handle matters that are not subject to ex ante verification.[13] Warranties can be used to add credibility to claims about the item under negotiation that cannot be reliably or cost-effectively assessed until after the deal is struck. "Defective products will be replaced or repaired at the manufacturer's expense." They also can be used to make explicit and reinforce promises of future performance. "If we ever fail to plow the snow from your driveway before 7 A.M., your full year's service contract is free."[14] They can even provide some assurance regarding settlement preferences. "If we sell this item to anyone at a lower price within six months, or if you can find another dealer who will beat our price on the item, we will pay you double the difference."[15] Metopians would use warranties to shift the risks inherent in a negotiation from the recipient of the warranty to the provider of the warranty.

It is not easy to write an enforceable and cost-effective warranty in Metopia. To be enforceable, it needs to clearly specify the conditions under which it applies, the remedies available to the recipient, and the process for bringing the remedies about. Otherwise, it invites costly and hard-to-resolve disputes between self-interested Metopians. Cost-effectiveness depends on the nature of the warranty's specific provisions, the ability and the incentives for the provider to make good, and tendencies for opportunistic behavior on the part of the recipient. For instance, a manufacturer's warranty that allows for replacement or repair only when a manufacturing defect is detected may not be very effective in cases where it is difficult to determine whether a discovered defect is due to poor manufacture, or misuse of the product by the buyer. A warranty that requires that the product be returned in person to a remote regional service center for lengthy evaluation and repair could well make the transaction costs involved in seeking remedy under the warranty so high as to make its application a non-issue. Likewise, a product service contract offered by a company with limited financial resources and a significantly understaffed service department provides little value to the buyer. On the other hand, an unconditional warranty of consumer satisfaction that is easy to invoke and offers generous remedies (e.g., satisfaction guaranteed, or all your money back, no questions asked) is likely to create opportunistic behavior on the part of self-interested Metopian consumers. They will buy products, get some valuable use out of them, and then make warranty claims.

Despite these difficulties, Metopians would work hard to construct enforceable and cost-effective warranties to secure their transactions, provide credibility to their claims, and reduce incentives for opportunism. Nonetheless, at its heart, a warranty is just another promise. Its credibility, in a Metopian world, rests on the availability of other enforcement mechanisms and on reputation effects (to be discussed shortly).

2. Bonds. Promises, including warranties, often need further reinforcement to be credible. Even if the promisor makes the promise in good faith, incentives can change before the promise is carried out. How can the promisee be reasonably confident of performance? Another way to provide credibility to claims about future action is to put in place mechanisms that will reinforce the promisor's incentives for good faith ex ante and compliance ex post. This can be done by posting a bond.

Posting a bond involves doing something at the time the deal is struck that allows the other party, or a third-party, to either exact a penalty from a negligent promisor, or compensate the harmed promisee, if the promise is not kept. The most common form of bonding mechanism is collateral. The promisor gives the promisee, in effect, a contingent claim on some of the promisor's assets. If the promise is not fulfilled, the assets revert to the promisee. In some cases, the promisee will hold the assets until the promise is fulfilled, but this need not be the case if a credible third-party can enforce the asset transfer when nonperformance is verified.

What if the promisor does not have assets to compensate the promisee for nonperformance? One way of handling this would be through insurance schemes. An insurer would evaluate promisors and charge a premium based on the insurance company's assessment of the probabilities of default. The insurer would pool premiums from a number of promisors to provide enough funds for paying expected claims. Such a scheme would have to be constructed carefully to avoid the problems of adverse selection and moral hazard. Another alternative for dealing with the problem of limited assets is the use of hostages. The agreement can be reinforced as long as the promisor has assets that she values as much as noncompliance with the promise. Hostages are items of value to the promisor that may not have value to the promisee. The incentive for compliance is the threat to destroy or transfer the hostages.

Creating the right bonding agreement is also difficult in Metopia.[16] A bond that requires too little from the promisor will result in nonperformance. A bond that provides too much value to the promisee may lead to a false claim of nonperformance, especially if the promisee is holding the collateral. Even with independent parties adjudicating disputes, it will be difficult to get the incentives just right for all three parties. Much rests on the reputation of the third party and on the clarity of conditions for nonperformance. Nonetheless, we would expect to find Metopians constructing a wide variety of bonding arrangements to off-set the problems raised by incentives to deceive.[17]

Contractual mechanisms, such as warranties and bonds, have limited application. In some cases, it will be impossible for Metopians to contract on relevant future actions. One reason it may not be possible is that one party's action may be unobservable to the other. Hence, the party may make false claims about the unobservable action. For example, a consultant may be hired to complete a project that has uncertain time requirements, promising to work hard to complete the project in the shortest possible time. If the consultant's effort is unobservable to the client, the consultant may have an incentive to renege on the promise of concerted effort. Likewise, a group sharing a common resource may agree to use the resource efficiently, but if the group cannot monitor individual use of the resource, individuals may overuse it. The difficulty of verifying compliance may make it impossible to write a contract that induces the efficient level of effort (Holmstrom, 1979). Even if it is possible to write a complete contract, it may prove too costly to enforce the contract, because the actions—while observable to the deceived party—may not be easily verified to the third-party attempting to enforce the contract. Furthermore, the effective application of contractual mechanisms often requires an independent third-party with the right incentives. Finally, these mechanisms can be costly. They can complicate contract writing, tie up assets that could be profitably used elsewhere, and divert value to third-parties who must be paid. If not constructed with great care, these contractual mechanisms can create new incentives for deceptive behavior.

Reputation Effects. To supplement ex ante verification and contractual mechanisms, Metopians would need to rely on reputation effects to induce honesty.[18] A person's reputation affects future opportunities by influencing the other's belief about what the person will do in the future. A negotiator with a reputation for being deceitful is likely to be disadvantaged in future negotiations. She may have a hard time finding negotiating partners and when she finds them, they will be on their guard. This is not because Metopians are morally offended by deceit. It is simply that negotiations tend to go better, other things being equal, when one is dealing with a person who has a reputation for honesty to maintain. Thus, when deciding to deceive, a Metopian negotiator must consider not only the short-run consequence of the decision, but also how the decision affects her reputation and hence future negotiations.

Adam Smith (1759, p. 350) was aware of the power of reputation, commenting, "The prudent man is always sincere, and feels horror at the very thought of exposing himself to the disgrace which attends upon the detection of falsehood." Smith overstates the case. An intelligent Metopian will know that some attempts at deception pose greater risks to one's reputation than others. Reputation works best when claims are explicit, ex post detection is likely, and information about deceptive practices can be credibly communicated to the culprit's future negotiating partners.

1. Reputations in On-Going Negotiations Between Two Parties. The setting in which reputation is most likely to be effective is that of two parties, *A* and *B*, who negotiate repeatedly over time. Suppose both parties have an incentive to deceive if a particular negotiation is considered in isolation. The incentive problem in an isolated negotiation is captured by the following Prisoner's Dilemma game:

		B's Choice	
		Honest	Deceive
A's Choice	Honest	2, 2	0, 3
	Deceive	3, 0	1, 1

Each cell in the matrix gives the payoffs to *A* and *B,* as a function of their choices. In this highly stylized representation, both parties decide independently whether to adopt a negotiation strategy based on open and honest communication or a strategy of deception. If both are honest, they find a point on the Pareto frontier that is both equitable and efficient (each gets 2). If both deceive, equity is preserved but efficiency is sacrificed (each gets 1). Finally, if one deceives an honest person, the deceiver gets the maximum payoff (3) and the honest person gets the worst payoff (0). A Metopian in the one-shot negotiation would choose to deceive, since it is a dominant strategy—deception is the preferred choice regardless of what the other person does. But if the parties face each other repeatedly in subsequent negotiations, the incentives change.

To see how reputations can work in our example, imagine that after each negotiation there is a probability p that the relationship will continue for at least one more period.[19] In such a setting, each party can adopt a reputational strategy that supports honest behavior, such as the following: "I will be open and honest so long as you reciprocate with honest behavior, but if ever you deceive me I will be deceitful forever after." Such a harsh and unforgiving strategy (Friedman, 1971) will prompt honest behavior provided the long-run benefit from honest behavior exceeds the short-run benefit that can be gained by deceiving an honest party. Assuming *B* is following the strategy above, *A* can get 2 in each period by being honest; whereas, deceit would result in a payoff of 3 in the current period and a payoff of 1 in all future periods. The payoff from honesty then is $2(1 + p + p^2 + \ldots) = 2/(1 - p)$; the payoff from deceit is $3 + (p + p^2 + \ldots) = 3 + p/(1 - p)$. It is better to be honest than to deceive so long as $2/(1-p) \geq 3 + p/(1-p)$, or $p \geq 1/2$. So long as there is at least a 50% chance that the parties will meet again, they are able to support honest behavior. The short-run benefit from deceiving an honest party is insufficient compensation for destroying a reputation for honesty.[20]

This story relies on the assumption that deception is uncovered after each negotiation and before any further encounters. What if deceptions are only occasionally observed? Can we still motivate honesty as self-interested behavior? The answer (and analysis) is roughly the same as before: honest behavior can be sustained, provided it is sufficiently likely that the parties will meet again and it is not too unlikely that a deception will be observed. Suppose each deception is detected with probability d. Is honesty better than a one-period deception? Honesty yields 2 in every period for an expected payoff of $2/(1-p)$; whereas, a one-period deception results in 3 in the current period and then either 1 or 2 thereafter, depending on whether the deception was detected, resulting in an expected payoff of $3 + p[d/(1-p) + (1-d)2/(1-p)]$. Simplifying, we find that honesty is better than deception, so long as $p \geq 1/(1+d)$. If there is a 50% chance of detection, then there must be a 2/3 chance of meeting again; if there is a 10% chance of detection, the continuation probability must be at least 10/11.

More interesting is the case where only a noisy signal of deception is observed. Reputations can help in this situation of imperfect observability. However, some punishment must take place even if no one is actually deceptive. Since deception cannot be distinguished from bad luck, *both* bad luck and deception must be punished. This unjust punishment might offend moral sensibilities in the real world, but Metopians would freely use it if it worked. One possible strategy is as follows: "If it is sufficiently likely that you have been honest in the last period, I will be honest this period; otherwise, I won't trust you for the next several periods, and then will revert to honesty." For a given continuation probability and level of noise in the observations of honesty, it is possible to specify exactly what "sufficiently likely" and "several" must be in order to support honesty as an equilibrium with this strategy.[21] There is some efficiency loss, since punishments occasionally are called for. However, to the extent that the continuation probability is large and the noise in observing defections is small, the efficiency loss will be small as well.

Continuing relationships provide an effective environment for using reputations to deter deception. However, we should note one limitation of this analysis. It assumes that the continuation probability is a given. But in fact a party's decision whether to continue the relationship may depend on what happened in the past. If there is a particular negotiation with unusually large stakes, it might make sense for a Metopian negotiator to adopt a "take the money and run" strategy: deceive the other and then move on to other things. This is precisely the strategy used by a double agent engaged in espionage (Sobel, 1985). For a time, the spy must gain the confidence of her superior by supplying accurate information, but when the value of deception is highest, the spy will double-cross her superior and move on.

2. Reputations Where Only One Party Has a Continuing Market Presence. Our story so far requires that the parties in the negotiation continue to interact with each other for an indefinite period. This seems plausible in a

number of situations, such as negotiations between a firm and a regular supplier, or between a manager and her immediate subordinate, but there are numerous situations where only one party is likely to be susceptible to reputation effects. This happens when one party continues to play an active role in a market, but does so with many one-shot (or infrequent) negotiating partners. A retail car dealer is an example of what we call an enduring negotiating party. The typical car buyer does not make car purchases frequently enough to develop much of a reputation. The dealer, however, provides an enduring presence to which a reputation can adhere.

Do reputation effects still work to induce honesty in these Metopian negotiations? They do only if the party that endures is also the party with the greatest opportunities for deception, and there is an efficient mechanism for conveying information about the enduring party's reputation in a credible way to future negotiating partners. In such cases, the threat of losing a good reputation prevents the enduring party from exploiting the other.

What if there is also some risk of the non-enduring party engaging in deception. For instance, the car buyer might pay for the car with a bad check. In our example of a one-shot negotiation, modelled as a Prisoner's Dilemma, both parties are at risk—each may be deceived by the other—so both parties must endure, if reputation effects are to inhibit deception. If only one party endures, then nothing is to stop the non-enduring party from deceiving the enduring party. As a defensive measure, the enduring party might be forced to be deceptive as well. However, this undesirable result can be avoided if we modify the example so that the non-enduring party moves first (or equivalently, that the non-enduring party's behavior is verifiable ex ante). For instance, the car dealer would not deliver the car until the buyer's check cleared the bank. In this case, the enduring party B is facing a sequence $\{A^1, A^2, \ldots, A^n, \ldots\}$ of A parties. B is not at risk, since she can condition her action on A's choice. Although each A only participates in one negotiation, so she cannot develop a reputation, she does observe the previous outcomes of others dealing with B; hence, she can condition her behavior on what B has done in the past. The following strategy by each A party will support honest behavior provided the future is sufficiently valuable to B: "I will be honest, so long as you have never deceived a previous A person. Otherwise, I will not trust you."

As before, we can introduce complications such as providing the A parties with only a noisy signal of B's behavior. The result is the same as with two enduring parties: to the extent each A party can observe B's past actions and so long as the future is sufficiently important to B, B will want to maintain a reputation for honesty. As before, we make the assumption that whether a party endures is a given. In reality, an enduring party might choose to leave a business. In this case, there would be an incentive for deception in the final transactions, provided that the non-enduring parties were in the dark about this termination decision. A case of this sort was mentioned earlier: the computer company offering warranties on its machines, even though it is secretly planning to go out of business.

3. Reputations in One-shot Negotiations. But what if neither party is likely to have a continued presence in a given negotiation market and the parties are likely to be negotiating together only a single time? This is the case of

the principals in many civil litigation cases. Can reputations be used to reduce the incentive for deception? The answer is clearly no, if we cannot create something to carry the reputation, but often it is possible to create a reputation bearer.

Metopians might do this by hiring an enduring agent to perform the negotiation. Lawyers in a litigation case might serve this purpose. Even if the plaintiff and defendant are antagonistic adversaries, their lawyers may have established reputations for the efficient and equitable resolution of disputes. The lawyers' use of deceptive tactics is limited to the extent such tactics would adversely affect their reputations. Similarly, when a firm hires an auditor to prepare a financial statement before a public stock offering, the firm is renting the reputation of the auditor to add credibility to the firm's statement to potential investors (Wilson, 1983). The firm cannot be trusted on its own, since deception would raise the proceeds from the offering. Hence, an auditor who maintains a valuable reputation for honest behavior is an essential ingredient of the transaction. In Metopia, we would expect to find a variety of reputational agents.

This strategy, however, is not always available. It may be difficult to motivate the agent to act in the principal's best interests. Divorce attorneys may be in an excellent position to settle rationally the dispute of an emotional and antagonistic couple, but if they are paid by the hour their financial incentive may be to magnify the conflict. Alternatives, such as a fixed-fee contract, may not be feasible, since it exposes the attorneys to adverse selection (only the most time consuming conflicts may be submitted to an attorney for a fixed fee) and threatens the couple with moral hazard (the attorneys may shirk on their responsibility to find an efficient and fair settlement in favor of a quick settlement).

An alternative to the use of reputational agents when the parties to a negotiation are not likely to interact again is suggested by Kreps (1990). Suppose the party, A, that puts the other, B, at risk can buy a name that indicates honest behavior because past holders of the name have been honest. After buying the name, A decides whether to act honestly, and then sells the name to another party. If the sale is delayed until A's honesty can be determined, the sale price of the name should depend on A's behavior. By acting honestly, A preserves the value of the name. Deceit would destroy the name's good reputation and hence its value. Viewing reputations as an asset that can be bought and sold enables the parties to make deals that require trust, even if they are involved in only a single negotiation. Of course, there are limits to this technique. It requires that the reputational names be protected and treated as property. Its effectiveness depends on the price of the name and on the probability that any deception would be detected before the name is sold. If the payoff from deception is too high, relative to the cost and potential worth of the name, A will forfeit the investment in the name in favor of deception. It is important for B, the party at risk, to know how the name's value depends on A's behavior.

Summary of Factors Affecting Deception in Metopia

Even in the self-centered world of Metopia, deception would be moderated by natural forces in a wide range of circumstances. To preserve fruitful transactions, Metopians will protect themselves (and their trading partners) from deception when they can do so in a cost-effective way. Since even the suspicion of deception can be harmful to potentially profitable negotiations, it is worthwhile for the negotiating parties to find means of reducing it.

Honesty, however, is not always the best policy by Metopian standards. Occasionally, Metopians will be able to gain from deceptive tactics. Based on the above analysis, we would predict that in Metopia, other things equal, deception is more likely to be a problem when the following conditions hold.

Information asymmetry is great. The greater the information disparity between the two parties, the more opportunity at least one of the parties has for profitable deception. Every negotiation involves some asymmetry. Each negotiator possesses some private information, such as information about her preferences, or about her intentions to keep future commitments.

Verification is difficult. Some questions, such as the physical condition of a simple, existing product, can be easily settled before the deal is consummated. Others, such as long-term maintenance costs for a new product, can only be confirmed afterwards. And some, such as a party's reservation price, are difficult to ever confirm. Deception is more likely with matters that are most difficult to verify, such as the other party's preferences, their commitment to future actions, and long-term performance claims about the good under negotiation. Because it makes verification to a third-party difficult, deception is also more likely to occur when claims are made verbally without independent witnesses.

The intention to deceive is difficult to establish. Deliberate deception is often hard to distinguish from a mistake or oversight. Deception is more likely when the deceiver has a plausible alternative explanation for her behavior. Deception about something one should clearly know is less likely than deception about matters for which one could innocently claim to be the victim of misinformation. Subtle forms of deception are more likely to occur than explicit lying. The use of negotiating agents may also make it difficult to detect intentional deception. The principal can claim that the deception was the result of poor communication, or an unscrupulous negotiating agent who acted without authority. Finally, vague or sweeping claims that are open to alternative interpretations make it difficult to establish intentional deception. In such cases, a negotiator can more plausibly claim that she never meant to give a false impression.

The parties have insufficient resources to adequately safeguard against deception.[22] Depending on the expected gains from the negotiation and on the initial endowments of the negotiating parties, there will be limits on the resources available to protect the parties against deception. Warranties, collateral, hostages, and other insurance devices use up resources. They may be potentially useful, but not sensible in transactions promising small gains. In larger, more risky transactions, the negotiators may have too few assets to create bonding devices sufficient to eliminate incentive problems.

Interaction between the parties is infrequent. Deception is more likely in one-shot negotiations than in long-term relationships. The expectation of continued interaction provides negotiators with more time and a greater incentive to confirm the reliability of information provided or signaled by the other party. It also provides more opportunities for retaliation in future transactions.

Ex post redress is too costly. If deception is uncovered after the deal is done, there may be means of seeking redress, either individually or through third-parties. One could track down the offender and threaten harm, unless adequate compensation is provided. Alternatively, one could take the offender to court. The deceived party may prefer such an effort, even when the costs of it exceed the expected compensation, if the action has enough reputation value. Aggressive action in one case may dissuade future negotiating partners from attempting deception. Sometimes, however, the costs and risks of seeking redress are too high,[23] even recognizing the reputation value. In other cases, such redress is not feasible, because the deceived party has little leverage over the deceiver, the deceiver cannot easily be found, or the deception cannot be adequately demonstrated to a third-party (a court, or future negotiators).

Reputation information is unavailable, unreliable, or very costly to communicate. When it is difficult to convey information about the past performance of negotiators, we can expect more deception. We should find less deception in small, close-knit communities, or in dense social networks, than we do in large, loosely connected populations. Even in Metopia, there may be situations in which handshake deals are possible, without formal contracting. We should also find less deception when there is a relatively low cost system for collecting and transmitting reputation information, such as a Better Business Bureau.

The circumstances are unusual in a way that limits inferences about future behavior. Some instances of deception are unlikely to damage future negotiations, because they occur in distinctly different circumstances. The question is whether future negotiating partners would regard a particular act of deception as relevant to predicting behavior in negotiations with them. For instance, deception in a game setting, such as bluffing in poker, may not be thought to have any bearing on expectations of behavior outside of the game setting. Deception of an enemy or of an outsider may not affect negotiations with a friend or an insider.

One party has little to lose (or much to gain) from attempting deception. The mechanisms discussed so far work only when each negotiator has expectations of a continuing economic life, places reasonably high value on future economic success, and has a reputation to protect. However, in some circumstances, a negotiator may not be concerned about the prospects of being caught at deception, provided she is not caught until after the deal is closed. The negotiator may have a reputation that is so bad that further deception would not hurt it. She may have a high discount rate, placing a low value on future transactions. She may be in desperate straits. Or, the payoff from this one negotiation may be sufficiently high.

These above conditions represent rough guidelines about when Metopians have greater incentives for profitable deception. Whether to attempt deception in a given situation requires a complex assessment of expected costs, benefits, and risks.

REAL WORLD DIFFERENCES

We have offered some specific hypotheses about incentives for deception in Metopia. To what extent do our findings about Metopia extend to the world we know? Human nature is not so simple or uniform as that of the Metopians.[24]

People are not as self-centered as Metopians. They are capable of a wide range of sentiments and commitments not available to Metopians. Some of these sentiments work to promote honesty; others encourage more deception.

People often care about others. Most people have some benevolent motivations and ethical commitments. Individuals have sympathy for the pains of others and take pleasure in others' well-being. However, this care does not typically extend to all of humankind, but only to a referent group (Hirschleifer, 1982). The size and nature of that group varies significantly from person to person. The care also varies in intensity, depending on such things as the closeness of the relationship with the other person. In addition to this passive care for others, people care about how they affect others (Arrow, 1974). They generally do not want to cause harm, and do want to cause pleasure or satisfaction. Individuals typically do not want to benefit from the misfortune of others, even when they have not caused the misfortune (Nagel, 1975).

Beyond concerns about the welfare of others, most have internalized rules of behavior so that they feel pangs of conscience, guilt, or shame when they resort to certain objectionable behaviors such as deception. They have preferences about how they act as well as preferences about the results of their actions. Many take pride in their sense of personal integrity. They take offense at any suggestion that they are not trustworthy. On a social level, people feel and express moral approbation and disapprobation about the behavior of others, even when the other's behavior is not a direct threat to them. They are willing to incur costs to shame, ostracize, and punish others who engage in questionable behavior.

On the other hand, people also have preferences that may encourage deception. Benevolence and moral commitments typically have limits. People are concerned about their own well-being and generally place more weight on their own welfare than on that of others. Furthermore, people tend to be competitive. Relative standing matters. People want to win, to do better than their peers. The harm they are willing to commit on their way to winning may be limited—each will draw the line somewhere—but many are willing to cause harm to have an advantage. For many people, moral commitments are contingent upon a belief that others share the same commitments. Many individuals, especially in competitive settings, are moral pragmatists, willing to do their part, but concerned not to be taken as a sucker or a fool. At the extreme, some people actually appear to take pleasure in harming other parties in a negotiation. People can carry grudges and vendettas beyond reason. They are capable of malevolence and spite. Some even take a particular pleasure in successful deception. The evidence for this is the large number of games where bluffing and deception play a role in the enjoyment of the game and in determining success. Some individuals carry the thrill of fooling others out of the game setting into other more serious negotiations.

People are not as smart as Metopians.   Individuals in the real world vary more in their ability to make rational calculations. None reach the level of intelligence found in Metopians. Consequently, people are more likely to make mistakes in reasoning about the costs and benefits of deception. Some opportunities for self-interested deception will be missed as a result of such mistakes. Also, because of the common affliction of myopia, the bias toward clear short-term gains, some individuals will see opportunities for deception even when they would disappear with a longer view. Hume (1751) identified the risk of opportunism by frail humans. Of those who attempt to selectively use deception only when it appears to be in their self-interest he says, "while they propose to cheat with moderation and secrecy, a tempting incident occurs, nature is frail, and they give in to the snare; whence they can never extricate themselves, without total loss of reputation, and the forfeiture of all future trust and confidence with mankind." Hume identifies a real risk, but exaggerates the repercussions of getting caught in a deception. As Bhide and Stevenson (1990, p. 192) observe, "Even unreconstructed scoundrels are tolerated in our world as long as they have something else to offer."

Because of the limits of human rationality and intelligence, judgments of trust may be made hastily without adequate supporting evidence. In some cases, individuals will not appreciate the powerful incentives for deception. As a result, individuals may be gullible and believe others when it would be more reasonable to discount their claims. This opens the door to more deception. However, sometimes people err in the other direction and exhibit more distrust than is rational. Bad experience in a negotiation can make people cynical about the trustworthiness of others. They may ignore the structural differences from one negotiation to the next, irrationally distrusting the other party regardless of the incentives. Such a person is likely to overinvest in protective measures.

What can we conclude from these differences? The main lessons can be summarized briefly. In the real world, mutual benevolence, moral commitment, and mutual trust are available as tools for promoting honesty in negotiations. However, there is so much variation in individual moral attitudes, characters, and abilities that it is hard to develop strategies for promoting honesty that are robust. People do not wear their characters on their sleeves. Negotiators often face significant uncertainty about the trustworthiness of the party on the other side of the table. The chances for honesty depend not only on the structural conditions that permit self-interested deception in Metopia, but also on the psychological forces in individuals and in the communities in which they live. A benevolent person supported by a community that reinforces that benevolence is less likely to engage in opportunistic deception than a Metopian would be. A more competitive person from a community of competitive persons is more likely to be deceptive. In either case, how the individual behaves may be a function of that individual's attitudes toward and expectations of the other party in the negotiation.

Despite the differences, we believe that the Metopian model presents a useful starting point for thinking about the problem of deception in real world negotiations. Self-interest plays an important role in the real world. Reputation, verification, and contractual mechanisms are viable means of reducing the inefficiencies caused by deception and providing a basis for trust.

PROMOTING HONESTY IN NEGOTIATION

Given that deception is a regrettable feature of negotiations, both morally and practically, what can be done by ethically concerned people to promote more honesty? Before describing individual strategies, it is useful to review how existing institutional arrangements work to support honesty.

Social and Institutional Support

Those who think social engineering for ethics is unwise or unnecessary should reflect on the many institutions (public and private) that already exist with this end in mind. Many of the mechanisms that we noticed in Metopia are part of standard practice in the real world.[25] Individuals deciding on strategies for promoting honesty should be aware of the support mechanisms already in place to promote honesty and trust. This is not to say that further institutional improvement is impossible. Something may be learned by reflecting on the strengths and weaknesses of existing mechanisms. Entrepreneurial extensions and innovations (both in the public and private sectors) may be possible.

Legal and Regulatory Protection. The most obvious social support mechanism is government enforcement of norms. Not only do we have civil and criminal law, but we have in this country elaborate regulatory mechanisms. Regulators not only set rules, but also do the research that individual consumers could ill afford. Examples of legal and regulatory protections are numerous. On the federal level, they range from the effort of the Federal Trade Commission to control deceptive advertising, to the Food and Drug Administration to screen medications before they can be sold to the public, and the National Labor Relations Board to adjudicate disputes between business and organized labor. State governments, for instance, enact "lemon" laws to protect car buyers, and seller disclosure requirements to protect house buyers. One can debate the effectiveness and efficiency of any of these mechanisms, but they are clearly intended to help reduce deception in the marketplace.

In commercial negotiations, contract law is an important source of support for policing deception in negotiation. Negotiators should understand potential legal remedies and protections relevant to their negotiations. They are more extensive than many negotiators realize.[26] Unfortunately, the civil law is a rather blunt instrument for the enforcement of norms. For it to be effective, negotiators need to be aware of its provisions, the deceptive behavior needs to be verifiable in a court of law, and the parties must be willing to spend the resources (time and money) to seek remedies.

In addition to governmental regulation and adjudication, industries often have their own regulatory mechanisms. Sometimes it is in the interest of an industry to provide assurance of honorable dealings with its customers, suppliers, employees, and the communities in which it does business. For instance, in the securities industry, a form of arbitration is used to settle disputes between brokers and their clients. A negotiator should know whether any relevant industry regulations or dispute resolution procedures apply.

Institutional Sources of Reputational Information. In addition to formal adjudication mechanisms and regulatory agencies, negotiators may have access to formal sources of reputational information. Two prominent examples of this are better business bureaus and credit rating bureaus. Better business bureaus keep records of customer complaints and can provide this information to potential customers. Credit rating bureaus provide information on past payment performance of individuals. Negotiators also can gain access to legal and news databases that contain information on prior legal actions against the other party. These and other reputational databases may help negotiators decide with whom to do business. With information technology advancing, the costs of maintaining reputational databases should decline and their use should increase.

These institutionalized reputational databases are controversial. Questions have been raised about the completeness and accuracy of the information they dispense. Reputations may be unfairly ruined. Parties whose reputations are threatened may not be given a fair opportunity to rebut the allegations, or to make a case for extenuating circumstances. These databases may provide inaccurate, thin, or inappropriate information. The challenge for these sources is to maintain the integrity of their information. The challenge for users is to keep in mind that the information is imperfect.

Independent Rating and Evaluation Services. There have arisen several private organizations that test products, survey consumers, rate company performance, and provide other information to potential buyers. These organizations capitalize on the economies of scale associated with product and service evaluation. By serving a large customer base, they can afford to engage in research that would be too costly for an individual.

One such organization is Consumers' Union, the publisher of *Consumer Reports* magazine. This organization evaluates products and services offered to consumers and makes the information available in its publications. Among other things, it provides information on dealer costs for new cars, price ranges for used cars, and information on the reliability and maintenance costs of various makes. Customers can use this information to make inferences about a car dealer's reservation price or to challenge any misleading assertions about the reliability of the car. Because Consumers' Union is independent from the manufacturers, it has credibility with buyers that manufacturers making quality claims about their own products would not have. Other examples of this sort of service are J.D. Power and Associates' customer satisfaction indexes, Lipper Analytical Services' mutual fund rating service, Underwriters' Laboratory's certification of electrical safety, Moody's and Standard and Poor's bond ratings, and A. M. Best's ratings of the financial strength of insurance companies. By providing an independent source of hard-to-get information, these organizations make it difficult for sellers to deceive about product quality, company financial strength, or the satisfaction of previous customers. Sometimes independent evaluators will even provide guarantees, as with the Good Housekeeping Seal of Approval. Of course, these services work most effectively in large markets. For many commercial negotiations, sufficient economies of scale are not present to justify the creation of such an organization.

Third-Party Professionals. Negotiators often have access to professionals to assist in specific negotiations. They may be used to act as reputational agents, to assess important facts, or to arbitrate disputes. Industries that are organized in part for this role include lawyers, accountants, arbitrators, investment bankers, and engineers. The challenge in using third parties is in assessing their qualifications and aligning their incentives properly.

Professional associations often have mechanisms for improving information and incentives, thereby reducing the risk to the buyer of third-buyer services. For instance, lawyers have strong norms to faithfully represent their clients' interests. These norms are supported by codes of ethics, which are enforced by the state's bar association. The bar also sets minimum quality standards.

Standardized Contractual Mechanisms. Norms are also established in certain industries to provide standard protections that go beyond legal requirements. Products and (increasingly) services often come with warranties. The use of collateral to secure certain types of loans against repayment risks is also a common institutionalized practice.

Affiliations and Credentials. It is also common in some industries for individual businesses to join together under a common name, or to purchase the rights to use a name for reputational purposes. Sears sells the use of its name to building contractors who install fencing, aluminum siding, and other home improvements. Consumers who trust Sears and who believe Sears stands behind the contractor's work may be more willing to trust a Sears affiliated contractor than an independent contractor with whom they will deal only once. In industries with many independent practitioners, industry associations can play a similar role. They provide members with a certification of credibility. Examples include Chartered Life Underwriter, Certified Financial Planner, and Certified Public Accountant. These designations assist consumers in evaluating the level of professional expertise, and, perhaps, the ethics of practitioners. Even when a specific designation or certification process is not involved, affiliation with a reputable industry group, such as the Better Business Bureau or Chamber of Commerce, may provide some sense of trustworthiness.

Society has been remarkably creative in developing mechanisms to promote honesty and secure business transactions from the risks of deception. However, these institutional safeguards are not present, nor are they effective, in all arenas of negotiation. Sometimes individual negotiators have to develop strategies for promoting honesty and for protecting themselves from opportunism.

Tactics and Strategies for Individual Negotiators

What can be done by individuals who wish to promote honesty in their negotiations? We cannot recommend a single strategy that will work effectively in all negotiations. We can offer some strategic and tactical suggestions. They are directed to negotiators who see the value of honesty and mutual trust and are willing to make some investment in them. They are based on a rather extensive literature in the field of negotiation and conflict resolution,[27] as well as our experiences teaching and studying negotiation and business ethics.

Negotiators face two kinds of risks: trusting too much and trusting too little. The first risk is all too familiar. Most people can think of situations in which their trust proved to be unfounded. Painful memories provide powerful lessons. The second risk is not so apparent, in part, because the cost, which may take the form of a foregone opportunity, is not so vivid. However, this risk is just as real. As the movie actress's agent in one of the Philip Marlowe detective stories comments, "One of these days . . . I'm going to make the mistake which a man in my business dreads above all other mistakes. I'm going to find myself doing business with a man I can trust and I'm going to be just too goddamn smart to trust him." (Chandler, 1955, p. 118; cited in Coleman, 1990). Coleman (1990, p. 100–101) points out that the mistake one should worry about most depends on the nature of the risks involved. A sensible strategy for dealing with the risks of deception is one that enhances trust in the negotiations and protects the participants from opportunistic exploitation. In specific situations, it is reasonable for one of these elements to be emphasized more than the other.

Assessing the Situation. No matter what strategy one pursues, the place to start is by doing one's homework. This seems like an obvious point, but it is surprising how many people cut this step short. Admittedly, it is not always cost-effective to do in-depth pre-negotiation research, but rarely should this step be skipped. There are many low-cost mechanisms for gathering information. For our purposes, pre-negotiation homework can be broken down into four steps.

1. Incentives for Deception. The questions here are based on what we learned about incentives in Metopia. The starting point in assessing vulnerabilities is to determine what sort of privileged information each side is likely to have. To what extent do you have to rely on them, and they on you, for important information? Are there natural incentives for either of you to exaggerate, deliberately suppress, or misrepresent any of this privileged information? Is there time pressure on either side? How important is a favorable outcome to each of the parties? This should be asked about principals and specific negotiating agents. It is generally thought to be a good thing if the other side in a negotiation is highly motivated to reach agreement. However, other things being equal, this creates a more powerful incentive for deception, both to cover up a weak bargaining position, and to persuade the other side to accept an agreement. It is also important to determine whether there are any factors to counterbalance these natural incentives. Are there easy means of verifying the information? How important is it for each of you to do business together in the future? How easy would it be for either of you to penalize or ruin the reputation of the other? These questions should be asked from your point of view and theirs. Do not expect them to fully appreciate the long-term and intangible benefits of honesty. Recognize that immediate payoffs can exert an inordinate amount of influence. Finally, you should assess how bad it would be for either side if the other attempts deception.

2. Competence and Character of the Other Side. Whether you can trust the claims and signals from the other party is a function of your assessment of their character[28] and their competence. Competence, in this context, speaks to whether the other party would be a reliable source of information, even if they were honest. With regard to information about the item under negotiation, the party you are negotiating with may lack technical expertise, have access only to limited information, or be susceptible to a natural bias. With regard to future actions, the party may not have a realistic perception of her own (or her firm's) abilities to fulfill the promise. With regard to settlement issues, if one is dealing with a new company representative, for instance, she may not know just how flexible she can be on price or terms. In cases of questionable competence, promoting honesty may not solve the problem of getting reliable information. Other steps my be required.

Evaluating the other party's character would not be necessary if we could simply observe when someone is attempting to deceive us. Though Ekman (1985) suggests that there are behavioral signs associated with lying, these are not so obvious and reliable as to relieve us of the need to think about the character of the parties with whom we are dealing. Assessing character is usually done first by reference to one's own past dealings with the other party, and second by checking on the other party's reputation in the marketplace. One should check not only for instances of dishonesty per se, but also for a general willingness to engage in objectionable behavior for selfish or competitive reasons. For the first, you must ask, how well do you know the other party? Are you really in a position to assess their character? If not, checking their reputation may be sensible. This can be done through any of the reputational sources of information mentioned in the previous section, or, more directly, by interviewing their prior negotiating partners. The latter step may help a great deal at little cost. It is important to attempt to get an unbiased list. Instead of asking for references in general, ask for a specific group that should be able to offer a fair and independent judgment, such as the landlord's last three tenants. In many cases, a candid assessment will be provided. However, in some situations, candor may be limited because of the fear of litigation or some other reason. For instance, one of the authors asked a group of mid-level executives whether they would provide an honest reference about a former employee who was dismissed for unethical conduct. The vast majority said they would not tell about the unethical conduct, unless the person requesting the information happened to be another manager within their company or a friend.

An inherent bias in evaluating someone's reputation is that reasons for distrusting someone are more convincing than reasons for trusting someone (Gambetta, 1988, pp. 233–5). Someone who lied in their last deal is not trustworthy, but is someone trustworthy because they appeared to be honest in their last deal? A further problem with reliance on reputational information is that it is often an inadequate gauge of character. One can find out about unsatisfactory performance, but usually not about extenuating circumstances. Past performance failures may be the result of factors beyond the individual's control, or the person may have changed significantly since then. Someone who defaulted on a loan because of the financial drain of a serious illness may not be a bad risk for a new loan. Someone convicted of stealing something twenty years ago may be a very different person now. Though reputation information is and should be valuable tool in assessing the trustworthiness and honesty of the other party, one should be careful not to place too much weight on it. Judgments about character based on this information must be tentative.

3. Attitudes and Perspective of the Other Side. The other party will enter the negotiation with a set of expectations and attitudes. Some of these will bear directly on their willingness to engage in deceptive behavior. One important matter concerns their attitude and beliefs about you. What is the other party likely to believe about you and your character? Will they identify with you? Will they trust you to be honest? Is there a history of animosity between the two of you, or between the other party and people like you? You also need to find out what they expect in the negotiation. This is especially crucial in cross-cultural negotiations. How do they expect information to be shared? How do they build trust with other negotiators? How adversarial or competitive are their negotiations? How are they likely to respond to different techniques of checking their veracity? Will your status as an "outsider" be a barrier to building trust?

4. Critical Self-Reflection. Finally, you must assess the biases and attitudes that you bring into the negotiation. You have a set of attitudes and presumptions, some of which may not be justified. Ask whether your attitudes are fair to the other side. Without critical reflection, there is a tendency toward cognitive inertia. This is a tendency to persist in certain prior beliefs by selecting and ignoring evidence. Both trust and distrust can persist beyond a reasonable point. Significant effort must be made to question your own beliefs and conclusions. Discussions with a third party whom you can trust to challenge your reasoning may be helpful.

The overall issue in all this "due diligence" is to establish a basis on which to craft an appropriate strategy. If the negotiating risks seem too high compared to the benefits, you may choose (if this is an option) not to negotiate with this particular party. On the other hand, if the risks are small, or the other side seems trustworthy and trusting, you may choose to simply negotiate in good faith. The costs of building trust or constructing protective mechanisms may not be justified. When the risks are moderate (or when they are high and you have no alternative but to negotiate), you must decide on a mix of building trust and protecting yourself from opportunistic, desperate, or defensive deception on the part of the other party. The mix will depend on the structure of the negotiation, time pressures, and whether you believe the other side is open to promoting honesty. If the other party is either highly opportunistic, or in desperate straits, attempting to build trust may be too risky.

Building Mutual Trust. In many cases, the incentive for deception in negotiation is defensive. It arises out of a suspicion that the other party is likely to be dishonest and out of a fear that the other party will unfairly exploit any weakness that is honestly revealed. This suspicion and fear may be overcome if a climate of mutual trust can be developed.

The level of trust with which a specific negotiation begins depends on the prior relationship of the parties, their individual reputations, their vulnerabilities to opportunism, and the established norms. We find some settings in which handshake deals are common, and others in which the distrust is so high that a lengthy and complex contracting process is required.[29]

The general principle behind the trust-building mechanisms is that one should demonstrate both trustworthiness and the ability to trust. The latter entails taking some moderate risks. As Adam Smith (1759, p. 531) observed. "We trust the [person] who seems willing to trust us." If we want to be trusted, we have to be able to show trust in return. In many cases, this trust will be reciprocated. It will promote honesty and reduce negotiating and contracting cost. In other cases, it will invite opportunistic exploitation. The process must be managed carefully. As long as the parties still have some divergent interests, it is unlikely that all deception, bluffing, or posturing can be eliminated.

The effort to build trust should match the opportunity. If the gains from trust are likely to be great and time and resources are available, a major investment in trust building may be justified. If not, trust-building activities may have to be constrained. The choice of techniques should also be tailored to the parties and the social context. Zucker (1986, p. 53) has identified three modes of trust production: "(1) process-based, where trust is tied to past or expected exchange such as in reputation or gift exchange; (2) characteristic-based, where trust is tied to a person, depending on characteristics such as family background or ethnicity; and (3) institutional-based, where trust is tied to formal societal structures depending on individual or firm-specific attributes, (e.g., certification as an accountant) or on intermediary mechanisms (e.g., use of escrow accounts)." Drawing on these modes, we outline some generic steps that might help business negotiators build trust.

1. Build Mutual Benevolence. One avenue available in the real world, but not in Metopia, is to build a personal or moral foundation for trust by creating a sense of mutual benevolence.[30] The key here is to get each party to include the other in the reference group toward whom they feel good will, or a sense of moral commitment. It is easier to maintain distrust as long as the other party is seen as an adversary. One strategy for accomplishing this is to create more characteristic-based trust by highlighting any common religious, ethnic, family, or community ties shared by the parties. Another approach is to create opportunities for face-to-face meetings, either to discuss issues related to the negotiation, or simply to socialize. The use of preliminary meetings before the actual negotiation (or between negotiations) to discuss issues of mutual concern is becoming a more common element in labor-management relations. For instance, contracts between CBS and the IBEW now stipulate that the parties "shall meet at least once every three months, unless waived by mutual consent, to discuss subjects of mutual concern or interest . . ." The experimental gaming literature suggests that the possibility of communication between the parties typically enhances the probability of cooperation (Good, 1988). The use of pre-negotiation social contact and gift giving is common in Japanese (March, 1989) and Chinese negotiations. It serves to build trust and good will. If face-to-face meetings are to be arranged, the choice of site and arrangements can be crucial.[31] For trust building, it would seem wise to hold the meetings at a neutral location, or on the home turf of the most vulnerable party.

This strategy is not suitable to all situations. Sometimes direct contact between the principles may be risky. It may provoke more conflict and animosity, or one party may manipulate the other into unreasonable concessions. The prospect for these untoward outcomes is a function of the prior relationship, relative power, and attitudes of the parties. Each has to be willing and able to treat the other with respect.

2. Create Opportunities for Displaying Trust. Taking Adam Smith's observation seriously, if you want to get the other side to trust you, you may want to show a willingness to trust them, within the bounds of prudence. If the negotiations will be on-going, or if the process can be broken into stages, this approach can be part of the early stages. Strategic trust building of this sort involves creating low (or moderate) risk opportunities, in the pre-contractual stage, to be trusting, and, thus, provide the other party with occasions to prove themselves trustworthy. This is a way of both testing their trustworthiness and sending a signal of respect. In creating these opportunities, it is important not to appear weak or naive. Mutual trust is not promoted by passively allowing yourself to be taken advantage of. The risk taken should be seen as reasonable, the other party's performance needs to be at least partially observable before final contracting, and you should be prepared to demonstrate dissatisfaction if the trust is abused.[32]

As Hirschman (1984, p. 94) hypothesizes, trust seems to be the kind of social asset that flourishes with moderate use, but declines when not adequately practiced, or when practiced to excess. Accordingly, we are not suggesting a strategy of complete unilateral trust. In some settings this may be fine, but too often it would be disastrous. It invites exploitation. Nonetheless, a reasonable willingness to trust can be a powerful tool in building mutual trust.

There are two risks, even with modest trusting steps. One risk is that the trust will be abused. If there were no risk of this, it would not be trust. However, if the abuse is observed before further commitments are made, this provides extremely valuable information for going forward. It may be worth the cost. A more serious risk is that you are dealing with a clever opportunist, who plays along until the stakes get high and then exploits the trust. You have to rely on the due diligence process and your own judgment to help screen out extreme opportunists.

3. Demonstrate Trustworthiness. In addition to showing a willingness to trust, you should also show that you are trustworthy.[33] This is best done in the early stages of the negotiation. Again, the trustworthiness must be at least partially observable before final contracting. To show your trustworthiness, you may have to facilitate the other party's verification. You may need to provide direct access to what would otherwise have been privileged information. Trustworthiness that will not be apparent until much later cannot help build mutual trust in the pre-contracting stage. One difficulty with this strategy is that you do not fully control the opportunities to demonstrate your trustworthiness. These opportunities will, in large part, be a function of the other party's decisions to trust you. It is essential for trust-building that negotiators create and vigilantly watch for opportunities to show that they can be trusted. It is wise to keep even small promises, and be candid about matters that the other side may already know (from their due diligence) or could verify before the deal is

complete. Anything short of this could undermine a trust built to that point. As Dasgupta (1988, p.62) points out, "although a reputation for honesty may be acquired slowly, it can generally be destroyed very quickly."

Of course, there are risks in being fully trustworthy. In some cases, it is not possible to conceal your negotiating vulnerabilities without being deceptive. If you are under time pressure and are asked, "How soon do you need to close the deal on this building?", it is hard to conceal your vulnerability without seeming shifty and evasive. The question is not out of line if timing is an important matter for the other party. Being trustworthy may require you to be trusting.

A variation on the strategy of being trustworthy is to offer to stand behind your claims, by using some of the contractual devices we discussed in Metopia (warranties, collateral, etc.) to show that you are willing to protect the other party from the risk and uncertainty of relying on your word. In contrast to visible trustworthy behavior, this can be done with claims that cannot easily be verified before the other side makes a commitment. The point of doing this is not to set a precedent of always using contractual mechanisms to secure the trust. This would defeat the purpose of building the trust. Rather, the purpose of such an offer is to signal good faith, in hopes that a sincere show of good faith on one important issue will alleviate the need for further contractual protection.

4. Place the Negotiation in a Longer-Term Context. When negotiating with someone for the first time, it may be tempting for both parties to think of the negotiation as a one-shot deal. We have seen the incentive problems this can create. When business people develop norms of constantly shopping for the best deal, with no long-term commitment to specific suppliers or customers, they invite this risk. It has been claimed that many of the recent problems on Wall Street result from a breakdown in investment bank and client relations. As investment banks get more aggressive and clients shop around for specialized services, it increases the incentives for drawing a client into a deal that will generate large fees for the bank today, but that might harm the client in the long run.[34] A wiser long-term strategy may be to demonstrate a willingness to be a loyal negotiating partner. By placing the negotiation in the context of being first among many, the incentive problem may be removed. Within an on-going relationship, the parties can invoke a number of strategies to encourage honest behavior. The fact that these strategies are available should provide some comfort.

Demonstrating loyalty to a relationship takes time. This is hard to do credibly in an initial negotiation. However, some contractual devices can promote this. For instance, making a follow-on service contract part of the deal may help. Alternatively, providing and asking for references can emphasize the importance of reputations and convince the other that you are interested in the long run.

5. Bring in Mutually Respected Intermediaries. A final possibility is to induce trust by involving a mutually trusted intermediary. This intermediary can serve as a conduit for trust and as a form of security. Though trust may not be perfectly transitive, finding an intermediary who can vouch for the reliability of each of the parties to the negotiation may provide some comfort. This comfort is strengthened when the third party is in a position to <u>reward honest be-havior, or punish dishonest behavior</u> (Brams, 1990, pp. 29–61). This practice is common in cross-cultural negotiations when the party from country X hires a respected consultant or representative in country Y to facilitate negotiations with another party in country Y.

This is not the same as hiring reputational agents, such as lawyers, to han-dle the negotiation. The use of lawyers, generally, does not build <u>mutual trust</u>, though it may reduce the incentives for certain forms of opportunistic behav-ior. It is not essential that the principals trust the other party's attorney. What is crucial in using the lawyers is that <u>their reputations are at stake</u> and that they can act to protect their clients from exploitation in that they have more expe-rience in <u>controlling opportunistic behavior</u>. The differences in these two strategies is apparent from the fact that in some cultures, it is proper to work through a <u>respected local agent, but outright offensive</u> to propose negotiating <u>through lawyers</u>.

Trust building requires time and puts the negotiator at some risk. By using a mutually trusted intermediary, one may be able to shorten the time require-ments, but costs and risks remain. Accordingly, trust building is only suitable when additional trust could have significant value, the stakes are high, the risks of trust building can be effectively managed, and the negotiation can be structured to provide sufficient time.

Self-Protection. Given the uncertainties associated with business negotia-tion, some element of self-protection and structuring of the incentives of the other party may be in order. *Caveat emptor* may not be a good legal rule, but it is reasonable advice for negotiators in many arm's length business transactions. In discussing Metopia, we identified several mechanisms that might be used to reduce the incentives for deception. Many of these will work just as effectively in the real world. However, when these mechanisms are proposed in the real world, the negotiator proposing them runs the risk of offending the other party: "Don't you trust me?" The offended party may respond irrationally by walking away or retaliating in some fashion. It may lead to an ever increasing spiral of mutual distrust.

Several techniques are available to make the proposals more palatable. Fortunately, many of the mechanisms serve multiple purposes. Many of them work to hedge against uncertainties that both parties face. They provide relia-bility. In some cases, they relieve the party with the information advantage of the pressure to decide what to disclose. The standard use of house inspectors in real estate transactions may be a relief to sellers who do not want to be liable for providing a comprehensive assessment of their house. To offset any unde-sirable implications, the individual proposing the use of protective mecha-nisms may need to offer the same sort of protection for the other side, or to pay for the added protection. Unless the other party has behaved particularly badly, it would be wiser to project an attitude of reasonable prudence, rather than moral superiority.

The following tactics can be effective in protecting against opportunistic deception when opportunities for trust-building are limited. Since many of these have been introduced earlier, we will keep our descriptions brief.

1. Select Your Negotiating Partners Wisely. The best protection is simply to avoid dealing with opportunists. Provide and ask for references. Consider their reputation, their relationship with you, and their incentives. When you decide to take a risk, do it with your eyes open.

2. Verify What You Can. Do your homework. Kick the tires. Tap into independent sources of information as available. Hire expert third-parties (e.g., inspectors, assessors, auditors, etc.) to assist. In many instances where there are incentive problems, this will be common practice. Request direct access to information that you need.

3. Get Important Claims in Writing. What you think the other party said and what they think they said (or claim they said) can be two different things, especially when a conflict arises. You should identify those areas in which you are relying most heavily on their word and ask for written clarification. If a written commitment is not feasible, see if you can get them to make their claims in front of an independent audience. Push for some precision. Vague claims and verbal assurances made in private make it difficult to confirm bad faith in court or to reputation channels. The claim should be clear and easily verifiable.

4. Request Bonds and Warranties. Warranties at least provide a written document to appeal to if difficulties arise later. They may be written so as to provide strong incentives for reliability. If the other party has enough resources, it may be wise to ask for collateral (or some other bond) to secure commitments and claims where their good faith will not be evident until after you have made irreversible investments. As noted in the Metopia discussion, these contractual mechanisms must be carefully crafted if they are to be effective and are not to induce more opportunistic behavior.

5. Hire a Skilled Intermediary. A skilled intermediary can serve many purposes. She can provide reputation value, negotiating expertise, legal or technical expertise, and a buffer from the other's manipulative tactics. Finding a suitable intermediary for self-protection is especially hard when you also are interested in building trust. As with any third party, the challenge is to find the right party and to provide them with the right incentives.

In general, we do not recommend that you go on the offensive. If you are vulnerable to exploitation and you have good reason to distrust the other party, it may be prudent to send deceptive signals to conceal your vulnerability. However, to engage in deception to level the playing field is a risky strategy. If you are discovered, it may lead to an escalation of questionable tactics and the loss of a good reputation. Unless the other party is widely recognized as a scoundrel who deserves to be dealt with in this way, future negotiating partners may be wary of dealing with you. Reputation channels may not be able to convey why your behavior was justified. In addition, deceit may affect your sense of integrity and cause stress. Deception must be used with caution, even when you believe it is morally justified.

Each of the steps we recommend for self-protection is costly. As with trust building, you need to weigh the costs against the benefits. Even when you have little reason to trust the other party, establishing protective mechanisms may be too costly. When the stakes are low, the wise course may be to accept the risk. Nonetheless, in many business negotiations, the stakes are sufficiently high and the level of trust sufficiently low, so that an investment in self-protection is worthwhile.

Many negotiations, particularly those at arms-length with strangers, require both trust building and self-protection. The former works to raise the moral climate, the latter to take the other party out of the path of temptation. The challenge is to strike the right balance. Too much self-protection can undermine the trust-building effort.[35] Care must be taken not to present inconsistent signals.

SUMMARY AND CONCLUSION

Deception is a regrettable, but common element in negotiations. In this paper, we have provided a practical response to the problem of deception in negotiation. The foundation of the response is built on our analysis of a self-interested world, Metopia. This analysis reveals that deception is not monolithic. Different types of deception have different characteristics that need to be considered in promoting honesty. The analysis also illustrates the insidious nature of deception, showing how the mere possibility of deception can rob good faith claims of their credibility. Finally, our exploration of Metopia suggests many steps that can be taken, even with amoral individuals, to promote honesty.

Real people have a wider range of sentiments and are less rational than Metopians. Accordingly, we propose options for promoting honesty that reflect the differences between Metopia and the real world. They are set within the context of social institutions, public and private, designed, at least in part, to promote honesty. The options draw heavily on a growing body of empirical and theoretical research on negotiation and conflict resolution.

Because of the diversity of negotiation contexts, it is not possible for us to offer a specific strategy that will be effective on all occasions. We hope that our presentation of options allows practitioners to craft strategies appropriate to their situations. These strategies cannot eliminate all deception in negotiation. It is not always wise to invest in building trust, or protecting oneself. Even when it is wise, strategies based on the options we have presented will not always achieve their objectives. Nonetheless, if we are to narrow the Machiavellian gap between the normative ideal of honesty and the practice of negotiation, we must encourage negotiators to identify and pursue opportunities for promoting trust and honesty. We must also encourage them to participate in and improve existing institutional support mechanisms. Some practitioners may even embark on institution building ventures, providing new and better support for doing the right thing. The fight to extend the moral frontier into remaining pockets of Hobbesian behavior (Dees and Cramton, 1991) is a difficult one. It requires creativity and prudent risk taking.

Notes

We are grateful to Howard Stevenson and Tom Piper for comments, and to the Harvard Business School, the National Science Foundation and the Hoover Institution for support.

1. For a description of a variety of deceptive practices in everyday business, see Blumberg (1989).

2. For more argument on this point, see Dees and Cramton (1992).

3. We invoke a narrow notion of self-interest specifically to avoid two dangers inherent in broader notions. One danger is reflected in the meaningless conception of self-interest characterized by revealed preference theory, according to which even the most blatant self-sacrificial behavior is by definition self-interested. Sen (1977) exposes the weaknesses inherent in this definition. The other danger is that posed by some philosophers (see Kavka, 1984) who wish to broaden the notion of self-interest in a specific way, so as to guarantee that ethical behavior is self-interested. Ethical behavior becomes its own reward. Both of these views trivialize real incentive problems.

4. For instance, an example of academic research in this vein is presented by Baiman and Lewis (1987), who conducted an experiment in which they found that though subjects exhibited some resistance to lying, modest monetary incentives were sufficient to overcome this resistence in a large number of cases.

5. This mutual trust perspective on morality in practice is developed further in Dees and Cramton (1991).

6. Though our definition is quite broad, it excludes unintended deception, even where that deception could be foreseen and prevented. Such deception raises interesting issues, but to discuss them would be a diversion from our main objective. For detailed treatments of some definitional complexities, see Chisholm and Feehan (1977) and Fried (1978, Ch. 3).

7. Some would suggest that honesty requires the disclosure of all relevant information, even when withholding that information would not qualify as deception on our account. We prefer to distinguish between honesty, i.e., the absence of deliberate deception, and candor, i.e., complete openness. For simplicity of analysis, we choose to focus on the former.

8. This may seem problematic, because the standard assumptions of game theory imply that deception is never successful. Game theory assumes that the agents are intelligent and rational. As a result, agents recognize when deception is in another's self-interest, and are not misled. By not allowing gullible negotiators, we understate the incentives to deceive. Nonetheless, game theory provides a rigorous and consistent framework for thinking about incentive problems.

9. For simplicity, we speak of one party having information that could be concealed, misrepresented, or truthfully shared. Technically, however, deception can occur even when the deceiver has no private information. It is enough that the other party to the negotiation believe that the first party has valuable private information.

10. This latter strategy is effective on issues where one party expects a conflict of interest when none exists. In a study of experienced and naive negotiators, Thompson (1990, p. 88) found that successful, experienced bargainers disguised their compatible interests to feign "making a concession for the purpose of gaining on another issue."

11. This is a rough statement of a theorem due to Myerson and Satterthwaite (1983). Cramton, Gibbons, and Klemperer (1987) show how the theorem depends on the distribution of the ownership rights when many parties share ownership. For an analysis of the inefficiencies caused by private information in dynamic bargaining models see, for example, Cramton (1992). Kennan and Wilson (1993) provide a survey of the literature on bargaining with private information.

12. For now, we set aside the problem of contracting with these third-parties in Metopia. In order to assure the reliability of a third-party verifier, Metopian negotiators would have to use the same mechanisms that they use for promoting honesty in their primary negotiations.

13. Under the broad heading of warranties we are including any promise to make an adjustment to the terms of exchange (provide a full or partial refund, repair or replace a product, etc.) based on what happens after the deal is consummated. This includes warranties against defects, performance guarantees, guarantees of satisfaction, price guarantees, and cancellation or refund policies.

14. For a discussion of the value of service guarantees see Heskett, Sasser, and Hart (1990).

15. It should be noted that price guarantees can have the effect of reducing price competition rather than assuring low prices.

16. See Kronman (1985) for a discussion of the limitations of these devices in the absence of third-party enforcement. Though we allow a role for third-parties, the basic structure of his arguments still applies.

17. We do not mean to suggest that warranties and bonds only serve to reduce incentives for deception. Even with universal due diligence and good faith, some uncertainties will remain in most negotiating contexts. These devices can be used to provide for a more efficient allocation of the associated risk.

18. See Fudenberg (1992) and Pearce (1992) for surveys of reputation models in game theory.

19. Alternatively, p could denote the discount factor in an infinitely repeated game or more generally the product of the discount factor and the continuation probability. In all cases, the analysis is the same.

20. More forgiving punishments, such as tit-for-tat (see Axelrod, 1984), work as well. Indeed, so long as the continuation probability is more than 50%, assuming detection is certain, tit-for-tat sustains honest behavior, since $2 + 2p \geq 3 + 0p$ for all $p \geq 1/2$. Dixit and Nalebuff (1991, pp. 113–5) suggest an even more forgiving strategy that takes into account the good will that might build up over time. In gaming experiments, Deutsch (1973, Ch. 12) found that a defensive, but non-punitive strategy could be quite effective in inducing cooperation.

21. See Porter (1983) for a detailed analysis of this strategy or Abreu, Pearce, Stacchetti (1986) for an analysis of the optimal collusive strategy.

22. For a more general discussion of limited transaction resources, in the context of contract law, see Maser and Coleman (1989).

23. See Maser and Coleman (1989), for a discussion of the costs and risks of third-party intervention.

24. Several of the differences we discuss are in Etzioni (1988).

25. We concentrate here on secular mechanisms relevant to all in our pluralistic society. However, we would be remiss if we failed to note the importance of religion in inspiring and reinforcing the moral conduct of many individuals. Religion often relies not only on inspiration and moral exhortation, but also on powerful incentive systems, including monitoring of behavior by an all-knowing third party. For a discussion of the importance of moral retribution in religion, see Green (1988), especially pp. 12–16.

26. See Shell (1991a and 1991b) and Farnsworth (1987) for discussions of the extent to which contract law applies to opportunism and fair dealing in the pre-contractual stages of negotiation.

27. Many of the suggestions we make appear in a number of sources. See Deutsch (1973), Fisher and Brown (1988), Fisher and Ury (1981), Lax and Sebenius (1986), Lewicki and Litterer (1985), Raiffa (1982), and Rubin and Brown (1975).

28. Fisher and Brown (1988) play down the importance of character, suggesting that reliability is largely a function of other things. We acknowledge other influences, but believe that perceptions of character are central to assessing the likelihood of honesty.

29. The practical difficulties of eliminating deception are seen in the distrust often present in labor negotiations. For example, according to the *New York Times* (28 October 1990, p. B1), "At the core of the stalled New York City municipal labor talks is the union leaders' growing distrust of the claims being made about the city's financial plight." This distrust persists despite the fact that the setting allows for reputations (labor and management deal with each other on a regular basis), contractual mechanisms (wage rates could be tied to financial performance) and verification (management can open its books).

30. Kronman (1985) suggests a highly specialized version of this called "union" in which the interests of the two parties are somehow united. He cites close family bonds as an example. Our recommendation is less extreme.

31. Rubin and Brown (1975, pp. 82–91) point out how important the site and arrangements at the site are to control and dominance.

32. This parallel's Lindskold's (1978) conclusion, in evaluating a proposal for tension reduction in a conflict situation, that one must be "both conciliatory and resistant to exploitation" (p. 788).

33. This is the linchpin of the Fisher and Brown (1988) plan for managing reliability and trust in a relationship, see especially their chapter 7.

34. This points to an interesting tension that we will not discuss in this paper between encouraging healthy competition by being willing to move your business from one hand to another, and losing the value to be gained in long-term relationships.

35. Ring and Van de Ven (1989) found that, in attempts to build relationships to pursue innovations, too much attention to formal protections of the individual parties could undermine trust created in the informal sharing processes.

Bibliography

Abreu, Dilip, David Pearce and Ennio Stacchetti: 1986, "Optimal Cartel Equilibria with Imperfect Monitoring." *Journal of Economic Theory* 39, 251–269.

Akerlof, George A.: 1970, "The Market for 'Lemons': Quality Uncertainty and the Market Mechanism." *Quarterly Journal of Economics* 84, 488–500.

Arrow, Kenneth J.: 1974, "Gifts and Exchanges." *Philosophy and Public Affairs* 1, 343–362.

Axelrod, Robert: 1984, *The Evolution of Cooperation* (Basic Books, New York).

Baiman, Stanley and Barry Lewis: 1989, "An Experiment Testing the Behavioral Equivalence of Strategically Equivalent Employment Contracts." *Journal of Accounting Research* 27, 1–20.

Bhide, Amar and Howard H. Stevenson: 1990, "Why Be Honest if Honesty Doesn't Pay." *Harvard Business Review* September–October, 121–129.

Blumberg, Paul: 1989, *The Predatory Society: Deception in the American Marketplace* (Oxford University Press, Oxford).

Boatright, John R.: 1992. "Morality in Practice: Dees, Cramton, and Brer Rabbit on a Problem of Applied Ethics." *Business Ethics Quarterly*. 2, 63–73.

Brams, Steven J.: 1990, *Negotiation Games: Applying Game Theory to Bargaining and Arbitration* (Foundation Press, New York).

Carr, Albert Z.: 1968, "Is Business Bluffing Ethical?" *Harvard Business Review* January–February, 143–159.

Chandler, R.: 1955, *The Little Sister* (Penguin Books, Harmondsworth).

Chisholm, Roderick, and Thomas D. Feehan: 1977, "The Intent to Deceive." *Journal of Philosophy* 74, 143–159.

Coleman, James S.: 1990, *Foundations of Social Theory* (Harvard University Press, Cambridge).

Cramton, Peter C.: 1992, "Strategic Delay in Bargaining with Two-Sided Uncertainty." *Review of Economic Studies* 59, 205–225.

Cramton, Peter, Robert Gibbons, and Paul Klemperer: 1987, "Dissolving a Partnership Efficiently." *Econometrica* 55, 615–632.

Dasgupta, Partha: 1988, "Trust as a Commodity." In Diego Gambetta (ed.), *Trust: Making and Breaking Cooperative Relations* (Basil Blackwell Ltd., Oxford).

Dees, J. Gregory, and Peter C. Cramton: 1991, "Shrewd Bargaining on the Moral Frontier: Toward a Theory of Morality in Practice." *Business Ethics Quarterly* 1, 135–167.

Deutsch, Morton: 1973, *The Resolution of Conflict: Constructive and Destructive Processes* (Yale University Press, New Haven).

Dixit, Avinash K. and Barry J. Nalebuff: 1991, *Thinking Strategically: The Competitive Edge in Business, Politics, and Everyday Life* (W. W. Norton and Company, New York).

Ekman, Paul: 1985, *Telling Lies* (W. W. Norton and Company, New York).

Etzioni, Amitai: 1988, *The Moral Dimension: Toward a New Economics* (The Free Press, New York).

Farnsworth, E. Allan: 1987, "Precontractual Liability and Preliminary Agreements: Fair Dealing and Failed Negotiations." *Columbia Law Review* 87, 218–293.

Fisher, Roger and Scott Brown: 1988, *Getting Together: Building a Relationship that Gets to Yes* (Houghton Mifflin Company, Boston).

Fisher, Roger and William Ury: 1981, *Getting to Yes: Negotiating Agreement Without Giving In* (Houghton Mifflin Company, Boston).

Fried, Charles: 1978, *Right and Wrong* (Harvard University Press, Cambridge).

Friedman, James W.: 1971, "A Noncooperative Equilibrium for Supergames." *Review of Economic Studies* 38, 1–12.

Fudenberg, Drew: 1992, "Explaining Cooperation and Commitment in Repeated Games." In J. J. Laffont (ed.), *Advances in Economic Theory: Sixth World Congress* (Cambridge University Press, Cambridge).

Gambetta, Diego: 1988, "Can We Trust Trust?" In Diego Gambetta (ed.), *Trust: Making and Breaking Cooperative Relations* (Basil Blackwell Ltd., Oxford).

Good, David: 1988, "Individuals, Interpersonal Relations, and Trust." In Diego Gambetta (ed.), *Trust: Making and Breaking Cooperative Relations* (Basil Blackwell Ltd., Oxford).

Green, Ronald M.: 1988, *Religion and Moral Reason: A New Method for Comparative Study* (Oxford University Press, Oxford).

Heskett, James L., W. Earl Sasser, Jr., and Christopher W. L. Hart: 1990, *Service Breakthroughs: Changing the Rules of the Game* (The Free Press, New York).

Hirschleifer, Jack: 1982, "Evolutionary Models in Economics and Law: Cooperation versus Conflict Strategies." In P. H. Rubin and R. O. Zerbe, Jr. (eds.), *Research in Law and Economics* 4, 1–60 (JAI Press, Greenwich).

Hirschman, Albert O.: 1984, "Against Parsimony: Three Easy Ways of Complicating Some Categories of Economic Discourse." *American Economic Review* Proceedings 74, 88–96.

Holmstrom, Bengt: 1979, "Moral Hazard and Observability." *Bell Journal of Economics* 10, 74–91.

Hume, David. 1751. *An Enquiry Concerning the Principle of Morals*. References are to the 1975 edition (Clarendon Press, Oxford).

Kavka, Gregory S.: 1984, "The Reconciliation Project." In D. Copp and D. Zimmerman (eds.), *Morality, Reason, and Truth* (Rowman and Allanheld, Totowa).

Kennan, John, and Robert Wilson: 1993, "Bargaining with Private Information." *Journal of Economic Literature* 31, 45–104.

Kreps, David M.: 1990, "Corporate Culture and Economic Theory." In James Alt and Kenneth Shepsle (eds.), *Perspectives on Positive Political Economy* (Cambridge University Press, Cambridge) 90–143.

Kronman, Anthony T.: 1985, "Contract Law and the State of Nature." *Journal of Law, Economics, and Organization* 1, 5–32.

Lax, David A. and Sebenius, James K.: 1986, *The Manager As Negotiator: Bargaining for Cooperation and Competitive Gain* (The Free Press, New York).

Lewicki, Roy J. and Joseph A. Litterer: 1985, *Negotiation* (Richard D. Irwin, Homewood).

Lindskold, Svenn: 1978, "Trust Development, the GRIT Proposal, and the Effects of Conciliatory Acts on Conflict and Cooperation." *Psychological Bulletin* 85, 772–793.

March, Robert M.: 1989, *The Japanese Negotiator: Subtlety and Strategy Beyond Western Logic* (Kodansha International, Tokyo).

Maser, Steven M. and Coleman, Jules L.: 1989, "A Bargaining Theory Approach to Default Provisions and Disclosure Rules in Contract Law." *Harvard Journal of Law and Public Policy* 12, 637–709.

Myerson, Roger B. and Mark A. Satterthwaite: 1983, "Efficient Mechanisms for Bilateral Trading." *Journal of Economic Theory* 28, 265–281.

Nagel, Thomas: 1975, "Comment." In E. S. Phelps (ed.), *Altruism, Morality, and Economic Theory* (Russell Sage Foundation, New York).

Pearce, David: 1992, "Repeated Games: Cooperation and Rationality." In J. J. Laffont (ed.), *Advances in Economic Theory: Sixth World Congress* (Cambridge University Press, Cambridge).

Porter, Robert H.: 1983, "Optimal Cartel Trigger Price Strategies." *Journal of Economic Theory* 29, 313–338.

Raiffa, Howard: 1982, *The Art and Science of Negotiation: How to Resolve Conflicts and Get the Best Out of Bargaining* (Harvard University Press, Cambridge).

Ring, Peter Smith and Andrew Van de Ven: 1989, "Formal and Informal Dimensions of Transactions." In Andrew H. Van de Ven, Harold L. Angle, and Marshall Scott Poole (eds.), *Research on the Management of Innovation* (Ballinger Publishing Company, New York).

Rubin, Jeffrey A. and Bert R. Brown: 1975, *The Social Psychology of Bargaining and Negotiation* (Academic Press, New York).

Sen, Amartya: 1977, "Rational Fools: A Critique of the Behavioural Foundations of Economic Theory." *Philosophy and Public Affairs* 6, 317–344.

Shell, G. Richard: 1991a, "When Is It Legal to Lie in Negotiations?" *Sloan Management Review* Spring: 93–101.

Shell G. Richard: 1991b, "Opportunism and Trust in the Negotiation of Commercial Contracts: Toward a New Cause of Action." *Vanderbilt Law Review* 44, 221–282.

Smith, Adam. 1759. *The Theory of Moral Sentiments.* Reprinted in 1976 (Liberty Classics, Indianapolis).

Sobel, Joel: 1985, "A Theory of Credibility." *Review of Economic Studies* 52, 557–574.

Thompson, Leigh: 1990, "An Examination of Naive and Experienced Negotiators." *Journal of Personality and Social Psychology* 59, 82–90.

White, James J.: 1980, "Machiavelli and the Bar: Ethical Limitations on Lying in Negotiation." *American Bar Foundation Research Journal* 1980, 926–934.

Wilson, Robert: 1983, "Auditing: Perspectives from Multiperson Decision Theory." *Accounting Review* 58, 305–318.

Zucker, Lynne G.: 1986, "The Production of Trust: Institutional Sources of Economic Structure." *Research in Organizational Behavior* 8, 53–111.

• PART TWO •

Property, Profit, and Justice
Introduction

TRADITIONAL THEORIES OF PROPERTY AND PROFIT

Issues about money and economics are often connected to those of ethics and values. If a friend borrows five dollars and later refuses to pay it, then the issue quickly becomes an ethical one: we say the friend really should repay the money. At all levels of economics, ethics plays an important role. For example, to decide how society should distribute wealth, one must know what ethical standards distinguish fair from unfair distributions. Thus it is not surprising that two well-known economists, Adam Smith and Karl Marx (both of whom are discussed in this section), began their careers as philosophers.

Two of the most volatile issues in economics have ethical implications: the importance of the profit motive, and whether restrictions should be placed on private ownership of property. The pursuit of profit and the existence of private property are said by some economists to be the foundations of a free society. The seventeenth-century philosopher John Locke argued that each person has a natural right to own property. However, others argue that the profit motive and private property are corrupting and result in labor abuses, unfair income distribution, monopolistic practices, and misuse of the environment.

A third issue involving both ethics and economics is the nature of justice. For example, is there such a thing as a just distribution of wealth, resources, and opportunities in society, and if so, what does that distribution look like? Is it fair that one person buys yachts and racehorses while another cannot even buy food? Or is it true, instead, that any time government attempts to insure "fairness" by interfering with the free accumulation of wealth, its attempt to redistribute wealth, resources, or opportunities commits a fundamental injustice by violating the liberty of those who have freely earned power, position, or property?

The Profit Motive

Although people today are more accepting of the profit motive than at any other period in history, it is still common to hear of a person or corporation condemned for being greedy. Such an attitude, which questions the morality of emphasizing profit, is not new. Prior to the nineteenth century, pursuing wealth or lending money with interest was condemned as being immoral. The first great defender of the profit motive was the eighteenth-century economist Adam Smith. Today, nearly two hundred years after Smith presented his ideas in *The Wealth of Nations* (excerpts of which are presented in this section), his name is almost synonymous with the defense of the free market or "laissez-faire" economic system. Smith asserted that the pursuit of profit, even for one's self-interest, is not always bad. In a famous quotation from *The Wealth of Nations* he writes,

> It is not from the benevolence of the butcher, the brewer, or the baker that we expect our dinner, but from their regard of their own interest. We address ourselves not to their humanity, but to their self-love and never talk to them of our own necessities, but of their advantage.

However, Smith did not believe that economic gain was our most noble goal; rather, he claimed that justice, not self-interest nor even benevolence, is the crowning virtue of humanity. Smith emphasized the way in which pursuing one's own economic interests in the free marketplace could enhance public welfare so long as one acted with prudence, engaged in fair play, and respected the rights of others. Smith believed that an economic system could function such that people's pursuing their own economic ends could generate, in the absence of government intervention, great public economic good, so long as those involved acted with restraint and respected basic principles of justice.

Criticisms of the Invisible Hand

By the time the Industrial Revolution was under way in the early nineteenth century, Smith's ideas dominated economic theory, and interestingly, many of the emerging inequities of that era were justified by appealing to his philosophy. The increased specialization, the reduction of quotas and tariffs, and the decreased roles of government in business were all justified by appealing to a reading of Smith's *Wealth of Nations*. Smith himself, however, did not live to see the changes or the human miseries rampant during the Industrial Revolution, and his worries about the poor pay of workers indicate that he would not have approved of the treatment of industrial laborers. In fact, labor was poorly paid, working conditions deplorable, and working hours long. One of the most depressing sights of all was children working in factories for sixteen hours a day, six days a week. For the children, such work was necessary to supplement their family's meager income.

Many witnesses to the Industrial Revolution were persuaded that the real villain was the economic system. The German philosopher and economist Karl Marx argued that the "free market" Smith championed was little more than a convenient fiction for capitalist property owners. Whereas Smith had praised the competitive market because of its ability to generate better products at lower prices, Marx argued that in the marketplace workers were mere commodities, available to the factory owners at the lowest possible wages. Indeed, he thought the pressures of the marketplace would force workers, who could not refuse to work without starving, to accept wages barely above a subsistence level. Meanwhile the owners of the means of production, the capitalists, could exploit workers by using their labor and then selling the resulting product at a profit. Marx identified the difference between the costs of production, including wages, and the selling price of products as "surplus value." For Marx, then, profits always meant exploitation of the worker by the capitalist. And he added that whenever technology develops, the economic gap between the capitalist and the worker must widen further, since technology allows products to be manufactured with less human labor and thus creates unemployment and lower wages.

In the selections taken from the *Economic and Philosophic Manuscripts of 1844*, Marx outlines his influential theory of alienation, in which he asserts that workers in capitalistic society are separated from, and deprived of, their own labor. When forced to work for the capitalist, workers are also forced to give the capitalist what most belongs to them: their own work. Factory employees toil away producing products that the factory owner will eventually sell, and they feel no connection to those products; rather, they have been alienated from the effects of their labor. Thus, through the concept of alienation, Marx offers a fundamental condemnation of the treatment of labor in early modern capitalism, a condemnation that was enormously influential in improving labor conditions, although less effective in its more revolutionary implications.

At the same time that Marx was developing his criticism of capitalism, another equally dramatic development occurred. In 1859 the English naturalist Charles Darwin published his monumental work on evolution, *The Origin of the Species*. Darwin argued, in short, that in the process of natural selection (1) organisms in the biological kingdom had evolved from simple to more complex species; and (2) during this process organisms less adaptable to the environment failed to survive, while the more adaptable ones flourished. This selection process maximizes benefits for individual organisms and species as well.

Darwin himself expressly stated that his ideas applied only to the biological kingdom, but many thinkers extended them to social and economic issues. The resulting theory of society, popularized by Herbert Spencer and industrialists such as Andrew Carnegie (whose article "Wealth" is reproduced in this section), was known as Social Darwinism.

Although Social Darwinism confronted the same issues dealt with by Adam Smith and Karl Marx, it agreed with neither. The Darwinists argued that the Industrial Revolution exemplified social evolution from simple to complex societies. In the evolution of capitalistic industrial systems, then, some individuals may suffer; but the system itself enhances human welfare, since it weeds out the unsuccessful, weak competitors while allowing the tougher ones to flourish. Thus, both marketplace and nature operate according to the same "natural" laws. Those who can, survive; those who cannot, perish. Consequently, Social Darwinists came to view the profit motive in business as the essential motivating force in the struggle for economic survival. Unfortunately, Social Darwinism was also touted by a few wealthy tycoons in the nineteenth century as a justification for deplorable working conditions and massive economic inequalities.

The key issues of Part Two—human motivation, human nature, and which economic system is preferable—are interrelated. For example, the ethical question of when, if at all, it is best for people to be motivated by profit is directly connected to the question of whether there is a common human nature. If, as some have argued, people must and will pursue their own self-interest because of their very *nature*, it is sometimes concluded that the pursuit of self-interest in the form of economic gain is often morally justified. In a similar fashion, both issues are tied to that of discovering the best economic system. If people are naturally self-interested and will inevitably act on the basis of self-interest in the marketplace, perhaps society needs an economic system that proscribes such economic pursuits. On the other hand, if self-interested people can regularly subordinate their interests to higher motives such as justice, then perhaps a free market can be a morally viable economic framework.

Locke

Private Ownership

Another issue closely connected to that of profit is public versus private ownership. A common argument used by those who criticize private property asserts that the elimination of private property makes it impossible for people to strive to accumulate wealth, and thus discourages them from acting from a bad motive, that is, the profit motive. Defenders of the institution of private property disagree, citing the incentive for hard work and creativity that private property provides. But by far the most ingenious argument in favor of private property is the classical one offered by the seventeenth-century English philosopher John Locke.

Locke believed that human beings have a fundamental right to own private property, and the basic premises that establish this right can be found in the selection from his *Second Treatise on Government*. Even today his "social contract" argument is commonly used in defending the right to own property. Locke asserts what he claims is a truism: in the absence of a formally structured society—that is, in the "state of nature"—all people may be said to own their bodies. It was upon this seemingly obvious premise that Locke rested his defense. If one admits that one has the right to own one's body, it follows that one owns the actions of that body, or in other words, one's own labor, and that one is free to do what one pleases with one's body, one's abilities, and one's labor. Finally, one may also be said to own, and to have a right to own, the things which one mixes with one's labor. For example, if in the state of nature a person picks fruit from wild bushes, that person may be said to own the fruit. And if we grant that property may be freely traded, given, and accumulated, we have the beginning of the basis for justification of vast ownership of capital and land.

In sharp contrast to Locke's seemingly benign defense of private property, Marx argued that it is actually an institution that perpetuates the class struggle. He denied that any such state of nature as Locke described ever existed, and he tried to give an accurate historical account of the evolution of the institution of property. He attempted to show how at every stage in the struggle for private property, one class succeeds in exploiting and alienating another. He argued that the institution of private property in a capitalistic economic system is nothing other than the means by which the privileged class—the capitalists—exploits the class of the less privileged, the workers.

We should remind ourselves that the immediate question confronting most people in the Western world is probably not whether to adopt a purely communistic or a purely free market economy. Moreover, one should be reminded that Marx's ideal was a communal society, not the more totalitarian socialist systems that the Soviet Union and other communistic nations developed in his name. Of more immediate practical significance is the question of how community issues should be handled by private corporations. Can private corporations, such as the "Dorrence Corporation" described in the book, combine the drive for profit with a sensitivity to human issues? The practical challenges of doing so are illustrated in the case "Dorrence Corporation," where profit targets are established by Dorrence's CEO, yet meeting those profit targets *appears* to have human cost.

PROFIT AND PROPERTY: MODERN DISCUSSIONS

One of the most outspoken critics of public ownership in the twentieth century is the economist Milton Friedman. Strongly opposing Marx, Friedman argues that the maintenance of the economic institution of private property is necessary to ensure basic political rights and freedoms. In his article "The Social Responsibility of Business Is to Increase Its Profits," Friedman denies the claim that businesses have obligations to society over and above their obligation to make a profit. In the spirit of Adam Smith, Friedman believes that the free market works best, and makes its greatest contribution, when companies compete for consumers' business and for the maximation of profits. Consequently, says Friedman, if a company were to make ethics or social responsibility a primary goal, it would be failing in its duty and hence, ironically, would not be fulfilling its real "social responsibility." Rather, the social responsibility of a corporate manager is simply to maximize profits on behalf of the corporation's owners, the shareholders.

Friedman strongly objects to placing society's major economic institutions in public ownership. Not only would the competitive marketplace be undermined, resulting in poorer products and services for the consumer, but a basic freedom would be denied insofar as the government would be interfering with the right to own property. In other of his writings, Friedman even argues that certain institutions that are now public, such as the post office and national parks, should be turned over to private investors.

How seriously one takes either Friedman's arguments or arguments asserting the opposite—that the railroads or oil industry, for example, should become publicly owned—will hinge on how seriously one takes the arguments of Locke and Marx. Is Locke correct in arguing that there is a natural right to private property? And how does his argument relate to Marx's claim that private property makes it possible for one class to exploit another?

Friedman's well-known edict that "the social responsibility of business is to increase its profits" is brought into questions by another eminent Nobel Prize economist, Kenneth Arrow. While being a strong proponent of free markets, Arrow argues that profit maximization alone does not always create an efficient market and may in fact produce some other negative side-effects. Unequal competition and the imbalance of information between the corporation and other stakeholders, such as employees or consumers, create inefficiencies that may be harmful to those stockholders. Moreover, even under perfect conditions or competition, profit maximization itself does not handle problems of poverty, pollution, and traffic congestion; in fact, a preoccupation with profit appears to aggrandize selfish motives at the expense of altruistic ones.

These social and market injuries, Arrow argues, could be adjudicated with regulations, taxation, and enforcement of legal liability. But, interestingly, Arrow finds that the adoption, proliferation, and enforcement of codes of ethics by corporations, codes analogous to those adopted by the medical profession, might do the work of regulation in a less intrusive and more flexible manner while preserving the benefits of an efficient competitive market.

In the case study "Merck & Co., Inc.," issues of profit and social welfare clash in the context of Merck's quandary over whether to test and produce a new drug designed to fight the disease River Blindness. Should Merck proceed with the development of a drug that promises to save hundreds of thousands from blindness, *even if* it will lose money in the process? Merck's corporate history stresses commitment to the health of the customer over profits (despite the fact that Merck has been enormously successful financially). But can it seriously pursue this philosophy in the instance of River Blindness?

JUSTICE

The subject of social justice, both for traditional and modern philosophers, is directly connected to economics and ethical theory. One important subcategory of justice dealt with in this section—namely, distributive justice—concerns the issue of how, and according to what principles, society's goods should be distributed. When thinking about justice, it is important to remember that the concept of "justice" cannot include all ethical and political values. Thus, no matter how desirable it may be to have justice established in society, we must acknowledge other ideals such as benevolence and charity. Justice refers to a minimal condition that should exist in a good society, a condition that traditionally has been interpreted as "giving each individual his or her due."

The notion of distributive justice, i.e., what constitutes justice in distributing goods to persons, is an evasive concept, as is illustrated by the following story: Once a group of soldiers found themselves defending a fort against an enemy. The soldiers were in desperate need of water, and the only source was 200 yards from the fort in enemy territory. Courageously, a small group sneaked outside the fort, filled their canteens with water, and returned safely. After showing the water to their fellow soldiers, the successful adventurers proposed that it should be distributed in accordance with the principles of justice. Since justice requires distribution on the basis of merit, they said, they themselves should get the water because they risked their lives in obtaining it. There was considerable disagreement. Although agreeing that justice requires distribution on the basis of deserving characteristics, a different group of soldiers, which had been longest without water, claimed they deserved it more because they *needed* it more than the others. After all, they were the thirstiest. And still a different group, agreeing with the same general principle of justice, argued that everyone deserved equal amounts of water because all human beings, considered generally, have equal worth. The moral, obviously, is that interpretations of justice have difficulty specifying a particular characteristic or set of characteristics which, when possessed by human beings, will serve as the basis for "giving each person his or her due."

Although the subject of distributive justice is a popular topic among modern philosophers, some thinkers, such as Robert Nozick, claim that the idea is prejudicial and controversial. If society's goods are to be distributed, this implies the existence of a distributing agency such as the government to enforce certain principles of distribution, thus taking away from those who have acquired holdings through voluntary exchanges and desert and giving them to those who have and deserve less. In attacking any principles of distribution, Nozick is arguing that the very existence of such a process violates basic principles of individual liberty, because it denies individuals the opportunity to do as they please without interference, and thus to engage freely in exchanges of goods and property. In this way, Nozick maintains, distributive and redistributive practices necessitate the violation of basic liberties and therefore no willful distribution can itself be just.

Another modern writer presented in this section, John Rawls, also considers questions of justice and the social order. Rawls believes that the idea of distributive justice can be coordinated with principles of individual rights and liberties. He argues that a just society is one in which agreements are freely made, in which no one is left out, and in which deserving people are not shortchanged. Rawls argues that a just society is based on two principles: (1) " . . . each person engaged in an institution or affected by it has an equal right to the most extensive liberty compatible with a like liberty for all . . ." and (2) " . . . inequalities as defined by the institutional structure . . . are arbitrary unless it is reasonable to expect that they will work out to everyone's advantage and provided that the positions and offices to which they attach or from which they may be gained are open to all." Thus, Rawls is not arguing that in a just society things would be structured so as to give all people an equal number of goods—for example, money, education, or status; and he allows that some people may have a great deal more than others. However, for a society to be · just, such inequalities are only acceptable if their existence is to the advantage of the least fortunate as well as to everybody else. Rawls further specifies that no form of distribution in any society is just unless it satisfies the first condition of justice: freedom. Rawls's article "Distributive Justice," excerpts of which are presented in this section, first appeared in 1967 and is a precursor of his influential book *A Theory of Justice* (Harvard University Press, 1971) in which he more fully develops the views presented here.

The contemporary debate over the interpretation of justice begun by thinkers such as Rawls and Nozick in the 1970s was joined in the 1980s by a variety of voices, many of them critical of the very assumptions underlying the debate. Perhaps, many have argued, the modern political mind-set is preoccupied with individual liberty and fair procedures at the expense of a fuller and more positive concept of social-personal good.

Issues of justice arise not only in large social systems, but in corporate organizations. We take for granted a considerable amount of inequality in the modern work place; inequality in salaries, working conditions, and status. But which inequalities are to be tolerated, and which are not? If the quality and availability of medical treatment is significantly different for managers than for ordinary workers, is the result injustice? To what extent should modern managers concerned with justice be attempting to "level" perks and advantages for all working in the corporation? In the case "The Oil Rig," we encounter dramatic disparities between expatriates and hired Angolan workers on an oil rig. The Angolans have dramatically lower salaries, fewer privileges, different clothing, limited access to medical treatment, and smaller quarters. Does justice require that the Tool Pusher (the boss of the oil rig) eliminate or substantially reduce inequalities?

Traditional Theories
of
Property and Profit

• *Case Study* •

Plasma International

T. W. ZIMMERER • P. L. PRESTON

The Sunday headline in the Tampa, Florida, newspaper read:

Blood Sales Result in Exorbitant Profits for Local Firm

The story went on to relate how the Plasma International Company, headquartered in Tampa, Florida, purchased blood in underdeveloped countries for as little a 90[1] cents a pint and resold the blood to hospitals in the United States and South America. A recent disaster in Nicaragua produced scores of injured persons and the need for fresh blood. Plasma International had 10,000 pints of blood flown to Nicaragua from West Africa and charged hospitals $150 per pint, netting the firm nearly 1.5 million dollars.

As a result of the newspaper story, a group of irate citizens, led by prominent civic leaders, demanded that the City of Tampa, and the State of Florida, revoke Plasma International's licenses to practice business. Others protested to their congressmen to seek enactment of legislation designed to halt the sale of blood for profit. The spokesperson was reported as saying, "What kind of people are these—selling life and death? These men prey on the needs of dying people, buying blood from poor, ignorant Africans for 90 cents worth of beads and junk, and selling it to injured people for $150 a pint. Well, this company will soon find out that the people of our community won't stand for their kind around here."

"I just don't understand it. We run a business just like any other business; we pay taxes and we try to make an honest profit," said Sol Levin as he responded to reporters at the Tampa International Airport. He had just returned home from testifying before the House Subcommittee on Medical Standards. The recent publicity surrounding his firm's activities during the recent earthquakes had once again fanned the flames of public opinion. An election year was an unfortunate time for the publicity to occur. The politicians and the media were having a field day.

Levin was a successful stockbroker when he founded Plasma International

"Plasma International," case prepared by T. W. Zimmerer and P. L. Preston, reprinted from *Business and Society: Cases and Text*, ed. by Robert D. Hay, Edmund R. Gray, and James E. Gates (Cincinnati: South-western Publishing Co., 1976). Reprinted with permission from the publisher and authors.

Company three years ago. Recognizing the world's need for safe, uncontaminated, and reasonably priced whole blood and blood plasma, Levin and several of his colleagues pooled their resources and went into business. Initially, most of the blood and plasma they sold was purchased through store-front operations in the southeast United States. Most of the donors were, unfortunately, men and women who used the money obtained from the sale of their blood to purchase wine. While sales increased dramatically on the basis of an innovative marketing approach, several cases of hepatitis were reported in recipients. The company wisely began a search for new sources.

Recognizing their own limitations in the medical-biological side of the business they recruited a highly qualified team of medical consultants. The consulting team, after extensive testing, and a worldwide search, recommended that the blood profiles and donor characteristics of several rural West African tribes made them ideal prospective donors. After extensive negotiations with the State Department and the government of the nation of Burami, the company was able to sign an agreement with several of the tribal chieftains.

As Levin reviewed these facts, and the many costs involved in the sale of a commodity as fragile as blood, he concluded that the publicity was grossly unfair. His thoughts were interrupted by the reporter's question: "Mr. Levin, is it necessary to sell a vitally needed medical supply, like blood, at such high prices especially to poor people in such a critical situation?" "Our prices are determined on the basis of a lot of costs that we incur that the public isn't even aware of," Levin responded. However, when reporters pressed him for details of these "relevant" costs, Levin refused any further comment. He noted that such information was proprietary in nature and not for public consumption.

Note

1. Prices have been adjusted in this article to allow for inflation occurring since the article was written (ed.).

Dorrence Corporation Trade-offs

HANS WOLF

Arthur Cunningham, Chief Executive Officer of the Dorrence Corporation, was reflecting on the presentations by the various divisions of the company of their operating plans and financial budgets for the next three years, which he had heard during the past several days. A number of critical decisions would have to be made at tomorrow's meeting of the nine senior executives who formed Dorrence's Corporate Operating Committee. Although Dorrence's tradition was one of consensus management, Cunningham knew that he was expected to exercise leadership and would have the final word, as well as the ultimate responsibility for the subsequent performance of the company.

Dorrence, a large U.S.-based pharmaceutical company with sales and operations throughout the world, had achieved an outstanding long-term record of growth in sales and profits. The company had not incurred a loss in any year since 1957 and profits had increased over the prior year in 28 out of the past 32 years. During the past 10 years, sales had grown at an average compound rate of 12% per year and profits had increased at a 15% average annual rate. Dorrence's profit as a percent of sales was considerably higher than that of the average U.S. industrial concern. (See Exhibit 1)

This growth had produced a huge increase in the value of Dorrence's stock. There are approximately 30,000 Dorrence shareholders, but as with many large American corporations, about 65% of Dorrence shares are held by a relatively small number of pension funds, mutual funds, university endowments and insurance companies. Dorrence grants stock options to its executives and permits employees in the U.S. and several other countries to purchase Dorrence stock through the company's savings plan. Dorrence executives own about 2% of the company's shares and all other employees about 1%. Thus, directly and indirectly, Dorrence is owned by millions of people who are affected to some degree by the marketplace of Dorrence shares.

Dorrence's fine record of growth had also brought benefits to the company's customers, employees and the communities in which the company had operations. Dorrence had steadily expanded its research expenditures at a greater rate than its sales growth and had developed important new products that extended life and improved the quality of life for millions of people. Because of its profitability, Dorrence was able to pay higher-than-average salaries to its employees, pay sizeable incentive awards to middle and upper management and bonuses to all employees based on the success of the company. Dorrence's growth also had provided unusual opportunities for career growth to many of its people. The company prided itself on being a good citizen in the communities in which its laboratories and factories were located. It contributed to local charities and encouraged its employees to work constructively in community organizations.

Cunningham felt that 1989 was, however, a very disappointing year. The company fell short of the goals management had established at the start of the year.

Growth in sales and profits was far below the rate of recent years and below the levels achieved by several of Dorrence's peers in the pharmaceutical industry. Management incentive awards and employee bonuses were, therefore, about 5% smaller than those distributed for 1988. The value of Dorrence stock was about 20% below its high point.

Consequently, Cunningham considered it important that Dorrence achieve at least a 13% profit growth in 1990, and higher rates in the two years beyond that. He recognized that such a goal would not be easy to reach. It would not only require the best efforts of the entire organization, but also force some tough decisions.

The 1990 budgets proposed by the divisions added up to a growth rate of only 8% in profit-after-taxes, five percentage points below what Cunningham considered a minimum acceptable level. As a rough rule of thumb he calculated that each percentage point increase in the profit growth rate required about $8 million additional profit-before-taxes. Thus, each percentage point improvement could be achieved in a number of ways: $13 million additional sales volume accompanied by normal incremental costs, or $8 million additional revenue from price increases, or $8 million reduction on expenditures. During the course of the three days of presentations he had identified several possibilities for such improvements about which decisions would have to be made. In his notes he had summarized them as follows.

1. Size of the research budget: Dorrence's total expenditures for research and development had climbed annually, not only in absolute dollars but also as a percent of sales. During the current year they totaled about 17% of sales, one of the higher levels in the pharmaceutical industry. The proposed budget included a further increase and Cunningham knew that many promising projects required additional funding if the company were to demonstrate the safety and efficacy of important new drugs in a timely manner.

Cunningham was keenly aware that pharmaceutical research and development was a very risky activity. The failure rate was high. Many years of effort were required before the success or failure of a new product could be known. Typically, it took seven to ten years from the identification of a potential new drug to receiving the approval to market it from the Food and Drug Administration and its sister bodies in other countries. On average, a pharmaceutical company brought to successful conclusion only one new drug development program for each $100 million of R&D expenditures.

Clearly, there was a trade-off between investing for future growth and achieving acceptable profits in the short run. On Cunningham's list of possible changes in the proposed 1990 budget was a $10 million reduction in the amount of money requested for R&D.

2. Export sales: The International Division had presented an opportunity for a $4 million sale to the Philippine government which was not included in the 1990 budget because of lack of product availability. It was for Savolene, a new Dorrence injectable drug for the treatment of serious viral infections, including measles. The drug was difficult and expensive to manufacture and had been in very short supply since its introduction.

A large lot, costing about $1 million, had been rejected for the U.S. market on the basis of a very sensitive new test for endotoxins recently required by the U.S. Food & Drug Administration in addition to another test that had been the FDA standard for many years. The new test had shown a very low level of endotoxins on this batch of Savolene, even though no endotoxins has been revealed by the older test.

Cunningham had asked whether this ruled out shipping the batch to the Philippines. The company's chief medical safety officer had answered, "Officially the Philippines and a lot of other countries still rely only on the old test. It always takes them a while to follow U.S. practice, and sometimes they never do. Endotoxins might cause a high fever when injected into patients, but I can't tell you that the level in this batch is high enough to cause trouble. But how can we have a double standard, one for the U.S. and one for Third World countries?"

However, when Cunningham asked Dorrence's export vice president the same question, she said, "It's not our job to over-protect other countries. The health authorities in the Philippines know what they're doing. Our FDA always takes an extreme position. Measles is a serious illness. Last year in the Philippines half the kids who had measles died. It's not only good business but also good ethics to send them the only batch of Savolene we have available."

3. Capital investments: Among the capital investments that had been included in the proposed budgets was a $200 million plant automation program for Dorrence's Haitian chemical plant. The purpose of the investment was to permit a dramatic reduction in the cost of Libam, Dorrence's principal product whose U.S. patent would expire in a couple of years. Patent protection had already ended in most other countries and chemical manufacturers in Italy, Hungary and India were selling Libam's active ingredient at very low prices. Once there was no longer patent protection in the U.S. these companies, and others, could capture a large share of Dorrence's existing sales unless Dorrence could match their low prices. Automating the Haitian plant was essential to achieving such lower cost. Successful implementation of the new technology would enable the plant to achieve the required output with far fewer people than currently employed at the plant. What to do about these surplus workers presented a difficult problem for which no solution had yet been worked out.

Dorrence was currently earning about 9% interest on its surplus funds. The proposed automation project would use up $200 million of those funds and thus reduce the interest income earned by the company. The 1990 impact of such a reduction was about $9 million. If the automation program were stretched out over a longer period, almost half of that interest income reduction would be postponed a year, thus adding $4 million to 1990 profits. The risk was that the automated plant would not be in operation in time to meet the expected competition.

4. Employee health insurance costs: Like all U.S. companies Dorrence was experiencing rapid escalation in the cost of its employee health insurance program. Dorrence paid 100% of the premium for its employees and 80% of the premiums for their dependents. After meeting certain deductibles, employees are reimbursed 80% to 90% of their medical and dental costs. The company's cost of maintaining the plan was budgeted to increase 22%, or $12 million in 1990. An important issue, therefore, was whether the plan should be changed to shift all or a portion of that cost increase to the employees through reducing the share of the premiums paid by the company, or increasing the deductibles, or reducing the percent reimbursement, or some combination of those changes.

5. Closing Dorrence's plant in Argentina: Dorrence had purchased a small pharmaceutical company in Argentina in the early 1950s when prospects for growth in the local market seemed excellent. However, in most years since then Argentina has been plagued by hyper-inflation. With rapidly rising wage rates and other local costs on the one hand, and strictly controlled selling prices for pharmaceuticals on the other hand, Dorrence's Argentine subsidiary had consistently lost money. The 1990 budget projected a loss of $4 million.

For the past year Dorrence had tried to find a buyer for its Argentine subsidiary who would utilize the existing Dorrence 120-person sales force and continue to operate Dorrence's Buenos Aires factory with its 250 employees. No such buyer had been found, but recently a local company had offered to purchase the rights to Dorrence's product line. It would manufacture them in its under-utilized plant and distribute them through its own sales force. If Dorrence accepted this offer, the 370 Dorrence employees in Argentina would be laid off. Dorrence had already created a financial reserve for the government-mandated severance payments. Thus if Dorrence decided to end its operations in Argentina, corporate profits would improve by $4 million in 1990.

6. *Price increase on principal product sold in the U.S.:* The budget proposed by Dorrence's U.S. pharmaceutical division already assumed a 5% price increase on all its current products at the end of the first quarter of the year, producing a $40 million increase in sales revenues. A substantially higher price increase on Libam, its largest selling product, could probably be implemented without adversely affecting sales volume. For example, if the budgeted price increase were 10% instead of 5%, an additional $12 million would be generated. Alternately, if two 5% price increases were implemented six months apart, Dorrence would earn $4 million above the proposed budget. Libam is used by chronically ill patients, many of them elderly. (See Exhibit 2 for a comparison of Libam's price with the prices of other drugs in the same therapeutic class.)

In most countries pharmaceutical prices are controlled by the government. The United States is one of the few countries in which pharmaceutical companies are free to decide what prices to charge for their drugs. Physicians generally prescribe the drug which they feel will be most beneficial to their patients regardless of price. Unless the patent on a drug has expired and a generic equivalent is available, the demand for a prescription drug is not very sensitive to its price. Consequently, drug prices in the United States are substantially higher than in most other countries. (See Exhibit 3)

Cunningham was, however, very conscious of the growing public concern about health care costs. Although drugs constitute only a small fraction of the nation's total health care bill, drug prices are an easily identified target and drug companies were coming increasingly under attack for their price increases. (See Exhibit 4)

7. *New Costa Rican manufacturing plant:* $10 million in sales of a new life-saving drug developed by Dorrence had been removed from the budget because of an unexpected problem at the new plant that had been constructed to produce the product.

Three years earlier Dorrence had chosen a small town in Costa Rica after evaluating various possible sites for the plant. The town had won the competition for the new plant because of the availability of inexpensive land, relatively low wages, certain tax concessions, and a promise by the local government to build a new municipal waste-treatment facility by the time the plant would be completed. In addition Dorrence felt it would be fulfilling its social responsibilities by providing jobs in an area of high unemployment.

A few days before Dorrence's budget meeting the company had learned that the completion of the municipal waste-treatment plant was delayed at least a year. Although Costa Rica's environmental regulations are less stringent than those of industrialized countries, local law does prohibit the discharge of untreated factory waste water into streams. Without a means of disposing of its waste water, the Dorrence plant could not operate.

A message from the Dorrence plant manager received yesterday seemed to solve the problem. The city sanitation commissioner had given Dorrence a special exemption which would allow it to discharge its waste water into a stream behind the plant until the city's waste-treatment facility was completed. Cunningham had immediately asked for a fuller report on the situation. The plant manager had sent the following additional details:

> The stream is used to irrigate sugarcane fields and small vegetable plots on which people in this area depend. There is, therefore, a chance that substances in the waste water would be absorbed by the crops that people are going to eat. I wonder if that is acceptable. On the other hand, I fear that all the good we have accomplished here will go down the drain if we don't begin manufacturing operations. Construction of the plant was completed on schedule three months ago. Building our own waste-treatment facility now would add $5 million to the cost of the plant and would take at least 12 months. I've already hired over 100 workers and have given them extensive training. We obviously can't pay the workers for a year to sit around in an idle plant. Losing their jobs would be devastating to them and the whole community. Besides, there is no other Dorrence facility or plant of another company which could accomplish the synthesis required for this product. Lots of people in the United States are anxiously waiting for this new drug.

8. Pricing of an important new product: Finally, there was the issue of what price to charge for another new Dorrence drug, Miracule, which was expected to be introduced late in the year. In most cases patients for whom Miracule was prescribed would require the drug for the rest of their lives, unless an even more effective drug became available. The budget had assumed a price which would result in a daily cost of $1.75 (including wholesaler and drugstore markups) for the average patient. A price of $2.50 would yield an additional $8 million profit to Dorrence during 1990 and far greater sums in subsequent years.

Despite the difficulties surrounding each of the issues Cunningham had identified, he felt it was critical that the 1990 budget be improved to call for 13% profit growth over 1989. He believed that a second year in a row of below-average profit growth would be viewed very negatively by the investment community, be demoralizing to the company's management, and could result in a substantial drop in the value of the company's stock as investors switched to pharmaceutical companies with better 1990 results. He also recognized that large institutional investors, such as pension funds, were taking a more active role in demanding better performance from the managements of the companies in which they invested the funds entrusted to them.

EXHIBIT 1. Dorrence Corporation: Financial & Other Data

	1979	1980	1981	1982	1983	1984	1985	1986	1987	1988	1989
Sales—$Millions	826	1,074	1,181	1,259	1,333	1,453	1,466	1,703	2,063	2,404	2,572
Profit*—$Millions	132	164	175	204	224	222	241	312	413	524	558
Profit* as % of Sales	16.0	15.3	14.8	16.2	16.8	15.3	16.4	18.3	20.0	21.8	21.7
Employees	12,500	12,900	13,500	13,600	13,800	14,000	13,300	13,100	13,500	13,900	14,700
Stockholders of Record	26,500	25,000	23,900	23,300	22,300	21,700	20,300	21,200	24,500	28,900	29,800

*After taxes.

193

EXHIBIT 2. Average* Daily Cost in the U.S. at Retail of Prescription Anti-inflammatory Drugs

Drug	Company	Average Daily Cost at Retail
Clinoril	Merck	$1.92
Ansaid	Upjohn	1.76
Feldene	Pfizer	1.67
Libam	Dorrence	1.61
Naprosyn	Syntex	1.59
Indocin	Merck	1.54
Voltaren	Ciba-Geigy	1.50
Motrin**	Upjohn	1.06
Ibuprofen (generic)	Boots	.67

*Assuming mid-range dosages.
**Branded form of ibuprofen.

EXHIBIT 3. Average Daily Cost of Libam at Retail in 10 Countries

United States	$1.61
Sweden	.96
Canada	.89
Italy	.86
Great Britain	.70
Japan	.70
France	.51
Spain	.40
Australia	.27
Mexico	.20

EXHIBIT 4. Price Increases for Major Drugs in the U.S. for the Past 12 Months

Company	Product	Price Versus One Year Ago ($ increase)
Pfizer	Procardia	20
Pfizer	Feldene	10
SmithKline Beecham	Dyazide	10
SmithKline Beecham	Tagamet	15
SmithKline Beecham	Augmentin	8
Syntex	Naprosyn	11
Merck	Vasotec	12
Merck	Mevacor	6
Marion	Cardizem	9
Marion	Carafate	7
Monsanto (Searle)	Calan SR	10
Bristol-Myers Squibb	Capoten	12
Bristol-Myers Squibb	Buspar	8
Ciba-Geigy	Voltaren	6
Glaxo	Zantac	6
Lilly	Prozac	19
Lilly	Ceclor	9
Upjohn	Xanax	22
Upjohn	Halcion	22
Warner-Lambert	Lopid	6

Source: Bear, Stearns & Co., Inc.

The Justification of Private Property

JOHN LOCKE

. . . God, who hath given the world to men in common, hath also given them reason to make use of it to the best advantage of life and convenience. The earth and all that is therein is given to men for the support and comfort of their being. And though all the fruits it naturally produces, and beasts it feeds, belong to mankind in common, as they are produced by the spontaneous hand of nature; and nobody has originally a private dominion exclusive of the rest of mankind in any of them as they are thus in their natural state; yet being given for the use of men, there must of necessity be a means to appropriate them some way or other before they can be of any use at all beneficial to any particular man. The fruit or venison which nourishes the wild Indian, who knows no enclosure, and is still a tenant in common, must be his, and so his,

Reprinted with the permission of Simon & Schuster, Inc. from the Macmillan College text *The Second Treatise of Government* by Locke, edited by Thomas P. Peardon. Copyright © 1952 by Macmillan College Publishing Company, Inc.

i.e., a part of him, that another can no longer have any right to it, before it can do any good for the support of his life.

Though the earth and all inferior creatures be common to all men, yet every man has a property in his own person; this nobody has any right to but himself. The labor of his body and the work of his hands we may say are properly his. Whatsoever, then, he removes out of the state that nature hath provided and left it in, he hath mixed his labor with, and joined to it something that is his own, and thereby makes it his property. It being by him removed from the common state nature placed it in, it hath by this labor something annexed to it that excludes the common right of other men. For this labor being the unquestionable property of the laborer, no man but he can have a right to what this is once joined to, at least where there is enough, and as good left in common for others.

He that is nourished by the acorns he picked up under an oak, or the apples he gathered from the trees in the wood, has certainly appropriated them to himself. Nobody can deny but the nourishment is his. I ask, then, When did they begin to be his—when he digested, or when he ate, or when he boiled, or when he brought them home, or when he picked them up? And 'tis plain if the first gathering made them not his, nothing else could. That labor put a distinction between them and common; that added something to them more than nature, the common mother of all, had done, and so they became his private right. And will anyone say he had no right to those acorns or apples he thus appropriated, because he had not the consent of all mankind to make them his? Was it robbery thus to assume to himself what belonged to all in common? If such a consent as that was necessary, man had starved, notwithstanding the plenty God had given him. We see in common which remains so by compact that 'tis the taking any part of what is common and removing it out of the state nature leaves it in, which begins the property; without which the common is of no use. And the taking of this or that does not depend on the express consent of all the commoners. Thus the grass my horse has bit, the turfs my servant has cut, the ore I have dug in any place where I have a right to them in common with others, become my property without the assignation or consent of anybody. The labor that was mine removing them out of that common state they were in, hath fixed my property in them. . . .

It will perhaps be objected to this, that if gathering the acorns, or other fruits of the earth, etc., makes a right to them, then anyone may engross as much as he will. To which I answer, Not so. The same law of nature that does by this means give us property, does also bound that property too. "God has given us all things richly" (1 Tim. vi. 17), is the voice of reason confirmed by inspiration. But how far has He given it us? To enjoy. As much as anyone can make use of any advantage of life before it spoils, so much he may by his labor fix a property in; whatever is beyond this, is more than his share, and belongs to others. Nothing was made by God for man to spoil or destroy. And thus considering the plenty of natural provisions there was a long time in the world, and the few spenders, and to how small a part of that provision the industry of one man could extend itself, and engross it to the prejudice of others—especially keeping within the bounds, set by reason, of what might serve for his use—there could be then little room for quarrels or contentions about property so established.

But the chief matter of property being now not the fruits of the earth, and the beasts that subsist on it, but the earth itself, as that which takes in and carries with it all the rest, I think it is plain that property in that, too, is acquired as the former. As much land as a man tills, plants, improves, cultivates, and can use the product of, so much is his property. He by his labor does as it were enclose it from the common. Nor will it invalidate his right to say, everybody else has an equal title to it; and therefore he cannot appropriate, he cannot enclose, without the consent of all his fellow-commoners, all mankind. God, when He gave the world in common to all mankind, commanded man also to labor, and the penury of his condition required it of him. God and his reason commanded him to subdue the earth, i.e., improve it for the benefit of life, and therein lay out something upon it that was his own, his labor. He that, in obedience to this command of God, subdued, tilled, and sowed any part of it, thereby annexed to it something that was his property, which another had no title to, nor could without injury take from him.

Nor was this appropriation of any parcel of land, by improving it, any prejudice to any other man, since there was still enough and as good left; and more than the yet unprovided could use. So that in effect, there was never the less left for others because of his enclosure for himself. For he that leaves as much as another can make use of, does as good as take nothing at all. Nobody could think himself injured by the drinking of another man, though he took a good draught, who had a whole river of the same water left him to quench his thirst; and the case of land and water, where there is enough of both, is perfectly the same.

God gave the world to men in common; but since He gave it them for their benefit, and the greatest conveniences of life they were capable to draw from it, it cannot be supposed He meant it should always remain common and uncultivated. He gave it to the use of the industrious and rational (and labor was to be his title to it), not to the fancy or coveteousness of the quarrelsome and contentious. He that had as good left for his improvement as was already taken up, needed not complain, ought not to meddle with what was already improved by another's labor; if he did, it is plain he desired the benefit of another's pains, which he had no right to, and not the ground which God had given him in common with others to labor on, and whereof there was as good left as that already possessed, and more than he knew what to do with, or his industry could reach to.

It is true, in land that is common in England, or any other country where there is plenty of people under Government, who have money and commerce, no one can enclose or appropriate any part without the consent of all his fellow-commoners: because this is left common by compact, i.e., by the law of the land, which is not to be violated. And though it be common in respect of some men, it is not so to all mankind; but is the joint property of this country, or this parish. Besides, the remainder, after such enclosure, would not be as good to the rest of the commoners as the whole was, when they could all make use of the whole, whereas in the beginning and first peopling of the great common of the world it was quite otherwise. The law man was under was rather for appropriating. God commanded, and his wants forced him, to labor. That was his property, which could not be taken from him wherever he had fixed it. And hence subduing or cultivating the earth, and having dominion, we see are joined together. The one gave title to the other. So that God, by commanding to subdue, gave authority so far to appropriate. And the condition of human life, which requires labor and materials to work on, necessarily introduces private possessions.

The measure of property nature has well set by the extent of men's labor and the conveniency of life. No man's labor could subdue or appropriate all, nor could his enjoyment consume more than a small part; so that it was impossible for any man, this way, to entrench upon the right of another or acquire to himself a property to the prejudice of his neighbor, who would still have room for as good and as large a possession (after the other had taken out his) as before it was appropriated. Which measure did confine every man's possession to a very moderate proportion, and such as he might appropriate to himself without injury to anybody in the first ages of the world, when men were more in danger to be lost, by wandering from their company, in the then vast wilderness of the earth than to be straitened for want of room to plant in. . . .

And thus, without supposing any private dominion and property in Adam over all the world, exclusive of all other men, which can no way be proved, nor any one's property be made out from it, but supposing the world, given as it was to the children of men in common, we see how labor could make men distinct titles to several parcels of it for their private uses, wherein there could be no doubt of right, no room for quarrel.

Nor is it so strange, as perhaps before consideration it may appear, that the property of labor should be able to overbalance the community of land. For it is labor indeed that puts the difference of value on everything; and let anyone consider what the difference is between an acre of land planted with tobacco or sugar, sown with wheat or barley, and an acre of the same land lying in common without any husbandry upon it, and he will find that the improvement of labor makes the far greater part of the value. I think it will be but a very modest computation to say that of the products of the earth useful to the life of man nine-tenths are the effects of labor; nay, if we will rightly estimate things as they come to our use, and cast up the several expenses about them—what in them is purely owing to nature, and what to labor—we shall find that in most of them ninety-nine hundredths are wholly to be put on the account of labor. . . .

From all which it is evident that, though the things of nature are given in common, yet man, by being master of himself and proprietor of his own person and the actions or labor of it, had still in himself the great foundation of property; and that which made up the great part of what he applied to the support or comfort of his being, when invention and arts had improved the conveniences of life, was perfectly his own, and did not belong in common to others.

Thus labor, in the beginning, gave a right of property, wherever anyone was pleased to employ it upon what was common, which remained a long while the far greater part, and is yet more than mankind makes use of. Men at first, for the most part, contented themselves with what unassisted nature offered to their necessities; and though afterwards, in some parts of the world (where the increase of people and stock, with the use of money, had made land scarce, and so of some value), the several communities settled the bounds of their distinct territories, and by laws within themselves, regulated the properties of the private men of their society, and so, by compact and agreement, settled the property which labor and industry began—and the leagues that have been made between several states and kingdoms, either expressly or tacitly disowning all claim and right to the land in the other's possession, have, by common consent, given up their pretenses to their natural common right, which originally they had to those countries; and so have, by positive agreement, settled a property amongst themselves in distant parts of the world—yet there are still great tracts of ground to be found which, the inhabitants thereof not having joined with the rest of mankind in the consent of the use of their common money, lie waste, and more than the people who dwell on it do or can make use of, and so still lie in common; though this can scarce happen amongst that part of mankind that have consented to the use of money.

The greatest part of things really useful to the life of man, and such as the necessity of subsisting made the first commoners of the world look after, as it doth the Americans now, are generally things of short duration, such as, if they are not consumed by use, will decay and perish of themselves: gold, silver, and diamonds are things that fancy or agreement have put the value on more than real use and the necessary support of life. Now of those good things which nature hath provided in common, everyone hath a right, as hath been said, to as much as he could use, and had a property in all he could effect with his labor—all that his industry could extend to, to alter from the state nature had put it in, was his. He that gathered a hundred bushels of acorns or apples had thereby a property in them; they were his goods as soon as gathered. He was only to look that he used them before they spoiled, else he took more than his share, and robbed others; and, indeed, it was a foolish thing, as well as dishonest, to hoard up more than he could make use of. If he gave away a part to anybody else, so that it perished not uselessly in his possession, these he also made use of; and if he also bartered away plums that would have rotted in a week, for nuts that would last good for his eating a whole year, he did no injury; he wasted not the common stock, destroyed no part of the portion of goods that belonged to others, so long as nothing perished uselessly in his hands. Again, if he would give his nuts for a piece of metal, pleased with its color, or exchange his sheep for shells, or wool for a sparkling pebble or a diamond, and keep those by him all his life, he invaded not the right of others; he might heap up as much as these durable things as he pleased, the exceeding of the bounds of his just property not lying in the largeness of his possessions, but the perishing of anything uselessly in it.

And thus came in the use of money—some lasting thing that men might keep without spoiling, and that, by mutual consent, men would take in exchange for the truly useful but perishable supports of life.

And as different degrees of industry were apt to give men possessions in different proportions, so this invention of money gave them the opportunity to continue and enlarge them; for supposing an island, separate from all possible commerce with the rest of the world, wherein there were but a hundred families—but there were sheep, horses, and cows, with other useful animals, wholesome fruits, and land enough for corn for a hundred thousand times as many, but nothing in the island, either because of its commonness or perishableness, fit to supply the place of money—what reason could anyone have there to enlarge his possessions beyond the use of his family and a plentiful supply to its consumption, either in what their own industry produced, or they could barter for like perishable useful commodities with others? Where there is not something both lasting and scarce, and so valuable to be hoarded up, there men will not be apt to enlarge their possessions of land, were it never so rich, never so free for them to take; for I ask, what would a man value ten thousand or a hundred thousand acres of excellent land, ready cultivated, and well stocked too with cattle, in the middle of the inland parts of America, where he had no hopes of commerce with other parts of the world, to draw money to him by the sale of the product? It would not be worth the enclosing, and we should see him give up again to the wild common of nature whatever was more than would supply the conveniences of life to be had there for him and his family.

Thus in the beginning all the world was America, and more so than that is now, for no such thing as money was anywhere known. Find out something that hath the use and value of money amongst his neighbors, you shall see the same man will begin presently to enlarge his possessions.

But since gold and silver, being little useful to the life of man in proportion to food, raiment, and carriage, has its value only from the consent of men, whereof labor yet makes, in great part, the measure, it is plain that the consent of men have agreed to a disproportionate and unequal possession of the earth—I mean out of the bounds of society and compact; for in governments the laws regulate it; they having, by consent, found out and agreed in a way how a man may rightfully and without injury possess more than he himself can make use of by receiving gold and silver, which may continue long in a man's possession, without decaying for the overplus, and agreeing those metals should have a value.

And thus, I think, it is very easy to conceive without any difficulty how labor could at first begin a title of property in the common things of nature, and how the spending it upon our uses bounded it; so that there could then be no reason of quarrelling about title, nor any doubt about the largeness of possession it gave. Right and conveniency went together; for as a man had a right to all he could employ his labor upon, so he had no temptation to labor for more than he could make use of. This left no room for controversy about the title, nor for encroachment on the right of others; what portion a man carved to himself was easily seen, and it was useless, as well as dishonest, to carve himself too much, or take more than he needed.

Alienated Labour

KARL MARX

We shall begin from a *contemporary* economic fact. The worker becomes poorer the more wealth he produces and the more his production increases in power and extent. The worker becomes an ever cheaper commodity the more goods he creates. The *devaluation* of the human world increases in direct relation with the *increase in value* of the world of things. Labour does not only create goods; it also produces itself and the worker as a *commodity*, and indeed in the same proportion as it produces goods. . . .

All these consequences follow from the fact that the worker is related to the *product of his labour* as to an *alien* object. For it is clear on this presupposition that the more the worker expends himself in work the more powerful becomes the world of objects which he creates in face of himself, the poorer he becomes in his inner life, and the less he belongs to himself. It is just the same as in religion. The more of himself man attributes to God the less he has left in himself. The worker puts his life into the object, and his life then belongs no longer to himself but to the object. The greater his activity, therefore, the less he possesses. What is embodied in the product of his labour is no longer his own. The greater this product is, therefore, the more he is diminished. The *alienation* of the worker in his product means not only that his labour becomes an object, assumes an *external* existence, but that it exists independently, *outside himself*, and alien to him, and that it stands opposed to him as an autonomous power. The life which he has given to the object sets itself against him as an alien and hostile force.

. . . The worker becomes a slave of the object; first, in that he receives an *object of work*, i.e. receives *work*, and secondly, in that he receives *means of subsistence*. Thus the object enables him to exist, first as a *worker* and secondly as a *physical subject*. The culmination of this enslavement is that he can only maintain himself as a *physical subject* so far as he is a *worker*, and that it is only as a *physical subject* that he is a worker. . . .

What constitutes the alienation of labour? First, that the work is *external* to the worker, and that it is not part of his nature; and that, consequently, he does not fulfill himself in his work but denies himself, has a feeling of misery rather than well-being, does not develop freely his mental and physical energies but is physically exhausted and mentally debased. The worker, therefore, feels himself at home only during his leisure time, whereas at work he feels homeless. His work is not voluntary but imposed, *forced labour*. It is not the satisfaction of a need, but only a *means* for satisfying other needs. Its alien character is clearly shown by the fact that as soon as there is no physical or other compulsion it is avoided like the plague. External labour, labour in which man alienates himself, is a labour of self-sacrifice, of mortification. Finally, the external character of work for the worker is shown by the fact that it is not his own work but work for someone else, that in work he does not belong to himself but to another person. . . .

We arrive at the result that man (the worker) feels himself to be freely active only in his animal functions—eating, drinking, and procreating, or at most also in his dwelling and in personal adornment—while in his human functions he is reduced to an animal. The animal becomes human and the human becomes animal.

Eating, drinking, and procreating are of course also genuine human functions. But abstractly considered, apart from the environment of human activities, and turned into final and sole ends, they are animal functions.

We have now considered the act of alienation of practical human activity, labour, from two aspects: (1) the relationship of the worker to the *product of labour* as an alien object which dominates him. This relationship is at the same time the relationship to the sensuous external world, to natural objects, as an alien and hostile world; (2) the relationship of labour to the *act of production* within *labour*. This is the relationship of the worker to his own activity as something alien and not belonging to him, activity as suffering (passivity), strength as powerlessness, creation as emasculation, the *personal* physical and mental energy of the worker, his personal life (for what is life but activity?), as an activity which is directed against himself, independent of him and not belonging to him. This is *self-alienation* as against the above-mentioned alienation of the *thing*.

We have now to infer a third characteristic of *alienated labour* from the two we have considered.

Man is a species-being not only in the sense that he makes the community (his own as well as those of other things) his object both practically and theoretically, but also (and this is simply another expression for the same thing) in the sense that he treats himself as the present, living species, as a *universal* and consequently free being.[1]

Species-life, for man as for animals, has its physical basis in the fact that man (like animals) lives from inorganic nature, and since man is more universal than an animal so the range of inorganic nature from which he lives is more universal. . . . The universality of man appears in practice in the universality which makes the whole of nature into his inorganic body: (1) as a direct means of life; and equally (2) as the material object and instrument of his life activity. Nature is the inorganic body of man; that is to say nature, excluding the human body itself. To say that man *lives* from nature means that nature is his *body* with which he must remain in a continuous interchange in order not to die. The statement that the physical and mental life of man, and nature, are interdependent means simply that nature is interdependent with itself, for man is a part of nature.

Since alienated labour: (1) alienates nature from man; and (2) alienates man from himself, from his own active function, his life activity; so it alienates him from the species. It makes *species-life* into a means of individual life. In the first place it alienates species-life and individual life, and secondly, it turns the latter, as an abstraction, into the purpose of the former, also in its abstract and alienated form.

For labour, *life activity, productive life*, now appear to man only as *means* for the satisfaction of a need, the need to maintain his physical existence. Productive life is, however, species-life. It is life creating life. In the type of life activity resides the whole character of a species, its species-character; and free, conscious activity is the species-character of human beings. Life itself appears only as a *means of life*.

The animal is one with its life activity. It does not distinguish the activity from itself. It is *its activity*. But man makes his life activity itself an object of his will and consciousness. He has a conscious life activity. It is not a determination with which he is completely identified. Conscious life activity distinguishes man from the life activity of animals. Only for this reason is he a species-being. Or rather, he is only a self-conscious being, i.e., for his own life is an object for him, because he is a species-being. Only for this reason is his activity free activity. Alienated labour reverses the relationship, in that man because he is a self-conscious being makes his life activity, his *being*, only a means for his *existence*.

The practical construction of an *objective world*, the *manipulation* of inorganic nature, is the confirmation of man as a conscious species-being, i.e., a being who treats the species as his own being or himself as a species-being. . . .

It is just in his work upon the objective world that man really proves himself as a *species-being*. This production is his active species-life. By means of it nature appears as *his* work and his reality. The object of labour is, therefore, the *objectification of man's species-life:* for he no longer reproduces himself merely intellectually, as in consciousness, but actively and in a real sense, and he sees his own reflection in a world which he has constructed. While, therefore, alienated labour takes away the object of production from man, it also takes away his *species-life*, his real objectivity as a species-being, and changes his advantage over animals into a disadvantage in so far as his inorganic body, nature, is taken from him.

Just as alienated labour transforms free and self-directed activity into a means, so it transforms the species-life of man into a means of physical existence.

Consciousness, which man has from his species, is transformed through alienation so that species-life becomes only a means for him. (3) Thus alienated labour turns the *species-life of man*, and also nature as his mental species-property, into an *alien* being and into a *means* for his *individual existence*. It alienates from man his own body, external nature, his mental life and his *human* life. (4) A direct consequence of the alienation of man from the product of his labour, from his life activity and from his species-life, is that *man is alienated* from other *men*. When man confronts himself he also confronts *other* men. What is true of man's relationship to his work, to the product of his work and to himself, is also true of his relationship to other men, to their labour and to the objects of their labour.

In general, the statement that man is alienated from his species-life means that each man is alienated from others, and that each of the others is likewise alienated from human life.

Human alienation, and above all the relation of man to himself, is first realized and expressed in the relationship between each man and other men. Thus in the relationship of alienated labour every man regards other men according to the standards and relationships in which he finds himself placed as a worker.

We began with an economic fact, the alienation of the worker and his production. We have expressed this fact in conceptual terms as *alienated labour*, and in analysing the concept we have merely analysed an economic fact. . . .

The *alien* being to whom labour and the product of labour belong, to whose service labour is devoted, and to whose enjoyment the product of labour goes, can only be *man* himself. If the product of labour does not belong to the worker, but confronts him as an alien power, this can only be because it belongs to *a man other than the worker*. . . .

Thus, through alienated labour the worker creates the relation of another man, who does not work and is outside the work process, to this labour. The relation of the workers to work also produces the relation of the capitalist (or whatever one likes to call the lord of labour) to work. *Private property* is, therefore, the product, the necessary result, of *alienated labour*, of the external relation of the worker to nature and to himself.

Private property is thus derived from the analysis of the concept of *alienated labor;* that is, alienated man, alienated labour, alienated life, and estranged man.

We have, of course, derived the concept of *alienated labour* (*alienated life*) from political economy, from the analysis of the *movement of private property*. But the analysis of this concept shows that although private property appears to be the basis and cause of alienated labour, it is rather a consequence of the latter, just as the gods are *fundamentally* not the cause but the product of confusion of human reason. At a later stage, however, there is a reciprocal influence.

Only in the final state of the development of private property is its secret revealed, namely, that it is on one hand the *product* of alienated labour, and on the other hand the *means* by which labour is alienated, *the realization of this alienation*. . . .

Just as *private property* is only the sensuous expression of the fact that man is at the same time an *objective* fact for himself and becomes an alien and non-human object for himself; just as his manifestation of life is also his alienation of life and his self-realization a loss of reality, the emergence of an *alien* reality; so the positive supersession of private property, i.e., the *sensuous* appropriation of the human essence and of human life, of objective man and of human *creations*, by and for man, should not be taken only in the sense of *immediate*, exclusive *enjoyment*, or only in the sense of *possession* or *having*. Man appropriates his manifold being in an all-inclusive way, and thus as a whole man. All his *human* relations to the world—seeing, hearing, smelling, tasting, touching, thinking, observing, feeling, desiring, acting, loving—in short, all the organs of his individuality, like the organs which are directly communal in form, are in their objective action (their *action in relation to the object*) the appropriation of this object, the appropriation of human reality. The way in which they react to the object is the confirmation of *human reality*. It is human effectiveness and human *suffering*, for suffering humanly considered is an enjoyment of the self for man.

Private property has made us so stupid and partial that an object is only *ours* when we have it, when it exists for us as capital or when it is directly eaten, drunk, worn, inhabited, etc., in short, *utilized* in some way. But private property itself only conceives these various forms of possession as *means of life*, and the life for which they serve as means is the life of *private property*—labour and creation of capital.

The supersession of private property is, therefore, the complete *emancipation* of all the human qualities and senses. It is such an emancipation because these qualities and senses have become *human*, from the subjective as well as the objective point of view. The eye has become a *human* eye when its *object* has become a *human*, social object, created by man and destined for him. The senses have, therefore, become directly theoreticians in practice. They relate themselves to the thing for the sake of the thing, but the thing itself is an *objective human* relation to itself and to man, and vice versa. Need and enjoyment have thus lost their *egoistic* character and nature has lost its mere *utility* by the fact that its utilization has become *human* utilization. . . .

Note

1. In this passage Marx reproduces Feuerbach's argument in *Das Wesen des Christentums.*

Benefits of the Profit Motive

ADAM SMITH

BOOK I

Of the causes of improvement in the productive powers of labor and of the order according to which its produce is naturally distributed among the different ranks of the people

Chapter I   Of the Division of Labor

The greatest improvement in the productive powers of labor, and the greater part of the skill, dexterity, and judgment with which it is anywhere directed, or applied, seem to have been the effects of the division of labor. . . .

To take an example, therefore, from a very trifling manufacture; but one in which the division of labor has been very often taken notice of, the trade of the pin-maker; a workman not educated to this business (which the division of labor has rendered a distinct trade), nor acquainted with the use of the machinery employed in it (to the invention of which the same division of labor has probably given occasion), could scarce, perhaps, with his utmost industry, make one pin in a day, and certainly could not make twenty. But in the way in which this business is now carried on, not only the whole work is a peculiar trade, but it is divided into a number of branches, of which the greater part are likewise peculiar trades. One man draws out the wire, another straights it, a third cuts it, a fourth points it, a fifth grinds it at the top for receiving the head; to make the head requires two or three distinct operations; to put it on is a peculiar business, to whiten the pins is another; it is even a trade by itself to put them into the paper; and the important business of making a pin is, in this manner, divided into about eighteen distinct operations, which in some manufactories, are all performed by distinct hands, though in others the same man will sometimes perform two or three of them. I have seen a small manufactory of this kind where ten men only were employed, and where some of them consequently performed two or three distinct operations. But though they were very poor, and therefore but indifferently accommodated with the necessary machinery, they could, when they exerted themselves, make among them about twelve pounds of pins a day. There are in a pound upwards of four thousand pins of a middling size. Those ten persons, therefore, could make among them upwards of forty-eight thousand pins in a day. Each person, therefore, making a tenth part of forty-eight thousand pins, might be considered as mak-

From Adam Smith, *The Wealth of Nations*, Books I and IV (1776; rpt. Chicago: University of Chicago Press, 1976).

ing four thousand eight hundred pins in a day. But if they had all wrought separately and independently, and without any of them having been educated to this peculiar business, they certainly could not each of them have made twenty, perhaps not one pin in a day; that is, certainly, not the two hundred and fortieth, perhaps not the four thousand eight hundredth part, of what they are at present capable of performing in consequence of a proper division and combination of their different operations.

In every other art and manufacture, the effects of the division of labor are similar to what they are in this very trifling one; though in many of them, the labor can neither be so much subdivided, nor reduced to so great a simplicity of operation. The division of labor, however, so far as it can be introduced, occasions, in every art, a proportionate increase of the productive powers of labor. . . .

This great increase of the quantity of work, which in consequence of the division of labor, the same number of people are capable of performing, is owing to three different circumstances: first, to the increase of dexterity in every particular workman; secondly, to the saving of the time which is commonly lost in passing from one species of work to another; and lastly, to the invention of a great number of machines which facilitate and abridge labor, and enable one man to do the work of many.

First, the improvement of the dexterity of the workman necessarily increases the quantity of the work he can perform; and the division of labor, by reducing every man's business to some one simple operation and by making this operation the sole employment of his life, necessarily increases very much the dexterity of the workman. A common smith, who, though accustomed to handle the hammer, has never been used to make nails, if upon some particular occasion he is obliged to attempt it, will scarce, I am assured, be able to make about two or three hundred nails in a day, and those too very bad ones. A smith who has been accustomed to make nails, but whose sole or principal business has not been that of a nailer, can seldom with his utmost diligence make more than eight hundred or a thousand nails in a day. I have seen several boys under twenty years of age who had never exercised any other trade but that of making nails, and who, when they exerted themselves, could make, each of them, upwards of two thousand three hundred nails in a day. The making of a nail, however, is by no means one of the simplest operations. The same person blows the bellows, stirs or mends the fire as there is occasion, heats the iron, and forges every part of the nail: In forging the head too he is obliged to change his tools. The different operations into which the making of a pin or of a metal button is subdivided, are all of them much more simple; and the dexterity of the person, of whose life it has been the sole business to perform them, is usually much greater. The rapidity with which some of the operations of those manufacturers are performed exceeds what the human hand could, by those who had never seen them, be supposed capable of acquiring.

Secondly, the advantage which is gained by saving the time commonly lost in passing from one sort of work to another is much greater than we should at first view be apt to imagine it. It is impossible to pass very quickly from one kind of work to another, that is carried on in a different place, and with quite different tools. A country weaver who cultivates a small farm must lose a good deal of time in passing from his loom to the field, and from the field to his loom. When the two trades can be carried on in the same workhouse, the loss of time is no doubt much less. It is even in this case, however, very considerable. . . .

Thirdly, and lastly, every body must be sensible how much labor is facilitated and abridged by the application of proper machinery. . . .

. . . A great part of the machines made use of in those manufactures in which labor is most subdivided were originally the inventions of common workmen, who, being each of them employed in some very simple operation, naturally turned their thoughts toward finding out easier and readier methods of performing it. Whoever has been much accustomed to visit such manufacturers must frequently have been shown very pretty machines which were inventions of such workmen in order to facilitate and quicken their own particular part of the work. In the first fire-engines, a boy was constantly employed to open and shut alternately the communication between the boiler and the cylinder, according as the piston either ascended or descended. One of those boys, who loved to play with his companions, observed that, by tying a string from the handle of the valve which opened this communication to another part of the machine, the valve would open and shut without his assistance, and leave him at liberty to divert himself with his play-fellows. One of the greatest improvements that has been made upon this machine, since it was first invented, was in this manner the discovery of a boy who wanted to save his own labor. . . .

It is the great multiplication of the productions of all the different arts, in consequence of the division of labor, which occasions, in a well-governed society, that universal opulence which extends itself to the lowest ranks of the people. Every workman has a great quantity of his own work to dispose of beyond what he himself has occasion for; and every other workman being exactly in the same situation, he is enabled to exchange a great quantity of his own goods for a great quantity, or, what comes to the same thing, for the price of a great quantity of theirs. He supplies them abundantly with what they have occasion for, and they accommodate him as amply with what he has occasion for, and a general plenty diffuses itself through all the different ranks of the society. . . .

Chapter II   Of the Principle Which Gives Occasion to the Division of Labor

This division of labor, from which so many advantages are derived, is not originally the effect of any human wisdom which forsees and intends that general opulence to which it gives occasion. It is the necessary, though very slow and gradual, consequence of a certain propensity in human nature which has in view no such extensive utility: the propensity to truck, barter, and exchange one thing for another.

. . . In almost every other race of animals each individual, when it is grown up to maturity, is entirely independent, and in its natural state has occasion for the assistance of no other living creature. But man has almost constant occasion for the help of his brethren, and it is in vain for him to expect it from their benevolence only. He will be more likely to prevail if he can interest their self-love in his favor, and show them that it is for their own advantage to do for him what he requires of them. Whoever offers to another a bargain of any kind, proposes to do this. Give me that which I want, and you shall have this which you want, is the meaning of every such offer; and it is in the manner that we obtain from one another the far greater part of those good offices which we stand in need of. It is not from the benevolence of the butcher, the brewer, or the baker, that we expect our dinner, but from their regard to their own interest. We address ourselves, not to their humanity but to their self-love, and never talk to them of our own necessities but of their advantages. Nobody but a beggar chooses to depend chiefly upon the benevolence of his fellow-citizens. Even a beggar does not depend upon it entirely. The charity of well-disposed people, indeed, supplies him with the whole fund of his subsistence. But though this principle ultimately provides him with all the necessaries of life which he has occasion for, it neither does nor can provide him with them as he has occasion for them. The greater part of his occasional wants are supplied in the same manner as those of other people, by treaty, by barter, and by purchase. With the money which one man gives him he purchases food. The old clothes which another bestows upon him he exchanges for other old clothes which suit him better, or for lodging, or for food, or for money, with which he can buy either food, clothes, or lodging, as he has occasion.

As it is by treaty, by barter, and by purchase that we obtain from one another the greater part of those mutual good offices which we stand in need of, so it is this same trucking disposition which originally gives occasion to the division of labor. In a tribe of hunters or shepherds a particular person makes bows and arrows, for example, with more readiness and dexterity than any other. He frequently exchanges them for cattle or for venison with his companions; and he finds at last that he can in this manner get more cattle and venison than if he himself went to the field to catch them. From a regard to his own interest, therefore, the making of bows and arrows grows to be his chief business, and he becomes a sort of armorer. Another excels in making the frames and covers of their little huts or moveable houses. He is accustomed to be of use in this way to his neighbors, who reward him in the same manner with cattle and with venison till at last he finds it his interest to dedicate himself entirely to this employment, and to become a sort of house carpenter. In the same manner a third becomes a smith or a brazier; a fourth a tanner or dresser of hides or skins, the principal part of the clothing of savages. And thus the certainty of being able to exchange all that surplus part of the produce of his own labor, which is over and above his own consumption, for such parts of the produce of other men's labor as he may have occasion for, encourages every man to apply himself to a particular occupation, and to cultivate and bring to perfection whatever talent or genius he may possess for that particular species of business.

The difference of natural talents in different men is, in reality, much less than we are aware of; and the very different genius which appears to distinguish men of different professions, when grown up to maturity, is not upon many occasions so much the cause as the effect of the division of labor. The difference between the most dissimilar characters, between a philosopher and a common street porter, for example, seems to arise not so much from nature as from habit, custom, and education. When they came into the world, and for the first six or eight years of their existence, they were, perhaps, very much alike, and neither their parents nor play-fellows could perceive any remarkable difference. About that age, or soon after, they come to be employed in very different occupations. The difference of talents comes then to be taken notice of, and widens by degrees, till at last the vanity of the philosopher is willing to acknowledge scarce any resemblance. But without the disposition to truck, barter, and exchange, every man must have procured to himself every necessary and conveniency of life which he wanted. All must have had the same duties to perform, and the same work to do, and there could have been no such difference of employment as could alone give occasion to any great difference of talents. . . .

BOOK IV

Chapter II

Every individual is continually exerting himself to find out the most advantageous employment for whatever capital he can command. It is his own advantage, indeed, and not that of the society, which he has in view. But the study of his own advantage, naturally, or rather necessarily, leads him to prefer that employment which is most advantageous to the society. . . .

As every individual, therefore, endeavours as much as he can both to employ his capital in the support of domestic industry, and so to direct that industry that its produce may be of the greatest value, every individual necessarily labors to render the annual revenue of the society as great as he can. He generally, indeed, neither intends to promote the public interest, nor knows how much he is promoting it. By preferring the support of domestic to that of foreign industry, he intends only his own security: and by directing that industry in such a manner as its produce may be of the greatest value, he intends only his own gain, and he is in this, as in many other cases, led by an invisible hand to promote an end which was no part of his intention. Nor is it always the worse for society that it was no part of it. By pursuing his own interest he frequently promotes that of the society more effectually than when he really intends to promote it. I have never known much good done by those who affected to trade for the public good. It is an affectation, indeed, not very common among merchants, and very few words need by employed in dissuading them from it.

Wealth

ANDREW CARNEGIE

This article is one of the clearest attempts to justify Social Darwinism. Written in 1889, it defends the pursuit of wealth by arguing that society is strengthened and

First published in the *North American Review,* June 1889.

improved through the struggle for survival in the marketplace. Interestingly, it was written by one of the world's wealthiest men, Andrew Carnegie, who came to the United States as a poor immigrant boy and quickly rose to enormous power. He began his career as a minor employee in a telegraph company, but emerged in a few years as a superintendent of the Pennsylvania Railroad. After the Civil War he entered the iron and steel business, and by 1889 he controlled eight companies, which he eventually consolidated into the Carnegie Steel Corporation. Shortly before he died, he merged the Carnegie Steel Corporation with the United States Steel Company.

Carnegie took seriously the task of managing his vast fortune, and he made use of many of the ideas which are presented in the following article. He gave generously to many causes, including public libraries, public education, and the development of international peace.

• • •

The problem of our age is the proper administration of wealth, so that the ties of brotherhood may still bind together the rich and poor in harmonious relationship. The conditions of human life have not only been changed, but revolutionized, within the past few hundred years. In former days there was little difference between the dwelling, dress, food, and environment of the chief and those of his retainers. The Indians are today where civilized man then was. When visiting the Sioux, I was led to the wigwam of the chief. It was just like the others in external appearance, and even within the difference was trifling between it and those of the poorest of his braves. The contrast between the palace of the millionaire and the cottage of the laborer with us today measures the change which has come into civilization.

This change, however, is not to be deplored, but welcomed as highly beneficial. It is well, nay essential, for the progress of the race, that the houses of some should be homes for all that is highest and best in literature and art, and for all the refinements of civilization, rather than that none should be so. Much better this great irregularity than universal squalor. Without wealth there can be no Maecenases. When these apprentices rose to be masters, there was little or no change in their mode of life, and they, in turn, educated in the same routine succeeding apprentices. There was, substantially, social equality, and even political equality, for those engaged in industrial pursuits had then little or no political voice in the State.

But the inevitable result of such a mode of manufacture was crude articles at high prices. Today the world obtains commodities of excellent quality at prices which even the generation preceding this would have deemed incredible. In the commercial world similar causes have produced similar results, and the race is benefited thereby. The poor enjoy what the rich could not before afford. What were the luxuries have become the necessaries of life. The laborer has now more comforts than the farmer had a few generations ago. The farmer has more luxuries than the landlord had, and is more richly clad and better housed. The landlord has books and pictures rarer, and appointments more artistic, than the King could then obtain.

The price we pay for this salutary change is, no doubt, great. We assemble thousands of operatives in the factory, in the mine, and in the counting-house, of whom the employer can know little or nothing, and to whom the employer is little better than a myth. All intercourse between them is at an end. Rigid Castes are formed, and, as usual, mutual ignorance breeds mutual distrust. Each Caste is without sympathy for the other, and ready to credit anything disparaging in regard to it. Under the law of competition, the employer of thousands is forced into the strictest economies, among which the rates paid to labor figure prominently, and often there is friction between the employer and the employed, between capital and labor, between rich and poor. Human society loses homogeneity.

The price which society pays for the law of competition, like the price it pays for cheap comforts and luxuries, is also great; but the advantages of this law are greater still, for it is to this law that we owe our wonderful material development, which brings improved conditions in its train. But, whether the law be benign or not, we must say of it, as we say of the change in the conditions of men to which we have referred: It is here; we cannot evade it; no substitutes for it have been found; and while the law may be sometimes hard for the individual, it is best for the race, because it insures the survival of the fittest in every department. We accept and welcome, therefore, as conditions to which we must accommodate ourselves, great inequality of environment, the concentration of business, industrial and commercial, in the hands of a few, and the law of competition between these, as being not only beneficial, but essential for the future progress of the race. Having accepted these, it follows that there must be great scope for the exercise of special ability in the merchant and in the manufacturer who has to conduct affairs upon a great scale. That this talent for organization and management is rare among men is proved by the fact that it invariably secures for its possessor enormous rewards, no matter where or under what laws or conditions. The experienced in affairs always rate the man whose services can be obtained as a partner as not only the first consideration, but such as to render the question of his capital scarcely worth considering, for such men soon create capital; while, without the special talent required, capital soon takes wings. Such men become interested in firms or corporations using millions; and estimating only simple interest to be made upon the capital invested, it is inevitable that their income must exceed their expenditures, and that they must accumulate wealth. Nor is there any middle ground which such men can occupy, because the great manufacturing or commercial concern which does not earn at least interest upon its capital soon becomes bankrupt. It must either go forward or fall behind: to stand still is impossible. It is a condition essential for its successful operation that it should be thus far profitable, and even that, in addition to interest on capital, it should make a profit. It is a law, as certain as any of the others named, that men possessed of this peculiar talent for affairs, under the free play of economic forces, must, of necessity, soon be in receipt of more revenue than can be judiciously expended upon themselves, and this law is as beneficial for the race as the others.

Objections to the foundations upon which society is based are not in order, because the condition of the race is better with these than it has been with any others which have been tried. Of the effect of any new substitutes proposed we cannot be sure. The Socialist or Anarchist who seeks to overturn present conditions is to be regarded as attacking the foundation upon which civilization itself rests, for civilization took its start from the day that the capable, industrious workman said to his incompetent and lazy fellow, "If thou dost not sow, thou shalt not reap," and thus ended primitive Communism by separating the drones from the bees. One who studies this subject will soon be brought face to face with the conclusion that upon the sacredness of property civilization itself depends—the right of the laborer to his hundred dollars in the savings bank, and equally the legal right of the millionaire to his millions. To those who propose to substitute Communism for this intense Individualism the answer, therefore, is: The race has tried that. All progress from that barbarous day to the present time has resulted from its displacement. Not evil, but good, has come to the race from the accumulation of wealth by those who have the ability and energy that produce it. But even if we admit for a moment that it might be better for the race to discard its present foundations, Individualism—that it is a nobler ideal that man should labor, not for himself alone, but in and for a brotherhood of his fellows, and share with them all in common, realizing Swedenborg's idea of Heaven, where, as he says, the angels derive their happiness, not from laboring for self, but for each other—even admit all this, and a sufficient answer is, This is not evolution, but revolution. It necessitates the changing of human nature itself—a work of aeons, even if it were good to change it, which we cannot know. It is not practicable in our day or in our age. Even if desirable theoretically, it belongs to another and long-succeeding sociological stratum. Our duty is with what is practicable now; with the next step possible in our day and generation. It is criminal to waste our energies in endeavoring to uproot, when all we can profitably or possibly accomplish is to bend the universal tree of humanity a little in the direction most favorable to the production of good fruit under existing circumstances. We might as well urge the destruction of the highest existing type of man because he failed to reach our ideal as to favor the destruction of Individualism, Private Property, the Law of Accumulation of Wealth, and the Law of Competition; for these are the highest results of human experience, the soil in which society so far has produced the best fruit. Unequally or unjustly, perhaps, as these laws sometimes operate, and imperfect as they appear to the Idealist, they are nevertheless, like the highest type of man, the best and most valuable of all that humanity has yet accomplished.

We start, then, with a condition of affairs under which the best interests of the race are promoted, but which inevitably gives wealth to the few. Thus far, accepting conditions as they exist, the situation can be surveyed and pronounced good. The question then arises—and, if the foregoing be correct, it is the only question with which we have to deal—What is the proper mode of administering wealth after the laws upon which civilization is founded have thrown it into the hands of the few? And it is of this great question that I believe I offer the true solution. It will be understood that *fortunes* are here spoken of, not moderate sums saved by many years of effort, the returns from which are required for the comfortable maintenance and education of families. This is not *wealth*, but only *competence*, which it should be the aim of all to acquire.

. . . Indeed, it is difficult to set bounds to the share of a rich man's estate which should go at his death to the public through the agency of the state, and by all means such taxes should be graduated, beginning at nothing upon moderate sums to dependents, and increasing rapidly as the amounts swell, until of the millionaire's hoard, as of Shylock's at least

"_____The other half
Comes to the privy coffer of the state."

This policy would work powerfully to induce the rich man to attend to the administration of wealth during his life, which is the end that society should always have in view, as being that by far most fruitful for the people. Nor need it be feared that this policy would sap the root of enterprise and render men less anxious to accumulate, for to the class whose ambition it is to leave great fortunes and be talked about after their death, it will attract more attention, and, indeed, be a somewhat nobler ambition to have enormous sums paid over to the state from their fortunes.

There remains, then, only one mode of using great fortunes; but in this we have the true antidote for the temporary unequal distribution of wealth, the reconciliation of the rich and the poor—a reign of harmony—another ideal, differing, indeed, from that of the Communist in requiring only the further evolution of existing conditions, not the total overthrow of our civilization. It is founded upon the present most intense individualism, and the race is prepared to put it in practice by degrees whenever it pleases. Under its sway we shall have an ideal state, in which the surplus wealth of the few will become, in the best sense, the property of the many, because administered for the common good, and this wealth, passing through the hands of the few, can be made a much more potent force for the elevation of our race than if it had been distributed in small sums to the people themselves. Even the poorest can be made to see this, and to agree that great sums gathered by some of their fellow-citizens and spent for public purposes, from which the masses reap the principal benefit, are more valuable to them than if scattered among them through the course of many years in trifling amounts.

The best uses to which surplus wealth can be put have already been indicated. Those who would administer wisely must, indeed, be wise, for one of the serious obstacles to the improvement of our race is indiscriminate charity. It were better for mankind that the millions of the rich were thrown into the sea than so spent as to encourage the slothful, the drunken, the unworthy. Of every thousand dollars spent in so-called charity today, it is probable that $950 is unwisely spent; so spent, indeed, as to produce the very evils which it proposes to mitigate or cure. A well-known writer of philosophic books admitted the other day that he had given a quarter of a dollar to a man who approached him as he was coming to visit the house of his friend. He knew nothing of the habits of this beggar; knew not the use that would be made of this money, although he had every reason to suspect that it would be spent improperly. This man professed to be a disciple of Herbert Spencer; yet the quarter-dollar given that night will probably work more injury than all the money which its thoughtless donor will ever be able to give in true charity will do good. He only gratified his own feelings, saved himself from annoyance—and this was probably one of the most selfish and very worst actions of his life, for in all respects he is most worthy.

In bestowing charity, the main consideration should be to help those who will help themselves; to provide part of the means by which those who desire to improve may do so; to give those who desire to rise the aids by which they may rise; to assist, but rarely or never to do all. Neither the individual nor the race is improved by alms-giving. Those worthy of assistance, except in rare cases, seldom require assistance. The really valuable men of the race never do, except in cases of accident or sudden change. Everyone has, of course, cases of individuals brought to his own knowledge where temporary assistance can do genuine good, and these he will not overlook. But the amount which can be wisely given by the individual for individuals is necessarily limited by his lack of knowledge of the circumstance connected with each. He is the only true reformer who is as careful and as anxious not to aid the unworthy as he is to aid the worthy, and perhaps, even more so, for in alms-giving more injury is probably done by rewarding vice than by relieving virtue.

Thus is the problem of Rich and Poor to be solved. The laws of accumulation will be left free; the laws of distribution free. Individualism will continue, but the millionaire will be but a trustee for the poor; entrusted for a season with a great part of the increased wealth of the community, but administrating it for the community far better than it could or would have done for itself. The best minds will thus have reached a stage in the development of the race in which it is clearly seen that there is no mode of disposing of surplus wealth creditable to thoughtful and earnest men into whose hands it flows save by using it year by year for the general mood. This day already dawns. But a little while, and although, without incurring the pity of their fellows, men may die sharers in great business enterprises from which their capital cannot be or has not been withdrawn, and is left chiefly at death for public uses, yet the man who dies leaving behind him millions of available wealth, which was his to administer during life, will pass away "unwept, unhonored, and unsung," no matter to what uses he leaves the dross which he cannot take with him. Of such as these the public verdict will then be: "The man who dies thus rich dies disgraced."

Such, in my opinion, is the true Gospel concerning Wealth, obedience to which is destined some day to solve the problems of the Rich and the Poor, and to bring "Peace on earth, among men Good-Will."

Property and Profit: Modern Discussions

• *Case Study* •

Merck & Co., Inc.

THE BUSINESS ENTERPRISE TRUST

In 1978, Dr. P. Roy Vagelos, then head of the Merck research labs, received a provocative memorandum from a senior researcher in parasitology, Dr. William C. Campbell. Dr. Campbell had made an intriguing observation while working with ivermectin, a new antiparasitic compound under investigation for use in animals.

Campbell thought that ivermectin might be the answer to a disease called river blindness that plagued millions in the Third World. But to find out if Campbell's hypothesis had merit, Merck would have to spend millions of dollars to develop the right formulation for human use and to conduct the field trials in the most remote parts of the world. Even if these efforts produced an effective and safe drug, virtually all of those afflicted with river blindness could not afford to buy it. Vagelos, originally a university researcher but by then a Merck executive, had to decide whether to invest in research for a drug that, even if successful, might never pay for itself.

River Blindness

River blindness, formally known as *onchocerciasis*, was a disease labeled by the World Health Organization (WHO) as a public health and socioeconomic problem of considerable magnitude in over 35 developing countries throughout the Third World. Some 85 million people in thousands of tiny settlements throughout Africa and parts of the Middle East and Latin America were thought to be at risk. The cause: a parasitic worm carried by a tiny black fly which bred along fast-moving rivers. When the flies bit humans—a single person could be bitten thousands of times a day—the larvae of a parasitic worm, *Onchocerca volvulus*, entered the body.

These worms grew to more than two feet in length, causing grotesque but relatively innocuous nodules in the skin. The real harm began when the adult worms reproduced, releasing millions of microscopic offspring, known as microfilariae, which swarmed through body tissue. A terrible itching resulted, so bad that some victims committed suicide. After several years, the microfilariae caused lesions and depigmentation of the skin. Eventually they invaded the eyes, often causing blindness.

The World Health Organization estimated in 1978 that some 340,000 people were blind because of onchocerciasis, and that a million more suffered from varying degrees of visual impairment. At that time, 18 million or more people were infected with the parasite, though half did not yet have serious symptoms. In some villages close to fly-breeding sites, nearly all residents were infected and a majority of those over age 45 were blind. In such places, it was said, children believed that severe itching, skin infections and blindness were simply part of growing up.

In desperate efforts to escape the flies, entire villages abandoned fertile areas near rivers, and moved to poorer land. As a result, food shortages were frequent. Community life disintegrated as new burdens arose for already impoverished families.

The disease was first identified in 1893 by scientists and in 1926 was found to be related to the black flies. But by the 1970s, there was still no cure that could safely be used for community-wide treatment. Two drugs, diethylcarbamazine (DEC) & Suramin, were useful in killing the parasite, but both had severe side effects in infected individuals, needed close monitoring, and had even caused deaths. In 1974, the Onchocerciasis Control Program was created to be administered by the World Health Organization, in the hope that the flies could be killed through spraying of larvacides at breeding sites, but success was slow and uncertain. The flies in many areas developed resistance to the treatment, and were also known to disappear and then reinfest areas.

Merck & Co., Inc.

Merck & Co., Inc. was, in 1978, one of the largest producers of prescription drugs in the world. Headquartered in Rahway, New Jersey, Merck traced its origins to Germany in 1668 when Friedrich Jacob Merck purchased an apothecary in the city of Darmstadt. Over three hundred years later, Merck, having become an American firm, employed over 28,000 people and had operations all over the world.

In the late 1970s, Merck was coming off a 10-year drought in terms of new products. For nearly a decade, the company had relied on two prescription drugs for a significant percentage of its approximately $2 billion in annual sales: Indocin, a treatment for rheumatoid arthritis, and Aldomet, a treatment for high blood pressure. Henry W. Gadsden, Merck's chief executive from 1965 to 1976, along with his successor, John J. Horan, were concerned that the 17-year patent protection on Merck's two big moneymakers would soon expire, and began investing an enormous amount in research.

Merck management spent a great deal of money on research because it knew that its success ten and twenty years in the future critically depended upon present investments. The company deliberately fashioned a corporate culture to nurture the most creative, fruitful research. Merck scientists were among the best-paid in the industry, and were given great latitude to pursue intriguing leads. Moreover, they were inspired to think of their work as a quest to alleviate human disease and suffering world-wide. Within certain proprietary constraints, researchers were encouraged to publish in academic journals and to share ideas with their scientific peers. Nearly a billion dollars was spent between 1975 and 1978, and the investment paid off. In that period, under the direction of head of research, Dr. P. Roy Vagelos, Merck introduced Clinoril, a painkiller for arthritis; a general antibiotic called Mefoxin; a drug for glaucoma named Timoptic; and Ivomec (ivermectin, MSD), an antiparasitic for cattle.

In 1978, Merck had sales of $1.98 billion and net income of $307 million. Sales had risen steadily between 1969 and 1978 from $691 million to almost $2 billion. Income during the same period rose from $106 million to over $300 million. (See Exhibit 1 for a 10-year summary of performance.)

At that time, Merck employed 28,700 people, up from 22,200 ten years earlier. Human and animal health products constituted 84% of the company's sales, with environmental health products and services representing an additional 14% of sales. Merck's foreign sales had grown more rapidly during the 1970s than had domestic sales, and in 1978 represented 47% of total sales. Much of the company's research operations were organized separately as the Merck Sharp & Dohme Research Laboratories, headed by Vagelos. Other Merck operations included the Merck Sharp & Dohme Division, the Merck Sharp & Dohme International Division, Kelco Division, Merck Chemical Manufacturing Division, Merck Animal Health Division, Calgon Corporation, Baltimore Aircoil Company, and Hubbard Farms.

The company had 24 plants in the United States, including one in Puerto Rico, and 44 in other countries. Six research laboratories were located in the United States and four abroad.

While Merck executives sometimes squirmed when they quoted the "unbusinesslike" language of George W. Merck, son of the company's founder and its former chairman, there could be no doubt that Merck employees found the words inspirational. "We try never to forget that medicine is for the people," Merck said. "It is not for the profits. The profits follow, and if we have remembered that, they have never failed to appear. The better we have remembered it, the larger they have been." These words formed the basis of Merck's overall corporate philosophy.

The Drug Investment Decision

Merck invested hundreds of millions of dollars each year in research. Allocating those funds amongst various projects, however, was a rather involved and inexact process. At a company as large as Merck, there was never a single method by which projects were approved or money distributed.

Studies showed that, on the average, it took 12 years and $200 million to bring a new drug to market. Thousands of scientists were continually working on new ideas and following new leads. Drug development was always a matter of trial and error; with each new iteration, scientists would close some doors and open others. When a Merck researcher came across an apparent breakthrough—either in an unexpected direction, or as a derivative of the original lead—he or she would conduct preliminary research. If the idea proved promising, it was brought to the attention of the department heads.

Every year, Merck's research division held a large review meeting at which all research programs were examined. Projects were coordinated and consolidated, established programs were reviewed and new possibilities were considered. Final approval on research was not made, however, until the head of research met later with a committee of scientific advisors. Each potential program was extensively reviewed, analyzed on the basis of the likelihood of success, the existing market, competition, potential safety problems, manufacturing feasibility and patent status before the decision was made whether to allocate funds for continued experimentation.

The Problem of Rare Diseases and Poor Customers

Many potential drugs offered little chance of financial return. Some diseases were so rare that treatments developed could never be priced high enough to recoup the investment in research, while other diseases afflicted only the poor in rural and remote areas of the Third World. These victims had limited ability to pay even a small amount for drugs or treatment.

In the United States, Congress sought to encourage drug companies to conduct research on rare diseases. In 1978 legislation had been proposed which would grant drug companies tax benefits and seven-year exclusive marketing rights if they would manufacture drugs for diseases afflicting fewer than 200,000 Americans. It was expected that this "orphan drug" program would eventually be passed into law.

There was, however, no U.S. or international program that would create incentives for companies to develop drugs for diseases like river blindness which afflicted millions of the poor in the Third World. The only hope was that some Third World government, foundation, or international organization might step in and partially fund the distribution of a drug that had already been developed.

The Discovery of Ivermectin

The process of investigating promising drug compounds was always long, laborious and fraught with failure. For every pharmaceutical compound that became a "product candidate," thousands of others failed to meet the most rudimentary pre-clinical tests for safety and efficacy. With so much room for failure, it became especially important for drug companies to have sophisticated research managers who could identify the most productive research strategies.

Merck had long been a pioneer in developing major new antibiotic compounds, beginning with penicillin and streptomycin in the 1940s. In the 1970s, Merck Sharp & Dohme Research Laboratories were continuing this tradition. To help investigate for new microbial agents of potential therapeutic value, Merck researchers obtained 54 soil samples from the Kitasato Institute of Japan in 1974. These samples seemed novel and the researchers hoped they might disclose some naturally occurring antibiotics.

As Merck researchers methodically put the soil through hundreds of tests, Merck scientists were pleasantly surprised to detect strong antiparasitic activity in Sample No. OS3153, a scoop of soil dug up at a golf course near Ito, Japan. The Merck labs quickly brought together an interdisciplinary team to try to isolate a pure active ingredient from the microbial culture. The compound eventually isolated—avermectin—proved to have an astonishing potency and effectiveness against a wide range of parasites in cattle, swine, horses and other animals. Within a year, the Merck team also began to suspect that a group of related compounds discovered in the same soil sample could be effective against many other intestinal worms, mites, ticks and insects.

After toxicological tests suggested that ivermectin would be safer than related compounds, Merck decided to develop the substance for the animal health market. In 1978 the first ivermectin-based animal drug, Ivomec, was nearing approval by the U.S. Department of Agriculture and foreign regulatory bodies. Many variations would likely follow: drugs for sheep and pigs, horses, dogs, and others. Ivomec had the potential to become a major advance in animal health treatment.

As clinical testing of ivermectin progressed in the late 1970s, Dr. William Campbell's ongoing research brought him face-to-face with an intriguing hypothesis. Ivermectin, when tested in horses, was effective against the microfilariae of an exotic, fairly unimportant gastrointestinal parasite, Onchocerca cervicalis. This particular worm, while harmless in horses, had characteristics similar to the insidious human parasite that causes river blindness, Onchocerca volvulus.

Dr. Campbell wondered: Could ivermectin be formulated to work against the human parasite? Could a safe, effective drug suitable for community-wide treatment of river blindness be developed? Both Campbell and Vagelos knew that it was very much a gamble that it would succeed. Furthermore, both knew that even if success were attained, the economic viability of such a project would be nil. On the other hand, because such a significant amount of money had already been invested in the development of the animal drug, the cost of developing a human formulation would be much less than that for developing a new compound. It was also widely believed at this point that ivermectin, though still in its final development stages, was likely to be very successful.

A decision to proceed would not be without risks. If a new derivative proved to have any adverse health effects when used on humans, its reputation as a veterinary drug could be tainted and sales negatively affected, no matter how irrelevant the experience with humans. In early tests, ivermectin had had some negative side effects on some specific species of mammals. Dr. Brian Duke of the Armed Forces Institute of Pathology in Washington, D.C., said the cross-species effectiveness of antiparasitic drugs are unpredictable, and there is "always a worry that some race or subsection of the human population" might be adversely affected.

Isolated instances of harm to humans or improper use in Third World settings might also raise some unsettling questions: Could drug residues turn up in meat eaten by humans? Would any human version of ivermectin distributed to the Third World be diverted into the black market, undercutting sales of the veterinary drug? Could the drug harm certain animals in unknown ways?

Despite these risks, Vagelos wondered what the impact might be of turning down Campbell's proposal. Merck had built a research team dedicated to alleviating human suffering. What would a refusal to pursue a possible treatment for river blindness do to morale?

Ultimately, it was Dr. Vagelos who had to make the decision whether or not to fund research toward a treatment for river blindness.

EXHIBIT 1. 10-Year Summary of Financial Performance

Merck & Co., Inc. and Subsidiaries (Dollar amounts in thousands except per-share figures)

Results for Year:	1978	1977	1976	1975	1974	1973	1972	1971	1970	1969
Sales	$1,981,440	$1,724,410	$1,561,117	$1,401,979	$1,260,416	$1,104,035	$942,631	$832,416	$761,109	$691,453
Materials and production costs	744,249	662,703	586,963	525,853	458,837	383,879	314,804	286,646	258,340	232,878
Marketing/administrative expenses	542,186	437,579	396,975	354,525	330,292	304,807	268,856	219,005	201,543	178,593
Research/development expenses	161,350	144,898	133,826	121,933	100,952	89,155	79,692	71,619	69,707	61,100
Interest expense	25,743	25,743	26,914	21,319	8,445	6,703	4,533	3,085	2,964	1,598
Income before taxes	507,912	453,487	416,439	378,349	361,890	319,491	274,746	252,061	228,555	217,284
Taxes on income	198,100	173,300	159,100	147,700	149,300	134,048	121,044	118,703	108,827	109,269
Net income**	307,534	277,525	255,482	228,778	210,492	182,681	151,180	131,381	117,878	106,645
Per common share**	$4.07	$3.67	$3.38	$3.03	$2.79	$2.43	$2.01	$1.75	$1.57	$1.43
Dividends declared on common stock	132,257	117,101	107,584	105,564	106,341	93,852	84,103	82,206	76,458	75,528
Per common share	$1.75	$1.55	$1.42-½	$1.40	$1.40	$1.23-½	$1.12	$1.10	$1.02-½	$1.02-½
Gross plant additions	155,853	177,167	153,894	249,015	159,148	90,194	69,477	67,343	71,540	48,715
Depreciation	75,477	66,785	58,198	52,091	46,057	40,617	36,283	32,104	27,819	23,973
Year-End Position:										
Working capital	666,817	629,515	549,840	502,262	359,591	342,434	296,378	260,350	226,084	228,296
Property, plant, and equipment (net)	924,179	846,784	747,107	652,804	459,245	352,145	305,416	274,240	239,638	197,220
Total assets	2,251,358	1,993,389	1,759,371	1,538,999	1,243,287	988,985	834,847	736,503	664,294	601,484
Stockholders' equity	1,455,135	1,277,753	1,102,154	949,991	822,782	709,614	621,792	542,978	493,214	451,030
Year-End Statistics:										
Average number of common shares outstanding (in thousands)	75,573	75,546	75,493	75,420	75,300	75,193	75,011	74,850	74,850	74,547
Number of stockholders	62,900	63,900	63,500	63,500	61,400	60,000	58,000	54,300	54,600	53,100
Number of employees	28,700	28,100	26,800	26,300	26,500	25,100	24,100	23,200	23,000	22,200

*The above data are as previously reported, restated for poolings-of-interests and stock splits.
**Net income for 1977 and related per-share amounts exclude gain on disposal of businesses of $13,225 and 18¢, respectively.

The Social Responsibility of Business
Is to Increase Its Profits

MILTON FRIEDMAN

When I hear businessmen speak eloquently about the "social responsibilities of business in a free-enterprise system," I am reminded of the wonderful line about the Frenchman who discovered at the age of 70 that he had been speaking prose all his life. The businessmen believe that they are defending free enterprise when they declaim that business is not concerned "merely" with profit but also with promoting desirable "social" ends; that business has a "social conscience" and takes seriously its responsibilities for providing employment, eliminating discrimination, avoiding pollution and whatever else may be the catchwords of the contemporary crop of reformers. In fact they are—or would be if they or anyone else took them seriously—preaching pure and unadulterated socialism. Businessmen who talk this way are unwitting puppets of the intellectual forces that have been undermining the basis of a free society these past decades.

The discussions of the "social responsibilities of business" are notable for their analytical looseness and lack of rigor. What does it mean to say that "business" has responsibilities? Only people can have responsibilities. A corporation is an artificial person and in this sense may have artificial responsibilities, but "business" as a whole cannot be said to have responsibilities, even in this vague sense. The first step toward clarity to examining the doctrine of the social responsibility of business is to ask precisely what it implies for whom.

Presumably, the individuals who are to be responsible are businessmen, which means individual proprietors or corporate executives. Most of the discussion of social responsibility is directed at corporations, so in what follows I shall mostly neglect the individual proprietors and speak of corporate executives.

In a free-enterprise, private-property system, a corporate executive is an employee of the owners of the business. He has direct responsibility to his employers. That responsibility is to conduct the business in accordance with their desires, which generally will be to make as much money as possible while conforming to the basic rules of the society, both those embodied in law and those embodied in ethical custom. Of course, in some cases his employers may have a different objective. A group of persons might establish a corporation for an eleemosynary purpose—for example, a hospital or a school. The manager of such a corporation will not have money profit as his objectives but the rendering of certain services.

In either case, the key point is that, in his capacity as a corporate executive, the manager is the agent of the individuals who own the corporation or establish the eleemosynary institution, and his primary responsibility is to them.

From *New York Times Magazine*, September 13, 1970. © 1970 by The New York Times Company. Reprinted by permission.

Needless to say, this does not mean that it is easy to judge how well he is performing his task. But at least the criterion of performance is straightforward, and the persons among whom a voluntary contractual arrangement exists are clearly defined.

Of course, the corporate executive is also a person in his own right. As a person, he may have many other responsibilities that he recognizes or assumes voluntarily—to his family, his conscience, his feelings of charity, his church, his clubs, his city, his country. He may feel impelled by these responsibilities to devote part of his income to causes he regards as worthy, to refuse to work for particular corporations, even to leave his job, for example, to join his country's armed forces. If we wish, we may refer to some of these responsibilities as "social responsibilities." But in these respects he is acting as a principal, not an agent; he is spending his own money or time or energy, not the money of his employers or the time or energy he has contracted to devote to their purposes. If these are "social responsibilities," they are the social responsibilities of individuals, not of business.

What does it mean to say that the corporate executive has a "social responsibility" in his capacity as businessman? If this statement is not pure rhetoric, it must mean that he is to act in some way that is not in the interest of his employers. For example, that he is to refrain from increasing the price of the product in order to contribute to the social objective of preventing inflation, even though a price increase would be in the best interests of the corporation. Or that he is to make expenditures on reducing pollution beyond the amount that is in the best interests of the corporation or that is required by law in order to contribute to the social objective of improving the environment. Or that, at the expense of corporate profits, he is to hire "hardcore" unemployed instead of better qualified available workmen to contribute to the social objective of reducing poverty.

In each of these cases, the corporate executive would be spending someone else's money for a general social interest. Insofar as his actions in accord with his "social responsibility" reduce returns to stockholders, he is spending their money. Insofar as his actions raise the price to customers, he is spending customers' money. Insofar as his actions lower the wages of some employees, he is spending their money.

The stockholders or the customers or the employees could separately spend their own money on the particular action if they wished to do so. The executive is exercising a distinct "social responsibility," rather than serving as an agent of the stockholders or the customers or the employees, only if he spends the money in a different way than they would have spent it.

But if he does this, he is in effect imposing taxes, on the one hand, and deciding how the tax proceeds shall be spent, on the other.

This process raises political questions on two levels: principle and consequences. On the level of political principle, the imposition of taxes and the expenditure of tax proceeds are governmental functions. We have established elaborate constitutional, parliamentary and judicial provisions to control these functions, to assure that taxes are imposed so far as possible in accordance with the preferences and desires of the public—after all, "taxation without representation" was one of the battle cries of the American Revolution. We have a system of checks and balances to separate the legislative function of imposing taxes and enacting expenditures from the executive function of collecting taxes and administering expenditure programs and from the judicial function of mediating disputes and interpreting the law.

Here the businessman—self-selected or appointed directly or indirectly by stockholders—is to be simultaneously legislator, executive and jurist. He is to decide whom to tax by how much and for what purpose, and he is to spend the proceeds—all this guided only by general exhortations from on high to restrain inflation, improve the environment, fight poverty and so on and on.

The whole justification for permitting the corporate executive to be selected by the stockholders is that the executive is an agent serving the interests of his principal. This justification disappears when the corporate executive imposes taxes and spends the proceeds for "social" purposes. He becomes in effect a public employee, a civil servant, even though he remains in name an employee of a private enterprise. On grounds of political principle, it is intolerable that such civil servants—insofar as their actions in the name of social responsibility are real and not just window dressing—should be selected as they are now. If they are to be civil servants, then they must be elected through a political process. If they are to impose taxes and make expenditures to foster "social" objectives, then political machinery must be set up to make the assessment of taxes and to determine through a political process the objectives to be served.

This is the basic reason why the doctrine of "social responsibility" involves the acceptance of the socialist view that political mechanisms, not market mechanisms, are the appropriate way to determine the allocation of scarce resources to alternative uses.

On the grounds of consequences, can the corporate executive in fact discharge his alleged "social responsibilities"? On the one hand, suppose he could get away with spending the stockholders' or customers' or employees' money. How is he to know how to spend it? He is told that he must contribute to fighting inflation. How is he to know what action of his will contribute to that end? He is presumably an expert in running his company—in producing a product or selling it or financing it. But nothing about his selection makes him an expert on inflation. Will his holding down the price of his product reduce inflationary pressure? Or, by leaving more spending power in the hands of his customers, simply divert it elsewhere? Or, by forcing him to produce less because of the lower price, will it simply contribute to shortages? Even if he could answer these questions, how much cost is he justified in imposing on his stockholders, customers, and employees for this social purpose? What is his appropriate share and what is the appropriate share of others?

And, whether he wants to or not, can he get away with spending his stockholders', customers' or employees' money? Will not the stockholders fire him? (Either the present ones or those who take over when his actions in the name of social responsibility have reduced the corporation's profits and the price of its stock.) His customers and his employees can desert him for other producers and employers less scrupulous in exercising their social responsibilities.

This facet of "social responsibility" doctrine is brought into sharp relief when the doctrine is used to justify wage restraint by trade unions. The conflict of interest is naked and clear when union officials are asked to subordinate the interest of their members to some more general purpose. If union officials try to enforce wage restraint, the consequence is likely to be wildcat strikes, rank-and-file revolts and the emergence of strong competitors for their jobs. We thus have the ironic phenomenon that union leaders—at least in the U.S.—have objected to Government interference with the market far more consistently and courageously than have business leaders.

The difficulty of exercising "social responsibility" illustrates, of course, the great virtue of private competitive enterprise—it forces people to be responsible for their own actions and makes it difficult for them to "exploit" other people for either selfish or unselfish purposes. They can do good—but only at their own expense.

Many a reader who has followed the argument this far may be tempted to remonstrate that it is all well and good to speak of Government's having the responsibility to impose taxes and determine expenditures for such "social" purposes as controlling pollution or training the hard-core unemployed, but that the problems are too urgent to wait on the slow course of political processes, that the exercise of social responsibility by businessmen is a quicker and surer way to solve pressing current problems.

Aside from the question of fact—I share Adam Smith's skepticism about the benefits that can be expected from "those who affect to trade for the public good"—this argument must be rejected on the grounds of principle. What it amounts to is an assertion that those who favor the taxes and expenditures in question have failed to persuade a majority of their fellow citizens to be of like mind and that they are seeking to attain by undemocratic procedures what they cannot attain by democratic procedures. In a free society it is hard for "evil" people to do "evil," especially since one man's good is another's evil.

I have, for simplicity, concentrated on the special case of the corporate executive, except only for the brief digression on trade unions. But precisely the same argument applies to the newer phenomenon of calling upon stockholders to require corporations to exercise social responsibility (the recent G.M. crusade for example). In most of these cases, what is in effect involved is some stockholders trying to get other stockholders (or customers or employees) to contribute against their will to "social" causes favored by the activists. Insofar as they succeed, they are again imposing taxes and spending the proceeds.

The situation of the individual proprietor is somewhat different. If he acts to reduce the returns of his enterprise in order to exercise his "social responsibility," he is spending his own money, not someone else's. If he wishes to spend his money on such purposes, that is his right, and I cannot see that there is any objection to his doing so. In the process, he, too, may impose costs on employees and customers. However, because he is far less likely than a large corporation or union to have monopolistic power, any such side effects will tend to be minor.

Of course, in practice the doctrine of social responsibility is frequently a cloak for actions that are justified on other grounds rather than a reason for those actions.

To illustrate, it may well be in the long-run interest of a corporation that is a major employer in a small community to devote resources to providing amenities to that community or to improving its government. That may make it easier to attract desirable employees, it may reduce the wage bill or lessen losses from pilferage and sabotage or have other worthwhile effects. Or it may be that, given the laws about the deductibility of corporate charitable contributions, the stockholders can contribute more to charities they favor by having the corporation make the gift than by doing it themselves, since they can in that way contribute an amount that would otherwise have been paid as corporate taxes.

In each of these—and many similar—cases, there is a strong temptation to rationalize these actions as an exercise of "social responsibility." In the present climate of opinion, with its widespread aversion to "capitalism," "profits," and the "soulless corporation" and so on, this is one way for a corporation to generate goodwill as a by-product of expenditures that are entirely justified in its own self-interest.

It would be inconsistent of me to call on corporate executives to refrain from this hypocritical window-dressing because it harms the foundations of a free society. That would be to call on them to exercise a "social responsibility"! If our institutions, and the attitudes of the public make it in their self-interest to cloak their actions in this way, I cannot summon much indignation to renounce them. At the same time, I can express admiration for those individual proprietors or owners of closely held corporations or stockholders of more broadly held corporations who disdain such tactics as approaching fraud.

Whether blameworthy or not, the use of the cloak of social responsibility, and the nonsense spoken in its name by influential and prestigious businessmen, does clearly harm the foundations of a free society. I have been impressed time and again by the schizophrenic character of many businessmen. They are capable of being extremely far-sighted and clearheaded in matters that are internal to their businesses. They are incredibly short-sighted and muddle-headed in matters that are outside their businesses but affect the possible survival of business in general. This short-sightedness is strikingly exemplified in the calls from many businessmen for wage and price guidelines or controls or income policies. There is nothing that could do more in a brief period to destroy a market system and replace it by a centrally controlled system than effective governmental control of prices and wages.

The short-sightedness is also exemplified in speeches by businessmen on social responsibility. This may gain them kudos in the short run. But it helps to strengthen the already too prevalent view that the pursuit of profits is wicked and immoral and must be curbed and controlled by external forces. Once this view is adopted, the external forces that curb the market will not be the social consciences, however highly developed, of the pontificating executives; it will be the iron fist of Government bureaucrats. Here, as with price and wage controls, businessmen seem to me to reveal a suicidal impulse.

The political principle that underlies the market mechanism is unanimity. In an ideal free market resting on private property, no individual can coerce any other, all cooperation is voluntary, all parties to such cooperation benefit or they need not participate. There are no values, no "social" responsibilities in any sense other than the shared values and responsibilities of individuals. Society is a collection of individuals and of the various groups they voluntarily form.

The political principle that underlies the political mechanism is conformity. The individual must serve a more general social interest—whether that be determined by a church or a dictator or a majority. The individual may have a vote and say in what is to be done, but if he is overruled, he must conform. It is appropriate for some to require others to contribute to a general social purpose whether they wish to or not.

Unfortunately, unanimity is not always feasible. There are some respects in which conformity appears unavoidable, so I do not see how one can avoid the use of the political mechanism altogether.

But the doctrine of "social responsibility" taken seriously would extend the scope of the political mechanism to every human activity. It does not differ in philosophy from the most explicitly collectivist doctrine. It differs only by professing to believe that collectivist ends can be attained without collectivist means. That is why, in my book *Capitalism and Freedom*, I have called it a "fundamentally subversive doctrine" in a free society, and I have said that in such a society, "there is one and only one social responsibility of business—to use its resources and engage in activities designed to increase its profits so long as it stays within the rules of the game, which is to say, engages in open and free competition without deception or fraud."

Social Responsibility and Economic Efficiency

KENNETH J. ARROW

This paper makes some observations on the widespread notion that the individual has some responsibility to others in the conduct of his economic affairs. It is held that there are a number of circumstances under which the economic agent should forgo profit or other benefits to himself in order to achieve some social goal, especially to avoid a disservice to other individuals. For the purpose of keeping the discussion within bounds, I shall confine my attention to the obligations that might be imposed on business firms. Under what circumstances is it reasonable to expect a business firm to refrain from maximizing its profits because it will hurt others by doing so? What institutions can we expect to serve the function not merely of limiting profits but of limiting them in just those ways that will avoid harm to others? Is it reasonable to expect that ethical codes will arise or be created? My purpose in discussing these questions is not so much to achieve definitive answers as to analyze the kinds of consideration that enter into discussing them.

First of all, it may be well to review what possible ways there are by which the economic activity of one firm may affect other members of the economy. A substantial list comes to mind; a few illustrations will serve. A firm affects others by competing with them in the product markets and in the factor markets, in the buying of labor, buying of other goods for its use, and in the selling of its products. It pays wages to others. It buys goods from others. It sets prices to its

Kenneth J. Arrow, Professor of Economics, Harvard University, *Public Policy*, Vol. XXI, No. 3, Summer, 1973. Reprinted by permission. This is a revised version of the Carl Synder Memorial Lecture delivered at the University of California, Santa Barbara, April 1972.

customers, and so enters into an economic relation with them. The firm typically sets working conditions, including—of greatest importance—conditions that affect the health and possibility for accident within the plant. We are reminded in recent years that the firm, as well as the private individual, is a contributor to pollution. Pollution has a direct effect on the welfare of other members of the economy. Less mentioned, but of the same type, are the effects of economic activity on congestion. Bringing a new plant into an already crowded area is bound to create costs, disservices, and disutilities to others in the area if by nothing else than by crowding the streets and the sidewalks and imposing additional burdens on the public facilities of the area. Indeed, although congestion has not been discussed as much as has pollution, it may have greater economic impact and probably even greater health costs. Certainly the number of automobile deaths arising from accidents far exceeds the health hazards arising from automobile pollution. The firm affects others through determining the quality of its products, and again, among the many aspects of product quality we may especially single out the qualities of the product with respect to its pollution-creating ability, as in the case of automobiles, and with respect to its safety, the hazards it poses to its user. The question of social responsibility takes very different forms with regard to the different items on this varied list. It is not a uniform characteristic at all.

Let us first consider the case against social responsibility: the assumption that the firms should aim simply to maximize their profits. One strand of that argument is empirical rather than ethical or normative. It simply states that firms *will* maximize their profits. The impulse to gain, it is argued, is very strong and the incentives for selfish behavior are so great that any kind of control is likely to be utterly ineffectual. This argument has some force but is by no means conclusive. Any mechanism for enforcing or urging social responsibility upon firms must of course reckon with a profit motive, with a desire to evade whatever response of controls are imposed. But it does not mean that we cannot expect any degree of responsibility at all.

One finds a rather different argument, frequently stated by some economists. It will probably strike the noneconomist as rather strange, at least at first hearing. The assertion is that firms *ought* to maximize profits; not merely do they like to do so but there is practically a social obligation to do so. Let me briefly sketch the argument:

Firms buy the goods and services they need for production. What they buy they pay for and therefore they are paying for whatever costs they impose upon others. What they receive in payment by selling their goods, they receive because the purchaser considers it worthwhile. This is a world of voluntary contracts; nobody *has* to buy the goods. If he chooses to buy it, it must be that he is getting a benefit measured by the price he pays. Hence, it is argued, profit really represents the net contribution that the firm makes to the social good, and the profits should therefore be made as large as possible. When firms compete with each other, in selling their goods or in buying labor or other services, they may have to lower their selling prices in order to get more of the market for themselves or raise their wages; in either case the benefits which the firm is deriving are in some respects shared with the population at large. The forces of competition prevent the firms from engrossing too large a share of the social benefit. For example, if a firm tries to reduce the quality of its goods, it will sooner or later have to lower the price which it charges because the purchaser will no longer find it worthwile to pay the high price. Hence, the consumers will gain from price reduction at the same time as they are losing through quality deterioration. On detailed analysis it appears the firm will find it privately profitable to reduce quality under these circumstances only if, in fact, quality reduction is a net social benefit, that is, if the saving in cost is worth more to the consumer than the quality reduction. Now, as far as it goes this argument is sound. The problem is that it may not go far enough.

Under the proper assumptions profit maximization is indeed efficient in the sense that it can achieve as high a level of satisfaction as possible for any one consumer without reducing the levels of satisfaction of other consumers or using more resources than society is endowed with. But the limits of the argument must be stressed. I want to mention two well-known points in passing without making them the principal focus of discussion. First of all, the argument assumes that the forces of competition are sufficiently vigorous. But there is no social justification for profit maximization by monopolies. This is an important and well-known qualification. Second, the distribution of income that results from unrestrained profit maximization is very unequal. The competitive maximizing economy is indeed efficient—this shows up in high average incomes—but the high average is accompanied by widespread poverty on the one hand and vast riches, at least for a few, on the other. To many of us this is a very undesirable consequence.

Profit maximization has yet another effect on society. It tends to point away from the expression of altruistic motives. Altruistic motives are motives whose gratification is just as legitimate as selfish motives, and the expression of those motives is something we probably wish to encourage. A profit-maximizing, self-centered form of economic behavior does not provide any room for the expression of such motives.

If the three problems above were set aside, many of the ways by which firms affect others should not be tampered with. Making profits by competition is, if anything, to be encouraged rather than discouraged. Wage and price bargains between the firm and uncoerced workers and customers represent mutually beneficial exchanges. There is, therefore, no reason within the framework of the discussion to interfere with them. But these examples far from exhaust the list of interactions with which we started. The social desirability of profit maximization does not extend to all the interactions on the list. There are two categories of effects where the arguments for profit maximization break down: The first is illustrated by pollution or congestion. Here it is no longer true (and this is the key to these issues) that the firm in fact does pay for the harm it imposes on others. When it takes a person's time and uses it at work, the firm is paying for this, and therefore the transaction can be regarded as a beneficial exchange from the point of view of both parties. We have no similar mechanism by which the pollution which a firm imposes upon its neighborhood is paid for. Therefore the firm will have a tendency to pollute more than is desirable. That is, the benefit to it or to its customers from the expanded activity is really not as great, or may not be as great, as the cost it is imposing upon the neighborhood. But since it does not pay that cost, there is no profit incentive to refrain.

The same argument applies to traffic congestion when no change is made for the addition of cars or trucks on the highway. It makes everybody less comfortable. It delays others and increases the probability of accidents; in short, it imposes a cost upon a large number of members of the society, a cost which is not paid for by the imposer of the cost, at least not in full. The person congesting is also congested, but the costs he is imposing on others are much greater than those he suffers himself. Therefore there will be a tendency to overutilize those goods for which no price is charged, particularly scarce highway space.

There are many other examples of this kind, but these two will serve to illustrate the point in question: some effort must be made to alter the profit-maximizing behavior of firms in those cases where it is imposing costs on others which are not easily compensated through an appropriate set of prices.

The second category of effects where profit maximization is not socially desirable is that in which there are quality effects about which the firm knows more than the buyer. In my examples I will cite primarily the case of quality in the product sold, but actually very much the same considerations apply to the quality of working conditions. The firm is frequently in a better position to know the consequences (the health hazards, for example) involved in working conditions than the worker is, and the considerations I am about to discuss in the case of sale of goods have a direct parallel in the analysis of working conditions in the relation of a firm to its workers. Let me illustrate by considering the sale of a used car. (Similar considerations apply to the sale of new cars.) A used car has potential defects and typically the seller knows more about the defects than the buyer. The buyer is not in a position to distinguish among used cars, and therefore he will be willing to pay the same amount for two used cars of differing quality because he cannot tell the difference between them. As a result, there is an inefficiency in the sale of used cars. If somehow or other the cars were distinguished as to their quality, there would be some buyers who would prefer a cheaper car with more defects because they intend to use it very little or they only want it for a short period, while others will want a better car at a higher price. In fact, however, the two kinds of car are sold indiscriminately to the two groups of buyers at the same price, so that we can argue that there is a distinct loss of consumer satisfaction imposed by the failure to convey information that is available to the seller. The buyers are not necessarily being cheated. They may be, but the problem of inefficiency would remain if they weren't. One can imagine a situation where, from past experience, buyers of used cars are aware that cars that look alike may turn out to be quite different. Without knowing whether a particular car is good or bad, they do know that there are good and bad cars, and of course their willingness to pay for the cars is influenced accordingly. The main loser from a monetary viewpoint may not be the customer, but rather the seller of the good car. The buyer will pay a price which is only appropriate to a lottery that gives him a good car or a bad car with varying probabilities, and therefore the seller of the good car gets less than the value of the car. The seller of the bad car is, of course, the beneficiary. Clearly then, if one could arrange to transmit the truth from the sellers to the buyers, the efficiency of the market would be greatly improved. The used-car illustration is an example of a very general phenomenon.

Consider now any newly produced complex product, such as a new automobile. The seller is bound to know considerably more about its properties than all but a very few of its buyers. In order to develop the car, the producer has had to perform tests of one kind or another. He knows the outcome of the tests. Failure to reveal this knowledge works against the efficiency of satisfying the consumers' tastes. The argument of course applies to any aspect of the quality of a product, durability or the ability to perform under trying circumstances or differing climatic conditions. Perhaps we are most concerned about the safety features of the automobile. The risks involved in the use of automobiles are not trivial, and the kind of withholding of safety information which has been revealed to exist in a number of cases certainly cannot be defended as a socially useful implication of profit maximization. The classical efficiency arguments for profit maximization do not apply here, and it is wrong to obfuscate the issue by invoking them.

Perhaps even more dramatic, though on a smaller scale, are the repeated examples of misleading information about the risks and use of prescription drugs and other chemicals. These again manifest the same point. Profit maximization can lead to consequences which are clearly socially injurious. This is the case if the buyers are on the average deceived—if, for example, they have higher expectations than are in fact warranted. They are also injured when on the average they are not deceived but merely uncertain, although here the argument is more subtle. One consequence may be the excessively limited use of some new drugs, for example. If the users of the drugs become fully aware of the risks involved but are not able to assess the risk with respect to any particular drug, the result may be an indiscriminate rejection of new treatments which is rational from the point of view of the user; this, in the long run, may be just as serious an error as the opposite.

Defenders of unrestricted profit maximization usually assume that the consumer is well informed or at least that he becomes so by his own experience, in repeated purchases, or by information about what has happened to other people like him. This argument is empirically shaky; even the ability of individuals to analyze the effects of their own past purchases may be limited, particularly with respect to complicated mechanisms. But there are two further defects. The risks, including death, may be so great that even one misleading experience is bad enough, and the opportunity to learn from repeated trials is not of much use. Also, in a world where the products are continually changing, the possibility of learning from experience is greatly reduced. Automobile companies are continually introducing new models which at least purport to differ from what they were in the past, though doubtless the change is more external than internal. New drugs are being introduced all the time; the fact that one has had bad experiences with one drug may provide very little information about the next one.

Thus there are two types of situation in which the simple rule of maximizing profits is socially inefficient: the case in which costs are not paid for, as in pollution, and the case in which the seller has considerably more knowledge about his product than the buyer, particularly with regard to safety. In these situations it is clearly desirable to have some idea of social responsibility, that is, to experience an obligation, whether ethical, moral, or legal. Now we cannot expect such an obligation to be created out of thin air. To be meaningful, any obligation of this kind, any feeling or rule of behavior has to be embodied in some definite social institution. I use that term broadly: a legal code is a social institution in a sense. Exhortation to do good must be made specific in some external form, a steady reminder and perhaps enforcer of desirable values. Part of the need is simply for factual information as a guide to individual behavior. A firm may need to be told what is right and what is wrong when in fact it is polluting, or which safety requirements are reasonable and which are too extreme or too costly to be worth consideration. Institutionalization of the social responsibility of firms also serves another very important function. It provides some assurance to any one firm that the firms with which it is in competition will also accept the same responsibility. If a firm has some code imposed from the outside, there is some expectation that other firms will obey it too and therefore there is some assurance that it need not fear any excessive cost to its good behavior.

Let me then turn to some alternative kinds of institutions that can be considered as embodying the possible social responsibilities of firms. First, we have legal regulation, as in the case of pollution where laws are passed about the kind of burning that may take place, and about setting maximum standards for emissions. A second category is that of taxes. Economists, with good reason, like to preach taxation as opposed to regulation. The movement to tax polluting emissions is getting under way and there is a fairly widely backed proposal in Congress to tax sulfur dioxide emissions from industrial smokestacks. That is an example of the second kind of institutionalization of social responsibility. The responsibility is made very clear: the violator pays for violations.

A third very old remedy or institution is that of legal liability—the liability of the civil law. One can be sued for damages. Such cases apparently go back to the Middle Ages. Regulation also extends back very far. There was an ordinance in London about the year 1300 prohibiting the burning of coal, because of the smoke nuisance.

The fourth class of institutions is represented by ethical codes. Restraint is achieved not by appealing to each individual's conscience but rather by having some generally understood definition of appropriate behavior. Let me discuss the advantages and disadvantages of these four institutions.

In regard to the first two, regulation and taxes, I shall be rather brief because these are the more familiar. We can have regulations governing pollution. We can also regulate product safety. We may even have standards to insure quality in dimensions other than safety. The chief drawback of direct regulation is associated with the fact that it is hard to make regulations flexible enough to meet a wide variety of situations and yet simple enough to be enforceable. In addition, there is a slowness in response to new situations. For example, if a new chemical, such as a pesticide, comes on the market and after a period of time is recognized as a danger, it requires a long and complicated process to get this awareness translated into legal action. One problem is that legislative time is a very scarce factor; a proposal to examine the problems involved in some pesticide may at any given time be competing with totally different considerations for the attention of the legislature or regulatory body. In short, there is considerable rigidity in most regulatory structures. For certain purposes it is clear that regulation is best but it is equally clear that it is not useful as a universal device. In the case of taxes on the effects, rather than on the causes, there is a little more built-in flexibility. To combat pollution, taxation is probably the most appropriate device; a tax is imposed on the emission by the plant, whether in water or in air. Now this means the plant is free to find its own way of minimizing the tax burden. It is not told it must do one thing, such as raising smokestacks to a certain height. It is free to try to find the cheapest way of meeting the pollution problem. It may well decide that the profitability situation is such that it will continue to pollute and sell the product presumably at a somewhat higher price. This decision is not necessarily bad; it implies that the product is in fact much desired and it provides an automatic test of the market to see whether it is worth polluting or not, because in effect the consumer is ultimately paying for the pollution he induces. However, it is difficult to see how this method, useful though it is in the case of pollution, would have any relevance to safety, to see how one could frame a tax which would make very much sense. Taxation appears to be a rather blunt instrument for controlling product safety.

Legal liability can be and has been applied; i.e., courts have allowed damages in cases arising out of pollution or out of injury or death due to unsafe products. The nature of the law in this area is still evolving; under our system this means that it is being developed by a sequence of court decisions. Just exactly what the company or its officers have to know before they can be regarded as liable for damages due to unsafe products is not yet clear. No doubt it would certainly be held even today that if officers of a company were aware that a product had a significant probability of a dangerous defect and they sold it anyway without saying so, and if the defect occurred, legal liability would be clear. But it is frequently hard to establish such knowledge. No doubt if society wants to use the route of legal liability as a way of imposing social responsibility, then it can change the principles on which the decision is based. For example, one might throw the burden of proof on the company, so that in the case of any new product they have to run tests to show positively that it is safe. Their failure to make such tests would be an indication of their liability. One could imagine changes of this kind which would bring the law more into line with what is desirable. But there are some intrinsic defects in the liability route which, in my opinion, make it unsuitable in its present form as a serious method of achieving social control or of imposing responsibility on profit-making firms. First, litigation is costly. In many cases there are social wrongs or social inefficiencies which are quite significant in the aggregate and are perceived by a large number of people, each of whom bears a small part of the cost. This is characteristic of pollution and may be the case with certain kinds of quality standards. It really does not pay any particular person to sue, and if a few people do sue it does not really do the company much harm.

Another problem is that the notion of liability in law is really too simple a concept. Legal liability tends to be an all-or-none proposition. Consider a product such as plastic bags. They are perfectly all right for storing clothes or food but there is a risk that small children will misuse them, with serious consequences. One would hardly want to say that there is any legal liability ascribable to the plastic-bag makers, for even the safest product can be misused. On the other hand, one might argue that a product that can be misused ought to be somewhat discouraged and perhaps some small degree of responsibility should be imposed, particularly if no adequate warning is issued. The law does not permit any such distinctions. Thus, in an automobile case, one party or the other must be found wrong, even though in fact a crash may clearly be due to the fact that both drivers were behaving erratically, and it would be reasonable to have some splitting of responsibility. At present, with some minor exceptions, the law does not permit this, and I suppose it would confuse legal proceedings irreparably to start introducing partial causation. Economists are accustomed to the idea that almost nothing happens without the cooperation of a number of factors, and we have large bodies of doctrine devoted to imputing in some appropriate way the consequences of an action to all of its causes. It is for these reasons that this kind of crude liability doctrine seems to be unsuitable in many cases.

A number of other problems with litigation could be mentioned. Consider very high-risk situations that involve a very low probability of death or other serious adverse consequence, as in the case of drugs, or possible radiation from nuclear power plants. The insurance companies are willing to insure because the probability is low. But once insurance is introduced the incentive to refrain from incurring the risk is dulled. If you are insured against a loss you have less of an incentive to prevent it. In the field of automobile liability, it has become clear that the whole system of liability has to a very great extent broken down. The result is a widespread movement toward no-fault insurance, which in effect means people are compensated for their losses but no attempt is made to charge damages to the persons responsible. Responsibility is left undecided.

Finally, litigation does not seem suitable for continuing problems. Pollution will be reduced but not eliminated; indeed it is essentially impossible to eliminate it. There remain continuous steady damages to individuals. These should still be charged to firms in order to prevent them from polluting more. But enforcement by continuous court action is a very expensive way of handling a repetitious situation. It is silly to keep on going to court to establish the same set of facts over and over again. For these reasons taxes which have the same incentive effects are superior.

Let me turn to the fourth possibility, ethical code. This may seem to be a strange possibility for an economist to raise. But when there is a wide difference in knowledge between the two sides of the market, recognized ethical codes can be, as has already been suggested, a great contribution to economic efficiency. Actually we do have examples of this in our everyday lives, but in very limited areas. The case of medical ethics is the most striking. By its very nature there is a very large difference in knowledge between the buyer and the seller. One is, in fact, buying precisely the service of someone with much more knowledge than you have. To make this relationship a viable one, ethical codes have grown up over the centuries, both to avoid the possibility of exploitation by the physician and to assure the buyer of medical services that he is not being exploited. I am not suggesting that these are universally obeyed, but there is a strong presumption that the doctor is going to perform to a large extent with your welfare in mind. Unnecessary medical expenses or other abuses are perceived as violations of ethics. There is a powerful ethical background against which we make this judgment. Behavior that we would regard as highly reprehensible in a physician is judged less harshly when found among businessmen. The medical profession is typical of professions in general. All professions involve a situation in which knowledge is unequal on two sides of the market by the very definition of the profession, and therefore there have grown up ethical principles that afford some protection to the client. Notice there is a mutual benefit in this. The fact is that if you had sufficient distrust of a doctor's services, you wouldn't buy them. Therefore the physician wants an ethical code to act as assurance to the buyer, and he certainly wants his competitors to obey this same code, partly because any violation may put him at a disadvantage but more especially because the violation will reflect on him, since the buyer of the medical services may not be able to distinguish one doctor from another. A close look reveals that a great deal of economic life depends for its viability on a certain limited degree of ethical commitment. Purely selfish behavior of individuals is really incompatible with any kind of settled economic life. There is almost invariably some element of trust and confidence. Much business is done on the basis of verbal assurance. It would be too elaborate to try to get written commitments on every possible point. Every contract depends for its observance on a mass of unspecified conditions which suggest that the performance will be carried out in good faith without insistence on sticking literally to its wording. To put the matter in its simplest form, in almost every economic transaction, in any exchange of goods for money, somebody gives up his valuable asset before he gets the other's, either the goods are given before the money or the money is given before the goods. Moreover there is a general confidence that there won't be any violation of the implicit agreement. Another example in daily life of this kind of ethics is the observance of queue discipline. People line up; there are people who try to break in ahead of you, but there is an ethic which holds that this is bad. It is clearly an ethic which is in everybody's interest to preserve; one waits at the end of the line this time, and one is protected against somebody's coming in ahead of him.

In the context of product safety, efficiency would be greatly enhanced by accepted ethical rules. Sometimes it may be enough to have an ethical compulsion to reveal all the information available and let the buyer choose. This is not necessarily always the best. It can be argued that under some circumstances setting minimum safety standards and simply not putting out products that do not meet them would be desirable and should be felt by the businessman to be an obligation.

Now I've said that ethical codes are desirable. It doesn't follow from that that they will come about. An ethical code is useful only if it is widely accepted. Its implications for specific behavior must be moderately clear, and above all it must be clearly perceived that the acceptance of these ethical obligations by everybody does involve mutual gain. Ethical codes that lack the latter property are unlikely to be viable. How do such codes develop? They may develop as a consensus out of lengthy public discussion of obligations, discussion which will take place in legislatures, lecture halls, business journals, and other public forums. The codes are communicated by the very process of coming to an agreement. A more formal alternative would be to have some highly prestigious group discuss ethical codes for safety standards. In either case to become and to remain a part of the economic environment, the codes have to be accepted by the significant operating institutions and transmitted from one generation of executives to the next through standard operating procedures, through education in business schools, and through indoctrination of one kind or another. If we seriously expect such codes to develop and to be maintained, we might ask how the agreements develop and, above all, how the codes remain stable. After all, an ethical code, however much it may be in the interest of all, is, as we remarked earlier, not in the interest of any one firm. The code may be of value to the running of the system as a whole, it may be of value to all firms if all firms maintain it, and yet it will be to the advantage of any one firm to cheat—in fact the more so, the more other firms are sticking to it. But there are some reasons for thinking that ethical codes can develop and be stable. These codes will not develop completely without institutional support. That is to say, there will be need for focal organizations, such as government agencies, trade associations, and consumer defense groups, or all combined to make the codes explicit, to iterate their doctrine and to make their presence felt. Given that help, I think the emergence of ethical codes on matters such as safety at least, is possible. One positive factor here is something that is a negative factor in other contexts, namely that our economic organization is to such a large extent composed of large firms. The corporation is no longer a single individual; it is a social organization with internal social ties and internal pressures for acceptability and esteem. The individual members of the corporation are not only parts of the corporation but also members of a larger society whose esteem is desired. Power in a large corporation is necessarily diffused; not many individuals in such organizations feel so thoroughly identified with the corporation that other kinds of social pressures become irrelevant. Furthermore, in a large, complex firm where many people have to participate in any decision, there are likely to be some who are motivated to call attention to violations of the code. This kind of check has been conspicuous in government in recent years. The Pentagon Papers are an outstanding illustration of the fact that within the organization there are those who recognize moral guilt and take occasion to blow the whistle. I expect the same sort of behavior to occur in any large organization when there are well-defined ethical rules whose violation can be observed.

One can still ask if the codes are likely to be stable. Since it may well be possible and profitable for a minority to cheat, will it not be true that the whole system may break down? In fact, however, some of the pressures work in the other direction. It is clearly in the interest of those who are obeying the codes to enforce them, to call attention to violations, to use the ethical and social pressures of the society at large against their less scrupulous rivals. At the same time the value of maintaining the system may well be apparent to all, and no doubt ways will be found to use the assurance of quality generated by the system as a positive asset in attracting consumers and workers.

One must not expect miraculous transformations in human behavior. Ethical codes, if they are to be viable, should be limited in their scope. They are not a universal substitute for the weapons mentioned earlier, the institutions, taxes, regulations, and legal remedies. Further, we should expect the codes to apply only in situations where the firm has superior knowledge of the situation. I would not want the firm to act in accordance with some ethical principles in regard to matters of which it has little knowledge. For example, with quality standards which consumers can observe, it may not be desirable that the firm decide for itself, at least on ethical grounds, because it is depriving the consumer of the freedom of choice between high-quality, high-cost and low-quality, low-cost products. It is in areas where someone is typically misinformed or imperfectly informed that ethical codes can contribute to economic efficiency.

The Moral Muteness of Managers

FREDERICK B. BIRD • JAMES A. WATERS

Many managers exhibit a reluctance to describe their actions in moral terms even when they are acting for moral reasons. They talk as if their actions were guided exclusively by organizational interests, practicality, and economic good sense even when in practice they honor morally defined standards codified in law, professional conventions, and social mores. They characteristically defend morally defined objectives such as service to customers, effective cooperation among personnel, and utilization of their own skills and resources in terms of the long-run economic objectives of their organizations. Ostensibly moral standards regarding colleagues, customers, and suppliers are passed off as "street smarts" and "ways to succeed."[1]

Many observers have called attention to this reluctance of managers to use moral expressions publicly to identify and guide their decision making even when they are acting morally. A century and a half ago, de Tocqueville noted the disinclination of American business people to admit they acted altruistically even when they did.[2] More recently, McCoy has observed that managers are constantly making value choices, privately invoking moral standards, which they in turn defend in terms of business interests. Silk and Vogel note that many managers simply take for granted that business and ethics have little relation except negatively with respect to obvious cases of illegal activities, like bribery or price-fixing. Solomon and Hanson observe that, although managers are often aware of moral issues, the public discussion of these issues in ethical terms is ordinarily neglected.[3]

Current research based on interviews with managers about how they experience ethical questions in their work reveals that mangers seldom discuss with their colleagues the ethical problems they routinely encounter.[4] In a very real sense, "Morality is a live topic for individual managers but it is close to a non-topic among groups of managers."[5]

This article explores this phenomenon of moral muteness and suggests ways that managers and organizations can deal openly with moral questions.

Actions, Speech, and Normative Expectations

To frame the exploration of moral muteness, it is useful to consider in general terms the relationships among managers' actions, their communicative exchanges, and relevant normative expectations. Normative expectations are standards for behavior that are sufficiently compelling and authoritative that people feel they must either comply with them, make a show of complying with them, or offer good reasons why not.

While normative expectations influence conduct in many areas of life from styles of dress to standards of fair treatment, in most societies certain types of activities are considered to be morally neutral. Choices of how to act with respect to morally neutral activities are considered to be matters of personal preference, practical feasibility, or strategic interest.[6]

Although managers often disagree regarding the extent to which business activities are morally neutral, their interactions in contemporary industrial societies are influenced by a number of normative expectations. These expectations are communicated by legal rulings, regulatory agencies' decrees, professional codes, organizational policies, and social mores.[7] Considerable consensus exists with respect to a number of general ethical principles bearing upon management regarding honest communication, fair treatment, fair competition, social responsibility, and provision of safe and worthwhile services and products.[8]

Through verbal exchanges people identify, evoke, and establish normative expectations as compelling cultural realities. Moral expressions are articulated to persuade others, to reinforce personal convictions, to criticize, and to justify decisions. Moral expressions are also invoked to praise and to blame, to evaluate and to rationalize. Moral discourse plays a lively role communicating normative expectations, seeking cooperation of others, and rendering judgments.

For those decisions and actions for which moral expectations are clearly relevant, it is possible to conceive of four different kinds of relationship between managers' actions and their verbal exchanges. These are depicted in Figure 1. One pattern (Quadrant I) identifies those situations in which speaking and acting correspond with each other in keeping with moral expectations. A second congruent pattern (Quadrant III) is the mirror image of the first: no discrepancy exists between speech and action, but neither is guided by moral expectations.

The other two patterns represent incongruence between speech and action. In Quadrant II, actual conduct falls short of what is expected. Verbal exchanges indicate a deference for moral standards that is not evident in actual conduct. Discrepancy here represents hypocrisy, when people intentionally act contrary to their verbalized commitments.[9] Discrepancy may also assume the form of moral backsliding or moral weakness. In this case, the failure to comply with verbalized commitments occurs because of moral fatigue, the inability to honor conflicting standards, or excusable exceptions.[10] Because they are intuitively understandable, none of these three patterns are our concern in this article.

Rather, our focus is on the more perplexing fourth pattern (Quadrant IV) which corresponds with situations of moral muteness: managers avoid moral expressions in their communicative exchanges but would be expected to use them either because their actual conduct reveals deference to moral standards, because they expect others to honor such standards, or because they

FIGURE 1. Relations Between Moral Action and Speech

	Actions Follow Normative Expectations	Actions Do Not Follow Normative Expectations
Moral Terms Used in Speech	**I** Congruent Moral Conduct	**II** Hypocrisy, Moral Weakness
Moral Terms Not Used in Speech	**IV** Moral Muteness	**III** Congruent Immoral or Amoral Conduct

privately acknowledge that those standards influence their decisions and actions. In other words, with respect to those instances where the managers involved feel that how they and others act ought to be and is guided by moral expectations, why do they avoid moral references in their work-related communications?

For example, a given manager may argue that the only ethic of business is making money, but then describe at length the non-remunerative ways she fosters organizational commitment from her co-workers by seeking their identification with the organization as a community characterized by common human objectives and styles of operation. In another example, managers may enter into formal and informal agreements among themselves. In the process they necessarily make promises and undertake obligations. Implicitly, they must use moral terms to enter and confirm such understandings even though explicitly no such expressions are voiced. This discrepancy occurs most pervasively in relation to countless existing normative standards regarding business practices that are passed off as common sense or good management—e.g., taking care of regular customers in times of shortage even though there is opportunity to capture new customers, respecting the bidding process in purchasing even though lower prices could be forced on dependent suppliers, and ensuring equitable pricing among customers even though higher prices could be charged to less-knowledgeable or less-aggressive customers.

Causes of Moral Muteness

Interviews with managers about the ethical questions they face in their work indicate that they avoid moral talk for diverse reasons.[11] In the particular pattern of moral muteness, we observe that in general they experience moral talk as dysfunctional. More specifically, managers are concerned that moral talk will threaten organizational harmony, organizational efficiency, and their own reputation for power and effectiveness.

Threat to Harmony—Moral talk may, on occasion, require some degree of interpersonal confrontation. In extreme cases, this may take the form of blowing the whistle on powerful persons in the organization who are involved in illegal or unethical practices and may involve significant personal risk for the whistleblower.[12] Even in less-extreme cases, moral talk may involve raising questions about or disagreeing with practices or decisions of superiors, colleagues, or subordinates. Managers typically avoid any such confrontation, experiencing it as difficult and costly—as witnessed, for example, by the frequent avoidance of candid performance appraisals. Faced with a situation where a subordinate or colleague is involved in an unethical practice, managers may "finesse" a public discussion or confrontation by publishing a general policy statement or drawing general attention to an existing policy.

In the case of moral questions, managers find confrontations particularly difficult because they experience them as judgmental and likely to initiate cycles of mutual finger-pointing and recrimination. They are aware of the small and not-so-small deceits which are pervasive in organizations, e.g., juggling budget lines to cover expenditures, minor abuses of organizational perks, favoritism, nepotism, and fear that if they "cast the first stone" an avalanche may ensue.[13]

Many managers conclude that it is disruptive to bring up moral issues at work because their organizations do not want public discussion of such issues. We interviewed or examined the interviews of sixty managers who in turn talked about nearly 300 cases in which they had faced moral issues in their work. In only twelve percent of these cases had public discussion of moral issues taken place and more than half of these special cases were cited by a single executive. Give-and-take discussions of moral issues typically took place in private conversations or not at all.

Threat to Efficiency—Many managers avoid or make little use of moral expressions because moral talk is associated with several kinds of exchanges that obstruct or distract from responsible problem-solving. In these instances, moral talk is viewed as being self-serving and obfuscating. Thus, for example, while moral talk may be legitimately used to praise and blame people for their conduct, praising and blaming do not facilitate the identification, analysis, and resolution of difficult moral conundrums. Similarly, while moral talk in the form of ideological exhortations may function to defend structures of authority and to rally support for political goals, it does not facilitate problem solving among people with varied ideological commitments.[14]

Because of the prevalence of such usages, many managers are loath to use moral talk in their work. Blaming, praising, and ideological posturing do not help to clarify issues. Moreover, such moral talk frequently seems to be narrowly self-serving. Those who praise, blame, or express ideological convictions usually do so in order to protect and advance their own interests.

In addition, managers shun moral talk because such talk often seems to result in burdening business decisions with considerations that are not only extraneous, but at times antagonistic to responsible management. Moral talk may distract by seeking simplistic solutions to complicated problems. For example, discussions of justice in business often divert attention to theoretical formulas for distributing rewards and responsibilities without first considering how resources as a whole might be expanded and how existing contractual relations might already have built-in standards of fair transactions and allocations.

Moral talk may also be experienced as a threat to managerial flexibility. In order to perform effectively, managers must be able to adapt to changes in their organizations and environments. They are correspondingly wary of contractual relations that seem to be too binding, that too narrowly circumscribe discretionary responses. They therefore seek out working agreements, when they legally can, that are informal, flexible, and can be amended easily. They assume that if the stipulations are formally articulated in terms of explicit promises, obligations, and rights, then flexibility is likely to be reduced. In order to preserve flexibility in all their relations, managers frequently seek verbal, handshake agreements that make minimal use of explicit moral stipulations.[15]

Many managers also associate moral talk with rigid rules and intrusive regulations. Too often, public talk about moral issues in business is felt to precede the imposition of new government regulations that are experienced as arbitrary, inefficient, and meddlesome. Complaints about particular immoral practices too often seem to lead to government harassment through procedures and rules that make little economic sense. Managers may therefore avoid using moral expressions in their exchanges so that they do not invite moralistic criticisms and rigid restrictions.[16]

Threat to Image of Power and Effectiveness—Ambitious managers seek to present themselves as powerful and effective. They avoid moral talk at times because moral arguments appear to be too idealistic and utopian. Without effective power, the uses of moral expressions are like empty gestures. Many managers experience futility after they attempt unsuccessfully to change corporate policies which they feel are morally questionable. They privately voice their objections but feel neither able to mount organized protests within their organization nor willing to quit in public outcry. De facto they express a loyalty they do not wholeheartedly feel.[17]

This sense of futility may even be occasioned by management seminars on ethics. Within these workshops managers are encouraged to discuss hypothetical cases and to explore potential action alternatives. Many find these workshops instructive and stimulating. However, when managers begin to consider problems that they actually face in their organizations, then the character of these discussions often changes. Moral expressions recede and are replaced by discussions of organizational politics, technical qualifications, competitive advantages, as well as costs and benefits measured solely in economic terms. In the midst of these kinds of practical considerations, moral terms are abandoned because they seem to lack robustness. They suggest ideals and special pleadings without too much organizational weight.

Managers also shun moral talk in order to not expose their own ethical illiteracy. Most managers neither know nor feel comfortable with the language and logic of moral philosophy. At best they received instruction in juvenile versions of ethics as children and young adults in schools and religious associations. They have little or no experience using ethical concepts to analyze issues. They may more readily and less self-consciously use some ethical terms to identify and condemn obvious wrongdoings, but do not know how to use ethical terms and theories with intellectual rigor and sophistication to identify and resolve moral issues.

Finally, the "value of autonomy places great weight on lower managers' ability to solve creatively all their own problems they regularly face."[18] They observe how this valuing of autonomy actually decreases the likelihood that managers will discuss with their superiors the ethical questions they experience. Figure 2 summarizes these three causes of moral muteness.

FIGURE 2. Causes of Moral Muteness

Moral talk is viewed as creating these negative effects . . .	. . . because of these assumed attributes of moral talk.
• Threat to Harmony	• Moral talk is intrusive and confrontational and invites cycles of mutual recrimination.
• Threat to Efficiency	• Moral talk assumes distracting moralistic forms (praising, blaming, ideological) and is simplistic, inflexible, soft and inexact.
• Threat to Image of Power and Effectiveness	• Moral talk is too esoteric and idealistic, and lacks rigor and force.

Consequences of Moral Muteness

The short-term benefits of moral muteness as perceived by managers (i.e., preservation of harmony, efficiency, and image of self-sufficiency) produce significant long-term costs for organizations. These costly consequences include:

- creation of moral amnesia;
- inappropriate narrowness in conceptions of morality;
- moral stress for individual managers;
- neglect of moral abuses; and
- decreased authority of moral standards.

Moral Amnesia—The avoidance of moral talk creates and reinforces a caricature of management as an amoral activity, a condition we describe as moral amnesia. Many business people and critics of business seem to be unable to recognize the degree to which business activities are in fact regulated by moral expectations. Critics and defenders of current business practices often debate about the legitimacy of bringing moral considerations to bear as if most business decisions were determined exclusively by considerations of profit and personal and organizational self-interest. In the process they ignore the degree to which actual business interactions are already guided by moral expectations communicated by law, professional codes, organizational conventions, and social mores.

When particular business practices seem not to honor particular standards, then it may be wrongly assumed that such actions are guided by no normative expectations whatsoever. Actually, specific business practices which are not, for example, guided primarily by particular standards such as social welfare and justice may in fact be determined in a large part by other moral expectations such as respect for fair contractual relations, the efficient and not wasteful use of human and natural resources, and responsiveness to consumer choices and satisfactions. Often, when businesses act in ways that are judged to be immoral, such as the unannounced closure of a local plant, they may well be acting in keeping with other normative standards, regarding, for example, organizational responsibility. To assume that conduct judged to be unethical because it is counter to particular standards necessarily springs solely from amoral consideration is to fail to grasp the extent to which such conduct may well be guided and legitimated by other, conflicting norms.

The moral amnesia regarding business practices is illustrated by the debate occasioned by an article by Friedman entitled "The Social Responsibility of Business is to Increase its Profit."[19] To many, Friedman seemed to conclude that business people had no moral responsibility other than to use any legal means to increase the returns on the investments of stockholders. He did argue that business people were ill-equipped to become social reformers and that such moral crusading might well lead them to do harm both to those they sought to help and to their own organizations. Both defenders and critics assumed the Friedman was defending an amoral position. However, although cloaked in the language of economic self-interest, Friedman's article alluded in passing to eight different normative standards relevant for business practices: namely, businesses should operate without fraud, without deception in interpersonal communications, in keeping with conventions regarding fair competition, in line with existing laws, with respect to existing contractual agreements, recognizing the given rights of employees and investors, seeking to maximize consumer satisfactions, and always in ways that allow for the free choices of the individual involved. It can be argued that Friedman invited misunderstanding by polarizing issues of profit and social responsibility. It cannot be argued that according to his position profits can be pursued without any other moral criteria than legality.

It is characteristic of this moral amnesia that business people often feel themselves moved by moral obligations and ideals and find no way to refer explicitly to these pushes and pulls except indirectly by invoking personal preferences, common sense, and long-term benefits. They remain inarticulate and unself-conscious of their convictions.

Narrowed Conception of Morality—In order to avoid getting bogged down in moral talk which threatens efficiency, managers who are convinced they are acting morally may argue that their actions are a morally neutral matter. They "stonewall" moral questions by arguing that the issues involved are ones of feasibility, practicality, and the impersonal balancing of costs and benefits, and that decisions on these matters are appropriately made by relevant managers and directors without public discussion.

We interviewed a number of managers who made these kinds of claims with respect to issues that others might consider contentious. A utilities executive argued, for example, that studies had exaggerated the impact of steam plants on water supplies. He also contended that no moral issues were relevant to the decisions regarding the domestic use of nuclear power. A pharmaceutical company manager criticized those who attempted to make a moral issue out of a leak in a rinse water pipe. An accountant criticized a colleague for arguing that the procedure recently used with a customer involved moral improprieties. These managers attempted to treat issues that had been questioned as if they were not publicly debatable.

Insofar as it is thought that moral issues are posed only by deviance from acceptable standards of behavior, then managers have a legitimate case to shun moral discussions of their actions which are neither illegal nor deviant. However, while appropriately claiming that their actions are not morally improper, managers stonewall whenever they insist, in addition, that their actions are constituted not only by deviance, but also by dilemmas (when two or more normative standards conflict) and by shortfalls (from the pursuit of high ideals). In the examples cited above, the managers were correct in asserting that no illegal nor blatantly deviant actions were involved. However, they were incorrect to argue that these actions were morally neutral.

Moral muteness in the form of stonewalling thus perpetuates a narrow conception of morality, i.e., as only concerned with blatant deviance from moral standards. Most importantly, moral muteness in this case prevents creative exploration of action alternatives that might enable the organization to balance better conflicting demands or to approximate better the highest ideals.

Moral Stress—Managers experience moral stress as a result of role conflict and role ambiguity in connection with moral expectations.[20] They treat their responsibility to their organizations as a moral standard and, when confronted with an ethical question, they frequently have difficulty deciding what kinds of costs will be acceptable in dealing with the question (e.g., it costs money to upgrade toilet facilities and improve working conditions). Moreover, moral expectations (for example, honesty in communications) are often very general and the manager is frequently faced with a decision on what is morally appropriate behavior in a specific instance. He or she may have to decide, for example, when legitimate entertainment becomes bribery or when legitimate bluffing or concealment of basic positions in negotiations with a customer or supplier becomes dishonesty in communication.

A certain degree of such moral stress is unavoidable in management life. However, it can be exacerbated beyond reasonable levels by the absence of moral talk. If managers are unable to discuss with others their problems and questions, they absorb the uncertainty and stress that would more appropriately be shared by colleagues and superiors. In the absence of moral talk, managers may cope with intolerable levels of moral stress by denying the relevance or importance of particular normative expectations. This may take the form of inappropriate idealism in which the legitimacy of the organization's economic objectives is given inadequate attention. Conversely, and perhaps more frequently, managers may cope with excessive moral stress by treating decisions as morally neutral, responding only to economic concerns and organizational systems of reward and censure. In either case, moral muteness eliminates any opportunity that might exist for creative, collaborative problem solving that would be best for the manager, as well as for the organization and its stakeholders.

Neglect of Abuses—The avoidance of moral talk by managers also means that many moral issues are simply not organizationally recognized and addressed. Consequently, many moral abuses are ignored, many moral ideals are not pursued, and many moral dilemmas remain unresolved. Managers we interviewed readily cited moral lapses of colleagues and competitors.[21] The popular press continually cites examples of immoral managerial conduct, often failing in the process to credit the extent to which managers actually adhere to moral standards.

Just as norms of confrontation contribute to moral muteness, in circular fashion that muteness reinforces those norms and leads to a culture of neglect. Organizational silence on moral issues makes it more difficult for members to raise questions and debate issues. What could and should be ordinary practice—i.e., questioning of the propriety of specific decisions and actions—tends to require an act of heroism and thus is less likely to occur.

Decreased Authority of Moral Standards—Moral arguments possess compelling authority only if the discourse in which these arguments are stated is socially rooted. It is an idealistic misconception to suppose that moral reasons by virtue of their logic alone inspire the feelings of obligation and desire that make people willingly adhere to moral standards. Blake and Davis refer to this assumption as the "fallacy of normative determinism."[22] The pushes and pulls which lead people to honor normative standards arise as much, if not more, from social relationships as from verbal communication of moral ideas. The articulations of moral ideas gain compelling authority to the degree that these expressions call to mind existing feelings of social attachments and obligations, build upon tacit as well as explicit agreements and promises, seem to be related to realistic rewards and punishments, and connect feelings of self-worth to moral compliance.[23] That is, moral expressions become authoritative, and therefore genuinely normative, to the degree that they both arouse such feelings and reveal such agreements, and also connect these feelings and recollections with moral action.

Moral ideas communicated without being socially rooted simply lack compelling authority. Such expressions are like inflated currency: because they possess little real authority, there is a tendency to use more and more of them in order to create hoped-for effects. Such language, unless it has become socially rooted, is experienced as disruptive, distracting, inflexible, and overblown. Simply attempting to talk more about moral issues in business is not likely to make these conversations more weighty and authoritative. What is needed is to find ways of realistically connecting this language with the experiences and expectations of people involved in business.

Indeed, in an even more general effect, the resolution of organizational problems through cooperation becomes more difficult to the extent that managers shun moral talk. Cooperation may be gained in several ways. For example, it may be inspired by charismatic leadership or achieved by forceful commands. Charisma and command are, however, limited temporary devices for gaining cooperation. Many managers do not have the gift for charismatic leadership. In any case, such leadership is best exercised in relation to crises and not ordinary operations. Commands may achieve compliance, but a compliance that is half-hearted, foot-dragging, and resentful. Cooperation is realized more enduringly and more fully by fostering commitments to shared moral values. Shared values provide a common vocabulary for identifying and resolving problems. Shared values constitute common cultures which provide the guidelines for action and the justifications for decisions.[24]

It is impossible to foster a sense of ongoing community without invoking moral images and normative expectations. Moral terms provide the symbols of attachment and guidelines for interactions within communities.[25] In the absence of such images and norms, individuals are prone to defend their own interests more aggressively and with fewer compromises. Longer range and wider conceptions of self-interest are likely to be abandoned. Without moral appeals to industry, organizational well-being, team work, craftsmanship, and service, it is much more difficult to cultivate voluntary rather than regimented cooperation.[26]

The Nature of Change Interventions

Several factors must be taken into account by those who wish to reduce this avoidance of moral talk by managers. Those who wish to "institutionalize ethics" in business, "manage values in organizations," or gain "the ethical edge"[27] must take into account the factors which give rise to this avoidance. It is impossible to foster greater moral responsibility by business people and organizations without also facilitating more open and direct conversations about these issues by managers.

First, business people will continue to shun open discussions of actual moral issues unless means are provided to allow for legitimate dissent by managers who will not be personally blamed, criticized, ostracized, or punished for their views. From the perspective of the managers we interviewed, their organizations seemed to expect from them unquestioning loyalty and deference. Although many had privately spoken of their moral objections to the practices of other managers and their own firms, few had publicly voiced these concerns within their own organizations. Full discussions of moral issues are not likely to take place unless managers and workers feel they can openly voice arguments regarding policies and practices that will not be held against them when alternatives are adopted.

Business organizations often do not tolerate full, open debate of moral issues because they perceive dissent as assuming the form either of carping assaults or of factional divisiveness. Carping is a way of airing personal grievances and frustrations, often using moral expressions in order to find fault.[28]

Ideally, managers ought to be able openly to voice dissent and then, once decisions have been made contrary to their views, either respectfully support such choices or formally protest. However, business organizations that stifle open discussions of moral concerns invite the carping they seek to avoid by limiting debate in the first place. Managers are most likely to complain, to express resentment, and to find personal fault in others if they feel they have no real opportunities to voice justifiable dissents.

Legitimate expressions of dissent may be articulated in ways that do not aggravate and reinforce factional divisiveness. Before considering recommendations for organizational change (about which various managers and workers are likely to have vested interests), it is useful to set aside time for all those involved to recognize the degree to which they both hold similar long-run objectives and value common ethical principles.[29] These exercises are valuable because they help to make shared commitments seem basic and the factional differences temporary and relative. In addition, factional differences are less likely to become contentious if these factions are accorded partial legitimacy as recognized functional sub-groups within larger organizations. Finally, legitimate dissent is less likely to aggravate factional divisiveness if ground rules for debate and dissent include mutual consultations with all those immediately involved. These rules can help reduce the chances of discussions turning into empty posturing and/or irresolute harangues.

Second, if business people are going to overcome the avoidance of moral talk, then they must learn how to incorporate moral expressions and arguments into their exchanges. Learning how to talk ethics is neither as simple nor as difficult as it seems to be to many managers. Initially, managers must learn to avoid as much as possible the ordinary abuses of moral talk. In particular, efforts must be made to limit the degree to which moral talk is used for publicly extolling the virtues or excoriating the vices of other managers. Evaluations of personal moral worth ought to remain as private as possible. Furthermore, the use of moral expressions to rationalize and to express personal frustrations ought to be censored. In addition, the use of moral expression to take ideological postures ought to be minimized. Moral talk ought to be used primarily to identify problems, to consider issues, to advocate and criticize policies, and to justify and explain decisions.

Managers should recognize and learn to use several of the typical forms in which moral arguments are stated. An elementary knowledge of moral logics as applied to business matters is a useful skill not only for defending one's own argument, but also for identifying the weaknesses and strengths in the arguments of others. It is important, however, to recognize that verbal skill at talking ethics is primarily a rhetorical and discursive skill and not a matter of philosophical knowledge. Like the skill of elocution, learning how to talk ethics involves learning how to state and criticize moral arguments persuasively. What is critical is that managers are able to use moral reasoning to deal with issues they actually face in their lives and to influence others to consider carefully their positions.

Managers must regularly and routinely engage with each other in reflection and dialogue about their own experiences with moral issues. The attempt to overcome the avoidance of moral talk by managers by introducing them to formal philosophical languages and logics not rooted in their social experiences is likely to fail. Philosophical ethics is indeed an instructive and critical tool that can be used to analyze moral arguments of business people and to propose creative solutions to perceived dilemmas. It is improbable, however, that many managers are likely to adopt philosophical discourse on a day-to-day basis to talk about moral issues. At best, this language might serve as a technical instrument, much like the specialized languages of corporate law and advanced accounting used by specialized experts in consultation with executives. Such technical use does not overcome the moral amnesia that infects ordinary communications among managers. To be compelling, moral discourse must be connected with, express, foster, and strengthen managers' feelings of attachment, obligation, promises, and agreements.

Moral ideas rarely possess compelling authority unless some group or groups of people so closely identify with these ideas as to become their articulate champions. Moral ideas are likely to gain widespread following by business people as smaller groups of managers and workers so closely identify with these ideas—which in turn express their own attachments, obligations, and desires—that they champion them. This identification is most likely to occur where business people with existing feelings of community, due to professional, craft, or organizational loyalties, begin to articulate their moral convictions and to discuss moral issues. It is precisely in these sorts of subgroups of people who have to work with each other as colleagues that managers will be willing to risk speaking candidly and see the benefits of such candor in fuller cooperation.

The role of senior managers in fostering such "good conversation" among managers in an organization cannot be overemphasized.[30] If they seek to provide moral leadership to an organization, senior managers must not only signal the importance they place on such conversations, but also demand that they take place. They need also to build such conversations into the fabric of organizational life through management mechanisms such as requiring that managers include in their annual plans a statement of the steps they will take to ensure that questionable practices are reviewed, or that new business proposals include an assessment of the ethical climate of any new business area into which entry is proposed.[31]

Finally, interventions require patience. Open conversations of the kind we have been describing will, in the short-run, be slow and time-consuming and thus reduce organizational efficiency. They will, in the short-run, be awkward and fumbling and appear futile, and thus they will be quite uncomfortable for managers used to smooth control of managerial discussions. Patience will be required to persevere until these short-run problems are overcome, until new norms emerge which encourage debate without carping and acrimony, until managers develop the skills necessary for efficient and reflective problem solving with respect to moral issues, until moral voices and commitments are heard clearly and strongly throughout their organizations.

Note

The research on which this article is based was made possible in part by a grant from the Social Science and Humanities Research Council of Canada. The Center for Ethics and Social Policy in Berkeley, California, aided this research by helping to arrange for interviews with executives. The authors wish to thank William R. Torbert and Richard P. Nielsen for their helpful comments on an earlier draft of this article.

References

1. Chester Barnard, *The Function of the Executive* (Cambridge, MA: Harvard University Press, 1938), p. 154; George E. Breen, "Middle Management Morale in the 80's," *An AMA Survey Report* (New York, NY: The American Management Association, 1983); Mark H. McCormick, *What They Don't Teach You at Harvard Business School* (Toronto: Bantam Books, 1984), chapter 2.

2. Alexis DeTocqueville, *Democracy in America*, Vol. 2., translated by Henry Reeve, revised by Francis Bowen (New York, NY: Mentor Books, 1945), pp. 129–132.

3. Charles McCoy, *Management of Values: The Ethical Differences in Corporate Policy and Performance* (Boston, MA: Pitman, 1985), pp. 8, 9, 16, 98; Leonard Silk and David Vogel, *Ethics and Profits: The Crisis of Confidence in American Business* (New York, NY: Simon and Schuster, 1976), chapter 8; Robert C. Solomon and Kristine R. Hanson, *It's Good Business* (New York, NY: Atheneum, 1985), p. xiv; see also, Mark Pastin, *The Hard Problems of Management: Gaining the Ethics Edge* (San Francisco, CA: Jossey-Bass, 1986), Introduction, Part One.

4. James A. Waters, Frederick Bird, and Peter D. Chant, "Everyday Moral Issues Experienced by Managers," *Journal of Business Ethics* (Fall 1986), pp. 373–384; Barbara Ley Toffler, *Tough Choices: Managers Talk Ethics* (New York, NY: John Wiley and Sons, 1986); Kathy E. Kram, Peter C. Yaeger, and Gary Reed, "Ethical Dilemmas in Corporate Context," paper presented at Academy of Management, August 1988; Robin Derry, "Managerial Perceptions of Ethical Conflicts and Conceptions of Morality: A Qualitative Interview Study," paper presented at Academy of Management, August 1988.

5. James A. Waters and Frederick B. Bird, "The Moral Dimension of Organizational Culture," *Journal of Business Ethics*, 6/1 (1987): 18.

6. Jurgen Habermas, *The Theory of Communicative Action*, Vol. I, translated by Thomas McCarthy (Boston, MA: The Beacon Press, 1984), Part I, chapter 3.

7. Mark L. Taylor, *A Study of Corporate Ethical Policy Statements* (Dallas, TX: The Foundation of the Southwestern Graduate School of Banking, 1980).

8. Frederick Bird and James A. Waters, "The Nature of Managerial Moral Standards," *Journal of Business Ethics*, 6 (1987): 1–13.

9. George Wilhelm Frederick Hegel, *Philosophy of Right*, translated by T.M. Knox (London: Oxford University Press, 1952, 1967), pp. 93–103.

10. Aristotle, *The Nichomachean Ethics*, translated by J. A. R. Rhomson (Middlesex, U.K.: Penguin Books, 1953), Book VII; Peter Winch, *Ethics and Action* (London: Routledge and Kegan Paul, 1972), chapters 4, 8.

11. Waters, Bird, and Chant, op. cit.; Frederick Bird, Frances Westley, and James A. Waters, "The Uses of Moral Talk: Why Do Managers Talk Ethics?" *Journal of Business Ethics* (1989).

12. Ralph Nader, Peter Petkas, and Kate Blackwell, eds., *Whistle Blowing* (New York, NY: Grossman, 1972); Richard P. Nielsen, "What Can Managers Do About Unethical Management?" *Journal of Business Ethics* 6/4 (1987).

13. Steven Kerr, "Integrity in Effective Leadership," in Suresh Srivastra and Associates, eds., *Executive Integrity* (San Francisco, CA: Jossey-Bass, 1988).

14. Clifford Geertz, *The Interpretation of Cultures* (New York, NY: Basic Books, 1973), chapter 9.

15. Oliver E. Williamson, "Transactional Cost Economics: The Governance of Contractual Relations," *Journal of Law and Economics* (1980), pp. 233–261.

16. Pastin, op. cit., chapter 3; Silk and Vogel, op. cit., chapter 2; Solomon and Hanson, op. cit., p. 5; Kerr, op. cit., p. 138.

17. Albert Hirschman, *Exit, Voice and Loyalty: Responses to Decline in Firms and States* (Cambridge, MA: Harvard University Press, 1970), chapter 7.

18. Kram, Yaeger, and Read, op. cit., p. 28.

19. Milton Friedman, "The Social Responsibility of Business Is to Increase its Profit," *New York Times Magazine*, September 13, 1970.

20. Waters and Bird, op. cit., pp. 16–18.

21. Waters, Bird, and Chant, op. cit.

22. Judith Blake and Kingsley Davis, "Norms, Values and Sanctions" in Dennis Wrong and Harry L. Gracey, *Readings in Introductory Sociology* (New York, NY: Macmillan Co., 1967).

23. Emile Durkheim, *Suicide*, translated by John A. Spaulding and George Simpson (New York, NY: The Free Press, 1974), chapter 2; Frederick Bird, "Morality and Society: An Introduction to Comparative Sociological Study of Moralities," unpublished manuscript, 1988, chapter 4.

24. Karl E. Weick, "Organizational Culture as a Source of High Reliability," *California Management Review*, 29/2 (Winter 1987): 112–127.

25. Basil Bernstein, *Class Codes, and Control* (St. Albans, NY: Palladin, 1973).

26. Frances Westley and Frederick Bird, "The Social Psychology of Organizational Commitment," unpublished paper, 1989.

27. Kirk Hanson, "Ethics and Business: A Progress Report," in Charles McCoy, ed., *Management of Values* (Boston, MA: Pitman, 1985), pp. 280–88; Fred Twining and Charles McCoy, "How to Manage Values in Organizations," unpublished manuscript, 1987; Pastin, op. cit.

28. Bird, Westley, and Waters, op. cit.

29. Twining and McCoy, op. cit.

30. James A. Waters, "Integrity Management: Learning and Implementing Ethical Principles in the Workplace," in S. Srivastva, ed., *Executive Integrity* (San Francisco, CA: Jossey-Bass, 1988).

31. James A. Waters and Peter D. Chant, "Internal Control of Management Integrity: Beyond Accounting Systems," *California Management Review*, 24/3 (Spring 1982): 60–66.

Justice

• *Case Study* •

The Oil Rig

JOANNE B. CIULLA

This description focuses on one of the three exploratory rigs which have been drilling for several years along the coast of Angola, under contract to a major U.S. multinational oil company. All three rigs are owned and operated by a large U.S. drilling company.

The "Explorer IV" rig is a relatively small jack-up (i.e., with legs) with dimensions of approximately 200 ft. by 100 ft. which houses a crew of 150 men. The crew comprises laborers, roustabouts (unskilled laborers) and maintenance staff, and 30 expatriate workers who work as roughnecks, drillers or in administrative or technical positions. The top administrator on the Explorer IV is the "tool pusher," an American Expat, who wields almost absolute authority over matters pertaining to life on the rig.

The crew quarters on the Explorer IV were modified for operations in Angola. A second galley was installed on the lower level and cabins on the upper level were enlarged to permit a dormitory style arrangement of 16 persons per room. The lower level is the "Angolan section" of the rig, where the 120 local workers eat, sleep, and socialize during their 28-day "hitch."

The upper level houses the 30 Expats in an area equal in square footage to that of the Angolan section. The Expat section's quarters are semi-private with baths and this section boasts its own galley, game room and movie room. Although it is nowhere explicitly written, a tacit regulation exists prohibiting Angolan workers from entering the Expat section of the rig, except in emergencies. The only Angolans exempt from this regulation are those assigned to the highly valued positions of cleaning or galley staff in the Expat section. These few positions are highly valued because of the potential for receiving gifts or recovering discarded razors, etc., from the Expats.

The separation of Angolan workers from Expats is reinforced by several other rig policies. Angolan laborers travel to and from the rig by boat (an eighteen-hour trip) whereas the expats are transported by helicopter. Also, medical attention is dispensed by the British R.N. throughout the day for Expats, but only during shift changes for the Angolans (except in emergencies). When there are serious injuries, the response is different for the two groups. If, for example, a finger is severed, Expats are rushed to Luanda for reconstructive surgery, whereas Angolan workers have the amputation operation performed on the rig by a medic.

From *Business Ethics Module*, 1990, pages 13–14, by Dr. Joanne B. Ciulla, University of Richmond. Reprinted with permission.

Angolan workers are issued grey overalls and Expats receive red coveralls. Meals in the two galleys are vastly different; they are virtually gourmet in the Expat galley and somewhat more proletarian in the Angolan section. The caterers informed the author that the two galleys' budgets were nearly equal (despite the gross disparity in numbers served).

Communication between Expats and Angolans is notable by its absence on the Explorer IV. This is principally because none of the Expats speaks Portuguese and none of the Angolans speaks more than a few words of English. Only the chef of the Portuguese catering company speaks both English and Portuguese, and consequently, he is required to act as interpreter in all emergency situations. In the working environment, training and coordination of effort is accomplished via sign language or repetition of example.

From time to time an entourage of Angolan government officials visits the Explorer IV. These visits normally last only for an hour or so, but invariably, the officials dine with the Expats and take a brief tour of the equipment before returning to shore via helicopter. Never has an entourage expressed concern about the disparity in living conditions on the rig, nor have the officials bothered to speak with the Angolan workers. Observers comment that the officials seem disinterested in the situation of the Angolan workers, most of whom are from outside the capital city.

The rig's segregated environment is little affected by the presence of an American black. The American black is assigned to the Expat section and is, of course, permitted to partake of all Expat privileges. Nevertheless, it should be noted that there are few American blacks in the international drilling business and those few are frequently less than completely welcomed into the rig's social activities.

Distributive Justice

John Rawls

We may think of a human society as a more or less self-sufficient association regulated by a common conception of justice and aimed at advancing the good of its members.[1] As a co-operative venture for mutual advantage, it is characterized by a conflict as well as an identity of interests. There is an identity of interests since social co-operation makes possible a better life for all than any would have if everyone were to try to live by his own efforts; yet at the same time men are not indifferent as to how the greater benefits produced by their joint labours are distributed, for in order to further their own aims each prefers a larger to a lesser share. A conception of justice is a set of principles

From John Rawls, "Distributive Justice," *Philosophy, Politics, and Society*, 3rd series, ed. by Peter Laslett and W. G. Runciman (Basil Blackwell, Oxford; Barnes & Noble Books, Div. Harper & Row, Publishers, New York, 1967). Reprinted by permission of the author and publisher.

for choosing between the social arrangements which determine this division and for underwriting a consensus as to the proper distributive shares.

Now at first sight the most rational conception of justice would seem to be utilitarian. For consider: each man in realizing his own good can certainly balance his own losses against his own gains. We can impose a sacrifice on ourselves now for the sake of a greater advantage later. A man quite properly acts, as long as others are not affected, to achieve his own greatest good, to advance his ends as far as possible. Now, why should not a society act on precisely the same principle? Why is not that which is rational in the case of one man right in the case of a group of men? Surely the simplest and most direct conception of the right, and so of justice, is that of maximizing the good. This assumes a prior understanding of what is good, but we can think of the good as already given by the interests of rational individuals. Thus just as the principle of individual choice is to achieve one's greatest good, to advance so far as possible one's own system of rational desires, so the principle of social choice is to realize the greatest good (similarly defined) summed over all the members of society. We arrive at the principle of utility in a natural way: by this principle a society is rightly ordered, and hence just, when its institutions are arranged so as to realize the greatest sum of satisfactions.

The striking feature of the principle of utility is that it does not matter, except indirectly, how this sum of satisfactions is distributed among individuals, any more than it matters, except indirectly, how one man distributes his satisfactions over time. Since certain ways of distributing things affect the total sum of satisfactions, this fact must be taken into account in arranging social institutions; but according to this principle the explanation of common-sense precepts of justice and their seemingly stringent character is that they are those rules which experience shows must be strictly respected and departed from only under exceptional circumstances if the sum of advantages is to be maximized. The precepts of justice are derivative from the one end of attaining the greatest net balance of satisfactions. There is no reason in principle why the greater gains of some should not compensate for the lesser losses of others; or why the violation of the liberty of a few might not be made right by a greater good shared by many. It simply happens, at least under most conditions, that the greatest sum of advantages is not generally achieved in this way. From the standpoint of utility the strictness of common-sense notions of justice has a certain usefulness, but as a philosophical doctrine it is irrational.

If, then, we believe that as a matter of principle each member of society has an inviolability founded on justice which even the welfare of everyone else cannot override, and that a loss of freedom for some is not made right by a greater sum of satisfactions enjoyed by many, we shall have to look for another account of the principles of justice. The principle of utility is incapable of explaining the fact that in a just society the liberties of equal citizenship are taken for granted, and the rights secured by justice are not subject to political bargaining nor to the calculus of social interests. Now, the most natural alternative to the principle of utility is its traditional rival, the theory of the social contract. The aim of the contract doctrine is precisely to account for the strictness of justice by supposing that its principles arise from an agreement among free and independent persons in an original position of equality and hence reflect the integrity and equal sovereignty of the rational persons who are the contractees. Instead of supposing that a conception of right, and so a conception of justice, is simply an extension of the principle of choice for one man to society as a whole, the contract doctrine assumes that the rational individuals who belong to society must choose together, in one joint act, what is to count among them as just and unjust. They are to decide among themselves once and for all what is to be their conception of justice. This decision is thought of as being made in a suitably defined initial situation one of the significant features of which is that no one knows his position in society, nor even his place in the distribution of natural talents and abilities. The principles of justice to which all are forever bound are chosen in the absence of this sort of specific information. A veil of ignorance prevents anyone from being advantaged or disadvantaged by the contingencies of social class and fortune; and hence the bargaining problems which arise in everyday life from the possession of this knowledge do not affect the choice of principles. On the contract doctrine, then, the theory of justice, and indeed ethics itself, is part of the general theory of rational choice, a fact perfectly clear in its Kantian formulation.

Once justice is thought of as arising from an original agreement of this kind, it is evident that the principle of utility is problematical. For why should rational individuals who have a system of ends they wish to advance agree to a violation of their liberty for the sake of a greater balance of satisfactions enjoyed by others? It seems more plausible to suppose that, when situated in an original position of equal right, they would insist upon institutions which returned compensating advantages for any sacrifices required. A rational man would not accept an institution merely because it maximized the sum of advantages irrespective of its effect on his own interests. It appears, then, that the principle of utility would be rejected as a principle of justice, although we shall not try to argue this important question here. Rather, our aim is to give a brief sketch of the conception of distributive shares implicit in the principles of justice which, it seems would be chosen in the original position. The philosophical appeal of utilitarianism is that it seems to offer a single principle on the basis of which a consistent and complete conception of right can be developed. The problem is to work out a contractarian alternative in such a way that it has comparable if not all the same virtues.

In our discussion we shall make no attempt to derive the two principles of justice which we shall examine; that is, we shall not try to show that they would be chosen in the original position.[2] It must suffice that it is plausible that they would be, at least in preference to the standard forms of traditional theories. Instead we shall be mainly concerned with three questions: first, how to interpret these principles so that they define a consistent and complete conception of justice; second, whether it is possible to arrange the institutions of a constitutional democracy so that these principles are satisfied, at least approximately; and third, whether the conception of distributive shares which they define is compatible with common-sense notions of justice. The significance of these principles is that they allow for the strictness of the claims of justice; and if they can be understood so as to yield a consistent and complete conception, the contractarian alternative would seem all the more attractive.

The two principles of justice which we shall discuss may be formulated as follows: first, each person engaged in an institution or affected by it has an equal right to the most extensive liberty compatible with a like liberty for all;

and second, inequalities as defined by the institutional structure or fostered by it are arbitrary unless it is reasonable to expect that they will work out to everyone's advantage and provided that the positions and offices to which they attach or from which they may be gained are open to all. These principles regulate the distributive aspects of institutions by controlling the assignment of rights and duties throughout the whole social structure, beginning with the adoption of a political constitution in accordance with which they are then to be applied to legislation. It is upon a correct choice of a basic structure of society, its fundamental system of rights and duties, that the justice of distributive shares depends.

The two principles of justice apply in the first instance to this basic structure, that is, to the main institutions of the social system and their arrangement, how they are combined together. Thus, this structure includes the political constitution and the principal economic and social institutions which together define a person's liberties and rights and affect his life-prospects, what he may expect to be and how well he may expect to fare. The intuitive idea here is that those born into the social system at different positions, say in different social classes, have varying life-prospects determined, in part, by the system of political liberties and personal rights, and by the economic and social opportunities which are made available to these positions. In this way the basic structure of society favours certain men over others, and these are the basic inequalities, the ones which affect their whole life-prospects. It is inequalities of this kind, presumably inevitable in any society, with which the two principles of justice are primarily designed to deal.

Now the second principle holds that an inequality is allowed only if there is reason to believe that the institution with the inequality, or permitting it, will work out for the advantage of every person engaged in it. In the case of the basic structure this means that all inequalities which affect life-prospects, say the inequalities of income and wealth which exist between social classes, must be to the advantage of everyone. Since the principle applies to institutions, we interpret this to mean that inequalities must be to the advantage of the representative man for each relevant social position; they should improve each such man's expectation. Here we assume that it is possible to attach to each position an expectation, and that this expectation is a function of the whole institutional structure: it can be raised and lowered by reassigning rights and duties throughout the system. Thus the expectation of any position depends upon the expectations of the others, and these in turn depend upon the pattern of rights and duties established by the basic structure. But it is not clear what is meant by saying that inequalities must be to the advantage of every representative man. . . . [One] . . . interpretation [of what is meant by saying that inequalities must be to the advantage of every representative man] . . . is to choose some social position by reference to which the pattern of expectations as a whole is to be judged, and then to maximize with respect to the expectations of this representative man consistent with the demands of equal liberty and equality of opportunity. Now, the one obvious candidate is the representative man of those who are least favoured by the system of institutional inequalities. Thus we arrive at the following idea: the basic structure of the social system affects the life-prospects of typical individuals according to their initial places in society, say the various income classes into which they are born, or depending upon certain natural attributes, as when institutions make discriminations between men and women or allow certain advantages to be gained by those with greater natural abilities. The fundamental problem of distributive justice concerns the differences in life-prospects which come about in this way. We interpret the second principle to hold that these differences are just if and only if the greater expectations of the more advantaged, when playing a part in the working of the whole social system, improve the expectations of the least advantaged. The basic structure is just throughout when the advantages of the more fortunate promote the well-being of the least fortunate, that is, when a decrease in their advantages would make the least fortunate even worse off than they are. The basic structure is perfectly just when the prospects of the least fortunate are as great as they can be.

In interpreting the second principle (or rather the first part of it which we may, for obvious reasons, refer to as the difference principle), we assume that the first principle requires a basic equal liberty for all, and that the resulting political system, when circumstances permit, is that of a constitutional democracy in some form. There must be liberty of the person and political equality as well as liberty of conscience and freedom of thought. There is one class of equal citizens which defines a common status for all. We also assume that there is equality of opportunity and a fair competition for the available positions on the basis of reasonable qualifications. Now, given this background, the differences to be justified are the various economic and social inequalities in the basic structure which must inevitably arise in such a scheme. These are the inequalities in the distribution of income and wealth and the distinctions in social prestige and status which attach to the various positions and classes. The difference principle says that these inequalities are just if and only if they are part of a larger system in which they work out to the advantage of the most unfortunate representative man. The just distributive shares determined by the basic structure are those specified by this constrained maximum principle.

Thus, consider the chief problem of distributive justice, that concerning the distribution of wealth as it affects the life-prospects of those starting out in the various income groups. These income classes define the relevant representative men from which the social system is to be judged. Now, a son of a member of the entrepreneurial class (in a capitalist society) has a better prospect than that of the son of an unskilled labourer. This will be true, it seems, even when the social injustices which presently exist are removed and the two men are of equal talent and ability; the inequality cannot be done away with as long as something like the family is maintained. What, then, can justify this inequality in life-prospects? According to the second principle it is justified only if it is to the advantage of the representative man who is worse off, in this case the representative unskilled labourer. The inequality is permissible because lowering it would, let's suppose, make the working man even worse off than he is. Presumably, given the principle of open offices (the second part of the second principle), the greater expectations allowed to entrepreneurs has the effect in the longer run of raising the life-prospects of the labouring class. The inequality in expectation provides an incentive so that the economy is more efficient, industrial advance proceeds at a quicker pace, and so on, the end result of which is that greater material and other benefits are distributed throughout the system. Of course, all of this is familiar, and whether true or not in particular cases, it is the sort of thing which must be argued if the inequality in income and wealth is to be acceptable by the difference principle.

We should now verify that this interpretation of the second principle gives a natural sense in which everyone may be said to be made better off. Let us suppose that inequalities are chain-connected: that is, if an inequality raises the expectations of the lowest position, it raises the expectations of all positions in between. For example, if the greater expectations of the representative entrepreneur raises that of the unskilled labourer, it also raises that of the semi-skilled. Let us further assume that inequalities are close-knit: that is, it is impossible to raise (or lower) the expectation of any representative man without raising (or lowering) the expectations of every other representative man, and in particular, without affecting one way or the other that of the least fortunate. There is no loose-jointedness, so to speak, in the way in which expectations depend upon one another. Now with these assumptions, everyone does benefit from an inequality which satisfies the difference principle, and the second principle as we have formulated it reads correctly. For the representative man who is better off in any pair-wise comparison gains by being allowed to have his advantage, and the man who is worse off benefits from the contribution which all inequalities make to each position below. Of course, chain-connection and close-knitness may not obtain; but in this case those who are better off should not have a veto over the advantages available for the least advantaged. The stricter interpretation of the difference principle should be followed, and all inequalities should be arranged for the advantage of the most unfortunate even if some inequalities are not to the advantage of those in middle positions. Should these conditions fail, then, the second principle would have to be stated in another way.

It may be observed that the difference principle represents, in effect, an original agreement to share in the benefits of the distribution of natural talents and abilities, whatever this distribution turns out to be, in order to alleviate as far as possible the arbitrary handicaps resulting from our initial starting places in society. Those who have been favoured by nature, whoever they are, may gain from their good fortune only on terms that improve the well-being of those who have lost out. The naturally advantaged are not to gain simply because they are more gifted, but only to cover the costs of training and cultivating their endowments and for putting them to use in a way which improved the position of the less fortunate. We are led to the difference principle if we wish to arrange the basic social structure so that no one gains (or loses) from his luck in the natural lottery of talent and ability, or from his initial place in society, without giving (or receiving) compensating advantages in return. (The parties in the original position are not said to be attracted by this idea and so agree to it; rather, given the symmetries of their situation, and particularly their lack of knowledge, and so on, they will find it to their interest to agree to a principle which can be understood in this way.) And we should note also that when the difference principle is perfectly satisfied, the basic structure is optimal by the efficiency principle. There is no way to make anyone better off without making someone worse off, namely, the least fortunate representative man. Thus the two principles of justice define distributive shares in a way compatible with efficiency, at least as long as we move on this highly abstract level. If we want to say (as we do, although it cannot be argued here) that the demands of justice have an absolute weight with respect to efficiency, this claim may seem less paradoxical when it is kept in mind that perfectly just institutions are also efficient.

Our second question is whether it is possible to arrange the institutions of a constitutional democracy so that the two principles of justice are satisfied, at least approximately. We shall try to show that this can be done provided the government regulates a free economy in a certain way. More fully, if law and government act effectively to keep markets competitive, resources fully employed, property and wealth widely distributed over time, and to maintain the appropriate social minimum, then if there is equality of opportunity underwritten by education for all, the resulting distribution will be just. Of course, all of these arrangements and policies are familiar. The only novelty in the following remarks, if there is any novelty at all, is that this framework of institutions can be made to satisfy the difference principle. To argue this, we must sketch the relations of these institutions and how they work together.

First of all, we assume that the basic social structure is controlled by a just constitution which secures the various liberties of equal citizenship. Thus the legal order is administered in accordance with the principle of legality, and liberty of conscience and freedom of thought are taken for granted. The political process is conducted, so far as possible, as a just procedure for choosing between governments and for enacting just legislation. From the standpoint of distributive justice, it is also essential that there be equality of opportunity in several senses. Thus, we suppose that, in addition to maintaining the usual social overhead capital, government provides for equal educational opportunities for all either by subsidizing private schools or by operating a public school system. It also enforces and underwrites equality of opportunity in commercial ventures and in the free choice of occupation. This result is achieved by policing business behaviour and by preventing the establishment of barriers and restriction to the desirable positions and markets. Lastly, there is a guarantee of a social minimum which the government meets by family allowances and special payments in times of unemployment, or by a negative income tax.

In maintaining this system of institutions the government may be thought of as divided into four branches. Each branch is represented by various agencies (or activities thereof) charged with preserving certain social and economic conditions. These branches do not necessarily overlap with the usual organization of government, but should be understood as purely conceptual. Thus the allocation branch is to keep the economy feasibly competitive, that is, to prevent the formation of unreasonable market power. Markets are competitive in this sense when they cannot be made more so consistent with the requirements of efficiency and the acceptance of the facts of consumer preferences and geography. The allocation branch is also charged with identifying and correcting, say by suitable taxes and subsidies wherever possible, the more obvious departures from efficiency caused by the failure of prices to measure accurately social benefits and costs. The stabilization branch strives to maintain reasonably full employment so that there is no waste through failure to use resources and the free choice of occupation and the deployment of finance is supported by strong effective demand. These two branches together are to preserve the efficiency of the market economy generally.

The social minimum is established through the operations of the transfer branch. Later on we shall consider at what level this minimum should be set, since this is a crucial matter; but for the moment, a few general remarks will suffice. The main idea is that the workings of the transfer branch take into account the precept of need and assign it an appropriate weight with respect to the other common-sense precepts of justice. A market economy ignores the claims of need altogether. Hence there is a division of labour between the parts of the social system as different institutions answer to different common-sense precepts. Competitive markets (properly supplemented by government operations) handle the problem of the efficient allocation of labour and resources and set a weight to the conventional precepts associated with wages and earnings (the precepts of each according to his work and experience, or responsibility and the hazards of the job, and so on), whereas the transfer branch guarantees a certain level of well-being and meets the claims of need. Thus it is obvious that the justice of distributive shares depends upon the whole social system and how it distributes total income, wages plus transfers. There is with reason strong objection to the competitive determination of total income, since this would leave out of account the claims of need and of a decent standard of life. From the standpoint of the original position it is clearly rational to insure oneself against these contingencies. But now, if the appropriate minimum is provided by transfers, it may be perfectly fair that the other part of total income is competitively determined. Moreover, this way of dealing with the claims of need is doubtless more efficient, at least from a theoretical point of view, than trying to regulate prices by minimum wage standards and so on. It is preferable to handle these claims by a separate branch which supports a social minimum. Henceforth, in considering whether the second principle of justice is satisfied, the answer turns on whether the total income of the least advantaged, that is, wages plus transfers, is such as to maximize their long-term expectations consistent with the demands of liberty.

Finally, the distribution branch is to preserve an approximately just distribution of income and wealth over time by affecting the background conditions of the market from period to period. Two aspects of this branch may be distinguished. First of all, it operates a system of inheritance and gift taxes. The aim of these levies is not to raise revenue, but gradually and continually to correct the distribution of wealth and to prevent the concentrations of power to the detriment of liberty and equality of opportunity. It is perfectly true, as some have said,[3] that unequal inheritance of wealth is no more inherently unjust than unequal inheritance of intelligence; as far as possible the inequalities founded on either should satisfy the difference principle. Thus, the inheritance of greater wealth is just as long as it is to the advantage of the worst off and consistent with liberty, including equality of opportunity. Now by the latter we do not mean, of course, the equality of expectations between classes, since differences in life-prospects arising from the basic structure are inevitable, and it is precisely the aim of the second principle to say when these differences are just. Indeed, equality of opportunity is a certain set of institutions which assures equally good education and chances of culture for all and which keeps open the competition for positions on the basis of qualities reasonably related to performance, and so on. It is these institutions which are put in jeopardy when inequalities and concentrations of wealth reach a certain limit; and the taxes imposed by the distribution branch are to prevent this limit from being exceeded. Naturally enough where this limit lies is a matter for political judgment guided by theory, practical experience, and plain hunch; on this question the theory of justice has nothing to say.

The second part of the distribution branch is a scheme of taxation for raising revenue to cover the costs of public goods, to make transfer payments, and the like. This scheme belongs to the distribution branch since the burden of taxation must be justly shared. Although we cannot examine the legal and economic complications involved, there are several points in favour of proportional expenditure taxes as part of an ideally just arrangement. For one thing, they are preferable to income taxes at the level of common-sense precepts of justice, since they impose a levy according to how much a man takes out of the common store of goods and not according to how much he contributes (assuming that income is fairly earned in return for productive efforts). On the other hand, proportional taxes treat everyone in a clearly defined uniform way (again assuming that income is fairly earned) and hence it is preferable to use progressive rates only when they are necessary to preserve the justice of the system as a whole, that is, to prevent large fortunes hazardous to liberty and equality of opportunity, and the like. If proportional expenditure taxes should also prove more efficient, say because they interfere less with incentives, or whatever, this would make the case for them decisive provided a feasible scheme could be worked out.[4] Yet these are questions of political judgment which are not our concern; and, in any case, a proportional expenditure tax is part of an idealized scheme which we are describing. It does not follow that even steeply progressive income taxes, given the injustice of existing systems, do not improve justice and efficiency all things considered. In practice we must usually choose between unjust arrangements and then it is a matter of finding the lesser injustice.

Whatever form the distribution branch assumes, the argument for it is to be based on justice: we must hold that once it is accepted the social system as a whole—the competitive economy surrounded by a just constitutional legal framework—can be made to satisfy the principles of justice with the smallest loss in efficiency. The long-term expectations of the least advantaged are raised to the highest level consistent with the demands of equal liberty. In discussing the choice of a distribution scheme we have made no reference to the traditional criteria of taxation according to ability to pay or benefits received; nor have we mentioned any of the variants of the sacrifice principle. These standards are subordinate to the two principles of justice; once the problem is seen as that of designing a whole social system, they assume the status of secondary precepts with no more independent force than the precepts of common sense in regard to wages. To suppose otherwise is not to take a sufficiently comprehensive point of view. In setting up a just distribution branch these precepts may or may not have a place depending upon the demands of the two principles of justice when applied to the entire system. . . .

The sketch of the system of institutions satisfying the two principles of justice is now complete. . . .

In order . . . to establish just distributive shares a just total system of institutions must be set up and impartially administered. Given a just constitution and the smooth working of the four branches of government, and so on, there exists a procedure such that the actual distribution of wealth, whatever it turns out to be, is just. It will have come about as a consequence of a just system of institutions satisfying the principles to which everyone would agree and against which no one can complain. The situation is one of pure procedural justice, since there is no independent criterion by which the outcome can be judged. Nor can we say that a particular distribution of wealth is just because it is one which could have resulted from just institutions although it has not, as this would be to allow too much. Clearly there are many distributions which may be reached by just institutions, and this is true whether we count patterns of distributions among social classes or whether we count distributions of particular goods and services among particular individuals. There are definitely many outcomes and what makes one of these just is that it has been achieved by actually carrying out a just scheme of co-operation as it is publicly understood. It is the result which has arisen when everyone receives that to which he is entitled given his and others' actions guided by their legitimate expectations and their obligations to one another. We can no more arrive at a just distribution of wealth except by working together within the framework of a just system of institutions than we can win or lose fairly without actually betting.

This account of distributive shares is simply an elaboration of the familiar idea that economic rewards will be just once a perfectly competitive price system is organized as a fair game. But in order to do this we have to begin with the choice of a social system as a whole, for the basic structure of the entire arrangement must be just. The economy must be surrounded with the appropriate framework of institutions, since even a perfectly efficient price system has no tendency to determine just distributive shares when left to itself. Not only must economic activity be regulated by a just constitution and controlled by the four branches of government, but a just saving-function must be adopted to estimate the provision to be made for future generations. . . .

Notes

1. In this essay I try to work out some of the implications of the two principles of justice discussed in "Justice as Fairness," which first appeared in the *Philosophical Review*, 1958, and which is reprinted in *Philosophy, Politics and Society*, Series II, pp. 132–57.

2. This question is discussed very briefly in "Justice as Fairness," see pp. 138–41. The intuitive idea is as follows. Given the circumstances of the original position, it is rational for a man to choose as if he were designing a society in which his enemy is to assign him his place. Thus, in particular, given the complete lack of knowledge (which makes the choice one uncertainty), the fact that the decision involves one's life-prospects as a whole and is constrained by obligations to third parties (e.g., one's descendants) and duties to certain values (e.g., to religious truth), it is rational to be conservative and so to choose in accordance with an analogue of the maximum principle. Viewing the situation in this way, the interpretation given to the principles of justice earlier is perhaps natural enough. Moreover, it seems clear how the principle of utility can be interpreted; it is the analogue of the Laplacean principle for choice uncertainty. (For a discussion of these choice criteria, see R. D. Luce and H. Raiffa, *Games and Decisions* [1957], pp. 275–98.)

3. Example F. von Hayek, *The Constitution of Liberty* (1960), p. 90.

4. See N. Kaldor, *An Expenditure Tax* (1955).

The Entitlement Theory

ROBERT NOZICK

The minimal state is the most extensive state that can be justified. Any state more extensive violates people's rights. Yet many persons have put forth reasons purporting to justify a more extensive state. It is impossible within the compass of this book to examine all the reasons that have been put forth. Therefore, I shall focus upon those generally acknowledged to be most weighty and influential, to see precisely wherein they fail. In this chapter we consider the claim that a more extensive state is justified, because necessary (or the best instrument) to achieve distributive justice; in the next chapter we shall take up diverse other claims.

The term "distributive justice" is not a neutral one. Hearing the term "distribution," most people presume that some thing or mechanism uses some principle or criterion to give out a supply of things. Into this process of distributing shares some error may have crept. So it is an open question, at least, whether *re*distribution should take place; whether we should do again what has already been done once, though poorly. However, we are not in the position of children who have been given portions of pie by someone who now makes last-minute adjustments to rectify careless cutting. There is no *central* distribution, no person or group entitled to control all the resources, jointly deciding how they are to be doled out. What each person gets, he gets from others who give to him in exchange for something, or as a gift. In a free society, diverse persons control different resources, and new holdings arise out of the voluntary exchanges and actions of persons. There is no more a distributing or distribution of shares than there is a distributing of mates in a society in which persons choose whom they shall marry. The total result is the product of many individual decisions which the different individuals involved are entitled to make. Some uses of the term "distribution," it is true, do not imply a previous distributing appropriately judged by some criteron (for example, "probability distribution"); nevertheless, despite the title of this chapter, it would be best to use a terminology that clearly is neutral. We shall speak of people's holdings; a principle of justice in holdings describes (part of) what justice tells us (requires) about holdings. I shall state first what I take to be the correct view about justice in holdings, and then turn to the discussion of alternate views.

I

The Entitlement Theory

The subject of justice in holdings consists of three major topics. The first is the *original acquisition of holdings,* the appropriation of unheld things. This includes the issues of how unheld things may come to be held, the process, or processes, by which unheld things may come to be held, the things that may come to be held by these processes, the extent of what comes to be held by a particular process, and so on. We shall refer to the complicated truth about this topic, which we shall not formulate here, as the principle of justice in acquisition. The second topic concerns the *transfer of holdings* from one person to another. By what processes may a person transfer holdings to another? How may a person acquire a holding from another who holds it? Under this topic come general descriptions of voluntary exchange, and gift and (on the other hand) fraud, as well as reference to particular conventional details fixed upon in a given society. The complicated truth about this subject (with placeholders for conventional details) we shall call the principle of justice in transfer. (And we shall suppose it also includes principles governing how a person may divest himself of a holding, passing it into an unheld state.)

If the world were wholly just, the following inductive definition would exhaustively cover the subject of justice in holdings.

1. A person who acquires a holding in accordance with the principle of justice in acquisition is entitled to that holding.
2. A person who acquires a holding in accordance with the principle of justice in transfer, from someone else entitled to the holding, is entitled to the holding.
3. No one is entitled to a holding except by (repeated) applications of 1 and 2.

The complete principle of distributive justice would say simply that a distribution is just if everyone is entitled to the holdings they possess under the distribution.

A distribution is just if it arises from another just distribution by legitimate means. The legitimate means of moving from one distribution to another are specified by the principle of justice in transfer. The legitimate first "moves" are specified by the principle of justice in acquisition.[1] Whatever arises from a just situation by just steps is itself just. The means of change specified by the principle of justice in transfer preserve justice. As correct rules of inference are truth-preserving, and any conclusion deduced via repeated application of such rules from only true premises is itself true, so the means of transition from one situation to another specified by the principle of justice in transfer are justice-preserving, and any situation actually arising from repeated transitions in accordance with the principle from a just situation is itself just. The parallel between justice-preserving transformations and truth-preserving transformations illuminates where it fails as well as where it holds. That a conclusion could have been deduced by truth-preserving means from premises that are true suffices to show its truth. That from a just situation a situation *could* have arisen via justice-preserving means does *not* suffice to show its justice. The fact that a thief's victims voluntarily *could* have presented him with gifts does not entitle the thief to his ill-gotten gains. Justice in holdings is historical; it depends upon what actually has happened. We shall return to this point later.

Not all actual situations are generated in accordance with the two principles of justice in holdings: the principle of justice in acquisition and the principle of justice in transfer. Some people steal from others, or defraud them, or enslave them, seizing their product and preventing them from living as they choose, or forcibly exclude others from competing in exchanges. None of these are permissible modes of transition from one situation to another. And some persons acquire holdings by means not sanctioned by the principle of justice in acquisition. The existence of past injustice (previous violations of the first two principles of justice in holdings) raises the third major topic under justice in holdings: the rectification of injustice in holdings. If past injustice has shaped present holdings in various ways, some identifiable and some not, what now, if anything, ought to be done to rectify these injustices? What obligations do the performers of injustice have toward those whose position is worse than it would have been had the injustice not been done? Or, than it would have been had compensation been paid promptly? How, if at all, do things change if the beneficiaries and those made worse off are not the direct parties in the act of injustice, but, for example, their descendants? Is an injustice done to someone whose holding was itself based upon an unrectified injustice? How far back must one go in wiping clean the historical slate of injustices? What may victims of injustice permissibly do in order to rectify the injustices being done to them, including the many injustices done by persons acting through their government? I do not know of a thorough or theoretically sophisticated treatment of such issues. Idealizing greatly, let us suppose theoretical investigation will produce a principle of rectification. This principle uses historical information about previous situations and injustices done in them (as defined by the first two principles of justice and rights against interference), and information about the actual course of events that flowed from these injustices, until the present, and it yields a description (or descriptions) of holdings in the society. The principle of rectification presumably will make use of its best estimate of subjunctive information about what would have occurred (or a probability distribution over what might have occurred, using the expected value) if the injustice had not taken place. If the actual description of holdings turns out not to be one of the descriptions yielded by the principle, then one of the descriptions yielded must be realized.

The general outlines of the theory of justice in holdings are that the holdings of a person are just if he is entitled to them by the principles of justice in acquisition and transfer, or by the principle of rectification of injustice (as specified by the first two principles). If each person's holdings are just, then the total set (distribution) of holdings is just. To turn these general outlines into a specific theory we would have to specify the details of each of the three principles of justice in holdings: the principle of acquisition of holdings, the principle of transfer of holdings, and the principle of rectification of violations of the first two principles. I shall not attempt that task here. (Locke's principle of justice in acquisition is discussed below.)

Historical Principles and End-Result Principles

The general outlines of the entitlement theory illuminate the nature and defects of other conceptions of distributive justice. The entitlement theory of justice in distribution is *historical;* whether a distribution is just depends upon how it came about. In contrast, *current time-slice principles* of justice hold that the justice of a distribution is determined by how things are distributed (who has what) as judged by some *structural* principle(s) of just distribution. A utilitarian who judges between any two distributions by seeing which has the greater sum of utility and, if the sums tie, applies some fixed equality criterion to choose the more equal distribution, would hold a current time-slice principle of justice. As would someone who had a fixed schedule of trade-offs between the sum of happiness and equality. According to a current time-slice principle, all that needs to be looked at, in judging the justice of a distribution, is who ends up with what; in comparing any two distributions one need look only at the matrix presenting the distributions. No further information need be fed into a principle of justice. It is a consequence of such principles of justice that any two structurally identical distributions are equally just. (Two distributions are structurally identical if they present the same profile, but perhaps have different persons occupying the particular slots. My having ten and your having five, and my having five and your having ten are structurally identical distributions.) Welfare economics is the theory of current time-slice principles of justice. The subject is conceived as operating on matrices representing only current information about distribution. This, as well as some of the usual conditions (for example, the choice of distribution is invariant under relabeling of columns), guarantees that welfare economics will be a current time-slice theory, with all of its inadequacies.

Most persons do not accept current time-slice principles as constituting the whole story about distributive shares. They think it relevant in assessing the justice of a situation to consider not only the distribution it embodies, but also how that distribution came about. If some persons are in prison for murder or war crimes, we do not say that to assess the justice of the distribution in the society we must look only at what this person has, and that person has, and that person has, . . . at the current time. We think it relevant to ask whether someone did something so that he *deserved* to be punished, deserved to have a lower share. Most will agree to the relevance of further information with regard to punishments and penalties. Consider also desired things. One traditional socialist view is that workers are entitled to the product and full fruits of their labor; they have earned it; a distribution is unjust if it does not give the workers what they are entitled to. Such entitlements are based upon some past history. No socialist holding this view would find it comforting to be told that because the actual distribution A happens to coincide structurally with the one he desires D, A therefore is no less just than D; it differs only in that the "parasitic" owners of capital receive under A what the workers are entitled to under D, and the workers receive under A what the owners are entitled to under D, namely very little. This socialist rightly, in my view, holds onto the notions of earning, producing, entitlement, desert, and so forth, and he rejects current time-slice principles that look only to the structure of the resulting set of holdings. (The set of holdings resulting from what? Isn't it implausible that how holdings are produced and come to exist has no effect at all on who should hold what?) His mistake lies in his view of what entitlements arise out of what sorts of productive processes.

We construe the position we discuss too narrowly by speaking of *current* time-slice principles. Nothing is changed if structural principles operate upon a time sequence of current time-slice profiles and, for example, give someone more now to counterbalance the less he has had earlier. A utilitarian or an egalitarian or any mixture of the two over time will inherit the difficulties of his more myopic comrades. He is not helped by the fact that *some* of the information others consider relevant in assessing a distribution is reflected, unrecoverably, in past matrices. Henceforth, we shall refer to such unhistorical principles of distributive justice, including the current time-slice principles, as *end-result principles* or *end-state principles.*

In contrast to end-result principles of justice, *historical principles* of justice hold that past circumstances or actions of people can create differential entitlements or differential deserts to things. An injustice can be worked by moving from one distribution to another structurally identical one, for the second, in profile the same, may violate people's entitlements or deserts; it may not fit the actual history.

• • •

How Liberty Upsets Patterns

It is not clear how those holding alternative conceptions of distributive justice can reject the entitlement conception of justice in holdings. For suppose a distribution favored by one of these nonentitlement conceptions is realized. Let us suppose it is your favorite one and let us call this distribution D_1; perhaps everyone has an equal share, perhaps shares vary in accordance with some dimension you treasure. Now suppose that Wilt Chamberlain is greatly in demand by basketball teams, being a great gate attraction. (Also suppose contracts run only for a year, with players being free agents.) He signs the following sort of contract with a team: In each home game, twenty-five cents from the price of each ticket of admission goes to him. (We ignore the question of whether he is "gouging" the owners, letting them look out for themselves.) The season starts, and people cheerfully attend his team's games; they buy their tickets, each time dropping a separate twenty-five cents of their admission price into a special box with Chamberlain's name on it. They are excited about seeing him play; it is worth the total admission price to them. Let us suppose that in one season one million persons attend his home games, and Wilt Chamberlain winds up with $250,000, a much larger sum than the average income and larger even than anyone else has. Is he entitled to this income? Is this new distribution D_2, unjust? If so, why? There is *no* question about whether each of the people was entitled to the control over the resources they held in D_1; because that was the distribution (your favorite) that (for the purposes of argument) we assumed was acceptable. Each of these persons *chose* to give twenty-five cents of their money to Chamberlain. They could have spent it on going to the movies, or on candy bars, or on copies of *Dissent* magazine, or of *Monthly Review.* But they all, at least one million of them, converged on giving it to Wilt Chamberlain in exchange for watching him play basketball. If D_1 was a just distribution, and people voluntarily moved from it to D_2, transferring parts of their shares they were given under D_1 (what was it for if not to do something with?), isn't D_2 also just? If the people were entitled to dispose of the resources to which they were entitled (under D_1), didn't this include their being entitled to give it to, or exchange it with, Wilt Chamberlain? Can anyone else complain on grounds of justice? Each other person already has his legitimate share under D_1. Under D_1, there is nothing that anyone has that anyone else has a claim of justice against. After someone transfers something to Wilt Chamberlain, third parties *still* have their legitimate shares; *their* shares are not changed. By what process could such a transfer among two persons give rise to a legitimate claim of distributive justice on a portion of what was transferred, by a third party who had no claim of justice on any holding of the others *before* the transfer? To cut off objections irrelevant here, we might imagine the exchanges occurring in a socialist society, after hours. After playing whatever basketball he does in his daily work, or doing whatever other daily work he does. Wilt Chamberlain decides to put in *overtime* to earn additional money. (First his work quota is set; he works time over that.) Or imagine it is a skilled juggler people like to see, who puts on shows after hours.

Why might someone work overtime in a society in which it is assumed their needs are satisfied? Perhaps because they care about things other than needs. I like to write in books that I read, and to have easy access to books for browsing at odd hours. It would be very pleasant and convenient to have the resources of Widener Library in my back yard. No society, I assume, will provide such resources close to each person who would like them as part of his regular allotment (under D_1). Thus, persons either must do without some extra things that they want, or be allowed to do something extra to get some of these things. On what basis could the inequalities that would eventuate be forbidden? Notice also that small factories would spring up in a socialist society, unless forbidden. I melt down some of my personal possessions (under D_1) and build a machine out of the material. I offer you, and others, a philosophy lecture once a week in exchange for your cranking the handle on my machine, whose products I exchange for yet other things, and so on. (The raw materials used by the machine are given to me by others who possess them under D_1, in exchange for hearing lectures.) Each person might participate to gain things over and above their allotment under D_1. Some persons even might want to leave their job in socialist industry and work full time in this private sector. I shall say something more about these issues in the next chapter. Here I wish merely to note how private property even in means of production would occur in a socialist society that did not forbid people to use as they wished some of the resources they are given under the socialist distribution D_1. The socialist society would have to forbid capitalist acts between consenting adults.

The general point illustrated by the Wilt Chamberlain example and the example of the entrepreneur in a socialist society is that no end-state principle or distributional patterned principle of justice can be continuously realized without continuous interference with people's lives. Any favored pattern would be transformed into one unfavored by the principle, by people choosing to act in various ways; for example, by people exchanging goods and services with other people, or giving things to other people, things the transferrers are entitled to under the favored distributional pattern. To maintain a pattern one must either continually interfere to stop people from transferring resources as they wish to, or continually (or periodically) interfere to take from some persons resources that others for some reason chose to transfer to them. (But if some time limit is to be set on how long people may keep resources others voluntarily transfer to them, why let them keep these resources for *any* period of time? Why not have immediate confiscation?) It might be objected that all persons voluntarily will choose to refrain from actions which would upset the pattern. This presupposes unrealistically (1) that all will most want to maintain the pattern (are those who don't, to be "reeducated" or forced to undergo "self-criticism"?), (2) that each can gather enough information about his own actions and the ongoing activities of others to discover which of his actions will upset the pattern, and (3) that diverse and far-flung persons can coordinate their actions to dove-tail into the pattern. Compare the manner in which the market is neutral among persons' desires, as it reflects and transmits widely scattered information via prices, and coordinates persons' activities.

It puts things perhaps a bit too strongly to say that every patterned (or end-state) principle is liable to be thwarted by the voluntary actions of the individual parties transferring some of their shares they receive under the principle. For perhaps some *very* weak patterns are not so thwarted. Any distributional pattern with any egalitarian component is overturnable by the voluntary actions of individual persons over time; as is every patterned condition with sufficient content so as actually to have been proposed as presenting the central core of distributive justice. Still, given the possibility that some weak conditions or patterns may not be unstable in this way, it would be better to formulate an explicit description of the kind of interesting and contentful patterns under discussion, and to prove a theorem about their instability. Since the weaker the patterning, the more likely it is that the entitlement system itself satisfies it, a plausible conjecture is that any patterning either is unstable or is satisfied by the entitlement system.

Note

1. Applications of the principle of justice in acquisition may also occur as part of the move from one distribution to another. You may find an unheld thing now and appropriate it. Acquisitions also are to be understood as included when, to simplify, I speak only of transitions by transfers.

Complex Equality

MICHAEL WALZER

PLURALISM

Distributive justice is a large idea. It draws the entire world of goods within the reach of philosophical reflection. Nothing can be omitted; no feature of our common life can escape scrutiny. Human society is a distributive community. That's not all it is, but it is importantly that: we come together to share, divide, and exchange. We also come together to make things that are shared, divided, and exchanged; but that very making—work itself—is distributed among us in a division of labor. My place in the economy, my standing in the political order, my reputation among my fellows, my material holdings: all these come to me from other men and women. It can be said that I have what I have rightly or wrongly, justly or unjustly; but given the range of distributions and the number of participants, such judgments are never easy.

The idea of distributive justice has as much to do with being and doing as with having, as much to do with production as with consumption, as much to do with identity and status as with land, capital, or personal possessions. Different political arrangements enforce, and different ideologies justify, different distributions of membership, power, honor, ritual eminence, divine grace, kinship and love, knowledge, wealth, physical security, work and leisure, rewards and punishments, and a host of goods more narrowly and materially conceived—food, shelter, clothing, transportation, medical care, commodities of every sort, and all the odd things (paintings, rare books, postage stamps) that human beings collect. And this multiplicity of goods is matched by a multiplicity of distributive procedures, agents, and criteria. There are such things as simple distributive systems—slave galleys, monasteries, insane asylums, kindergartens (though each of these, looked at closely, might show unexpected complexities); but no full-fledged human society has ever avoided the multiplicity. We must study it all, the goods and the distributions, in many different times and places.

There is, however, no single point of access to this world of distributive arrangements and ideologies. There has never been a universal medium of exchange. Since the decline of the barter economy, money has been the most common medium. But the old maxim according to which there are some things that money can't buy is not only normatively but also factually true. What should and should not be up for sale is something men and women always have to decide and have decided in many different ways. Throughout history, the market has been one of the most important mechanisms for the distribution of social goods; but it has never been, it nowhere is today, a complete distributive system.

Similarly, there has never been either a single decision point from which all distributions are controlled or a single set of agents making decisions. No state power has ever been so pervasive as to regulate all the patterns of sharing, dividing, and exchanging out of which a society takes shape. Things slip away from the state's grasp; new patterns are worked out—familial networks, black markets, bureaucratic alliances, clandestine political and religious organizations. State officials can tax, conscript, allocate, regulate, appoint, reward, punish, but they cannot capture the full range of goods or substitute themselves for every other agent of distribution. Nor can anyone else do that: there are market coups and cornerings, but there has never been a fully successful distributive conspiracy.

And finally, there has never been a single criterion, or a single set of interconnected criteria, for all distributions. Desert, qualification, birth and blood, friendship, need, free exchange, political loyalty, democratic decision: each has had its place, along with many others, uneasily coexisting, invoked by competing groups, confused with one another.

In the matter of distributive justice, history displays a great variety of arrangements and ideologies. But the first impulse of the philosopher is to resist the displays of history, the world of appearances, and to search for some underlying unity: a short list of basic goods, quickly abstracted to a single good; a single distributive criterion or an interconnected set; and the philosopher himself standing, symbolically at least, at a single decision point. I shall argue that to search for unity is to misunderstand the subject matter of distributive justice. Nevertheless, in some sense the philosophical impulse is unavoidable. Even if we choose pluralism, as I shall do, that choice still requires a coherent defense. There must be principles that justify the choice and set limits to it, for pluralism does not require us to endorse every proposed distributive criteria or to accept every would-be agent. Conceivably, there is a single principle and a single legitimate kind of pluralism. But this would still be a pluralism that encompassed a wide range of distributions. By contrast, the deepest assumption of most of the philosophers who have written about justice, from Plato onward, is that there is one, and only one, distributive system that philosophy can rightly encompass.

Today this system is commonly described as the one that ideally rational men and women would choose if they were forced to choose impartially, knowing nothing of their own situation, barred from making particularist claims, confronting an abstract set of goods.[1] If these constraints on knowing and claiming are suitably shaped, and if the goods are suitably defined, it is probably true that a singular conclusion can be produced. Rational men and women, constrained this way or that, will choose one, and only one, distributive system. But the force of that singular conclusion is not easy to measure. It is surely doubtful that those same men and women, if they were transformed into ordinary people, with a firm sense of their own identity, with their own goods in their hands, caught up in everyday troubles, would reiterate their hypothetical choice or even recognize it as their own. The problem is not, most importantly, with the particularism of interest, which philosophers have always assumed they could safely—that is, uncontroversially—set aside. Ordinary people can do that too, for the sake, say, of the public interest. The greater problem is with the particularism of history, culture, and membership. Even if they are committed to impartiality, the question most likely to arise in the minds of the members of a political community is not, What would rational individuals choose under universalizing conditions of such-and-such a sort? But rather, What would individuals like us choose, who are situated as we are, who share a culture and are determined to go on sharing it? And this is a question that is readily transformed into, What choices have we already made in the course of our common life? What understandings do we (really) share?

Justice is a human construction, and it is doubtful that it can be made in only one way. At any rate, I shall begin by doubting, and more than doubting, this standard philosophical assumption.The questions posed by the theory of distributive justice admit of a range of answers, and there is room within the range for cultural diversity and political choice. It's not only a matter of implementing some singular principle or set of principles in different historical settings. No one would deny that there is a range of morally permissible implementations. I want to argue for more than this: that the principles of justice are themselves pluralistic in form; that different social goods ought to be distributed for different reasons, in accordance with different procedures, by different agents; and that all these differences derive from different understandings of the social goods themselves—the inevitable product of historical and cultural particularism.

A THEORY OF GOODS

Theories of distributive justice focus on a social process commonly described as if it had this form:

People distribute goods to (other) people.

Here, "distribute" means give, allocate, exchange, and so on, and the focus is on the individuals who stand at either end of these actions: not on producers and consumers, but on distributive agents and recipients of goods. We are as always interested in ourselves, but, in this case, in a special and limited version of ourselves, as people who give and take. What is our nature? What are our rights? What do we need, want, deserve? What are we entitled to? What would we accept under ideal conditions? Answers to these questions are turned into distributive principles, which are supposed to control the movement of goods. The goods, defined by abstraction, are taken to be movable in any direction.

But this is too simple an understanding of what actually happens, and it forces us too quickly to make large assertions about human nature and moral agency—assertions unlikely, ever, to command general agreement. I want to propose a more precise and complex description of the central process.

People conceive and create goods, which they then distribute among themselves.

Here, the conception and creation precede and control the distribution. Goods don't just appear in the hands of distributive agents who do with them as they like or give them out in accordance with some general principle.[2] Rather, goods with their meanings—because of their meanings—are the crucial medium of social relations; they come into people's minds before they come into their hands; distributions are patterned in accordance with shared conceptions of what the goods are and what they are for. Distributive agents are constrained by the goods they hold; one might almost say that goods distribute themselves among people.

Things are in the saddle
And ride mankind.[3]

But these are always particular things and particular groups of men and women. And, of course, we make the things—even the saddle. I don't want to deny the importance of human agency, only to shift our attention from distribution itself to conception and creation: the naming of the goods, and the giving of meaning, and the collective making. What we need to explain and limit the pluralism of distributive possibilities is a theory of goods. For our immediate purposes, that theory can be summed up in six propositions.

1. All the goods with which distributive justice is concerned are social goods. They are not and they cannot be idiosyncratically valued. I am not sure that there are any other kinds of goods; I mean to leave the question open. Some domestic objects are cherished for private and sentimental reasons, but only in cultures where sentiment regularly attaches to such objects. A beautiful sunset, the smell of new-mown hay, the excitement of an urban vista: these perhaps are privately valued goods, though they are also, and more obviously, the objects of cultural assessment. Even new inventions are not valued in accordance with the ideas of their inventors; they are subject to a wider process of conception and creation. God's goods, to be sure, are exempt from this rule—as in the first chapter of Genesis: "and God saw every thing that He had made, and, behold, it was very good" (1:31). That evaluation doesn't require the agreement of mankind (who might be doubtful), or of a majority of men and women, or of any group of men and women meeting under ideal conditions (though Adam and Eve in Eden would probably endorse it). But I can't think of any other exemptions. Goods in the world have shared meanings because conception and creation are social processes. For the same reason, goods have different meanings in different societies. The same "thing" is valued for different reasons, or it is valued here and disvalued there. John Stuart Mill once complained that "people like in crowds," but I know of no other way to like or to dislike social goods.[4] A solitary person could hardly understand the meaning of the goods or figure out the reasons for taking them as likable or dislikable. Once people like in crowds, it becomes possible for individuals to break away, pointing to latent or subversive meanings, aiming at alternative values—including the values, for example, of notoriety and eccentricity. An easy eccentricity has sometimes been one of the privileges of the aristocracy: it is a social good like any other.

 2. Men and women take on concrete identities because of the way they conceive and create, and then possess and employ social goods. "The line between what is me and mine," wrote William James, "is very hard to draw."[5] Distributions can not be understood as the acts of men and women who do not yet have particular goods in their minds or in their hands. In fact, people already stand in a relation to a set of goods; they have a history of transactions, not only with one another but also with the moral and material world in which they live. Without such a history, which begins at birth, they wouldn't be men and women in any recognizable sense, and they wouldn't have the first notion of how to go about the business of giving, allocating, and exchanging goods.

 3. There is no single set of primary or basic goods conceivable across all moral and material worlds—or, any such set would have to be conceived in terms so abstract that they would be of little use in thinking about particular distributions. Even the range of necessities, if we take into account moral as well as physical necessities, is very wide, and the rank orderings are very different. A single necessary good, and one that is always necessary—food, for example—carries different meanings in different places. Bread is the staff of life, the body of Christ, the symbol of the Sabbath, the means of hospitality, and so on. Conceivably, there is a limited sense in which the first of these is primary, so that if there were twenty people in the world and just enough bread to feed the twenty, the primacy of bread-as-staff-of-life would yield a sufficient distributive principle. But that is the only circumstance in which it would do so; and even there, we can't be sure. If the religious uses of bread were to conflict with its nutritional uses—if the gods demanded that bread be baked and burned rather than eaten—it is by no means clear which use would be primary. How, then, is bread to be incorporated into the universal list? The question is even harder to answer, the conventional answers less plausible, as we pass from necessities to opportunities, powers, reputations, and so on. These can be incorporated only if they are abstracted from every particular meaning—hence, for all practical purposes, rendered meaningless.

4.   But it is the meaning of goods that determines their movement. Distributive criteria and arrangements are intrinsic not to the good-in-itself but to the social good. If we understand what it is, what it means to those for whom it is a good, we understand how, by whom, and for what reasons it ought to be distributed. All distributions are just or unjust relative to the social meanings of the goods at stake. This is in obvious ways a principle of legitimation, but it is also a critical principle.* When medieval Christians, for example, condemned the sin of simony, they were claiming that the meaning of a particular social good, ecclesiastical office, excluded its sale and purchase. Given the Christian understanding of office, it followed—I am inclined to say, it necessarily followed—that office holders should be chosen for their knowledge and piety and not for their wealth. There are presumably things that money can buy, but not this thing. Similarly, the words *prostitution* and *bribery*, like *simony*, describe the sale and purchase of goods that, given certain understandings of their meaning, ought never to be sold or purchased.

5.   Social meanings are historical in character; and so distributions, and just and unjust distributions, change over time. To be sure, certain key goods have what we might think of as characteristic normative structures, reiterated across the lines (but not all the lines) of time and space. It is because of this reiteration that the British philosopher Bernard Williams is able to argue that goods should always be distributed for "relevant reasons"—where relevance seems to connect to essential rather than to social meanings.[7] The idea that offices, for example, should go to qualified candidates—though not the only idea that has been held about offices—is plainly visible in very different societies where simony and nepotism, under different names, have similarly been thought sinful or unjust. (But there has been a wide divergence of views about what sorts of position and place are properly called "offices.") Again, punishment has been widely understood as a negative good that ought to go to people who are judged to deserve it on the basis of a verdict, not of a political decision. (But what constitutes a verdict? Who is to deliver it? How, in short, is justice to be done to accused men and women? About these questions there has been significant disagreement.) These examples invite empirical investigation. There is no merely intuitive or speculative procedure for seizing upon relevant reasons.

6.   When meanings are distinct, distributions must be autonomous. Every social good or set of goods constitutes, as it were, a distributive sphere within which only certain criteria and arrangements are appropriate. Money is inappropriate in the sphere of ecclesiastical office; it is an intrusion from an-

---

*Aren't social meanings, as Marx said, nothing other than "the ideas of the ruling class," "the dominant material relationships grasped as ideas"?[6] I don't think that they are ever only that or simply that, though the members of the ruling class and the intellectuals they patronize may well be in a position to exploit and distort social meanings in their own interests. When they do that, however, they are likely to encounter resistance, rooted (intellectually) in those same meanings. A people's culture is always a joint, even if it isn't an entirely cooperative, production; and it is always a complex production. The common understanding of particular goods incorporates principles, procedures, conceptions of agency, that the rulers would not choose if they were choosing *right now*—and so provides the terms of social criticism. The appeal to what I shall call "internal" principles against the usurpations of powerful men and women is the ordinary form of critical discourse.

other sphere. And piety should make for no advantage in the marketplace, as the marketplace has commonly been understood. Whatever can rightly be sold ought to be sold to pious men and women and also to profane, heretical, and sinful men and women (else no one would do much business). The market is open to all comers; the church is not. In no society, of course, are social meanings entirely distinct. What happens in one distributive sphere affects what happens in the others; we can look, at most, for relative autonomy. But relative autonomy, like social meaning, is a critical principle—indeed, as I shall be arguing throughout this book, a radical principle. It is radical even though it doesn't point to a single standard against which all distributions are to be measured. There is no single standard. But there are standards (roughly knowable even when they are also controversial) for every social good and every distributive sphere in every particular society; and these standards are often violated, the goods usurped, the spheres invaded, by powerful men and women.

DOMINANCE AND MONOPOLY

In fact, the violations are systematic. Autonomy is a matter of social meaning and shared values, but it is more likely to make for occasional reformation and rebellion than for everyday enforcement. For all the complexity of their distributive arrangements, most societies are organized on what we might think of as a social version of the gold standard: one good or one set of goods is dominant and determinative of value in all the spheres of distribution. And that good or set of goods is commonly monopolized, its value upheld by the strength and cohesion of its owners. I call a good dominant if the individuals who have it, because they have it, can command a wide range of other goods. It is monopolized whenever a single man or woman, a monarch in the world of value—or a group of men and women, oligarchs—successfully hold it against all rivals. Dominance describes a way of using social goods that isn't limited by their intrinsic meanings or that shapes those meanings in its own image. Monopoly describes a way of owning or controlling social goods in order to exploit their dominance. When goods are scarce and widely needed, like water in the desert, monopoly itself will make them dominant. Mostly, however, dominance is a more elaborate social creation, the work of many hands, mixing reality and symbol. Physical strength, familial reputation, religious or political office, landed wealth, capital, technical knowledge: each of these, in different historical periods, has been dominant; and each of them has been monopolized by some group of men and women. And then all good things come to those who have the one best thing. Possess that one, and the others come in train. Or, to change the metaphor, a dominant good is converted into another good, into many others, in accordance with what often appears to be a natural process but is in fact magical, a kind of social alchemy.

No social good ever entirely dominates the range of goods; no monopoly is ever perfect. I mean to describe tendencies only, but crucial tendencies. For we can characterize whole societies in terms of the patterns of conversion that are established within them. Some characterizations are simple: in a capitalist society, capital is dominant and readily converted into prestige and power; in a technocracy, technical knowledge plays the same part. But it isn't difficult to imagine, or to find, more complex social arrangements. Indeed, capitalism and technocracy are more complex than their names imply, even if the names do convey real information about the most important forms of sharing, dividing, and exchanging. Monopolistic control of a dominant good makes a ruling class, whose members stand atop the distributive system—much as philosophers, claiming to have the wisdom they love, might like to do. But since dominance is always incomplete and monopoly imperfect, the rule of every ruling class is unstable. It is continually challenged by other groups in the name of alternative patterns of conversion.

Distribution is what social conflict is all about. Marx's heavy emphasis on productive processes should not conceal from us the simple truth that the struggle for control of the means of production is a distributive struggle. Land and capital are at stake, and these are goods that can be shared, divided, exchanged, and endlessly converted. But land and capital are not the only dominant goods; it is possible (it has historically been possible) to come to them by way of other goods—military or political power, religious office and charisma, and so on. History reveals no single dominant good and no naturally dominant good, but only different kinds of magic and competing bands of magicians.

The claim to monopolize a dominant good—when worked up for public purposes—constitutes an ideology. Its standard form is to connect legitimate possession with some set of personal qualities through the medium of a philosophical principle. So aristocracy, or the rule of the best, is the principle of those who lay claim to breeding and intelligence: they are commonly the monopolists of landed wealth and familial reputation. Divine supremacy is the principle of those who claim to know the word of God: they are the monopolists of grace and office. Meritocracy, or the career open to talents, is the principle of those who claim to be talented: they are most often the monopolists of education. Free exchange is the principle of those who are ready, or who tell us they are ready, to put their money at risk: they are the monopolists of movable wealth. These groups—and others, too, similarly marked off by their principles and possessions—compete with one another, struggling for supremacy. One group wins, and then a different one; or coalitions are worked out, and supremacy is uneasily shared. There is no final victory, nor should there be. But that is not to say that the claims of the different groups are necessarily wrong, or that the principles they invoke are of no value as distributive criteria; the principles are often exactly right within the limits of a particular sphere. Ideologies are readily corrupted, but their corruption is not the most interesting thing about them.

It is in the study of these struggles that I have sought the guiding thread of my own argument. The struggles have, I think, a paradigmatic form. Some group of men and women—class, caste, strata, estate, alliance, or social formation—comes to enjoy a monopoly or a near monopoly of some dominant good; or, a coalition of groups comes to enjoy, and so on. This dominant good is more or less systematically converted into all sorts of other things—opportunities, powers, and reputations. So wealth is seized by the strong, honor by the wellborn, office by the well educated. Perhaps the ideology that justifies the seizure is widely believed to be true. But resentment and resistance are (almost) as pervasive as belief. There are always some people, and after a time there are a great many, who think the seizure is not justice but usurpation. The ruling group does not possess, or does not uniquely possess, the qualities it claims; the conversion process violates the common understanding of the goods at stake. Social conflict is intermittent, or it is endemic; at some point, counterclaims are put forward. Though these are of many different sorts, three general sorts are especially important:

1. The claim that the dominant good, whatever it is, should be redistributed so that it can be equally or at least more widely shared: this amounts to saying that monopoly is unjust.
2. The claim that the way should be opened for the autonomous distribution of all social goods: this amounts to saying that dominance is unjust.
3. The claim that some new good, monopolized by some new group, should replace the currently dominant good: this amounts to saying that the existing pattern of dominance and monopoly is unjust.

The third claim is, in Marx's view, the model of every revolutionary ideology—except, perhaps, the proletarian or last ideology. Thus, the French Revolution in Marxist theory: the dominance of noble birth and blood and of feudal landholding is ended, and bourgeois wealth is established in its stead. The original situation is reproduced with different subjects and objects (this is never unimportant), and then the class war is immediately renewed. It is not my purpose here to endorse or to criticize Marx's view. I suspect, in fact, that there is something of all three claims in every revolutionary ideology, but that, too, is not a position that I shall try to defend here. Whatever its sociological significance, the third claim is not philosophically interesting—unless one believes that there is a naturally dominant good, such that its possessors could legitimately claim to rule the rest of us. In a sense, Marx believed exactly that. The means of production is the dominant good throughout history, and Marxism is a historicist doctrine insofar as it suggests that whoever controls the prevailing means legitimately rules.[8] After the communist revolution, we shall all control the means of production: at that point, the third claim collapses into the first. Meanwhile, Marx's model is a program of ongoing distributive struggle. It will matter, of course, who wins at this or that moment, but we won't know why or how it matters if we attend only to the successive assertions of dominance and monopoly.

SIMPLE EQUALITY

It is with the first two claims that I shall be concerned, and ultimately with the second alone, for that one seems to me to capture best the plurality of social meanings and the real complexity of distributive systems. But the first is the more common among philosophers; it matches their own search for unity and singularity; and I shall need to explain its difficulties at some length.

Men and women who make the first claim challenge the monopoly but not the dominance of a particular social good. This is also a challenge to monopoly in general; for if wealth, for example, is dominant and widely shared, no other good can possibly be monopolized. Imagine a society in which everything is up for sale and every citizen has as much money as every other call this the "regime of simple equality." Equality is multiplied throu conversion process, until it extends across the full range of social good regime of simple equality won't last for long, because the further progress of conversion, free exchange in the market, is certain to bring inequalities in its train. If one wanted to sustain simple equality over time, one would require a "monetary law" like the agrarian laws of ancient times or the Hebrew sabbatical, providing for a periodic return to the original condition. Only a centralized and activist state would be strong enough to force such a return; and it isn't clear that state officials would actually be able or willing to do that, if money were the dominant good. In any case, the original condition is unstable in another way. It's not only that monopoly will reappear, but also that dominance will disappear.

In practice, breaking the monopoly of money neutralizes its dominance. Other goods come into play, and inequality takes on new forms. Consider again the regime of simple equality. Everything is up for sale, and everyone has the same amount of money. So everyone has, say, an equal ability to buy an education for his children. Some do that, and others don't. It turns out to be a good investment: other social goods are, increasingly, offered for sale only to people with educational certificates. Soon everyone invests in education; or, more likely, the purchase is universalized through the tax system. But then the school is turned into a competitive world within which money is no longer dominant. Natural talent or family upbringing or skill in writing examinations is dominant instead, and educational success and certification are monopolized by some new group. Let's call them (what they call themselves) the "group of the talented." Eventually the members of this group claim that the good they control should be dominant outside the school: offices, titles, prerogatives, wealth too, should all be possessed by themselves. This is the career open to talents, equal opportunity, and so on. This is what fairness requires; talent will out; and in any case, talented men and women will enlarge the resources available to everyone else. So Michael Young's meritocracy is born, with all its attendant inequalities.[9]

What should we do now? It is possible to set limits to the new conversion patterns, to recognize but constrain the monopoly power of the talented. I take this to be the purpose of John Rawls's difference principle, according to which inequalities are justified only if they are designed to bring, and actually do bring, the greatest possible benefit to the least advantaged social class.[10] More specifically, the difference principle is a constraint imposed on talented men and women, once the monopoly of wealth has been broken. It works in this way: Imagine a surgeon who claims more than his equal share of wealth on the basis of the skills he has learned and the certificates he has won in the harsh competitive struggles of college and medical school. We will grant the claim if, and only if, granting it is beneficial in the stipulated ways. At the same time, we will act to limit and regulate the sale of surgery—that is, the direct conversion of surgical skill into wealth.

This regulation will necessarily be the work of the state, just as monetary laws and agrarian laws are the work of the state. Simple equality would require continual state intervention to break up or constrain incipient monopolies and to repress new forms of dominance. But then state power itself will become the central object of competitive struggles. Groups of men and women will seek to monopolize and then to use the state in order to consolidate their control of other social goods. Or, the state will be monopolized by its own agents in accordance with the iron law of oligarchy. Politics is always the most direct path to dominance, and political power (rather than the means of production) is probably the most important, and certainly the most dangerous, good in human history.* Hence the need to constrain the agents of constraint, to establish constitutional checks and balances. There are limits imposed on political monopoly, and they are all the more important once the various social and economic monopolies have been broken.

One way of limiting political power is to distribute it widely. This may not work, given the well-canvassed dangers of majority tyranny; but these dangers are probably less acute than they are often made out to be. The greater danger of democratic government is that it will be weak to cope with re-emerging monopolies in society at large, with the social strength of plutocrats, bureaucrats, technocrats, meritocrats, and so on. In theory, political power is the dominant good in a democracy, and it is convertible in any way the citizens choose. But in practice, again, breaking the monopoly of power neutralizes its dominance. Political power cannot be widely shared without being subjected to the pull of all the other goods that the citizens already have or hope to have. Hence democracy is, as Marx recognized, essentially a reflective system, mirroring the prevailing and emerging distribution of social goods.[11] Democratic decision making will be shaped by the cultural conceptions that determine or underwrite the new monopolies. To prevail against these monopolies, power will have to be centralized, perhaps itself monopolized. Once again, the state must be very powerful if it is to fulfill the purposes assigned to it by the difference principle or by any similarly interventionist rule.

Still, the regime of simple equality might work. One can imagine a more or less stable tension between emerging monopolies and political constraints, between the claim to privilege put forward by the talented, say, and the enforcement of the difference principle, and then between the agents of enforcement and the democratic constitution. But I suspect that difficulties will recur, and that at many points in time the only remedy for private privilege will be statism, and the only escape from statism will be private privilege. We will mobilize power to check monopoly, then look for some way of checking the power we have mobilized. But there is no way that doesn't open opportunities for strategically placed men and women to seize and exploit important social goods.

These problems derive from treating monopoly, and not dominance, as

---

*I should note here what will become more clear as I go along, that political power is a special sort of good. It has a twofold character. First, it is like the other things that men and women make, value, exchange, and share: sometimes dominant, sometimes not; sometimes widely held, sometimes the possession of very few. And, second, it is unlike all the other things because, however it is had and whoever has it, political power is the regulative agency for social goods generally. It is used to defend the boundaries of all the distributive spheres, including its own, and to enforce the common understandings of what goods are and what they are for. (But it can also be used, obviously, to invade the different spheres and to override those understandings.) In this second sense, we might say, indeed, that political power is always dominant—at the boundaries, but not within them. The central problem of political life is to maintain that crucial distinction between "at" and "in." But this is a problem that cannot be solved given the imperatives of simple equality.

the central issue in distributive justice. It is not difficult, of course, to understand why philosophers (and political activists, too) have focused on monopoly. The distributive struggles of the modern age begin with a war against the aristocracy's singular hold on land, office, and honor. This seems an especially pernicious monopoly because it rests upon birth and blood, with which the individual has nothing to do, rather than upon wealth, or power, or education, all of which—at least in principle—can be earned. And when every man and woman becomes, as it were, a smallholder in the sphere of birth and blood, an important victory is indeed won. Birthright ceases to be a dominant good; henceforth, it purchases very little; wealth, power, and education come to the fore. With regard to these latter goods, however, simple equality cannot be sustained at all, or it can only be sustained subject to the vicissitudes I have just described. Within their own spheres, as they are currently understood, these three tend to generate natural monopolies that can be repressed only if state power is itself dominant and if it is monopolized by officials committed to the repression. But there is, I think, another path to another kind of equality.

TYRANNY AND COMPLEX EQUALITY

I want to argue that we should focus on the reduction of dominance—not, or not primarily, on the break-up or the constraint of monopoly. We should consider what it might mean to narrow the range within which particular goods are convertible and to vindicate the autonomy of distributive spheres. But this line of argument, though it is not uncommon historically, has never fully emerged in philosophical writing. Philosophers have tended to criticize (or to justify) existing or emerging monopolies of wealth, power, and education. Or, they have criticized (or justified) particular conversions—of wealth into education or of office into wealth. And all this, most often, in the name of some radically simplified distributive system. The critique of dominance will suggest instead a way of reshaping and then living with the actual complexity of distributions.

Imagine now a society in which different social goods are monopolistically held—as they are in fact and always will be, barring continual state intervention—but in which no particular good is generally convertible. As I go along, I shall try to define the precise limits on convertibility, but for now the general description will suffice. This is a complex egalitarian society. Though there will be many small inequalities, inequality will not be multiplied through the conversion process. Nor will it be summed across different goods, because the autonomy of distributions will tend to produce a variety of local monopolies, held by different groups of men and women. I don't want to claim that complex equality would necessarily be more stable than simple equality, but I am inclined to think that it would open the way for more diffused and particularized forms of social conflict. And the resistance to convertibility would be maintained, in large degree, by ordinary men and women within their own spheres of competence and control, without large-scale state action.

This is, I think, an attractive picture, but I have not yet explained just why it is attractive. The argument for complex equality begins from our understanding—I mean, our actual, concrete, positive, and particular understanding—of the various social goods. And then it moves on to an account of the way we relate to one another through those goods. Simple equality is a simple distributive condition, so that if I have fourteen hats and you have fourteen hats, we are equal. And it is all to the good if hats are dominant, for then our equality is extended through all the spheres of social life. On the view that I shall take here, however, we simply have the same number of hats, and it is unlikely that hats will be dominant for long. Equality is a complex relation of persons, mediated by the goods we make, share, and divide among ourselves; it is not an identity of possessions. It requires, then, a diversity of distributive criteria that mirrors the diversity of social goods.

The regime of complex equality is the opposite of tyranny. It establishes a set of relationships such that domination is impossible. In formal terms, complex equality means that no citizen's standing in one sphere or with regard to one social good can be undercut by his standing in some other sphere, with regard to some other good. Thus, citizen X may be chosen over citizen Y for political office, and then the two of them will be unequal in the sphere of politics. But they will not be unequal generally so long as X's office gives him no advantages over Y in any other sphere—superior medical care, access to better schools for his children, entrepreneurial opportunities, and so on. So long as office is not a dominant good, is not generally convertible, office holders will stand, or at least can stand, in a relation of equality to the men and women they govern.

But what if dominance were eliminated, the autonomy of the spheres established—and the same people were successful in one sphere after another, triumphant in every company, piling up goods without the need for illegitimate conversions? This would certainly make for an inegalitarian society, but it would also suggest in the strongest way that a society of equals was not a lively possibility. I doubt that any egalitarian argument could survive in the face of such evidence. Here is a person whom we have freely chosen (without reference to his family ties or personal wealth) as our political representative. He is also a bold and inventive entrepreneur. When he was younger, he studied science, scored amazingly high grades in every exam, and made important discoveries. In war, he is surpassingly brave and wins the highest honors. Himself compassionate and compelling, he is loved by all who know him. Are there such people? Maybe so, but I have my doubts. We tell stories like the one I have just told, but the stories are fictions, the conversion of power or money or academic talent into legendary fame. In any case, there aren't enough such people to constitute a ruling class and dominate the rest of us. Nor can they be successful in every distributive sphere, for there are some spheres to which the idea of success doesn't pertain. Nor are their children likely, under conditions of complex equality, to inherit their success. By and large, the most accomplished politicians, entrepreneurs, scientists, soldiers, and lovers will be different people; and so long as the goods they possess don't bring other goods in train, we have no reason to fear their accomplishments.

The critique of dominance and domination points toward an open-ended distributive principle. *No social good* x *should be distributed to men and women who possess some other good* y *merely because they possess* y *and without regard to the meaning of* x. This is a principle that has probably been reiterated, at one time or another, for every y that has ever been dominant. But it has not often been stated in general terms. Pascal and Marx have suggested the application of the principle against all possible *y*'s, and I shall attempt to work out that application. I shall be looking, then, not at the members of Pascal's companies—the strong or the weak, the handsome or the plain—but at the goods they share and divide. The purpose of the principle is to focus our attention; it doesn't determine the shares or the division. The principle directs us to study the meaning of social goods, to examine the different distributive spheres from the inside. . . .

THREE DISTRIBUTIVE PRINCIPLES

The theory that results is unlikely to be elegant. No account of the meaning of a social good, or of the boundaries of the sphere within which it legitimately operates, will be uncontroversial. Nor is there any neat procedure for generating or testing different accounts. At best, the arguments will be rough, reflecting the diverse and conflict-ridden character of the social life that we seek simultaneously to understand and to regulate—but not to regulate until we understand. I shall set aside, then, all claims made on behalf of any single distributive criteron, for no such criterion can possibly match the diversity of social goods. Three criteria, however, appear to meet the requirements of the open-ended principle and have often been defended as the beginning and end of distributive justice, so I must say something about each of them. Free exchange, desert, and need: all three have real force, but none of them has force across the range of distributions. They are part of the story, not the whole of it.

Free Exchange

Free exchange is obviously open-ended; it guarantees no particular distributive outcome. At no point in any exchange process plausibly called "free" will it be possible to predict the particular division of social goods that will obtain at some later point.[12] (It may be possible, however, to predict the general structure of the division.) In theory at least, free exchange creates a market within which all goods are convertible into all other goods through the neutral medium of money. There are no dominant goods and no monopolies. Hence the successive divisions that obtain will directly reflect the social meanings of the goods that are divided. For each bargain, trade, sale, and purchase will have been agreed to voluntarily by men and women who know what that meaning is, who are indeed its makers. Every exchange is a revelation of social meaning. By definition, then, no *x* will ever fall into the hands of someone who possesses *y*, merely because he possesses *y* and without regard to what *x* actually means to some other member of society. The market is radically pluralistic in its operations and its outcomes, infinitely sensitive to the meanings that individuals attach to goods. What possible restraints can be imposed on free exchange, then, in the name of pluralism?

But everyday life in the market, the actual experience of free exchange, is very different from what the theory suggests. Money, supposedly the neutral medium, is in practice a dominant good, and it is monopolized by people who

possess a special talent for bargaining and trading—the green thumb of bourgeois society. Then other people demand a redistribution of money and the
establishment of the regime of simple equality, and the search begins for some
way to sustain that regime. But even if we focus on the first untroubled moment of simple equality—free exchange on the basis of equal shares—we will
still need to set limits on what can be exchanged for what. For free exchange
leaves distributions entirely in the hands of individuals, and social meanings
are not subject, or are not always subject, to the interpretative decisions of individual men and women.

Consider an easy example, the case of political power. We can conceive of
political power as a set of goods of varying value, votes, influence, offices, and
so on. Any of these can be traded on the market and accumulated by individuals willing to sacrifice other goods. Even if the sacrifices are real, however, the
result is a form of tyranny—petty tyranny, given the conditions of simple equality. Because I am willing to do without my hat, I shall vote twice; and you who
value the vote less than you value my hat, will not vote at all. I suspect that the
result is tyrannical even with regard to the two of us, who have reached a voluntary agreement. It is certainly tyrannical with regard to all the other citizens
who must now submit to my disproportionate power. It is not the case that
votes can't be bargained for; on one interpretation, that's what democratic
politics is all about. And democratic politicians have certainly been known to
buy votes, or to try to buy them, by promising public expenditures that benefit
particular groups of voters. But this is done in public, with public funds, and
subject to public approval. Private trading is ruled out by virtue of what politics, or democratic politics, is—that is, by virtue of what we did when we constituted the political community and of what we still think about what we did.

Free exchange is not a general criterion, but we will be able to specify the
boundaries within which it operates only through a careful analysis of particular social goods. And having worked through such an analysis, we will come up
at best with a philosophically authoritative set of boundaries and not necessarily with the set that ought to be politically authoritative. For money seeps
across all boundaries—this is the primary form of illegal immigration; and just
where one ought to try to stop it is a question of expediency as well as of principle. Failure to stop it at some reasonable point has consequences throughout the range of distributions, but consideration of these belongs in a later
chapter.

Desert

Like free exchange, desert seems both open-ended and pluralistic. One
might imagine a single neutral agency dispensing rewards and punishments,
infinitely sensitive to all the forms of individual desert. Then the distributive
process would indeed be centralized, but the results would still be unpredictable and various. There would be no dominant good. No x would ever be
distributed without regard to its social meaning; for, without attention to what
x is, it is conceptually impossible to say that x is deserved. All the different companies of men and women would receive their appropriate reward. How this
would work in practice, however, is not easy to figure out. It might make sense
to say of this charming man, for example, that he deserves to be loved. It

makes no sense to say that he deserves to be loved by this (or any) particular woman. If he loves her while she remains impervious to his (real) charms, that is his misfortune. I doubt that we would want the situation corrected by some outside agency. The love of particular men and women, on our understanding of it, can only be distributed by themselves, and they are rarely guided in these matters by considerations of desert.

The case is exactly the same with influence. Here, let's say, is a woman widely thought to be stimulating and encouraging to others. Perhaps she deserves to be an influential member of our community. But she doesn't deserve that I be influenced by her or that I follow her lead. Nor would we want my followership, as it were, assigned to her by any agency capable of making such assignments. She may go to great lengths to stimulate and encourage me, and do all the things that are commonly called stimulating or encouraging. But if I (perversely) refuse to be stimulated or encouraged, I am not denying her anything that she deserves. The same argument holds by extension for politicians and ordinary citizens. Citizens can't trade their votes for hats; they can't individually decide to cross the boundary that separates the sphere of politics from the marketplace. But within the sphere of politics, they do make individual decisions; and they are rarely guided, again, by considerations of desert. It's not clear that offices can be deserved—another issue that I must postpone; but even if they can be, it would violate our understanding of democratic politics were they simply distributed to deserving men and women by some central agency.

Similarly, however we draw the boundaries of the sphere within which free exchange operates, desert will play no role within those boundaries. I am skillful at bargaining and trading, let's say, and so accumulate a large number of beautiful pictures. If we assume, as painters mostly do, that pictures are appropriately traded in the market, then there is nothing wrong with my having the pictures. My title is legitimate. But it would be odd to say that I deserve to have them simply because I am good at bargaining and trading. Desert seems to require an especially close connection between particular goods and particular persons, whereas justice only sometimes requires a connection of that sort. Still, we might insist that only artistically cultivated people, who deserve to have pictures, should actually have them. It's not difficult to imagine a distributive mechanism. The state could buy all the pictures that were offered for sale (but artists would have to be licensed, so that there wouldn't be an endless number of pictures), evaluate them, and then distribute them to artistically cultivated men and women, the better pictures to the more cultivated. The state does something like this, sometimes, with regard to things that people need—medical care, for example—but not with regard to things that people deserve. There are practical difficulties here, but I suspect a deeper reason for this difference. Desert does not have the urgency of need, and it does not involve having (owning and consuming) in the same way. Hence, we are willing to tolerate the separation of owners of paintings and artistically cultivated people, or we are unwilling to require the kinds of interference in the market that would be necessary to end the separation. Of course, public provision is always possible alongside the market, and so we might argue that artistically cultivated people deserve not pictures but museums. Perhaps they do, but they don't deserve that the rest of us contribute money or appropriate public funds for the purchase of pictures and the construction of buildings. They will have to persuade us that art is worth the money; they will have to stimulate and encourage our own artistic cultivation. And if they fail to do that, their own love of art may well turn out to be "impotent and a misfortune."

Even if we were to assign the distribution of love, influence, offices, works of art, and so on, to some omnipotent arbiters of desert, how would we select them? How could anyone deserve such a position? Only God, who knows what secrets lurk in the hearts of men, would be able to make the necessary distributions. If human beings had to do the work, the distributive mechanism would be seized early on by some band of aristocrats (so they would call themselves) with a fixed conception of what is best and most deserving, and insensitive to the diverse excellences of their fellow citizens. And then desert would cease to be a pluralist criterion; we would find ourselves face to face with a new set (of an old sort) of tyrants. We do, of course, choose people as arbiters of desert—to serve on juries, for example, or to award prizes; it will be worth considering later what the prerogatives of a juror are. But it is important to stress here that he operates within a narrow range. Desert is a strong claim, but it calls for difficult judgments; and only under very special conditions does it yield specific distributions.

Need

Finally, the criterion of need. "To each according to his needs" is generally taken as the distributive half of Marx's famous maxim: we are to distribute the wealth of the community so as to meet the necessities of its members.[13] A plausible proposal, but a radically incomplete one. In fact, the first half of the maxim is also a distributive proposal, and it doesn't fit the rule of the second half. "From each according to his ability" suggests that jobs should be distributed (or that men and women should be conscripted to work) on the basis of individual qualifications. But individuals don't in any obvious sense need the jobs for which they are qualified. Perhaps such jobs are scarce, and there are a large number of qualified candidates: which candidates need them most? If their material needs are already taken care of, perhaps they don't need to work at all. Or if, in some non-material sense, they all need to work, then that need won't distinguish among them, at least not to the naked eye. It would in any case be odd to ask a search committee looking, say, for a hospital director to make its choice on the basis of the needs of the candidates rather than on those of the staff and the patients of the hospital. But the latter set of needs, even if it isn't the subject of political disagreement, won't yield a single distributive decision.

Nor will need work for many other goods. Marx's maxim doesn't help at all with regard to the distribution of political power, honor and fame, sailboats, rare books, beautiful objects of every sort. These are not things that anyone, strictly speaking, needs. Even if we take a loose view and define the verb *to need* the way children do, as the strongest form of the verb *to want*, we still won't have an adequate distributive criterion. The sorts of things that I have listed cannot be distributed equally to those with equal wants because some of them are generally, and some of them are necessarily, scarce, and some of them can't be possessed at all unless other people, for reasons of their own, agree on who is to possess them.

Need generates a particular distributive sphere, within which it is itself the appropriate distributive principle. In a poor society, a high proportion of social wealth will be drawn into this sphere. But given the great variety of goods that arises out of any common life, even when it is lived at a very low material level, other distributive criteria will always be operating alongside of need, and it will always be necessary to worry about the boundaries that mark them off from one another. Within its sphere, certainly, need meets the general distributive rule about *x* and *y*. Needed goods distributed to needy people in proportion to their neediness are obviously not dominated by any other goods. It's not having *y*, but only lacking *x* that is relevant. But we can now see, I think, that every criterion that has any force at all meets the general rule within its own sphere, and not elsewhere. This is the effect of the rule: different goods to different companies of men and women for different reasons and in accordance with different procedures. And to get all this right, or to get it roughly right, is to map out the entire social world.

Notes

1. See John Rawls, *A Theory of Justice* (Cambridge, Mass., 1971); Jürgen Habermas, *Legitimation Crisis*, trans. Thomas McCarthy (Boston, 1975), esp. p. 113; Bruce Ackerman, *Social Justice in the Liberal State* (New Haven, 1980).

2. Robert Nozick makes a similar argument in *Anarchy, State, and Utopia* (New York, 1974), pp. 149–50, but with radically individualistic conclusions that seem to me to miss the social character of production.

3. Ralph Waldo Emerson, "Ode," in *The Complete Essays and Other Writings*, ed. Brooks Atkinson (New York, 1940), p. 770.

4. John Stuart Mill, *On Liberty*, in *The philosophy of John Stuart Mill*, ed. Marshall Cohen (New York, 1961), p. 255. For an anthropological account of liking and not liking social goods, see Mary Douglas and Baron Isherwood, *The World of Goods* (New York, 1979).

5. William James, quoted in C. R. Snyder and Howard Fromkin, *Uniqueness: The Human Pursuit of Difference* (New York, 1980), p. 108.

6. Karl Marx, *The German Idology*, ed. R. Pascal (New York, 1947), p. 89.

7. Bernard Williams, *Problems of the Self: Philosophical Papers, 1956–1972* (Cambridge, England, 1973), pp. 230–49 ("The Idea of Equality"). This essay is one of the starting points of my own thinking about distributive justice. See also the critique of Williams's argument (and of an earlier essay of my own) in Amy Gutmann, *Liberal Equality* (Cambridge, England, 1980), chap. 4.

8. See Alan W. Wood, "The Marxian Critique of Justice," *Philosophy and Public Affairs* 1 (1972): 244–82.

9. Michael Young, *The Rise of the Meritocracy, 1870–2033* (Hammondsworth, England, 1961)—a brilliant piece of social science fiction.

10. Rawls, *Theory of Justice* [1], pp. 75ff.

11. See Marx's comment, in his "Critique of the Gotha Program," that the democratic republic is the "form of state" within which the class struggle will be fought to a conclusion: the struggle is immediately and without distortion reflected in political life (Marx and Engels, *Selected Works* [Moscow, 1951], vol. II, p. 31).

12. Cf. Nozick on "patterning," *Anarchy, State, and Utopia* [2], pp. 155 ff.

13. Marx, "Gotha Program" [11], p. 23.

PART THREE

Corporations, Persons, and Morality
Introduction

People eat, sleep, vote, love, hate, and suffer guilt. They also go to work for corporations that do none of these. Yet corporations are considered "persons" under the law and have many of the same rights as humans: to sue, to own property, to conduct business and conclude contracts, and to enjoy freedom of speech, of the press, and freedom from unreasonable searches and seizures. Corporations are legal citizens of the state in which they are chartered. They even possess two rights not held by humans: unlimited longevity and limited liability. This means that corporations have unlimited charters—they never "die"—and their shareholders are liable for corporate debts only up to the extent of their personal investment. Are corporations, then, morally responsible in the ways in which people are?

The Moral Responsibility of Corporations

One of the most stubborn ethical issues surrounding the corporation is not what it should do, but how it should be understood. *What* is a corporation? Is it a distinct individual in its own right, or merely an aggregate of individuals, for example, stockholders, managers, and employees? The answer to this question is crucial for understanding corporations and their activities. We already know that individual members of a corporation can be held morally responsible. For example, if a chemical engineer intentionally puts a dangerous chemical in a new cosmetic product, he is morally blameworthy. But can we hold the corporation, considered as something distinct from its individual members, morally blameworthy too?

The very concept of a corporation seems to involve more than the individual actions of specific persons. The corporation is understood to exist even after all its original members are deceased; it is said to hire or fire employees when only a handful of the corporate members are involved in the decision; and it is said to have obligations through its charter that override the desires of its individual members. Let us grant that the corporation is a distinct entity whose actions are not reducible—at least in a straightforward way—to the actions of individuals. Does it follow that the corporation has moral characteristics that are not reducible to the moral characteristics of its members? Philosophers have addressed this issue by asking whether the corporation is a "moral agent." Rocks, trees, and machines are clearly not moral agents. People clearly are. What are we to say about corporations?

When discussing whether corporations are moral agents, a good place to begin is with corporate legal history, that is, with the series of legislative acts and court decisions that have defined the corporation's existence. From its beginning in the Middle Ages, the corporation has been subject to differing legal interpretations. In the Middle Ages the law did not recognize any profit-making organizations as corporations; instead, it granted corporate status only to guilds, boroughs, and the church. In some instances the law decreed that corporations follow strict guidelines; for example, in 1279 the French Statute of Mortmain declared that a corporation's property could not exceed a specified amount. Even hundreds of years after its beginning, the corporation remained subject to strict legal sanctions on the conditions of its charter. As late as the nineteenth century, some U.S. corporations were granted charters only on the condition that they restrict land purchases to a certain geographic location and to a maximum number of acres. Thus corporations were viewed merely as artificial beings, created by the state and owing their very existence to a decree by the government.

But in the latter part of the nineteenth century and in the twentieth century, especially in the United States, this view changed dramatically. Instead of treating corporations as mere creations of the state, the courts began to see them as natural outcomes of the habits of business persons. It saw them as the predictable results of the actions of business persons who, exercising their inalienable right to associate freely with others, gathered together to conduct business and pursue a profit. As such, incorporation came to be seen less as a privilege granted by the state and more as a right to be protected by the state. Chartering a corporation became easier, and government restrictions less severe. Even so, the traditional view of a corporation continues to influence the law. The most accepted legal definition of a corporation remains the one offered by Chief Justice John Marshall in 1819: "A corporation," he wrote, "is an artificial being, invisible, intangible, and existing only in the contemplation of law. Being the mere creation of law, it possesses only those properties which the charter of its creation confers upon it . . . ."

Throughout the evolution of corporation law, the problem of whether and how to ascribe responsibility to the corporation persisted. In the sixteenth century the large trading corporations were not held responsible when one ship collided with another; instead, the individual boat owners, who participated in the corporation only to secure special trading rights, were held individually responsible. By the seventeenth century, the notion of "corporate" responsibility was thoroughly established in the law, but some sticky issues remained. Could a corporation be criminally liable? What rights, if any, did corporations share with ordinary persons? In the early twentieth century and again in recent years, U.S. corporations have been charged with homicide—one such case involved the Ford Pinto's exploding gas tank—but in every instance so far, the court has stopped short of entering a verdict of homicide, although it has been willing to impose stiff fines.

In 1978 the U.S. Supreme Court delivered a landmark verdict in the case of *First National Bank of Boston v. Bellotti.* The fundamental issue was whether a corporation should be allowed the right to free speech even when exercising that right by spending corporate money to promote political causes not directly related to corporate profits. Should corporations have full-fledged first amendment rights to free speech even when that means that they can use their vast financial reserves to support partisan political ends? In a split decision the Supreme Court decided in favor of recognizing such a right, although the decision itself remains controversial.

Whatever the courts eventually decide about the legal status of a corporation, questions about its moral status will remain. While courts have upheld corporate rights to free speech, the federal government has tried to devise ways to hold corporations accountable for wrongdoing. As the article, "The 'New' U.S. Sentencing Commission Guidelines," explains, in 1991 the United States Sentencing Commission instituted guidelines in order to encourage corporate compliance through the institution of ethics programs, establishing codes of conduct, the installation of ombudspeople, and other activities within the corporation to elicit appropriate managerial behavior. The idea is to encourage good corporate citizenship through internal standards of compliance. The Sentencing Guidelines pressure companies to develop standards of conduct, and they also help to protect other stakeholders and the public from corporate wrongdoing by imposing stiff financial penalties for noncompliance. In the years to follow, their effectiveness will be tested, demonstrated, and challenged.

Whether a corporation is a moral agent or not, it must adhere to certain norms of behavior. For example, at a minimum a corporation must not deliberately murder or systematically harm others. But beyond specifying a bare minimum, what can one say? How can one *evaluate* corporate behavior from a moral perspective?

In the *Harvard Business Review* article "Uncommon Decency: Pacific Bell Responds to AIDS," we find a California corporation, after a great deal of foot dragging, moving to develop one of the most respected AIDS programs in the country. At one point the company even decided to enter the political fray, taking a stand to oppose a measure that would have eliminated anonymous AIDS testing throughout the state.

How are we to understand the moral responsibility of a corporation? Does it extend, as Pacific Bell seems to believe, to creating exemplary programs to deal with broad problems of public interest? Does it extend to fighting proposed laws that the corporation opposes? In this section we find three articles that help answer such questions. Evan and Freeman's article, "A Stakeholder Theory of the Modern Corporation," develops an increasingly popular concept in business ethics literature, namely, that of the corporate "stakeholder." Defined as any group or individual who can afford or is affected by a business, the "stakeholder" can be a shareholder, an employee, a supplier, a customer, other individuals or groups, or the community. Notice that the stakeholder concept conflicts with the assumption that the moral responsibility of business is nothing other than profit maximization for shareholders (a view associated with Milton Friedman and examined in the previous section). It assumes, rather, that the job of the manager is to weigh and balance the interests of a variety of stakeholders including, but not limited to, those of investors.

In an article challenging Evan and Freeman, Kenneth Goodpaster argues that stakeholder *analysis* merely identifies stakeholders. He suggests that one must engage in stakeholder *synthesis*—that is, processes of moral reasoning—to elicit moral judgment. Moreover, Goodpaster questions Evan and Freeman's multi-fiduciary approach to stakeholder analysis. Returning to Friedman's argument that managers have fiduciary responsibilities to shareholders, Goodpaster enriches that analysis by claiming that managers have equally important non-fiduciary obligations to other stakeholders. This division of fiduciary and non-fiduciary responsibilities, Goodpaster contends, preserves the differences between various stakeholder relationships while enriching the moral dialogue that stakeholder analysis is designed to encourage.

In retelling a dramatic true-to-life episode in which he played a role, a Wall Street financier, Bowen McCoy, attempts to establish an analogy between personal and corporate ethics. When mountain climbing in the Himalaya Mountains, McCoy and his climbing party left a Sadhu, an Indian holy man, behind in the snow in order to achieve their goal of reaching the summit. What similarities, he asks, are there between this episode and decisions facing corporate managers? Equally important, what lessons from the behavior of McCoy's climbing party extend to the corporate organization and its obligations to its stakeholders?

Employee Rights and Responsibilities

A number of years ago the B. F. Goodrich Corporation became involved in serious ethical problems over the testing procedures it used in the fulfillment of a government contract for jet aircraft brakes. According to an account written by one of the company's employees, the pressures in this incident upon corporate employees, including those of job security and advancement, were so strong that they resulted in the falsifying of engineering specifications so that Goodrich could market dangerous and defective aircraft brakes. The dilemma of Kermit Vandivier, who finally "blew the whistle" on Goodrich, is a revealing illustration of some of the conflicts that can occur between self-interest, job responsibility, and one's sense of right and wrong.

This case illustrates a pressing contemporary concern: the relationship between employers and employees, especially in the area of employee rights. Do employees have rights in the workplace despite having voluntarily entered into a formal employee-employer relationship? For example, does a worker have the right to blow the whistle on a dangerous product without reprisal from management? Does he or she have a right to refuse a lie detector or polygraph test without being fired? Does he or she have the right to participate, directly or indirectly, in the management of the organization for which he or she works? And what are the concomitant rights of employers vis-à-vis their employees? What might an employer justifiably and reasonably expect in terms of loyalty and trust from his or her employees? These questions are among those falling under the heading of "employee rights," and their discussion has become one of the most heated and controversial in the field of business ethics.

When talking about employee rights, a few philosophical distinctions about the concept of rights are in order. We take the concept of "rights" for granted, often forgetting that it was unknown only a few centuries ago. The first instance of the word in English appeared during the sixteenth century in the phrase "the rights of Englishmen." But these "rights" referred literally to Englishmen, not Englishwomen, and included only those who owned property. History waited for the English philosopher John Locke to provide the word "right" with its present, far-reaching significance. In Locke's writings the word came to refer to something which, by definition, is possessed unconditionally by all rational adult human beings. The talk of rights in our own Declaration of Independence and Constitution owes much to Locke's early doctrine of rights.

Philosophers disagree about the precise definition of a right. Three of the most widely used definitions are (1) a right is a justified claim (for example, the right to freedom); (2) a right is an entitlement to something, held against someone else (for example, the right to equal protection is an entitlement which requires positive action on the part of others, including government); and (3) a right is a "trump" over a collective goal. The right to worship as one pleases, for example, overrides or "trumps" the collective goal of ideological unity within our society, and thus overrides any claims by certain groups or by a government that certain religions must be suppressed for the sake of the common good.

Rights may be divided into legal rights and moral rights. The former are rights that are either specified formally by law or protected by it. In the United States, the right to sue, to have a jury trial, to own property, and to have a free public education are legal rights. Not all such rights were included in the founding documents of the U.S. government: The right to free publication, the right of women and blacks to vote, and the right of workers to form unions were historical additions made in the nineteenth and twentieth centuries. Moral rights, on the other hand, are rights that are not necessarily protected and specified by the law. Moral rights are rights everyone has or should have—that is, they are normative claims about what people are entitled to—but they may not be universally recognized or incorporated into law. They would include, for example, the right to be treated with equal respect, the right to equal freedom, and the right not to be systematically deceived or harmed. The law might stop short of preventing private clubs, for instance, from excluding Jews and blacks, yet most of us would agree that Jews and blacks have a moral right in such situations not to be excluded. Similarly, for many years South African law perpetuated the apartheid system, yet few of us think that those laws were morally correct.

Turning to employee rights, although the Constitution and Bill of Rights protect the political rights of citizens, as late as 1946 the Supreme Court argued that the protection of the right to due process under the Fourteenth Amendment does not extend to private industry unless that particular business is performing a public function.[1] It is not that some rights are denied to employees in private industry, but rather that they are not always explicitly protected, nor are employers always restrained when rights are abrogated.

One of the most controversial issues in the area of employee rights, then, is whether, given that employees have some moral rights, those rights should remain only as *moral* rights or also be protected as *legal* rights. Until recently, the lack of protection of employee rights has been rationalized by appealing to the common-law doctrine of the principle of Employment at Will (EAW). This principle states that, in the absence of law or a specific contract, an employer may hire, fire, demote, or promote an employee whenever the employer wishes—and without having to give reasons or justify that action. In raising some issues about Employment at Will in the article "Employment at Will and Due Process," Patricia Werhane and Tara Radin assert that the three grounds upon which Employment at Will are typically defended are also grounds on which it can be attacked. Considerations of equal freedom, efficiency, and freedom of contract are often introduced in support of the prerogative of employers to fire "at will." But the doctrine of Employment at Will, Werhane asserts, can reflect inequality of freedom between employee and employer, can produce inefficient outcomes, and can be inconsistent with the employee's freedom of contract. The problem is not so much the doctrine of EAW per se but the way in which it is interpreted to imply that managers, when dealing with "at will" employees, can act without having to give reasons for their actions, a phenomenon that is inexcusable in the exercise of other managerial decision-making. At a minimum, Werhane and Radin argue, the reasonable free exercise of management requires that employees be given reasons, publicly stated and verifiable, for firing decisions. Due process is a means to institutionalize that requirement while protecting the employer from not being able to fire someone for *good* reasons.

Sissela Bok takes a hard look at one of the most difficult issues affecting Employment at Will and workplace freedom: whistleblowing. While she notes that the topic is rife with moral conflicts, she concludes that whistleblowing is often the only course available to a concerned employee. It is important, in turn, for any potential whistleblower to understand the broader panorama of issues against which whistleblowing occurs, for example, of group loyalty, openness authority, and the public interest. Equally important is the need for the employee to first exhaust less dramatic remedies before crying "foul" to the world. Only with such understanding, and by exploring alternative remedies, can an employee make an informed and correct decision about whether or not to blow the whistle.

One of the most serious issues facing late twentieth-century business is the question of job security. It has often been argued that long-time good employees and managers have rights to their jobs. In a number of European countries and in Japan companies often grant these rights, while in the United States "at will" employment has been the norm. In an interesting short article, Rosabeth Moss Kanter, an early defender of employee rights, introduces a new and challenging concept: "employability." While she does not make the case for lifetime employment in any one corporation, she argues that companies have obligations to train and retrain employees and managers so that they are *employable* in the changing markets of this and the next century. Thus while managers may move from company to company with skills enhancement, they become flexible and adaptable to changing work environments.

Diversity

One important moral right that directly concerns business is the right of every person to be treated equally in matters of hiring, pay, and promotion. If a person may be said to have such rights, business managers presumably have corresponding obligations not to pursue discriminatory policies. For example, business organizations should be obliged to hire on the basis of applicant competence without being swayed by irrelevant factors such as gender, religion, race, or ethnic origin. Most business people today recognize this obligation, one which is enforced fully in the law. By the year 2000 less than 25% of all new hires will be white males. So how one integrates the workforce and treats an increasingly diverse population of employees is no longer merely a matter of philosophical or legal interest.

A more controversial issue is whether business has an obligation to go beyond the point of merely not discriminating, to pursue what is called affirmative action. Affirmative action programs are of at least three sorts:

1. those which pursue a policy of deliberately hiring and promoting equally qualified minorities and women when considering candidates for a position;
2. those which pursue a policy of deliberately favoring qualified, but not necessarily equally qualified, minorities and women when hiring or promoting; and
3. those which establish quota systems to regulate the percentage of minority members hired or promoted in accordance with an ideal distribution of race, sex, creed, or ethnicity.

Although affirmative action is often misidentified as (3) above, i.e., as promoting quota systems, in fact most policies of affirmative action seek (1), to hire *equally* qualified minorities and women.

Perhaps the most common objection to affirmative action programs is that they are inconsistent, that is, that they make the same mistakes they hope to remedy. If discrimination entails using a morally irrelevant characteristic, such as a person's skin color, as a factor in hiring, is affirmative action itself perpetuating unjust discrimination? In giving preference to, say, blacks over whites, are such programs using the same morally irrelevant characteristic previously used in discriminatory practices, thus themselves committing discrimination?

Defenders of affirmative action argue that these programs are, all things considered, fair and consistent. They are not merely necessary to compensate past injustices in employment practices, injustices which clearly damaged the well-being and prospects of many members of society. Rather, they are also necessary to guarantee fairness in hiring and promotion for future generations. How will minority applicants ever seriously compete for positions in, say, medical school unless the educational and economic opportunities for minorities and non-minorities are equalized? And how will educational and economic opportunities be equalized unless minorities are able to attain a fair share of society's highest level of jobs?

While extremely important, affirmative action is only one of the issues at the center of the constellation of issues involving race and sex, and discussions of affirmative action tend to focus on a narrow range of equal opportunity, that of hiring. In a controversial article that sheds new light on affirmative action, Peggy McIntosh points out that affirmative action argues for the equalizing of disadvantages. Seldom, however, do we recognize how being white or male is an advantage. Being white gives one implicit privileges that are neither acknowledged nor taken into account when questioning affirmative action programs. Being white *and* male offers more such privileges, all of which are simply due to one's race or gender, none of which is earned or deserved. Privilege is often accompanied by power, thus creating inevitable advantages that are hard to dismantle. McIntosh argues that race and gender inequalities will persist even with affirmative action programs until or unless we recognize, acknowledge, and work at changing unearned privileges of being white or white and male. McIntosh's analysis of privilege can also explain how gays in our society are disadvantaged by the fact of sexual preference. The case "Is This the Right Time to Come Out?" illustrates the fact of privilege for heterosexuals in corporate America.

The case "Foreign Assignment" illustrates the existence of male privilege in another culture, and raises another concern, the changing role of women in corporate America. Felice N. Schwartz's "Management Women and the New Facts of Life" discusses aspects of this problem. It is one of the most-discussed and controversial pieces to appear in the *Harvard Business Review*. It quickly became known as the "mommy-track" article for its recommendation that women managers should be identified early by upper management as falling into one of two tracks: "career primary" and "career and family." This way, argues Schwartz, everyone gets what she wants. Career-primary women are not blamed for the fact that some women have more family-oriented commitments; career and family women are not blamed for not putting in lots of overtime hours; and corporate managers are able effectively to tap the full talent of the labor pool. In the responses to Schwartz's view that were printed later in the *Harvard Business Review,* many people, including active feminists, criticized Schwartz's view as reactionary and wrong-headed. Not the least of their concerns is that such a view mistakenly turns an issue that is properly a *parenting* issue into something that is only a *women's* issue.

Sexual harassment has probably existed since the advent of employment, and to imagine that men and women working together will never produce sexual tension is naive at best. The existence of sexual harassment has been identified as a "women's issue," although male managers have been subject to this phenomenon as well. With more women entering the workplace and assuming management positions, awareness of the existence of harassment has received a great deal of attention. One of the problems is in defining sexual harassment and distinguishing it from friendliness or harmless but verbally suggestive behavior. The article "Sexual Harassment" gives a number of examples of possible harassment incidents and suggests that it is, at best, difficult to equate sexual harassment with motives, with whether or not the person allegedly being harassed objects to the act, or whether or not the harassment produces negative consequences. Rather, sexual harassment is best evaluated on what counts as acceptable or unacceptable behavior. By specifying this behavior the activity of sexual harassment is clearly defined, thus avoiding the pitfalls of misunderstandings. The series of cases in John Hasnas' "Confronting Harassment" asks the reader to take the point of view of different people in cases of possible sexual harassment where the disparity between intentions and behavior produced some misunderstandings and negative consequences.

Note

1. *Marsh v. State of Alabama,* 66 S. Ct. 276 (1946).

The Moral
Responsibility
of Corporations

• *Case Study* •

Uncommon Decency:
Pacific Bell Responds to AIDS

DAVID L. KIRP

Sitting nervously in the public health clinic that Friday before Labor Day in 1986, awaiting word on his AIDS test, Pacific Bell repairman Dave Goodenough already half knew what he would be told: he had AIDS. He'd suspected as much for seven months, ever since he first noticed the markings on his chest. His doctor dismissed them as bruises picked up at work, but when the purplish markings started showing up all over his body, Goodenough sought another opinion. It had taken the second doctor only moments to identify the symptoms as "KS"—Kaposi's sarcoma, a type of cancer frequently associated with AIDS—and the test results confirmed that diagnosis.

Suspicions of AIDS are one thing, certainty something very different. "I was wiped out," Goodenough recalls. As he began to sort out the implications of the news, one question kept recurring: Would he—could he—go back to work?

Goodenough had been with Pacific for a decade, and working meant a lot to him. He liked what he did and liked the crew he worked with; he appreciated the fact that he didn't have to hide his homosexuality. Back in Ohio, Goodenough had been sacked from a probation officer's job when word leaked out he was gay. But San Francisco was different. And even though the phone company had a reputation as a bastion of mid-America, operating with a rule book as thick as a phone directory, by the late 1970s Pacific had just begun learning how to cope with the reality that a sizable number of its employees were gay.

To Goodenough, confirmation of AIDS only reinforced how important it was to him to stay on the job. "If I left the job," he recalls thinking, "it would be like putting a limit on the amount of time I have to live." His friend, Tim O'Hara, a long-time Communication Workers of America steward and a spokesman for gay concerns in the union, encouraged Goodenough not to quit—and to tell company officials that he had AIDS.

Initially, Goodenough resisted this last bit of advice. "I won't let anybody know," he insisted. But a few days later he changed his mind. "I can't hold something like this inside," he decided. "It'd be like being in the closet all over again."

On Goodenough's behalf, O'Hara went to Chuck Woodman, supervisor of the 750 people in Operations who keep the phone system in San Francisco up and running. Woodman's response was, "We'll do everything we need to do to keep Dave working," and he called Goodenough's immediate superior to enlist his support. Later that week, Goodenough phoned Woodman to thank him. "You could hear in his tone of voice how much Chuck cared," Goodenough remembers. "What he said kept me going. He told me, 'You've always got a job here.'"

Chuck Woodman hadn't always been so concerned about people with AIDS. To his subordinates Woodman had a reputation as a tough guy, a self-described redneck whose heroes included John Wayne and George Patton. A devout Mormon, father of 8, and grandfather of 20, Woodman's attitude about AIDS began to change in 1985 when he was transferred to San Francisco. He remembers how he was affected by a funeral for a worker who had died of AIDS.

"As I listened to that minister talking about how angry it made him that people with AIDS were shunned, I began to feel some of that anger," Woodman says. "The whole moral question of homosexuality got put aside."

To learn more, Woodman turned to Tim O'Hara, whom he knew and liked. With O'Hara's assistance, Woodman got a thorough education on AIDS. Information brought understanding, and understanding gradually eased the fear. After that first funeral, Woodman started asking questions. "What can we do for the people with AIDS on the job?" he wondered.

"They need to keep working," O'Hara answered. "It gives them a reason to stay alive."

Woodman began talking with supervisors and visiting workers with AIDS when they were too sick to work. Out of those talks with Woodman and Michael Eriksen, the company's director of preventative medicine and health education, came Pacific's first steps toward dealing with AIDS in the workplace: an AIDS Education Task Force, with company nurses and volunteering union members trained by the San Francisco AIDS Foundation giving presentations in offices and company garages all around the city. Woodman's bosses in the Pacific hierarchy were pleased with his AIDS initiatives. But peers who knew him from his earlier days were stunned. "I got maybe half a dozen calls from guys around the state. 'What are you doing, Woodman,' they'd say, 'do you love those gay guys?' I told them, 'Until you've walked in these tracks, you can't understand. You start buying in when it's someone you know.' And here's something. Each of those guys called me back later to say, 'I've got someone with AIDS. Now what do I do?'"

Chuck Woodman talks about AIDS as a managerial challenge, the toughest in his nearly 40 years at Pacific. "When I look at where I was and where I am now, AIDS has had a bigger impact on my thinking about people than anything I've come up against."

• • •

This comment about the impact of AIDS is no hyperbole; that isn't Woodman's style. And Woodman's remark applies not just to himself, not even just to Pacific, but to business generally. Just as AIDS has already changed American society, it will reshape American corporations.

That is not the conventional wisdom. To most managers, AIDS is a medical and social epidemic of still-unknown dimensions—the federal Centers for Disease Control conservatively estimate that 1.5 million Americans now carry the AIDS virus and that by 1991 every county in the United States will have at least one AIDS case. Much less common is a managerial awareness that American business must reckon with AIDS. Managers in general regard AIDS as a problem not for workers but for homosexuals and drug users and their promiscuous sexual partners, as a disease that attacks people outside the office and factory walls.

Such denial, however understandable, doesn't fit the facts. Among 273 companies responding to a 1987 American Society for Personnel Administration survey, one-third acknowledged having workers with AIDS. This was more than triple the percentage reported two years earlier and a figure that will steadily grow, if only because of AIDS's long incubation period (it can take seven years or more for symptoms to develop). Furthermore, those numbers represent only the most direct impact of AIDS, and this is not necessarily its most important dimension to the corporation.

AIDS molds behavior in many ways. In the worst, usually hushed-up incidents, employees afraid of AIDS-carrying coworkers have walked off the job. More common are dances of avoidance—workers refusing to share tools or even sit in the cafeteria with a stricken coworker. And then there is a very different reaction—grief at the loss of a friend and colleague. In a society where, for many, the workplace isn't merely the source of a paycheck but also a source of community, where fellow workers are also friends, there is simply no way for business to wall out AIDS.

How does a company respond to something as alien as AIDS? The best answer, as Pacific learned, is to recognize AIDS as a legitimate part of the corporate environment and to tailor a response that is of a piece with all that the company stands for and is doing. Pacific's reaction to AIDS was affected by the fact that the utility is headquartered in San Francisco—with its large gay community—and that telecommunications is a highly regulated industry. Nevertheless, the remarkable turnaround of this unlikely innovator tells an instructive tale for every major U.S. corporation.

• • •

Three years after AIDS was first identified, in 1984, Pacific's preventative medicine and health education director, Michael Eriksen, began hearing stories about Pacific employees worried about getting AIDS on the job. There was the coin collector who refused to touch the phone booths in the predominantly gay Castro district of San Francisco. One Los Angeles crew balked at installing phones in the offices of the L.A. AIDS Foundation, and another San Francisco crew insisted on being issued head-to-toe covering before installing phones in General Hospital's AIDS ward. And there was the lineman who refused to use the truck of a fellow employee, rumored to have died of AIDS, until it was sterilized.

As the number of crisis phone calls mounted, Eriksen resolved to determine the dimensions of Pacific's AIDS problem, to conscript other activists in shaping a plan—and to act. Later, one colleague recalled, "Eriksen became our AIDS guru." Bearded, mid-thirties, casual, fresh out of a Johns Hopkins Ph.D. program, Eriksen had been hired several years earlier to move the company toward a "wellness" approach. Already he had developed an in-house program to help employees quit smoking and to enable women to spot the first signs of breast cancer. Eriksen brought an activist's impatience to Pacific. In a company where going by the book is the instinctive response of lifetime employees, he equated going through corporate channels with death by memo.

Eriksen's work on AIDS began with the facts. He reviewed the company's 1984 death certificates and turned up 20 employees who had died of the disease. This meant that, after cancer, AIDS was the most frequent cause of death among active Pacific employees. Pacific officials, who hadn't considered AIDS a workplace issue, were startled; but the data made sense, since the nearly 70,000 employees and 250,000 people in Pacific's larger "family" were concentrated in San Francisco and Los Angeles, two cities with a high incidence of AIDS cases.

Moreover, Eriksen knew that the figure of 20 was decidedly conservative since it excluded workers who had gone on the permanent disability rolls before dying and cases where the doctor had not specified AIDS on the death certificate as the cause of death. In the general population, the number of AIDS cases was doubling every year; this meant Pacific was seeing just the beginning of the epidemic. Add those deaths among the company's work force to the stories of Pacific workers' fears about encountering AIDS while serving customers, and something had to be done. But what, and by whom?

If AIDS had been a garden-variety disease, tracing the path of corporate response would be easy. Policy would have been designed by the company's human resources division, with the medical director, Ralph Alexander, having the final say. But because AIDS was new and frightening, it demanded the kind of cross-the-boundaries effort that is hard for a company to marshal on any issue, let alone on a subject so loaded with bias, contention, and misinformation.

The corporate medical group needed to sift prevailing medical wisdom— but that was just the start. The human resources division, drawing on corporate-safety and labor-relations experts, had to determine how AIDS would be treated in the workplace—whether prospective employees would be screened for the virus, whether workers with AIDS could continue on the job—and what benefits to offer people with AIDS. Potentially every manager in the company needed help in handling workplace fears, and not just in San Francisco and in Los Angeles. Phone operators in California's decidedly unswinging Central Valley had no personal fears about contracting AIDS, but expressed real concern for their children. And because the AIDS issue was so hot, whatever the company did was potentially news—that made the corporate communications division a player as well.

Urged on by Michael Eriksen, the lawyers and medics and corporate-safety staffers determined that workers with AIDS would be treated like anyone with a life-threatening illness. The culture of the phone company, with its strong emphasis on two-way commitment and loyalty, kept Pacific from seriously considering the option of revoking the medical coverage of employees with AIDS—a policy that some companies followed. Jim Henderson, the company's executive director of human resources policy and services, says bluntly, "People with AIDS are sick. We don't fire sick people."

This policy was not only humane but also affordable, a vital consideration for any business. Reviewing the company's 20 AIDS-related deaths, Michael Eriksen estimated that the lifetime cost of medical treatment for an AIDS patient ran about $30,000, about the same as costs for treating other life-threatening illness such as cancer. To Pacific, whose escalating health costs were subject to review by California's Public Utilities Commission, that news was reassuring.

In practice, AIDS forced the company to make much-needed reforms that went beyond this one disease. For example, Pacific was already searching for ways to reduce reliance on hospitalization. The company sought less expensive alternatives, and its sick workers considered less impersonal ones. Both preferred new options, like at-home or hospice care, which offered more personal settings and attention at reduced costs. These quickly became part of corporate health coverage. Pacific's capacity for individual case management also needed strengthening so it could better determine—on a case-by-case basis—which regimen of care made best sense. Moreover, since many drugs used to treat AIDS patients were most readily available by mail, the company extended its health plan to cover mail-order drugs.

None of these innovations applied to AIDS alone. Indeed, business organizations like the Washington Business Group on Health have preached for years that case management is the best way for a company to tame the costs of catastrophic diseases. But AIDS treatment demonstrated the efficacy of the approach. One Southeastern public utility, relying heavily on hospitalization for AIDS patients, reported that its first eight AIDS cases cost the company $1 million—almost four times Pacific's per-patient cost. At Pacific, AIDS was a catalyst for reshaping many employee health benefits. The resulting package offered better treatment at markedly lower costs.

• • •

Pacific was drawing from its own tradition in defining benefits for employees with AIDS. But in dealing with workers' fears about being exposed to AIDS through casual contact, Pacific had to determine entirely new responses.

The accounts that Eriksen and Jean Taylor, director of employee counseling, had collected—installers shunning customers, workers avoiding AIDS-stricken associates—hinted at a dangerous level of anxiety in the field. And those employees' misgivings mirrored feelings in the society. In 1984, when AIDS fears had first begun to surface at Pacific, far less was known about the disease than today, and uncertainty left ample room for fearfulness and misinformation.

Managers had to wrestle with difficult questions. How would Pacific allay its employees' worries and thereby ensure that an AIDS incident didn't escalate into a fiasco? How could it protect the confidentiality of disclosures about

AIDS while attending to the concerns of employees with the disease? What changes were needed to Pacific's detailed rule book to help managers deal with the special needs of employees with AIDS?

The way Pacific handled the 1985 case of the phone installer who refused an assignment in San Francisco's Castro district suggests the delicacy of the issue and the need for new and nonpunitive approaches—educational approaches—to win over frightened workers. When the balking phone installer was suspended, he went to Shop Steward Tim O'Hara. But instead of lodging a grievance, O'Hara struck a deal. The workers would return to the job and a joint union-management AIDS education program would begin immediately at the site. The idea was feasible because Pacific and its union had developed an unusually cooperative and nonadversarial relationship during the last contract talks.

O'Hara's evenhanded approach respected the workers' fears and met the needs of the company's customers. Meanwhile, the shop steward put together a list of 30 volunteering workers, whose lifestyles ran the gamut from the most traditional heterosexual middle American to the openly gay. If other workers were ever unwilling to make an installation where there was an AIDS victim, this squad was ready to handle the job. Here again, preparation and education worked: no supervisor has ever had to turn to O'Hara's list.

But despite early agreement on nondiscrimination as the broad company policy, corporate AIDS education at Pacific did not advance beyond crisis intervention. Yes, several hundred employees did show up in April 1985 at the company's headquarters downtown for a question-and-answer session with Michael Eriksen and a San Francisco AIDS Foundation representative. But that was a one-time occasion. For all the other employees—the San Francisco work crews who wouldn't dream of coming all the way downtown; the 7,200 back-room personnel working in "San Remote," a Pentagon-like fortress 35 miles outside the city in suburban San Ramon; the employees in Los Angeles and throughout California and Nevada—there was essentially no AIDS education.

Within Pacific's medical department, there was disagreement about the adequacy of the company's approach thus far. The dispute reflected deep differences in perspective between the classic medical approach and the newer views of wellness specialists.

For longtime medical director Ralph Alexander—a consistently conservative official who believed that, as an M.D., he should have the last say—what Pacific was doing sufficed. In discussions with other divisions, Alexander regularly stressed the need to keep a sense of proportion when responding to AIDS, which he viewed as a relatively minor health concern for the company. "There's danger of offending a hell of a lot of people," said Alexander. It was better, he argued, for the company to devote more attention to heart disease and cancer, far bigger killers and diseases that wouldn't "raise eyebrows."

Wellness specialist Michael Eriksen saw matters differently. AIDS, he believed, deserved special attention because it was new and unnerving. He began to hook up with other like-minded colleagues, most of them mid-level managers involved in communications both inside and outside the company. These middle-level policy entrepreneurs believed that acting decisively on AIDS was the right thing to do; moreover, such a stance would benefit the company. It was these middle managers who took the lead in shaping Pacific's response to AIDS, exercising leadership from below.

One opening salvo was an article on AIDS that slipped into Pacific's newspaper, *Update,* moving the issue higher on the corporate agenda. In early 1985, Eriksen had suggested to *Update* editor Diane Olberg that she run an AIDS story; coincidentally, the organizers of the company's blood drive made the same request. They were troubled by reports of workers refusing to donate blood for fear that they could get AIDS—reports that showed the workers' generally low level of knowledge about the disease. Higher-ups would balk at the idea of an article on AIDS, Olberg knew, insisting that this was really just a San Francisco issue. But sensing the importance of the topic, Olberg went ahead on her own.

That first article focused entirely on the facts about AIDS in the workplace, avoiding the sensitive matter of company policy. It appeared on July 22, 1985—the same day Rock Hudson went public with the fact that he had AIDS—and demand for that issue of *Update* was unprecedented. The newspaper had to run reprints. To corporate tea-leaf readers, the coverage said that AIDS was something Pacific cared about; the strong employee response showed that AIDS was something employees cared about, and that paved the way for other AIDS-related stories. This reaction and the increasing demand for AIDS education sessions in the field sent another message up the corporate ladder: informing those who were healthy but worried might be as important to Pacific as ministering to those with the disease.

• • •

On March 20, 1986, the conference room at Levi Strauss's downtown San Francisco headquarters was packed. Over 230 managers from 100 companies were there for the first-ever conference on "AIDS in the Workplace." The demand so exceeded the organizers' expectations that 100 would-be participants had to be turned away. Reporters from leading daily newspapers were in the audience and TV crews from as far away as France recorded the event.

It came as no surprise to California executives that Levi Strauss had a big part in organizing this conference. The company had a long history of social activism, and CEO Bob Haas had personally acquired a reputation for dealing forthrightly with AIDS. Back in 1982, when several Levi employees told him that they were nervous about distributing AIDS information leaflets on company property, Haas had responded by stationing himself in the headquarters lobby, handing out leaflets to passersby.

But sharing the spotlight with Levi Strauss was Pacific—and this *was* surprising, for here was a company that usually made itself invisible on provocative topics. The corporation's name was prominent among the conference sponsors because the Pacific Telesis Foundation (established by Pacific's parents) had underwritten—and in conjunction with the San Francisco AIDS Foundation, Pacific's corporate TV group had produced—the first AIDS video aimed at U.S. business.

First screened at a breakfast session attended by 20 CEOs and then shown at the conference, "An Epidemic of Fear" pulled no punches: in telling detail it presented the panic, the medical evidence, the emotional tugs. Present on camera was Todd Shuttlesworth, who had been fired from his job by Broward

County, Florida when he was diagnosed with AIDS. Shuttlesworth's case served to remind managers how expensive a wrongheaded AIDS policy could be to a business; after his dismissal Shuttlesworth had taken his employer to court and secured a six-figure settlement.

Outsiders weren't the only ones surprised at Pacific's prominent visibility. Some high-ranking Pacific officials were amazed and decidedly uncomfortable about this unusual corporate position. It was appropriate for the company to treat its AIDS-stricken workers decently, they agreed. But to link AIDS with the corporation in the public mind was entirely different: that would associate Pacific with gays, drugs, and contagion, potentially driving away prospective employees, conceivably scaring creditors and customers who depended on the company's stability. There was every reason for the company to avoid sticking its neck out, said the advocates of a low corporate profile.

But Pacific did stick its neck out with AIDS-related decisions—decisions that in part reflected the company's determination to change its corporate culture to fit its new competitive realities. Gradually but steadily, Pacific went beyond the nondiscrimination policies that suited the old character of the company to real leadership that helped define the company Pacific was becoming.

• • •

Pacific Telesis Group is a holding company for Pacific Bell, the regional phone company that accounts for over 90 percent of the entire business's revenue and PacTel Corporation, which manages the company's diversified businesses. When it was launched after the 1984 AT&T breakup, many viewed Pacific as the weakest of the Baby Bells. "Of all the Bell regional holding companies, Pacific Telephone holds the most risk for investors," declared the *New York Times.* "The company's record of poor earnings and its long-running feud with the California Public Utilities Commission make it a risky investment at best."

Like other AT&T offspring, Pacific had to learn how to respond to the discipline of the marketplace. And in California, the company found itself in the nation's most hotly contested, fiercely competitive telecommunications markets. Other Bell companies, including Nynex and Southwestern Bell, as well as a host of new entrants, were all clamoring for a piece of the action, advertising heavily to an urbanized population with a reputation for buying whatever is new.

To respond to these changed conditions, Pacific had to meet three challenges: to be financially successful where smart investors were betting against Pacific's likely financial performance; to create an innovative and forward-looking organization, where tradition dictated that long-standing employees had to mold themselves until they gradually developed "Bell-shaped heads"; and to adopt corporate positions responsive to new constituencies that were socially conscious, where the company had always been seen as socially and politically backward. Together these challenges called on Pacific to redefine itself. It was under these conditions that AIDS became a measure of the company's transformation—and a vehicle for it. And it did so at a time when the company's efforts at change consistently misfired, reminding managers just how difficult large-scale change really is.

In its enthusiasm to demonstrate its newfound competitive hustle, for example, Pacific launched aggressive marketing campaigns. But what came to light were dubious sales tactics, like selling unneeded phone services to non-English-speaking customers who didn't understand what they were buying. Morale suffered among employees who didn't expect the phone company to behave like a used car dealership.

Pacific's effort at organizational transformation also ran into problems. To become more innovative, top management realized, the company would need to shake up its rigidly hierarchical structure, a steep pyramid with 14 precisely delineated levels. The problem was, how to change?

Looking for direction, Pacific contracted with an outside consultant for $40 million worth of leadership-development and personal-growth training. The system was called Kroning, after Charles Krone, the consultant who developed the training material. It backfired. Instead of opening up communication, it sharpened divisions between the "in" group, who claimed to fathom Kroning, and everyone else in the company. Instead of easing relations with the Public Utilities Commission, the controversial corporate expenditure triggered a "cease and desist" recommendation from the Commission's advocacy arm. Instead of improving Pacific's public image, the fiasco yielded a harvest of journalistic ridicule.

A big part of becoming competitive was learning about the state's shifting political environment—and that meant becoming more socially conscious. Historically, Pacific's idea of responsiveness was to join all the Rotary Clubs in California. While that approach might have worked in the 1950s, in the 1980s California's shifting coalitions of interest groups—blacks, Hispanics, consumer-oriented organizations—increasingly wielded political power. Pacific had long treated these groups as if they were the enemy. Now, however, these same groups were major purchasers of telecommunications services, and they had the ear of the most aggressive state Public Utilities Commission in the country. For the phone company to prosper on its own, it somehow had to co-opt these groups—to reach a mutually workable level of understanding and accommodation.

Steve Coulter, Pacific's director of consumer affairs, had the job of handling these troubling concerns. Coulter was a former Nevada legislator in his mid-thirties, a man who had made a political career out of enlisting constituencies to his cause. His collegial style and political savvy enabled him to get away with being a corporate guerrilla warrior. "A 'no' from above isn't necessarily the end of things," Coulter explains. "I'd ask 'Where's the block?' Then I'd go look for allies."

Working under Jim Moberg, then the vice president for corporate communications, Coulter had been devising company approaches to such new issues as minority procurement and multilingual services. Coulter was also involved in negotiations over minority hiring and procurement with the NAACP and HACER, a consortium of some of California's major Hispanic groups organized by Pacific. To Coulter, a visible Pacific presence on AIDS was appropriate: it was politically astute, operationally important, and morally right. In collaboration with Michael Eriksen and other allies, Coulter became a leading advocate for an AIDS policy inside Pacific.

The politics were particularly interesting. Pacific had long been in open warfare with San Francisco's affluent and influential gay community, and the company badly needed to mend its fences. In the early 1970s, Jim Henderson, now executive director of human resources policy and services, had helped draft the company's policy on homosexuals. Back then, Henderson recalls, "Some managers were afraid that gay activists would show up to work wearing dresses." In 1973, those fears prompted Pacific to adopt a policy against employing "manifest homosexuals." In practice, this rule meant that anyone who publicly acknowledged his or her homosexuality couldn't get a job with the phone company.

Although Pacific formally revoked its "manifest homosexuals" policy in 1976, it wasn't until 1986 that the then-defunct policy's earlier existence came to light. By then, Pacific had tangled with the City of San Francisco, refusing to subscribe to a city ordinance barring discrimination against homosexuals. In 1979, the company lost an employee-discrimination lawsuit in the California Supreme Court, which ruled that the state's human rights law prohibited public utilities from refusing to hire gays. Shortly before a trial for damages was scheduled to begin, Pacific lawyers produced a previously undisclosed 1973 job application that confirmed the company's former anti-homosexual policy. In December 1986, the company negotiated a $3 million settlement, the biggest ever in a gay discrimination case.

All this recent history—the disclosures of shoddy business practices, the troubles with Kroning, the acknowledged need to reach out to outsiders, the mishandling of the gay community—was artfully deployed by those within Pacific who pushed to make AIDS a visible corporate concern.

Eriksen provided the substantive information on AIDS, Coulter spoke mostly of politics and positioning. What Pacific needed, he argued to his bosses, was a winner, an issue on which the company could do well by doing good. AIDS could be the issue. Confronted with considerable internal opposition, it took all of Coulter's political experience and lots of help from other insiders to carry the day.

In March 1985, at a meeting of San Francisco's Business Leadership Task Force, Levi Strauss CEO Bob Haas raised the AIDS issue for the CEOs to discuss. The group's agenda already covered items like the role of the elderly worker and health-care cost containment. It was time, Haas said, to put AIDS on the list. Everyone else in the room, top officers from Wells Fargo, Chevron, Bank of America, and McKesson—and Pacific—said nothing, as if they could make something very embarrassing go away by being quiet.

Yet despite the CEOs' initial unease, AIDS did not disappear from the agenda. Haas continued to push the matter. So did Leslie Luttgens, organizer of the Leadership Task Force, who served on the boards of several important local foundations and blue-chip corporations, including Pacific. A one-time president of the United Way, Luttgens combined a strong commitment to social causes with a persuasive but diplomatic style. She had learned about AIDS as an overseer of the University of California-San Francisco Medical School; now she was convinced that trouble in the workplace was inevitable if businesses continued to deny the scary reality of the disease. After Haas made his proposal to the CEO group, Luttgens spent the next few months talking up the need to promote AIDS education, imparting a sense of urgency that kept the issue alive.

Making the rounds about this time was a request from the San Francisco

AIDS Foundation asking for corporate financial support for an AIDS education video. Pacific Telesis Foundation officials expressed considerable interest in funding the video; the in-house filmmakers added their enthusiasm for actually producing it. But at the top of corporate communications, Jim Moberg was unpersuaded. For advice, Moberg turned to Pacific's medical director, Ralph Alexander—and what he heard was conservative medical and corporate policy. According to Alexander, Pacific's role on industrial health issues was as a "national weather vane—and that's why we need to be doubly cautious about having a public profile."

Steve Coulter, like Mike Eriksen, equated caution with timidity. An AIDS video was clearly needed by businesses. Moreover, as Coulter argued in a memo to Alexander, getting the phone company publicly involved in AIDS education might just bolster its position in the pending gay discrimination lawsuit. Such a stance might provide some sorely needed good publicity. It was responsive to the AIDS-related concerns of other stakeholder groups including the NAACP, which, as Coulter pointed out, identified AIDS as a top national health priority. It could also improve relations with California's Congressman Henry Waxman, a powerhouse in telecommunications policy who was historically no friend of Pacific's and the congressmember most knowledgeable about AIDS.

As a savvy corporate politician, Coulter knew that he could not realistically expect Moberg to reverse his decision against the video project. The idea had to be repackaged, and that meant reviving the notion of Leadership Task Force involvement. Perhaps if the AIDS video proposal appeared in a different guise from a different sponsor, the answer would be different. Working with Michael Eriksen and the AIDS Foundation, Coulter sharpened the video proposal, waiting for another chance to bring up the matter with Moberg.

The occasion came on the eve of a December 1985 meeting of the Leadership Task Force. Coulter had been designated to sit in for Moberg as Pacific's representative at the session. On the table was a plan put forth by Leslie Luttgens for an "AIDS in the Workplace" conference. Hoping that he could now deliver Pacific's support for the AIDS video, Coulter phoned Moberg in New York, where Pacific had just signed a statement of mutual cooperation with the NAACP. Coulter's pitch to his boss noted the internal support for the AIDS video—from Luttgens, corporate TV, and the Foundation—as well as the endorsement of enterprises like Bank of America, Chevron, and Levi Strauss. "I need to be able to say, 'We have $25,000 on the table,'" Coulter argued.

Jim Moberg, euphoric after his successful NAACP negotiation, gave his cautious go-ahead—"as long as we don't seek publicity and don't stand alone." Leslie Luttgens's quiet advocacy had reassured him that AIDS activism was not a far-out idea; after all, here was a Pacific board member offering encouragement and a degree of protection if things misfired.

Then Moberg took up the matter with his fellow VPs, who had questions of their own. "Anytime you do something different from what's normal in the business community," Moberg says, "questions will be raised: 'Why only us?'" Some of these officers wondered aloud whether AIDS wasn't just a passing phenomenon, but Moberg set them straight. "In the end, they accepted the proposal on faith . . . it was enough that someone they trusted advocated it."

Now AIDS had become something "owned" by corporate Pacific—not just by some of its more enterprising staffers.

With that corporate approval, Coulter's group went to work. In less than three months, they prepared the video and an inch thick managers' workbook on AIDS and organized and publicized the conference.

The reaction to the March 1986 gathering was more enthusiastic than even Steve Coulter could have hoped for. Pacific, a company that lately had seen little but media brickbats, was now getting raves; a company known for its habit of avoiding social issues had gone out front, to considerable applause. The thank-you letters and the press clips circulated inside the company. At the next meeting of the Pacific board, Leslie Luttgens made a point of noting that the AIDS video that Pacific had produced was being aired nationally on PBS, as well as in France and Japan.

There was one internal casualty of the struggle to promote AIDS education: Michael Eriksen was abruptly fired by Ralph Alexander immediately after the AIDS conference. "I no longer have any need for you," the medical director had told Eriksen. There had been continuing disagreements between the two men. For his part, Alexander says, "Some programs he was supposed to run didn't work out."

The loss of Eriksen was deeply troubling to his colleagues, who had relied on his expertise. But his loss at this point was sustainable. There was product and momentum. With the video in hand and the AIDS Education Task Force functioning, the internal education efforts began to pick up. Success led to success. Responding to a request from the union that Pacific require AIDS education, Operations Vice President Lee Cox sent a letter to all supervisors, not insisting but recommending that they show the video as part of an AIDS education session.

• • •

Producing the video pushed Pacific into the public arena on AIDS. What came next was even further removed from corporate tradition and even more dangerous: taking a public position on a statewide AIDS ballot proposition.

An organization led by political extremist Lyndon LaRouche, whose motto, "Spread panic, not AIDS," became the rallying cry for a cause, had garnered enough signatures to force a statewide vote on a measure—Proposition 64—that, if passed by the electorate in the November 1986 election, would turn panic into law. The implications of the badly drafted measure were that thousands of workers who had AIDS could be fired, hundreds of students who carried the virus could be removed from school and college; moreover, people with AIDS could be quarantined. It appealed to people's emotions and played on their fears—yet had the simple allure of seeming to offer voters their chance to do something to protect themselves from the dread AIDS virus.

Most of California's chief public figures—politicians, church leaders, educators—opposed the measure. Steve Coulter wanted Pacific to add its voice to the opposition. Yet the huge number of signatures—it took nearly half a million to qualify the measure for the ballot—testified to the proposition's popular appeal. And some of the state's leading political conservatives voiced their strong support for the measure.

Like most companies, Pacific seldom took a stand on any ballot measure that did not directly affect its business. This political principle gave the company an easy and clear dividing line and protected it from needlessly making enemies over extraneous issues. Instead, Pacific preferred to exert its political influence through quieter relationships between lobbyists and lawmakers in the state capital. On the ballot measure, Pacific's lobbyists in Sacramento adamantly urged the company to remain mute.

For months, the debate over Proposition 64 continued inside Pacific. The conservatives from government relations and human resources insisted that opposing the measure would only earn Pacific powerful political enemies. The corporate communications activists countered that silence would put Pacific in league with those who proposed quarantining AIDS carriers and would also offend key external stakeholders, who might then "find additional avenues to criticize the company."

The stalemate was finally broken at the officers' level. Art Latno and Gary McBee, the two top external-affairs officials, determined that the company would publicly urge the defeat of Proposition 64. McBee, who had come to know the human cost of AIDS when a member of his staff died from the disease, became a strong voice for taking on LaRouche. "Given our internal position on AIDS," he says, "it would have been unconscionable for us not to oppose Prop. 64." The officers authorized a $5,000 corporate contribution to the campaign, the biggest single donation from any California business.

The stance was different—a decided shift from business as usual. Yet it reflected a fact of life about the shifting relationship between business and politics. In California—and increasingly across the country—voters are deciding more and more significant policy questions, rather than leaving matters to the elected officials. If a company wants to have a say on those matters, it must go public.

In the November 1986 election, California's voters resoundingly rejected Proposition 64. Although some Sacramento lawmakers grumbled at Pacific's lobbyists, the feared retaliation never occurred; and when LaRouche put the same measure on the ballot in June 1988, Pacific officials opposed it without thinking twice.

But the real test of how far Pacific had come on the issue took place in November 1988, when Proposition 102 hit the ballot. This was no kooky extremists' handiwork but a proposal authored by GOP Congressman William Dannemeyer that would essentially abolish anonymous AIDS testing. While leading public health figures opposed the measure, fearing that its reporting requirements would drive those at risk for AIDS underground, the proposition did not threaten quarantining. It had modest support among doctors—and, more important, an endorsement from the popular Republican governor, George Deukmejian. Pacific risked political wrath—facing down a barrage of appeals from Dannemeyer—by opposing the measure. McBee again championed that position. The proposition was defeated.

• • •

Now there were other constituencies enlisting Pacific in their efforts to combat AIDS. Prompted by Lynn Jiménez in corporate communications, Pacific spent nearly $100,000 in 1987 to promote a Spanish-language AIDS *videonovela*. This venture too had its risks, for the story line dealt candidly with homosexuality and drug use, two topics anathema to the conservative Hispanic community. But HACER, the coalition of Hispanic groups, urged the company to go ahead—despite the opposition of religious and political leaders in the community. The videonovela was yet another success story, with local TV stations reporting larger than usual audiences. Pacific Telesis Foundation proceeded with its plans to underwrite a dubbed-into-English version.

In 1988, Pacific and the Foundation received a presidential citation for their AIDS initiative. And there was more recognition: the *Wall Street Journal*, *Newsweek*, and *Business Week* lauded the company as enlightened; Sam Puckett and Alan Emery's book, *Managing AIDS in the Workplace*, called it a "role model for the rest of the nation" (along with other companies, including Dayton-Hudson, Bank of America, Digital Equipment Corporation, and Westinghouse). AIDS policy had become a winner inside Pacific. And more begat more, with new corporate enthusiasts for AIDS education emerging. "People love favorable recognition," points out Terry Mulready, Moberg's successor as corporate communications vice president. The company produced a video aimed at families, "Talking to Your Family About AIDS," and planned a video for the black community. The making of AIDS policy had taken on a life of its own.

• • •

On a sunny Wednesday afternoon in July 1988, 11 Pacific employees with the AIDS virus gather in the medical department's conference room for their weekly support group session. Three-piece suits sit amicably alongside flannel shirts. Janice Dragotta, a counselor who spends about a quarter of her company time on AIDS, encourages group members to check in.

As the talk moves around the table, members share information on drug treatments, describe their medical condition, offer advice, complain about a benefits nurse "who went to Auschwitz U," dish up tales of life in the gay bars, commiserate with those who tell how exhausted the preceding Sunday's group-sponsored picnic left them. There is an edgy humor, gallows humor, in the talk. One man, off to visit his parents in Ohio, imagines the local headlines if he were to die—Gay Comes Home To Die—and his mother's reaction: "How can you do this to us—again?" The employees also talk about the strength they draw from the group, about how it helps to have a place to discuss questions that arise on the job, conflicts with colleagues, and guilt about not being able to work as hard as they once could.

Until recently, no one at Pacific would have imagined such a group on company premises and on company time. "When I first proposed it in 1985, there were no takers," says Dragotta. Employees with AIDS were afraid to come forward. "At the time I started doing AIDS education," counselor Jean Taylor recalls, "an embarrassed official buttonholed me and said, 'Do anything you want, Jean, just don't talk about condoms.'" Now everything related to AIDS is open to discussion. Union Steward Tim O'Hara, relying on a poll detailing workers' interests, is pushing the idea of a corporate-produced video on the correct use of condoms. The concern that some employees might be offended by frank talk about sex is receding.

In organizing discussions of safe sexual practices or running AIDS support groups, Pacific, like any company, has to walk a fine line. AIDS is still encased in moral debate, but discussions of private morality have no place in the business setting. What is relevant are sound business practices and sensible personal precautions. The AIDS support group is both a humane gesture and an appropriate business move. Taylor says, "We started seeing people with the AIDS virus, and those who were well but worried, going out on disability. These groups are a way to help people stay productive, a way for people to begin processing their own grief."

New evidence of Pacific's support for AIDS education is clear not only in these groups but also throughout the organization. At the second annual AIDS Walk, a citywide fund-raising event in July 1988, over 400 Pacific employees sporting company T-shirts walked together under the company's banner. Elsewhere in the company, AIDS-related causes have become almost as familiar and noncontroversial as the United Way. At Pacific Telesis Foundation, the staff has made AIDS causes a top priority for charitable giving.

Still, there remain important and unresolved AIDS issues on Pacific's agenda. AIDS education is not a part of an overall corporatewide strategy. Whether employees ever see the AIDS video or get to talk through their concerns about AIDS depends entirely on whether a supervisor volunteers to organize such a session. This bottom-up approach means that, where such education is least needed—in San Francisco and Los Angeles, two cities where public knowledge about the disease is high—it is most likely to be provided. But elsewhere in California, in the fortress at San Ramon and the outposts beyond, where a majority of phone company workers are employed, many managers still treat AIDS as someone else's problem.

Those supervisors who phoned their colleague Chuck Woodman, asking how to handle an AIDS case on their work force, may still regard it as just a once-in-a-career concern; and their workers are still unwilling to talk openly about AIDS. "Whenever I get an AIDS call from Fresno," says counselor Jean Taylor at San Francisco headquarters, "it's always like Deep Throat, and it's always, 'Someone I know was wondering. . . .'"

For Pacific, an AIDS education effort pitched to the varying concerns of its employees is not only enlightened practice. It is sound business, Pacific may be among the companies with the most AIDS cases in the country. As those numbers continue to mount—and they will—the work force problem will become more critical. Already, Chuck Woodman has some 25 workers with AIDS, requiring regular shuffling of his 750-person roster. According to company sources, a 1987 estimate prepared by medical director Ralph Alexander—but never made public—indicated that as few as 200 and as many as 2,000 employees might be infected with the AIDS virus.

There is little that the company can do for these employees with AIDS that it isn't already doing—treating them just as it would treat anyone with a life-threatening illness—but it can do more to slow the spread of the disease. If Pacific can strengthen and expand the scope of its in-house AIDS education, intelligently implementing a program that will reach a quarter-of-a-million lives, then this unlikely corporate pioneer will continue to enlighten others coming to terms with AIDS.

• • •

Across the country, the corporate time clock of AIDS policy has run quickly if unevenly, with wide variations in responses reported. According to the 1987

American Society for Personnel Administration survey, some companies persist in punishing workers with AIDS, firing them or limiting their health benefits. A majority of companies offer no AIDS education and have no contingency plans for handling employees refusing to work with an AIDS victim. Barely one business in ten has a written AIDS policy. As discouraging as these data are, they probably exaggerate the degree of corporate responsiveness, since companies that deny the corporate reality of AIDS are unlikely to answer such a survey.

On the other side of the ledger, since the landmark 1986 Bay Area "AIDS in the Workplace" conference, there have been dozens of similar conferences across the country. In February 1988, 30 prominent corporations—among them, IBM, Warner-Lambert, Time Inc., Chemical Bank, Johnson & Johnson—endorsed an AIDS "bill of rights," ensuring that employees with AIDS would receive evenhanded treatment.

For the CEOs in Knoxville or Kansas City still wondering whether their companies should deal with AIDS, the answer should be plain: there is little choice. Nor can handling AIDS be just the province of corporate doctors or human resources specialists. Everyone has a stake in this boundary-crossing issue—that's one of the things that makes AIDS both so hard to manage and so important.

There is considerable help available to business. The groundbreaking experience at Pacific is instructive, AIDS educational materials are now widely marketed, and groups like the Red Cross and local AIDS organizations can assist. But to confront AIDS intelligently means having a new look at a wide range of business practices. It means rethinking a company's approach to medical benefits. Those issues Pacific found readily manageable several years ago have become tougher now because recent scientific advances have reshaped the equation. Medication like the antiviral drug AZT is now prolonging the productive lives of workers, but at a cost—one insurance company estimates that AIDS-related illnesses will make up between 2% and 5% of all group-health claims by 1991.

Devising an AIDS policy also means reexamining the company's approach to wellness education, its concern for prevention, and its willingness to talk about once-forbidden subjects like sex. It means rethinking relations between employer and employee, rethinking relations among units within the company, rethinking the boundaries between the company and the public domain.

The outcome of that reanalysis will likely reach far beyond AIDS education to produce a telling portrait of the corporation. For American business, as for Americans generally, AIDS is something like a mirror that, unwillingly and unexpectedly, we have come upon. The meaning of Chuck Woodman's, and Pacific's, odyssey is this: in our reactions to AIDS, something of significance about ourselves and about the character of our enterprises is revealed.

A Stakeholder Theory of the Modern Corporation: Kantian Capitalism

WILLIAM M. EVAN • R. EDWARD FREEMAN

During the 1960s, the Stanford Research Institute coined the term "stakeholders" to describe the various groups that provide critical support to a business firm. The following article develops the stakeholder theory as an alternative to the traditional legal viewpoint that officers and directors must manage a corporation for the benefit of shareholders. The authors base their theory on the ethical principle articulated by Immanuel Kant that all human beings should be treated as persons, not merely as means to ends. Although the stakeholder theory has not supplanted the traditional principles of corporate law, the basic concepts of the theory are used by many managers to analyze issues of ethics and social responsibility.[1]

[S]cholars and managers alike continue to hold sacred the view that managers bear a special relationship to the stockholders in the firm. Since stockholders own shares in the firm, they have certain rights and privileges, which must be granted to them by management, as well as others. Since the greatest good of all results from the self-interested pursuit of business, managers must be free to respond quickly to market forces. Sanctions, in the form of "the law of corporations," and other protective mechanisms in the form of social custom, accepted management practice, myth, and ritual, serve to reinforce the assumption of the primacy of the stockholder.

The purpose of this paper is to pose several challenges to this assumption, from within the framework of managerial capitalism, and to suggest the bare bones of an alternative theory, *a stakeholder theory of the modern corporation.* . . .

Our thesis is that we can revitalize the concept of managerial capitalism by replacing the notion that managers have a duty to stockholders with the concept that managers bear a fiduciary relationship to stakeholders. Stakeholders are those groups who have a stake in or claim on the firm. Specifically, we include suppliers, customers, employees, stockholders, and the local community, as well as management in its role as agent for these groups. We argue that the legal, economic, political, and moral challenges to the currently received theory of the firm, as a nexus of contracts among the owners of the factors of production and customers, require us to revise this concept along essentially Kantian lines. That is, each of these stakeholder groups has a right not to be treated as a means to some end, and therefore must participate in determining the future direction of the firm in which they have a stake. . . .

The crux of our argument is that we must reconceptualize the firm around the following question: For whose benefit and at whose expense should the firm be managed? We shall set forth such a reconceptualization in the form of a *stakeholder theory of the firm.* . . .

From *Ethical Theory and Business*, 3rd ed., T. Beauchamp and N. Bowie, eds. (Englewood Cliffs: Prentice Hall, 1988), pp. 97, 101–105. Reprinted by permission.

Stakeholders in the Modern Corporation

Figure 1 depicts the stakeholders in a typical large corporation. The stakes of each are reciprocal, since each can affect the other in terms of harms and benefits as well as rights and duties. The stakes of each are not univocal and would vary by particular corporation. We merely set forth some general notions that seem to be common to many large firms.

Owners have some financial stake in the form of stocks, bonds, and so on, and expect some kind of financial return. Either they have given money directly to the firm, or they have some historical claim made through a series of morally justified exchanges. The firm affects their livelihood or, if a substantial portion of their retirement income is in stocks or bonds, their ability to care for themselves when they can no longer work. Of course, the stakes of owners will differ by type of owner, preferences for money, moral preferences, and so on, as well as by type of firm. The owners of AT&T are quite different from the owners of Ford Motor Company, with stock of the former company being widely dispersed among 3 million stockholders and that of the latter being held by a small family group, as well as a large group of public stockholders.

Employees have their jobs and usually their livelihood at stake; they often have specialized skills for which there is usually no perfectly elastic market. In return for their labor, they expect some security, wages, and benefits, and meaningful work. Where they are used as means to an end, they must participate in decisions affecting such use. In return for their loyalty, the corporation is expected to provide for them and carry them through difficult times. Employees are expected to follow the instructions of management most of the time, to speak favorably about the company, and to be responsible citizens in the local communities in which the company operates. The evidence that such policies and values as described here lead to productive company-employee relationships is compelling. It is equally compelling to realize that the opportunities for "bad faith" on the part of both management and employees are enormous. "Mock participation" in quality circles, singing the company song, and wearing the company uniform solely to please management, as well as management by authoritarian supervisors, all lead to distrust and unproductive work.

Suppliers, interpreted in a stakeholder sense, are vital to the success of the firm, for raw materials will determine the final product quality and price. In turn the firm is a customer of the supplier and is therefore vital to the success

Figure 1. A Stakeholder Model of the Corporation

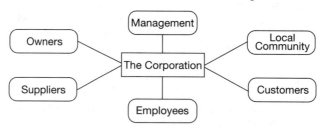

and survival of the supplier. When the firm treats the supplier as a valued member of the stakeholder network, rather than simply as a source of materials, the supplier will respond when the firm is in need. Chrysler traditionally had very close ties to its suppliers, even to the extent that led some to suspect the transfer of illegal payments. And when Chrysler was on the brink of disaster, the suppliers responded with price cuts, accepting late payments, financing, and so on. Supplier and company can rise and fall together. Of course, again, the particular supplier relationships will depend on a number of variables such as the number of suppliers and whether the supplies are finished goods or raw materials.

Customers exchange resources for the products of the firm and in return receive the benefits of the products. Customers provide the lifeblood of the firm in the form of revenue. Given the level of reinvestment of earnings in large corporations, customers indirectly pay for the development of new products and services. . . . By paying attention to customers' needs, management automatically addresses the needs of suppliers and owners. Moreover, it seems that the ethic of customer service carries over to the community. . . .

The local community grants the firm the right to build facilities and benefits from the tax base and economic and social contributions of the firm. In return for the provision of local services, the firm is expected to be a good citizen, as is any person, either "natural or artificial." The firm cannot expose the community to unreasonable hazards in the form of pollution, toxic waste, and so on. If for some reason the firm must leave a community, it is expected to work with local leaders to make the transition as smooth as possible. Of course, the firm does not have perfect knowledge, but when it discovers some danger or runs afoul of new competition, it is expected to inform the local community and to work with the community to overcome any problem. When the firm mismanages its relationship with the local community, it is in the same position as a citizen who commits a crime. It has violated the implicit social contract with the community and should expect to be distrusted and ostracized. It should not be surprised when punitive measures are invoked.

We have not included "competitors" as stakeholders in the narrow sense, since strictly speaking they are not necessary for the survival and success of the firm; the stakeholders theory works equally well in monopoly contexts. However, competitors and government would be the first to be included in an extension of this basic theory. It is simply not true that the interests of competitors in an industry are always in conflict. There is no reason why trade associations and other multi-organizational groups cannot band together to solve common problems that have little to do with how to restrain trade. Implementation of stakeholder management principles, in the long run, mitigates the need for industrial policy and an increasing role for government intervention and regulation.

The Role of Management

Management plays a special role, for it too has a stake in the fiction that is the modern corporation. On the one hand, management's stake is like that of employees, with some kind of explicit or implicit employment contract. But, on the other hand, management has a duty of safeguarding the welfare of the abstract entity that is the corporation, which can override a stake as employee. In short, management, especially top management, must look after the health of the corporation, and this involves balancing the multiple claims of conflicting stakeholders. Owners want more financial returns, while customers want more money spent on research and development. Employees want higher wages and better benefits, while the local community wants better parks and day-care facilities.

The task of management in today's corporation is akin to that of King Solomon. The stakeholder theory does not give primacy to one stakeholder group over another, though there will surely be times when one group will benefit at the expense of others. In general, however, management must keep the relationships among stakeholders in balance. When these relationships become unbalanced, the survival of the firm is in jeopardy.

When wages are too high and product quality is too low, customers leave, suppliers suffer, and owners sell their stocks and bonds, depressing the stock price and making it difficult to raise new capital at favorable rates. Note, however, that the reason for paying returns to owners is not that they "own" the firm, but that their support is necessary for the survival of the firm, and that they have a legitimate claim on the firm. Similar reasoning applies in turn to each stakeholder group.

A stakeholder theory of the firm must redefine the purpose of the firm. The stockholder theory claims that the purpose of the firm is to maximize the welfare of the stockholders, perhaps subject to some moral or social constraints, either because such maximization leads to the greatest good or because of property rights. The purpose of the firm is quite different in our view. If a stakeholder theory is to be consistent with the principles of corporate effects and rights, then its purpose must take into account Kant's dictum of respect for persons. The very purpose of the firm is, in our view, to serve as a vehicle for coordinating stakeholder interests. It is through the firm that each stakeholder group makes itself better off through voluntary exchanges. The corporation serves at the pleasure of its stakeholders, and none may be used as a means to the ends of another without full rights of participation in that decision. . . . [Two] stakeholder management principles will serve as a foundation for articulating the theory. They are guiding ideals for the immortal corporation as it endures through generations of particular mortal stakeholders.

Stakeholder Management Principles

P1: The corporation should be managed for the benefit of its stakeholders: its customers, suppliers, owners, employees, and local communities. The rights of these groups must be ensured, and, further, the groups must participate, in some sense, in decisions that substantially affect their welfare.

P2: Management bears a fiduciary relationship to stakeholders and to the corporation as an abstract entity. It must act in the interests of the stakeholders as their agent, and it must act in the interests of the corporation to ensure the survival of the firm, safeguarding the long-term stakes of each group.

P1, which we might call The Principle of Corporate Legitimacy, redefines the purpose of the firm to be in line with the principles of corporate effects and rights. It implies the legitimacy of stakeholder claims on the firm. Any social contract that justifies the existence of the corporate form includes the notion that stakeholders are a party to that contract. Further, stakeholders have some inalienable rights to participate in decisions that substantially affect their welfare or involve their being used as a means to another's ends. We bring to bear our arguments for the incoherence of the stockholder view as justification for P1. If in fact there is no good reason for the stockholder theory, and if in fact there are harms, benefits, and rights of stakeholders involved in running the modern corporation, then we know of no other starting point, for a theory of the corporation than P1.

P2, which we might call The Stakeholder Fiduciary Principle, explicitly defines the duty of management to recognize these claims. It will not always be possible to meet all claims of all stakeholders all the time, since some of these claims will conflict. Here P2 recognizes the duty of management to act in the long-term best interests of the corporation, conceived as a forum of stakeholder interaction, when the interests of the group outweigh the interests of the individual parties to the collective contract. The duty described in P2 is a fiduciary duty, yet it does not suffer from the difficulties surrounding the fiduciary duty to stockholders, for the conflicts involved there are precisely those that P2 makes it mandatory for management to resolve. Of course, P2 gives no instructions for a magical resolution of the conflicts that arise from prima facie obligations to multiple parties. An analysis of such rules for decision making is a subject to be addressed on another occasion, but P2 does give these conflicts a legitimacy that they do not enjoy in the stockholder theory. It gives management a clear and distinct directive to pay attention to stakeholder claims.

P1 and P2 recognize the eventual need for changes in the law of corporations and other governance mechanisms if the stakeholder theory is to be put into practice. P1 and P2, if implemented as a major innovation in the structure of the corporation, will make manifest the eventual legal institutionalization of sanctions. . . .

The law of corporations needs to be redefined to recognize the legitimate purpose of the corporation as stated in P1. This has in fact developed in some areas of the law, such as products liability, where the claims of customers to safe products have emerged, and labor law, where the claims of employees have been safeguarded. . . . We envision that a body of case law will emerge to give meaning to "the proper claims of stakeholders," and in effect that the "wisdom of Solomon" necessary to make the stakeholder theory work will emerge naturally through the joint action of the courts, stakeholders, and management.

Note

1. Introduction by Beauchamp & Bowie, eds. *Ethical Theory in Business* 97, 101–105 (3d ed., 1988).

Business Ethics and Stakeholder Analysis

KENNETH E. GOODPASTER

Abstract: Much has been written about stakeholder analysis as a process by which to introduce ethical values into management decision-making. This paper takes a critical look at the assumptions behind this idea, in an effort to understand better the meaning of ethical management decisions.

A distinction is made between stakeholder analysis and stakeholder synthesis. The two most natural kinds of stakeholder synthesis are then defined and discussed: strategic and multi-fiduciary. Paradoxically, the former appears to yield business without ethics and the latter appears to yield ethics without business. The paper concludes by suggesting that a third approach to stakeholder thinking needs to be developed, one that avoids the paradox just mentioned and that clarifies for managers (and directors) the legitimate role of ethical considerations in decision-making.

> *So we must think through what management should be accountable for; and how and through whom its accountability can be discharged. The stockholders' interest, both short- and long-term, is one of the areas. But it is only one.*
>
> PETER DRUCKER, 1988
> *Harvard Business Review*

What is ethically responsible management? How can a corporation, given its economic mission, be managed with appropriate attention to ethical concerns? These are central questions in the field of business ethics. One approach to answering such questions that has become popular during the last two decades is loosely referred to as "stakeholder analysis." Ethically responsible management, it is often suggested, is management that includes careful attention not only to stockholders *but to stakeholders generally* in the decision-making process.

This suggestion about the ethical importance of stakeholder analysis contains an important kernel of truth, but it can also be misleading. Comparing the ethical relationship between managers and stockholders with their relationship to other stakeholders is, I will argue, almost as problematic as ignoring stakeholders (ethically) altogether—presenting us with something of a "stakeholder paradox."

Reprinted by permission of the author Kenneth E. Goodpaster, University of St. Thomas, and *Business Ethics Quarterly,* January 1991, Vol. 1, No. 1, the Journal of the Society for Business Ethics.

Definition

The term "stakeholder" appears to have been invented in the early '60s as a deliberate play on the word "stockholder" to signify that there are other parties having a "stake" in the decision-making of the modern, publicly-held corporation in addition to those holding equity positions. Professor R. Edward Freeman, in his book *Strategic Management: A Stakeholder Approach* (Pitman, 1984), defines the term as follows:

> A stakeholder in an organization is (by definition) any group or individual who can affect or is affected by the achievement of the organization's objectives. (46)

Examples of stakeholder groups (beyond stockholders) are employees, suppliers, customers, creditors, competitors, governments, and communities. . . .

Another metaphor with which the term "stakeholder" is associated is that of a "player" in a game like poker. One with a "stake" in the game is one who plays and puts some economic value at risk.[1]

Much of what makes responsible decision-making difficult is understanding how there can be an ethical relationship between management and stakeholders that avoids being too weak (making stakeholders mere means to stockholders' ends) or too strong (making stakeholders quasi-stockholders in their own right). To give these issues life, a case example will help. So let us consider the case of General Motors and Poletown.

The Poletown Case[2]

In 1980, GM was facing a net loss in income, the first since 1921, due to intense foreign competition. Management realized that major capital expenditures would be required for the company to regain its competitive position and profitability. A $40 billion five-year capital spending program was announced that included new, state-of-the-art assembly techniques aimed at smaller, fuel-efficient automobiles demanded by the market. Two aging assembly plants in Detroit were among the ones to be replaced. Their closure would eliminate 500 jobs. Detroit in 1980 was a city with a black majority, an unemployment rate of 18% overall and 30% for blacks, a rising public debt and a chronic budget deficit, despite high tax rates.

The site requirements for a new assembly plant included 500 acres, access to long-haul railroad and freeways, and proximity to suppliers for "just-in-time" inventory management. It needed to be ready to produce 1983 model year cars beginning in September 1982. The only site in Detroit meeting GM's requirements was heavily settled, covering a section of the Detroit neighborhood of Poletown. Of the 3,500 residents, half were black. The whites were mostly of Polish descent, retired or nearing retirement. An alternative "green field" site was available in another midwestern state.

Using the power of eminent domain, the Poletown area could be acquired and cleared for a new plant within the company's timetable, and the city government was eager to cooperate. Because of job retention in Detroit, the leadership of the United Auto Workers was also in favor of the idea. The Poletown

Neighborhood Council strongly opposed the plan, but was willing to work with the city and GM.

The new plant would employ 6,150 workers and would cost GM $500 million wherever it was built. Obtaining and preparing the Poletown site would cost an additional $200 million, whereas alternative sites in the midwest were available for $65–80 million.

The interested parties were many—stockholders, customers, employees, suppliers, the Detroit community, the midwestern alternative, the Poletown neighborhood. The decision was difficult. GM management needed to consider its competitive situation, the extra costs of remaining in Detroit, the consequences to the city of leaving for another part of the midwest, and the implications for the residents of choosing the Poletown site if the decision was made to stay. The decision about whom to talk to and *how* was as puzzling as the decision about *what* to do and *why*.

I. STAKEHOLDER ANALYSIS AND STAKEHOLDER SYNTHESIS

Ethical values enter management decision-making, it is often suggested, through the gate of stakeholder analysis. But the suggestion that introducing "stakeholder analysis" into business decisions is the same as introducing ethics into those decisions is questionable. To make this plain, let me first distinguish between two importantly different ideas: stakeholder analysis and stakeholder synthesis. I will then examine alternative kinds of stakeholder synthesis with attention to ethical content.

The decision-making process of an individual or a company can be seen in terms of a sequence of six steps to be followed after an issue or problem presents itself for resolution.[3] For ease of reference and recall, I will name the sequence PASCAL, after the six letters in the name of the French philosopher-mathematician Blaise Pascal (1623–62), who once remarked in reference to ethical decision-making that "the heart has reasons that reason knows not of."

(1) PERCEPTION or fact-gathering about the options available and their short- and long-term implications;
(2) ANALYSIS of these implications with specific attention to affected parties and to the decision-maker's goals, objectives, values, responsibilities, etc.;
(3) SYNTHESIS of this structured information according to whatever fundamental priorities obtain in the mindset of the decision-maker;
(4) CHOICE among the available options based on the synthesis;
(5) ACTION or implementation of the chosen option through a series of specific requests to specific individuals or groups, resource allocation, incentives, controls, and feedback;
(6) LEARNING from the outcome of the decision, resulting in either reinforcement or modification (for future decisions) of the way in which the above steps have been taken.

We might simplify this analysis, of course, to something like "input," "decision," and "output," but distinguishing interim steps can often be helpful. The main point is that the path from the presentation of a problem to its resolution must somehow involve gathering, processing, and acting on relevant information.

Now, by *stakeholder analysis* I simply mean a process that does not go beyond the first two steps mentioned above. That is, the affected parties caught up in each available option are identified and the positive and negative impacts on each stakeholder are determined. But questions having to do with processing this information into a decision and implementing it are *left unanswered*. These steps are not part of the *analysis* but of the *synthesis, choice,* and *action*.

Stakeholder analysis may give the initial appearance of a decision-making process, but in fact it is only a *segment* of a decision-making process. It represents the preparatory or opening phase that awaits the crucial application of the moral (or nonmoral) values of the decision-maker. So, to be informed that an individual or an institution regularly makes stakeholder analysis part of decision-making or takes a "stakeholder approach" to management is to learn little or nothing about the ethical character of that individual or institution. It is to learn only that stakeholders are regularly identified—*not why and for what purpose*. To be told that stakeholders are or must be "taken into account" is, so far, to be told very little. Stakeholder analysis is, as a practical matter, morally neutral. It is therefore a mistake to see it as a substitute for normative ethical thinking.[4]

What I shall call "stakeholder synthesis" goes further into the sequence of decision-making steps mentioned above to include actual decision-making and implementation (S, C, A). The critical point is that stakeholder synthesis offers *a pattern or channel by which to move from stakeholder identification to a practical response or resolution*. Here we begin to join stakeholder analysis to questions of substance. But we must now ask: What kind of substance? And how does it relate to *ethics*? The stakeholder idea, remember, is typically offered as a way of integrating *ethical* values into management decision-making. When and how does substance become *ethical* substance?

Strategic Stakeholder Synthesis

We can imagine decision-makers doing "stakeholder analysis" for different underlying reasons, not always having to do with ethics. A management team, for example, might be careful to take positive and (especially) negative stakeholder effects into account for no other reason than that offended stakeholders might resist or retaliate (e.g., through political action or opposition to necessary regulatory clearances). It might not be *ethical* concern for the stakeholders that motivates and guides such analysis, so much as concern about potential impediments to the achievement of strategic objectives. Thus positive and negative effects on relatively powerless stakeholders may be ignored or discounted in the synthesis, choice, and action phases of the decision process.[5]

In the Poletown case, General Motors might have done a stakeholder analysis using the following reasoning: our stockholders are the central stakeholders here, but other key stakeholders include our suppliers, old and new plant employees, the City of Detroit, and the residents of Poletown. These other stakeholders are not our direct concern as a corporation with an economic mission, but since they can influence our short- or long-term strategic interests, they must be taken into account. Public relation's costs and benefits, for example, or concerns about union contracts or litigation might well have influenced the choice between staying in Detroit and going elsewhere.

I refer to this kind of stakeholder synthesis as "strategic" since stakeholders outside the stockholder group are viewed instrumentally, as factors potentially affecting the overarching goal of optimizing stockholder interests. They are taken into account in the decision-making process, but as external environmental forces, as potential sources of either good will or retaliation. "We" are the economic principals and management; "they" are significant players whose attitudes and future actions might affect our short-term or long-term success. We must respect them in the way one "respects" the weather—as a set of forces to be reckoned with.[6]

It should be emphasized that managers who adopt the strategic stakeholder approach are not necessarily *personally* indifferent to the plight of stakeholders who are "strategically unimportant." The point is that *in their role as managers,* with a fiduciary relationship that binds them as agents to principals, their basic outlook subordinates other stakeholder concerns to those of stockholders. Market and legal forces are relied upon to secure the interests of those whom strategic considerations might discount. This reliance can and does take different forms, depending on the emphasis given to market forces on the one hand and legal forces on the other. A more conservative, market-oriented view acknowledges the role of legal compliance as an environmental factor affecting strategic choice, but thinks stakeholder interests are best served by minimal interference from the public sector. Adam Smith's "invisible hand" is thought to be the most important guarantor of the common good in a competitive economy. A more liberal view sees the hand of government, through legislation and regulation, as essential for representing stakeholders that might otherwise not achieve "standing" in the strategic decision process.

What both conservatives and liberals have in common is the conviction that the fundamental orientation of management must be toward the interests of stockholders. Other stakeholders (customers, employees, suppliers, neighbors) enter the decision-making equation either directly as instrumental economic factors or indirectly as potential legal claimants. Both see law and regulation as providing a voice for stakeholders that goes beyond market dynamics. They differ about how much government regulation is socially and economically desirable.

During the Poletown controversy, GM managers as individuals may have cared deeply about the potential lost jobs in Detroit, or about the potential dislocation of Poletown residents. But in their role as agents for the owners (stockholders) they could only allow such considerations to "count" if they served GM's strategic interests (or perhaps as legal constraints on the decision).

Professor Freeman (1984, cited above) appears to adopt some form of strategic stakeholder synthesis. After presenting his definition of stakeholders, he remarks about its application to any group or individual "who can *affect* or is *affected by*" a company's achievement of its purposes. The "affect" part of the definition is not hard to understand; but Freeman clarifies the "affected by" part:

The point of strategic management is in some sense to chart a direction for the firm. Groups which can affect that direction and its implementation must be considered in the strategic management process. However, it is less obvious why "those groups who are affected by the corporation" are stakeholders as well . . . I make the definition symmetric because of the changes which the firm has undergone in the past few years. Groups which 20 years ago had no effect on the actions of the firm, can affect it today, largely because of the actions of the firm which ignored the effects on these groups. Thus, by calling those affected groups "stakeholders," the ensuing strategic management model will be sensitive to future change . . . (46)

Freeman might have said "who can actually or potentially affect" the company, for the mind-set appears to be one in which attention to stakeholders is justified in terms of actual or potential impact on the company's achievement of its strategic purposes. <u>Stakeholders (other than stockholders) are actual or potential means/obstacles to corporate objectives</u>. A few pages later, Freeman writes:

From the standpoint of strategic management, or the achievement of organizational purpose, we need an inclusive definition. We must not leave out any group or individual who can affect or is affected by organizational purpose, *because that group may prevent our accomplishments*. (52) [Emphasis added.]

The sense of a strategic view of stakeholders is not that stakeholders are ignored, but that all but a special group (stockholders) are considered on the basis of their actual or potential influence on management's central mission. The basic normative principle is fiduciary responsibility (organizational prudence), supplemented by legal compliance.

Is the Substance Ethical?

The question we must ask in thinking about a strategic approach to stakeholder synthesis is this: Is it really an adequate rendering of the *ethical* component in managerial judgment? Unlike mere stakeholder *analysis*, this kind of synthesis does go beyond simply *identifying* stakeholders. It integrates the stakeholder information by using a single interest group (stockholders) as its basic normative touchstone. If this were formulated as an explicit rule or principle, it would have two parts and would read something like this: (1) Maximize the benefits and minimize the costs to the stockholder group, short- and long-term, and (2) <u>Pay close attention to the interests of other stakeholder</u> groups that might <u>potentially influence the achievement of</u> (1). But while expanding the list of stakeholders may be a way of "enlightening" self-interest for the organization, is it really a way of <u>introducing ethical values into business decision-making</u>?

There are really two possible replies here. The first is that as an account of how ethics enters the managerial mind-set, the strategic stakeholder approach fails not because it is *im*moral; but because it is *non*moral. By most accounts of the nature of ethics, a strategic stakeholder synthesis would not qualify as an ethical synthesis, even though it does represent a substantive view. The point is simply that while there is nothing necessarily *wrong* with strategic reasoning about the consequences of one's actions for others, the kind of concern exhibited should not be confused with what most people regard as *moral* concern.

Moral concern would avoid injury or unfairness to those affected by one's actions because it is wrong, regardless of the retaliatory potential of the aggrieved parties.[7]

The second reply does question the morality (*vs.* immorality) of strategic reasoning as the ultimate principle behind stakeholder analysis. It acknowledges that strategy, when placed in a highly effective legal and regulatory environment and given a time-horizon that is relatively long-term, may well avoid significant forms of anti-social behavior. But it asserts that as an operating principle for managers under time pressure in an imperfect legal and regulatory environment, strategic analysis is insufficient. In the Poletown case, certain stakeholders (e.g., the citizens of Detroit or the residents of Poletown) may have merited more *ethical* consideration than the strategic approach would have allowed. Some critics charged that GM only considered these stakeholders *to the extent that* serving their interests also served GM's interests, and that as a result, their interests were undermined.

Many, most notably Nobel Laureate Milton Friedman, believe that market and legal forces are adequate to translate or transmute ethical concerns into straightforward strategic concerns for management. He believes that in our economic and political system (democratic capitalism), direct concern for stakeholders (what Kant might have called "categorical" concern) is unnecessary, redundant, and inefficient, not to mention dishonest:

> In many cases, there is a strong temptation to rationalize actions as an exercise of "social responsibility." In the present climate of opinion, with its widespread aversion to "capitalism," "profits," the "soulless corporation" and so on, this is one way for a corporation to generate good will as a by-product of expenditures that are entirely justified in its own self-interest. If our institutions, and the attitudes of the public make it in their self-interest to cloak their actions in this way, I cannot summon much indignation to denounce them. At the same time, I can express admiration for those individual proprietors or owners of closely held corporations or stockholders of more broadly held corporations who disdain such tactics as approaching fraud.

Critics respond, however, that absent a pre-established harmony or linkage between organizational success and ethical success, some stakeholders, some of the time, will be affected a lot but will be able to affect in only a minor way the interests of the corporation. They add that in an increasingly global business environment, even the protections of law are fragmented by multiple jurisdictions.

At issue then is (1) defining ethical behavior partly in terms of the (non-strategic) decision-making values *behind* it, and (2) recognizing that too much optimism about the correlation between strategic success and virtue runs the risk of tailoring the latter to suit the former.

Thus the move toward substance (from analysis to synthesis) in discussions of the stakeholder concept is not necessarily a move toward ethics. And it is natural to think that the reason has to do with the instrumental status accorded to stakeholder groups other than stockholders. If we were to treat all stakeholders by strict analogy with stockholders, would we have arrived at a more ethically satisfactory form of stakeholder synthesis? Let us now look at this alternative, what I shall call a "multi-fiduciary" approach.

Multi-Fiduciary Stakeholder Synthesis

In contrast to a strategic view of stakeholders, one can imagine a management team processing stakeholder information by giving the same care to the interests of, say, employees, customers, and local communities as to the economic interests of stockholders. This kind of substantive commitment to stakeholders might involve trading off the economic advantages of one group against those of another, e.g., in a plant closing decision. I shall refer to this way of integrating stakeholder analysis with decision-making as "multi-fiduciary" since all stakeholders are treated by management as having equally important interests, deserving joint "maximization" (or what Herbert Simon might call "satisficing").

Professor Freeman, quoted earlier, contemplates what I am calling the multi-fiduciary view at the end of his 1984 book under the heading *The Manager As Fiduciary To Stakeholders:*

> Perhaps the most important area of future research is the issue of whether or not a theory of management can be constructed that uses the stakeholder concept to enrich "managerial capitalism," that is, can the notion that managers bear a fiduciary relationship to stockholders or the owners of the firm, be replaced by a concept of management whereby the manager *must* act in the interests of the stakeholders in the organization? (249)

As we have seen, the strategic approach pays attention to stakeholders as to factors that might affect economic interests, so many market forces to which companies must pay attention for competitive reasons. They become actual or potential legal challenges to the company's exercise of economic rationality. The multi-fiduciary approach, on the other hand, views stakeholders apart from their instrumental, economic, or legal clout. It does not see them merely as what philosopher John Ladd once called "limiting operating conditions" on management attention.[8] On this view, the word "stakeholder" carries with it, by the deliberate modification of a single phoneme, a dramatic shift in managerial outlook.

In 1954, famed management theorist Adolf Berle conceded a longstanding debate with Harvard law professor E. Merrick Dodd that looks in retrospect very much like a debate between what we are calling strategic and multi-fiduciary interpretations of stakeholder synthesis. Berle wrote:

> Twenty years ago, [I held] that corporate powers were powers in trust for shareholders while Professor Dodd argued that these powers were held in trust for the entire community. The argument has been settled (at least for the time being) squarely in favor of Professor Dodd's contention. (Quoted in Ruder, see below.)

The intuitive idea behind Dodd's view, and behind more recent formulations of it in terms of "multiple constituencies" and "stakeholders, not just stockholders," is that by expanding the list of those in whose trust corporate management must manage, we thereby introduce ethical responsibility into business decision-making.

In the context of the Poletown case, a multi-fiduciary approach by GM management might have identified the same stakeholders. But it would have considered the interests of employees, the city of Detroit, and the Poletown residents *alongside* stockholder interests, not solely in terms of how they might *influence* stockholder interests. This may or may not have entailed a different outcome. But it probably would have meant a different approach to the decision-making process in relation to the residents of Poletown (talking with them, for example).

We must now ask, as we did of the strategic approach: How satisfactory is multi-fiduciary stakeholder synthesis as a way of giving ethical substance to management decision-making? On the face of it, and in stark contrast to the strategic approach, it may seem that we have at last arrived at a truly moral view. But we should be cautious. For no sooner do we think we have found the proper interpretation of ethics in management than a major objection presents itself. And, yes, it appears to be a *moral* objection!

It can be argued that multi-fiduciary stakeholder analysis is simply incompatible with widely held moral convictions about the special fiduciary obligations owed by management to stockholders. At the center of the objection is the belief that the obligations of agents to principals are stronger or different in kind from those of agents to third parties.

The Stakeholder Paradox

Managers who would pursue a multi-fiduciary stakeholder orientation for their companies must face resistance from those who believe that a strategic orientation is the only *legitimate* one for business to adopt, given the economic mission and legal constitution of the modern corporation. This may be disorienting since the word "illegitimate" has clear negative ethical connotations, and yet the multi-fiduciary approach is often defended on ethical grounds. I will refer to this anomalous situation as the *Stakeholder Paradox*:

> It seems essential, yet in some ways illegitimate, to orient corporate decisions by ethical values that go beyond strategic stakeholder considerations to multi-fiduciary ones.

I call this a paradox because it says there is an ethical problem whichever approach management takes. Ethics seems both to forbid and to demand a strategic, profit-maximizing mind-set. The argument behind the paradox focuses on management's *fiduciary* duty to the stockholder, essentially the duty to keep a profit-maximizing promise, and a concern that the "impartiality" of the multi-fiduciary approach simply cuts management loose from certain well-defined bonds of stockholder accountability. On this view, impartiality is thought to be a *betrayal of trust*. Professor David S. Ruder, a former chairman of the Securities and Exchange Commission, once summarized the matter this way:

> Traditional fiduciary obligation theory insists that a corporate manager owes an obligation of care and loyalty to shareholders. If a public obligation theory unrelated to profit maximization becomes the law, the corporate manager who is not able to act in his own self interest without violating his fiduciary obligation, may nevertheless act in the public interest without violating that obligation.[9] (226)

Ruder continued:

> Whether induced by government legislation, government pressure, or merely by

enlightened attitudes of the corporation regarding its long range potential as a unit in society, corporate activities carried on in satisfaction of public obligations can be consistent with profit maximization objectives. In contrast, justification of public obligations upon bold concepts of public need without corporate benefit will merely serve to reduce further the owner's influence on his corporation and to create additional demands for public participation in corporate management. (228–9).

Ruder's view appears to be that (a) multi-fiduciary stakeholder synthesis *need not* be used by management because the strategic approach is more accommodating than meets the eye; and (b) multi-fiduciary stakeholder synthesis should not be invoked by management because such a "bold" concept could threaten the private (*vs.* public) status of the corporation.

In response to (a), we saw earlier that there were reasonable questions about the tidy convergence of ethics and economic success. Respecting the interests and rights of the Poletown residents might really have meant incurring higher costs for GM (short-term as well as long-term).

Appeals to corporate self-interest, even long-term, might not always support ethical decisions. But even on those occasions where they will, we must wonder about the disposition to favor economic and legal reasoning "for the record." If Ruder means to suggest that business leaders can often *reformulate* or *re-present* their reasons for certain morally grounded decisions in strategic terms having to do with profit maximization and obedience to law, he is perhaps correct. In the spirit of our earlier quote from Milton Friedman, we might not summon much indignation to denounce them. But why the fiction? Why not call a moral reason a moral reason?

This issue is not simply of academic interest. Managers must confront it in practice. In one major public company, the C.E.O. put significant resources behind an affirmative action program and included the following explanation in a memo to middle management:

> I am often asked why this is such a high priority at our company. There is, of course, the obvious answer that it is in our best interest to seek out and employ good people in all sectors of our society. And there is the answer that enlightened self-interest tells us that more and more of the younger people, whom we must attract as future employees, choose companies by their social records as much as by their business prospects. *But the one overriding reason for this emphasis is because it is right.* Because this company has always set for itself the objective of assuming social as well as business obligations. Because that's the kind of company we have been. And with your participation, that's the kind of company we'll continue to be.[10]

In this connection, Ruder reminds us of what Professor Berle observed over twenty-five years ago:

> The fact is that boards of directors or corporation executives are often faced with situations in which they quite humanly and simply consider that such and such is the decent thing to do and ought to be done . . . They apply the potential profits or public relations tests later on, a sort of left-handed justification in this curious free-market world where an obviously moral and decent or humane action has to be apologized for on the ground that, conceivably, you may somehow make money by it. (*Ibid.*)

The Problem of Boldness

What appears to lie at the foundation of Ruder's cautious view is a concern about the "boldness" of the multi-fiduciary concept [(b) above].[11] It is not that he thinks the strategic approach is always satisfactory; it is that the multi-fiduciary approach is, in his eyes, much worse. For it questions the special relationship between the manager as agent and the stockholder as principal.

Ruder suggests that what he calls a "public obligation" theory threatens the private status of the corporation. He believes that what we are calling multi-fiduciary stakeholder synthesis *dilutes* the fiduciary obligation to stockholders (by extending it to customers, employees, suppliers, etc.) and he sees this as a threat to the "privacy" of the private sector organization. If public obligations are understood on the model of public sector institutions with their multiple constituencies, Ruder thinks, the stockholders lose status.

There is something profoundly *right* about Ruder's line of argument here, I believe, and something profoundly *wrong*. What is right is his intuition that if we treat other stakeholders on the model of the fiduciary relationship between management and the stockholder, we will, in effect, make them into quasi-stockholders. We can do this, of course, if we choose to as a society. But we should be aware that it is a radical step indeed. For it blurs traditional goals in terms of entrepreneurial risk-taking, pushes decision-making towards paralysis because of the dilemmas posed by divided loyalties and, in the final analysis, represents nothing less than the conversion of the modern private corporation into a public institution and probably calls for a corresponding restructuring of corporate governance (e.g., representatives of each stakeholder group on the board of directors). Unless we believe that the social utility of a private sector has disappeared, not to mention its value for individual liberty and enterprise, we will be cautious about an interpretation of stakeholder synthesis that transforms the private sector into the public sector.

On the other hand, I believe Ruder is mistaken if he thinks that business ethics requires this kind of either/or: either a private sector with a strategic stakeholder synthesis (business without ethics) or the effective loss of the private sector with a multi-fiduciary stakeholder synthesis (ethics without business).

Recent debates over state laws protecting companies against hostile takeovers may illustrate Ruder's concern as well as the new challenge. According to one journalist, a recent Pennsylvania anti-takeover law

> does no less than redefine the fiduciary duty of corporate directors, enabling them to base decisions not merely on the interests of shareholders, but on the interests of customers, suppliers, employees and the community at large. Pennsylvania is saying that it is the corporation that directors are responsible to. Shareholders say they always thought they themselves were the corporation.

Echoing Ruder, one legal observer quoted by Elias *(ibid.)* commented with reference to this law that it "undermines and erodes free markets and property rights. From this perspective, this is an anticapitalist law. The management can take away property from the real owners."

In our terms, the state of Pennsylvania is charged with adopting a multi-fiduciary stakeholder approach in an effort to rectify deficiencies of the strategic approach which (presumably) corporate raiders hold.

The challenge that we are thus presented with is to develop an account of the moral responsibilities of management that (i) avoids surrendering the moral relationship between management and stakeholders as the strategic view does, while (ii) not transforming stakeholder obligations into fiduciary obligations (thus protecting the uniqueness of the principal-agent relationship between management and stockholder).

II. TOWARD A NEW STAKEHOLDER SYNTHESIS

We all remember the story of the well-intentioned Doctor Frankenstein. He sought to improve the human condition by designing a powerful, intelligent force for good in the community. Alas, when he flipped the switch, his creation turned out to be a monster rather than a marvel! Is the concept of the ethical corporation like a Frankenstein monster?

Taking business ethics seriously need not mean that management bears *additional* fiduciary relationships to third parties (nonstockholder constituencies) as multi-fiduciary stakeholder synthesis suggests. It may mean that there are morally significant *nonfiduciary* obligations to third parties surrounding any fiduciary relationship (See Figure 1.) Such moral obligations may be owed by private individuals as well as private-sector organizations to those whose freedom and well-being is affected by their economic behavior. It is these very obligations in fact (the duty not to harm or coerce and duties not to lie, cheat, or steal) that are cited in regulatory, legislative, and judicial arguments for constraining profit-driven business activities. These obligations are not "hypothetical" or contingent or indirect, as they would be on the strategic model, wherein they are only subject to the corporation's interests being met. They are "categorical" or direct. They are not rooted in the *fiduciary* relationship, but in other relationships at least as deep.

	Fiduciary	Non-fiduciary
Stockholders	●	
Other Stakeholders		●

Figure 1. Direct Managerial Obligations

It must be admitted in fairness to Ruder's argument that the jargon of "stakeholders" in discussions of business ethics can seem to threaten the notion of what corporate law refers to as the "undivided and unselfish loyalty" owed by managers and directors to stockholders. For this way of speaking can suggest a multiplication of management duties *of the same kind* as the duty to stockholders. What we must understand is that the responsibilities of management toward stockholders are of a piece with the obligations that *stockholders themselves* would be expected to honor in their own right. As an old Latin proverb has it, *nemo dat quod non habet*, which literally means "nobody gives what he doesn't have." Freely translating in this context we can say: No one can expect of an *agent* behavior that is ethically less responsible than what he would expect of himself. I cannot (ethically) *hire* done on my behalf what I would not (ethically) *do* myself. We might refer to this as the "Nemo Dat Principle" (NDP) and consider it a formal requirement of consistency in business ethics (and professional ethics generally):

> (NDP) Investors cannot expect of managers (more generally, principals cannot expect of their agents) behavior that would be inconsistent with the reasonable ethical expectations of the community.[13]

The NDP does not, of course, resolve in advance the many ethical challenges that managers must face. It only indicates that these challenges are of a piece with those that face us all. It offers a different kind of test (and so a different kind of stakeholder synthesis) that management (and institutional investors) might apply to policies and decisions.

The foundation of ethics in management—and the way out of the stakeholder paradox—lies in understanding that the conscience of the corporation is a logical and moral extension of the consciences of its principals. It is *not* an expansion of the *list* of principals, but a gloss on the principal-agent relationship itself. Whatever the structure of the principal-agent relationship, neither principal nor agent can ever claim that an agent has "moral immunity" from the basic obligations that would apply to any human being toward other members of the community.

Indeed, consistent with Ruder's belief, the introduction of moral reasoning (distinguished from multi-fiduciary stakeholder reasoning) into the framework of management thinking may *protect* rather than threaten private sector legitimacy. The conscientious corporation can maintain its private economic mission, but in the context of fundamental moral obligations owed by any member of society to others affected by that member's actions. Recognizing such obligations does *not* mean that an institution is a public institution. Private institutions, like private individuals, can be and are bound to respect moral obligations in the pursuit of private purposes.

Conceptually, then, we can make room for a moral posture toward stakeholders that is both *partial* (respecting the fiduciary relationship between managers and stockholders) and *impartial* (respecting the equally important non-fiduciary relationships between management and other stakeholders). As philosopher Thomas Nagel has said, "In the conduct of life, of all places, the rivalry between the view from within and the view from without must be taken seriously."[14]

Whether this conceptual room can be used *effectively* in the face of enormous pressures on contemporary managers and directors is another story, of course. For it is one thing to say that "giving standing to stakeholders" in managerial reasoning is conceptually coherent. It is something else to say that it is practically coherent.

Yet most of us, I submit, believe it. Most of us believe that management at General Motors *owed* it to the people of Detroit and to the people of Poletown to take their (nonfiduciary) interests very seriously, to seek creative solutions to the conflict, to do more than use or manipulate them in accordance with GM's needs only. We understand that managers and directors have a special obligation to provide a financial return to the stockholders, but we also understand that the word "special" in this context needs to be tempered by an appreciation of certain fundamental community norms that go beyond the demands of both laws and markets. There are certain class-action suits that stockholders ought not to win. For there is sometimes a moral defense.

CONCLUSION

The relationship between management and stockholders is ethically different in kind from the relationship between management and other parties (like employees, suppliers, customers, etc.), a fact that seems to go unnoticed by the multi-fiduciary approach. If it were not, the corporation would cease to be a private sector institution—and what is now called business ethics would become a more radical critique of our economic system than is typically thought. On this point, Milton Friedman must be given a fair and serious hearing.

This does not mean, however, that "stakeholders" lack a morally significant relationship to management, as the strategic approach implies. It means only that the relationship in question is different from a fiduciary one. Management may never have promised customers, employees, suppliers, etc., a "return on investment," but management is nevertheless obliged to take seriously its extra-legal obligations not to injure, lie to or cheat these stakeholders *quite apart from* whether it is in the stockholders' interests.

As we think through the *proper* relationship of management to stakeholders, fundamental features of business life must undoubtedly be recognized: that corporations have a principally economic mission and competence; that fiduciary obligations to investors and general obligations to comply with the law cannot be set aside; and that abuses of economic power and disregard of corporate stewardship in the name of business ethics are possible.

But these things must be recognized as well: that corporations are not solely financial institutions; that fiduciary obligations go beyond short-term profit and are in any case subject to moral criteria in their execution; and that mere compliance with the law can be unduly limited and even unjust.

The *Stakeholder Paradox* can be avoided by a more thoughtful understanding of the nature of moral obligation and the limits it imposes on the principal-agent relationship. Once we understand that there is a practical "space" for identifying the ethical values shared by a corporation and its stockholders—a space that goes beyond strategic self-interest but stops short of impartiality—the hard work of filling that space can proceed.

Notes

This paper derives from a conference in Applied Ethics, *Moral Philosophy in the Public Domain*, held at the University of British Columbia, in June 1990. It will also appear in an anthology currently in preparation at the UBC Centre of Applied Ethics.

1. Strictly speaking the historical meaning of "stakeholder" in this context is someone who literally *holds* the stakes during play.

2. See Goodpaster and Piper, *Managerial Decision Making and Ethical Values*, Harvard Business School Publishing Division, 1989.

3. See Goodpaster, PASCAL: A Framework For Conscientious Decision Making (1989).

4. Actually, there are subtle ways in which even the stakeholder identification or inventory process might have *some* ethical content. The very process of *identifying* affected parties involves the use of the imagination in a way that can lead to a natural empathetic or caring response to those parties in the synthesis, choice and action phases of decision-making. This is a contingent connection, however, not a necessary one.

5. Note that including powerless stakeholders in the analysis phase may indicate whether the decision-maker cares about "affecting" them or "being affected by" them. Also, the inclusion of what might be called secondary stakeholders as advocates for primary stakeholders (e.g., local governments on behalf of certain citizen groups) may signal the values that will come into play in any synthesis.

6. It should be mentioned that some authors, most notably Kenneth R. Andrews in *The Concept of Corporate Strategy* (Irwin, Third Edition, 1987), employ a broader and more social definition of "strategic" decision-making than the one implied here.

7. Freeman writes: "Theoretically, 'stakeholder' must be able to capture a broad range of groups and individuals, even though when we put the concept to practical tests we must be willing to ignore certain groups who will have little or no impact on the corporation at this point in time." (52–3).

8. Ladd observed in a now-famous essay entitled "Morality and the Ideal of Rationality in Formal Organizations" (*The Monist*, 54, 1970) that organizational "rationality" was defined solely in terms of economic objectives: "The interests and needs of the individuals concerned, as individuals, must be considered only insofar as they establish limiting operating conditions. Organizational rationality dictates that these interests and needs must not be considered in their own right or on their own merits. If we think of an organization as a machine, it is easy to see why we cannot reasonably expect it to have any moral obligations to people or for them to have any to it." (507)

9. "Public Obligations of Private Corporations," *U. of Pennsylvania Law Review*, 114 (1965). Ruder recently (1989) reaffirmed the views in his 1965 article.

10. "Business Products Corporation—Part 1," HBS Case Services 9-377-077.

11. "The Business Judgement Rule" gives broad latitude to officers and directors of corporations, but calls for reasoning on the basis of the long-term economic interest of the company. And corporate case law ordinarily allows exceptions to profit-maximization criteria only when there are actual or potential *legal* barriers, and limits charitable and humanitarian gifts by the logic of long-term self-interest. The underlying rationale is accountability to investors. Recent work by the American Law Institute, however, suggests a rethinking of these matters.

12. Christopher Elias, "Turning Up the Heat on the Top," *Insight*, July 23, 1990.

13. We might consider the NDP in broader terms that would include the relationship between "client" and "professional" in other contexts, such as law, medicine, education, government, and religion, where normally the community's expectations are embodied in ethical standards.

14. T. Nagel, *The View from Nowhere*, Oxford U. Press (1986), p. 163.

The "New" U.S. Sentencing Commission Guidelines: A Wake-Up Call for Corporate America

Dan R. Dalton • Michael B. Metzger • John W. Hill

We recognize that some will interpret the title of this article as a bit of hyperbole. Until recently—November 1, 1991, to be exact—we might have agreed. On that day the United States Sentencing Commission's[1] guidelines for sentencing organizations found guilty of violating federal law became effective.[2] In our view, expectations for reasonable business conduct will never be the same. Perhaps more important, the potential consequences of behavior outside those expectations have never been greater. In fact, the ability of the U.S. Sentencing Commission to create such an emphatic threat to business organizations has been described as an "awesome power."[3] It has been reported, for example, that a number of lobbying groups tried—unsuccessfully—to have the sentencing guidelines abated or made voluntary.[4] Those efforts having failed, we believe that rational business organizations are now compelled to sharply intensify their attention to managerial ethics.

We focus here on what might be referred to as the pragmatics of the sentencing guidelines. By this focus, we do not abandon our view that ethical managerial practice has value that transcends purely prudential concerns. Neither do we indicate any sympathy with those who dismiss programs of managerial ethics and corporate social responsibility because they have not been positively associated with organizational performance. It is not that we disagree that the extant literature on this point is articulate, but that we view it as largely irrelevant.[5]

Suppose, for example, that it has been unequivocally determined that the number of capital crimes in a given geographical area was unrelated to the vitality of the local economy. At the risk of some understatement, we would be uncomfortable concluding from such a report that our concerns about capital crime rates were misplaced. In response to such arguments in a business context prior to November 1, 1991, we might have argued that "economists know the price of everything and the value of nothing."[6] or that "... there are now numerous examples illustrating the choice of whether or not to do good is a moral, and not an economic, decision."[7] We might also have recalled that:

> It is irresponsible to imply that acting responsibly is always costless, and it is unethical to base the case for ethics on economic self interest ... *The market has many worthwhile features, but setting an appropriate price on virtue is not among them.*[8]

While the U.S. Sentencing Commission similarly failed to set a price on virtue, it plainly enhanced the economic value of organizational efforts to encourage virtuous behavior while, at the same time, increasing the potential costs of misbehavior. The new guidelines, therefore, are a virtual mandate for organizational investment in ethics and compliance programs. This is not to say that the Commission has ordered organizations to adopt such programs; it has not.

Academy of Management Executive, 1994, Vol. 8, No. 1. Reprinted by permission.

It does suggest, however, that for an organization not to do so borders on recklessness. We, therefore, agree with the assertion that "any general counsel not now reviewing his company's compliance programs could be engaged in professional malpractice."[9]

U.S. Sentencing Commission Guidelines for Organizational Defendants

In early 1991, the U.S. Sentencing Commission sent Congress its proposed guidelines for the sentencing of organizational offenders. However, the imposition of these guidelines is not limited to corporations. Partnerships, labor unions, pension funds, trusts, joint stock companies, unincorporated organizations and associations, and non-profit organizations are included as well.[10] It would seem that no business enterprise is exempt. Since November 1, 1991, these guidelines have governed the sentencing of organizations in the federal courts. Perhaps the most prominent feature of these guidelines is their provision for more lenient sentencing if, at the time of the offense, the convicted organization had implemented an "effective program to prevent and detect violations of the law." In the absence of such a program, a substantially more severe sentence may be imposed. It is notable—and a matter to which we devote more attention in a succeeding section—that such a program need not actually detect, or prevent the violation. The very existence of a reasonable program may entitle the corporation to leniency in subsequent sentencing.[11]

How Much Leniency?[12]

The actual sentencing under the guidelines for an offense committed by an organization depends on a number of factors. There are elements that aggravate an offense; conversely, there are elements that mitigate an offense. Having considered these various factors, the court must determine the "offense level" under the guidelines. Associated with any given offense level is a corresponding range from which the penalty must be assessed.

The first exacerbating issue is the nature of the crime itself. The more serious the crime, the higher the offense level. A second consideration is the amount of loss suffered by the victim(s) of the crime. Fraud, for example, is a level six offense; a fraud causing harm in excess of $5 million is increased by fourteen levels—to a level twenty offense. The amount of planning evidenced by the offense is also at issue. Anything beyond minimal planning, for instance, will increase the level of the crime by two levels. For the fraud example, the crime is now at level twenty-two. The different in offense level is hardly trivial. Crimes at level six or lower involve a base fine of $5,000; offense levels of thirty-eight or higher involve a base fine of $72.5 million, a ruinous penalty for most organizations.

Having set the offense level, the court must determine the defendant's "culpability score." This culpability score is essentially a multiplier. A number of conditions associated with the crime can have the effect of increasing or decreasing this multiplier. First, if the organization employs more than 5,000 people, the multiplier is increased. Further, suppose that high-level organizational personnel were involved in or tolerated the criminal activity. Also, suppose that the organization had a prior history of similar criminal conduct. Assume, too, that the organization had violated a judicial order or injunction, or had obstructed justice during the investigation or prosecution stages of the offense. Activities such as these would almost certainly establish the multiplier at four, the maximum. The $72.5 million fine to which we earlier referred would now be $290 million (i.e., the base fine times the multiplier: $72.5 million x 4).

Consider, instead, an organization that—unlike the one previously profiled—did nothing to exacerbate the crime. Instead, this organization is aware of the only two circumstances that actually reduce the culpability score. One is the existence—prior to the crime—of an effective program to prevent and detect violations of the law. The second is self-reporting, cooperation, and acceptance of responsibility. The reduction for self-reporting of the crime assumes that the report is made on a timely basis—within a reasonable period after the discovery of the offense. Also, the self-report must not have been made in consideration of an imminent threat of governmental investigation, indictment, or some threat of exposure through other means.

A company that has such a program and does self-report an offense in a timely manner could have a culpability score of less than zero. The minimum multiplier in such a case would be 0.05; the maximum multiplier for a sub-zero culpability score would be 0.2. Consider a simple example. Suppose that a company faced a $40 million base fine. The worst-case scenario (a four multiplier) would result in the actual assessment of a $160 million fine (four multiplier times $40 million base fine). A company with an effective program and a self-reported crime could receive a 0.05 multiplier. This would result in a fine of $2 million (0.05 multiplier times $40 million base fine). The difference between $160 million and $2 million should persuasively illustrate the potential impact of ethical managerial practice and attention to factors which reduce culpability scores under the sentencing guidelines. Such practices and attention can be "the difference between bankruptcy and salvation for a company that gets into trouble."[13] Further, it should be obvious that an effective compliance program should reduce the probability that an organization would "get into trouble" in the first place.

Given the gross differences in these outcomes, it might be expected that organizations would have immediately embraced compliance programs. Curiously, there is some indication that this is not the case. A recent commentary on the federal sentencing guidelines suggested that "few companies seem to be responding," and that "several major companies, lawyers and executives said they hadn't heard about the guidelines."[14] A general counsel acknowledged only a "vague idea of the guidelines" and remarked of the guidelines, "I don't think it has had a high profile." Another corporate spokesperson noted that "everybody I have asked in our area said, 'Huh?'"

What Constitutes Compliance?

Fortunately, there is little need to speculate on what exactly is meant by an "effective program to prevent and detect violations of law." The Sentencing Commission's commentary suggests that to qualify for a reduction in the culpability score, a program must be "reasonably designed, implemented and enforced so that it will generally be effective in preventing criminal conduct."[15] Minimum standards for such a program include a number of elements:

- An organization must have established standards and procedures for its employees and agents which are "reasonably capable of reducing the prospect of criminal conduct."
- Specific high-level officer(s) of the organization must be assigned the responsibility for compliance.
- An organization must use due care not to assign substantial discretionary authority to any individual whom the organization knew, or should have known, might have a propensity to engage in criminal activities.
- An organization must effectively communicate its standards and procedures to all employees or agents through appropriate training programs and publications.
- An organization must take reasonable steps to ensure compliance with its standards and procedures. This might be accomplished through the use of monitoring and auditing systems. Also, the organization should maintain and publicize a reporting system so that employees can disclose criminal activities without fear of retribution.
- Standards and procedures should be enforced through appropriate disciplinary mechanisms.
- Following detection of an offense, an organization should take all reasonable steps "to respond appropriately to the offense" and to prevent further, similar offenses.[16]

Clearly, there are ambiguous components in these guidelines. What exactly is "substantial discretionary authority"? What are "reasonable steps"? What is an "appropriate disciplinary mechanism"? Inasmuch as the sentencing guidelines became effective in November 1991, we know of no cases on which we could rely to answer such questions. The total lack of empirical data on trends in corporate sentencing has been noted.[17] Even so, it has been wisely suggested that ". . . while the letter of these guidelines may be indistinct in parts, their spirit is clear: to encourage organizations to establish, monitor, and enforce programs that detect and prevent violations of the law."

Given the consequences of criminal activity with and without such programs, we would strongly recommend being an early adopter. Consider an example:[18] A $25,000 bribe has been paid to a city official to ensure an award of a cable television franchise. This is a level eighteen offense with a base penalty of a $350,000 fine. Based on a variety of factors (e.g., culpability, multipliers), that penalty is now increased to $1.4 million. The minimum fine with mitigating circumstances (e.g., company has a compliance plan, no high-level involvement) would have placed this fine in the $17,500 to $70,000 range. We do not mean to trivialize such offenses or penalties in this range. We will note, however, that the comparison of a $1.4 million fine to one of $70,000 does provide a stark—and we think persuasive—contrast.

Accordingly, it appears that the cost of waiting for the courts to define in some detail what constitutes these various elements could be enormous. We cannot resist noting the irony of an organization waiting for such guidance becoming a participant—as a defendant—in the court's determination of these guidelines. Moreover, our guess would be that a defense based on "Well, we were not sure exactly what to do with regard to the sentencing guidelines, so we opted to do nothing" would be less than compelling.

Conclusion

In many ways we rue the necessity of—and the opportunity provided by—the sentencing guidelines. We are sensitive to the cynicism expressed by some about the motives of those companies that will adopt ethics programs to capitalize on the "rewards" provided by such compliance.[19] We confess, however, that we think it is more important that organizations adopt effective compliance programs than that they do so for altruistic reasons. While we would always have argued that the principles set forth by the Sentencing Commission for a responsible compliance program were exemplary from an ethical perspective, we suggest that adherence to these principles—as a practical matter—is now imperative. Managers should also be aware that the Justice Department has recently announced similar guidelines. Companies with in-place environmental compliance audits that promptly report violations will qualify for "prosecution leniency."[20]

The sentencing guidelines address criminal behavior and sanctions. For us, legal compliance is a necessary, but insufficient, standard for the conduct of the modern organization. It is possible that an organization could behave legally on every dimension, yet demonstrate a near total disregard for managerial ethics and social responsibility. This sentiment may never have been stated more definitively than by Alexander Solzhenitsyn:

> I have spent all my life under a communist regime, and I will tell you that society without any objective legal scale is a terrible one indeed. But, a society with no other scale but the legal one is not quite worthy of man either . . . Life organized legalistically has shown its inability to defend itself against the corrosion of evil.[21]

We would hope that the U.S. sentencing guidelines do provide an incentive for organizations to establish compliance programs or to review and amend existing programs. Also, we hope that attention to these opportunities will acquaint employees at all levels with the commitment of the organization to establish, monitor, and enforce these programs. Beyond that, we would hope that programs consistent with the culpability guidelines of the Sentencing Commission will produce ripple effects that go beyond curbing illegal behavior to reach behavior that is "only" unethical.

There may be another aspect of the sentencing guidelines which may lead—somewhat more indirectly—to improved attention to ethical outcomes in the organization. A fascinating, and troublesome, point has recently been made. It seems that many managers are reluctant to recount their actions in moral terms even when, in fact, they are morally motivated. Instead, they adopt postures that justify such moral behavior only on the basis of "organizational interests, practicality, and economic good sense."[22]

Such postures are evidently of long standing as they echo de Tocqueville's observation that Americans in business enterprise were disinclined to admit altruistic behavior, even while engaging in it.[23] Certainly, the sentencing guidelines afford ethically motivated managers with additional prudential arguments in favor of corporate attention to ethical concerns. Perhaps the sentencing guidelines, by establishing a pretext for the discussion of ethical issues, will help lure morality out of the organizational closet.

Perhaps three matters bear repeating. First, any programs which may entitle an organization to decreases in the critical culpability index must be in place prior to any infraction. Second, it is not necessary that these programs actually lead to the discovery of prohibited behavior to qualify for culpability reduction. The Sentencing Commission commentary emphasizes that the "hallmark" of a meaningful program is that the organization exercised "due diligence" in seeking to prevent and detect criminal conduct by its employees and other agents.[24] Judge William W. Wilkins, chairman of the Sentencing Commission, noted that "Even the best efforts to prevent crime may not be successful in every case. But we have to reward the corporation that was trying to be a good corporate citizen."[25] Last, if attention to these sentencing guidelines, multipliers, culpability scores, and related issues are not "imperative" for the contemporary organization as we have suggested, it must be something very close to it.

Notes

1. The Sentencing Reform Act of 1984 (U.S.C. §3551 & 28 U.S.C. §§991–998) established the U.S. Sentencing Commission. This commission was created as an independent body of the judicial branch and empowered to provide guidelines for federal judges to follow in the sentencing of criminals. It is fair to say that these "guidelines" are not advisory, but determinate and binding on federal courts. While always referred to as "guidelines," departures from the standards set forth by the Sentencing Commission are subject to appeal by either the defendant or the government. For general commentary on the Sentencing Commission, see M.A. Cohen, "Explaining Judicial Behavior or What's 'Unconstitutional' About the Sentencing Commission," *Journal of Law, Economics, & Organization, 7,* 1991. 183–199. In *Mistretta v. U.S.* (682 F. Supp. 1033) the Supreme Court upheld (8–1; January 18, 1989) the constitutionality of the Sentencing Commission.

2. U.S. Sentencing Commission, "Sentencing Guidelines for Organizational Defendants," *Federal Register, 56,* 1991, 22786–22797.

3. L. Chambliss, "Hang 'em High." *Financial World,* July 9, 1991, 20–21.

4. T. Smart, "The Crackdown on Crime in the Suites," *Business Week,* April 23, 1991, 102–104.

5. There is virtually no evidence that managerial ethics/social responsibility is associated with improved financial performance of the firm. See: K.E. Aupperle, A.B. Carroll, and J.D. Hatfield, *Academy of Management Journal, 28,* 1985, 446–463; P.L. Cochran and R.A. Wood, "Corporate Social Responsibility and Financial Performance," *Academy of Management Journal, 27,* 1984, 42–56; J.B. McGuire, A. Sundren, and T. Schneeweis, "Corporate Social Responsibility and Firm Financial Performance," *Academy of Management Journal, 31,* 1988, 854–872.

6. See Paul T. Mentzler in *Medical Costs, Moral Choices* (New Haven, CT: Yale University Press, 1987), vi. We should note, however, that it is cited there as an "aphorism." Despite our efforts, we do not know the original source of this comment. No disrespect is meant to economists as a group; our point is that all things may not be subject to cost/benefit analysis.

7. J. O'Toole, "Doing Good by Doing Well: The Business Enterprise Trust Awards," *California Management Review, 33,* 1991, 21.

8. D. Vogel, "Ethics and Profits Don't Always Go Hand in Hand," *Ethics: Easier Said than Done, 2,* 1988, 63 (emphasis is ours).

9. See J.M. Kaplan, "Now is the Time to Review Corporate Compliance Programs," *Ethikos, 5,* 1991, 8–9; 11. The statement is by law professor John Coffee of Columbia University, p. 11.

10. Kaplan, *op. cit.*

11. For some discussion of this point, see G.J. Wallance, "Guidelines on Corporate Crime Emphasize Prevention Programs," *The National Law Journal,* July 1, 1991, 22–23.

12. See Wallance, *op. cit.*, and Kaplan, *op. cit.*, for more detail on the derivation of offense levels and multipliers on which we rely for the examples in the text.

13. A.W. Singer, "Ethics Programs Could Save Companies Millions under New Sentencing Guidelines," *Ethikos, 4,* 1991, 1.

14. A.S. Hayes, "Corporate Sentencing Guidelines Trigger Limited Initial Response," *Wall Street Journal,* Nov. 1, 1991, B1, col. 4–5.

15. See Sec. 8A1.2. Also, quoted text in this section is from the Sentencing Guidelines' commentary.

16. We derive these guidelines from Wallance, *op. cit.* and Kaplan, *op. cit.*

17. See, for example, A.J. Chaset, and B.B. Weintraub, "New Guidelines for Sentencing Corporations," *Trial, 28,* 4, 1992, 41–44.

18. See Chaset and Weintraub, *op. cit.* 42.

19. See B. Hager, "What's Behind Business' Sudden Fervor for Ethics?" *Business Week,* September 23, 1991, 65.

20. J. Moses and W. Lambert, "Companies Given Spur to Uncover Own Environmental Wrongdoing," *The Wall Street Journal,* Sept. 25, 1991, B2. Environmental violations are not included in the U.S. Sentencing Commission Guidelines. Therefore, this opinion of the Justice Department could be an important indicator of sentencing under the various environmental statutes. See Wallance, *op. cit.* for more detail on sentencing under environmental statutes.

21. Alexander Solzhenitsyn, "A World Split Apart," commencement address delivered at Harvard University, June 8, 1983, from G. Starling, *The Changing Environment of Business* (Boston, MA: Kent Publishing Company, 1984).

22. F.B. Bird and J.A. Waters, "The Moral Muteness of Managers," *California Management Review, 32,* 1989, 73. This point is also nicely made in R. Jackall, *Moral Mazes: The World of Corporate Managers* (New York, NY: Oxford University Press, 1988), see especially, Ch. 4. It is noted, for example, that managers who attend to ethical/moral considerations not associated with pragmatism in the workplace are at serious risk of breaking a "cardinal rule" of managerial circles: "you . . . don't play holier than thou," p. 97.

23. Alexis de Tocqueville, *Democracy in America,* Vol. 2, translated by Henry Reeve, revised by Francis Bowen (New York, NY: Mentor Books, 1945), 129–132. We acknowledge Bird and Waters, *op. cit.* for bringing this insight to our attention.

24. See Wallance, *op. cit.*, Kaplan, *op. cit.*, and Singer, *op. cit.*, for more detail on this point.

25. See Hager, *op. cit.*, p. 65 for these comments by Judge Wilkins.

The Parable of the Sadhu

BOWEN H. McCOY

It was early in the morning before the sun rose, which gave them time to climb the treacherous slope to the pass at 18,000 feet before the ice steps melted. They were also concerned about their stamina and altitude sickness, and felt the need to press on. Into the chance collection of climbers on that Himalayan slope an ethical dilemma arose in the guise of an unconscious, almost naked sadhu, an Indian holy man. Each climber gave the sadhu help but none made sure he would be safe. Should somebody have stopped to help the sadhu to safety? Would it have done any good? Was the group responsible? Since leaving the sadhu on the mountain slope, the author, who was one of the climbers, has pondered these issues. He sees many parallels for business people as they face ethical decisions at work.

Last year, as the first participant in the new six-month sabbatical program that Morgan Stanley has adopted, I enjoyed a rare opportunity to collect my thoughts as well as do some traveling. I spent the first three months in Nepal, walking 600 miles through 200 villages in the Himalayas and climbing some 120,000 vertical feet. On the trip my sole Western companion was an anthropologist who shed light on the cultural patterns of the villages we passed through.

During the Nepal hike, something occurred that has had a powerful impact on my thinking about corporate ethics. Although some might argue that the experience has no relevance to business, it was a situation in which a basic ethical dilemma suddenly intruded into the lives of a group of individuals. How the group responded I think holds a lesson for all organizations no matter how defined.

The Sadhu

The Nepal experience was more rugged and adventuresome than I had anticipated. Most commercial treks last two or three weeks and cover a quarter of the distance we traveled.

My friend Stephen, the anthropologist, and I were halfway through the 60-day Himalayan part of the trip when we reached the high point, an 18,000-foot pass over a crest that we'd have to traverse to reach the village of Muklinath, an ancient holy place for pilgrims.

Six years earlier I had suffered pulmonary edema, an acute form of altitude sickness, at 16,500 feet in the vicinity of Everest base camp, so we were understandably concerned about what would happen at 18,000 feet. Moreover, the Himalayas were having their wettest spring in 20 years; hip-deep powder and ice had already driven us off one ridge. If we failed to cross the pass, I feared that the last half of our "once in a lifetime" trip would be ruined.

The night before we would try the pass, we camped at a hut at 14,500 feet. In the photos taken at that camp, my face appears wan. The last village we'd passed through was a sturdy two-day walk below us, and I was tired.

During the late afternoon, four backpackers from New Zealand joined us, and we spent most of the night awake, anticipating the climb. Below we could see the fires of two other parties, which turned out to be two Swiss couples and a Japanese hiking club.

To get over the steep part of the climb before the sun melted the steps cut in the ice, we departed at 3:30 A.M. The New Zealanders left first, followed by Stephen and myself, our porters and Sherpas, and then the Swiss. The Japanese lingered in their camp. The sky was clear, and we were confident that no spring storm would erupt that day to close the pass.

At 15,500 feet, it looked to me as if Stephen were shuffling and staggering a bit, which are symptoms of altitude sickness. (The initial stage of altitude sickness brings a headache and nausea. As the condition worsens, a climber may encounter difficult breathing, disorientation, aphasia, and paralysis.) I felt strong, my adrenaline was flowing, but I was very concerned about my ultimate ability to get across. A couple of our porters were also suffering from the height, and Pasang, our Sherpa sirdar (leader), was worried.

Just after daybreak, while we rested at 15,500 feet, one of the New Zealanders, who had gone ahead, came staggering down toward us with a body slung across his shoulders. He dumped the almost naked, barefoot body of an Indian holy man—a sadhu—at my feet. He had found the pilgrim lying on the ice, shivering and suffering from hypothermia. I cradled the sadhu's head and laid him out on the rocks. The New Zealander was angry. He wanted to get across the pass before the bright sun melted the snow. He said, "Look, I've done what I can. You have porters and Sherpa guides. You care for him. We're going on!" He turned and went back up the mountain to join his friends.

I took a carotid pulse and found that the sadhu was still alive. We figured he had probably visited the holy shrines at Muklinath and was on his way home. It was fruitless to question why he had chosen this desperately high route instead of the safe, heavily traveled caravan route through the Kali Gandaki gorge. Or why he was almost naked and with no shoes, or how long he had been lying in the pass. The answers weren't going to solve our problem.

Stephen and the four Swiss began stripping off outer clothing and opening their packs. The sadhu was soon clothed from head to foot. He was not able to walk, but he was very much alive. I looked down the mountain and spotted below the Japanese climbers marching up with a horse.

Without a great deal of thought, I told Stephen and Pasang that I was concerned about withstanding the heights to come and wanted to get over the pass. I took off after several of our porters who had gone ahead.

On the steep part of the ascent where, if the ice steps had given way, I would have slid down about 3,000 feet, I felt vertigo. I stopped for a breather, allowing the Swiss to catch up with me. I inquired about the sadhu and Stephen. They said that the sadhu was fine and that Stephen was just behind. I set off again for the summit.

Stephen arrived at the summit an hour after I did. Still exhilarated by victory, I ran down the snow slope to congratulate him. He was suffering from altitude sickness, walking 15 steps, then stopping, walking 15 steps, then stopping, Pasang accompanied him all the way up. When I reached them, Stephen glared at me and said: "How do you feel about contributing to the death of a fellow man?"

I did not fully comprehend what he meant.

"Is the sadhu dead?" I inquired.

"No," replied Stephen, "but he surely will be!"

After I had gone, and the Swiss had departed not long after, Stephen had remained with the sadhu. When the Japanese had arrived, Stephen had asked to use their horse to transport the sadhu down to the hut. They had refused. He had then asked Pasang to have a group of our porters carry the sadhu. Pasang had resisted the idea, saying that the porters would have to exert all their energy to get themselves over the pass. He had thought they could not carry a man down 1,000 feet to the hut, reclimb the slope, and get across safely before the snow melted. Pasang had pressed Stephen not to delay any longer.

The Sherpas had carried the sadhu down to a rock in the sun at about 15,000 feet and had pointed out the hut another 500 feet below. The Japanese had given him food and drink. When they had last seen him he was listlessly throwing rocks at the Japanese party's dog, which had frightened him.

We do not know if the sadhu lived or died.

For many of the following days and evenings Stephen and I discussed and debated our behavior toward the sadhu. Stephen is a committed Quaker with deep moral vision. He said, "I feel that what happened with the sadhu is a good example of the breakdown between the individual ethic and the corporate ethic. No one person was willing to assume ultimate responsibility for the sadhu. Each was willing to do his bit just so long as it was not too inconvenient. When it got to be a bother, everyone just passed the buck to someone else and took off. Jesus was relevant to a more individualistic stage of society, but how do we interpret his teaching today in a world filled with large, impersonal organizations and groups?"

I defended the larger group, saying, "Look, we all cared. We all stopped and gave aid and comfort. Everyone did his bit. The New Zealander carried him down below the snow line. I took his pulse and suggested we treat him for hypothermia. You and the Swiss gave him clothing and got him warmed up. The Japanese gave him food and water. The Sherpas carried him down to the sun and pointed out the easy trail toward the hut. He was well enough to throw rocks at a dog. What more could we do?"

"You have just described the typical affluent Westerner's response to a problem. Throwing money—in this case food and sweaters—at it, but not solving the fundamentals!" Stephen retorted.

"What would satisfy you?" I said. "Here we are, a group of New Zealanders, Swiss, Americans, and Japanese who have never met before and who are at the apex of one of the most powerful experiences of our lives. Some years the pass is so bad no one gets over it. What right does an almost naked pilgrim who chooses the wrong trail have to disrupt our lives? Even the Sherpas had no interest in risking the trip to help him beyond a certain point."

Stephen calmly rebutted, "I wonder what the Sherpas would have done if the sadhu had been a well-dressed Nepali, or what the Japanese would have done if the sadhu had been a well-dressed Asian, or what you would have done, Buzz, if the sadhu had been a well-dressed Western woman?"

"Where, in your opinion," I asked instead, "is the limit of our responsibility in a situation like this? We had our own well-being to worry about. Our Sherpa guides were unwilling to jeopardize us or the porters for the sadhu. No one else on the mountain was willing to commit himself beyond certain self-imposed limits."

Stephen said, "As individual Christians or people with a Western ethical tradition, we can fulfill our obligations in such a situation only if (1) the sadhu dies in our care, (2) the sadhu demonstrates to us that he could undertake the two-day walk down to the village, or (3) we carry the sadhu for two days down to the village and convince someone there to care for him."

"Leaving the sadhu in the sun with food and clothing, while he demonstrated hand-eye coordination by throwing a rock at a dog, comes close to fulfilling items one and two," I answered. "And it wouldn't have made sense to take him to the village where the people appeared to be far less caring than the Sherpas, so the third condition is impractical. Are you really saying that, no matter what the implications, we should, at the drop of a hat, have changed our entire plan?"

The Individual vs. the Group Ethic

Despite my arguments, I felt and continue to feel guilt about the sadhu. I had literally walked through a classic moral dilemma without fully thinking through the consequences. My excuses for my actions include a high adrenaline flow, a superordinate goal, and a once-in-a-lifetime opportunity—factors in the usual corporate situation, especially when one is under stress.

Real moral dilemmas are ambiguous, and many of us hike right through them, unaware that they exist. When, usually after the fact, someone makes an issue of them, we tend to resent his or her bringing it up. Often, when the full import of what we have done (or not done) falls on us, we dig into a defensive position from which it is very difficult to emerge. In rare circumstances we may contemplate what we have done from inside a prison.

Had we mountaineers been free of physical and mental stress caused by the effort and the high altitude, we might have treated the sadhu differently. Yet isn't stress the real test of personal and corporate values? The instant decisions executives make under pressure reveal the most about personal and corporate character.

Among the many questions that occur to me when pondering my experience are: What are the practical limits of moral imagination and vision? Is there a collective or institutional ethic beyond the ethics of the individual? At what level of effort or commitment can one discharge one's ethical responsibilities?

Not every ethical dilemma has a right solution. Reasonable people often disagree; otherwise there would be no dilemma. In a business context, however, it is essential that managers agree on a process for dealing with dilemmas.

The sadhu experience offers an interesting parallel to business situations. An immediate response was mandatory. Failure to act was a decision in itself. Up on the mountain we could not resign and submit our résumés to a headhunter. In contrast to philosophy, business involves action and implementation—getting things done. Managers must come up with answers to problems based on what they see and what they allow to influence their decision-making processes. On the mountain, none of us but Stephen realized the true dimensions of the situation we were facing.

One of our problems was that as a group we had no process for developing a consensus. We had no sense of purpose or plan. The difficulties of dealing with the sadhu were so complex that no one person could handle it. Because it did not have a set of preconditions that could guide its action to an acceptable resolution, the group reacted instinctively as individuals. The cross-cultural nature of the group added a further layer of complexity. We had no leader with whom we could all identify and in whose purpose we believed. Only Stephen was willing to take charge, but he could not gain adequate support to care for the sadhu.

Some organizations do have a value system that transcends the personal values of the managers. Such values, which go beyond profitability, are usually revealed when the organization is under stress. People throughout the organization generally accept its values, which, because they are not presented as a rigid list of commandments, may be somewhat ambiguous. The stories people tell, rather than printed materials, transmit these conceptions of what is proper behavior.

For 20 years I have been exposed at senior levels to a variety of corporations and organizations. It is amazing how quickly an outsider can sense the tone and style of an organization and the degree of tolerated openness and freedom to challenge management.

Organizations that do not have a heritage of mutually accepted, shared values tend to become unhinged during stress, with each individual bailing out for himself. In the great takeover battles we have witnessed during past years, companies that had strong cultures drew the wagons around them and fought it out, while other companies saw executives, supported by their golden parachutes, bail out of the struggles.

Because corporations and their members are interdependent, for the corporation to be strong the members need to share a preconceived notion of what is correct behavior, a "business ethic," and think of it as a positive force, not a constraint.

As an investment banker I am continually warned by well-meaning lawyers, clients, and associates to be wary of conflicts of interest. Yet if I were to run away from every difficult situation, I wouldn't be an effective investment banker. I have to feel my way through conflicts. An effective manager can't run from risk either; he or she has to confront and deal with risk. To feel "safe" in doing this, managers need the guidelines of an agreed-on process and set of values within the organization.

After my three months in Nepal, I spent three months as an executive-in-residence at both Stanford Business School and the Center for Ethics and Social Policy at the Graduate Theological Union at Berkeley. These six months away from my job gave me time to assimilate 20 years of business experience. My thoughts turned often to the meaning of the leadership role in any large organization. Students at the seminary thought of themselves as antibusiness. But when I questioned them they agreed that they distrusted all large organizations, including the church. They perceived all large organizations as impersonal and opposed to individual values and needs. Yet we all know of organizations where peoples' values and beliefs are respected and their expressions encouraged. What makes the difference? Can we identify the difference and, as a result, manage more effectively?

The word "ethics" turns off many and confuses more. Yet the notions of shared values and an agreed-on process for dealing with adversity and change—what many people mean when they talk about corporate culture—seem to be at the heart of the ethical issue. People who are in touch with their own core beliefs and the beliefs of others and are sustained by them can be more comfortable living on the cutting edge. At times, taking a tough line or a decisive stand in a muddle of ambiguity is the only ethical thing to do. If a manager is indecisive and spends time trying to figure out the "good" thing to do, the enterprise may be lost.

Business ethics, then, has to do with the authenticity and integrity of the enterprise. To be ethical is to follow the business as well as the cultural goals of the corporation, its owners, its employees, and its customers. Those who cannot serve the corporate vision are not authentic business people and, therefore, are not ethical in the business sense.

At this stage of my own business experience I have a strong interest in organizational behavior. Sociologists are keenly studying what they call corporate stories, legends, and heroes as a way organizations have of transmitting the value system. Corporations such as Arco have even hired consultants to perform an audit of their corporate culture. In a company, the leader is the person who understands, interprets, and manages the corporate value system. Effective managers are then action-oriented people who resolve conflict, are tolerant of ambiguity, stress, and change, and have a strong sense of purpose for themselves and their organizations.

If all this is true, I wonder about the role of the professional manager who moves from company to company. How can he or she quickly absorb the values and culture of different organizations? Or is there, indeed, an art of management that is totally transportable? Assuming such fungible managers do exist, is it proper for them to manipulate the values of others?

What would have happened had Stephen and I carried the sadhu for two days back to the village and become involved with the villagers in his care? In four trips to Nepal my most interesting experiences occurred in 1975 when I lived in a Sherpa home in the Khumbu for five days recovering from altitude sickness. The high point of Stephen's trip was an invitation to participate in a family funeral ceremony in Manang. Neither experience had to do with climbing the high passes of the Himalayas. Why were we so reluctant to try the lower path, the ambiguous trail? Perhaps because we did not have a leader who could reveal the greater purpose of the trip to us.

Why didn't Stephen with his moral vision opt to take the sadhu under his personal care? The answer is because, in part, Stephen was hard-stressed physically himself, and because, in part, without some support system that involved our involuntary and episodic community on the mountain, it was beyond his individual capacity to do so.

I see the current interest in corporate culture and corporate value systems as a positive response to Stephen's pessimism about the decline of the role of the individual in large organizations. Individuals who operate from a thoughtful set of personal values provide the foundation for a corporate culture. A corporate tradition that encourages freedom of inquiry, supports personal values, and reinforces a focused sense of direction can fulfill the need for individuality along with the prosperity and success of the group. Without such corporate support, the individual is lost.

That is the lesson of the sadhu. In a complex corporate situation, the individual requires and deserves the support of the group. If people cannot find such support from their organization, they don't know how to act. If such support is forthcoming, a person has a stake in the success of the group, and can add much to the process of establishing and maintaining a corporate culture. It is management's challenge to be sensitive to individual needs, to shape them, and to direct and focus them for the benefit of the group as a whole.

For each of us the sadhu lives. Should we stop what we are doing and comfort him; or should we keep trudging up toward the high pass? Should I pause to help the derelict I pass on the street each night as I walk by the Yale Club en route to Grand Central Station? Am I his brother? What is the nature of our responsibility if we consider ourselves to be ethical persons? Perhaps it is to change the values of the group so that it can, with all its resources, take the other road.

Employee Rights
and
Responsibilities

• *Case Study* •

The Aircraft Brake Scandal

KERMIT VANDIVIER

The B. F. Goodrich Company is what business magazines like to refer to as "a major American corporation." It has operations in a dozen states and as many foreign countries; and of these far-flung facilities, the Goodrich plant at Troy, Ohio, is not the most imposing. It is a small, one-story building, once used to manufacture airplanes. Set in the grassy flatlands of west-central Ohio, it employs only about six hundred people. Nevertheless, it is one of the three largest manufacturers of aircraft wheels and brakes, a leader in a most profitable industry. Goodrich wheels and brakes support such well-known planes as the F111, the C5A, the Boeing 727, the XB70, and many others.

Contracts for aircraft wheels and brakes often run into millions of dollars, and ordinarily a contract with a total value of less than $70,000, though welcome, would not create any special stir of joy in the hearts of Goodrich sales personnel. But purchase order P-237138—issued on June 18, 1967, by the LTV Aerospace Corporation, ordering 202 brake assemblies for a new Air Force plane at a total price of $69,417—was received by Goodrich with considerable glee. And there was good reason. Some ten years previously, Goodrich had built a brake for LTV that was, to say the least, considerably less than a rousing success. The brake had not lived up to Goodrich's promises, and after experiencing considerable difficulty, LTV had written off Goodrich as a source of brakes. Since that time, Goodrich salesmen had been unable to sell so much as a shot of brake fluid to LTV. So in 1967, when LTV requested bids on wheels and brakes for the new A7D light attack aircraft it proposed to build for the Air Force, Goodrich submitted a bid that was absurdly low, so low that LTV could not, in all prudence, turn it down.

Goodrich had, in industry parlance, "bought into the business." The company did not expect to make a profit on the initial deal; it was prepared, if necessary, to lose money. But aircraft brakes are not something that can be ordered off the shelf. They are designed for a particular aircraft, and once an aircraft manufacturer buys a brake, he is forced to purchase all replacement parts from the brake manufacturer. The $70,000 that Goodrich would get for making the brake would be a drop in the bucket when compared with the cost of the linings and other parts the Air Force would have to buy from Goodrich during the lifetime of the aircraft.

There was another factor, besides the low bid, that had undoubtedly influenced LTV. All aircraft brakes made today are of the disk type, and the bid submitted by Goodrich called for a relatively small brake, one containing four disks and weighing only 106 pounds. The weight of any aircraft is extremely important: the lighter a part is, the heavier the plane's payload can be.

The brake was designed by one of Goodrich's most capable engineers, John Warren. A tall, lanky, blond graduate of Purdue, Warren had come from the Chrysler Corporation seven years before and had become adept at aircraft brake design. The happy-go-lucky manner he usually maintained belied a temper that exploded whenever anyone ventured to offer criticism of his work, no matter how small. On these occasions, Warren would turn red in the face, often throwing or slamming something and then stalking from the scene. As his coworkers learned the consequences of criticizing him, they did so less and less readily, and when he submitted his preliminary design for the A7D brake, it was accepted without question.

Warren was named project engineer for the A7D, and he, in turn, assigned the task of producing the final production design to a newcomer to the Goodrich engineering stable, Searle Lawson. Just turned twenty-six, Lawson had been out of the Northrop Institute of Technology only one year when he came to Goodrich in January, 1967. He had been assigned to various "paper projects" to break him in, and after several months spent reviewing statistics and old brake designs, he was beginning to fret at the lack of challenge. When told he was being assigned to his first "real" project, he was elated and immediately plunged into his work.

The major portion of the design had already been completed by Warren, and major subassemblies for the brake had already been ordered from Goodrich suppliers. Naturally, however, before Goodrich could start making the brakes on a production basis, much testing would have to be done. Lawson would have to determine the best materials to use for the linings and discover what minor adjustments in the design would have to be made.

Then, after the preliminary testing and after the brake was judged ready for production, one whole brake assembly would undergo a series of grueling, simulated braking stops and other severe trials called qualification tests. These tests are required by the military, which gives very detailed specifications on how they are to be conducted, the criteria for failure, and so on. They are performed in the Goodrich plant's test laboratory, where huge machines called dynamometers can simulate the weight and speed of almost any aircraft.

Searle Lawson was well aware that much work had to be done before the A7D brake could go into production, and he knew that LTV had set the last two weeks of June 1968 as the starting dates for flight tests. So he decided to begin testing immediately. Goodrich's suppliers had not yet delivered the brake housing and other parts, but the brake disks had arrived, and using the housing from a brake similar in size and weight to the A7D brake, Lawson built a prototype. The prototype was installed in a test wheel and placed on one of the big dynamometers in the plant's test laboratory. Lawson began a series of tests, "landing" the wheel and brake at the A7D's landing speed and braking it to a stop. The main purpose of these preliminary tests was to learn what temperatures would develop within the brake during the simulated stops and to evaluate lining materials tentatively selected for use.

During a normal aircraft landing the temperatures inside the brake may reach 1,000 degrees, and occasionally a bit higher. During Lawson's first simulated landings, the temperature of his prototype brake reached 1,500 degrees. The brake glowed a bright cherry-red and threw off incandescent particles of metal and lining material as the temperature reached its peak. After a few such stops, the brake was dismantled and the linings were found to be almost completely disintegrated. Lawson chalked this first failure up to chance, and ordering new lining materials, tried again.

The second attempt was a repeat of the first. The brake became extremely hot, causing the lining materials to crumble into dust.

After the third such failure, Lawson, inexperienced though he was, knew that the <u>fault</u> lay not in defective parts or unsuitable lining material but in the <u>basic design of the brake itself</u>. Ignoring Warren's original computations, Lawson made his own, and it didn't take him long to discover where the trouble lay—<u>the brake was too small</u>. There simply was not enough surface area on the disks to stop the aircraft without generating the excessive heat that caused the linings to fail.

The answer to the problem was obvious, but far from simple—the four-disk brake would have to be scrapped, and a new design, using five disks, would have to be developed. The implications were not lost on Lawson. Such a step would require junking the four-disk-brake subassemblies, many of which had now begun to arrive from the various suppliers. It would also mean several weeks of preliminary design and testing and many more weeks of waiting while the suppliers made and delivered the new subassemblies.

Yet, several weeks had already gone by since LTV's order had arrived, and the date for delivery of the first production brakes for flight testing was only a few months away.

Although John Warren had more or less turned the A7D over to Lawson, he knew of the difficulties Lawson had been experiencing. He had assured the younger engineer that the problem revolved around getting the right kind of <u>lining material</u>. Once that was found, he said, the difficulties would end.

Despite the evidence of the abortive tests and Lawson's careful computations, Warren rejected the suggestion that the four-disk brake was too light for the job. He knew that his superior had already told LTV, in rather glowing terms, that the preliminary tests on the A7D brake were very successful. Indeed, Warren's superiors weren't aware at this time of the troubles on the brake. It would have been difficult for Warren to admit not only that he had made a serious error in his calculations and original design but that his mistakes had been caught by a green kid, barely out of college.

Warren's reaction to a five-disk brake was not unexpected by Lawson, and, seeing that the four-disk brake was not to be abandoned so easily, he took his calculations and dismal test results one step up the <u>corporate ladder</u>.

At Goodrich, the man who supervises the engineers working on projects slated for production is called, predictably, the projects manager. The job was held by a short, chubby, bald man named Robert Sink. Some fifteen years before, Sink had begun working at Goodrich as a lowly draftsman. Slowly, he worked his way up. Despite his geniality, Sink was neither respected nor liked by the majority of the engineers, and his appointment as their supervisor did not improve their feelings toward him. He possessed only a high-school diploma, and it quite naturally rankled those who had gone through years of college to be commanded by a man whom they considered their intellectual inferior. But, though Sink had no college training, he had something even more useful: a fine working knowledge of company politics.

Puffing on a Meerschaum pipe, Sink listened gravely as young Lawson confided his fears about the four-disk brake. Then he examined Lawson's calculations and the results of the abortive tests. Despite the fact that he was not a qualified engineer, in the strictest sense of the word, it must certainly have been obvious to Sink that Lawson's calculations were correct and that a four-disk brake would never work on the A7D.

But other things of equal importance were also obvious. First, to concede that Lawson's calculations were correct would also mean conceding that Warren's calculations were incorrect. As projects manager, not only was he responsible for Warren's activities, but in admitting that Warren had erred he would also have to admit that he had erred in trusting Warren's judgment. It also meant that, as projects manager, it would be he who would have to explain the whole messy situation to the Goodrich hierarchy, not only at Troy but possibly on the corporate level at Goodrich's Akron offices. And having taken Warren's judgment of the four-disk brake at face value, he had assured LTV, not once but several times, that about all there was left to do on the brake was pack it in a crate and ship it out the door.

There's really no problem at all, he told Lawson. After all, Warren was an experienced engineer, and if he said the brake would work, it would work. Just keep on testing and probably, maybe even on the very next try, it'll work out just fine.

Lawson was far from convinced, but without the support of his superiors there was little he could do except keep on testing. By now, housings for the four-disk brake had begun to arrive at the plant, and Lawson was able to build a production model of the brake and begin the formal qualification tests demanded by the military.

The first qualification attempts went exactly as the tests on the prototype had. Terrific heat developed within the brakes, and after a few short, simulated stops the linings crumbled. A new type of lining material was ordered and once again an attempt to qualify the brake was made. Again, failure.

Experts were called in from lining manufacturers, and new lining "mixes" were tried, always with the same result. Failure.

It was now the last week of March 1968, and flight tests were scheduled to begin in seventy days. Twelve separate attempts had been made to qualify the brake, and all had failed. It was no longer possible for anyone to ignore the glaring truth that the brake was a dismal failure and that nothing short of a major design change could ever make it work.

On April 4, the thirteenth attempt at qualification was begun. This time no attempt was made to conduct the tests by the methods and techniques spelled out in the military specifications. Regardless of how it had to be done, the brake was to be "nursed" through the required fifty simulated stops.

Fans were set up to provide special cooling. Instead of maintaining pressure on the brake until the test wheel had come to a complete stop, the pressure was reduced when the wheel had decelerated to around 15 mph, allowing it to "coast" to a stop. After each stop, the brake was disassembled and carefully cleaned, and after some of the stops, internal brake parts were machined in order to remove warp and other disfigurations caused by the high heat.

By these and other methods, all clearly contrary to the techniques established by the military specifications, the brake was coaxed through the fifty stops. But even using these methods, the brake could not meet all the requirements. On one stop the wheel rolled for a distance of 16,000 feet, or over three miles, before the brake could bring it to a stop. The normal distance required for such a stop was around 3,500 feet.

On April 11, the day the thirteenth test was completed, I became personally involved in the A7D situation.

I had worked in the Goodrich test laboratory for five years, starting first as an instrumentation engineer, then later becoming a data analyst and technical writer. As part of my duties, I analyzed the reams and reams of instrumentation data that came from the many testing machines in the lab, then transcribed all of it to a more usable form for the engineering department. When a new-type brake had successfully completed the required qualification tests, I would issue a formal qualification report.

Qualification reports are an accumulation of all the data and test logs compiled during the qualification tests and are documentary proof that a brake has met all the requirements established by the military specifications and is therefore presumed safe for flight testing. Before actual flight tests are conducted on a brake, qualification reports have to be delivered to the customer and to various government officials.

On April 11, I was looking over the data from the latest A7D test, and I noticed that many irregularities in testing had been noted on the test logs.

Technically, of course, there was nothing wrong with conducting tests in any manner desired, so long as the test was for research purposes only. But qualification test methods are clearly delineated by the military, and I knew that this test had been a formal qualification attempt. One particular notation on the test logs caught my eye. For some of the stops, the instrument that recorded the brake pressure had been deliberately miscalibrated so that, while the brake pressure used during the stops was recorded as 1,000 psi (pounds per square inch)—the maximum pressure that would be available on the A7D aircraft—the pressure had actually been 1,100 psi.

I showed the test logs to the test lab supervisor, Ralph Gretzinger, who said he had learned from the technician who had miscalibrated the instrument that he had been asked to do so by Lawson. Lawson, said Gretzinger, readily admitted asking for the miscalibration, saying he had been told to do so by Sink.

I asked Gretzinger why anyone would want to miscalibrate the data-recording instrument.

"Why? I'll tell you why," he snorted. "That brake is a failure. It's way too small for the job, and they're not ever going to get it to work. They're getting desperate, and instead of scrapping the damned thing and starting over, they figure they can horse around down here in the lab and qualify it that way."

An expert engineer, Gretzinger had been responsible for several innovations in brake design. It was he who had invented the unique brake system used on the famous XB70. "If you want to find out what's going on," said Gretzinger, "ask Lawson; he'll tell you."

Curious, I did ask Lawson the next time he came into the lab. He seemed eager to discuss the A7D and gave me the history of his months of frustrating efforts to get Warren and Sink to change the brake design. "I just can't believe this is really happening," said Lawson, shaking his head slowly. "This isn't engineering, at least not what I thought it would be. Back in school, I thought that when you were an engineer you tried to do your best, no matter what it cost. But this is something else."

He sat across the desk from me, his chin propped in his hand. "Just wait," he warned. "You'll get a chance to see what I'm talking about. You're going to get in the act too, because I've already had the word that we're going to make one more attempt to qualify the brake, and that's it. Win or lose, we're going to issue a qualification report!"

I reminded him that a qualification report could be issued only after a brake had successfully met all military requirements, and therefore, unless the next qualification attempt was a success, no report would be issued.

"You'll find out," retorted Lawson. "I was already told that regardless of what the brake does on test, it's going to be qualified." He said he had been told in those exact words at a conference with Sink and Russell Van Horn.

This was the first indication that Sink had brought his boss, Van Horn, into the mess. Although Van Horn, as manager of the design engineering section, was responsible for the entire department, he was not necessarily familiar with all phases of every project, and it was not uncommon for those under him to exercise the what-he-doesn't-know-won't-hurt-him philosophy. If he was aware of the full extent of the A7D situation, it meant that Sink had decided not only to call for help but to look toward that moment when blame must be borne and, if possible, shared.

Also, if Van Horn had said, "regardless of what the brake does on test, it's going to be qualified," then it could only mean that, if necessary, a false qualification report would be issued. I discussed this possibility with Gretzinger, and he assured me that under no circumstances would such a report ever be issued.

"If they want a qualification report, we'll write them one, but we'll tell it just like it is," he declared emphatically. "No false data or false reports are going to come out of this lab."

On May 2, 1968, the fourteenth and final attempt to qualify the brake was begun. Although the same improper methods used to nurse the brake through the previous tests were employed, it soon became obvious that this too would end in failure.

When the tests were about half completed, Lawson asked if I would start preparing the various engineering curves and graphic displays that were normally incorporated in a qualification report. I flatly refused to have anything to do with the matter and immediately told Gretzinger what I had been asked to do. He was furious and repeated his previous declaration that under no circumstances would any false data or other matter be issued from the lab.

"I'm going to get this settled right now, once and for all," he declared.

"I'm going to see Line [Russell Line, manager of the Goodrich Technical Services Section, of which the test lab was a part] and find out just how far this thing is going to go!" He stormed out of the room.

In about an hour, he returned and called me to his desk. He sat silently for a few moments, then muttered, half to himself, "I wonder what the hell they'd do if I just quit?" I didn't answer and I didn't ask him what he meant. I knew. He had been beaten down. He had reached the point when the decision had to be made. Defy them now while there was still time—or knuckle under, sell out.

"You know," he went on uncertainly, looking down at his desk, "I've been an engineer for a long time, and I've always believed that ethics and integrity were every bit as important as theorems and formulas, and never once has anything happened to change my beliefs. Now this . . . Hell I've got two sons I've got to put through school and I just . . ." His voice trailed off.

He sat for a few more minutes, then, looking over the top of his glasses, said hoarsely, "Well, it looks like we're licked. The way it stands now, we're to go ahead and prepare the data and other things for the graphic presentation in the report, and when we're finished, someone upstairs will actually write the report.

"After all," he continued, "we're just drawing some curves, and what happens to them after they leave here—well, we're not responsible for that."

I wasn't at all satisfied with the situation and decided that I too would discuss the matter with Russell Line, the senior executive in our section.

Tall, powerfully built, his teeth flashing white, his face tanned to a coffee-brown by a daily stint with a sunlamp, Line looked and acted every inch the executive. He had been transferred from the Akron offices some two years previously, and he commanded great respect and had come to be well liked by those of us who worked under him.

He listened sympathetically while I explained how I felt about the A7D situation, and when I had finished, he asked me what I wanted him to do about it. I said that as employees of the Goodrich Company we had a responsibility to protect the company and its reputation if at all possible. I said I was certain that officers on the corporate level would never knowingly allow such tactics as had been employed on the A7D.

"I agree with you," he remarked, "but I still want to know what you want me to do about it."

I suggested that in all probability the chief engineer at the Troy plant, H. C. "Bud" Sunderman, was unaware of the A7D problem and that he, Line, could tell him what was going on.

Line laughed, good-humoredly. "Sure, I could, but I'm not going to. Bud probably already knows about this thing anyway, and if he doesn't, I'm sure not going to be the one to tell him."

"But why?"

"Because it's none of my business, and it's none of yours. I learned a long time ago not to worry about things over which I had no control. I have no control over this."

I wasn't satisfied with this answer, and I asked him if his conscience wouldn't bother him if, say, during flight tests on the brake, something should happen resulting in death or injury to the test pilot.

"Look," he said, becoming somewhat exasperated. "I just told you I have no control over this. Why should my conscience bother me?"

His voice took on a quiet, soothing tone as he continued. "You're just getting all upset over this thing for nothing. I just do as I'm told, and I'd advise you to do the same."

I made no attempt to rationalize what I had been asked to do. It made no difference who would falsify which part of the report or whether the actual falsification would be by misleading numbers or misleading words. Whether by acts of commission or omission, all of us who contributed to the fraud would be guilty. The only question left for me to decide was whether or not I would become a party to the fraud.

Before coming to Goodrich in 1963, I had held a variety of jobs, each a little more pleasant, a little more rewarding than the last. At forty-two, with seven children, I had decided that the Goodrich Company would probably be my "home" for the rest of my working life. The job paid well, it was pleasant and challenging, and the future looked reasonably bright. My wife and I had bought a home and we were ready to settle down into a comfortable, middle-age, middle-class rut. If I refused to take part in the A7D fraud, I would have either to resign or be fired. The report would be written by someone anyway, but I would have the satisfaction of knowing I had had no part in the matter. But bills aren't paid with personal satisfaction, nor house payments with ethical principles. I made my decision. The next morning, I telephoned Lawson and told him I was ready to begin on the qualification report.

I had written dozens of qualification reports, and I knew what a "good" one looked like. Resorting to the actual test data only on occasion, Lawson and I proceeded to prepare page after page of elaborate, detailed engineering curves, charts, and test logs, which purported to show what had happened during the formal qualification tests. Where temperatures were too high, we deliberately chopped them down a few hundred degrees, and where they were too low, we raised them to a value that would appear reasonable to the LTV and military engineers. Brake pressure, torque values, distances, times—everything of consequence was tailored to fit.

Occasionally, we would find that some test either hadn't been performed at all or had been conducted improperly. On those occasions, we "conducted" the test—successfully, of course—on paper.

For nearly a month we worked on the graphic presentation that would be a part of the report. Meanwhile, the final qualification attempt had been completed, and the brake, not unexpectedly, had failed again.

We finished our work on the graphic portion of the report around the first of June. Altogether, we had prepared nearly two hundred pages of data, containing dozens of deliberate falsifications and misrepresentations. I delivered the data to Gretzinger, who said he had been instructed to deliver it personally to the chief engineer, Bud Sunderman, who in turn would assign someone in the engineering department to complete the written portion of the report. He gathered the bundle of data and left the office. Within minutes, he was back with the data, his face white with anger.

"That damned Sink's beat me to it," he said furiously. "He's already talked to Bud about this, and now Sunderman says no one in the engineering department has time to write the report. He wants us to do it, and I told him we couldn't."

The words had barely left his mouth when Russell Line burst in the door. "What the hell's all the fuss about this damned report?" he demanded.

Patiently, Gretzinger explained. "There's no fuss. Sunderman just told me that we'd have to write the report down here, and I said we couldn't. Russ," he went on, "I've told you before that we weren't going to write the report. I made my position clear on that a long time ago."

Line shut him up with a wave of his hand and, turning to me, bellowed "I'm getting sick and tired of hearing about this damned report. Now, write the goddamn thing and shut up about it!" He slammed out of the office.

Gretzinger and I just sat for a few seconds looking at each other. Then he spoke.

"Well, I guess he's made it pretty clear, hasn't he? We can either write the thing or quit. You know, what we should have done was quit a long time ago. Now, it's too late."

Somehow I wasn't at all surprised at this turn of events, and it didn't really make that much difference. As far as I was concerned, we were all up to our necks in the thing anyway, and writing the narrative portion of the report couldn't make me more guilty than I already felt myself to be.

Within two days, I had completed the narrative, or written portion, of the report. As a final sop to my own self-respect, in the conclusion of the report I wrote, "The B. F. Goodrich P/N 2–1162–3 brake assembly does not meet the intent or the requirements of the applicable specification documents and therefore is not qualified."

This was a meaningless gesture, since I knew that this would certainly be changed when the report went through the final typing process. Sure enough, when the report was published, the negative conclusion had been made positive.

One final and significant incident occurred just before publication.

Qualification reports always bear the signature of the person who has prepared them. I refused to sign the report, as did Lawson. Warren was later asked to sign the report. He replied that he would "when I receive a signed statement from Bob Sink ordering me to sign it."

The engineering secretary who was delegated the responsibility of "dogging" the report through publication told me later that after I, Lawson, and Warren had all refused to sign the report, she had asked Sink if he would sign. He replied, "On something of this nature, I don't think a signature is really needed."

On June 5, 1968, the report was officially published and copies were delivered by hand to the Air Force and LTV. Within a week flight tests were begun at Edwards Air Force Base in California. Searle Lawson was sent to California as Goodrich's representative. Within approximately two weeks, he returned because some rather unusual incidents during the tests had caused them to be canceled.

His face was grim as he related stories of several near crashes during landings—caused by brake troubles. He told me about one incident in which, upon landing, one brake was literally welded together by the intense heat developed during the test stop. The wheel locked, and the plane skidded for nearly 1,500 feet before coming to a halt. The plane was jacked up and the wheel removed. The fused parts within the brake had to be pried apart.

That evening I left work early and went to see my attorney. After I told him the story, he advised that, while I was probably not actually guilty of fraud, I was certainly part of a conspiracy to defraud. He advised me to go to the Federal Bureau of Investigation and offered to arrange an appointment. The following week he took me to the Dayton office of the FBI and after I had been warned that I would not be immune from prosecution, I disclosed the A7D matter to one of the agents. The agent told me to say nothing about the episode to anyone and to report any further incidents to him. He said he would forward the story to his superiors in Washington.

A few days later, Lawson returned from a conference with LTV in Dallas and said that the Air Force, which had previously approved the qualification report, had suddenly rescinded that approval and was demanding to see some of the raw test data. I gathered that the FBI had passed the word.

Omitting any reference to the FBI, I told Lawson I had been to an attorney and that we were probably guilty of conspiracy.

"Can you get me an appointment with your attorney?" he asked. Within a week, he had been to the FBI and told them of his part in the mess. He too was advised to say nothing but to keep on the job reporting any new development.

Naturally, with the rescinding of Air Force approval and the demand to see raw test data, Goodrich officials were in a panic. A conference was called for July 27, a Saturday morning affair at which Lawson, Sink, Warren, and I were present. We met in a tiny conference room in the deserted engineering department. Lawson and I, by now openly hostile to Warren and Sink, ranged ourselves on one side of the conference table while Warren sat on the other side. Sink, chairing the meeting, paced slowly in front of a blackboard, puffing furiously on a pipe.

The meeting was called, Sink began, "to see where we stand on the A7D." What we were going to do, he said, was to "level" with LTV and tell them the "whole truth" about the A7D. "After all," he said, "they're in this thing with us, and they have the right to know how matters stand."

"In other words," I asked, "we're going to tell them the truth?"

"That's right," he replied. "We're going to level with them and let them handle the ball from there."

"There's one thing I don't quite understand," I interjected. "Isn't it going to be pretty hard for us to admit to them that we've lied?"

"Now, wait a minute," he said angrily. "Let's don't go off half-cocked on this thing. It's not a matter of lying. We've just interpreted the information the way we felt it should be."

"I don't know what you call it," I replied, "but to me it's lying, and it's going to be damned hard to confess to them that we've been lying all along."

He became very agitated at this and repeated, "We're not lying," adding, "I don't like this sort of talk."

I dropped the matter at this point, and he began discussing the various discrepancies in the report.

We broke for lunch, and afterward, I came back to the plant to find Sink sitting alone at his desk, waiting to resume the meeting. He called me over and said he wanted to apologize for his outburst that morning. "This thing has kind of gotten me down," he confessed, "and I think you've got the wrong picture. I don't think you really understand everything about this."

Perhaps so, I conceded, but it seemed to me that if we had already told LTV one thing and then had to tell them another, changing our story completely, we would have to admit we were lying.

"No," he explained patiently, "we're not really lying. All we were doing was interpreting the figures the way we knew they should be. We were just exercising engineering license."

During the afternoon session, we marked some forty-three discrepant points in the report; forty-three points that LTV would surely spot as occasions where we had exercised "engineering license."

After Sink listed those points on the blackboard, we discussed each one individually. As each point came up, Sink would explain that it was probably "too minor to bother about," or that perhaps it "wouldn't be wise to open that can of worms," or that maybe this was a point that "LTV just wouldn't understand." When the meeting was over, it had been decided that only three points were "worth mentioning."

Similar conferences were held during August and September, and the summer was punctuated with frequent treks between Dallas and Troy and demands by the Air Force to see the raw test data. Tempers were short, and matters seemed to grow worse.

Finally, early in October 1968, Lawson submitted his resignation, to take effect on October 25. On October 18, I submitted my own resignation, to take effect on November 1. In my resignation, addressed to Russell Line, I cited the A7D report and stated: "As you are aware, this report contains numerous deliberate and willful misrepresentations which, according to legal counsel, constitute fraud and expose both myself and others to criminal charges of conspiracy to defraud . . . The events of the past seven months have created an atmosphere of deceit and distrust in which it is impossible to work . . ."

On October 25, I received a sharp summons to the office of Bud Sunderman. Tall and graying, impeccably dressed at all times, he was capable of producing a dazzling smile or a hearty chuckle or immobilizing his face into marble hardness, as the occasion required.

I faced the marble hardness when I reached his office. He motioned me to a chair. "I have your resignation here," he snapped, "and I must say you have made some rather shocking, I might even say irresponsible, charges. This is very serious."

Before I could reply, he was demanding an explanation. "I want to know exactly what the fraud is in connection with the A7D and how you can dare accuse this company of such a thing!"

I started to tell some of the things that had happened during the testing, but he shut me off saying, "There's nothing wrong with anything we've done here. You aren't aware of all the things that have been going on behind the scenes. If you had known the true situation, you would never have made these charges." He said that in view of my apparent "disloyalty" he had decided to accept my resignation "right now," and said it would be better for all concerned if I left the plant immediately. As I got up to leave he asked me if I intended to "carry this thing further."

I answered simply, "Yes," to which he replied, "Suit yourself." Within twenty minutes, I had cleaned out my desk and left. Forty-eight hours later, the B. F. Goodrich Company recalled the qualification report and the four-disk brake, announcing that it would replace the brake with a new, improved, five-disk brake at no cost to LTV.

Ten months later, on August 13, 1969, I was the chief government witness at a hearing conducted before Senator William Proxmire's Economy in Government Subcommittee. I related the A7D story to the committee, and my testimony was supported by Searle Lawson, who followed me to the witness stand. Air Force officers also testified, as well as a four-man team from the General Accounting Office, which had conducted an investigation of the A7D brake at the request of Senator Proxmire. Both Air Force and GAO investigators declared that the brake was dangerous and had not been tested properly.

Testifying for Goodrich was R. G. Jeter, vice-president and general counsel of the company, from the Akron headquarters. Representing the Troy plant was Robert Sink. These two denied any wrongdoing on the part of the Goodrich Company, despite expert testimony to the contrary by Air Force and GAO officials. Sink was quick to deny any connection with the writing of the report or directing of any falsifications, claiming to have been on the West Coast at the time. John Warren was the man who had supervised its writing, said Sink.

As for me, I was dismissed as a high-school graduate with no technical training, while Sink testified that Lawson was a young, inexperienced engineer. "We tried to give him guidance," Sink testified, "but he preferred to have his own convictions."

About changing the data to figures in the report, Sink said: "When you take data from several different sources, you have to rationalize among those data what is the true story. This is part of your engineering know-how." He admitted that changes had been made in the data, "but only to make them more consistent with the overall picture of the data that is available."

Jeter pooh-poohed the suggestion that anything improper occurred, saying: "We have thirty-odd engineers at this plant . . . and I say to you that it is incredible that these men would stand idly by and see reports changed or falsified . . . I mean you just do not have to do that working for anybody . . . Just nobody does that."

The four-hour hearing adjourned with no real conclusion reached by the subcommittee. But the following day the Department of Defense made sweeping changes in its inspection, testing, and reporting procedures. A spokesman for the DOD said the changes were a result of the Goodrich episode.

The A7D is now in service, sporting a Goodrich-made five-disk brake, a brake that works very well, I'm told. Business at the Goodrich plant is good. Lawson is now an engineer for LTV and has been assigned to the A7D project, possibly explaining why the A7D's new brakes work so well. And I am now a newspaper reporter.

At this writing, those remaining at Goodrich—including Warren—are still secure in the same positions, all except Russell Line and Robert Sink.

Line has been rewarded with a promotion to production superintendent, a large step upward on the corporate ladder. As for Sink, he moved up into Line's old job.

Whistleblowing and Professional Responsibility

• SISSELA BOK •

"Whistleblowing" is a new label generated by our increased awareness of the ethical conflicts encountered at work. Whistleblowers sound an alarm from within the very organization in which they work, aiming to spotlight neglect or abuses that threaten the public interest.

The stakes in whistleblowing are high. Take the nurse who alleges that physicians enrich themselves in her hospital through unnecessary surgery; the engineer who discloses safety defects in the braking systems of a fleet of new rapid-transit vehicles; the Defense Department official who alerts Congress to military graft and overspending: all know that they pose a threat to those whom they denounce and that their own careers may be at risk.

Moral Conflicts

Moral conflicts on several levels confront anyone who is wondering whether to speak out about abuses or risks or serious neglect. In the first place, he must try to decide whether, other things being equal, speaking out is in fact in the public interest. This choice is often made more complicated by factual uncertainties: Who is responsible for the abuse or neglect? How great is the threat? And how likely is it that speaking out will precipitate changes for the better?

In the second place, a would-be whistleblower must weigh his responsibility to serve the public interest against the responsibility he owes to his colleagues and the institution in which he works. While the professional ethic requires collegial loyalty, the codes of ethics often stress responsibility to the public over and above duties to colleagues and clients. Thus the United States Code of Ethics for Government Servants asks them to "expose corruption wherever uncovered" and to "put loyalty to the highest moral principles and to country above loyalty to persons, party, or government."[1] Similarly, the largest professional engineering association requires members to speak out against abuses threatening the safety, health, and welfare of the public.[2]

A third conflict for would-be whistleblowers is personal in nature and cuts across the first two: even in cases where they have concluded that the facts warrant speaking out, and that their duty to do so overrides loyalties to colleagues and institutions, they often have reason to fear the results of carrying out such a duty. However strong this duty may seem in theory, they know that, in practice, retaliation is likely. As a result, their careers and their ability to support themselves and their families may be unjustly impaired.[3] A government handbook issued during the Nixon era recommends reassigning "undesirables" to places so remote that they would prefer to resign. Whistleblowers may also be downgraded or given work without responsibility or work for which they are not qualified; or else they may be given many more tasks than they can possibly

From Sissela Bok, "Whistleblowing and Professional Responsibility," *New York University Education Quarterly*, 11 (Summer 1980): 2–7. Reprinted with permission.

perform. Another risk is that an outspoken civil servant may be ordered to undergo a psychiatric fitness-for-duty examination,[4] declared unfit for service, and "separated" as well as discredited from the point of view of any allegations he may be making. Outright firing, finally, is the most direct institutional response to whistleblowers.

Add to the conflicts confronting individual whistleblowers the claim to self-policing that many professions make, and professional responsibility is at issue in still another way. For an appeal to the public goes against everything that "self-policing" stands for. The question for the different professions, then, is how to resolve, insofar as it is possible, the conflict between professional loyalty and professional responsibility toward the outside world. The same conflicts arise to some extent in all groups, but professional groups often have special cohesion and claim special dignity and privileges.

The plight of whistleblowers has come to be documented by the press and described in a number of books. Evidence of the hardships imposed on those who chose to act in the public interest has combined with a heightened awareness of professional malfeasance and corruption to produce a shift toward greater public support of whistleblowers. Public service law firms and consumer groups have taken up their cause; institutional reforms and legislation have been proposed to combat illegitimate reprisals.[5]

Given the indispensable services performed by so many whistleblowers, strong public support is often merited. But the new climate of acceptance makes it easy to overlook the dangers of whistleblowing: of uses in error or in malice; of work and reputations unjustly lost for those falsely accused; of privacy invaded and trust undermined. There comes a level of internal prying and mutual suspicion at which no institution can function. And it is a fact that the disappointed, the incompetent, the malicious, and the paranoid all too often leap to accusations in public. Worst of all, ideological persecution throughout the world traditionally relies on insiders willing to inform on their colleagues or even on their family members, often through staged public denunciations or press campaigns.

No society can count itself immune from such dangers. But neither can it risk silencing those with a legitimate reason to blow the whistle. How then can we distinguish between different instances of whistleblowing? A society that fails to protect the right to speak out even on the part of those whose warnings turn out to be spurious obviously opens the door to political repression. But from the moral point of view there are important differences between the aims, messages, and methods of dissenters from within.

Nature of Whistleblowing

Three elements, each jarring, and triply jarring when conjoined, lend acts of whistleblowing special urgency and bitterness: dissent, breach of loyalty, and accusation.

Like all dissent, whistleblowing makes public a disagreement with an authority or a majority view. But whereas dissent can concern all forms of disagreement with, for instance, religious dogma or government policy or court decisions, whistleblowing has the narrower aim of shedding light on negligence or abuse, or alerting to a risk, and of assigning responsibility for this risk.

Would-be whistleblowers confront the conflict inherent in all dissent: between conforming and sticking their necks out. The more repressive the authority they challenge, the greater the personal risk they take in speaking out. At exceptional times, as in times of war, even ordinarily tolerant authorities may come to regard dissent as unacceptable and even disloyal.[6]

Furthermore, the whistleblower hopes to stop the game; but since he is neither referee nor coach, and since he blows the whistle on his own team, his act is seen as a violation of loyalty. In holding his position, he has assumed certain obligations to his colleagues and clients. He may even have subscribed to a loyalty oath or a promise of confidentiality. Loyalty to colleagues and to clients comes to be pitted against loyalty to the public interest, to those who may be injured unless the revelation is made.

Not only is loyalty violated in whistleblowing, hierarchy as well is often opposed, since the whistleblower is not only a colleague but a subordinate. Though aware of the risks inherent in such disobedience, he often hopes to keep his job.[7] At times, however, he plans his alarm to coincide with leaving the institution. If he is highly placed, or joined by others, resigning in protest may effectively direct public attention to the wrongdoing at issue.[8] Still another alternative, often chosen by those who wish to be safe from retaliation, is to leave the institution quietly, to secure another post, and then to blow the whistle. In this way, it is possible to speak with the authority and knowledge of an insider without having the vulnerability of that position.

It is the element of accusation, of calling a "foul," that arouses the strongest reactions on the part of the hierarchy. The accusation may be of neglect, of willfully concealed dangers, or of outright abuse on the part of colleagues or superiors. It singles out specific persons or groups as responsible for threats to the public interest. If no one could be held responsible—as in the case of an impending avalanche—the warning would not constitute whistleblowing.

The accusation of the whistleblower, moreover, concerns a present or an imminent threat. Past errors or misdeeds occasion such an alarm only if they still affect current practices. And risks far in the future lack the immediacy needed to make the alarm a compelling one, as well as the close connection to particular individuals that would justify actual accusations. Thus an alarm can be sounded about safety defects in a rapid-transit system that threaten or will shortly threaten passengers, but the revelation of safety defects in a system no longer in use, while of historical interest, would not constitute whistleblowing. Nor would the revelation of potential problems in a system not yet fully designed and far from implemented.[9]

Not only immediacy, but also specificity, is needed for there to be an alarm capable of pinpointing responsibility. A concrete risk must be at issue rather than a vague foreboding or a somber prediction. The act of whistleblowing differs in this respect from the lamentation or the dire prophecy. An immediate and specific threat would normally be acted upon by those at risk. The whistleblower assumes that his message will alert listeners to something they do not know, or whose significance they have not grasped because it has been kept secret.

The desire for openness inheres in the temptation to reveal any secret, sometimes joined to an urge for self-aggrandizement and publicity and the hope for revenge for past slights or injustices. There can be pleasure, too—righteous or malicious—in laying bare the secrets of co-workers and in setting the record straight at last. Colleagues of the whistleblower often suspect his motives: they may regard him as a crank, as publicity-hungry, wrong about the facts, eager for scandal and discord, and driven to indiscretion by his personal biases and shortcomings.

For whistleblowing to be effective, it must arouse its audience. Inarticulate whistleblowers are likely to fail from the outset. When they are greeted by apathy, their message dissipates. When they are greeted by disbelief, they elicit no response at all. And when the audience is not free to receive or to act on the information—when censorship or fear of retribution stifles response—then the message rebounds to injure the whistleblower. Whistleblowing also requires the possibility of concerted public response: the idea of whistleblowing in an anarchy is therefore merely quixotic.

Such characteristics of whistleblowing and strategic considerations for achieving an impact are common to the noblest warnings, the most vicious personal attacks, and the delusions of the paranoid. How can one distinguish the many acts of sounding an alarm that are genuinely in the public interest from all the petty, biased, or lurid revelations that pervade our querulous and gossip-ridden society? Can we draw distinctions between different whistleblowers, different messages, different methods?

We clearly can, in a number of cases. Whistleblowing may be starkly inappropriate when in malice or error, or when it lays bare legitimately private matters having to do, for instance, with political belief or sexual life. It can, just as clearly, be the only way to shed light on an ongoing unjust practice such as drugging political prisoners or subjecting them to electroshock treatment. It can be the last resort for alerting the public to an impending disaster. Taking such clear-cut cases as benchmarks, and reflecting on what it is about them that weighs so heavily for or against speaking out, we can work our way toward the admittedly more complex cases in which whistleblowing is not so clearly the right or wrong choice, or where different points of view exist regarding its legitimacy—cases where there are moral reasons both for concealment and for disclosure and where judgments conflict. Consider the following cases[10]:

A. As a construction inspector for a federal agency, John Samuels (not his real name) had personal knowledge of shoddy and deficient construction practices by private contractors. He knew his superiors received free vacations and entertainment, had their homes remodeled and found jobs for their relatives—all courtesy of a private contractor. These superiors later approved a multimillion no-bid contract with the same "generous" firm.

Samuels also had evidence that other firms were hiring nonunion laborers at a low wage while receiving substantially higher payments from the government for labor costs. A former superior, unaware of an office dictaphone, had incautiously instructed Samuels on how to accept bribes for overlooking sub-par performance.

As he prepared to volunteer this information to various members of Congress, he became tense and uneasy. His family was scared and the fears were valid. It might cost Samuels thousands of dollars to protect his job. Those who had freely provided Samuels with information would probably recant or withdraw their friendship. A number of people might object to his using a dictaphone to gather information. His agency would start covering up and vent its collective wrath upon him. As for reporters and writers, they would gather for a few days, then move on to the next story. He would be left without a job, with fewer friends, with massive battles looming, and without the financial means of fighting them, Samuels decided to remain silent.

B. Engineers of Company "A" prepared plans and specifications for machinery to be used in a manufacturing process and Company "A" turned them over to Company "B" for production. The engineers of Company "B," in reviewing the plans and specifications, came to the conclusion that they included certain miscalculations and technical deficiencies of a nature that the final product might be unsuitable for the purposes of the ultimate users, and that the equipment, if built according to the original plans and specifications, might endanger the lives of persons in proximity to it. The engineers of Company "B" called the matter to the attention of appropriate officials of their employer who, in turn, advised Company "A." Company "A" replied that its engineers felt that the design and specifications for the equipment were adequate and safe and that Company "B" should proceed to build the equipment as designed and specified. The officials of Company "B" instructed its engineers to proceed with the work.

C. A recently hired assistant director of admissions in a state university begins to wonder whether transcripts of some applicants accurately reflect their accomplishments. He knows that it matters to many in the university community, including alumni, that the football team continue its winning tradition. He has heard rumors that surrogates may be available to take tests for a fee, signing the names of designated applicants for admission, and that some of the transcripts may have been altered. But he has no hard facts. When he brings the question up with the director of admissions, he is told that the rumors are unfounded and asked not to inquire further into the matter.

Individual Moral Choice

What questions might those who consider sounding an alarm in public ask themselves? How might they articulate the problem they see and weigh its injustice before deciding whether or not to reveal it? How can they best try to make sure their choice is the right one? In thinking about these questions it helps to keep in mind the three elements mentioned earlier: dissent, breach of loyalty, and accusation. They impose certain requirements—of accuracy and judgment in dissent; of exploring alternative ways to cope with improprieties that minimize the breach of loyalty; and of fairness in accusation. For each, careful articulation and testing of arguments are needed, to limit error and bias.

Dissent by whistleblowers, first of all, is expressly claimed to be intended to benefit the public. It carries with it, as a result, an obligation to consider the nature of this benefit and to consider also the possible harm that may come from speaking out: harm to persons or institutions and, ultimately, to the public interest itself. Whistleblowers must, therefore, begin by making every effort to consider the effects of speaking out versus those of remaining silent. They must assure themselves of the accuracy of their reports, checking and rechecking the facts before speaking out; specify the degree to which there is genuine impropriety; consider how imminent is the threat they see, how serious, and how closely linked to those accused of neglect and abuse.

If the facts warrant whistleblowing, how can the second element—breach of loyalty—be minimized? The most important question here is whether the existing avenues for change within the organization have been explored. It is a waste of time for the public as well as harmful to the institution to sound the loudest alarm first. Whistleblowing has to remain a last alternative because of its destructive side effects: it must be chosen only when other alternatives have been considered and rejected. They may be rejected if they simply do not apply to the problem at hand, or when there is not time to go through routine channels or when the institution is so corrupt or coercive that steps will be taken to silence the whistleblower should he try the regular channels first.

What weight should an oath or a promise of silence have in the conflict of loyalties? One sworn to silence is doubtless under a stronger obligation because of the oath he has taken. He has bound himself, assumed specific obligations beyond those assumed in merely taking a new position. But even such promises can be overridden when the public interest at issue is strong enough. They can be overridden if they were obtained under duress or through deceit. They can be overridden, too, if they promise something that is in itself wrong or unlawful. The fact that one has promised silence is no excuse for complicity in covering up a crime or a violation of the public's trust.

The third element in whistleblowing—accusation—raises equally serious ethical concerns. They are concerns of fairness to the persons accused of impropriety. Is the message one to which the public is entitled in the first place? Or does it infringe on personal and private matters that one has no right to invade? Here, the very notion of what is in the public's best "interest" is at issue: "accusations" regarding an official's unusual sexual or religious experiences may well appeal to the public's interest without being information relevant to "the public interest."

Great conflicts arise here. We have witnessed excessive claims to executive privilege and to secrecy by government officials during the Watergate scandal in order to cover up for abuses the public had every right to discover. Conversely, those hoping to profit from prying into private matters have become adept at invoking "the public's right to know." Some even regard such private matters as threats to the public: they voice their own religious and political prejudices in the language of accusation. Such a danger is never stronger than when the accusation is delivered surreptitiously. The anonymous accusations made during the McCarthy period regarding political beliefs and associations often injured persons who did not even know their accusers or the exact nature of the accusations.

From the public's point of view, accusations that are openly made by identifiable individuals are more likely to be taken seriously. And in fairness to those criticized, openly accepted responsibility for blowing the whistle should be preferred to the denunciation or the leaked rumor. What is openly stated can more easily be checked, its source's motives challenged, and the underlying information examined. Those under attack may otherwise be hard put to defend themselves against nameless adversaries. Often they do not even know that they are threatened until it is too late to respond. The anonymous denunciation, moreover, common to so many regimes, places the burden of investigation on government agencies that may thereby gain the power of a secret police.

From the point of view of the whistleblower, on the other hand, the anonymous message is safer in situations where retaliation is likely. But it is also often less likely to be taken seriously. Unless the message is accompanied by indications of how the evidence can be checked, its anonymity, however safe for the source, speaks against it.

During the process of weighing the legitimacy of speaking out, the method used, and the degree of fairness needed, whistleblowers must try to compensate for the strong possibility of bias on their part. They should be scrupulously aware of any motive that might skew their message: a desire for self-defense in a difficult bureaucratic situation, perhaps, or the urge to seek revenge, or inflated expectations regarding the effect their message will have on the situation. (Needless to say, bias affects the silent as well as the outspoken. The motive for holding back important information about abuses and injustice ought to give similar cause for soul-searching.)

Likewise, the possibility of personal gain from sounding the alarm ought to give pause. Once again there is then greater risk of a biased message. Even if the whistleblower regards himself as incorruptible, his profiting from revelations of neglect or abuse will lead others to question his motives and to put less credence in his charges. If, for example, a government employee stands to make large profits from a book exposing the iniquities in his agency, there is danger that he will, perhaps even unconsciously, slant his report in order to cause more of a sensation.

A special problem arises when there is a high risk that the civil servant who speaks out will have to go through costly litigation. Might he not justifiably try to make enough money on his public revelations—say, through books or public speaking—to offset his losses? In so doing he will not strictly speaking have *profited* from his revelations: he merely avoids being financially crushed by their sequels. He will nevertheless still be suspected at the time of revelation, and his message will therefore seem more questionable.

Reducing bias and error in moral choice often requires consultation, even open debate[11]: methods that force articulation of the moral arguments at stake and challenge privately held assumptions. But acts of whistleblowing present special problems when it comes to open consultation. On the one hand, once the whistleblower sounds his alarm publicly, his arguments will be subjected to open scrutiny; he will have to articulate his reasons for speaking out and substantiate his charges. On the other hand, it will then be too late to retract the alarm or to combat its harmful effects, should his choice to speak out have been ill-advised.

For this reason, the whistleblower owes it to all involved to make sure of two things: that he has sought as much and as objective advice regarding his choice as he can *before* going public; and that he is aware of the arguments for and against the practice of whistleblowing in general, so that he can see his own choice against as richly detailed and coherently structured a background as possible. Satisfying these two requirements once again has special problems because of the very nature of whistleblowing: the more corrupt the circumstances, the more dangerous it may be to seek counsultation before speaking out. And yet, since the whistleblower himself may have a biased view of the state of affairs, he may choose not to consult others when in fact it would be not only safe but advantageous to do so; he may see corruption and conspiracy where none exists.

Notes

1. Code of Ethics for Government Service passed by the U.S. House of Representatives in the 85th Congress (1958) and applying to all government employees and office holders.

2. Code of Ethics of the Institute of Electrical and Electronics Engineers, Article IV.

3. For case histories and descriptions of what befalls whistleblowers, see Rosemary Chalk and Frank von Hippel, "Due Process for Dissenting Whistle-Blowers," *Technology Review* 81 (June–July 1979): 48–55; Alan S. Westin and Stephen Salisbury, eds., *Individual Rights in the Corporation* (New York: Pantheon, 1980); Helen Dudar, "The Price of Blowing the Whistle," *New York Times Magazine,* 30 October 1979, pp. 41–54; John Edsall, *Scientific Freedom and Responsibility* (Washington, D.C.: American Association for the Advancement of Science, 1975), p. 5; David Ewing, *Freedom Inside the Organization* (New York: Dutton, 1979); Ralph Nader, Peter Petkas, and Kate Blackwell, *Whistle Blowing* (New York: Grossman, 1972); Charles Peter and Taylor Branch, *Blowing the Whistle* (New York: Praeger, 1972).

4. Congressional hearings uncovered a growing resort to mandatory psychiatric examinations.

5. For an account of strategies and proposals to support government whistleblowers, see Government Accountability Project, *A Whistleblower's Guide to the Federal Bureaucracy* (Washington, D.C.: Institute for Policy Studies, 1977).

6. See, e.g., Samuel Eliot Morison, Frederick Merk, and Frank Friedel, *Dissent in Three American Wars* (Cambridge: Harvard University Press, 1970).

7. In the scheme worked out by Albert Hirschmann in *Exit, Voice and Loyalty* (Cambridge: Harvard University Press, 1970), whistleblowing represents "voice" accompanied by a preference not to "exit," though forced "exit" is clearly a possibility and "voice" after or during "exit" may be chosen for strategic reasons.

8. Edward Weisband and Thomas N. Franck, *Resignation in Protest* (New York: Grossman, 1975).

9. Future developments can, however, be the cause for whistleblowing if they are seen as resulting from steps being taken or about to be taken that render them inevitable.

10. Case A is adapted from Louis Clark, "The Sound of Professional Suicide," *Barrister,* Summer 1978, p. 10; Case B is Case 5 in Robert J. Baum and Albert Flores, eds., *Ethical Problems of Engineering* (Troy, N.Y.: Rensselaer Polytechnic Institute, 1978), p. 186.

11. I discuss these questions of consultation and publicity with respect to moral choice in chapter 7 of Sissela Bok, *Lying* (New York: Pantheon, 1978); and in *Secrets* (New York: Pantheon Books, 1982), Ch. IX and XV.

Employment at Will and Due Process

PATRICIA H. WERHANE   •   TARA J. RADIN

In 1980, Howard Smith III was hired by the American Greetings Corporation as a materials handler at the plant in Osceola, Arkansas. He was promoted to forklift driver and held that job until 1989, when he became involved in a dispute with his shift leader. According to Smith, he had a dispute with his shift leader at work. After work he tried to discuss the matter, but according to Smith, the shift leader hit him. The next day Smith was fired.

Smith was an <u>"at will" employee</u>. He did not belong to, nor was he protected by, <u>any union or union agreement</u>. He did not have any special legal protection, for there was no apparent question of age, gender, race, or handicap discrimination.

And he was not alleging any type of problem with worker safety on the job. The American Greetings Employee Handbook stated that "We believe in working and thinking and planning to provide a stable and growing business, to give such service to our customers that we may provide maximum job security for our employees." It did not state that employees could not be fired without due process or reasonable cause. According to the common law principle of Employment at Will (EAW), Smith's job at American Greetings could, therefore, legitimately be terminated at any time without cause, by either Smith or his employer, as long as that termination did not violate any law, agreement, or public policy.

Smith challenged his firing in the Arkansas court system as a "tort of outrage." A "tort of outrage" occurs when employer engages in "extreme or outrageous conduct" or intentionally inflicts terrible emotional stress. If such a tort is found to have occurred, the action, in this case, the dismissal, can be overturned.

Smith's case went to the Supreme Court of Arkansas in 1991. In court the management of American Greetings argued that Smith was fired for provoking management into a fight. The Court held that the firing was not in violation of law or a public policy, that the employee handbook did not specify restrictions on at will terminations, and that the alleged altercation between Smith and his shift leader "did not come close to meeting" criteria for a tort of outrage. Howard Smith lost his case and his job.[1]

The principle of EAW is a common-law doctrine that states that, in the absence of law or contract, employers have the right to hire, promote, demote, and fire whomever and whenever they please. In 1887, the principle was stated explicitly in a document by H. G. Wood entitled *Master and Servant*. According to Wood, "A general or indefinite hiring is prima facie a hiring at will."[2] Although the term "master-servant," a medieval expression, was once used to characterize employment relationships, it has been dropped from most of the recent literature on employment.[3]

In the United States, EAW has been interpreted as the rule that, when employees are not specifically covered by union agreement, legal statute, public policy, or contract, employers "may dismiss their employees at will . . . for good cause, for no cause, *or even for causes morally wrong*, without being thereby guilty of legal wrong."[4] At the same time, "at will" employees enjoy rights parallel to employer prerogatives, because employees may quit their jobs for any reason whatsoever (or no reason) without having to give any notice to their employers. "At will" employees range from part-time contract workers to CEOs, including all those workers and managers in the private sector of the economy not covered by agreements, statutes, or contracts. Today at least 60% of all employees in the private sector in the United States are "at will" employees. These employees have no rights to due process or to appeal employment decisions, and the employer does not have any obligation to give reasons for demotions, transfers, or dismissals. Interestingly, while employees in the *private* sector of the economy tend to be regarded as "at will" employees, *public*-sector employees have guaranteed rights, including due process, and are protected from demotion, transfer, or firing without cause.

Due process is a means by which a person can appeal a decision in order to get an explanation of that action and an opportunity to argue against it. Procedural due process is the right to a hearing, trial, grievance procedure, or appeal when a decision is made concerning oneself. Due process is also substantive. It is the demand for rationality and fairness: for good reasons for decisions. EAW has been widely interpreted as allowing employees to be demoted, transferred or dismissed without due process, that is, without having a hearing and without requirement of good reasons or "cause" for the employment decision. This is not to say that employers do not have reasons, usually good reasons, for their decisions. But there is no moral or legal obligation to state or defend them. EAW thus sidesteps the requirement of procedural and substantive due process in the workplace, but it does not preclude the institution of such procedures or the existence of good reasons for employment decisions.

EAW is still upheld in the state and federal courts of this country, as the Howard Smith case illustrates, although exceptions are made when violations of public policy and law are at issue. According to the *Wall Street Journal,* the court has decided in favor of the employees in 67% of the wrongful discharge suits that have taken place during the past three years. These suits were won not on the basis of a rejection of the principle of EAW but, rather, on the basis of breach of contract, lack of just cause for dismissal when a company policy was in place, or violations of public policy. The court has carved out the "public policy" exception so as not to encourage fraudulent or wrongful behavior on the part of employers, such as in cases where employees are asked to break a law or to violate state public policies, and in cases where employees are not allowed to exercise fundamental rights, such as the rights to vote, to serve on a jury, and to collect worker compensation. For example, in one case, the court reinstated an employee who was fired for reporting theft at his plant on the grounds that criminal conduct requires such reporting.[5] In another case, the court reinstated a physician who was fired from the Ortho Pharmaceutical Corporation for refusing to seek approval to test a certain drug on human subjects. The court held that safety clearly lies in the interest of public welfare, and employees are not to be fired for refusing to jeopardize public safety.[6]

During the last ten years, a number of positive trends have become apparent in employment practices and in state and federal court adjudications of employment disputes. Shortages of skilled managers, fear of legal repercussions, and a more genuine interest in employee rights claims and reciprocal obligations have resulted in a more careful spelling out of employment contracts, the development of elaborate grievance procedures, and in general less arbitrariness in employee treatment.[7] While there has not been a universal revolution in thinking about employee rights, an increasing number of companies have qualified their EAW prerogatives with restrictions in firing without cause. Many companies have developed grievance procedures and other means for employee complaint and redress.

Interestingly, substantive due process, the notion that employers should give good reasons for their employment actions, previously dismissed as legal and philosophical nonsense, has also recently developed positive advocates. Some courts have found that it is a breach of contract to fire a long-term employee when there is not sufficient cause—under normal economic conditions even when the implied contract is only a verbal one. In California, for example, 50% of the implied contract cases (and there have been over 200) during the last five years have been decided in favor of the employee, again, without challenging EAW.[8] In light of this recognition of implicit contractual obligations between employees and employers, in some unprecedented court cases *employees* have been held liable for good faith breaches of contract, particularly in cases of quitting without notice in the middle of a project and/or taking technology or other ideas to another job.[9]

These are all positive developments. At the same time, there has been neither an across-the-board institution of due process procedures in all corporations nor any direct challenges to the *principle* (although there have been challenges to the practice) of EAW as a justifiable and legitimate approach to employment practices. Moreover, as a result of mergers, downsizing, and restructuring, hundreds of thousands of employees have been laid off summarily without being able to appeal those decisions.

"At will" employees, then, have no rights to demand an appeal to such employment decisions except through the court system. In addition, no form of due process is a requirement preceding any of these actions. Moreover, unless public policy is violated, the law has traditionally protected employers from employee retaliation in such actions. It is true that the scope of what is defined as "public policy" has been enlarged so that "at will" dismissals without good reason are greatly reduced. It is also true that many companies have grievance procedures in place for "at will" employees. But such procedures are voluntary, procedural due process is not *required,* and companies need not give any reasons for their employment decisions.

In what follows we shall present a series of arguments defending the claim that the right to procedural and substantive due process should be extended to all employees in the private sector of the economy. We will defend the claim partly on the basis of human rights. We shall also argue that the public/private distinction that precludes the application of constitutional guarantees in the private sector has sufficiently broken down so that the absence of a due process requirement in the workplace is an anomaly.

Employment at Will

EAW is often justified for one or more of the following reasons:

1. The proprietary rights of employers guarantee that they may employ or dismiss whomever and whenever they wish.
2. EAW defends employee and employer rights equally, in particular the right to freedom of contract, because an employee voluntarily contracts to be hired and can quit at any time.
3. In choosing to take a job, an employee voluntarily commits herself to certain responsibilities and company loyalty, including the knowledge that she is an "at will" employee.
4. Extending due process rights in the workplace often interferes with the efficiency and productivity of the business organization.
5. Legislation and/or regulation of employment relationships further undermine an already overregulated economy.

Let us examine each of these arguments in more detail. The principle of EAW is sometimes maintained purely on the basis of proprietary rights of employers and corporations. In dismissing or demoting employees, the employer is not denying rights to *persons.* Rather, the employer is simply excluding that person's *labor* from the organization.

This is not a bad argument. Nevertheless, accepting it necessitates consideration of the proprietary rights of employees as well. To understand what is meant by "proprietary rights of employees" it is useful to consider first what is meant by the term "labor." "Labor" is sometimes used collectively to refer to the workforce as a whole. It also refers to the activity of working. Other times it refers to the productivity or "fruits" of that activity. Productivity, labor in the third sense, might be thought of as a form of property or at least as something convertible into property, because the productivity of working is what is traded for remuneration in employee-employer work agreements. For example, suppose an advertising agency hires an expert known for her creativity in developing new commercials. This person trades her ideas, the product of her work (thinking), for pay. The ideas are not literally property, but they are tradable items because, when presented on paper or on television, they are sellable by their creator and generate income. But the activity of working (thinking in this case) cannot be sold or transferred.

Caution is necessary, though, in relating productivity to tangible property, because there is an obvious difference between productivity and material property. Productivity requires the past or present activity of working, and thus the presence of the person performing this activity. Person, property, labor, and productivity are all different in this important sense. A person can be distinguished from his possessions, a distinction that allows for the creation of legally fictional persons such as corporations or trusts that can "own" property. Persons cannot, however, be distinguished from their working, and this activity is necessary for creating productivity, a tradable product of one's working.

In dismissing an employee, a well-intentioned employer aims to rid the corporation of the costs of generating that employee's work products. In ordinary employment situations, however, terminating that cost entails terminating that employee. In those cases the justification for the "at will" firing is presumably proprietary. But treating an employee "at will" is analogous to considering her a piece of property at the disposal of the employer or corporation. Arbitrary firings treat people as things. When I "fire" a robot, I do not have to give reasons, because a robot is not a rational being. It has no use for reasons. On the other hand, if I fire a person arbitrarily, I am making the assumption that she does not need reasons either. If I have hired people, then, in firing them, I should treat them as such, with respect, throughout the termination process. This does not preclude firing. It merely asks employers to give reasons for their actions, because reasons are appropriate when people are dealing with other people.

This reasoning leads to a second defense and critique of EAW. It is contended that EAW defends employee and employer rights equally. An employer's right to hire and fire "at will" is balanced by a worker's right to accept or reject employment. The institution of any employee right that restricts "at will" hiring and firing would be unfair unless this restriction were balanced by a similar restriction controlling employee job choice in the workplace. Either program would do irreparable damage by preventing both employees and employers from continuing in voluntary employment arrangements. These arrangements are guaranteed by "freedom of contract," the right of persons or organizations to enter into any voluntary agreement with which all parties of the agreement are in accord.[10] Limiting EAW practices or requiring due

process would negatively affect freedom of contract. Both are thus clearly coercive, because in either case persons and organizations are forced to accept
behavioral restraints that place unnecessary constraints on voluntary employment agreements.[11]

This second line of reasoning defending EAW, like the first, presents some
solid arguments. A basic presupposition upon which EAW is grounded is that
of protecting equal freedoms of both employees and employers. The purpose
of EAW is to provide a guaranteed balance of these freedoms. But arbitrary
treatment of employees extends prerogatives to managers that are not equally
available to employees, and such treatment may unduly interfere with a fired
employee's prospects for future employment if that employee has no avenue
for defense or appeal. This is also sometimes true when an employee quits
without notice or good reason. Arbitrary treatment of employees *or* employers
therefore violates the spirit of EAW—that of protecting the freedoms of both
employees and employers.

The third justification of EAW defends the voluntariness of employment
contracts. If these are agreements between moral agents, however, such agreements imply reciprocal obligations between the parties in question for which
both are accountable. It is obvious that, in an employment contract, people
are rewarded for their performance. What is seldom noticed is that, if part of
the employment contract is an expectation of loyalty, trust, and respect on the
part of an employee, the employer must, in return, treat the employee with respect as well. The obligations required by employment agreements, if these
are free and noncoercive agreements, must be equally obligatory and mutually restrictive on both parties. Otherwise one party cannot expect—morally expect—loyalty, trust, or respect from the other.

EAW is most often defended on practical grounds. From a utilitarian perspective, hiring and firing "at will" is deemed necessary in productive organizations to ensure maximum efficiency and productivity, the goals of such organizations. In the absence of EAW unproductive employees, workers who are
no longer needed, and even troublemakers, would be able to keep their jobs.
Even if a business *could* rid itself of undesirable employees, the lengthy procedure of due process required by an extension of employee rights would be
costly and time-consuming, and would likely prove distracting to other employees. This would likely slow production and, more likely than not, prove
harmful to the morale of other employees.

This argument is defended by Ian Maitland, who contends,

> [I]f employers were generally to heed business ethicists and institute workplace
> due process in cases of dismissals and take the increased costs or reduced efficien-
> cy out of workers' paychecks—then they would expose themselves to the pirating
> of their workers by other employers who would give workers what they wanted in-
> stead of respecting their rights in the workplace. . . . In short, there is good reason
> for concluding that the prevalence of EAW does accurately reflect workers' prefer-
> ences for wages over contractually guaranteed protections against unfair dis-
> missal.[12]

Such an argument assumes (a) that due process increases costs and reduces efficiency, a contention that is not documented by the many corporations that
have grievance procedures, and (b) that workers will generally give up some
basic rights for other benefits, such as money. The latter is certainly sometimes

true, but not always so, particularly when there are questions of unfair dismissals or job security. Maitland also assumes that an employee is on the same level and possesses the same power as her manager, so that an employee can choose her benefit package in which grievance procedures, whistleblowing protections, or other rights are included. Maitland implies that employers might include in that package of benefits their rights to practice the policy of unfair dismissals in return for increased pay. He also at least implicitly suggests that due process precludes dismissals and layoffs. But this is not true. Procedural due process demands a means of appeal, and substantive due process demands good reasons, both of which are requirements for other managerial decisions and judgments. Neither demands benevolence, lifetime employment, or prevents dismissals. In fact, having good reasons gives an employer a justification for getting rid of poor employees.

In summary, arbitrariness, although not prohibited by EAW, violates the managerial ideal of rationality and consistency. These are independent grounds for not abusing EAW. Even if EAW itself is justifiable, the practice of EAW, when interpreted as condoning arbitrary employment decisions, is not justifiable. Both procedural and substantive due process are consistent with, and a moral requirement of, EAW. The former is part of recognizing obligations implied by freedom of contract, and the latter, substantive due process, conforms with the ideal of managerial rationality that is implied by a consistent application of this common law principle.

Employment at Will, Due Process, and the Public/Private Distinction

The strongest reasons for allowing abuses of EAW and for not instituting a full set of employee rights in the workplace, at least in the private sector of the economy, have to do with the nature of business in a free society. Businesses are privately owned voluntary organizations of all sizes from small entrepreneurships to large corporations. As such, they are not subject to the restrictions governing public and political institutions. Political procedures such as due process, needed to safeguard the public against the arbitrary exercise of power by the state, do not apply to private organizations. Guaranteeing such rights in the workplace would require restrictive legislation and regulation. Voluntary market arrangements, so vital to free enterprise and guaranteed by freedom of contract, would be sacrificed for the alleged public interest of employee claims.

In the law, courts traditionally have recognized the right of corporations to due process, although they have not required due process for employees in the private sector of the economy. The justification put forward for this is that since corporations are public entities acting in the public interest, they, like people, should be afforded the right to due process.

Due process is also guaranteed for permanent full-time workers in the public sector of the economy, that is, for workers in local, state and national government positions. The Fifth and Fourteenth Amendments protect liberty and property rights such that any alleged violations or deprivation of those rights may be challenged by some form of due process. According to recent Supreme Court decisions, when a state worker is a permanent employee, he has a property interest in his employment. Because a person's productivity contributes to the place of employment, a public worker is entitled to his job unless there is good reason to question it, such as poor work habits, habitual absences, and the like. Moreover, if a discharge would prevent him from obtaining other employment, which often is the case with state employees who, if fired, cannot find further government employment, that employee has a right to due process before being terminated.[13]

This justification for extending due process protections to public employees is grounded in the public employee's proprietary interest in his job. If that argument makes sense, it is curious that private employees do not have similar rights. The basis for this distinction stems from a tradition in Western thinking that distinguishes between the public and private spheres of life. The public sphere contains that part of a person's life that lies within the bounds of government regulation, whereas the private sphere contains that part of a person's life that lies outside those bounds. The argument is that the portion of a person's life that influences only that person should remain private and outside the purview of law and regulation, while the portion that influences the public welfare should be subject to the authority of the law.

Although interpersonal relationships on any level—personal, family, social, or employee-employer—are protected by statutes and common law, they are not constitutionally protected unless there is a violation of some citizen claim against the state. Because entrepreneurships and corporations are privately owned, and since employees are free to make or break employment contracts of their choice, employee-employer relationships, like family relationships, are treated as "private." In a family, even if there are no due process procedures, the state does not interfere, except when there is obvious harm or abuse. Similarly, employment relationships are considered private relationships contracted between free adults, and so long as no gross violations occur, positive constitutional guarantees such as due process are not enforceable.

The public/private distinction was originally developed to distinguish individuals from the state and to protect individuals and private property from public—i.e., governmental—intrusion. The distinction, however, has been extended to distinguish not merely between the individual or the family and the state, but also between universal rights claims and national sovereignty, public and private ownership, free enterprise and public policy, publicly and privately held corporations, and even between public and private employees. Indeed, this distinction plays a role in national and international affairs. Boutros Boutros-Ghali, the head of the United Nations, recently confronted a dilemma in deciding whether to go into Somalia without an invitation. His initial reaction was to stay out and to respect Somalia's right to "private" national sovereignty. It was only when he decided that Somalia had fallen apart as an independent state that he approved U.N. intervention. His dilemma parallels that of a state, which must decide whether to intervene in a family quarrel, the alleged abuse of a spouse or child, the inoculation of a Christian Scientist, or the blood transfusion for a Seventh-Day Adventist.

There are some questions, however, with the justification of the absence of due process with regard to the public/private distinction. Our economic system is allegedly based on private property, but it is unclear where "private" property and ownership end and "public" property and ownership begin. In the workplace, ownership and control is often divided. Corporate assets are held by an ever-changing group of individual and institutional shareholders. It is no longer true that owners exercise any real sense of control over their property and its management. Some do, but many do not. Moreover, such complex property relationships are spelled out and guaranteed by the state. This has prompted at least one thinker to argue that "private property" should be defined as "certain patterns of human interaction underwritten by public power."[14]

This fuzziness about the "privacy" of property becomes exacerbated by the way we use the term "public" in analyzing the status of businesses and in particular corporations. For example, we distinguish between privately owned business corporations and government-owned or -controlled public institutions. Among those companies that are not government owned, we distinguish between regulated "public" utilities whose stock is owned by private individuals and institutions; "publicly held" corporations whose stock is traded publicly, who are governed by special SEC regulations, and whose financial statements are public knowledge; and privately held corporations and entrepreneurships, companies and smaller businesses that are owned by an individual or group of individuals and not available for public stock purchase.

There are similarities between government-owned, public institutions and privately owned organizations. When the air controllers went on strike in the 1980s, Ronald Reagan fired them, and declared that, as public employees, they could not strike because it jeopardized the public safety. Nevertheless, both private and public institutions run transportation, control banks, and own property. While the goals of private and public institutions differ in that public institutions are allegedly supposed to place the public good ahead of profitability, the simultaneous call for businesses to become socially responsible and the demand for governmental organizations to become efficient and accountable further question the dichotomy between "public" and "private."

Many business situations reinforce the view that the traditional public/private dichotomy has been eroded, if not entirely, at least in large part. For example, in 1981, General Motors (GM) wanted to expand by building a plant in what is called the "Poletown" area of Detroit. Poletown is an old Detroit Polish neighborhood. The site was favorable because it was near transportation facilities and there was a good supply of labor. To build the plant, however, GM had to displace residents in a nine-block area. The Poletown Neighborhood Council objected, but the Supreme Court of Michigan decided in favor of GM and held that the state could condemn property for private use, with proper compensation to owners, when it was in the public good. What is particularly interesting about this case is that GM is not a government-owned corporation; its primary goal is *profitability*, not the common good. The Supreme Court nevertheless decided that it was in the *public* interest for Detroit to use its authority to allow a company to take over property despite the protesting of the property owners. In this case the public/private distinction was thoroughly scrambled.

The overlap between private enterprise and public interests is such that at least one legal scholar argues that "developments in the twentieth century have significantly undermined the 'privateness' of modern business corporations, with the result that the traditional bases for distinguishing them from public corporations have largely disappeared."[15] Nevertheless, despite the blurring of the public and private in terms of property rights and the status and functions of corporations, the subject of employee rights appears to remain immune from conflation.

The expansion of employee protections to what we would consider just claims to due process gives to the state and the courts more opportunity to interfere with the private economy and might thus further skew what is seen by some as a precarious but delicate balance between the private economic sector and public policy. We agree. But if the distinction between public and private institutions is no longer clear-cut, and the traditional separation of the public and private spheres is no longer in place, might it not then be better to recognize and extend constitutional guarantees so as to protect all citizens equally? If due process is crucial to political relationships between the individual and the state, why is it not central in relationships between employees and corporations since at least some of the companies in question are as large and powerful as small nations? Is it not in fact inconsistent with our democratic tradition *not* to mandate such rights?

The philosopher T. M. Scanlon summarizes our intuitions about due process. Scanlon says,

> The requirement of due process is one of the conditions of the moral acceptability of those institutions that give some people power to control or intervene in the lives of others.[16]

The institution of due process in the workplace is a moral requirement consistent with rationality and consistency expected in management decision-making. It is not precluded by EAW, and it is compatible with the overlap between the public and private sectors of the economy. Convincing business of the moral necessity of due process, however, is a task yet to be completed.

Notes

1. *Howard Smith III* v. *American Greetings Corporation*, 304 Ark. 596; 804 S.W. 2d 683.

2. H. G. Wood, *A Treatise on the Law of Master and Servant* (Albany, N.Y.: John D. Parsons, Jr., 1877), p. 134.

3. Until the end of 1980 the *Index of Legal Periodicals* indexed employee-employer relationships under this rubric.

4. Lawrence E. Blades, "Employment at Will versus Individual Freedom: On Limiting the Abusive Exercise of Employer Power," *Columbia Law Review*, 67 (1967), p. 1405, quoted from *Payne* v. *Western*, 81 Tenn. 507 (1884), and *Hutton* v. *Watters*, 132 Tenn. 527, S.W. 134 (1915).

5. *Palmateer* v. *International Harvester Corporation*, 85 Ill. App. 2d 124 (1981).

6. *Pierce* v. *Ortho Pharmaceutical Corporation* 845 NJ 58 (NJ 1980), 417 A.2d 505. See also Brian Heshizer, "The New Common Law of Employment: Changes in the Concept of Employment at Will," *Labor Law Journal*, 36 (1985), pp. 95–107.

7. See David Ewing, *Justice on the Job: Resolving Grievances in the Nonunion Workplace* (Boston: Harvard Business School Press, 1989).

8. See R. M. Bastress, "A Synthesis and a Proposal for Reform of the Employment at Will Doctrine," *West Virginia Law Review*, 90 (1988), pp. 319–51.

9. See "Employees' Good Faith Duties," *Hastings Law Journal,* 39 (198). See also *Hudson* v. *Moore Business Forms,* 609 Supp. 467 (N.D. Cal. 1985).

10. See *Lockner* v. *New York,* 198 U.S. (1905), and Adina Schwartz, "Autonomy in the Workplace," in Tom Regan, ed., *Just Business* (New York: Random House, 1984), pp. 129–40.

11. Eric Mack, "Natural and Contractual Rights," *Ethics,* 87 (1977), pp. 153–59.

12. Ian Maitland, "Rights in the Workplace: A Nozickian Argument," in Lisa Newton and Maureen Ford, eds., *Taking Sides* (Guilford, CT: Dushkin Publishing Group), 1990, pp. 34–35.

13. Richard Wallace, "Union Waiver of Public Employees' Due Process Rights," *Industrial Relations Law Journal,* 8 (1986), pp. 583–87.

14. Morris Cohen, "Dialogue on Private Property," *Rutgers Law Review* 9 (1954), pp. 357. See also *Law and the Social Order* (1933) and Robert Hale, "Coercion and Distribution in a Supposedly Non-Coercive State," *Political Science Quarterly,* 38 (1923), pp. 470; John Brest, "State Action and Liberal Theory," *University of Pennsylvania Law Review* (1982), pp. 1296–1329.

15. Gerald Frug, "The City As a Legal Concept," *Harvard Law Review,* 93 (1980), p. 1129.

16. T. M. Scanlon, "Due Process," in J. Roland Pennock and John W. Chapman, eds., *Nomos XVIII: Due Process* (New York: New York University Press, 1977), p. 94.

Employability Security

• ROSABETH MOSS KANTER •

For many people in the twentieth century, careers were constituted by institutions. Large employers were expected to provide—and guarantee—jobs, benefits, and upward mobility. Long-term employment has long been considered a central component of high-commitment, high-productivity work systems. And corporate entitlements, from health benefits to pensions, were based on an assumption of longevity, especially as U.S. employers were expected to offer benefits guaranteed by governments in other countries.

Now recessionary pressures and sweeping industrial transformations are forcing large companies to downsize—a euphemism that masks the human turmoil involved. Even in Japan, the bastion of life-time employment in big businesses where nearly three quarters of the country's 60 million workers stayed with one employer throughout their working life, cutbacks and layoffs beginning in 1992 have been shaking the social contract.

The job-tenure ideal of the past is colliding with the job-insecurity reality of the present. Institutionally dependent careers are declining; self-reliant careers as professionals and entrepreneurs are proliferating, increasing the burdens on people. And women are joining men as peers in nearly every corner of the labor market, bringing new issues—inclusion, empowerment, accommodation to family needs—at a time when companies are struggling to stay afloat.

Churn and Displacement

The United States has been fortunate in not depending solely on large enterprises. America has a vibrant entrepreneurial economy, a small business sector that creates a higher proportion of jobs than are similarly created in European nations. But employment in smaller organizations is inherently less secure, especially given the high failure rate of new small businesses, and such jobs often come without the benefits and safeguards mandated for companies with more than fifty employees. Some Americans count on entrepreneurs to pull the country out of the economic doldrums as large companies sputter and downsize. But an entrepreneurial economy is full of churn and displacement—and the fate of small companies is often linked to the fate of big ones which they supply and service.

New policies must reflect new forms of security while embracing the emerging realities of flexibility, mobility, and change.

"We promise to increase opportunity and power for our entire, diverse work force. We will:

- Recruit for the potential to increase in competence, not simply for narrow skills to fill today's slots.
- Offer ample learning opportunities, from formal training to lunchtime seminars—the equivalent of three weeks a year.
- Provide challenging jobs and rotating assignments that allow growth in skills even without promotion to higher jobs.
- Measure performance beyond accounting numbers and share the data to allow learning by doing and continuous improvement—turning everyone into self-guided professionals.
- Retrain employees as soon as jobs become obsolete.
- Emphasize team building, to help our diverse work force appreciate and utilize fully each other's skills.
- Recognize and reward individual and team achievements, thereby building external reputations and offering tangible indicators of value.
- Provide three-month educational sabbaticals, external internships, or personal time-out every five years.
- Find growth opportunities in our network of suppliers, customers, and venture partners.
- Ensure that pensions and benefits are portable, so that people have safety nets for the future even if they seek employment elsewhere.
- Help people be productive while carrying family responsibilities, through flex-time, provision for sick children, and renewal breaks between major assignments.
- Measure the building of human capital and the capabilities of our people as thoroughly and frequently as we measure the building and use of financial capital.
- Encourage entrepreneurship—new ventures within our company or outside that help our people start businesses and create alternative sources of employment.

- Tap our people's ideas to develop innovations that lower costs, serve customers, and create new markets—the best foundation for business growth and continuing employment, and the source of funds to reinvest in continuous learning."

Policies like these could renew loyalty, commitment, and productivity for all men and women, of corporations both large and small, as they struggle to create jobs, wealth, and well-being in the global economy.

Diversity

• *Case Study* •

Foreign Assignment

THOMAS DUNFEE • DIANA ROBERTSON

Sara Strong graduated with an MBA from UCLA four years ago. She immediately took a job in the correspondent bank section of the Security Bank of the American Continent. Sara was assigned to work on issues pertaining to relationships with correspondent banks in Latin America. She rose rapidly in the section and received three good promotions in three years. She consistently got high ratings from her superiors, and she received particularly high marks for her professional demeanor.

In her initial position with the bank, Sara was required to travel to Mexico on several occasions. She was always accompanied by a male colleague even though she generally handled similar business by herself on trips within the United States. During her trips to Mexico she observed that Mexican bankers seemed more aware of her being a woman and were personally solicitous to her, but she didn't discern any major problems. The final decisions on the work that she did were handled by male representatives of the bank stationed in Mexico.

A successful foreign assignment was an important step for those on the "fast track" at the bank. Sara applied for a position in Central or South America and was delighted when she was assigned to the bank's office in Mexico City. The office had about twenty bank employees and was headed by William Vitam. The Mexico City office was seen as a preferred assignment by young executives at the bank.

After a month, Sara began to encounter problems. She found it difficult to be effective in dealing with Mexican bankers—the clients. They appeared reluctant to accept her authority and they would often bypass her in important matters. The problem was exacerbated by Vitam's compliance in her being bypassed. When she asked that the clients be referred back to her, Vitam replied, "Of course that isn't really practical." Vitam made matters worse by patronizing her in front of clients and by referring to her as "my cute assistant" and "our lady banker." Vitam never did this when only Americans were present, and in fact treated her professionally and with respect in internal situations.

Sara finally complained to Vitam that he was undermining her authority and effectiveness; she asked him in as positive a manner as possible to help her. Vitam listened carefully to Sara's complaints, then replied: "I'm glad that you brought this up, because I've been meaning to sit down and talk to you about my little game-playing in front of the clients. Let me be frank with you.

Case study by Thomas Dunfee and Diana Robertson, "Foreign Assignment," the Wharton School of Business, The University of Pennsylvania. Reprinted by permission of the authors.

Our clients think you're great, but they just don't understand a woman in authority, and you and I aren't going to be able to change their attitudes overnight. As long as the clients see you as my assistant and deferring to me, they can do business with you. I'm willing to give you as much responsibility as they can handle your having. I *know* you can handle it. But we just have to tread carefully. You and I know that my remarks in front of clients don't mean anything. They're just a way of playing the game Latin style. I know it's frustrating for you, but I really need you to support me on this. It's not going to affect your promotions, and for the most part you really will have responsibility for these clients' accounts. You just have to act like it's my responsibility." Sara replied that she would try to cooperate, but that basically she found her role demeaning.

As time went on, Sara found that the patronizing actions in front of clients bothered her more and more. She spoke to Vitam again, but he was firm in his position, and urged her to try to be a little more flexible, even a little more "feminine."

Sara also had a problem with Vitam over policy. The Mexico City office had five younger women who worked as receptionists and secretaries. They were all situated at work stations at the entrance to the office. They were required to wear standard uniforms that were colorful and slightly sexy. Sara protested the requirement that uniforms be worn because (1) they were inconsistent to the image of the banking business and (2) they were demeaning to the women who had to wear them. Vitam just curtly replied that he had received a lot of favorable comments about the uniforms from clients of the bank.

Several months later, Sara had what she thought would be a good opportunity to deal with the problem. Tom Fried, an executive vice present who had been a mentor for her since she arrived at the bank, was coming to Mexico City; she arranged a private conference with him. She described her problems and explained that she was not able to be effective in this environment and that she worried that it would have a negative effect on her chance of promotion within the bank. Fried was very careful in his response. He spoke of certain "realities" that the bank had to respect and he urged her to "see it through" even though he could understand how she would feel that things weren't fair.

Sara found herself becoming more aggressive and defensive in her meetings with Vitam and her clients. Several clients asked that other bank personnel handle their transactions. Sara has just received an Average rating, which noted "the beginnings of a negative attitude about the bank and its policies."

• *Case Study* •

Is This the Right Time to Come Out?

ALISTAIR D. WILLIAMSON

George Campbell, assistant vice president in mergers and acquisitions at Kirkham McDowell Securities, a St. Louis underwriting and financial advisory firm, looked up as Adam Lawson, one of his most promising associates, entered his office. Adam, 29 years old, had been with the firm for only two years but had already distinguished himself as having great potential. Recently, he had helped to bring in an extremely lucrative deal, and in six weeks, he and several other associates would be honored for their efforts at the firm's silver anniversary dinner.

As Adam closed the door and sat down, he said, "George, I'd like to talk to you about the banquet. I've thought about this very carefully, and I want you to know that I plan to bring my partner, Robert Collins, as my escort."

George was taken aback. "Well, Adam," he said, "I don't quite know what to say. I have to be honest with you; I'm a little surprised. I had no idea that you were gay. I would never have guessed." He looked at Adam for clues on how to proceed: his subordinate did seem nervous but not defiant or hostile.

Though only a 50-person operation, Kirkham McDowell had long since secured its status as one of the region's leading corporate financial advisers. The firm's client roster included established and successful regional companies as well as one of the country's largest defense contractors, a very conservative company for which the firm managed part of an impressive pension portfolio. Representatives of Kirkham McDowell's major clients and many of the area's most influential political and business leaders were expected to attend the banquet. All this raced through George's mind as he asked Adam, "Why do you want to do this? Why do you want to mix your personal and professional lives?"

"For the same reason that you bring your wife to company social events," Adam replied.

A look of confusion flickered across George's face while Adam continued. "Think about it for a moment, George. Success in this business depends in great part on the relationships you develop with your clients and the people you work with. An important part of those relationships is letting people know about your life away from the office, and that includes the people who are important to you. Some of the other associates already know Robert. Whenever his schedule permits, he accompanies me when I'm invited by one of my colleagues to have dinner with his or her spouse. Granted, that isn't very often—Robert is a corporate attorney, and his work is very demanding—but he joins me whenever he can."

"But, Adam, a wife isn't the same thing as a—"

"It *is* the same thing, George. Robert and I have made a commitment to each other. We have been together for almost five years now, and I would feel very uncomfortable telling him that I was going to a major social event alone—on a weekend, no less."

"Well, I'm sure you'd agree that it wouldn't be appropriate for an associate to bring a date—someone he barely knows—to such an event."

"Come on, George. I think you know me well enough to realize that I have better judgment than that. If Robert and I had known each other for only six months, I wouldn't be having this conversation with you right now. But, as I said, we've been together for over five years!"

George thought for a moment. "Adam," he said slowly, "I'm just not sure you should try to make an issue of this at such an important time for the company. Why bring it up now? Think of our clients. We work with some very conservative companies. They could very well decide to give their business to a firm whose views seem to agree more with their own. You're not just making a personal statement here. You're saying something about the culture at Kirkham McDowell, something that some of our clients might fundamentally oppose. How are they going to react?"

Adam leaned forward. "This is only an issue if people make it an issue," he said. "I have resolved never to lie about myself or about anything that is important to me—and that includes my sexuality. Since I joined the firm, as I've become comfortable sharing details of my personal life with certain colleagues, I've come out to them and often introduced them to Robert. If people ask me if I'm gay, I'm honest with them. Likewise, if people ask me if I have a girlfriend, I tell them about my relationship with Robert. With the silver anniversary celebration coming up, I thought the time was right to speak with you. This is the first large social event the company has held since I started working here. And after a lot of discussion with Robert and some of the associates here, I've decided that I need to be as open at the banquet as I have tried to be in other areas within the organization.

"It's not a decision that I've taken lightly. I've seen what has happened to some of my gay friends who have come out at work. Even at much less conservative companies, some are never invited to important social events with colleagues and customers, no matter how much business they bring in. They'll never know whether or not their bonuses have been affected by prejudice related to their sexuality. I know my career could be adversely influenced by this decision, but I believe that my work should stand on its own merits. George, I've been a top contributor at this firm since I walked in the door. I hope I can rely on you to back me up on this."

Adam stood up but waited for George to reply. "You've given me a lot to think about," George said. "And I don't want to say anything until I've had a chance to consider all the implications. I appreciate the confidence you've shown in me by being so open. I wish I had something conclusive to say at this point, but the fact of the matter is that I have never had to face this issue before. I am one of your biggest supporters here at the firm. Your work has been exemplary. And, until today, I would have said that you could look forward to a very successful career here. But I'm concerned about how this will play with our clients and, as a result, about how senior management will react. I personally don't have any problems with your being gay, but I'd hate to see you torpedo your career over this. It's possible that this could jeopardize some of our relationships with significant clients. Let me think about it for a few days. We can have lunch next week and map out a strategy."

After Adam left his office, George sat in silence for a few minutes, trying to make sense of the conversation. He was unsure of his next move. Adam clearly had *not* come into his office looking for permission to bring his lover to the banquet. George realized that he could do nothing and let events simply unfold. After all, Adam had not asked that Robert be included in his benefits coverage nor had he requested a specific managerial decision. There was no company policy on paper to guide him through his dilemma. But Adam wouldn't have come to him if he hadn't wanted a response of some kind. And shouldn't he at least tell his superior in order to head off any awkward moments at the banquet?

Just how negative an effect could Robert have on Adam's career with the firm and on the firm's relationship with its clients? Wasn't it possible, even likely, that the party would come off without incident? That the issue would blow over? That even the firm's most conservative clients wouldn't realize the significance of Adam's guest or would simply decide that it was a personal issue, not a business one? Or would George's worst fears be realized? Adam had to recognize that the potential risks were great. It was one thing for him to come out of the closet at the office. But wasn't he pushing things too far?

Management Women and the New Facts of Life

Felice N. Schwartz

The cost of employing women in management is greater than the cost of employing men. This is a jarring statement, partly because it is true, but mostly because it is something people are reluctant to talk about. A new study by one multinational corporation shows that the rate of turnover in management positions is 2½ times higher among top-performing women than it is among men. A large producer of consumer goods reports that one half of the women who take maternity leave return to their jobs late or not at all. And we know that women also have a greater tendency to plateau or to interrupt their careers in ways that limit their growth and development. But we have become so sensitive to charges of sexism and so afraid of confrontation, even litigation, that we rarely say what we know to be true. Unfortunately, our bottled-up awareness leaks out in misleading metaphors ("glass ceiling" is one notable example), veiled hostility, lowered expectations, distrust, and reluctant adherence to Equal Employment Opportunity requirements.

Career interruptions, plateauing, and turnover are expensive. The money corporations invest in recruitment, training, and development is less likely to produce top executives among women than among men, and the invaluable company experience that developing executives acquire at every level as they move up through management ranks is more often lost.

The studies just mentioned are only the first of many, I'm quite sure. Demographic realities are going to force corporations all across the country to analyze the cost of employing women in managerial positions, and what they will discover is that women cost more.

But here is another startling truth: The greater cost of employing women is not a function of inescapable gender differences. Women *are* different from men, but what increases their cost to the corporation is principally the clash of their perceptions, attitudes, and behavior with those of men, which is to say, with the policies and practices of male-led corporations.

It is terribly important that employers draw the right conclusions from the studies now being done. The studies will be useless—or worse, harmful—if all they teach us is that women are expensive to employ. What we need to learn is how to reduce that expense, how to stop throwing away the investments we make in talented women, how to become more responsive to the needs of the women that corporations *must* employ if they are to have the best and the brightest of all those now entering the work force.

The gender differences relevant to business fall into two categories: those related to maternity and those related to the differing traditions and expectations of the sexes. Maternity is biological rather than cultural. We can't alter it, but we can dramatically reduce its impact on the workplace and in many cases eliminate its negative effect on employee development. We can accomplish this by addressing the second set of differences, those between male and female socialization. Today, these differences exaggerate the real costs of maternity and can turn a relatively slight disruption in work schedule into a serious business problem and a career derailment for individual women. If we are to overcome the cost differential between male and female employees, we need to address the issues that arise when female socialization meets the male corporate culture and masculine rules of career development—issues of behavior and style, of expectation, of stereotypes and preconceptions, of sexual tension and harassment, of female mentoring, lateral mobility, relocation, compensation, and early identification of top performers.

• • •

The one immutable, enduring difference between men and women is maternity. Maternity is not simply childbirth but a continuum that begins with an awareness of the ticking of the biological clock, proceeds to the anticipation of motherhood, includes pregnancy, childbirth, physical recuperation, psychological adjustment, and continues on to nursing, bonding, and child rearing. Not all women choose to become mothers, of course, and among those who do, the process varies from case to case depending on the health of the mother and baby, the values of the parents, and the availability, cost, and quality of child care.

In past centuries, the biological fact of maternity shaped the traditional roles of the sexes. Women performed the home-centered functions that related to the bearing and nurturing of children. Men did the work that required great physical strength. Over time, however, family size contracted, the community assumed greater responsibility for the care and education of children, packaged foods and household technology reduced the work load in the home, and technology eliminated much of the need for muscle power at the workplace. Today, in the developed world, the only role still uniquely gender related is childbearing. Yet men and women are still socialized to perform their traditional roles.

Men and women may or may not have some innate psychological disposition toward these traditional roles—men to be aggressive, competitive, self-reliant, risk taking; women to be supportive, nurturing, intuitive, sensitive, communicative—but certainly both men and women are capable of the full range of behavior. Indeed, the male and female roles have already begun to expand and merge. In the decades ahead, as the socialization of boys and girls and the experience and expectations of young men and women grow steadily more androgynous, the differences in workplace behavior will continue to fade. At the moment, however, we are still plagued by disparities in perception and behavior that make the integration of men and women in the workplace unnecessarily difficult and expensive.

Let me illustrate with a few broadbrush generalizations. Of course, these are only stereotypes, but I think they help to exemplify the kinds of preconceptions that can muddy the corporate waters.

Men continue to perceive women as the rearers of their children, so they find it understandable, indeed appropriate, that women should renounce their careers to raise families. Edmund Pratt, CEO of Pfizer, once asked me in all sincerity, "Why would any woman choose to be a chief financial officer rather than a full-time mother?" By condoning and taking pleasure in women's traditional behavior, men reinforce it. Not only do they see parenting as fundamentally female, they see a career as fundamentally male—either an unbroken series of promotions and advancements toward CEOdom or stagnation and disappointment. This attitude serves to legitimize a woman's choice to extend maternity leave and even, for those who can afford it, to leave employment altogether for several years. By the same token, men who might want to take a leave after the birth of a child know that management will see such behavior as a lack of career commitment, even when company policy permits parental leave for men.

Women also bring counterproductive expectations and perceptions to the workplace. Ironically, although the feminist movement was an expression of women's quest for freedom from their home-based lives, most women were remarkably free already. They had many responsibilities, but they were autonomous and could be entrepreneurial in how and when they carried them out. And once their children grew up and left home, they were essentially free to do what they wanted with their lives. Women's traditional role also included freedom from responsibility for the financial support of their families. Many of us were socialized from girlhood to expect our husbands to take care of us, while our brothers were socialized from an equally early age to complete their educations, pursue careers, climb the ladder of success, and provide dependable financial support for their families. To the extent that this tradition of freedom lingers subliminally, women tend to bring to their employment a sense that they can choose to change jobs or careers at will, take time off, or reduce their hours.

Finally, women's traditional role encouraged particular attention to the quality and substance of what they did, specifically to the physical, psychological, and intellectual development of their children. This traditional focus may explain women's continuing tendency to search for more than monetary reward—intrinsic significance, social importance, meaning—in what they do. This too makes them more likely than men to leave the corporation in search of other values.

The misleading metaphor of the glass ceiling suggests an invisible barrier constructed by corporate leaders to impede the upward mobility of women beyond the middle levels. A more appropriate metaphor, I believe, is the kind of cross-sectional diagram used in geology. The barriers to women's leadership occur when potentially counterproductive layers of influence on women—maternity, tradition, socialization—meet management strata pervaded by the largely unconscious preconceptions, stereotypes, and expectations of men. Such interfaces do not exist for men and tend to be impermeable for women.

One result of these gender differences has been to convince some executives that women are simply not suited to top management. Other executives feel helpless. If they see even a few of their valued female employees fail to return to work from maternity leave on schedule or see one of their most promising women plateau in her career after the birth of a child, they begin to fear there is nothing they can do to infuse women with new energy and enthusiasm and persuade them to stay. At the same time, they know there is nothing they can do to stem the tide of women into management ranks.

Another result is to place every working woman on a continuum that runs from total dedication to career at one end to a balance between career and family at the other. What women discover is that the male corporate culture sees both extremes as unacceptable. Women who want the flexibility to balance their families and their careers are not adequately committed to the organization. Women who perform as aggressively and competitively as men are abrasive and unfeminine. But the fact is, business needs all the talented women it can get. Moreover, as I will explain, the women I call career-primary and those I call career-and-family each have particular value to the corporation.

• • •

Women in the corporation are about to move from a buyer's to a seller's market. The sudden, startling recognition that 80% of new entrants in the work force over the next decade will be women, minorities, and immigrants has stimulated a mushrooming incentive to "value diversity."

Women are no longer simply an enticing pool of occasional creative talent, a thorn in the side of the EEO officer, or a source of frustration to corporate leaders truly puzzled by the slowness of their upward trickle into executive positions. A real demographic change is taking place. The era of sudden population growth of the 1950s and 1960s is over. The birth rate has dropped about 40%, from a high of 25.3 live births per 1,000 population in 1957, at the peak of the baby boom, to a stable low of a little more than 15 per 1,000 over the last 16 years, and there is no indication of a return to a higher rate. The tidal wave of baby boomers that swelled the recruitment pool to overflowing seems to have been a one-time phenomenon. For 20 years, employers had the pick of a very large crop and were able to choose males almost exclusively for the executive track. But if future population remains fairly stable while the economy continues to expand, and if the new information society simultaneously creates a greater need for creative, educated managers, then the gap between supply and demand will grow dramatically and, with it, the competition for managerial talent.

The decrease in numbers has even greater implications if we look at the traditional source of corporate recruitment for leadership positions—white males from the top 10% of the country's best universities. Over the past decade, the increase in the number of women graduating from leading universities has been much greater than the increase in the total number of graduates, and these women are well represented in the top 10% of their classes.

The trend extends into business and professional programs as well. In the old days, virtually all MBAs were male. I remember addressing a meeting at the Harvard Business School as recently as the mid-1970s and looking out at a sea of exclusively male faces. Today, about 25% of that audience would be women. The pool of male MBAs from which corporations have traditionally drawn their leadership has shrunk significantly.

Of course, this reduction does not have to mean a shortage of talent. The top 10% is at least as smart as it always was—smarter, probably, since it's now drawn from a broader segment of the population. But it now consists increasingly of women. Companies that are determined to recruit the same number of men as before will have to dig much deeper into the male pool, while their competitors will have the opportunity to pick the best people from both the male and female graduates.

• • •

Under these circumstances, there is no question that the management ranks of business will include increasing numbers of women. There remains, however, the question of how these women will succeed—how long they will stay, how high they will climb, how completely they will fulfill their promise and potential, and what kind of return the corporation will realize on its investment in their training and development.

There is ample business reason for finding ways to make sure that as many of these women as possible will succeed. The first step in this process is to recognize that women are not all alike. Like men, they are individuals with differing talents, priorities, and motivations. For the sake of simplicity, let me focus on the two women I referred to earlier, on what I call the career-primary woman and the career-and-family woman.

Like many men, some women put their careers first. They are ready to make the same trade-offs traditionally made by the men who seek leadership positions. They make a career decision to put in extra hours, to make sacrifices in their personal lives, to make the most of every opportunity for professional development. For women, of course, this decision also requires that they remain single or at least childless or, if they do have children, that they be satisfied to have others raise them. Some 90% of executive men but only 35% of executive women have children by the age of 40. The *automatic* association of all women with babies is clearly unjustified.

The secret to dealing with such women is to recognize them early, accept them, and clear artificial barriers from their path to the top. After all, the best of these women are among the best managerial talent you will ever see. And career-primary women have another important value to the company that men and other women lack. They can act as role models and mentors to younger women who put their careers first. Since upwardly mobile career-primary women still have few role models to motivate and inspire them, a company with women in its top echelon has a significant advantage in the competition for executive talent.

Men at the top of the organization—most of them over 55, with wives who tend to be traditional—often find career women "masculine" and difficult to accept as colleagues. Such men miss the point, which is not that these women are just like men but that they are just like the *best* men in the organization. And there is such a shortage of the best people that gender cannot be allowed to matter. It is clearly counterproductive to disparage in a woman with executive talent the very qualities that are most critical to the business and that might carry a man to the CEO's office.

Clearing a path to the top for career-primary women has four requirements:

1. Identify them early.
2. Give them the same opportunity you give to talented men to grow and develop and contribute to company profitability. Give them client and customer responsibility. Expect them to travel and relocate, to make the same commitment to the company as men aspiring to leadership positions.
3. Accept them as valued members of your management team. Include them in every kind of communication. Listen to them.
4. Recognize that the business environment is more difficult and stressful for them than for their male peers. They are always a minority, often the only woman. The male perception of talented, ambitious women is at best ambivalent, a mixture of admiration, resentment, confusion, competitiveness, attraction, skepticism, anxiety, pride, and animosity. Women can never feel secure about how they should dress and act, whether they should speak out or grin and bear it when they encounter discrimination, stereotyping, sexual harassment, and paternalism. Social interaction and travel with male colleagues and with male clients can be charged. As they move up, the normal increase in pressure and responsibility is compounded for women because they are women.

Stereotypical language and sexist day-to-day behavior do take their toll on women's career development. Few male executives realize how common it is to call women by their first names while men in the same group are greeted with surnames, how frequently female executives are assumed by men to be secretaries, how often women are excluded from all-male social events where business is being transacted. With notable exceptions, men are still generally more comfortable with other men, and as a result women miss many of the career and business opportunities that arise over lunch, on the golf course, or in the locker room.

• • •

The majority of women, however, are what I call career-and-family women, women who want to pursue serious careers while participating actively in the rearing of children. These women are a precious resource that has yet to be mined. Many of them are talented and creative. Most of them are willing to trade some career growth and compensation for freedom from the constant pressure to work long hours and weekends.

Most companies today are ambivalent at best about the career-and-family women in their management ranks. They would prefer that all employees were willing to give their all to the company. They believe it is in their best interests for all managers to compete for the top positions so the company will have the largest possible pool from which to draw its leaders.

"If you have both talent and motivation," many employers seem to say, "we want to move you up. If you haven't got that motivation, if you want less pressure and greater flexibility, then you can leave and make room for a new generation." These companies lose on two counts. First, they fail to amortize the investment they made in the early training and experience of management women who find themselves committed to family as well as to career. Second, they fail to recognize what these women could do for their middle management.

The ranks of middle managers are filled with people on their way up and people who have stalled. Many of them have simply reached their limits, achieved career growth commensurate with or exceeding their capabilities, and they cause problems because their performance is mediocre but they still want to move ahead. The career-and-family woman is willing to trade off the pressures and demands that go with promotion for the freedom to spend more time with her children. She's very smart, she's talented, she's committed to her career, and she's satisfied to stay at the middle level, at least during the early child-rearing years. Compare her with some of the people you have there now.

Consider a typical example, a woman who decides in college on a business career and enters management at age 22. For nine years, the company invests in her career as she gains experience and skills and steadily improves her performance. But at 31, just as the investment begins to pay off in earnest, she decides to have a baby. Can the company afford to let her go home, take another job, or go into business for herself? The common perception now is yes, the corporation can afford to lose her unless, after six or eight weeks or even three months of disability and maternity leave, she returns to work on a full-time schedule with the same vigor, commitment, and ambition that she showed before.

But what if she doesn't? What if she wants or needs to go on leave for six months or a year or, heaven forbid, five years? In this worst-case scenario, she works full-time from age 22 to 31 and from 36 to 65—a total of 38 years as opposed to the typical male's 43 years. That's not a huge difference. Moreover, my typical example is willing to work part-time while her children are young, if only her employer will give her the opportunity. There are two rewards for companies responsive to this need: higher retention of their best people and greatly improved performance and satisfaction in their middle management.

The high-performing career-and-family woman can be a major player in your company. She can give you a significant business advantage as the competition for able people escalates. Sometimes too, if you can hold on to her, she will switch gears in mid-life and reenter the competition for the top. The price you must pay to retain these women is threefold: you must plan for and manage maternity, you must provide the flexibility that will allow them to be maximally productive, and you must take an active role in helping to make family supports and high-quality, affordable child care available to all women.

• • •

The key to managing maternity is to recognize the value of high-performing women and the urgent need to retain them and keep them productive. The first step must be a genuine partnership between the woman and her boss. I know this partnership can seem difficult to forge. One of my own senior executives came to me recently to discuss plans for her maternity leave and subsequent return to work. She knew she wanted to come back. I wanted to make certain that she would. Still, we had a somewhat awkward conversation, because I knew that no woman can predict with certainty when she will be able to return to work or under what conditions. Physical problems can lengthen her leave. So can a demanding infant, a difficult family or personal adjustment, or problems with child care.

I still don't know when this valuable executive will be back on the job full-time, and her absence creates some genuine problems for our organization. But I do know that I can't simply replace her years of experience with a new recruit. Since our conversation, I also know that she wants to come back, and that she *will* come back—part-time at first—unless I make it impossible for her by, for example, setting an arbitrary date for her full-time return or resignation. In turn, she knows that the organization wants and needs her and, more to the point, that it will be responsive to her needs in terms of working hours and child-care arrangements.

In having this kind of conversation it's important to ask concrete questions that will help to move the discussion from uncertainty and anxiety to some level of predictability. Questions can touch on everything from family income and energy level to child care arrangements and career commitment. Of course you want your star manager to return to work as soon as possible, but you want her to return permanently and productively. Her downtime on the job is a drain on her energies and a waste of your money.

• • •

For all the women who want to combine career and family—the women who want to participate actively in the rearing of their children and who also want to pursue their careers seriously—the key to retention is to provide the flexibility and family supports they need in order to function effectively.

Time spent in the office increases productivity if it is time well spent, but the fact that most women continue to take the primary responsibility for child care is a cause of distraction, diversion, anxiety, and absenteeism—to say nothing of the persistent guilt experienced by all working mothers. A great many women, perhaps most of all women who have always performed at the highest levels, are also frustrated by a sense that while their children are babies they cannot function at their best either at home or at work.

In its simplest form, flexibility is the freedom to take time off—a couple of hours, a day, a week—or to do some work at home and some at the office, an arrangement that communication technology makes increasingly feasible. At the complex end of the spectrum are alternative work schedules that permit the woman to work less than full-time and her employer to reap the benefits of her experience and, with careful planning, the top level of her abilities.

Part-time employment is the single greatest inducement to getting women back on the job expeditiously and the provision women themselves most desire. A part-time return to work enables them to maintain responsibility for critical aspects of their jobs, keeps them in touch with the changes constantly occurring at the workplace and in the job itself, reduces stress and fatigue, often eliminates the need for paid maternity leave by permitting a return to the office as soon as disability leave is over, and, not least, can greatly enhance company loyalty. The part-time solution works particularly well when a work load can be reduced for one individual in a department or when a full-time job can be broken down by skill levels and apportioned to two individuals at different levels of skill and pay.

I believe, however, that shared employment is the most promising and will be the most widespread form of flexible scheduling in the future. It is feasible at every level of the corporation except at the pinnacle, for both the short and the long term. It involves two people taking responsibility for one job.

Two red lights flash on as soon as most executives hear the words "job sharing": continuity and client-customer contact. The answer to the continuity question is to place responsibility entirely on the two individuals sharing the job to discuss everything that transpires—thoroughly, daily, and on their own time. The answer to the problem of client-customer contact is yes, job sharing requires reeducation and a period of adjustment. But as both client and supervisor will quickly come to appreciate, two contacts means that the customer has continuous access to the company's representative, without interruptions for vacation, travel, or sick leave. The two people holding the job can simply cover for each other, and the uninterrupted, full-time coverage they provide together can be a stipulation of their arrangement.

Flexibility is costly in numerous ways. It requires more supervisory time to coordinate and manage, more office space, and somewhat greater benefits costs (though these can be contained with flexible benefits plans, prorated benefits, and, in two-paycheck families, elimination of duplicate benefits). But the advantages of reduced turnover and the greater productivity that results from higher energy levels and greater focus can outweigh the costs.

A few hints:

- Provide flexibility selectively. I'm not suggesting private arrangements subject to the suspicion of favoritism but rather a policy that makes flexible work schedules available only to high performers.
- Make it clear that in most instances (but not all) the rates of advancement and pay will be appropriately lower for those who take time off or who work part-time than for those who work full-time. Most career-and-family women are entirely willing to make that trade-off.
- Discuss costs as well as benefits. Be willing to risk accusations of bias. Insist, for example, that half time is half of whatever time it takes to do the job, not merely half of 35 or 40 hours.

The woman who is eager to get home to her child has a powerful incentive to use her time effectively at the office and to carry with her reading and other work that can be done at home. The talented professional who wants to have it all can be a high performer by carefully ordering her priorities and by focusing on objectives rather than on the legendary 15-hour day. By the time professional women have their first babies—at an average age of 31—they have already had nine years to work long hours at a desk, to travel, and to relocate. In the case of high performers, the need for flexibility coincides with what has gradually become the goal-oriented nature of responsibility.

• • •

Family supports—in addition to maternity leave and flexibility—include the provision of parental leave for men, support for two-career and single-parent families during relocation, and flexible benefits. But the primary ingredient is child care. The capacity of working mothers to function effectively and without interruption depends on the availability of good, affordable child care. Now that women make up almost half the work force and the growing percentage of managers, the decision to become involved in the personal lives of employees is no longer a philosophical question but a practical one. To make matters worse, the quality of child care has almost no relation to technology, inventiveness, or profitability but is more or less a pure function of the quality of child care personnel and the ratio of adults to children. These costs are irreducible. Only by joining hands with government and the public sector can corporations hope to create the vast quantity and variety of child care that their employees need.

Until quite recently, the response of corporations to women has been largely symbolic and cosmetic, motivated in large part by the will to avoid litigation and legal penalties. In some cases, companies were also moved by a genuine sense of fairness and a vague discomfort and frustration at the absence of women above the middle of the corporate pyramid. The actions they took were mostly quick, easy, and highly visible—child care information services, a three-month parental leave available to men as well as women, a woman appointed to the board of directors.

When I first began to discuss these issues 26 years ago, I was sometimes able to get an appointment with the assistant to the assistant in personnel, but it was only a courtesy. Over the past decade, I have met with the CEOs of many large corporations, and I've watched them become involved with ideas they had never previously thought much about. Until recently, however, the shelf life of that enhanced awareness was always short. Given pressing, short-term concerns, women were not a front-burner issue. In the past few months, I have seen yet another change. Some CEOs and top management groups now take the initiative. They call and ask us to show them how to shift gears from a responsive to a proactive approach to recruiting, developing, and retaining women.

I think this change is more probably a response to business needs—to concern for the quality of future profits and managerial talent—than to uneasiness about legal requirements, sympathy with the demands of women and minorities, or the desire to do what is right and fair. The nature of such business motivation varies. Some companies want to move women to higher positions as role models for those below them and as beacons for talented young recruits. Some want to achieve a favorable image with employees, customers, clients, and stockholders. These are all legitimate motives. But I think the companies that stand to gain most are motivated as well by a desire to capture competitive advantage in an era when talent and competence will be in increasingly short supply. These companies are now ready to stop being defensive about their experience with women and to ask incisive questions without preconceptions.

Even so, incredibly, I don't know of more than one or two companies that have looked into their own records to study the absolutely critical issue of maternity leave—how many women took it, when and whether they returned, and how this behavior correlated with their rank, tenure, age, and performance. The unique drawback to the employment of women is the physical reality of maternity and the particular socializing influence maternity has had. Yet to make women equal to men in the workplace we have chosen on the whole not to discuss this single most significant difference between them. Unless we do, we cannot evaluate the cost of recruiting, developing, and moving women up.

Now that interest is replacing indifference, there are four steps every company can take to examine its own experience with women:

1. Gather quantitative data on the company's experience with management-level women regarding turnover rates, occurrence of and return from maternity leave, and organizational level attained in relation to tenure and performance.
2. Correlate this data with factors such as age, marital status, and presence and age of children, and attempt to identify and analyze why women respond the way they do.
3. Gather qualitative data on the experience of women in your company and on how women are perceived by both sexes.
4. Conduct a cost-benefit analysis of the return on your investment in high-performing women. Factor in the cost to the company of women's negative reactions to negative experience, as well as the probable cost of corrective measures and policies. If women's value to your company is greater than the cost to recruit, train, and develop them—and of course I believe it will be—then you will want to do everything you can to retain them.

• • •

We have come a tremendous distance since the days when the prevailing male wisdom saw women as lacking the kind of intelligence that would allow them to succeed in business. For decades, even women themselves have harbored an unspoken belief that they couldn't make it because they couldn't be just like men, and nothing else would do. But now that women have shown themselves the equal of men in every area of organizational activity, now that they have demonstrated that they can be stars in every field of endeavor, now we can all venture to examine the fact that women and men are different.

On balance, employing women is more costly than employing men. Women can acknowledge this fact today because they know that their value to employers exceeds the additional cost and because they know that changing attitudes can reduce the additional cost dramatically. Women in management are no longer an idiosyncrasy of the arts and education. They have always matched men in natural ability. Within a very few years, they will equal men in numbers as well in every area of economic activity.

The demographic motivation to recruit and develop women is compelling. But an older question remains: Is society better for the change?

Women's exit from the home and entry into the work force has certainly creat-ed problems—an urgent need for good, affordable child care; troubling ques-tions about the kind of parenting children need; the costs and difficulties of diversity in the workplace; the stress and fatigue of combining work and family responsibilities. Wouldn't we all be happier if we could turn back the clock to an age when men were in the workplace and women in the home, when male and female roles were clearly differentiated and complementary?

Nostalgia, anxiety, and discouragement will urge many to say yes, but my answer is emphatically no. Two fundamental benefits that were unattainable in the past are now within our reach. For the individual, freedom of choice—in this case the freedom to choose career, family, or a combination of the two. For the corporation, access to the most gifted individuals in the country. These benefits are neither self-indulgent nor insubstantial. Freedom of choice and self-realization are too deeply American to be cast aside for some wistful vision of the past. And access to our most talented human resources is not a luxury in this age of explosive international competition but rather the barest minimum that prudence and national self-preservation require.

White Privilege and Male Privilege: A Personal Account of Coming to See Correspondences Through Work in Women's Studies[1]

Peggy McIntosh

Through work to bring materials and perspectives from Women's Studies into the rest of the curriculum, I have often noticed men's unwillingness to grant that they are over-privileged in the curriculum, even though they may grant that women are disadvantaged. Denials which amount to taboos surround the subject of advantages which men gain from women's disadvantages. These de-nials protect male privilege from being fully recognized, acknowledged, less-ened, or ended.

Thinking through unacknowledged male privilege as a phenomenon with a life of its own, I realized that since hierarchies in our society are interlocking, there was most likely a phenomenon of white privilege which was similarly de-nied and protected but alive and real in its effects. As a white person, I realized I had been taught about racism as something which puts others at a disadvan-tage, but had been taught not to see one of its corollary aspects, white privi-lege, which puts me at an advantage.

I think whites are carefully taught not to recognize white privilege, as males are taught not to recognize male privilege. So I have begun in an untutored way to ask what it is like to have white privilege. This paper is a partial record of my personal observations, and not a scholarly analysis. It is based on my daily experiences within my particular circumstances.

I have come to see white privilege as an invisible package of unearned assets which I can count on cashing in each day, but about which I was "meant" to remain oblivious. White privilege is like an invisible weightless knapsack of special provisions, assurances, tools, maps, guides, codebooks, passports, visas, clothes, compass, emergency gear, and blank checks.

Since I have had trouble facing white privilege and describing its results in my life, I saw parallels here with men's reluctance to acknowledge male privilege. Only rarely will a man go beyond acknowledging that women are disadvantaged to acknowledging that men have unearned advantage, or that unearned privilege has not been good for men's development as human beings, or for society's development, or that privilege systems might ever be challenged and *changed.*

I will review here several types or layers of denial which I see at work protecting, and preventing awareness about, entrenched male privilege. Then I will draw parallels, from my own experience, with the denials which veil the facts of white privilege. Finally, I will list 46 ordinary and daily ways in which I experience white privilege within my life and its particular social and political frameworks.

Writing this paper has been difficult, despite warm receptions for the talks on which it is based.[2] For describing white privilege makes one newly accountable. As we in Women's Studies work reveal male privilege and ask men to give up some of their power, so one who writes about having white privilege must ask, "Having described it, what will I do to lessen or end it?"

The denial of men's overprivileged status takes many forms in discussions of curriculum change work. Some claim that men must be central in the curriculum because they have done most of what is important or distinctive in life or in civilization. Some recognize sexism in the curriculum but deny that it makes male students seem unduly important in life. Others agree that certain *individual* thinkers are blindly male-oriented but deny that there is any systemic tendency in disciplinary frameworks or epistemology to overempower men as a group. Those men who do grant that male privilege takes institutionalized and embedded forms are still likely to deny that male hegemony has opened doors for them personally. Virtually all men deny that male overreward alone can explain men's centrality in all the inner sanctums of our most powerful institutions. Moreover, those few who will acknowledge that male privilege systems have overempowered them usually end up doubting that these privilege systems could ever be dismantled. They may say they will work to improve women's status in society or in the university, but they can't or won't support the idea of lessening men's. In curricular terms, this is the point at which men say that they regret they cannot use any of the interesting new scholarship on women because the syllabus is full. When the talk turns to giving men less cultural room, even the most thoughtful and fair-minded of the men I know well tend to reflect or fall back on conservative assumptions about the inevitability of present gender relations and distributions of power, calling on precedent or sociobiology and psychobiology to demonstrate that male domination is natural and follows inevitably from evolutionary pressures. Others resort to arguments from "experience," religion, social responsibility or wishing and dreaming.

After I realized, through faculty development work in Women's Studies, the extent to which men work from a base of unacknowledged privilege, I understood that much of their oppressiveness was unconscious. Then I remembered the frequent charges from women of color that white women whom they encounter are oppressive. I began to understand why we are justly seen as oppressive, even when we don't see ourselves that way. At the very least, obliviousness of one's privileged state can make a person or group irritating to be with. I began to count the ways in which I enjoy unearned skin privilege and have been conditioned into oblivion about its existence, unable to see that it put me "ahead" in any way, or put my people ahead, overrewarding us and yet also paradoxically damaging us, or that it could or should be changed.

My schooling gave me no training in seeing myself as an oppressor, as an unfairly advantaged person, or as a participant in a damaged culture. I was taught to see myself as an individual whose moral state depended on her individual moral will. At school, we were not taught about slavery in any depth; we were not taught to see slaveholders as damaged people. Slaves were seen as the only group at risk of being dehumanized. My schooling followed the pattern which Elizabeth Minnich has pointed out: whites are taught to think of their lives as morally neutral, normative, and average, and also ideal, so that when we work to benefit others, this is seen as work which will allow "them" to be more like "us." I think many of us know how obnoxious this attitude can be in men.

After frustration with men who would not recognize male privilege, I decided to try to work on myself at least by identifying some of the daily effects of white privilege in my life. It is crude work, at this stage, but I will give here a list of special circumstances and conditions I experience which I did not earn but which I have been made to feel are mine by birth, by citizenship, and by virtue of being a conscientious law-abiding "normal" person of good will. I have chosen those conditions which I think in my case *attach somewhat more to skin-color privilege* than to class, religion, ethnic status, or geographical location, though of course all these other factors are intricately intertwined. As far as I can see, my African-American co-workers, friends, and acquaintances with whom I come into daily or frequent contact in this particular time, place, and line of work cannot count on most of these conditions.

1. I can if I wish arrange to be in the company of people of my race most of the time.
2. I can avoid spending time with people whom I was trained to mistrust and who have learned to mistrust my kind or me.
3. If I should need to move, I can be pretty sure of renting or purchasing housing in an area which I can afford and in which I would want to live.
4. I can be pretty sure that my neighbors in such a location will be neutral or pleasant to me.
5. I can go shopping alone most of the time, pretty well assured that I will not be followed or harassed.
6. I can turn on the television or open to the front page of the newspaper and see people of my race widely represented.
7. When I am told about our national heritage or about "civilization," I am shown that people of my color made it what it is.

8. I can be sure that my children will be given curricular materials that testify to the existence of their race.

9. If I want to, I can be pretty sure of finding a publisher for this piece on white privilege.

10. I can be pretty sure of having my voice heard in a group in which I am the only member of my race.

11. I can be casual about whether or not to listen to another woman's voice in a group in which she is the only member of her race.

12. I can go into a music shop and count on finding the music of my race represented, into a supermarket and find the staple foods which fit with my cultural traditions, or into a hairdresser's shop and find someone who can cut my hair.

13. Whether I use checks, credit cards, or cash, I can count on my skin color not to work against the appearance of financial reliability.

14. I can arrange to protect my children most of the time from people who might not like them.

15. I do not have to educate my children to be aware of systemic racism for their own daily physical protection.

16. I can be pretty sure that my children's teachers and employers will tolerate them if they fit school and workplace norms; my chief worries about them do not concern others' attitudes toward their race.

17. I can talk with my mouth full and not have people put this down to my color.

18. I can swear, dress in second-hand clothes, or not answer letters without having people attribute these choices to the bad morals, poverty, or the illiteracy of my race.

19. I can speak in public to a powerful male group without putting my race on trial.

20. I can do well in a challenging situation without being called a credit to my race.

21. I am never asked to speak for all the people of my racial group.

22. I can remain oblivious of the language and customs of persons of color who constitute the world's majority without feeling in my culture any penalty for such oblivion.

23. I can criticize our government and talk about how much I fear its policies and behavior without being seen as a cultural outsider.

24. I can be pretty sure that if I ask to talk to "the person in charge," I will be facing a person of my race.

25. If a traffic cop pulls me over or if the IRS audits my tax return, I can be sure I haven't been singled out because of my race.

26. I can easily buy posters, post-cards, picture books, greeting cards, dolls, toys, and children's magazines featuring people of my race.

27. I can go home from most meetings of organizations I belong to feeling somewhat tied in, rather than isolated, out-of-place, outnumbered, unheard, held at a distance, or feared.

28. I can be pretty sure that an argument with a colleague of another race is more likely to jeopardize her chances for advancement than to jeopardize mine.

29. I can be pretty sure that if I argue for the promotion of a person of another race, or a program centering on race, this is not likely to cost me heavily within my present setting, even if my colleagues disagree with me.

30. If I declare there is a racial issue at hand, or there isn't a racial issue at hand, my race will lend me more credibility for either position than a person of color will have.

31. I can choose to ignore developments in minority writing and minority activist programs, or disparage them, or learn from them, but in any case, I can find ways to be more or less protected from negative consequences of any of these choices.

32. My culture gives me little fear about ignoring the perspectives and powers of peoples of other races.

33. I am not made acutely aware that my shape, bearing, or body odor will be taken as a reflection on my race.

34. I can worry about racism without being seen as self-interested or self-seeking.

35. I can take a job with an affirmative action employer without having my co-workers on the job suspect that I got it because of my race.

36. If my day, week, or year is going badly, I need not ask of each negative episode or situation whether it has racial overtones.

37. I can be pretty sure of finding people who would be willing to talk with me and advise me about my next steps, professionally.

38. I can think over many options, social, political, imaginative, or professional, without asking whether a person of my race would be accepted or allowed to do what I want to do.

39. I can be late to a meeting without having the lateness reflect on my race.

40. I can choose public accommodation without fearing that people of my race cannot get in or will be mistreated in the places I have chosen.

41. I can be sure that if I need legal or medical help, my race will not work against me.

42. I can arrange my activities so that I will never have to experience feelings of rejection owing to my race.

43. If I have low credibility as a leader, I can be sure that my race is not the problem.

44. I can easily find academic courses and institutions which give attention only to people of my race.

45. I can expect figurative language and imagery in all of the arts to testify to experiences of my race.

46. I can choose blemish cover or bandages in "flesh" color and have them more or less match my skin.

   I repeatedly forgot each of the realizations on this list until I wrote it down. For me, white privilege has turned out to be an elusive and fugitive subject. The pressure to avoid it is great, for in facing it I must give up the myth of meritocracy. If these things are true, this is not such a free country; one's life is not what one makes it; many doors open for certain people through no virtues of their own. These perceptions mean also that my moral condition is not what I had been led to believe. The appearance of being a good citizen rather than a troublemaker comes in large part from having all sorts of doors open automatically because of my color.

   A further paralysis of nerve comes from literary silence protecting privilege. My clearest memories of finding such analysis are in Lillian Smith's unparalleled *Killers of the Dream* and Margaret Andersen's review of Karen and Mamie Fields' *Lemon Swamp*. Smith, for example, wrote about walking toward black children on the street and knowing they would step into the gutter; Andersen contrasted the pleasure which she, as a white child, took on summer driving trips to the south with Karen Fields' memories of driving in a closed car stocked with all necessities lest, in stopping, her black family should suffer "insult, or worse." Adrienne Rich also recognizes and writes about daily experiences of privilege, but in my observation, white women's writing in this area is far more often on systemic racism than on our daily lives as light-skinned women.[3]

In unpacking this invisible knapsack of white privilege, I have listed conditions of daily experience which I once took for granted as neutral, normal, and universally available to everybody, just as I once thought of a male-focused curriculum as the neutral or accurate account which can speak for all. Nor did I think of any of these perquisites as bad for the holder. I now think that we need a more finely differentiated taxonomy of privilege, for some of these varieties are only what one would want for everyone in a just society, and others give license to be ignorant, oblivious, arrogant and destructive. Before proposing some more finely tuned categorization, I will make some observations about the general effects of these conditions on my life and expectations.

In this potpourri of examples, some privileges make me feel at home in the world. Others allow me to escape penalties or dangers which others suffer. Through some, I escape fear, anxiety, or a sense of not being welcome or not being real. Some keep me from having to hide, to be in disguise, to feel sick or crazy, to negotiate each transaction from the position of being an outsider or, within my group, a person who is suspected of having too close links with a dominant culture. Most keep me from having to be angry.

I see a pattern running through the matrix of white privilege, a pattern of assumptions which were passed on to me as a white person. There was one main piece of cultural turf; it was my own turf, and I was among those who could control the turf. I could measure up to the cultural standards and take advantage of the many options I saw around me to make what the culture would call a success of my life. *My skin color was an asset for any move I was educated to want to make.* I could think of myself as "belonging" in major ways, and of making social systems work for me. I could freely disparage, fear, neglect, or be oblivious to anything outside of the dominant cultural forms. Being of the main culture, I could also criticize it fairly freely. My life was reflected back to me frequently enough so that I felt, with regard to my race, if not to my sex, like one of the real people.

Whether through the curriculum or in the newspaper, the television, the economic system, or the general look of people in the streets, we received daily signals and indications that my people counted, and that others *either didn't exist or must be trying, not very successfully, to be like people of my race.* We were given cultural permission not to hear voices of people of other races, or a tepid cultural tolerance for hearing or acting on such voices. I was also raised not to suffer seriously from anything which darker-skinned people might say about my group, "protected," though perhaps I should more accurately say *prohibited,* through the habits of my economic class and social group, from living in racially mixed groups or being reflective about interactions between people of differing races.

In proportion as my racial group was being made confident, comfortable, and oblivious, other groups were likely being made inconfident, uncomfortable, and alienated. Whiteness protected me from many kinds of hostility, distress, and violence, which I was being subtly trained to visit in turn upon people of color.

For this reason, the word "privilege" now seems to me misleading. Its connotations are too positive to fit the conditions and behaviors which "privilege systems" produce. We usually think of privilege as being a favored state, whether earned or conferred by birth or luck. School graduates are reminded that they are privileged and urged to use their (enviable) assets well. The word "privilege" carries the connotation of being something everyone must want. Yet some of the conditions I have described here work to systemically overempower certain groups. Such privilege simply *confers dominance,* gives permission to control, because of one's race or sex. The kind of privilege which gives license to some people to be, at best, thoughtless and, at worst, murderous should not continue to be referred to as a desirable attribute. Such "privilege" may be widely desired without being in any way beneficial to the whole society.

Moreover, though "privilege" may confer power, it does not confer moral strength. Those who do not depend on conferred dominance have traits and qualities which may never develop in those who do. Just as Women's Studies courses indicate that women survive their political circumstances to lead lives which hold the human race together, so "underprivileged" people of color who are the world's majority have survived their oppression and lived survivors' lives from which the white global minority can and must learn. In some groups, those dominated have actually become strong through *not* having all of these unearned advantages, and this gives them a great deal to teach the others. Members of so-called privileged groups can seem foolish, ridiculous, infantile or dangerous by contrast.

I want, then, to distinguish between earned strength and unearned power conferred systemically. Power from unearned privilege can look like strength when it is in fact permission to escape or to dominate. But not all of the privileges on my list are inevitably damaging. Some, like the expectation that neighbors will be decent to you, or that your race will not count against you in court, should be the norm in a just society and should be considered as the entitlement of everyone. Others, like the privilege not to listen to less powerful people, distort the humanity of the holders as well as the ignored groups. Still others, like finding one's staple foods everywhere, may be a function of being a member of a numerical majority in the population. Others have to do with not having to labor under pervasive negative stereotyping and mythology.

We might at least start by distinguishing between positive advantages which we can work to spread, to the point where they are not advantages at all but simply part of the normal civic and social fabric, and negative types of advantage which unless rejected will always reinforce our present hierarchies. For example, the positive "privilege" of belonging, the feeling that one belongs within the human circle, as Native Americans say, fosters development and should not be seen as privilege for a few. It is, let us say, an entitlement which none of us should have to earn; ideally it is an *unearned entitlement*. At present, since only a few have it, it is an *unearned advantage* for them. The negative "privilege" which gave me cultural permission not to take darker-skinned Others seriously can be seen as arbitrarily conferred dominance and should not be desirable for anyone. This paper results from a process of coming to see that some of the power which I originally saw as attendant on being a human being in the U.S. consisted in *unearned advantage* and *conferred dominance,* as well as other kinds of special circumstances not universally taken for granted.

In writing this paper I have also realized that white identity and status (as well as class identity and status) give me considerable power to choose whether to broach this subject and its trouble. I can pretty well decide whether to disappear and avoid and not listen and escape the dislike I may engender in other people through this essay, or interrupt, take over, dominate, preach, direct, criticize, or control to some extent what goes on in reaction to it. Being white, I am given considerable power to escape many kinds of danger or penalty as well as to choose which risks I want to take.

There is an analogy here, once again, with Women's Studies. Our male colleagues do not have a great deal to lose in supporting Women's Studies, but they do not have a great deal to lose if they oppose it either. They simply have the power to decide whether to commit themselves to more equitable distributions of power. They will probably feel few penalties whatever the choice they make; they do not seem, in any obvious short-term sense, the ones at risk, though they and we are all at risk because of the behaviors which have been rewarded in them.

Through Women's Studies work I have met very few men who are truly distressed about systemic, unearned male advantage and conferred dominance. And so one question for me and others like me is whether we will be like them, or whether we will get truly distressed, even outraged, about unearned race advantage and conferred dominance and if so, what we will do to lessen them. In any case, we need to do more work in identifying how they actually affect our daily lives. We need more down-to-earth writing by people about these taboo subjects. We need more understanding of the ways in which white "privilege" damages white people, for these are not the same ways in which it damages the victimized. Skewed white psyches are an inseparable part of the picture, though I do not want to confuse the kinds of damage done to the holders of special assets and to those who suffer the deficits. Many, perhaps most, of our white students in the U.S. think that racism doesn't affect them because they are not people of color; they do not see "whiteness" as a racial identity. Many men likewise do not see themselves as having gendered identities. Insisting on the universal *effects* of "privilege" systems, then, becomes one of our chief tasks, and being more explicit about the *particular* effects in particular contexts is another. Men need to join us in this work.

In addition, since race and sex are not the only advantaging systems at work, we need to similarly examine the daily experience of having age advantage, or ethnic advantage, or physical ability, or advantage related to nationality, religion, or sexual orientation. Professor Marnie Evans suggested to me that in many ways the list I made also applies directly to heterosexual privilege. This is a still more taboo subject than race privilege: the daily ways in which heterosexual privilege makes married persons comfortable or powerful, providing supports, assets, approvals, and rewards to those who live or expect to live in heterosexual pairs. Unpacking that content is still more difficult, owing to the deeper imbeddedness of heterosexual advantage and dominance, and stricter taboos surrounding these.

But to start such an analysis I would put this observation from my own experience: The fact that I live under the same roof with a man triggers all kinds of societal assumptions about my worth, politics, life, and values, and triggers a host of unearned advantages and powers. After recasting many elements from the original list I would add further observations like these:

1. My children do not have to answer questions about why I live with my partner (my husband).
2. I have no difficulty finding neighborhoods where people approve of our household.
3. My children are given texts and classes which implicitly support our kind of family unit and do not turn them against my choice of domestic partnership.
4. I can travel alone or with my husband without expecting embarrassment or hostility in those who deal with us.
5. Most people I meet will see my marital arrangements as an asset to my life or as a favorable comment on my likability, my competence, or my mental health.
6. I can talk about the social events of a weekend without fearing most listeners' reactions.
7. I will feel welcomed and "normal" in the usual walks of public life, institutional, and social.
8. In many contexts, I am seen as "all right" in daily work on women because I do not live chiefly with women.

Difficulties and dangers surrounding the task of finding parallels are many. Since racism, sexism, and heterosexism are not the same, the advantaging associated with them should not be seen as the same. In addition, it is hard to disentangle aspects of unearned advantage which rest more on social class, economic class, race, religion, sex and ethnic identity than on other factors. Still, all of the oppressions are interlocking, as the Combahee River Collective statement of 1977 continues to remind us eloquently.[4]

One factor seems clear about all of these interlocking oppressions. They take both active forms which we can see and embedded forms which as a member of the dominant group one is taught not to see. In my class and place, I did not see myself as racist because I was taught to recognize racism only in individual acts of meanness by members of my group, never in invisible systems conferring unsought racial dominance on my group from birth. Likewise, we are taught to think that sexism or heterosexism is carried on only through individual acts of discrimination, meanness, or cruelty toward women, gays, and lesbians, rather than in invisible systems conferring unsought dominance on certain groups. Disapproving of the systems won't be enough to change them. I was taught to think that racism could end if white individuals changed their attitudes; many men think sexism can be ended by individual changes in daily behavior toward women. But a man's sex provides advantage for him whether or not he approves of the way in which dominance has been conferred on his group. A "white" skin in the United States opens many doors for whites whether or not we approve of the way dominance has been conferred on us. Individual acts can palliate, but cannot end, these problems. To redesign social systems we need first to acknowledge their colossal unseen dimensions. The silences and denials surrounding privilege are the key political tool here. They keep the thinking about equality or equity incomplete, protecting unearned advantage and conferred dominance by making these taboo subjects. Most talk by whites about equal opportunity seems to me now to be about equal opportunity to try to get into a position of dominance while denying that *systems* of dominance exist.

It seems to me that obliviousness about white advantage, like obliviousness about male advantage, is kept strongly inculturated in the United States so as to maintain the myth of meritocracy, the myth that democratic choice is equally available to all. Keeping most people unaware that freedom of confident action is there for just a small number of people props up those in power and serves to keep power in the hands of the same groups that have most of it already. Though systemic change takes many decades, there are pressing questions for me and I imagine for some others like me if we raise our daily consciousness on the perquisites of being light-skinned. What will we do with such knowledge? As we know from watching men, it is an open question whether we will choose to use unearned advantage to weaken hidden systems of advantage, and whether we will use any of our arbitrarily awarded power to try to reconstruct power systems on a broader base.

Notes

1. This paper was funded by the Anna Wilder Phelps Fund through the generosity of Anna Emery Hanson. I have appreciated commentary on this paper from the Working Papers Committee of the Wellesley College Center for Research on Women, from members of the Dodge seminar, and from many individuals, including Margaret Andersen, Sorel Berman, Joanne Braxton, Johnella Butler, Sandra Dickerson, Marnie Evans, Beverly Guy-Sheftall, Sandra Harding, Eleanor Hinton Hoytt, Pauline Houston, Paul Lauter, Joyce Miller, Mary Norris, Gloria Oden, Beverly Smith, and John Walter.

2. This paper was presented at the Virginia Women's Studies Association conference in Richmond in April, 1986 and the American Educational Research Association conference in Boston in October, 1986 and discussed with two groups of participants in the Dodge Seminars for Secondary School Teachers in New York and Boston in the spring of 1987.

3. Margaret Andersen, "Race and the Social Science Curriculum: A Teaching and Learning Discussion." *Radical Teacher,* November, 1984, pp. 17–20. Lillian Smith, *Killers of the Dream,* New York, 1949.

4. "A Black Feminist Statement," The Combahee River Collective, pp. 13–22. In Hull, Scott, Smith, eds., *All the Women Are White, All the Blacks Are Men, But Some of Us Are Brave: Black Women's Studies.* The Feminist Press, 1982.

Sexual Harassment

• *Case Study* •

Confronting Harassment

JOHN HASNAS

Dominique Francon

You are Dominique Francon, a senior account representative in the advertising department of the successful architecture magazine *Your House*. In this position, you supervise the junior account reps who directly contact potential advertisers to sell advertising space. You and Peter Keating, the other senior account representative, are each responsible for half the staff, although your half consistently out-performs Keating's. Both of you report directly to Henry Cameron, the manager of the advertising department. Recently, you were excited to learn that Cameron will soon be promoted to the magazine's editorial board. Since by any performance standard, your results are greatly superior to Keating's, you feel sure that you are slated to replace Cameron.

You think of yourself as a self-assured and assertive woman and have a strong desire to succeed in what you view as the male-dominated publishing industry. Accordingly, you behave in what you consider a professional manner at all times. Although somewhat demanding, you are never unfair to your subordinates, a combination that you believe helps account for your staff's superior bottom-line performance. You feel some regret that this posture prevents you from developing the kind of work-place friendships that others do, but you see this as part of the price you have to pay to make it as a woman manager. You keep a strict separation between your social and professional lives and would never consider pursuing a personal relationship with any of your co-workers. In addition, you are a hard worker, typically putting in many hours beyond the 40 per week required by your position.

You get along fairly well with everyone at the magazine except Ellsworth Toohey, one of the senior editors. Even before the run-in you had with him last year, you considered Toohey to be a typical "male chauvinist pig." Toohey, a man in his mid-fifties from Lubbock, Texas, habitually engages in behavior that you find offensive and demeaning to the women who work at the magazine. Regardless of their position, he typically addresses the women on the staff as "Honey" or "Dear" and refers to them collectively as the magazine's "Fillies." In addition, he will invariably greet them with some comment on

"Confronting Harassment," by permission of John Hasnas, School of Business, Georgetown University.

their appearance such as "Looking good today, Dear" or "Nice dress. I don't know how I'll keep my mind on my work while you're around, Honey."

Last year, after a private meeting in his office concerning the advertising budget, Toohey asked you to go out with him. You told him that since he was a superior of yours whose judgment could have an effect on your future career, you thought it would be inappropriate and that you had a personal policy of never dating co-workers. Rather than accept your refusal, Toohey responded to this by saying, "Oh, loosen up. People go out with co-workers all the time. Let your hair down. I guarantee you won't be disappointed." Although you found this to be both condescending and offensive, you retained your calm and said, "Mr. Toohey, you are putting me in a very awkward situation. I don't think it would be a good idea and I'd appreciate it if you would drop the subject."

A few days following this, you overheard two of the female secretaries discussing Toohey at lunch. Upon inquiring, you learned that he had propositioned many of the single women at the magazine, something that upset several of them. The final straw, however, came the following week when you were leaning over to take a drink from the water fountain. Toohey, who was passing by at the time, said, "Whoa, nice view!" and when you stood up, "Have you reconsidered my proposal of last week? You should get to know me better. I can really be of help to you in this business."

Following this incident, you went immediately to the manager of personnel, Howard Roark, to complain. Roark listened to your description of both incidents and your claim that other female employees had had similar experiences and told you he would look into it. Less than a week later, he came by your office to say that the problem had been taken care of and if you had any further trouble with Toohey to inform him immediately. Although you have no idea what action Roark took, it was clear something had been done. From that point on, Toohey never said a word to you that was not strictly business related. His manner toward you had become completely cold and formal, and he seemed to try to avoid you whenever possible.

This state of affairs suited you fine until today. Yesterday afternoon, you were shocked to learn that the editorial board had voted to promote Peter Keating to manager of the advertising department. The editorial board is made up of the senior managers and editors and is empowered to fill any opening at the managerial level by majority vote. The board presently has 9 members, none of whom are women.

Upset, you had gone to Roark's office to ask why you had been passed over. He informed you that although the vote was as close as it possibly could be, the board elected to go with Keating because it was impressed with his "people skills." However, when you came in this morning, one of your account reps asked you what you had ever done to Toohey. When you asked her what she meant, she said that she had been talking to the secretary who had kept the minutes of yesterday's Board meeting, and she had said that Toohey really had it in for you. Before you could stop yourself, you heard yourself saying, "Why, that son of bitch. I'll sue him for sexual harassment and the entire board for sex discrimination."

When you calmed down, you found yourself wondering whether this was, in fact, a case of sexual harassment or sex discrimination. You also found yourself wondering what would be the best steps for you to take in this situation. What should you do?

Ellsworth Toohey

You are Ellsworth Toohey, a senior editor of the successful architecture magazine *Your House*. This position has both editorial and managerial responsibilities. As an editor, you both decide which articles will be printed in the magazine and make editorial recommendations regarding them. However, as a senior editor, you are also a member of the editorial board, which makes the important managerial decisions for the magazine. The board is comprised of the 9 men who are senior managers or editors. It has responsibility for planning the magazine's budget, establishing editorial policy, and selecting those who are to be hired or promoted to managerial positions.

You were born in 1937 in Lubbock, Texas. Your family was extremely poor and you always had to work as a boy, but you managed to put yourself through college, getting a B.A. in English. Following graduation, you married your college sweetheart, got a position as a reporter for the *Dallas Morning News,* and began your career. By 1982, you had worked your way up to editor. At that time, you left Dallas to join the staff of *Your House,* then a new magazine just starting out. You were quite happy with your new position and things were going very well for you until your wife died 18 months ago. After a very rough 6 or 7 months, you began to put your life back together and have rededicated yourself to your work, perhaps in order to compensate for some of the emptiness in your personal life.

You think of yourself as a skilled professional, but one who has never forgotten the importance of a friendly demeanor that your Southern upbringing impressed upon you. Accordingly, you try to maintain an informal and friendly manner with your co-workers and subordinates. You will often chat with the male employees about sports or politics. You also try to make small talk with the female employees, although you find this more difficult since your upbringing and life experience seems to have left you ignorant of what subjects are of interest to women. You have a personal policy of attempting to greet all co-workers with a complimentary comment in an effort to overcome the intimidating effect your high-level position can have on lower-level employees. Even when you don't know their names, you might greet an employee with a comment such as, "Nice suit, son," or "Looking good today, dear."

You believe you get along fairly well with everyone at the magazine except Dominique Francon, one of the two senior account representatives in the advertising department. A senior account representative supervises the junior account reps who directly contact potential advertisers to sell advertising space. Even before the run-in you had with her last year, you considered Francon to be an example of an "uptight feminist bitch"—cold, aloof, and demanding. She had the reputation for driving the account reps under her unmercifully hard while hardly ever dispensing a "Nice job" or "Well done." Although her section usually sold the most advertising, in your opinion these results came at the expense of a happy workforce.

Last year, about 6 months after your wife's death, you made what you now consider some terrible errors in judgment. Seeking an escape from your loneliness, you asked several of the single women at the magazine to go out with you. Since you had not asked a woman out in over 35 years, you were not particularly good at it and felt foolish and inept trying to do so.

One day last year, you were having a private meeting with Francon in your office concerning the advertising budget. It was one of those days when you were feeling particularly lonely and couldn't stand the thought of going home to an empty house again. As a result, you asked Francon to go out with you despite the negative impression you had of her personality. To your surprise, she did not turn you down directly, but simply stated that she had a policy against dating people from the office. At the time, you interpreted this to mean that she would like to go out with you, but was concerned with the appearance of impropriety. Rather than let the matter drop, you said something to the effect that she should not be so concerned with appearances and that people on the magazine's staff go out with each other all the time. However, Francon responded by saying that she thought it would create an awkward situation and that she would rather not.

A week later, Francon was getting a drink at the water fountain when you passed by. After saying hello, you said, "Have you reconsidered my proposal of last week? I would really like to get to know you better. I know you're trying to make a career in publishing. I have a lot of experience in the field. Maybe I can be of some help to you." To your surprise, she just stormed off.

The next thing you knew, Howard Roark, the manager of personnel, was in your office telling you that Francon had complained to him that you were sexually harassing her as well as other women on the magazine's staff. Angry and extremely embarrassed, you admitted to Roark that you had been lonely since your wife's death and had asked several women out. You assured him that since these actions had apparently been misinterpreted, you would not do so again. Since then, although you still have endeavored to remain on friendly terms with most of the women at the magazine, you have never been familiar with Francon again. You have kept all your dealings with her on a formal and professional level.

Yesterday, the editorial board met to vote on who should be named manager of the advertising department now that the former manager, Henry Cameron, had been promoted to senior manager and member of the editorial board. Although 4 members of the board wanted to promote Francon because of her section's superior sales performance, Cameron, now a board member, recommended Peter Keating, the other senior account representative. Cameron stated that he thought Keating had more "people skills" than did Francon and would make a better manager. You certainly agreed with this and said so. In the end, the board voted 5–4 to promote Keating.

Today, you learned that upon hearing that Keating had been promoted rather than her, Francon had told one of her account reps that she was going to sue you and the magazine for sexual harassment and sex discrimination. Your initial reaction to this was to exclaim, "Isn't that just like the bitch." However, after you calmed down, you realized that this could present a damaging situation both for you and the magazine. What should you do?

Howard Roark

You are Howard Roark, personnel manager at *Your House,* a successful architecture magazine. In this position, you are responsible for arranging the employee benefit package, overseeing hiring and promotion decisions below the level of senior management to ensure compliance with all legal requirements, and equitably resolving grievances involving members of the magazine's staff. The magazine is managed by the editorial board, which has responsibility for planning the magazine's budget, establishing editorial policy, and selecting those who are to be hired or promoted to managerial positions. The board is made up of all senior editors and managers and is presently comprised of the 9 men who hold these positions. Your position is not a senior position and you are not a member of the board.

At present, you are greatly concerned by a situation involving Ellsworth Toohey, one of the senior editors, and Dominique Francon, a senior account representative in the advertising department. Toohey, a man in his mid-fifties, has been with the magazine since its inception 10 years ago. Originally from Lubbock, Texas, his "good old boy" manner can strike people as either quaint and friendly or overly familiar and crude. He has a habit of greeting coworkers with comments concerning their appearance and often refers to them as "son" or "dear," something some of the women staff members resent. Although he went through some rough times following the death of his wife 18 months ago, recently he seems to have gotten back to his former gregarious self.

Francon, a woman in her early thirties, is one of the two senior account representatives whose job it is to supervise the junior account reps who directly contact potential advertisers to sell advertising space. Unlike Toohey, Francon is reserved in manner and can strike people as either highly professional or cold and aloof. She is quite demanding of the junior reps she supervises, which accounts for both the superior revenues generated by her section and her lack of personal friends among the staff.

Your present problem arises out of an incident that took place a year ago. At that time, Francon came to your office to complain about sexual harassment by Toohey. She claimed that Toohey had repeatedly asked her out, would not take "no" for an answer, had made a sexually offensive comment to her, and had offered to help advance her career if she went out with him. She further claimed that Toohey had also propositioned several other women at the magazine. When you confronted Toohey with Francon's accusation, he was obviously both angry and embarrassed. He admitted that he had been quite lonely since his wife's death and that he had asked Francon and some of the other women on the magazine's staff to go out with him. He vehemently denied exerting pressure on any woman, however, and stated that, "If Francon says that I offered to help advance her career, then she's a lying bitch." After he calmed down, he assured you that there would be no further incidents involving either Francon or any of the other women on staff. A few days following this meeting, you informed Francon that the problem had been dealt with and that if she had any further trouble with Toohey she should inform you immediately.

Until yesterday, you thought the matter had been successfully resolved.

That's when the editorial board met to replace Henry Cameron, the manager of the advertising department who had just been promoted to senior manager and member of the editorial board. The only two candidates for the position were Francon and Peter Keating, the other senior account representative. Although not privy to the board's deliberations, you were told that the board voted for Keating 5–4 despite the fact that Francon's section consistently sold more advertising space than Keating's. Apparently, the board was impressed with Keating's "people skills." Somehow, Francon found out that Toohey had both voted and spoken out against her at the meeting. You have just learned that today she told one of her account reps that she intends to sue both Toohey and the magazine for sexual harassment and sex discrimination.

You realize that such a suit could be extremely damaging to the magazine and find yourself wondering whether your handling of things last year might be responsible for the present situation. What should you do?

Sexual Harassment

SUSAN M. DODDS • LUCY FROST
ROBERT PARGETTER • ELIZABETH W. PRIOR

Mary has a problem. Her boss, Bill, gives her a bad time. He is constantly making sexual innuendoes and seems always to be blocking her way and brushing against her. He leers at her, and on occasions has made it explicitly clear that it would be in her own best interests to go to bed with him. She is the one woman in the office now singled out for this sort of treatment, although she hears that virtually all other attractive women who have in the past worked for Bill have had similar experiences. On no occasion has Mary encouraged Bill. His attentions have all been unwanted. She has found them threatening, unpleasant and objectionable. When on some occasions she has made these reactions too explicit, she has been subjected to unambiguously detrimental treatment. Bill has no genuinely personal feelings for Mary, is neither truly affectionate nor loving: his motivation is purely sexual.

Surely this is a paradigmatic case of sexual harassment. Bill discriminates against Mary, and it seems that he would also discriminate against any other attractive woman who worked for him. He misuses his power as an employer when he threatens Mary with sex she does not want. His actions are clearly against her interests. He victimizes her at present and will probably force her to leave the office, whatever the consequences to her future employment.

Not all cases of sexual harassment are so clear. Indeed, each salient characteristic of the paradigmatic case may be missing and yet sexual harassment may still occur. Even if all the features are missing, it could still be a case of sexual harassment.

We aim to explicate the notion of sexual harassment. We note that our aim is not to provide an analysis of the ordinary language concept of sexual harassment. Rather we aim to provide a theoretical rationale for a more behavioral stipulative definition of sexual harassment. For it is an account of this kind which proves to be clearly superior for policy purposes. It provides the basis for a clear, just and enforceable policy, suitable for the workplace and for society at large. Of course ordinary language intuitions provide important touchstones. What else could we use to broadly determine the relevant kind of behavior? But this does not mean that all ordinary language considerations are to be treated as sacrosanct. Sexual harassment is a concept with roots in ordinary language, but we seek to develop the concept as one suitable for more theoretical purposes, particularly those associated with the purposes of adequate policy development.

In brief we aim to provide an account which satisfies three desiderata. The account should:

a. show the connection between harassment in general and sexual harassment
b. distinguish between sexual harassment in general and legitimate sexual interaction
c. be useful for policy purposes.

1. Sexual Harassment and Sexual Discrimination

It seems plausible that minimally harassment involves discrimination, and more particularly, sexual harassment involves sexism. Sexual discrimination was clearly part of the harassment in the case of Mary and Bill.

The pull towards viewing sexual harassment as tied to sexual discrimination is strengthened by consideration of the status of most harassers and most harassees. In general, harassers are men in a position of power over female harassees. The roles of these men and women are reinforced by historical and cultural features of systematic sexual discrimination against women. Generally, men have control of greater wealth and power in our society, while women are economically dependent on men. Men are viewed as having the (positive) quality of aggression in sexual and social relations, while women are viewed as (appropriately) passive. These entrenched attitudes reflect an even deeper view of women as fundamentally unequal, that is in some sense, less fully persons than men. Sexual harassment, then, seems to be just one more ugly manifestation of the sexism and sexual inequality which is rampant in public life.

MacKinnon sees this connection as sufficient to justify treating cases of sexual harassment as cases of sexual discrimination.[1] Sexual discrimination, for MacKinnon, can be understood through two approaches. The first is the "difference approach," under which a "differentiation is based on sex when it can be shown that a person of the opposite sex in the same position is not treated the same." The other is the "inequality approach," which "requires no comparability of situation, only that a rule or practice disproportionately burden one sex because of sex."[2] Thus, even when no comparison can be made between the situation of male and female employees (for example, if the typing pool is composed entirely of women, then the treatment a woman in the pool receives cannot be compared with the treatment of a man in the same situation), if a rule or practice disproportionately burdens women, because they are women, that rule or practice is sexually discriminatory. For MacKinnon all cases of sexual harassment will be cases of sexual discrimination on one or other of these approaches.

Closer consideration reveals, however, that while discrimination may be present in cases of harassment, it need not be. More specifically, while sexual discrimination may be (and often is) present in cases of sexual harassment, it is not a necessary feature of sexual harassment.

The fact that in most cases women are (statistically, though not necessarily) the objects of sexual harassment, is an important feature of the issue of sexual harassment, and it means that in many cases where women are harassed, the harassment will involve sexual discrimination. However, sexual harassment need not entail sexual discrimination.

Consider the case of Mary A and Bill A, a case very similar to that of Mary and Bill. The only relevant difference is that Bill A is bisexual and is sexually attracted to virtually everyone regardless of sex, appearance, age or attitude. Perhaps all that matters is that he feels that he has power over them (which is the case no matter who occupies the position now occupied by Mary A). Mary A or anyone who filled her place would be subjected to sexual harassment.

The point of this variant case is that there appears to be no discrimination, even though there clearly is harassment. Even if it is argued that there is discrimination against the class of those over whom Bill A has power, we can still describe a case where no one is safe. Bill A could sexually harass anyone. This particular case clearly defeats both of MacKinnon's conceptual approaches to sexual discrimination; it is neither the case that Bill A treats a man in Mary A's position differently from the way in which he treats Mary A, nor is it the case that (in Bill A's office) the burden of Bill A's advances is placed disproportionately on one sex, because of that person's sex (for the purpose of sex, perhaps, but not on account of chromosomes).[3]

A different point, but one worth making here, is that there is a difference between sexual harassment and sexist harassment. A female academic whose male colleagues continually ridicule her ideas and opinions may be the object of sexist harassment, and this sexist harassment will necessarily involve sexual discrimination. But she is not, on this basis, the object of sexual harassment.

2. Negative Consequences and Interests

Perhaps sexual harassment always involves action by the harasser which is against the interests of the harassee, or has overall negative consequences for the harassee.

However consider Mary B who is sexually harassed by Bill B. Mary B gives in, but as luck would have it, things turn out extremely well; Mary B is promoted by Bill B to another department. The long term consequences are excellent, so clearly it has been in Mary B's best interests to be the object of Bill B's attentions. One could also imagine a case where Mary B rejects Bill B, with the (perhaps unintentional) affect that the overall consequences for Mary B are very good.

Crosthwaite and Swanton argue for a modification of this view. They urge that, in addition to being an action of a sexual nature, an act of sexual harassment is an action where there is <u>no adequate consideration of the interests of the harassee</u>. They in fact suggest that this is both a <u>necessary and sufficient condition for sexual harassment</u>.[4]

We think it is not sufficient. Consenting to sex with an AIDS carrier is not in an antibody-negative individual's best interests. If the carrier has not informed the other party, the antibody-positive individual has not given adequate consideration to those interests. But this case need not be one of sexual harassment.

Nor is this condition necessary for sexual harassment. Of course Bill B may believe that it is in Mary B's interests to come across. (A sexual harasser can be deceitful or just intensely egotistical.) Bill B may believe that it would conform with Mary B's conception of her interests. And, as we noted earlier, it may even be objectively in her own best interests. Yet still we think this would not prevent the action of Bill B against Mary B—which is in other ways similar to Bill's actions against Mary—being a case of sexual harassment.

In general, harassment need not be against the interests of the harassee. You can be harassed to stop smoking, and harassed to give up drugs. In these cases the consequences may well be good, and the interests of the harassee adequately considered and served, yet it is still harassment. This general feature seems equally applicable to sexual harassment.

3. Misuse of Power

Bill has power over Mary and it is the <u>misuse of this power</u> which plays an important role in making his treatment of Mary particularly immoral. For, on almost any normative theory, to <u>misuse power is immoral</u>. But is this misuse of power what makes this action one of sexual harassment?

If it is, then it must not be restricted to the formal power of the kind which Bill has over Mary—the power to dismiss her, demote her, withhold benefits from her, and so on. We also usually think of this sort of formal power in cases of police harassment. But consider the harassment of women at an abortion clinic by Right-To-Lifers. They cannot prevent the women having abortions and indeed lack any formal power over them. Nonetheless, they do possess important powers—to dissuade the faint-hearted (or even the over-sensitive), and to increase the unpleasantness of the experience of women attending the clinic.

Now consider the case of Mary C. Bill C and Mary C are co-workers in the office, and Bill C lacks formal power over Mary C. He sexually harasses her—with sexual innuendoes, touches, leers, jokes, suggestions, and unwanted invitations. To many women Bill C's actions would be unpleasant. But Mary C is a veteran—this has happened to her so many times before that she no longer responds. It is not that she desires or wants the treatment, but it no longer produces the unpleasant mental attitudes it used to produce—it just rolls off her. She gives the negative responses automatically, and goes on as though nothing had happened.

It would still seem to us that Mary C has been sexually harassed. But what power has Bill C misused against Mary C? He has not used even some informal power which has caused her some significantly unpleasant experience.

Crosthwaite and Swanton also argue against the necessary connection between misuse of power and sexual harassment. They note that one case where there is a lack of power and yet harassment takes place (like the Mary C and Bill C case), is the case where there is a use of pornographic pictures and sexist language by work colleagues. They also note that there are cases in which a sexually motivated misuse of power leads to events advantaging the women in the long run. Misuse of power cannot in itself therefore constitute sexual harassment.[5]

4. Attitudes, Intentions and Experiences

In our discussions so far, it seems that we have not taken into account, to any significant extent, how Mary and Bill feel about things. It may be argued that what defines or characterizes sexual harassment is the mental state of the harasser, or harassee, or both.

Bill wanted to have sex with Mary. He perceived her as a sex object. He failed to have regard for her as a person. He failed to have regard for how she might feel about things. And his actions gave him egotistical pleasure. These attitudes, intentions and experiences may help constitute Bill's action as a case of sexual harassment.

Mary also had very specific kinds of mental states. She found Bill's actions unpleasant, and unwanted. She wished Bill would not act in that way towards her, and she disliked him for it. She was angry that someone would treat her in that way, and she resented being forced to cope with the situation. So again we have attributed attitudes and mental experiences to Mary in describing this case as one of sexual harassment.

We do not want to have to label as sexual harassment all sexual actions or approaches between people in formally structured relationships. Cases of sexual harassment and non-harassing sexual interaction may appear very similar (at least over short time intervals). It seems that in the two kinds of cases only the mental features differ. That is, we refer to attitudes, intentions or experiences in explaining the difference between the two cases. But attention to this feature of sexual harassment is not enough in itself to identify sexual harassment.

We will now consider one of the more salient features of the mental attitudes of Bill and Mary, and show that sexual harassment is not dependent on these or similar features. Then we shall describe a case where the mental experiences are very different, but where sexual harassment does, in fact, still occur.

Consider the claim that Bill uses (or tries to use) Mary as a sex object. The notion of sex object is somewhat vague and ill-defined, but we accept that it is to view her as merely an entity for sexual activity or satisfaction, with no interests in her attributes as a person and without any intention of developing any personal relationship with her.

This will not do as a sufficient condition for sexual harassment. We normally do not think of a client sexually harassing a prostitute. And surely there can be a relationship between two people where each sees the other merely as a sex object without there being harassment. Nor is viewing her merely as a sex object a necessary condition.[6] For surely Bill could love Mary deeply, and yet by pursuing her against her wishes, still harass her.

Now consider the claim that what is essential is that Mary not want the attentions of Bill. This is not a sufficient condition—often the most acceptable of sexual approaches is not wanted. Also a woman may not want certain attentions, and even feel sexually harassed, in situations which we would not want to accept as ones of sexual harassment.

Imagine that Mary D is an abnormally sensitive person. She feels harassed when Bill D comments that the color she is wearing suits her very well, or even that it is a cold day. Bill D is not in the habit of making such comments, nor is he in the habit of harassing anyone. He is just making conversation and noting something (seemingly innocuous) that has caught his attention. Mary D feels harassed even though she is not being harassed.

Perhaps this condition is a necessary one. But this too seems implausible. Remember Mary C, the veteran. She is now so immune to Bill C that she has no reaction at all to his approaches. He does not cause unpleasantness for her; she does not care what he does. Yet nonetheless Bill C is harassing Mary C.

Mary E and Bill E interact in a way which shows that sexual harassment is not simply a matter of actual attitudes, intentions or experiences. Bill E is infatuated with Mary E and wants to have sex with her. In addition to this, he genuinely loves her and generally takes an interest in her as a person. But he is hopeless on technique. He simply copies the brash actions of those around him and emulates to perfection the actions of the sexual harasser. Most women who were the object of his infatuation (for instance, someone like our original Mary) would feel harassed and have all the usual emotions and opinions concerning the harasser. But Mary E is different. Outwardly, to all who observe the public interactions between them, she seems the typical harassee—doing her best to politely put off Bill E, seeming not to want his attentions, looking as though she is far from enjoying it. That is how Bill E sees it too, but he thinks that that is the way women are.

Inwardly Mary E's mental state is quite different. Mary E is indifferent about Bill E personally, and is a veteran like Mary C in that she is not distressed by his actions. But she decides to take advantage of the situation and make use of Bill E's attentions. By manipulating the harassing pressures and invitations, she believes she can obtain certain benefits that she wants and can gain certain advantages over others. The attention from Bill E is thus not unwanted, nor is the experience for her unpleasant. In this case neither the harasser nor the harassee have mental states in any way typical of harassers and harassees, yet it is a case of sexual harassment.

Such a case, as hypothetical and unlikely as it is, demonstrates that the actual mental states of the people involved cannot be what is definitive of sexual harassment. They are not even necessary for sexual harassment.

5. A Behavioral Account of Sexual Harassment

The case of Mary E and Bill E persuades us that we require a behavioral account of sexual harassment. For a harasser to sexually harass a harassee is for the harasser to behave in a certain way towards the harassee. The causes of that behavior are not important, and what that behavior in turn causes is not important. The behavior itself constitutes the harassment.

But how then are we to specify the behavior that is to count as sexual harassment? We shall borrow a technique from the functionalist theory of the mind.

Functionalists usually identify mental states in terms of the functional roles they play. However some functionalist theories allow a variation on this. If we talk instead of the kind of mental state which *typically* fills a functional role or the functional role *typically* associated with a mental state, we maintain the functionalist flavor, but allow unusual combinations of kinds of inner states and kinds of functional roles to be accommodated. We shall follow a similar technique when describing the kinds of behavior associated with sexual harassment.

Consider the behavior which is typically associated with a mental state representing an attitude which seeks sexual ends without any concern for the person from whom those ends are sought, and which typically produces an unwanted and unpleasant response in the person who is the object of the behavior. Such behavior we suggest is what constitutes sexual harassment. Instances of the behavior are instances of sexual harassment even if the mental states of the harasser or harassee (or both) are different from those typically associated with such behavior. The behavior constitutes a necessary and sufficient condition for sexual harassment.

According to this view, the earlier suggestion that attitudes, intentions and experience are essential to an adequate characterization of sexual harassment is correct. It is correct to the extent that we need to look at the mental states typical of the harasser, rather than those present in each actual harasser, and at those typical of the harassee, rather than those present in each actual harassee. The empirical claim is that connecting these typical mental states is a kind of behavior—behavior not incredibly different from instance to instance, but with a certain sameness to it. Thus it is a behavior of a definite characteristic *type*. This type of behavior is sexual harassment.

This proffered account may at first appear surprising. But let us look at some of its features to alleviate the surprise, and at the same time increase the plausibility of the account.

Most importantly, the account satisfies our three desiderata: to show the connection between harassment in general and sexual harassment, to distinguish between sexual harassment and legitimate sexual interaction, and to assist in guiding policy on sexual harassment.

The relationship between harassment and sexual harassment is to be accounted for in terms of a behavioral similarity. This at first may seem to be a sweeping suggestion, since *prima facie,* there need be no descriptive similarity between sexual harassment, harassment by police, harassment of homosexuals, harassment of Jews, and so on. But the behavioral elements on which each kind of harassment supervenes will have enough in common to explain our linking them all as harassment, while at the same time being sufficiently different to allow for their differentiation into various kinds of harassment. The most plausible similarity, as we shall argue later, will be in the presence of certain behavioral dispositions, though the bases for these dispositions may differ.

Our approach allows for an adequate distinction between sexual harassment and legitimate sexual approaches and interactions. The approach requires that this be a behavioral difference. There is something intrinsically different about the two kinds of activity. Given that the typical causal origin of each of the kinds of behavior is different and so too is the typical reaction it in turn produces, it is to be expected that there would be a difference in the behavior itself. It is important to note that the constitutive behavior will be within a particular context, in particular circumstances. (The importance of this is well illustrated in cases such as a student and her lecturer at a university.[7]) Further it will include both overt and covert behavior (subtle differences count). In many cases it will also be behavior over a time interval, not just behavior at a time.

From the policy guiding perspective the account is very attractive. It is far easier to stipulate a workable, practical, defensible, and legally viable policy on harassment if it is totally definable in behavioral terms. Definition in terms of mental experiences, intentions and attitudes spells nothing but trouble for a viable social policy on sexual harassment.

The analysis we have offered entails that if there were no such characteristic kind of behavior there would be no sexual harassment. This seems to be right. In this case no legislation to ground a social policy would be possible. We would instead condemn individual actions on other moral grounds—causing pain and distress, acting against someone's best interests, misusing power, and so on.

In addition to satisfying these three desiderata, our account has numerous other positive features. First our account is culturally relative. It is highly likely that the kind of behavior constitutive of sexual harassment will vary from culture to culture, society to society. That is, it will be a culture-relative kind of behavior that determines sexual harassment. In any culture our reference to the typical mental states of the harasser and harassee will identify a kind of behavior that is constitutive of sexual harassment in that culture. This kind of behavior matches well with the empirical observations. There is so much variation in human behavior across cultures that behavior which may be sexual harassment in one need not be in another. The same is true of other kinds of human behavior. In the Middle East, belching indicates appreciation of a meal. In Western society, it is considered bad manners. The practice of haggling over the price of a purchase is acceptable (indeed expected) in some societies, and unacceptable in others. But in almost any culture, some kind of behavior may reasonably be judged to be sexual harassment.

Second, while we have cast our examples in terms of a male harasser and female harassee, there is nothing in the account which necessitates any gender restriction on sexual harassment. All that is required is that the behavior is sexual in nature and has other behavioral features which make it an instance of sexual harassment. The participants could be of either sex in either role, or of the same sex.

We acknowledge that we use the notion of an action being sexual in nature without attempting any explication of that notion. Such an explication is a separate task, but we believe that for our purposes there is no problem in taking it as primitive.

Third, the account allows for the possibility of sexual harassment without the presence of the mental states typical of the harasser or the harassee. There is an important connection between these typical mental states and sexual harassment, but it does not restrict instances of sexual harassment to instances where we have these typical mental states.

Further as the account focuses on behavior, rather than mental states, it explains why we feel so skeptical about someone who behaves as Bill behaves, yet pleads innocence and claims he had no bad intentions. The intentions are not essential for the harassment, and such a person has an obligation to monitor the responses of the other person so that he has an accurate picture of what is going on. Moreover, he has an obligation to be aware of the character of his own behavior. He also has an obligation to give due consideration to the strength and the weight of the beliefs upon which he is operating before he makes a decision to act in a manner that may have unpleasant consequences for others. Strength of belief concerns the degree of confidence it is rational to have in the belief, given the evidence available. Weight of belief concerns the quality of the evidential basis of the belief, and the reasonableness of acting on the evidence available.[8] If a person is acting in a way which has a risk of bad consequences for others, that person has an obligation to be aware of the risks and to refrain from acting unless he has gained evidence of sufficient strength and weight to be confident that the bad consequences will not arise. In the case of someone who wishes to engage in legitimate sexual interaction and to avoid sexual harassment, he must display a disposition to be alive to the risks and to seek appropriate evidence from the other person's behavior, as to whether that person welcomes his attentions. He must also display a disposition to refrain from acting if such evidence is lacking.

In the case of Mary E and Bill E, Bill E relies on the harassing behavior of other men as a guide to his actions regarding Mary E. Mary E has displayed standard forms of avoidance behavior (although she has ulterior motives). Bill E does not pay sufficient heed to the strength and weight of the beliefs which guide his actions, and it is just fortunate that Mary E is not harmed by what he does. Given Bill E's total disregard of Mary E's interests and reactions, it seems that his behavior could have caused, just as easily, significant distress to any other Mary who might have filled that role. A policy intended to identify sexual harassment should not rely on such luck, although the actual mental states (where they are as atypical as Mary E's) may mitigate blameworthiness. Bill E's harassing behavior should be checked and evaluated, regardless of any of Mary's actual mental states.[9]

Consider an example taken from an actual case[10] which highlights this obligation. Suppose Tom is married to Jane. He invites Dick (an old friend who has never met Jane) home to have sex with Jane. He tells Dick that Jane will protest, but that this is just part of the game (a game she very much enjoys). Dick forces Jane, who all the time protests violently, to have sex with him. Jane later claims to have been raped. Dick has acted culpably because he has acted without giving due consideration to the weight of the belief which guided his action, that is, to how rational it was to act on the belief given such a minimal evidential base. The only evidence he had that Jane did consent was Tom's say-so, and the consequences of acting on the belief were very serious. All of Jane's actions indicated that she did not consent.

In the case of Bill E and Mary E, Bill has an obligation to consider the strength and weight of the beliefs which guide his action before he acts. He is not justified in claiming that he is innocent, when he has been provided with signals that indicate that Mary does not welcome his attentions.

We acknowledge that it will be difficult in many situations to obtain sufficient evidence that a proposed act will not be one of sexual harassment. This will be true especially in cases where the potential harassee may believe that any outward indication of her displeasure would have bad consequences for her. The awareness of this difficulty is probably what has led others to promote the policy of a total ban on sexual relationships at the office or work place. While we acknowledge the problem, we feel that such a policy is both unrealistic and overrestrictive.

Fourth, the account allows an interesting stance on the connection between sexual harassment and morality. For consequentialist theories of morality, it is possible (though unlikely) that an act of sexual harassment may be, objectively, morally right. This would be the case if the long term good consequences outweighed the bad effects (including those on the harassee at the time of the harassment). For other moral theories it is not clear that this is a possibility, except where there are sufficiently strong overriding considerations present, such as to make the sexual harassment morally permissible. From the agent's point of view, it would seem that the probable consequences of sexual harassment (given the typical attitude of the typical harasser and the typical effects on the typical harassee) will be bad. Hence it is very likely, on any moral theory, that the agent evaluation for a harasser will be negative. The possible exceptions are where the harasser's actual mental state is not typical of a harasser, or the harassee's is not typical of a harassee.

Further, on this account many of the salient features of the case of Mary and Bill—such as misuse of power, discrimination, unfair distribution of favors, and so on—are not essential features of sexual harassment. They are usually immoral in their own right, and their immorality is not explained by their being part of the harassment. But the behavior characteristic of sexual harassment will be constituted by features which we commonly find in particular instances of sexual harassment. For sexual harassment must supervene on the behavioral features which constitute its instances, but there is a range of such behavior, no one element of which need be present on any particular occasion. Similarly the morality of an instance of sexual harassment (at least for the consequentialist) will supervene on the morality of those same features of behavior.

6. Objections to the Behavioral Account

It may be objected that we have made no significant progress. We acknowledged at the beginning of the paper that many different kinds of behavior were instances of sexual harassment, even though there seemed to be no specific kind of behavior commonly present in all these instances.

Our reply is to concede the point that there is no first order property commonly possessed by all the behaviors. However, other important similarities do exist.

The property of being an instance of sexual harassment is a second order property of a particular complex piece of behavior. It is a property of the relevant specific behavioral features, and these features may be from a list of disjunctive alternatives (which may be altered as norms of behavior change). Also, the behavior of a typical harassee will possess the property of being an instance of avoidance behavior. Avoidance behavior is a disposition. Hence, even if two lots of behavior are descriptively similar they may differ in their dispositional properties. Finally the behavior of the typical harasser will possess the property of being sexually motivated, which again is dispositional in nature.

A second objection goes as follows: couldn't we have the very same piece of behavior and yet have no sexual harassment? To take the kind of example well tried as an objection to behaviorism, what would we say about the case of two actors, acting out a sexual harassment sequence?

There are a variety of replies we may make here. We could "bite the bullet" and admit the case to be one of sexual harassment. On the model proposed, we may do this while still maintaining that the behavior in this case is not morally wrong. Or, instead, we could insist that certain kinds of behavior only become harassment when they are carried on over a sufficiently lengthy time interval, the circumstances surrounding the behavior also being relevant. The case of the actors would not count as an instance of harassment because the behavior has not been recurrent over a sufficiently long period of time, especially as the behavior before and after the acting period are significantly different. Also the circumstances surrounding an acting exercise would be typically different from those of an instance of sexual harassment.

Still another response to the acting example is to argue that if the actual mental states of "harasser" and "harassee" are sufficiently different from those of the prototypical harasser and harassee, there can be no sexual harassment as there will be behavioral differences. This is not a logical necessity, but a physical one given the causal relations which hold between the mental states and the behavior. We should also keep in mind that many of the features of sexual harassment are dispositional. Thus, even if such features of sexual harassment are not manifested in particular circumstances, they would in other circumstances, and it is in these other circumstances that the observable behavior would be significantly different if it is the manifestation of harassment from that which would be associated with non-harassment.[11]

A third objection to our behavioral account focuses on our use of the mental state *typical* of harassers and harassees. We have noted that it is possible that some instances of harassment will involve a harasser or harassee with mental states significantly different from those of the typical harasser or harassee. So it is possible that the harassee is not even offended or made to feel uncomfortable, and it is possible that the harasser did not have intentions involving misuse of power against, and disregard for the interests of, the harassee. It is even possible that one or both of the harasser and harassee could know about the atypical mental states of the other. Why, at least in this last case, insist that the behavior is sufficient for sexual harassment?

From our concern to provide an account of sexual harassment adequate for policy purposes, we would be inclined to resist this kind of objection, given the clear advantage in policy matters of a behavioral account. But there is more to say in reply to this objection. Policy is directed at the action of agents, and in all cases except where at least one of the agents involved has justified beliefs about the atypical actual mental states of the agents involved, it is clearly appropriate to stipulate behavior associated with the states of mind typical of harassers and harassees as sexual harassment. For agents ought to be guided by what it is reasonable to predict, and rational prediction as to the mental states of those involved in some kind of behavior will be determined by the mental states typically associated with that behavior. So only in cases where we have reliable and justified knowledge of atypical mental states does the objection have any substance at all.

But even in these cases it seems the behavior should not be regarded as innocuous. Instances of behavior all form parts of behavioral patterns. People are disposed to behave similarly in similar circumstances. Hence we ought not to overlook instances of behavior which would typically be instances of sexual harassment. Agents ought not be involved in such patterns of behavior. It is for similar reasons that while we allow for cultural relativity in the behavior constitutive of sexual harassment, this relativity should not be taken to legitimate patterns of behavior which do constitute sexual harassment but which are taken as the standard mode of behavior by a culture.[12]

There are three final notes about our account of sexual harassment. Provided that the kind of behavior so specified is characteristically different from behavior having other typical causes and effects, the desired distinction between sexual harassment and other kinds of sexual activity is assured.

The required connection between sexual harassment and other forms of harassment seems assured by a kind of behavioral similarity. Other forms of harassment are not sexual and vary in many ways from the pattern of behavior characteristic of sexual harassment. But there will be corresponding accounts for each kind of harassment in terms of typical causes and typical effects. The connection between all the different kinds of harassment may well be revealed by looking at these typical causes and typical effects. But despite the noted differences, the contention is that there will be an empirically verifiable behavioral similarity, and this will justify the claim that they are all forms of harassment. It may be that the relevant features of the behavior characteristic of the various forms of harassment are dispositional.

We have made two claims about behavior constitutive of sexual harassment, and we should now see how they relate. The behavior is identified in terms of its typical causes and typical effects, that is, in terms of the typical mental states of harassers and harassees. But harassment is recognized by reference to features of the behavior itself, and any legislation to ground social policy will also refer to such features. The philosophical claim is that there will be a range of such behavior features some combination of which will be present in each case of sexual harassment. The empirical job is to tell us more about the nature of such behavior and help determine the practical social policy and legislation.[13]

Notes

1. Catherine MacKinnon, *Sexual Harassment of Working Women*, (London: Yale University Press, 1979), Ch. 6.

2. MacKinnon, p. 225.

3. Given that sexual harassment is possible between men, by a woman harassing a man, among co-workers, and so on, MacKinnon's view of sexual harassment as nothing but one form of sexual discrimination is even less persuasive. It is also interesting that the problems which MacKinnon recognizes in trying to characterize the "offence" of sexual harassment (p. 162 ff.), indicate a need for a behavioral analysis of sexual harassment, like the one we offer.

4. Jan Crosthwaite and Christine Swanton, "On the Nature of Sexual Harassment," *Women and Philosophy: Australasian Journal of Philosophy,* supplement to 64 (1986): 91–106; pp. 100–101.

5. Crosthwaite and Swanton, p. 99.

6. If it is, it needs to be connected to a general view that women are sex objects, for pornographic pin-ups and sexist jokes and language may harass a women without anyone viewing *that* woman as a sex object. (See Nathalie Hadjifotiou, *Women and Harassment at Work,* (London: Pluto Press, 1983), p. 14.) Note that we have urged that sexual harassment should be a special case of harassment. But what is the general form of the sex object account? It seems implausible that for each form of harassment there is something corresponding to the notion of sex object.

7. See, for example, Billie Wright Dzeich and Linda Weiner, *The Lecherous Professor: Sexual Harassment on Campus,* (Boston: Beacon Press, 1984).

8. For a discussion of this concept of weight see Barbara Davidson and Robert Pargetter, "Weight," *Philosophical Studies* 49 (1986): 219–30.

9. Some might say that this behavioristic account of sexual harassment is similar to having strict liability for murder, that is to say, that mental states do need to be taken into account when judging and penalizing someone's actions. What we are arguing for is a way of *identifying* sexual harassment, not how (or even if) it should be *penalized.* The appropriate response to a case of sexual harassment may very well take mental states into account, along with the harm caused, or likely to be caused, and so forth. One advantage of our account is that it demands that potential harassers become aware of their behavior and to be alert to the responses of those around them. The response of Bill E (that he thought women liked to be treated that way) ought not be considered adequate especially in public life where a person's livelihood could hang in the balance.

10. This example is based on the British case, D.P.P. v. Morgan (1975), 2 All E.R. 347 (House of Lords): Morgan (1975), 1 All E.R. 8 (Court of Appeal); see also Frank Jackson, "A Probabilistic Approach to Moral Responsibility," in Ruth Barcam Marcus, *et al.* (eds.), *Logic, Methodology and Philosophy of Science VII,* (North Holland, 1986), pp. 351–66.

11. For a useful account of dispositional properties, their manifestations, and their categorical bases, see Elizabeth Prior, Robert Pargetter and Frank Jackson, "Three Theses about Dispositions," *American Philosophical Quarterly* 19 (1982): 251–58.
    The case of pressing solicitation by a prostitute towards a reluctant john can be viewed in the same manner as that of the actors. It is quite likely that there would be sufficient difference in the mental states of the pressing prostitute and the typical harasser to yield behavioral differences (for instance the prostitute is more interested in making money than having sex, so her behavior will reflect this insofar as, say, she would not keep on pressing if the john proved to have no money). The pressing behavior of the prostitute may be seen as a nuisance by the reluctant john, but it is not sexual harassment.

12. What will be culturally relative are types of behavior incidental to their being viewed as constituting sexual harassment in a particular culture. Acceptable standards concerning modes of address, physical proximity, touching, and so forth will vary among cultures, so the behavior patterns which will constitute sexual harassment will also vary. Of course we must be careful not to confuse socially accepted behavior with behavior which is not sexually harassing, especially in cultures where men have much greater power to determine what is to count as socially acceptable behavior. However, so long as there are typical mental states of harassers and harassees, the behavior which constitutes sexual harassment will be identifiable in each culture.

13. We acknowledge useful comments from Robert Young and various readers for this journal.

• PART FOUR •

Contemporary Business Issues
Introduction

Modern business is undergoing dramatic changes. Smaller companies find it harder to compete as large corporations take bigger and bigger pieces of the economic pie. Today the 1,000 largest U.S. firms account for over 70 percent of the sales, over 85 percent of the employees, and approximately 85 percent of the profits of all U.S. industrial corporations. Fewer than 150 corporations now hold the same share of manufacturing assets as did the 1,000 largest corporations in 1941. Other changes include mergers and acquisitions, downsizing, reengineering (usually in the form of alterations in corporate organizational structure and managerial responsibilities), expansion into multinational markets, consumer unrest over advertising, and fears about pollution and the loss of natural resources. While these changes have been taking place, business has become more aware of itself not only as an economic institution but as an active participant in the surrounding community.

From an ethical standpoint, the transformation of business is significant. Changes in the goals and structure of the corporation have caused changes in the expectations of employees and consumers. For example, the shift away from the domination of the corporation by a single person has prompted greater participation by employees in corporate decisions. Professional managers, many of whom do not even own stock in the companies they manage, now control most of the largest and most influential corporations in the world. Technological changes, too, have played their role, generating a wider array of products and vastly more efficient means, such as television, for advertising them. With these advances have come moral doubts about the content of advertisements and the psychological impact of advertising on society.

Society has also changed its views about economic growth. It was once routinely assumed that economic growth should be pursued at every turn: greater production, higher incomes, and larger gross national products. Now critics complain that clean air, abundant wildlife, and adequate energy sources will vanish if we persist unreflectively in our search for greater economic prosperity. We seem to be driven to the point of asking whether an ever-increasing standard of living is possible without endangering the ecological systems that support technology and human life. And more and more people are also asking whether the unabated quest for economic prosperity doesn't erode human values such as freedom and creativity.

The Environment

In recent years attention has been drawn to the fact that we live on a planet which, despite its apparent abundance, possesses finite natural resources. Never-ending economic growth involves either a never-ending consumption of these resources or a discovery of substitutes. Is it wise, then, to persist in our goal of technological and economic expansion when our stocks of natural resources are continually dwindling? Critics of economic growth argue that we may soon approach the limits of those natural resources, and human needs may outstrip the technological know-how required to develop substitutes. To avoid this disaster such critics propose a radical reordering of the economy so that we actively control growth and work to replace lost resources. In contrast, a number of other economists argue that economic growth is both necessary and valuable. It enhances human life, it is necessary to provide for the growth of less developed economies, and it allows us to develop the technologies necessary to repair our previous ecological errors.

In his article "Why Political Questions Are Not All Economic," Mark Sagoff questions the claim that environmental problems are merely economic problems concerning distribution of costs and benefits. The identification of environmental problems as economic ones implies the conclusion that if consumers prefer and are willing to pay for a clean environment, for recycled products, and national parks, then it is efficient to develop these assets. It follows that if consumers find it more efficient and less costly to pollute or waste, then one should not interfere with their market preferences. The difficulty with this thesis, Sagoff argues, is that many of our preferences are not market preferences. Sagoff questions economic preferences as the ultimate judge of worthiness, challenges the neutrality of economic claims, and cogently defends the importance of noneconomic value. Sagoff points out that we find value in clean air, the preservation of the spotted owl, and virgin national forests despite their costs. Sagoff challenges us to take into account these nonmarket values which, more than market values, play a central role in human choice.

Much of the analysis of environmental degradation and improvement is conducted in terms of its costs and benefits. Steven Kelson questions the cost-benefit analysis as a general rule for the evaluation of environmental concerns. Like Sagoff, Kelson argues that there are nonmarket values that cannot be measured quantitatively, such as life, health, and liberty. Thus, in approaching environmental issues, we must clarify what we hold to be invaluable in calculating the risks of pollution, the harm to future generations, and questions of sustainability. The case study "AES Corporation" (A and B) presents a company that is concerned with its profitability and its impact on the environment in a situation where the congruence of these two goals is not obvious. The "B" case should not be read until the "A" case is first discussed. How companies resolve these sorts of dilemmas is part of the new challenge presented by the finite nature of the planet and the continuing demand for economic growth.

Advertising

Until the latter part of the nineteenth century, many articles of consumption, such as soap and clothing, were made at home. Products were in short supply, and religious leaders habitually preached against the vanity of materialism even in this country. But after 1875 many consumer industries were fully mechanized, an event which resulted in an explosion of items for daily use. This expansion of inexpensive production led to an obvious new task: someone had to persuade the public that these consumer products were worth having. Thus began the growth of advertising. Once complete, the transformation that advertising helped create ushered in a dramatic new age. Today advertising is big business. It accounts for one-fifth of the total selling costs of American industry, lagging behind only sales promotion and direct sales in its total cost.

A standard criticism of advertising is that it deceives. At least two major theories of advertising can be appealed to in making this criticism, the first relying on a conception of advertising as "persuasion," the second as "information." If the principal function of advertising is to establish the consumer's desire for a product (and hence willingness to pay), advertising may be equated with persuasion. Just as Tom Sawyer encouraged his friends to help him whitewash his famous fence, so modern advertisers encourage consumers to buy their toothpaste, chewing gum, and deodorants. In both cases, clever salesmanship makes an item more attractive than it would be otherwise; but in both cases there is no guarantee that the listeners are better off with their new desires than they were without them.

A second theory sees advertising not as persuasion but as information. How, its defenders ask, can you persuade people without telling them something? Furthermore, since a market economy relies on information to help consumers make choices that maximize their welfare, advertising's service to society is to provide consumers with two essential kinds of information about products: their characteristics (including quality) and their price. Yet insofar as advertising is seen as information, one can easily doubt the information values of many television and magazine advertisements. Advertisements frequently rely on mere association; for example, an advertisement for whiskey reads: "Increase the value of your holdings. Old Charter Bourbon Whiskey—The Final Step Up." This, and many advertisements like it, seem to provide little or no hard information about price or quality. Furthermore, the source of an advertisement may be "tainted," since the persons responsible for generating it have a vested interest in persuading consumers; they have a vested interest, in short, in making profits, not in being objective.

Yet another view, sometimes called the competitive efficiency view, defends the social importance of advertising. This view affirms the information value of advertising while granting that advertisements frequently contain little specific information about price or quality and, moreover, often "puff" or exaggerate the worth of products. But puffery, notes the theory, is an accepted part of salesmanship, and it would be a mistake to view the public as a collection of gullible fools. No one really believes an advertisement that suggests drinking Old Charter Bourbon will increase one's stock-market holdings. Specific product information, furthermore, is only one kind of information important for market efficiency: another is information about the existence ⸰⸱ availability of the product, and advertising supplies this kind of information in abundance. Competition in the marketplace is efficient only when consumers are able to compare rival products; and this is possible only if they know what products are available.

In his article "Advertising and Behavior Control," Robert Arrington defends the information value of advertising and denies that in most instances it controls behavior or threatens autonomy. Advertising does not so much create desires, he argues, as redirect them. Hence, if we are to accept this account, our desires for Grecian Formula 16, Mazda Rx-7s, and Pongo Peach lipstick depend ultimately upon our prior hopes for youth, power, adventure, or ravishing beauty, not upon desires that Madison Avenue creates.

In his response to Arrington, Roger Crisp questions the thesis that advertising does not affect one's autonomy. Persuasive advertising, in particular, creates desires, it distracts from making clear choices, and can create images about lifestyles and values that at least peripherally affect one's self-image and choices.

Whatever one thinks about the information value of advertising, the issue of children's advertising poses special problems. How, if at all, should advertisers shift their approach in light of the fact that children lack the judgment and experience required to even understand, much less evaluate, information? Also, are there limits to the amount of puffery or violence that should appear in children's advertising? These questions, along with the more standard ones about advertising, are raised in the case study "Toy Wars."

Organizations and Business in the Twenty-First Century

We are entering a new age. Global markets, organizational reengineering, environmental crises, and a more diverse workplace are only a few examples of some of the changes that are taking place. As we move into this new century managers will have to begin to think more creatively about every aspect of management and business. Leading organizations under new paradigms will be the order of the day.

In her *Harvard Business Review* article "Managing for Organizational Integrity," Lynn Sharp Paine outlines the role of organizational ethics in corporate strategy. When a common set of values drives an organization and its managerial behavior, this not only reduces incidents of misconduct, but more importantly, fosters a competitve long-term strategy that sustains the organization through the turmoil of change.

The book concludes by presenting the results of a survey of company ethics codes and programs prepared by the Conference Board. As readers will see, American corporations are beginning to take seriously the central role of ethics in corporate sensibility, decision-making, and accountability. This surge in ethics as a key part of managerial decision-making is part of the increasing recognition that ethics and values are part of, and cannot be separated from, economics. Managers who see values as the core of corporate culture and the driving force behind management decision-making may better prepare their companies for the challenges of the twenty-first century.

Environment

• *Case Study* •

The AES Corporation

MANAGEMENT INSTITUTE FOR ENVIRONMENT AND BUSINESS

A*

On an afternoon in mid-1987, Roger W. Sant was in a rush to get back to his office. As Chairman of the Board and CEO of the AES Corporation, and a board member of several environmental organizations, Sant felt the company ought to assume more accountability for its contribution to the build-up of greenhouse gases in the atmosphere. He had just spent another day as a member of a World Resources Institute global warming panel where he had become more convinced than ever that excessive carbon dioxide in the lower layer of the earth's atmosphere would be one of the main causes of global warming, should global warming occur.

As one of the nation's leading independent power producers, AES had a commitment to meeting the energy needs of its customers at the lowest possible cost, a strategy which Sant and his colleagues had developed and written about while with the Mellon Institute ten years previously. Although they had successfully operationalized their mission on "least cost," they felt a competing responsibility to minimize the company's impact on the environment. This accountability for social costs was integral to AES's value system, which put social responsibility as the first, and conditional order of business. Unfortunately, the least cost option for power generation in the U.S. does not have the lowest environmental impact. Coal-fired cogeneration plants are significant emitters of carbon dioxide, a gas which is not regulated by law, but which is the key greenhouse gas. As soon as he arrived at the office, Sant called Roger Naill, Vice President of Planning Services, and Sheryl Sturges, Director of Strategic Planning, to discuss the problem of how to offset these carbon dioxide emissions so that AES could bring its cost strategy in line with its value system.

---

*This case was prepared by Marcy Trent of the Management Institute for Environment and Business (MEB) and reviewed by James E. Post (Boston University School of Management), Forest Reinhardt (Harvard Business School), and Walter D. Scott (Kellogg Graduate School of Business at Northwestern University). Copyright © 1992 by MEB.

The Company

The AES Corporation was co-founded in 1981 by Roger W. Sant and Dennis W. Bakke to capitalize on the market potential for cogeneration (the sequential generation of steam for industrial uses and electricity for sale to utilities). The company entered the business of developing, owning and operating independent (i.e., non-utility) cogeneration facilities in 1981, and in 1983 began the construction of its first plant. By 1987, AES had grown to 215 employees with annual revenues of over $40 million (see Exhibit 1) and two operating cogeneration facilities: AES Deepwater, a 140-megawatt petroleum coke-fired facility and AES Beaver Valley, a 120-megawatt coal-fired cogeneration facility (see Exhibits 2 and 3).

AES's primary objective in 1987 was to meet the growing need for electricity by being a safe, reliable and efficient power supplier in the independent power market. AES used a six-part strategy to develop its core cogeneration business and maintained a critical corporate value system to achieve this objective. The six-part strategy was as follows:

- *Project Size:* AES typically focused on larger projects, generally greater than 100 megawatts in size and $100 million in construction costs. The customer base for the electricity produced from these projects was electric utilities.
- *Least Cost:* AES offered its customers the "least cost" supply of energy. In the company's judgment, coal generally provided the best alternative to meeting this criteria. Coal is expected to be abundant and available from U.S. reserves for over 200 years. Also, prices for coal are less likely to rise than those of other fuels due to threatened shortages or political disruptions, enabling the company to obtain long-term coal supply contracts at competitive rates.
- *Long-term Contracts:* AES entered into long-term power sales contracts with electric utilities (i.e., 30 years) at a set electric rate with escalators that match those of the projected fixed and variable costs of operating the plant.
- *Careful Site Selection:* The company attempted to find appropriate facility sites before extensive capital commitment by optimizing the following key variables: access to fuel and waste transportation, water availability, potential steam or thermal markets, and local government and community acceptance.
- *Stand-alone Financing:* Each project, to the maximum extent possible, was financed without recourse to the Company or to other projects.
- *Commitment to Operations:* Because of the Company's commitment to the electric utility customer, it emphasized excellence in operations and believed strongly that it should operate all projects which it developed or acquired.

Key to AES meeting their stated objective apart from the above six-part strategy was maintaining a strong corporate value system integral to all operating decisions. The four shared corporate values at AES included:

- *Integrity:* To act with integrity and honor its commitments.
- *Fairness:* To treat fairly its employees, customers, suppliers and the governments and communities in which it operates.
- *Fun:* To create and maintain an atmosphere where employees can advance in their skills while enjoying their time at work.

- *Social Responsibility:* To undertake projects that provide social benefits, such as lower costs to customers, a high degree of safety and reliability, increased employment, and a cleaner environment.

This value system was created by and represented the personal values of Roger Sant and Dennis Bakke. They were of such importance to the founding members of AES that the company would adhere to these values even at the cost of a lost profit opportunity.

The Thames Plant

During 1987, the company competed in and won the bidding competition to furnish Connecticut Power & Light 181 megawatts of base load power on an annual basis. Montville, Connecticut, on the Thames River was chosen as the site for the new "Thames" coal-fired cogeneration plant—estimated to begin commercial operation in 1990.

The 181 megawatts to be furnished under the 25-year contract was enough power to provide electricity to over 100,000 homes. The Thames plant would also supply up to 100,000 pounds per hour of steam to Stone Container Corporation's Uncasville paper recycling plant under a 15-year contract.

The fuel source for the plant was planned to be West Virginia coal, supplied by CSX Transportation, Inc., under a 15-year contract. The coal would be burned in two state-of-the-art circulating fluidized bed boilers, which produce lower stack emissions than conventional boilers, and are significantly cleaner than all current and proposed federal, state, and local standards (see section "Coal Technology").

The forecasted capital investment of the project was $275 million, with AES holding 100% of the economic interest. By the end of 1987, the project was beyond the planning stage and under construction. However, limiting carbon dioxide emissions had not been incorporated into the project planning or original cost estimates. AES estimated that the Thames plant would emit over 15 million tons of carbon over its expected 40-year life.

The Independent Power Industry

Historically, electricity-generating plants were constructed almost exclusively by regulated utilities, municipalities and rural electric cooperatives. In 1978, Congress passed the Public Utility Regulatory Policies Act of 1978 (PURPA) that fostered a new market of electricity generation produced by independent producers. The legislation required utilities to purchase power from independent power producers (IPP's) at a price at or below the utilities' "avoided" or incremental supply cost. By the late 1980's competition for these supply contracts was driving down the prices for electricity, making it difficult for small IPP's to compete. AES relied on its proactive environmental position as a means of setting it apart from its competitors.

In the *1987 AES Strategic Outlook,* the following statement summed up the state of competition in the independent power industry:

Our best guess is that over the long-term, the utility industry will restructure towards competitive (deregulated) generation . . . When this happens we want to be the least-cost (and most reliable) producers of electricity in order to survive in a deregulated market. Even in the near term, we are facing stiff competition from utilities and other IPP's in our bids to obtain electric contracts. We therefore need to lower our costs to obtain new electric contracts and maintain all of our plants profitably.

Coal Technology

Since World War I, over half of the electricity in the U.S. has been generated by coal-fired power plants. With the uncertainty of nuclear power and oil supply, coal-fired power plants in 1987 were expected to contribute up to 70% of electric power in the U.S by the end of the century.[1]

The U.S. is estimated to have coal reserves for over 200 years, and long-term contracts can be arranged with coal producers. This economic advantage of locking in a low-cost fuel supply as on offset to fixed price electricity contracts has been a leading cause for the U.S. power producers to continue building coal-fired power plants.

Most coal-fired power plants are used for larger "base load" facilities, rather than "peak load" facilities. Base load power plants are used 24 hours a day, and shut down for maintenance only about every two years. Peak load facilities run during intervals of high usage, such as mid-day during the summer months when air conditioning loads are high. The variable operating costs drive the profitability of a base load plant; coal and nuclear power are the most common base load fuel because the fuel costs are so low.

Despite the fact that coal has long been a major source of U.S. electricity, coal has never been considered a very efficient fuel for power plants. Coal contains less energy per unit of weight than natural gas or oil; it is expensive to transport; and there are many hidden environmental costs to using it. Coal-burning plants generate emissions of sulfur dioxide, oxides of nitrogen, and carbon dioxide, gases which may fall back to the earth as acid rain or contribute to global warming. Of the various sources of air pollution in the U.S., coal-fired power plants account for about 70% of all sulfur dioxide emissions, 30% of all oxides of nitrogen emissions, and 35% of all carbon dioxide emissions.[2]

Development of new technologies for burning coal cleanly was a key issue during the 1980's for the utility industry and AES. Congress created a national initiative to demonstrate and deploy clean coal technologies to industry. Emission control systems accounted for as much as 40% of the capital cost of a new plant, and 35% of its operational costs.[3] Maintaining the lead in clean coal technology was inherent to AES's commitment to social responsibility. Creating the most energy-efficient and low-cost pollution-controlled plants was also critical to maintaining their competitive advantage in the bidding process to win new electric contracts.

AES used a circulating fluidized bed (CFB) combustion technolgy to capture 90% or more of the sulfur released from coal during combustion while minimizing the formation of oxides of nitrogen by operating at a lower temperature. The advantages of this technology are its energy efficiencies and the flexibility for AES to purchase a range of coal qualities in the marketplace, reducing operating costs. In 1987, 78% of utilities were considering implementing the CFB combustion technology, making the technology less unique to AES and threatening their competitive cost advantage.[4] Thirty-six coal-fired cogeneration plants out of a total of 78 power plants were either under construction or planned through the year 2000 (see Exhibit 4) to satisfy a 1.5% to 3.6% forecasted growth in electricity demand (see Exhibit 5).

Global Climate Change

The earth's temperature is a function of the rate at which the sun's rays reach the earth's surface and the rate at which the warmed earth sends infrared radiation back into the atmosphere. "Greenhouse" gases such as carbon dioxide and methane trap this infrared radiation in the lower atmosphere, resulting in warmer temperatures (see Exhibit 6). Human activities during the last century have increased the concentrations of these naturally occurring greenhouse gases primarily through the burning of fossil fuels. Powerful new gases such as chlorofluorocarbons (CFC's) that are released through chemical processes have also intensified the "greenhouse effect" of the earth's lower atmosphere.

In 1987, the link between growing atmospheric concentrations of greenhouse gases and eventual global warming was becoming of greater interest world-wide to scientists and policymakers. The Environmental and Energy Study Institute, established by Congress and chaired by Robert Sant of AES, published a Special Report in 1987 summarizing the state of the global warming controversy:

> Recent studies support projections that the earth's surface temperature will climb in the next century by several degrees—to a level never experienced by humans. For virtually every effect, the amplitude, timing, and, in some cases, even direction of the projected changes are uncertain.[5]

Since scientists began measuring the mean global temperature over a hundred years ago, 1987 was the warmest year on record, and the 1980's the warmest decade on record.[6] Nevertheless, there were questions about the cause of leveling and slight downward trend of temperatures between 1940 and 1965, and the reliability of earlier measurements. Some scientists were also skeptical that these temperature trends represented simply a normal fluctuation from the thirty-year climate average rather than any link to the greenhouse effect.

The Department of Energy created climate models that estimated a 1.5 to 4.5 degrees Celsius (3 to 8 degrees Fahrenheit) increase in average global temperatures over the next 75 to 150 years using current carbon dioxide emission rates, and potentially double that increase with the other greenhouse gases included.[7] However, both the magnitude and the timing of global warming remain uncertain, and many related determinants of future climate change are still inadequately understood. For instance, climate models cannot predict how the thermal inertia of oceans may slow any temperature changes caused by increased greenhouse gases over the next several decades.

Roger Sant at AES thought the linkage between greenhouse gas buildup and global climate change was plausible. He also knew that carbon dioxide emissions were a primary contributor to the greenhouse gas buildup: global emissions of carbon dioxide in 1987 contributed to 57% of all greenhouse gas emissions. His research showed that the United States annually generated approximately 23% of global carbon dioxide emissions, and that U.S. energy producing plants alone generated over 6%.[8]

Although carbon dioxide emissions can be tied directly to industry smoke stacks, they are also an intergral part of virtually all natural and combustion processes. There is no single, identifiable source of carbon dioxide emissions, making the control of carbon dioxide through legislation particularly difficult.[9] Due to this fact, the Clean Air Act and its amendments never have included regulation of carbon dioxide emissions. By 1987 no legislation had been proposed to control carbon dioxide emissions, nor was there any expected to be considered in the near future.

Offsetting the Thames Plant Carbon Dioxide Emissions

Roger Sant presented the problem of carbon dioxide emissions from the Thames power plant and their possible relationship to global warming to Naill and Sturges. He asked them both to come up with some options to offset the carbon dioxide emissions for the next operating committee meeting in two weeks.

Neither Naill nor Sturges had a great deal of background knowledge on greenhouse gases nor the natural carbon cycle process. They did, however, know what kind of project would meet AES operational needs. Sitting in Naill's office, they developed the following criteria to evaluate the various alternatives:

a) **Cost of the alternative must not exceed 1% of capital cost of project (approximately $275 million).** If greater than this amount, the pool of investors would need to be advised and the electric sales contract would need to be modified. Such action would undermine AES's credibility and competitiveness.

b) **Carbon dioxide must be disposed of permanently.** For example, selling it to beverage companies to enhance the carbonation in their drinks would not permanently remove the carbon dioxide from the atmosphere.

c) **The alternative must be technologically feasible.** A solution is needed that solves the problem but maintains the viability of AES as a business.

d) **The alternative preferably has other positive social benefits aside from carbon sequestration.** The project itself is assured greater sustainability over the long-term and can be enhanced by financial leverage from other investor-related parties if it has further humanistic value than simply carbon sequestration.

The Alternatives

After developing these criteria, Naill passed the problem onto Sturges. After extensive investigation into the issue, Sturges came up with the following alternatives. The first three could be implemented for the Thames plant specifically, and then repeated for other coal-fired power plants. The last dealt with a strategy shift for AES, that would not only affect the carbon dioxide emissions but would drastically change the way AES does business.

1) Promote energy conservation of 180 megawatts per annum to offset the carbon dioxide emissions from the Thames plant. The Electric Power Research Institute estimated in 1986 that a 50,000-megawatt reduction in energy use was achievable during peak hours through industrial, commercial, and residential conservation and load management.[10] However, at that time, only a handful of utilities were focused on demand side energy conservation. Part of the problem of energy conservation programs was that, to assure project conservation goals were achieved, each individual user's old and new electricity utilization rates needed to be measured and aggregated. This made monitoring costs extremely high in relation to total conservation program costs.

Because utility companies had direct access to the residential market, their incremental cost of conservation marketing was minimal. AES did not have this access, so the company was limited to commercial and industrial sectors to target energy conservation. These sectors represented over 70% of all electricity and use in 1986 (see Exhibit 7).

A means of promoting conservation in these sectors was through "lighting retrofits." On average, one-third of commercial/industrial electricity costs were attributed to lighting. Lighting retrofits replaced short-lived fluorescent lights with longer-life fluorescents that lasted up to ten years. The customer would not only save on operation costs for replacement of the lights, they would also save 30 to 40% on their electricity bills. In order to obtain 180 megawatts of conservation, AES would need to form partnerships with several utility and industrial companies to establish in excess of 100 lighting retrofit contracts with individual end-users. As well, a monitoring system would need to be implemented to guarantee that the end-users remain faithful to the lighting retrofits, the cost of which at this point was unknown, but thought to be very expensive.

2) Employ a technology that scrubs carbon dioxide from plant exhaust gases. Find a means to permanently remove them from the atmosphere. Carbon dioxide can be removed from smokestack emissions using liquid solvents or solid absorbents and converted into gas, liquid or solid blocks. A variety of new systems were available, at a very high cost, to perform this task. For instance, the Brookhaven National Laboratory uses the chemical solvent monoethanolamine to separate the carbon dioxide. The system, however, costs \$50–300 million per plant in 1980 dollars. Also, extra energy capacity would be needed to run the removal system, lowering the overall efficiency of the plant. At the Shady Point plant currently operated by AES, the capital cost of 4% carbon dioxide removal was approximately \$10 million.

A secondary market for carbon dioxide existed; however, the price of purified carbon dioxide kept the market small. The only potential market for captured carbon dioxide emissions that would not cause the emissions to be re-released into the atmosphere was enhanced oil recovery (EOR). This process injected carbon dioxide into rock formations during exploration and production of crude oil, pushing out excess crude otherwise unattainable. The carbon dioxide was then recycled by the oil company.

According to the authors of EPRI 4631 *Chemistry and Uses of Carbon Dioxide:*

> The [EOR] activity is intense; probably the only reason that more projects are not in place is the shortage of Carbon Dioxide. This has been a problem for years and awaits a solution.[11]

In developing a market for carbon dioxide, AES had three major considerations:

- the volume of carbon dioxide it would capture and resell could exceed the market demand.
- a sudden increase in carbon dioxide supply could drive current inflated prices down.
- the company had to be sure that the carbon dioxide would not be re-released into the atmosphere (criterion b).

An alternative to selling the carbon dioxide in the EOR market would be to store the gas deep in the bottom of the ocean so that it could never be re-released. The cost of this process, in addition to the carbon capturing technology installed in the plant, would be considerable.

3) Halt deforestation or encourage reforestation to increase amount of carbon removed from atmosphere by trees. AES determined that the Thames plant would emit 15.5 million tons of carbon over the plant's 40-year life. Rather than attempting to capture or conserve the carbon dioxide using man-made processes, this third option utilizes the natural carbon cycle to absorb or "sequestrate" the carbon dioxide emissions. The natural carbon cycle consists of plants/ forests and oceans absorbing and emitting carbon particles as part of a natural process (see Exhibit 7). The man-made portion (combustion processes, deforestation, etc.) repesents only a small fraction of the carbon flows moving through this cycle. However, this intervention permanently affects the magnitude of the total process. By planting more trees or minimizing deforestation, for instance, the influence of the coal-fired combustion process can be minimized, returning the carbon process back to its more natural order.

Sturges came up with the following table to determine how many trees would need to be planted to offset the 15.5 million tons of carbon from the Thames plant. The numbers vary based on the type of tree (planting density and growth rates are critical factors), and the health of the soil being planted.

Area per 180-megawatt plant

Acres	32,400 to 127,800
Hectares	12,960 to 51,120
Square Miles	54 to 200

This table compares to nearly 410 million hectares (1 billion acres) of land that is currently recovering from "slash and burn" agricultural techniques in developing countries which could greatly benefit from reforestation work. Sturges also learned that trees in tropical areas grow more quickly thereby absorbing carbon more rapidly in the earlier years. Based on these figures, and discussions with various international development agencies, Sturges determined that the cost of such a project would be between $1.5 to $8.0 million in a tropical developing country, assuming that the reforested land would not need to be purchased. The development agencies believed that AES could leverage its financial input by collaborating with local groups that may provide cheap sources of labor or contribute to the funding of the reforestation project. The company could find land for reforestation near Connecticut, where the plant was to be located; however, the costs of the labor would be prohibitive. As it was, labor costs were projected to be 50% to 75% of the total project cost.

4) Reevaluate current strategy of coal-fired power plants as least cost technology. What are other long-term strategic options open to AES that may represent a least "social" cost?

Natural Gas

The most efficient technology for the natural gas fuel source in 1987 was combined cycle plants. These plants use combustion turbines which can burn natural gas, distillate, and residual oils allowing the risk of shortage or price variations to be spread across three products. The combustion turbines produced few or no sulfur dioxide emissions if the quality of the fuels burned is controlled. Nitrogen oxides are emitted, but could be mitigated through a secondary process of injecting water or steam into the system. Still, the amount of nitrogen oxide produced by natural gas is, per unit of energy, equal to or greater than that of coal. Carbon dioxide emissions from natural gas plants are approximately two-thirds that of coal.

Capital costs were approximately $600 per kilowatt for a combined cycle plant, as compared to $1000 per kilowatt for a coal-fired plant with CFB technology. However, fuel for the combined cycle technology was very expensive comparatively and subject to price swings; operating costs for natural gas ranged two to three times greater than that of coal. Also, plant profitability was at risk because the cost of the natural gas fuel could exceed the fixed price electric power sales contract developed by an independent power producer. Conservatively, the combined cycle option might add as much as 15% to AES real economic cost of doing business if gas price forecasts were to be realized.[12]

Renewables: Biomass, Wind, Hydro and Solar

Biomass refers to energy stored in plant and animal organic matter. The primary resources of biomass energy include wood wastes, agricultural residues, animal manures, the organic portions of municipal solid waste, landfill gas and sewage. Utilization of available biomass for energy production was estimated at only 25% in 1985.[13] However, biomass primarily provides energy for individual use rather than electricity sales. For instance, the lumber industry derives almost 75% of its energy from direct wood combustion and the pulp and paper industry derives 51% of its energy needs from wood.

The most promising biomass technology is waste-to-energy, which converts solid waste into saleable energy through incineration. Capacities typically of these plants are only 1 to 80 megawatts, with capita costs ranging from $500–$1600 per kilowatt. Most waste-to-energy projects must be developed through an alliance between a developer and municipality. The plants must also be located close to waste centers and to population centers, raising environmental concerns. Pollution from waste-to-energy plants varies based on the combustion method of the plant and the composition of the waste. However, little data exists as to the danger of the pollutants produced, and few regulatory standards have been established to monitor the emissions.

Wind energy is one of the fastest growing renewable technologies in the 1980's due to tax incentives passed in the Wind Energy Systems Act of 1980. However, these incentives expired during 1985, making wind energy production less appealing to investors. Over 95% of the U.S. development in wind energy production has been in California, in part due to state incentives. Wind is a clean, free and renewable source of energy with short lead times and few off-site environmental impacts. Major disadvantages are that wind is an intermittent energy source subject to unforeseen variations; it requires extensive land use potentially leading to land erosion, generates noise pollution for nearby home dwellers, and interrupts bird and wildlife migrations. The capital costs for wind technology range from $900 to $1200 per kilowatt, with most project size under 20 megawatts.

Hydropower harnesses the kinetic energy in falling water to produce electricity. The total capacity in the United States in 1985 was 79,000 megawatts or one-eighth of the nation's total generating supply. Because of the competing uses of rivers as water sources, and the depletion of available rivers for damming, most domestic development would need to be concentrated at existing dam sites with generating potential of 25 megawatts or less. In comparison with other renewable energy sources, hydropower's potential is limited due to its past high exploitation. A primary environmental advantage of hydropower is that it does not require combustion, therefore limiting any damage to air quality. However, the dams can have negative effects on wildlife, scenic river valleys and recreational uses of rivers, inhibiting future growth of hydropower. The process of obtaining a hydropower license has therefore become extremely expensive, arduous and time consuming.

Solar energy refers to technologies that convert energy from sunlight into thermal energy, which eventually becomes electricity. With tax incentives expiring year-end 1985, the solar industry could not maintain the financial support to continue growing as did the other renewables. As a result, capital costs of solar are higher than other renewable alternatives ($2000 to $3000 per kilowatt) and operating costs are burdensome. Most solar projects are under 30 megawatts of power.

The Operating Committee Meeting

Roger Sant had asked Naill and Sturges to present their recommendations at an upcoming operating committee meeting in October—two weeks away. Sturges knew that the operating committee members would be receptive to creative solutions that enhanced the company's commitment to social responsibility. She also realized that the fourth option, changing the long-term strategy of AES from coal-fired power plants to natural gas or renewable energy, could not be applied to the Thames plant which was already under construction. For the board meeting, she needed to present one of the first three options as a means to offset the carbon dioxide emissions.

Understanding the value structure at AES, she knew that eventually the company would need to reevaluate its least-cost strategy of coal-fired power plants to incorporate environmental externalities and generate a "total cost" strategy. For right now, she would have to leave that to later strategic planning meetings. Sturges turned to her computer and started working on the presentation of an alternative she knew was the right choice for the Thames plant and for AES.

B*

The Choice: The Guatemala Reforestation Project

With some trepidation, Sturges approached the 2:00 pm Operating Committee Meeting with her presentation materials. Sturges ran through the implications of the greenhouse gas buildup in the ozone and its potential link to global climate change. Then, she recommended that AES should fund a reforestation project in a tropical developing country to offset the carbon dioxide emissions that may be contributing to that buildup. She defended the project as being the most technically feasible, potentially coming under the 1% of capital costs of Thames, having positive social implications, and ensuring AES's position as the least cost supplier of clean coal-fired power plant energy. She paused to let the idea sink in, and was greeted with an exclamation from Dennis Bakke, President and Chief Operating Officer of AES: "Great idea Sheryl!"

The company asked the World Resources Institute (WRI) to advise them on the implementation of a reforestation, or tree-planting, program in a developing country. Over the next six months, WRI convened a panel of foresters and development experts to analyze various proposals from development agencies to implement the reforestation program. A project with CARE, an international relief and development organization, was chosen to help 40,000 smallholder farmers in Guatemala plant more than 52 million trees over a ten-year period. A total of 385 square miles of trees will be planted, one megawatt worth of carbon emissions for each two square miles planted. The forty year sequestration would amount to 19 million tons of carbon in the following manner:

> *35% Carbon mitigated by developing managed woodlots*
> * wood harvested would be used for building materials and firewood
> * 15% new growth; 20% protecting existing forest
> *60% Carbon mitigated by argo forestry planting*
> * trees help stabilize farm land, add nutrients to soil
> * all 60% of mitigation is from protecting existing forests
> *3% Carbon mitigated by preventing forest fires*
> *2% Carbon mitigated by adding carbon to soil*

AES was able to leverage its $2 million grant into $14.5 million worth of funding from the following sources:

U.S. Peace Corps (labor value)	$ 7.5 million
U.S. AID (food aid)	$ 1.8 million
Guatemalan Government	$ 1.2 million
CARE	$ 2.0 million
AES	$ 2.0 million
Total	$14.5 million

*This case was prepared by the Management Institute for Environment and Business (MEB) and reviewed by James E. Post (Boston University School of Management), Forest Reinhardt (Harvard Business School), and Walter D. Scott (Kellogg Graduate School of Business at Northwestern University). Copyright © 1992 by MEB.

WRI announced the project in a press release on October 11, 1988. Reaction to the carbon offset initiative was mixed. The *New Yorker* ran a cartoon depicting a sooth-sayer absolving a corporation of its pollution sins by telling the corporation how many trees to plant. On the other hand *Time* ran a short article calling the project "a healthy environmental equation." Two other publications, one an environmental advocacy magazine and the other an academic research journal, described the project in a very positive light and expressed a hope that the project would be emulated by other companies in the future. Because the feedback from the press was overall quite positive for AES, the small independent power producer in the United States gained international recognition, helping their eventual expansion overseas.

Investors in AES were worried and confused over the non-profit project, and the utilities, AES' primary customers, felt threatened that the initiative might force them to invest similarly to offset their carbon dioxide emissions. Some consumer groups where Thames was being built were also disappointed that the reforestation project would not involve their local community.

The company, and in particular Roger Sant, was not interested in the initiative as a public relations tool. Rather, Sant wanted to fulfill his commitment to the AES four corporate values (integrity, fairness, fun, and social responsibility) through the project. The total costs of the Guatemala project contributed approximately one-tenth of one cent per kilowatt to the cost of producing electricity at the Thames plant. AES' share was about one-seventh of that cost. Even in light of increased competition driving down the potential profitability in the independent power industry, the company took the risk and sponsored the project, maintaining its commitment to social and environmental responsibility.

The Sustainability Task Force

During the annual AES strategic planning process, the sustainability of coal-fired power plants, and its long-term viability in comparison with other fuel alternatives, was continually being analyzed. In early 1991, Roger Sant requested that Roger Naill spearhead a Sustainability Task Force that would extensively investigate alternative forms of fuel supply for AES new power plants. The company had not yet signed an electric contract to develop a new power plant since the Thames project, so the door was wide open to encouraging a realignment of AES basic business strategy of "least cost" through coal-fired power plants.

The charge of the task force was to find an energy fuel that was steady-state and 100% sustainable from an economic and environmental aspect. The task force, not surprisingly, found no fuel that would have both cost stability in the long-run (such as coal) and zero environmental externalities. What they did find is that the best means for AES to approach the sustainability issue would be to "hedge" their portfolio and begin looking into alternative fuels other than coal. In looking at a 50–100 year period, which includes the extended life of a power plant, it made sense to begin development of natural gas projects as well as coal. Incorporating this vision of a "total cost" strategy, the company is in fact now developing natural gas contracts both internationally and in the U.S.

Notes

1. Balzhiser, R.E., and Yeager, K.E., "Coal-fired Power Plants for the Future," *Scientific American,* vol. 257 (September 1987), pp. 100–107.
2. Corcoran, E., "Cleaning up Coal," *Scientific American,* May 1991, pp. 107–116.
3. Balzhiser, R.E. and Yeager, K. E., supra note 1.
4. "*1987 AES Strategic Plan:* Background Data and Issues," 1987.
5. Robock. A., "The Greenhouse Effect: Global Warming Raises Fundamental Issues," Environmental and Energy Study Institute Conference Special Report, September 1987.
6. "The Global Greenhouse Finally Has Leaders Sweating," *Business Week,* Aug. 1, 1988, p. 74.
7. Robock, A., supra note 5.
8. "The Looming Crisis in Electric Power Generation," April 4, 1989, Dennis P. Meany, Booz-Allen & Hamilton Inc.
9. Peters, M. B., "An International Approach to the Greenhouse Effect: The Problem of Increased Atmospheric Carbon Dioxide Can Be Approached by an Innovative International Agreement," *California Western International Law Journal,* Winter 1989, pp. 67–89.
10. Keelin, T. W. and Gellings, C. W., *Impact of Demand-Side Management on Future Customer Electricity Demand,* Electric Power Research Institute Report EM-4815-SR, October 1986.
11. *Chemistry and Uses of Carbon Dioxide,* Electric Power Research Institute Paper 4631, 1987.
12. *1987 AES Strategic Plan:* Background Data and Issues.
13. Fenn, S., Williams, S., and Cogan, D., *Power Plays: Profiles of America's Leading Renewable Electricity Developers,* Washington DC: Investor Responsibility Research Center Inc. (1986).

EXHIBIT 1. Projected AES Net Income

	($ millions)			
	1987	*1988*	*1989*	*1990*
OPERATING REVENUES				
Steam and Electricity Sales	40.8	80.5	125.8	220.3
OPERATING EXPENSES				
Costs of Production	24.1	44.0	68.4	112.6
Other Expenses	14.1	25.7	39.9	65.6
Total Expenses	38.2	69.7	108.3	178.2
INCOME BEFORE TAX	2.6	10.8	17.5	42.1
Taxes	1.0	4.2	6.4	16.1
NET INCOME AFTER TAX	1.6	6.6	11.1	26.0
MEMO:				
Earnings Per Share	1.1	4.6	7.7	18.1
Projected Cash Generation	5.7	10.0	14.4	27.7
Projected Cash Cumulative	6.1	16.1	30.5	58.2

Source: *1987 AES Strategic Plan: Background Data and Issues.*

EXHIBIT 2. Plant Descriptions

	Utility Customer	Fuel	Electricity (Megawatts)	Capital Cost ($MM)	AES Interest
In Operation:					
Deepwater	Houston Lighting & Power	Petroleum Coke	140.0	275.0	(1)
Beaver Valley	West Penn Power Co.	Coal	120	120	80%
Under Construction:					
Placerita	Southern California Edison Co.	Natural Gas	99	140	97.5%
Thames	Connecticut Light & Power Co.	Coal	181	275	100%

(1) Operated under management agreement

Source: *1991 Prospectus for the AES Corporation Common Stock.*

EXHIBIT 3. Operations Goals and Results

AES PLANTS IN OPERATION	1988 Goal	1988 Actual
Deepwater		
Capacity Factor	90%	100.2%
Operations & Maintenance Costs	$15.7 MM	$15.7 MM
Total Cost/kilowatt-hour	4.7 cents/kwh	4.7 cents
Beaver Valley		
Capacity Factor	87%	84.2%
Operations & Maintenance Costs	$35 MM	$35 MM
Total Cost/kilowatt-hour	5.3 cents/kwh	5.3 cents

Source: *1988 AES Strategic Plan: Background Data and Issues.*

EXHIBIT 4. Existing Capacity and Projected Expansion by Fuel Type.
Source: *Energy Information Administration: Annual Energy Outlook 1986,
February 1987.*

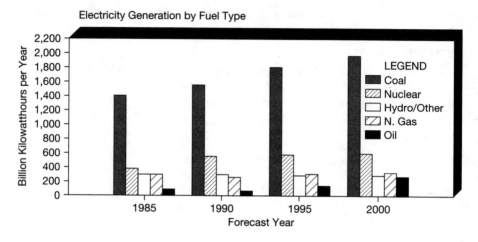

EXHIBIT 5. Uncommitted Utility Capacity Needs.
Source: *1987 AES Strategic Plan: Background Data and Issues.*

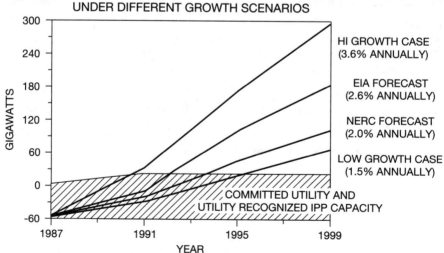

EXHIBIT 6. Greenhouse Effect. Source: *Environmental and Energy Study Institute, Special Report: The Greenhouse Effect, September 1987.*

Now...

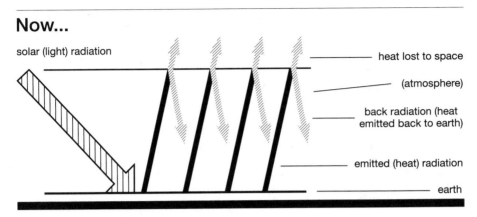

solar (light) radiation

heat lost to space

(atmosphere)

back radiation (heat emitted back to earth)

emitted (heat) radiation

earth

Mid-21st century...

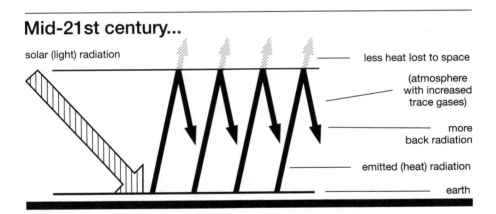

solar (light) radiation

less heat lost to space

(atmosphere with increased trace gases)

more back radiation

emitted (heat) radiation

earth

EXHIBIT 7. Electricity and Total Energy Use, 1986, 1985, and 1980, and Selected Growth Rates (Quadrillion Btu)

Sector	1986	1985[a]	1980	Growth Rate	
				1985–1986 (percent)	1980–1985 (percent)
Residential End Use					
Electricity	2.8	2.7	2.4	4.0	2.0
Total Energy	9.0	8.9	9.1	0.8	-0.5
Commercial/Other End Use					
Electricity[a]	2.5	2.4	1.9	5.2	4.4
Total Energy	6.1	6.0	6.0	0.7	0.3
Industrial End Use					
Electricity	2.8	2.9	2.8	-2.1	0.5
Total Energy	19.6	20.4	23.9	-4.2	-3.1
Total Electricity End Use[b]	8.1	7.9	7.1	2.2	2.1
Total Energy End Use[c]	55.2	55.4	58.6	-0.3	-1.1

[a]1985 data for electricity demand are collected from all U.S. electric utilities and published in the January 1987 *Electric Power Monthly*. The 1985 data for electricity demand used for projections in Chapter 2 are consistent with earlier data published in the *Annual Energy Outlook 1986*, based on data for sales of electricity collected from a sample of utilities.
[b]Includes electricity use in the transportation sector.
[c]Includes end-use energy in the transportation sector.
Note: Data include energy loss in electricity production.
Note: Totals may not equal sum of components because of independent rounding. Growth rates are calculated before rounding.
Sources: Energy Information Administration. 1986 and 1980 data: *Monthly Energy Review,* December 1986 and preceding issues. 1985 data: Estimates prepared by the Electric Power Division.

Source: *Energy Information Administration: Annual Energy Outlook for U.S. Electric Power 1987.*

At the Shrine of Our Lady of Fatima
or Why Political Questions Are Not All Economic

MARK SAGOFF

Lewiston, New York, a well-to-do community near Buffalo, is the site of the Lake Ontario Ordinance Works, where years ago the federal government disposed of the residues of the Manhattan Project. These radioactive wastes are buried but are not forgotten by the residents who say that when the wind is southerly, radon gas blows through the town. Several parents at a recent Lewiston conference I attended described their terror on learning that cases of leukemia had been found among area children. They feared for their own lives as well. On the other side of the table, officials from New York State and

"At the Shrine of Our Lady of Fatima *or* Why Political Questions Are Not All Economic" by Mark Sagoff, *Ariz. Law Rev.* 1283–98 (1981). Copyright © 1981 by the Arizona Board of Regents. Reprinted by permission.

from local corporations replied that these fears were ungrounded. People who smoke, they said, take greater risks than people who live close to waste disposal sites. One speaker talked in terms of "rational methodologies of decisionmaking." This aggravated the parents' rage and frustration.

The speaker suggested that the townspeople, were they to make their decision in a free market and if they knew the scientific facts, would choose to live near the hazardous waste facility. He told me later they were irrational— "neurotic"—because they refused to recognize or to act upon their own interests. The residents of Lewiston were unimpressed with his analysis of their "willingness to pay" to avoid this risk or that. They did not see what risk-benefit analysis had to do with the issues they raised.

If you take the Military Highway (as I did) from Buffalo to Lewiston, you will pass through a formidable wasteland. Landfills stretch in all directions and enormous trucks—tiny in that landscape—incessantly deposit sludge which great bulldozers then push into the ground. These machines are the only signs of life, for in the miasma that hangs in the air, no birds, not even scavengers, are seen. Along colossal power lines which criss-cross this dismal land, the dynamos at Niagra send electric power south, where factories have fled, leaving their remains to decay. To drive along this road is to feel, oddly, the mystery and awe one experiences in the presence of so much power and decadence.

Political and Economic Decisionmaking

This essay concerns the economic decisions we make about the environment. It also concerns our political decisions about the environment. Some people have suggested that ideally these should be the same, that all environmental problems are problems in distribution. According to this view, there is an environmental problem only when some resource is not allocated in equitable and efficient ways.[1]

This approach to environmental policy is pitched entirely at the level of the consumer. It is his or her values that count, and the measure of these values is the individual's willingness to pay. The problem of justice or fairness in society becomes, then, the problem of distributing goods and services so that more people get more of what they want to buy: a condo on the beach, a snowmobile for the mountains, a tank full of gas, a day of labor. The only values we have, according to this view, are those that a market can price.[2]

How much do you value open space, a stand of trees, an "unspoiled" landscape? Fifty dollars? A hundred? A thousand? This is one way to measure value. You could compare the amount consumers would pay for a townhouse or coal or a landfill to the amount they would pay to preserve an area in its "natural" state. If users would pay more for the land with the house, the coal mine, or the landfill, than without—less construction and other costs of development—then the efficient thing to do is to improve the land and thus increase its value. This is why we have so many tract developments, pizza stands, and gas stations. How much did you spend last year to preserve open space? How much for pizza and gas? "In principle, the ultimate measure of environmental quality," as one basic text assures us, "is the value people place on these . . . services or their *willingness to pay*."[3]

Willingness to pay: what is wrong with that? The rub is this: not all of us think of ourselves simply as *consumers*. Many of us regard ourselves *as citizens* as well. We act as consumers to get what we want *for ourselves*. We act as citizens to achieve what we think is right or best *for the community*. This question arises, then, whether what we want for ourselves individually as consumers is consistent with the goals we would set for ourselves collectively as citizens. Would I vote for the sort of things I shop for? Are my preferences as a consumer consistent with my judgments as a citizen?

They are not. I am schizophrenic. Last year, I fixed a couple of tickets and was happy to do so since I saved fifty dollars. Yet, at election time, I helped to vote the corrupt judge out of office. I speed on the highway; yet I want the police to enforce laws against speeding. I used to buy mixers in returnable bottles—but who can bother to return them? I buy only disposables now, but to soothe my conscience, I urge my state senator to outlaw one-way containers. I love my car; I hate the bus. Yet I vote for candidates who promise to tax gasoline to pay for public transporation. And of course I applaud the Endangered Species Act, although I have no earthly use for the Colorado squawfish or the Indiana bat. I support almost any political cause that I think will defeat my consumer interests. This is because I have contempt for—although I act upon—those interests. I have an "Ecology Now" sticker on a car that leaks oil everywhere it's parked.

The distinction between consumer and citizen preferences has long vexed the theory of public finance. Should the public economy serve the same goals as the household economy? May it serve, instead, goals emerging from our association as citizens? The question asks if we may collectively strive for and achieve only those items we individually compete for and consume. Should we aspire, instead, to public goals we may legislate as a nation?

The problem, insofar as it concerns public finance, is stated as follows by R. A. Musgrave, who reports a conversation he had with Gerhard Colm:

> He [Colm] holds that the individual voter dealing with political issues has a frame of reference quite distinct from that which underlies his allocation of income as a consumer. In the latter situation the voter acts as a private individual determined by self-interest and deals with his personal wants; in the former, he acts as a political being guided by his image of a good society. The two, Colm holds, are different things.[4]

Are these two different things? Stephen Marglin suggests that they are. He writes:

> the preferences that govern one's unilateral market actions no longer govern his actions when the form of reference is shifted from the market to the political arena. The Economic Man and the Citizen are for all intents and purposes two different individuals. It is not a question, therefore, of rejecting individual . . . preference maps; it is, rather, that market and political preference maps are inconsistent.[5]

Marglin observes that if this were true, social choices optimal under one set of preferences would not be optimal under another. What, then, is the meaning of "optimality?" He notices that if we take a person's true preferences to be those expressed in the market, we may neglect or reject the preferences that person reveals in advocating a political cause or position. "One might argue on welfare grounds," Marglin speculates, "for authoritarian rejection of individuals' politically revealed preferences in favor of their market revealed preferences!"[6]

Cost-Benefit Analysis vs. Regulation

On February 19, 1981, President Reagan published Executive Order 12,291[7] requiring all administrative agencies and departments to support every new major regulation with a cost-benefit analysis establishing that the benefits of the regulation to society outweigh its costs. The order directs the Office of Management and Budget (OMB) to review every such regulation on the basis of the adequacy of the cost-benefit analysis supporting it. This is a departure from tradition. Historically, regulations have been reviewed not by OMB but by the courts on the basis of the relation of the regulation to authorizing legislation, not to cost-benefit analysis.

A month earlier, in January, 1981, the Supreme Court heard lawyers for the American Textile Manufacturers Institute argue against a proposed Occupational Safety and Health Administration (OSHA) regulation which would have severely restricted the acceptable levels of cotton dust in textile plants.[8] The laywers for industry argued that the benefits of the regulation would not equal the costs.[9] The lawyers for the government contended that the law required the tough standard.[10] OSHA, acting consistently with Executive Order 12,291, asked the Court not to decide the cotton dust case in order to give the agency time to complete the cost-benefit analysis required by the textile industry.[11] The Court declined to accept OSHA's request and handed down its opinion in *American Textile Manufacturers v. Donovan* on June 17, 1981.[12]

The Supreme Court, in a 5–3 decision, found that the actions of regulatory agencies which conform to the OSHA law need not be supported by cost-benefit analysis.[13] In addition, the Court asserted that Congress, in writing a statute, rather than the agencies in applying it, has the primary responsibility for balancing benefits and costs.[14] The Court said:

> When Congress passed the Occupational Health and Safety Act in 1970, it chose to place pre-eminent value on assuring employees a safe and healthful working environment, limited only by the feasibility of achieving such an environment. We must measure the validity of the Secretary's actions against the requirements of that Act.[15]

The opinion upheld the finding of the District of Columbia Court of Appeals that "Congress itself struck the balance between costs and benefits in the mandate to the agency."[16]

The Appeals Courts opinion in *American Textile Manufacturers v. Donovan* supports the principle that legislatures are not necessarily bound to a particular conception of regulatory policy. Agencies that apply the law therefore may not need to justify on cost-benefit grounds the standards they set. These standards may conflict with the goal of efficiency and still express our political will as a nation. That is, they may reflect not the personal choices of self-interested individuals, but the collective judgments we make on historical, cultural, aesthetic, moral, and ideological grounds.[17]

The appeal of the Reagan Administration to cost-benefit analysis, however, may arise more from political than economic considerations. The intention, seen in the most favorable light, may not be to replace political or ideological goals with economic ones, but to make economic goals more apparent in regulation. This is not to say that Congress should function to reveal a collective willingness-to-pay just as markets reveal an individual willingness-to-pay. It is to suggest that Congress should do more to balance economic with ideological, aesthetic, and moral goals. To think that environmental or worker safety policy can be based exclusively on aspiration for a "natural" and "safe" world is as foolish as to hold that environmental law can be reduced to cost-benefit accounting. The more we move to one extreme, as I found in Lewiston, the more likely we are to hear from the other.

Substituting Efficiency for Safety

The labor unions won an important political victory when Congress passed the Occupational Safety and Health Act of 1970.[18] That Act, among other things, severely restricts worker exposure to toxic substances. It instructs the Secretary of Labor to set "the standard which most adequately assures, to the extent feasible . . . that no employee will suffer material impairment of health or funcitonal capacity even if such employee has regular exposure to the hazard . . . for the period of his working life."[19]

Pursuant to this law, the Secretary of Labor in 1977 reduced from ten to one part per million (ppm) the permissable ambient exposure level for benzene, a carcinogen for which no safe threshold is known. The American Petroleum Institute thereupon challenged the new standard in court.[20] It argued, with much evidence in its favor, that the benefits (to workers) of the one ppm standard did not equal the costs (to industry).[21] The standard therefore did not appear to be a rational response to a market failure in that it did not strike an efficient balance between the interests of workers in safety and the interests of industry and consumers in keeping prices down.

The Secretary of Labor defended the tough safety standard on the ground that the law demanded it.[22] An efficient standard might have required safety until it cost industry more to prevent a risk than it cost workers to accept it. Had Congress adopted this vision of public policy—one which can be found in many economics texts[23]—it would have treated workers not as ends-in-themselves but as means for the production of overall utility. This, as the Secretary saw it, was what Congress refused to do.[24]

The United States Court of Appeals for the Fifth Circuit agreed with the American Petroleum Institute and invalidated the one ppm benzene standard.[25] On July 2, 1980, the Supreme Court affirmed the decision in *American Petroleum Institute v. Marshall*[26] and remanded the benzene standard back to OSHA for revision. The narrowly based Supreme Court decision was divided over the role economic considerations should play in judicial review. Justice Marshall, joined in dissent by three other justices, argued that the Court had undone on the basis of its own theory of regulatory policy an act of Congress inconsistent with that theory.[27] He concluded that the plurality decision of the Court "requires the American worker to return to the political arena to win a victory that he won before in 1970."[28]

The decision of the Supreme Court is important not because of its consequences, which are likely to be minimal, but because of the fascinating questions it raises. Shall the courts uphold only those political decisions that can be defended on economic grounds? Shall we allow democracy only to the extent that it can be construed either as a rational response to a market failure or as an attempt to redistribute wealth? Should the courts say that a regulation is not "feasible" or "reasonable"—terms that occur in the OSHA law[29]—unless it is supported by a cost-benefit analysis?

The problem is this: An efficiency criterion, as it is used to evaluate public policy, assumes that the goals of our society are contained in the preferences individuals reveal or would reveal in markets. Such an approach may appear attractive, even just, because it treats everyone as equal, at least theoretically, by according to each person's preferences the same respect and concern. To treat a person with respect, however, is also to listen and to respond intelligently to his or her views and opinions. This is not the same thing as to ask how much he or she is willing to pay for them. The cost-benefit analyst does not ask economists how much they are willing to pay for what they believe, that is, that the workplace and the environment should be made efficient. Why, then, does the analyst ask workers, environmentalists, and others how much they are willing to pay for what they believe is right? Are economists the only ones who can back their ideas with reasons while the rest of us can only pay a price? The cost-benefit approach treats people as of equal worth because it treats them as of no worth, but only as places or channels at which willingness to pay is found.[30]

Liberty: Ancient and Modern

When efficiency is the criterion of public safety and health, one tends to conceive of social relations on the model of a market, ignoring competing visions of what we as a society should be like. Yet it is obvious that there are competing conceptions of what we should be as a society. There are some who believe on principle that worker safety and environmental quality ought to be protected only insofar as the benefits of protection balance the costs. On the other hand, people argue—also on principle—that neither worker safety nor environmental quality should be treated merely as a commodity to be traded at the margin for other commodities, but rather each should be valued for its own sake. The conflict between these two principles is logical or moral, to be resolved by argument or debate. The question whether cost-benefit analysis should play a decisive role in policymaking is not to be decided by cost-benefit analysis. A contradiction between principles—between contending visions of the good society—cannot be settled by asking how much partisans are willing to pay for their beliefs.

The role of the *legislator*, the political role, may be more important to the individual than the role of *consumer*. The person, in other words, is not to be treated merely as a bundle of preferences to be juggled in cost-benefit analyses. The individual is to be respected as an advocate of ideas which are to be judged according to the reasons for them. If health and environmental statutes reflect a vision of society as something other than a market by requiring protections beyond what are efficient, then this may express not legislative ineptitude but legislative responsiveness to public values. To deny this vision because it is economically inefficient is simply to replace it with another vision.

It is to insist that the ideas of the citizen be sacrificed to the psychology of the consumer.

We hear on all sides that government is routinized, mechanical, entrenched, and bureaucratized; the jargon alone is enough to dissuade the most mettlesome meddler. Who can make a difference? It is plain that for many of us the idea of a national political community has an abstract and suppositious quality. We have only our private conceptions of the good, if no way exists to arrive at a public one. This is only to note the continuation, in our time, of the trend Benjamin Constant described in the essay *De La Liberte des Anciens Comparee a Celle des Modernes.*[31] Constant observes that the modern world, as opposed to the ancient, emphasizes civil over political liberties, the rights of privacy and property over those of community and participation. "Lost in the multitude," Constant writes, "the individual rarely perceives the influence that he exercises," and, therefore, must be content with "the peaceful enjoyment of private independence."[32] The individual asks only to be protected by laws common to all in his pursuit of his own self-interest. The citizen has been replaced by the consumer; the tradition of Rousseau has been supplanted by that of Locke and Mill.

Nowhere are the rights of the moderns, particularly the rights of privacy and property, less helpful than in the area of the natural environment. Here the values we wish to protect—cultural, historical, aesthetic, and moral—are public values. They depend not so much upon what each person wants individually as upon what he or she thinks is right for the community. We refuse to regard worker health and safety as commodities; we regulate hazards as a matter of right. Likewise, we refuse to treat environmental resources simply as public goods in the economist's sense. Instead, we prevent significant deterioration of air quality not only as a matter of individual self-interest but also as a matter of collective self-respect. How shall we balance efficiency against moral, cultural, and aesthetic values in policy for the workplace and the environment? No better way has been devised to do this than by legislative debate ending in a vote. This is very different from a cost-benefit analysis terminating in a bottom line.

Values Are Not Subjective

It is the characteristic of cost-benefit analysis that it treats all value judgments other than those made on its behalf as nothing but statements of preference, attitude, or emotion, insofar as they are value judgments. The cost-benefit analyst regards as true the judgment that we should maximize efficiency or wealth. The analyst believes that this view can be backed by reasons,[33] but does not regard it as a preference or want for which he or she must be willing to pay. The cost-benefit analyst tends to treat all other normative views and recommendations as if they were nothing but subjective reports of mental states. The analyst supposes in all such cases that "this is right" and "this is what we ought to do" are equivalent to "I want this" and "this is what I prefer." Value judgments are beyond criticism if, indeed, they are nothing but expressions of personal preference; they are incorrigible since every person is in the best position to know what he or she wants. All valuation, according to this approach, happens *in foro interno;* debate *in foro publico* has no point. With this approach, the reasons that people give for their views do not count; what does count is how much they are willing to pay to satisfy their wants. Those who are willing to pay the most, for all intents and purposes, have the right view; theirs is the more informed opinion, the better aesthetic judgment, and the deeper moral insight.

The assumption that valuation is subjective, that judgments of good and evil are nothing but expressions of desire and aversion, is not unique to economic theory.[34] There are psychotherapists—Carl Rogers is an example—who likewise deny the objectivity or cognitivity of valuation.[35] For Rogers, there is only one criterion of worth: it lies in "the subjective world of the individual. Only he knows it fully."[36] The therapist shows his or her client that a "value system is not necessarily something imposed from without, but is something experienced."[37] Therapy succeeds when the client perceives himself in such a way that no self-experience can be discriminated as more or less worthy of positive self-regard than any other. . . ."[38] The client then "tends to place the basis of standards within himself, recognizing that the 'goodness' or 'badness' of any experience or perceptual object is not something inherent in that object, but is a value placed in it by himself."[39]

Rogers points out that "some clients make strenuous efforts to have the therapist exercise the valuing function, so as to provide them with guides for action."[40] The therapist, however, "consistently keeps the locus of evaluation with the client."[41] As long as the therapist refuses to "exercise the valuing function" and as long as he or she practices an "unconditional positive regard"[42] for all the affective states of the client, then the therapist remains neutral among the client's values or "sensory and visceral experiences."[43] The role of the therapist is legitimate, Rogers suggests, because of this value neutrality. The therapist accepts all felt preferences as valid and imposes none on the client.

Economists likewise argue that their role as policy-makers is legitimate because they are neutral among competing values in the client society. The political economist, according to James Buchanan, "is or should be ethically neutral: the indicated results are influenced by his own value scale only insofar as this reflects his membership in a larger group."[44] The economist might be most confident of the impartiality of his or her policy recommendations if he or she could derive them formally or mathematically from individual preferences. If theoretical difficulties make such a social welfare function impossible,[45] however, the next best thing, to preserve neutrality, is to let markets function to transform individual preference orderings into a collective ordering of social states. The analyst is able then to base policy on preferences that exist in society and are not necessarily his own.

Economists have used this impartial approach to offer solutions to many significant social problems, for example, the controversy over abortion. An economist argues that "there is an optimal number of abortions, just as there is an optimal level of pollution, or purity. . . . Those who oppose abortion could eliminate it entirely, if their intensity of feeling were so strong as to lead to payments that were greater at the margin than the price anyone would pay to have an abortion."[46] Likewise, economists, in order to determine whether the war in Vietnam was justified, have estimated the willingness to pay of those who demonstrated against it.[47] Following the same line of reasoning, it should be possible to decide whether Creationism should be taught in the public schools, whether black and white people should be segregated, whether the death penalty should be enforced, and whether the square root of six is three. All of these questions arguably depend upon how much people are willing to pay for their subjective preferences or wants. This is the beauty of cost-benefit analysis: no matter how relevant or irrelevant, wise or stupid, informed or uninformed, responsible or silly, defensible or indefensible wants may be, the analyst is able to derive a policy from them—a policy which is legitimate because, in theory, it treats all of these preferences as equally valid and good.

Preference or Principle?

In contrast, consider a Kantian conception of value.[48] The individual, for Kant, is a judge of values, not a mere haver of wants, and the individual judges not for himself or herself, merely, but as a member of a relevant community or group. The central idea in a Kantian approach to ethics is that some values are more reasonable than others and therefore have a better claim upon the assent of members of the community as such.[49] The world of obligation, like the world of mathematics or the world of empirical fact, is public not private, and objective standards of argument and criticism apply. Kant recognized that values, like beliefs, are subjective states of mind which have an objective content as well. Therefore, both values and beliefs are either correct or mistaken. A value judgment is like an empirical or theoretical judgment in that it claims to be *true* not merely to be *felt*.

We have, then, two approaches to public policy before us. The first, the approach associated with normative versions of welfare economics, asserts that the only policy recommendation that can or need be defended on objective grounds is efficiency or wealth-maximization. The Kantian approach, on the other hand, assumes that many policy recommendations may be justified or refuted on objective grounds. It would concede that the approach of welfare economics applies adequately to some questions, for example, those which ordinary consumer markets typically settle. How many yo-yos should be produced as compared to how many frisbees? Shall pens have black ink or blue? Matters such as these are so trivial it is plain that markets should handle them. It does not follow, however, that we should adopt a market or quasi-market approach to every public question.

A market or quasi-market approach to arithmetic, for example, is plainly inadequate. No matter how much people are willing to pay, three will never be the square root of six. Similarly, segregation is a national curse and the fact that we are willing to pay for it does not make it better, but only us worse. The case for abortion must stand on the merits; it cannot be priced at the margin. Our failures to make the right decisions in these matters are failures in arithmetic, failures in wisdom, failures in taste, failures in morality—but not market failures. There are no relevant markets which have failed.

What separates these questions from those for which markets are appropriate is that they involve matters of knowledge, wisdom, morality, and taste that admit of better or worse, right or wrong, true or false, and not mere economic optimality. Surely environmental questions—the protection of wilderness, habitats, water, land, and air as well as policy toward environmental safety and health—involve moral and aesthetic principles and not just economic ones. This is consistent, of course, with cost-effectiveness and with a sensible recognition of economic constraints.

The neutrality of the economist is legitimate if private preferences or subjective wants are the only values in question. A person should be left free to choose the color of his or her necktie or necklace, but we cannot justify a theory of public policy or private therapy on that basis. If the patient seeks moral advice or tries to find reasons to justify a choice, the therapist, according to Rogers' model, would remind him or her to trust his visceral and sensory experiences. The result of this is to deny the individual status as a cognitive being capable of responding intelligently to reasons; it reduces him or her to a bundle of affective states. What Rogers' therapist does to the patient the cost-benefit analyst does to society as a whole. The analyst is neutral among our "values"—having first imposed a theory of what value is. This is a theory that is impartial among values and for that reason fails to treat the persons who have them with respect or concern. It does not treat them even as persons but only as locations at which wants may be found. The neutrality of economics is not a basis for its legitimacy. We recognize it as an indifference toward value—an indifference so deep, so studied, and so assured that at first one hesitates to call it by its right name.

The Citizen as Joseph K.

The residents of Lewiston at the conference I attended demanded to know the truth about the dangers that confronted them and the reasons for those dangers. They wanted to be convinced that the sacrifice asked of them was legitimate even if it served interests other than their own. One official from a large chemical company dumping wastes in the area told them in reply that corporations were people and that people could talk to people about their feelings, interests, and needs. This sent a shiver through the audience. Like Joseph K. in *The Trial*,[50] the residents of Lewiston asked for an explanation, justice, and truth, and they were told that their wants would be taken care of. They demanded to know the reasons for what was continually happening to them. They were given a personalized response instead.

This response, that corporations are "just people serving people," is consisent with a particular view of power. This is the view that identifies power with the ability to get what one wants as an individual, that is, to satisfy one's personal preferences. When people in official positions in corporations or in the government put aside their personal interests, it would follow that they put aside their power as well. Their neutrality then justifies them in directing the resources of society in ways they determine to be best. This managerial role serves not their own interests but those of their clients. Cost-benefit analysis may be seen as a pervasive form of this paternalism. Behind this paternalism, as William Simon observes of the lawyer-client relationship, lies a theory of value that tends to personalize power. "It resists understanding power as a product of class, property, or institutions and collapses power into the personal needs and dispositions of the individuals who command and obey."[51] Once the economist, the therapist, the lawyer, or the manager abjures his own interests and acts wholly on behalf of client individuals, he appears to have no power of his own and thus justifiably manipulates and controls everything. "From this perspective it becomes difficult to distinguish the powerful from the powerless. In every case, both the exercise of power and submission to it are portrayed as a matter of personal accommodation and adjustment."[52]

The key to the personal interest or emotive theory of value, as one commentator has rightly said, "is the fact that emotivism entails the obliteration of any genuine distinction between manipulative and nonmanipulative social relations."[53] The reason is that once the affective self is made the source of all value, the public self cannot participate in the exercise of power. As Philip Reiff remarks, "the public world is constituted as one vast stranger who appears at inconvenient times and makes demands viewed as purely external and therefore with no power to elicit a moral response."[54] There is no way to distinguish the legitimate authority that public values and public law create from tyranny.[55]

"At the rate of progress since 1900," Henry Adams speculates in his *Education*, "every American who lived into the year 2000 would know how to control unlimited power."[56] . . . Yet in the 1980s, the citizens of Lewiston, surrounded by dynamos, high tension lines, and nuclear wastes, are powerless. They do not know how to criticize power, resist power, or justify power—for to do so depends on making distinctions between good and evil, right and wrong, innocence and guilt, justice and injustice, truth and lies. These distinctions cannot be made out and have no signficance within an emotive or psychological theory of value. To adopt this theory is to imagine society as a market in which individuals trade voluntarily and without coercion. No individual, no belief, no faith has authority over them. To have power to act as a nation we must be able to act, at least at times, on a public philosophy, conviction, or faith. We cannot abandon the moral function of public law. The antinomianism of cost-benefit analysis is not enough.

Notes

1. *See, e.g.,* W. Baxter, *People or Penguins: The Case for Optimal Pollution* ch. 1 (1974). *See generally* A. Freeman, R. Haveman, A. Kneese, *The Economics of Environmental Policy* (1973) [hereinafter A. Freeman].

2. Posner makes this point well in discussing wealth maximization as an ethical concept. "The only kind of preference that counts in a system of wealth-maximization," he writes, "is . . . one that is backed up by money—in other words, that is registered in a market." Posner, *Utilitarianism, Economics, and Legal Theory,* 8 J. Legal Stud. 103, 119 (1979).

3. A. Freeman, *supra* note 6, at 23.

4. R. Musgrave, *The Theory of Public Finance* 87–88 (1959).

5. Marglin, *The Social Rate of Discount and the Optimal Rate of Investment,* 77 Q.J. Econ. 95, 98 (1963).

6. *Id.*

7. 46 Fed. Reg. 13,193 (1981). The order specifies that the cost-benefit requirement shall apply "to the extent permitted by law."

8. American Fed'n of Labor, etc. v. Marshall, 617 F.2d 636 (D.C. Cir. 1979), *cert. granted sub nom.* American Textile Mfrs. Inst., Inc. v. Marshall, 49 U.S.L.W. 3208 (1981).

9. 49 U.S.L.W. 3523–24.

10. *Id.*

11. *Id.*

12. American Textile Mfrs. Inst., Inc. v. Donovan, 49 U.S.L.W. 4720 (1981).

13. *Id.* at 4724–29.

14. Id. at 4726–29.

15. *Id.* at 4733–34.

16. *Id.* at 4726–29.

17. To reject cost benefit analysis as a basis for policymaking is not necessarily to reject cost-effectiveness analysis which is an altogether different thing. For this difference, *see* Baram, *Cost-Benefit Analysis: An Inadequate Basis for Health, Safety, and Environmental Regulatory Decisionmaking*, 8 *Ecology L. Q.* 473 (1980). "*Cost-benefit analysis . . .* is used by the decisionmaker to establish societal goals as well as the means for achieving these goals, whereas *cost-effectiveness analysis* only compares alternative means for achieving 'given' goals." *Id.* at 478 (footnote omitted). In practice, regulatory uses of cost-benefit analysis stifle and obstruct the achievement of legislated health, safety, and environmental goals. *Id.* at 473. Further, to the extent that economic factors are permissible considerations under enabling statutes, agencies should engage in cost-effectiveness analysis, which aids in determining the least costly means to designated goals, rather than cost-benefit analysis, which improperly determines regulatory ends as well as means. *Id.* at 474.

18. Pub. L. No. 91–596, 84 Stat. 1596 (1970) (codified at 29 U.S.C. §§ 651–678 (1970)).

19. 29 U.S.C. § 655(b)(5) (1970).

20. American Petroleum Inst. v. Marshall, 581 F.2d 493 (5th Cir. 1978), *aff'd*, 448 U.S. 607 (1980).

21. 581 F.2d at 501–05.

22. *Id.* at 501.

23. *See, e.g.*, R. Posner, *Economic Analysis of Law I & II* (1973). In G. Calabresi, *The Costs of Accidents passim* (1970), the author argues that accident law balances two goals, "efficiency" and "equality" or "justice."

24. American Petroleum Inst. v. Marshall, 581 F.2d 493, 503–05 (5th Cir. 1978).

25. *Id.* at 505.

26. 448 U.S. 607 (1980).

27. *Id.* at 719.

28. *Id.*

29. 29 U.S.C. §§ 655(b)(5) & 652(8) (1975).

30. For a similar argument against utilitarianism, *see* Hart, *Between Utility and Rights*, 79 *Colum. L. Rev.* 838, 829–31 (1979).

31. B. Constant, *De La Liberte des Anciens Comparee a Celle des Modernes* (1819).

32. *Oeuvres Politiques de Benjamin Constant*, 269 (C. Louandre, ed. 1874), *quoted in* S. Wolin, *Politics and Vision* 281 (1960).

33. There are arguments that whatever reasons may be given are not good. *See generally* Dworkin, *Why Efficiency?* 8 *Hofstra L. Rev.* 563 (1980); Dworkin, *Is Wealth a Value?* 9 *J. Legal Stud.* 191 (1980); Kennedy, *Cost-Benefit Analysis of Entitlement Problems: A Critique*, 33 *Stan. L. Rev.* 387 (1980); Rizzo, *The Mirage of Efficiency*, 8 *Hofstra L. Rev.* 641 (1980); Sagoff, *Economic Theory and Environmental Law*, 79 *Mich. L. Rev.* 1393 (1981).

34. This is the emotive theory of value. For the classic statement, *see* C. Stevenson, *Ethics and Language* chs. 1 & 2 (144). For criticism, *see* Blanshard, *The New Subjectivism in Ethics*, 9 *Philosophy & Phenomenological Research* 504 (1949). For a statement of the related interest theory of value, *see generally* R. Perry, *General Theory of Value* (1926); E. Westermarck, *Ethical Relativity* chs. 3–5 (1932). For criticisms of subjectivism in ethics and a case for the objective theory

presupposed here, *see generally* P. Edwards, *The Logic of Moral Discourse* (1955) and W. Ross, *The Right and the Good* (1930).

35. My account is based on C. Rogers, *On Becoming a Person* (1961); C. Rogers, *Client Centered Therapy* (1965); and Rogers, *A Theory of Therapy, Personality, and Interpersonal Relationships, as Developed in the Client Centered Framework, 3 Psychology: A Study of a Science* 184 (1959). For a similar account used as a critique of the lawyer-client relation, *see* Simon, *Homo Psychologicus: Notes on a New Legal Formalism, 32 Stan. L. Rev.* 487 (1980).

36. Rogers, *supra* note 40, at 210.

37. C. Rogers, *Client Centered Therapy* 150 (1965).

38. Rogers, *supra* note 40, at 208.

39. C. Rogers, *supra* note 42, at 139.

40. *Id.* at 150.

41. *Id.*

42. Rogers, *supra* note 40, at 208.

43. *Id.* at 523–24.

44. Buchanan, *Positive Economics, Welfare Economics, and Political Economy 2 J.L. & Econ.* 124, 127 (1959).

45. K. Arrow, *Social Choice and Individual Values* I–V (2d ed. 1963).

46. H. Macaulay & B. Yandle, *Environmental Use and the Market* 120–21 (1978).

47. *See generally* Cicchetti, Freeman, Haveman, & Knetsch, *On the Economics of Mass Demonstrations: A Case Study of the November 1969 March on Washington, 61 Am. Econ. Rev.* 719 (1971).

48. I. Kant, *Foundations of the Metaphysics of Morals* (1969). I follow the interpretation of Kantian ethics of W. Sellars, *Science and Metaphysics* ch. vii (1968) and Sellars, *On Reasoning About Values, 17 Am. Phil. Q.* 81 (1980).

49. *See* A. Macintyre, *After Virtue* 22 (1981).

50. F. Kafka, *The Trial* (rev. ed. trans. 1957). Simon applies this analogy to the lawyer-client relationship. Simon, *supra* note 40, at 524.

51. Simon, *supra* note 40, at 495.

52. *Id.*

53. A. Macintyre, *supra* note 54, at 22.

54. P. Reiff, *The Triumph of the Therapeutic: Uses of Faith After Freud* 52 (1966).

55. That public law regimes inevitably lead to tyranny seems to be the conclusion of H. Arendt, *The Human Condition* (1958); K. Popper, *The Open Society and Its Enemies* (1966); L. Strauss, *Natural Right and History* (1953). For an important criticism of this conclusion in these authors, *see generally* Holmes, *Aristippus In and Out of Athens, 73 Am. Pol. Sci. Rev.* 113 (1979).

56. H. Adams, *supra* note 1, at 476.

Cost-Benefit Analysis: An Ethical Critique

STEVEN KELMAN

I

At the broadest and vaguest level, cost-benefit analysis may be regarded simply as systematic thinking about decision-making. Who can oppose, economists sometimes ask, efforts to think in a systematic way about the consequences of different courses of action? The alternative, it would appear, is unexamined decision-making. But defining cost-benefit analysis so simply leaves it with few implications for actual regulatory decision-making. Presumably, therefore, those who urge regulators to make greater use of the technique have a more extensive prescription in mind. I assume here that their prescription includes the following views:

1. There exists a strong presumption that an act should not be undertaken unless its benefits outweigh its costs.

2. In order to determine whether benefits outweigh costs, it is desirable to attempt to express all benefits and costs in a common scale or denominator, so that they can be compared with each other, even when some benefits and costs are not traded on markets and hence have no established dollar values.

3. Getting decision-makers to make more use of cost-benefit techniques is important enough to warrant both the expense required to gather the data for improved cost-benefit estimation and the political efforts needed to give the activity higher priority compared to other activities, also valuable in and of themselves.

My focus is on cost-benefit analysis as applied to environmental, safety, and health regulation. In that context, I examine each of the above propositions from the perspective of formal ethical theory, that is, the study of what actions it is morally right to undertake. My conclusions are:

1. In areas of environmental, safety, and health regulation, there may be many instances where a certain decision might be right even though its benefits do not outweigh its costs.

2. There are good reasons to oppose efforts to put dollar values on non-marketed benefits and costs.

3. Given the relative frequency of occasions in the areas of environmental, safety, and health regulation where one would not wish to use a benefits-outweigh-costs test as a decision rule, and given the reasons to oppose the monetizing of nonmarketed benefits of costs that is a prerequisite for cost-benefit analysis, it is not justifiable to devote major resources to the generation of data for cost-benefit calculations or to undertake efforts to "spread the gospel" of cost-benefit analysis further.

II

In order for cost-benefit calculations to be performed the way they are supposed to be, all costs and benefits must be expressed in a common measure, typically dollars, including things not normally bought and sold on markets,

Regulation (Jan., Feb. 1981), pp. 74–82. Reprinted with the permission of The American Enterprise Institute for Public Policy Research, Washington, D.C.

and to which dollar prices are therefore not attached. The most dramatic example of such things is human life itself; but many of the other benefits achieved or preserved by environmental policy—such as peace and quiet, fresh-smelling air, swimmable rivers, spectacular vistas—are not traded on markets either.

Economists who do cost-benefit analysis regard the quest after dollar values for nonmarket things as a difficult challenge—but one to be met with relish. They have tried to develop methods for imputing a person's "willingness to pay," for such things, their approach generally involving a search for bundled goods that *are* traded on markets and that vary as to whether they include a feature that is, *by itself,* not marketed. Thus, fresh air is not marketed, but houses in different parts of Los Angeles that are similar except for the degree of smog are. Peace and quiet is not marketed, but similar houses inside and outside airport flight paths are. The risk of death is not marketed, but similar jobs that have different levels of risk are. Economists have produced many often ingenious efforts to impute dollar prices to nonmarketed things by observing the premiums accorded homes in clean air areas over similar homes in dirty areas or the premiums paid for risky jobs over similar nonrisky jobs.

These ingenious efforts are subject to criticism on a number of technical grounds. It may be difficult to control for all the dimensions of quality other than the presence or absence of the nonmarketed thing. More important, in a world where people have different preferences and are subject to different constraints as they make their choices, the dollar value imputed to the non-market things that most people would wish to avoid will be lower than otherwise, because people with unusually weak aversion to those things or unusually strong constraints on their choices will be willing to take the bundled good in question at less of a discount than the average person. Thus, to use the property value discount of homes near airports as a measure of people's willingness to pay for quiet means to accept as a proxy for the rest of us the behavior of those least sensitive to noise, of airport employees (who value the convenience of a near-airport location) or of others who are susceptible to an agent's assurances that "it's not so bad." To use the wage premiums accorded hazardous work as a measure of the value of life means to accept as proxies for the rest of us the choices of people who do not have many choices or who are exceptional risk-seekers.

A second problem is that the attempts of economists to measure people's willingness to pay for nonmarketed things assume that there is no difference between the price a person would require for *giving up* something to which he has a preexisting right and the price he would pay to *gain* something to which he enjoys no right. Thus, the analysis assumes no difference between how much a homeowner would need to be paid in order to give up an unobstructed mountain view that he already enjoys and how much he would be willing to pay to get an obstruction moved once it is already in place. Available evidence suggests that most people would insist on being paid far more to assent to a worsening of their situation than they would be willing to pay to improve their situation. The difference arises from such factors as being accustomed to and psychologically attached to that which one believes one enjoys by right. But this creates a circularity problem for any attempt to use cost-benefit analysis to determine *whether* to assign to, say, the homeowner the right to an unobstructed mountain view. For willingness to pay will be different depending on whether the right is assigned initially or not. The value judgment about whether to assign the right must thus be made first. (In order to set an upper bound on the value of the benefit, one might hypothetically assign the right to the person and determine how much he would need to be paid to give it up.)

Third, the efforts of economists to impute willingness to pay invariably involve bundled goods exchanged in *private* transactions. Those who use figures garnered from such analysis to provide guidance for *public* decisions assume no difference between how people value certain things in private individual transactions and how they would wish those same things to be valued in public collective decisions. In making such assumptions, economists insidiously slip into their analysis an important and controversial value judgment, growing naturally out of the highly individualistic microeconomic tradition—namely, the view that there should be no difference between private behavior and the behavior we display in public social life. An alternate view—one that enjoys, I would suggest, wide resonance among citizens—would be that public, social decisions provide an opportunity to give certain things a higher valuation than we choose, for one reason or another, to give them in our private activities.

Thus, opponents of stricter regulation of health risks often argue that we show by our daily risk-taking behavior that we do not value life infinitely, and therefore our public decisions should not reflect the high value of life that proponents of strict regulation propose. However, an alternative view is equally plausible. Precisely because we fail, for whatever reasons, to give life-saving the value in everyday personal decisions that we in some general terms believe we should give it, we may wish our social decisions to provide us the occasion to display the reverence for life that we espouse but do not always show. By this view, people do not have fixed unambiguous "preferences" to which they give expression through private activities and which therefore should be given expression in public decisions. Rather, they may have what they themselves regard as "higher" and "lower" preferences. The latter may come to the fore in private decisions, but people may want the former to come to the fore in public decisions. They may sometimes display racial prejudice, but support anti-discrimination laws. They may buy a certain product after seeing a seductive ad, but be skeptical enough of advertising to want the government to keep a close eye on it. In such cases, the use of private behavior to impute the values that should be entered for public decisions, as is done by using willingness to pay in private transactions, commits grievous offense against a view of the behavior of the citizen that is deeply engrained in our democratic tradition. It is a view that denudes politics of any independent role in society, reducing it to a mechanistic, mimicking recalculation based on private behavior.

Finally, one may oppose the effort to place prices on a nonmarket thing and hence in effect incorporate it into the market system out of a fear that the very act of doing so will reduce the thing's perceived value. To place a price on the benefit may, in other words, reduce the value of that benefit. Cost-benefit analysis thus may be like the thermometer that, when placed in a liquid to be measured, itself changes the liquid's temperature.

Examples of the perceived cheapening of a thing's value by the very act of buying and selling it abound in everyday life and language. The disgust that accompanies the idea of buying and selling human beings is based on the sense that this would dramatically diminish human worth. Epithets such as "he prostituted himself," applied as linguistic analogies to people who have sold something, reflect the view that certain things should not be sold because doing so diminishes their value. Praise that is bought is worth little, even to the person buying it. A true anecdote is told of an economist who retired to another university community and complained that he was having difficulty making friends. The laconic response of a critical colleague—"If you want a friend why don't you buy yourself one"—illustrates in a pithy way the intuition that, for some things, the very act of placing a price on them reduces their perceived value.

The first reason that pricing something decreases its perceived value is that, in many circumstances, nonmarket exchange is associated with the production of certain values not associated with market exchange. These may include spontaneity and various other feelings that come from personal relationships. If a good becomes less associated with the production of positively valued feelings because of market exchange, the perceived value of the good declines to the extent that those feelings are valued. This can be seen clearly in instances where a thing may be transferred both by market and by nonmarket mechanisms. The willingness to pay for sex bought from a prostitute is less than the perceived value of the sex consummating love. (Imagine the reaction if a practitioner of cost-benefit analysis computed the benefits of sex based on the price of prostitute services.)

Furthermore, if one values in a general sense the existence of a nonmarket sector because of its connection with the production of certain valued feelings, then one ascribes added value to any nonmarketed good simply as a repository of values represented by the nonmarket sector one wishes to preserve. This seems certainly to be the case for things in nature, such as pristine streams or undisturbed forests: for many people who value them, part of their value comes from their position as repositories of values the nonmarket sector represents.

The second way in which placing a market price on a thing decreases its perceived value is by removing the possibility of proclaiming that the thing is "not for sale," since things on the market by definition are for sale. The very statement that something is not for sale affirms, enhances, and protects a thing's value in a number of ways. To begin with, the statement is a way of showing that a thing is valued for its own sake, whereas selling a thing for money demonstrates that it was valued only instrumentally. Furthermore, to say that something cannot be transferred in that way places it in the exceptional category—which requires the person interested in obtaining that thing to be able to offer something else that is exceptional, rather than allowing him the easier alternative of obtaining the thing for money that could have been obtained in an infinity of ways. This enhances its value. If I am willing to say "You're a really kind person" to whoever pays me to do so, my praise loses the value that attaches to it from being exchangeable only for an act of kindness.

In addition, if we have already decided we value something highly, one way of stamping it with a cachet affirming its high value is to announce that it is "not for sale." Such an announcement does more, however, than just reflect a preexisting high valuation. It signals a thing's distinctive value to others and helps us persuade them to value the thing more highly than they otherwise might. It also expresses our resolution to safeguard that distinctive value. To state that something is not for sale is thus also a source of value for that thing, since if a thing's value is easy to affirm or protect, it will be worth more than an otherwise similar thing without such attributes.

If we proclaim that something is not for sale, we make a once-and-for-all judgment of its special value. When something is priced, the issue of its perceived value is constantly coming up, as a standing invitation to reconsider that original judgment. Were people constantly faced with questions such as "how much money could get you to give up your freedom of speech?" or "how much would you sell your vote for if you could?" the perceived value of the freedom to speak or the right to vote would soon become devastated as, in moments of weakness, people started saying "maybe it's not worth *so much* after all." Better not to be faced with the constant questioning in the first place. Something similar did in fact occur when the slogan "better red than dead" was launched by some pacifists during the Cold War. Critics pointed out that the very posing of this stark choice—in effect, "would you *really* be willing to give up your life in exchange for not living under communism?"—reduced the value people attached to freedom and thus diminished resistance to attacks on freedom.

Finally, of some things valued very highly it is stated that they are "priceless" or that they have "infinite value." Such expressions are reserved for a subset of things not for sale, such as life or health. Economists tend to scoff at talk of pricelessness. For them, saying that something is priceless is to state a willingness to trade off an infinite quantity of all other goods for one unit of the priceless good, a situation that empirically appears highly unlikely. For most people, however, the word priceless is pregnant with meaning. Its value-affirming and value-protecting functions cannot be bestowed on expressions that merely denote a determinate, albeit high, valuation. John Kennedy in his inaugural address proclaimed that the nation was ready to "pay any price [and] bear any burden . . . to assure the survival and the success of liberty." Had he said instead that we were willing to "pay a high price" or "bear a large burden" for liberty, the statement would have rung hollow.

III

An objection that advocates of cost-benefit analysis might well make to the preceding argument should be considered. I noted earlier that, in cases where various non-utility-based duties or rights conflict with the maximization of utility, it is necessary to make a deliberative judgment about what act is finally right. I also argued earlier that the search for commensurability might not always be a desirable one, that the attempt to go beyond expressing benefits in terms of (say) lives saved and costs in terms of dollars is not something devoutly to be wished.

In situations involving things that are not expressed in a common measure, advocates of cost-benefit analysis argue that people making judgments "in effect" perform cost-benefit calculations anyway. If government regulators promulgate a regulation that saves 100 lives at a cost of $1 billion, they are "in effect" valuing a life at (a minimum of) $10 million, whether or not they say that they are willing to place a dollar value on a human life. Since, in this view, cost-benefit analysis "in effect" is inevitable, it might as well be made specific.

This argument misconstrues the real difference in the reasoning processes involved. In cost-benefit analysis, equivalencies are established *in advance* as one of the raw materials for the calculation. One determines costs and benefits, one determines equivalencies (to be able to put various costs and benefits into a common measure), and then one sets to toting things up—waiting, as it were, with bated breath for the results of the calculation to come out. The outcome is determined by the arithmetic; if the outcome is a close call or if one is not good at long division, one does not know how it will turn out until the calculation is finished. In the kind of deliberative judgment that is performed without a common measure, no estabishment of equivalencies occurs in advance. Equivalencies are not aids to the decision process. In fact, the decision-maker might not even be aware of what the "in effect" equivalencies were, at least before they are revealed to him afterwards by someone pointing out what he had "in effect" done. The decision-maker would see himself as simply having made a deliberate judgment; the "in effect" equivalency number did not play a causal role in the decision but at most merely reflects it. Given this, the argument against making the process explicit is the one discussed earlier in the discussion of problems with putting specific values on things that are not normally quantified—that the very act of doing so may serve to reduce the value of those things.

My own judgment is that modest efforts to assess levels of benefits and costs are justified, although I do not believe that government agencies ought to sponsor efforts to put dollar prices on nonmarket things. I also do not believe that the cry for more cost-benefit analysis in regulation is, on the whole, justified. If regulatory officials were so insensitive about regulatory costs that they did not provide acceptable raw material for deliberative judgments (even if not of a strictly cost-benefit nature), my conclusion might be different. But a good deal of research into costs and benefits already occurs—actually, far more in the U.S. regulatory process than in that of any other industrial society. The danger now would seem to come more from the other side.

Marketing

• *Case Study* •

Toy Wars

MANUEL G. VELASQUEZ

Early in 1986, Tom Daner, president of the advertising company of Daner Associates, was contacted by the sales manager of Crako Industries, Mike Teal.[1]
Crako Industries is a family-owned company that manufactures children's toys
and had long been a favorite and important client of Daner Associates. The
sales manager of Crako Industries explained that the company had just developed a new toy helicopter. The toy was modeled on the military helicopters
that had been used in Vietnam and that had appeared in the "Rambo" movies.
Mike Teal explained that the toy was developed in response to the craze for
military toys that had been sweeping the nation in the wake of the Rambo
movies. The family-owned toy company had initially resisted moving into military toys, since members of the family objected to the violence associated with
such toys. But as segments of the toy market were increasingly taken over by
military toys, the family came to feel that entry into the military toy market was
crucial for their business. Consequently, they approved development of a line
of military toys, hoping that they were not entering the market too late. Mike
Teal now wanted Daner Associates to develop a television advertising campaign for the toy.

The toy helicopter Crako designers had developed was about one and
one-half feet long, battery-operated, and made of plastic and steel. Mounted
to the sides were detachable replicas of machine guns and a detachable
stretcher modeled on the stretchers used to lift wounded soldiers from a bat-
tlefield. Mike Teal of Crako explained that they were trying to develop a toy
that had to be perceived as "more macho" than the top-selling "G. I. Joe" line
of toys. If the company was to compete successfully in today's toy market, according to the sales manager, it would have to adopt an advertising approach
that was even "meaner and tougher" than what other companies were doing.
Consequently, he continued, the advertising clips developed by Daner Associates would have to be "mean and macho." Television advertisements for the
toy, he suggested, might show the helicopter swooping over buildings and
blowing them up. The more violence and mayhem the ads suggested, the better. Crako Industries was relying heavily on sales from the new toy, and some
Crako managers felt that the company's future might depend on the success
of this toy.

Tom Daner was unwilling to have his company develop television advertisements that would increase what he already felt was too much violence in
television aimed at children. In particular, he recalled a television ad for a tri-

cycle with a replica machine gun mounted on the handlebars. The commercial showed the tricycle being pedaled through the woods by a small boy as he chased several other boys fleeing before him over a dirt path. At one point the camera closed in over the shoulder of the boy, focused through the gun sight, and showed the gun sight apparently trying to aim at the backs of the boys as they fled before the tricycle's machine gun. Ads of that sort had disturbed Tom Daner and had led him to think that advertisers should find other ways of promoting these toys. He suggested, therefore, that instead of promoting the Crako helicopter through violence, it should be presented in some other manner. When Teal asked what he had in mind, Tom was forced to reply that he didn't know. But at any rate, Tom pointed out, the three television networks would not accept a violent commercial aimed at children. All three networks adhered to an advertising code that prohibited violent, intense, or unrealistic advertisements aimed at children.

This seemed no real obstacle to Teal, however. Although the networks might turn down children's ads when they were too violent, local television stations were not as squeamish. Local television stations around the country regularly accepted ads aimed at children that the networks had rejected as too violent. The local stations inserted the ads as spots on their non-network programming, thereby circumventing the Advertising Codes of the three national networks. Daner Associates would simply have to place the ads they developed for the Crako helicopter through local television stations around the country. Mike Teal was firm: if Daner Associates would not or could not develop a "mean and tough" ad campaign, the toy company would move their account to an advertiser who would. Reluctantly, Tom Daner agreed to develop the advertising campaign. Crako Industries accounted for $1 million of Daner's total revenues.

Like Crako Industries, Daner Associates is also a family-owned business. Started by his father almost fifty years ago, the advertising firm that Tom Daner now ran had grown dramatically under his leadership. In 1975 the business had grossed $3 million; ten years later it had revenues of $25 million and provided a full line of advertising services. The company was divided into three departments (Creative, Media, and Account Executive), each of which had about 12 employees. Tom Daner credited much of the company's success to the many new people he had hired, especially a group with M.B.A.s who had developed new marketing strategies based on more thorough market and consumer analyses. Most decisions, however, were made by a five-person executive committee consisting of Tom Daner, the Senior Account Manager, and the three department heads. As owner-president, Tom's view tended to color most decisions, producing what one of the members called a "benevolent dictatorship." Tom himself was an enthusiastic, congenial, intelligent, and widely read person. During college he had considered becoming a missionary priest but had changed his mind and was now married and the father of three daughters. His personal heros included Thomas Merton, Albert Schweitzer, and Tom Dooley.

When Tom Daner presented the Crako deal to his Executive Committee, he found they did not share his misgivings. The other Committee members felt that Daner Associates should give Crako exactly the kind of ad Crako wanted: one with a heavy content of violence. Moreover, the writers and artists in the Creative Department were enthused with the prospect of letting their imaginations loose on the project, several feeling that they could easily produce an attention-grabbing ad by "out-violencing" current television programming. The Creative Department, in fact, quickly produced a copy-script that called for videos showing the helicopter "flying out of the sky with machine guns blazing" at a jungle village below. This kind of ad, they felt, was exactly what they were being asked to produce by their client, Crako Industries.

But after viewing the copy, Tom Daner refused to use it. They should produce an ad, he insisted, that would meet their client's needs but that would also meet the guidelines of the national networks. The ad should not glorify violence and war but should somehow support cooperation and family values. Disappointed and somewhat frustrated, the Creative Department went back to work. A few days later they presented a second proposal: an ad that would show the toy helicopter flying through the family room of a home as a little boy plays with it; then the scene shifts to show the boy on a rock rising from the floor of the family room; the helicopter swoops down and picks up the boy as though rescuing him from the rock where he had been stranded. Although the Creative Department was mildly pleased with their attempt, they felt it was too "tame." Tom liked it, however, and a version of the ad was filmed.

A few weeks later Tom Daner met with Mike Teal and his team and showed them the film. The viewing was not a success. Teal turned down the ad. Referring to the network regulations, which other toy advertisements were breaking as frequently as motorists broke the 55 mile per hour speed law, he said, "That commercial is going only 55 miles an hour when I want one that goes 75." If the next version was not "tougher and meaner," Crako Industries would be forced to look elsewhere.

Disappointed, Tom Daner returned to the people in his Creative Department and told them to go ahead with designing the kind of ad they had originally wanted. "I don't have any idea what else to do." In a short time the Creative Department had an ad proposal on his desk that called for scenes showing the helicopter blowing up villages. Shortly afterwards a small set was constructed depicting a jungle village sitting next to a bridge stretching over a river. The ad was filmed using the jungle set as a background.

When Tom saw the result he was not happy. He decided to meet with his Creative Department and air his feelings. "The issue here," he said, "is basically the issue of violence. Do we really want to present toys as instruments for beating up people? This ad is going to promote aggression and violence. It will glorify dominance and do it with kids who are terrifically impressionable. Do we really want to do this?" The members of the Creative Department, however, responded that they were merely giving their client what the client wanted. That client, moreover, was an important account. The client wanted an aggressive "macho" ad, and that was what they were providing. The ad might violate the regulations of the television networks, but there were ways to get around the networks. Moreover, they said, every other advertising firm in the business was breaking the limits against violence set by the networks. Tom made one last try: why not market the toy as an adventure and fantasy toy? Film the ad again, he suggested, using the same jungle backdrop. But instead of showing the helicopter shooting at a burning village, show it flying in to rescue people from the burning village. Create an ad that shows excitement, adventure, and fantasy, but no aggression. "I was trying," he said later, "to figure out a new way of approaching this kind of advertising. We have to follow the market or we can go out of business trying to moralize to the market. But why not try a new approach? Why not promote toys as instruments that expand the child's imagination in a way that is positive and that promotes cooperative values instead of violence and aggression?"

A new film version of the ad was made, now showing the helicopter flying over the jungle set. Quick shots and heightened background music give the impression of excitement and danger. The helicopter flies dramatically through the jungle and over a river and bridge to rescue a boy from a flaming village. As lights flash and shoot haphazardly through the scene the helicopter rises and escapes into the sky. The final ad was clearly exciting and intense. And it promoted saving of life instead of violence against life.

It was clear when the final version was shot, however, that it would not clear the network censors. Network guidelines require that sets in children's ads must depict things that are within the reach of most children so that they do not create unrealistic expectations. Clearly the elaborate jungle set (which cost $25,000 to construct) was not within the reach of most children, and consequently most children would not be able to recreate the scene of the ad by buying the toy. Moreover, network regulations stipulate that in children's ads scenes must be filmed with normal lighting that does not create undue intensity. Again clearly the helicopter ad, which created excitement by using quick changes of light and fast cuts, did not fall within these guidelines.

After reviewing the film Tom Daner reflected on some last-minute instructions Crako's sales manager had given him when he had been shown the first version of the ad: The television ad should show things being blown up by the guns of the little helicopter and perhaps even some blood on the fuselage of the toy; the ad had to be violent. Now Tom had to make a decision. Should he risk the account by submitting only the rescue mission ad? Or should he let Teal also see the ad that showed the helicopter shooting up the village, knowing that he would probably prefer that version if he saw it? And was the rescue mission ad really that much different from the ad that showed the shooting of the village? Did it matter that the rescue mission ad still violated some of the network regulations? What if he offered Teal only the rescue mission ad and Teal accepted the "rescue approach" but demanded he make it more violent; should he give in? And should Tom risk launching an ad campaign that was based on this new untested approach? What if the ad failed to sell the Crako toy? Was it right to experiment with a client's product, especially a product that was so important to the future of the client's business? Tom was unsure what he should do. He wanted to show Teal only the rescue mission commercial, but he first had to resolve these questions in his own mind.

Note

1. Although the events described in this case are real, all names of the individuals and the companies involved are fictitious; in addition, several details have been altered to disguise the identity of participants.

Advertising and Behavior Control

ROBERT L. ARRINGTON

Consider the following advertisements:

1. "A Woman in *Distinction Foundations* is so beautiful that all other women want to kill her."
2. Pongo Peach color from Revlon comes "from east of the sun . . . west of the moon, where each tomorrow dawns." It is "succulent on your lips" and "sizzling on your finger tips (And on your toes, goodness knows)." Let it be your "adventure in paradise."
3. "Musk by English Leather—The Civilized Way to Roar."
4. "Increase the value of your holdings. Old Charter Bourbon Whiskey—The Final Step Up."
5. Last Call Smirnoff Style: "They'd never really miss us, and it's kind of late already, and its quite a long way, and I could build a fire, and you're looking very beautiful, and we could have another martini, and it's awfully nice just being home . . . you think?"
6. A Christmas Prayer. "Let us pray that the blessings of peace be ours—the peace to build and grow, to live in harmony and sympathy with others, and to plan for the future with confidence." New York Life Insurance Company.

These are instances of what is called puffery—the practice by a seller of making exaggerated, highly fanciful, or suggestive claims about a product or service. Puffery, within ill-defined limits, is legal. It is considered a legitimate, necessary, and very successful tool of the advertising industry. Puffery is not just bragging; it is bragging carefully designed to achieve a very definite effect. Using the techniques of so-called motivational research, advertising firms first identify our often hidden needs (for security, conformity, oral stimulation) and our desires (for power, sexual dominance and dalliance, adventure) and then they design ads which respond to these needs and desires. By associating a product, for which we may have little or no direct need or desire, with symbols reflecting the fulfillment of these other, often subterranean interests, the advertisement can quickly generate large numbers of consumers eager to purchase the product advertised. What woman in the sexual race of life could resist a foundation which would turn other women envious to the point of homicide? Who can turn down an adventure in paradise, east of the sun where tomorrow dawns? Who doesn't want to be civilized and thoroughly libidinous at the same time? Be at the pinnacle of success—drink Old Charter. Or stay at home and dally a bit—with Smirnoff. And let us pray for a secure and predictable future, provided for by New York Life, God willing. It doesn't take very much motivational research to see the point of these sales pitches. Others are perhaps a little less obvious. The need to feel secure in one's home at night can be used to sell window air conditioners, which drown out small noises and provide a friendly, dependable companion. The fact that baking a cake is sym-

Robert L. Arrington, "Advertising and Behavior Control," *Journal of Business Ethics*, Vol. 1, No. 1, February 1982, pp. 3–12. Copyright © 1982 by D. Reidel Publishing Co., Dordrecht, Holland and Boston, U.S.A. Reprinted by permission of Kluwer Academic Publishers.

bolic of giving birth to a baby used to prompt advertisements for cake mixes which glamorized the "creative" housewife. And other strategies, for example involving cigar symbolism, are a bit too crude to mention, but are nevertheless very effective.

Don't such uses of puffery amount to manipulation, exploitation, or downright control? In his very popular book *The Hidden Persuaders,* Vance Packard points out that a number of people in the advertising world have frankly admitted as much:

> As early as 1941 Dr. Dichter (an influential advertising consultant) was exhorting ad agencies to recognize themselves for what they actualy were—"one of the most advanced laboratories in psychology." He said the successful ad agency "manipulates human motivations and desires and develops a need for goods with which the public has at one time been unfamiliar—perhaps even undesirous of purchasing." The following year *Advertising Agency* carried an ad man's statement that psychology not only holds a promise for understanding people but "ultimately for controlling their behavior."[1]

Such statements lead Packard to remark: "With all this interest in manipulating the customer's subconscious, the old slogan 'let the buyer beware' began taking on a new and more profound meaning."[2]

B. F. Skinner, the high priest of behaviorism, has expressed a similar assessment of advertising and related marketing techniques. Why, he asks, do we buy a certain kind of car?

> Perhaps our favorite TV program is sponsored by the manufacturer of that car. Perhaps we have seen pictures of many beautiful or prestigeful persons driving it— in pleasant or glamorous places. Perhaps the car has been designed with respect to our motivational patterns: the device on the hood is a phallic symbol; or the horsepower has been stepped up to please our competitive spirit in enabling us to pass other cars swiftly (or, as the advertisements say, 'safely'). The concept of freedom that has emerged as part of the cultural practice of our group makes little or no provision for recognizing or dealing with these kinds of control.[3]

In purchasing a car we may think we are free, Skinner is claiming, when in fact our act is completely controlled by factors in our environment and in our history of reinforcement. Advertising is one such factor.

A look at some other advertising techniques may reinforce the suspicion that Madison Avenue controls us like so many puppets. T.V. watchers surely have noticed that some of the more repugnant ads are shown over and over again, *ad nauseam.* My favorite, or most hated, is the one about A-1 Steak Sauce which goes something like this: Now, ladies and gentlemen, what *is* hamburger? It has succeeded in destroying my taste for hamburger, but it has surely drilled the name of A-1 Sauce into my head. And that is the point of it. Its very repetitiousness has generated what ad theorists call *information.* In this case it is indirect information, information derived not from the content of what is said but from the fact that it is said so often and so vividly that it sticks in one's mind—i.e., the information yield had increased. And not only do I always remember A-1 Sauce when I go to the grocers, I tend to assume that any product advertised so often has to be good—and so I usually buy a bottle of the stuff.

Still another technique: On a recent show of the television program "Hard

Choices" it was demonstrated how subliminal suggestion can be used to control customers. In a New Orleans department store, messages to the effect that shoplifting is wrong, illegal, and subject to punishment were blended into the Muzak background music and masked so as not to be consciously audible. The store reported a dramatic drop in shoplifting. The program host conjectured whether a logical extension of this technique would be to broadcast subliminal advertising messages to the effect that the store's $15.99 sweater special is the "bargain of a lifetime." Actually, this application of subliminal suggestion to advertising has already taken place. Years ago in New Jersey a cinema was reported to have flashed subthreshold ice cream ads onto the screen during regular showings of the film—and, yes, the concession stand did a landslide business.

Puffery, indirect information transfer, subliminal advertising—are these techniques of manipulation and control whose success shows that many of us have forfeited our autonomy and become a community, or herd, of packaged souls?[4] The business world and the advertising industry certainly reject this interpretation of their efforts. *Business Week,* for example, dismissed the charge that the science of behavior, as utilized by advertising, is engaged in human engineering and manipulation. It editorialized to the effect that "it is hard to find anything very sinister about a science whose principle conclusion is that you get along with people by giving them what they want.[5] The theme is familiar: businesses just give the consumer what he/she wants; if they didn't they wouldn't stay in business very long. Proof that the consumer wants the products advertised is given by the fact that he buys them, and indeed often returns to buy them again and again.

The techniques of advertising we are discussing have had their more intellectual defenders as well. For example, Theodore Levitt, Professor of Business Administration at the Harvard Business School, has defended the practice of puffery and the use of techniques depending on motivational research.[6] What would be the consequences, he asks us, of deleting all exaggerated claims and fanciful associations from advertisements? We would be left with literal descriptions of the empirical characteristics of products and their functions. Cosmetics would be presented as facial and bodily lotions and powders which produce certain odor and color changes; they would no longer offer hope or adventure. In addition to the fact that these products would not then sell as well, they would not, acccording to Levitt, please us as much either. For it is hope and adventure we want when we buy them. We want automobiles not just for transportation, but for the feelings of power and status they give us. Quoting T. S. Eliot to the effect that "Human kind cannot bear very much reality," Levitt argues that advertising is an effort to "transcend nature in the raw," to "augment what nature has so crudely fashioned." He maintains that "everybody everywhere wants to modify, transform, embellish, enrich and reconstruct the world around him." Commerce takes the same liberty with reality as the artist and the priest—in all three instances the purpose is "to influence the audience by creating illusions, symbols, and implications that promise more than pure functionality." For example, "to amplify the temple in men's eyes, (men of cloth) have, very realistically, systematically sanctioned the embellishment of the houses of the gods with the same kind of luxurious design and expensive decoration that Detroit puts into a Cadillac." A poem, a temple, a

Cadillac—they all elevate our spirits, offering imaginative promises and symbolic interpretations of our mundane activities. Seen in this light, Levitt claims, "Embellishment and distortion are among advertising's legitimate and socially desirable purposes." To reject these techniques of advertising would be "to deny man's honest needs and values."

Phillip Nelson, a Professor of Economics at SUNY-Binghamton, has developed an interesting defense of indirect information advertising.[7] He argues that even when the message (the direct information) is not credible, the fact that the brand is advertised, and advertised frequently, is valuable indirect information for the consumer. The reason for this is that the brands advertised most are more likely to be better buys—losers won't be advertised a lot, for it simply wouldn't pay to do so. Thus even if the advertising claims made for a widely advertised product are empty, the consumer reaps the benefit of the indirect information which shows the product to be a good buy. Nelson goes so far as to say that advertising, seen as information and especially as indirect information, does not require an intelligent human response. If the indirect information has been received and has had its impact, the consumer will purchase the better buy even if his explicit reason for doing so is silly, e.g., he naively believes an endorsement of the product by a celebrity. Even though his behavior is overtly irrational, by acting on the indirect information he is nevertheless doing what he ought to do, i.e, getting his money's worth. "'Irrationality' is rational," Nelson writes, "if it is cost-free."

I don't know of any attempt to defend the use of subliminal suggestion in advertising, but I can imagine one form such an attempt might take. Advertising information, even if perceived below the level of conscious awareness, must appeal to some desire on the part of the audience if it is to trigger a purchasing response. Just as the admonition not to shoplift speaks directly to the superego, the sexual virtues of Rx-7's, Pongo Peach, and Betty Crocker cake mix present themselves directly to the id, bypassing the pesky reality principle of the ego. With a little help from our advertising friends, we may remove a few of the discontents of civilization and perhaps even enter into the paradise of polymorphous perversity.

The defense of advertising which suggests that advertising simply is information which allows us to purchase what we want, has in turn been challenged. Does business, largely through its advertising efforts, really make available to the consumer what he/she desires and demands? John Kenneth Galbraith has denied that the matter is as straightforward as this.[8] In his opinion the desires to which business is supposed to respond, far from being original to the consumer, are often themselves created by business. The producers make both the product and the desire for it, and the "central function" of advertising is "to create desires." Galbraith coins the term "The Dependence Effect" to designate the way wants depend on the same process by which they are satisfied.

David Braybrooke has argued in similar and related ways.[9] Even though the consumer is, in a sense, the final authority concerning what he wants, he may come to see, according to Braybrooke, that he was mistaken in wanting what he did. The statement "I want x," he tells us, is not incorrigible but is "ripe for revision." If the consumer had more objective information than he is provided by product puffing, if his values had not been mixed up by motivational research strategies (e.g., the confusion of sexual and automotive values), and if he had an expanded set of choices instead of the limited set offered by profit-hungry corporations, then he might want something quite different from what he presently wants. This shows, Braybrooke thinks, the extent to which the consumer's wants are a function of advertising and not necessarily representative of his real or true wants.

The central issue which emerges between the above critics and defenders of advertising is this: do the advertising techniques we have discussed involve a violation of human autonomy and a manipulation and control of consumer behavior, *or* do they simply provide an efficient and cost-effective means of giving the consumer information on the basis of which he or she makes a free choice? Is advertising information, or creation of desire?

To answer this question we need a better conceptual grasp of what is involved in the notion of autonomy. This is a complex, multifaceted concept, and we need to approach it through the more determinate notions of (a) autonomous desire, (b) rational desire and choice, (c) free choice, and (d) control or manipulation. In what follows I shall offer some tentative and very incomplete analyses of these concepts and apply the results to the case of advertising.

(a) Autonomous Desire

Imagine that I am watching T.V. and see an ad for Grecian Formula 16. The thought occurs to me that if I purchase some and apply it to my beard, I will soon look younger—in fact I might even be myself again. Suddenly I want to be myself! I want to be young again! So I rush out and buy a bottle. This is our question: was the desire to be younger manufactured by the commercial, or was it 'original to me' and truly mine? Was it autonomous or not?

F. A. von Hayek has argued plausibly that we should not equate nonautonomous desires, desires which are not orignal to me or truly mine, with those which are culturally induced.[10] If we did equate the two, he points out, then the desires for music, art, and knowledge could not properly be attributed to a person as original to him, for these are surely induced culturally. The only desires a person would really have as his own in this case would be the purely physical ones for food, shelter, sex, etc. But if we reject the equation of the nonautonomous and the culturally induced, as von Hayek would have us do, then the mere fact that my desire to be young again is caused by the T.V. commercial—surely an instrument of popular culture transmission—does not in and of itself show that this is not my own, autonomous desire. Moreover, even if I never before felt the need to look young, it doesn't follow that this new desire is any less mine. I haven't always liked 1969 Aloxe Corton Burgundy or the music of Satie, but when the desires for these things first hit me, they were truly mine.

This shows that there is something wrong in setting up the issue over advertising and behavior control as a question whether our desires are truly ours *or* are created in us by advertisements. Induced and autonomous desires do not separate into two mutually exclusive classes. To obtain a better understanding of autonomous and nonautonomous desires, let us consider some cases of a desire which a person does not *acknowledge* to be his own even though he *feels* it. The kleptomaniac has a desire to steal which in many instances he repudiates, seeking by treatment to rid himself of it. And if I were suddenly overtaken by a desire to attend an REO concert, I would immediately disown this desire, claiming possession or momentary madness. These are examples of desires which one might have but with which one would not identify. They are experienced as foreign to one's character or personality. Often a person will have what Harry Frankfurt calls a second-order desire, that is to say, a desire *not* to have another desire.[11] In such cases, the first-order desire is thought of as being nonautonomous, imposed on one. When on the contrary a person has a second-order desire to maintain and fulfill a first-order desire, then the first-order desire is truly his own, autonomous, original to him. So there is in fact a distinction between desires which are the agent's own and those which are not, but this is not the same as the distinction between desires which are innate to the agent and those which are externally induced.

If we apply the autonomous/nonautonomous distinction derived from Frankfurt to the desires brought about by advertising, does this show that advertising is responsible for creating desires which are not truly the agent's own? Not necessarily, and indeed not often. There may be some desires I feel which I have picked up from advertising and which I disown—for instance, my desire for A-1 Steak Sauce. If I act on these desires it can be said that I have been led by advertising to act in a way foreign to my nature. In these cases my autonomy has been violated. But most of the desires induced by advertising I fully accept, and hence most of these desires are autonomous. The most vivid demonstration of this is that I often return to purchase the same product over and over again, without regret or remorse. And when I don't, it is more likely that the desire has just faded than that I have repudiated it. Hence, while advertising may violate my autonomy by leading me to act on desires which are not truly mine, this seems to be the exceptional case.

Note that this conclusion applies equally well to the case of subliminal advertising. This may generate subconscious desires which lead to purchases, and the act of purchasing these goods may be inconsistent with other conscious desires I have, in which case I might repudiate my behavior and by implication the subconscious cause of it. But my subconscious desires may not be inconsistent in this way with my conscious ones; my id may be cooperative and benign rather than hostile and malign. Here again, then, advertising may or may not produce desires which are 'not truly mine.'

What are we to say in response to Braybrooke's argument that insofar as we might choose differently if advertisers gave us better information and more options, it follows that the desires we have are to be attributed more to advertising than to our own real inclinations? This claim seems empty. It amounts to saying that if the world we lived in, and we ourselves, were different, then we would want different things. This is surely true, but it is equally true of our desire for shelter as of our desire for Grecian Formula 16. If we lived in a tropical paradise, we would not need or desire shelter. If we were immortal, we would not desire youth. What is true of all desires can hardly be used as a basis for criticizing some desires by claiming that they are nonautonomous.

(b) Rational Desire and Choice

Braybrooke might be interpreted as claiming that the desires induced by advertising are often irrational ones in the sense that they are not expressed by an agent who is in full possession of the facts about the products advertised or about the alternative products which might be offered him. Following this line of thought, a possible criticism of advertising is that it leads us to act on irrational desires or to make irrational choices. It might be said that our autonomy has been violated by the fact that we are prevented from following our rational wills or that we have been denied the 'positive freedom' to develop our true, rational selves. It might be claimed that the desires induced in us by advertising are false desires in that they do not reflect our essential, i.e., rational essence.

The problem faced by this line of criticism is that of determining what is to count as rational desire or rational choice. If we require that the desire or choice be the product of an awareness of *all* the facts about the product, then surely every one of us is always moved by irrational desires and makes nothing but irrational choices. How could we know all the facts about a product? If it be required only that we possess all of the *available* knowledge about the product advertised, then we still have to face the problem that not all available knowledge is *relevant* to a rational choice. If I am purchasing a car, certain engineering features will be, and others won't be, relevant, *given what I want in a car.* My prior desires determine the relevance of information. Normally a rational desire or choice is thought to be one based upon relevant information, and information is relevant if it shows how other, prior desires may be satisfied. It can plausibly be claimed that it is such prior desires that advertising agencies acknowledge, and that the agencies often provide the type of information that is relevant in light of these desires. To the extent that this is true, advertising does not inhibit our rational wills or our autonomy as rational creatures.

It may be urged that much of the puffery engaged in by advertising does not provide relevant information at all but rather makes claims which are not factually true. If someone buys Pongo Peach in anticipation of an adventure in paradise, or Old Charter in expectation of increasing the value of his holdings, then he/she is expecting purely imaginary benefits. In no literal sense will the one product provide adventure and the other increased capital. A purchasing decision based on anticipation of imaginary benefits is not, it might be said, a rational decision, and a desire for imaginary benefits is not a rational desire.

In rejoinder it needs to be pointed out that we often wish to purchase subjective effects which in being subjective are nevertheless real enough. The feeling of adventure or of enhanced social prestige and value are examples of subjective effects promised by advertising. Surely many (most?) advertisements directly promise subjective effects which their patrons actually desire (and obtain when they purchase the product), and thus the ads provide relevant information for rational choice. Moreover, advertisements often provide accurate indirect information on the basis of which a person who wants a certain subjective effect rationally chooses a product. The mechanism involved here is as follows.

To the extent that a consumer takes an advertised product to offer a subjective effect and the product does not, it is unlikely that it will be purchased again. If this happens in a number of cases, the product will be taken off the market. So here the market regulates itself, providing the mechanism whereby misleading advertisements are withdrawn and misled customers are no longer misled. At the same time, a successful bit of puffery, being one which leads to large and repeated sales, produces satisfied customers and more advertising of the product. The indirect information provided by such large-scale advertising efforts provides a measure of verification to the consumer who is looking for certain kinds of subjective effect. For example, if I want to feel well dressed and in fashion, and I consider buying an Izod Alligator shirt which is advertised in all of the magazines and newspapers, then the fact that other people buy it and that this leads to repeated advertisements shows me that the desired subjective effect is real enough and that I indeed will be well dressed and in fashion if I purchase the shirt. The indirect information may lead to a rational decision to purchase a product because the information testifies to the subjective effect that the product brings about.

Some philosophers will be unhappy with the conclusion of this section, largely because they have a concept of true, rational, or ideal desire which is not the same as the one used here. A Marxist, for instance, may urge that any desire felt by alienated man in a capitalistic society is foreign to his true nature. Or an existentialist may claim that the desires of inauthentic men are themselves inauthentic. Such concepts are based upon general theories of human nature which are unsubstantiated and perhaps incapable of substantiation. Moreover, each of these theories is committed to a concept of an ideal desire which is normatively debatable and which is distinct from the ordinary concept of a rational desire as one based upon relevant information. But it is in the terms of the ordinary concept that we express our concern that advertising may limit our autonomy in the sense of leading us to act on irrational desires, and if we operate with this concept we are driven again to the conclusion that advertising may lead, but probably most often does not lead, to an infringement of autonomy.

(c) Free Choice

It might be said that some desires are so strong or so covert that a person cannot resist them, and that when he acts on such desires he is not acting freely or voluntarily but is rather the victim of irresistible impulse or an unconscious drive. Perhaps those who condemn advertising feel that it produces this kind of desire in us and consequently reduces our autonomy.

This raises a very difficult issue. How do we distinguish between an impulse we *do* not resist and one we *could* resist, between freely giving in to a desire and succumbing to one? I have argued elsewhere that the way to get at this issue is in terms of the notion of acting for a reason.[12] A person acts or chooses freely if he does so for a reason, that is, if he can adduce considerations which justify in his mind the act in question. Many of our actions are in fact free because this condition frequently holds. Often, however, a person will act from habit, or whim, or impulse, and on these occasions he does not have a reason in mind. Nevertheless he often acts voluntarily in these instances, i.e., he could have acted otherwise. And this is because if there *had been* a reason for acting otherwise of which he was aware, he would in fact have done so. Thus acting from habit or impulse is not necessarily to act in an involuntary manner. If, however, a person is aware of a good reason to do x and still follows his impulse to do y, then he can be said to be impelled by irresistible impulse and hence to act involuntarily. Many kleptomaniacs can be said to act involuntarily, for in spite of their knowledge that they likely will be caught and their awareness that the goods they steal have little utilitarian value to them, they nevertheless steal. Here their "out of character" desires have the upper hand, and we have a case of compulsive behavior.

Applying these notions of voluntary and compulsive behavior to the case of behavior prompted by advertising, can we say that consumers influenced by advertising act compulsively? The unexciting answer is: sometimes they do, sometimes not. I may have an overwhelming, T.V.-induced urge to own a Mazda Rx-7 and all the while realize that I can't afford one without severely reducing my family's caloric intake to a dangerous level. If, aware of this good reason not to purchase the car, I nevertheless do so, this shows that I have been the victim of T.V. compulsion. But if I have the urge, as I assure you I do, and don't act on it, or if in some other possible world I could afford an Rx-7, then I have not been the subject of undue influence by Mazda advertising. Some Mazda Rx-7 purchasers act compulsively; others do not. The Mazda advertising effort *in general* cannot be condemned, then, for impairing its customers' autonomy in the sense of limiting free or voluntary choice. Of course the question remains what should be done about the fact that advertising may and does *occasionally* limit free choice.

In the case of subliminal advertising we may find an individual whose subconscious desires are activated by advertising into doing something his calculating, reasoning ego does not approve. This would be a case of compulsion. But most of us have a benevolent subconsciousness which does not overwhelm our ego and its reasons for action. And therefore most of us can respond to subliminal advertising without thereby risking our autonomy. To be sure, if some advertising firm developed a subliminal technique which drove all of us to purchase Lear jets, thereby reducing our caloric intake to the zero point, then we would have a case of advertising which could properly be censured for infringing our right to autonomy. We should acknowledge that this is possible, but at the same time we should recognize that it is not an inherent result of subliminal advertising.

(2) Control or Manipulation

Briefly let us consider the matter of control and manipulation. Under what conditions do these activities occur? In a recent paper on "Forms and Limits of Control" I suggested the following criteria.[13]

A person C controls the behavior of another person P *if*

1. C intends P to act in a certain way A;
2. C's intention is causally effective in bringing about A; and
3. C intends to ensure that all of the necessary conditions of A are satisfied.

These criteria may be elaborated as follows. To control another person it is not enough that one's actions produce certain behavior on the part of that person; additionally one must intend that this happen. Hence control is the intentional production of behavior. Moreover, it is not enough just to have the intention; the intenton must give rise to the conditions which bring about the intended effect. Finally, the controller must intend to establish by his actions any otherwise unsatisfied necessary conditions for the production of the intended effect. The controller is not just influencing the outcome, not just having input; he is as it were guaranteeing that the sufficient conditions for the intended effect are satisfied.

Let us apply these criteria of control to the case of advertising and see what happens. Conditions (1) and (3) are crucial. Does the Mazda manufacturing company or its advertising agency intend that I buy an Rx-7? Do they intend that a certain number of people buy the car? *Prima facie* it seems more appropriate to say that they *hope* a certain number of people will buy it, and hoping and intending are not the same. But the difficult term here is "intend." Some philosophers have argued that to intend *A* it is necessary only to desire that *A* happen and to believe that it will. If this is correct, and if marketing analysis gives the Mazda agency a reasonable belief that a cetain segment of the population will buy its product, then, assuming on its part the desire that this happen, we have the conditions necessary for saying that the agency intends that a certain segment purchase the car. If I am a member of this segment of the population, would it then follow that the agency intends that I purchase an Rx-7? Or is control referentially opaque? Obviously we have some questions here which need further exploration.

Let us turn to the third condition of control, the requirement that the controller intend to activate or bring about any otherwise unsatisfied necessary conditions for the production of the intended effect. It is in terms of this condition that we are able to distinguish brainwashing from liberal education. The brainwasher arranges all of the necessary conditions for belief. On the other hand, teachers (at least those of liberal persuasion) seek only to influence their students—to provide them with information and enlightenment which they may absorb *if they wish*. We do not normally think of teachers as controlling their students, for the students' performances depend as well on their own interests and inclinations.

Now the advertiser—does he control, or merely influence, his audience? Does he intend to ensure that all of the necessary conditions for purchasing behavior are met, or does he offer information and symbols which are intended to have an effect only *if* the potential purchaser has certain desires? Undeniably advertising induces some desires, and it does this intentially, but more often than not it intends to induce a desire for a particular object, *given* that the purchaser already has other desires. Given a desire for youth, or power, or adventure, or ravishing beauty, we are led to desire Grecian Formula 16, Mazda Rx-7s, Pongo Peach, and Distinctive Foundations. In this light, the advertiser is influencing us by appealing to independent desires we already have. He is not creating those basic desires. Hence it seems appropriate to deny that he intends to produce all of the necessary conditions for our purchases, and appropriate to deny that he controls us.

Let me summarize my argument. The critics of advertising see it as having a pernicious effect on the autonomy of consumers, as controlling their lives and manufacturing their very souls. The defense claims that advertising only offers information and in effect allows industry to provide consumers with what they want. After developing some of the philosophical dimensions of this dispute, I have come down tentatively in favor of the advertisers. Advertising may, but certainly does not always or even freuqently, control behavior, produce compulsive behavior, or create wants which are not rational or are not truly those of the consumer. Admittedly it may in individual cases do all of these things, but it is innocent of the charge of intrinsically or necessarily doing them or even, I think, of often doing so. This limited potentiality, to be sure, leads to the question whether advertising should be abolished or severely curtailed or regulated because of its potential to harm a few pour souls in the above ways. This is a very difficult question, and I do not pretend to have the answer. I only hope that the above discussion, in showing some of the kinds of harm that can be done by advertising and by indicating the likely limits of this harm, will put us in a better position to grapple with the question.

Notes

1. Vance Packard, *The Hidden Persuaders* (Pocket Books, New York, 1958), pp. 20–21.
2. *Ibid.,* p. 21.
3. B. F. Skinner, "Some Issues Concerning the Control of Human Behavior: A Symposium," in Karlins and Andrews (eds.), *Man Controlled* (The Free Press, New York, 1972).
4. I would like to emphasize that in what follows I am discussing these techniques of advertising from the standpoint of the issue of control and not from that of deception.
5. Quoted by Packard, *op. cit.,* p. 200.
6. Theodore Levitt, "The Morality (?) of Advertising," *Harvard Business Review* (1970), 84–92.
7. Phillip Nelson, "Advertising and Ethics," in Richard T. De George and Joseph A. Pichler (eds.), *Ethics, Free Enterprise, and Public Policy* (Oxford University Press, New York, 1978), pp. 187–98.
8. John Kenneth Galbraith, "The Dependence Effect," *The Affluent Society.*
9. David Braybrooke, "Skepticism of Wants, and Certain Subversive Effects of Corporations on American Values," in Sidney Hook (ed.), *Human Values and Economic Policy* (New York University Press, New York, 1967).
10. F. A. von Hayek, "The *Non Sequitur* of the 'Dependence Effect,'" *Southern Economic Journal* (1961).
11. Harry Frankfurt, "Freedom of the Will and the Concept of a Person," *Journal of Philosophy* LXVII (1971), 5–20.
12. Robert L. Arrington, "Practical Reason, Responsibility and the Psychopath," *Journal for the Theory of Social Behavior* 9 (1979), 71–89.
13. Robert L. Arrington, "Forms and Limits of Control," delivered in the annual meeting of the Southern Society for Philosophy and Psychology, Birmingham, Alabama, 1980.

Persuasive Advertising, Autonomy, and the Creation of Desire

ROGER CRISP

In this paper, I shall argue that all forms of a certain common type of advertising are morally wrong, on the ground that they override the autonomy of consumers.

One effect of an advertisement might be the creation of a desire for the advertised product. How such desires are caused is highly relevant as to whether we would describe the case as one in which the autonomy of the subject has been overridden. If I read an advertisement for a sale of clothes, I may rush down to my local clothes store and purchase a jacket I like. Here, my desire for the jacket has arisen partly out of my reading the advertisement. Yet, in an ordinary sense, it is based on or answers to certain properties of the jacket—its colour, style, material. Although I could not explain to you why my tastes are as they are, we still describe such cases as examples of autonomous action, in that all the decisions are being made by me: What kind of jacket do I like? Can I afford one? And so on. In certain other cases, however, the causal history of a desire may be different. Desires can be caused, for instance, by subliminal suggestion. In New Jersey, a cinema flashed sub-threshold advertisements for ice cream onto the screen during movies, and reported a dramatic increase in sales during intermissions. In such cases, choice is being deliberately ruled out by the method of advertising in question. These customers for ice cream were acting "automatonously," rather than autonomously. They did not buy the ice cream because they happened to like it and decided they would buy some, but rather because they had been subjected to subliminal suggestion. Subliminal suggestion is the most extreme form of what I shall call, adhering to a popular dichotomy, persuasive, as opposed to informative, advertising, Other techniques include puffery, which involves the linking of the product, through suggestive language and images, with the unconscious desires of consumers for power, wealth, status, sex, and so on; and repetition, which is self-explanatory, the name of the product being "drummed into" the mind of the consumer.

The obvious objection to persuasive advertising is that it somehow violates the autonomy of consumers. I believe that this objection is correct, and that, if one adopts certain common-sensical standards for autonomy, non-persuasive forms of advertising are not open to such an objection. Very high standards for autonomy are set by Kant, who requires that an agent be entirely external to the causal nexus found in the ordinary empirical world, if his or her actions are to be autonomous. These standards are too high, in that it is doubtful whether they allow *any* autonomous action. Standards for autonomy more congenial to common sense will allow that my buying the jacket is autonomous, although continuing to deny that the people in New Jersey were acting autonomously. In the former case, we have what has come to be known

Journal of Business Ethics 6 (1987) 413–418. © 1987 by D. Reidel Publishing Company. Reprinted by permission of Kluwer Academic Publishers.

in recent discussions of freedom of the will as *both* free will *and* free action. I both decide what to do, and am not obstructed in carrying through my decision into action. In the latter case, there is free action, but not free will. No one prevents the customers buying their ice cream, but they have not themselves made any genuine decision whether or not to do so. In a very real sense, decisions are made for consumers by persuasive advertisers, who occupy the motivational territory properly belonging to the agent. If what we mean by autonomy, in the ordinary sense, is to be present, the possibility of decision must exist alongside.

Arrington (1982) discusses, in a challenging paper, the techniques of persuasive advertising I have mentioned, and argues that such advertising does not override the autonomy of consumers. He examines four notions central to autonomous action, and claims that, on each count, persuasive advertising is exonerated on the charge we have made against it. I shall now follow in the footsteps of Arrington, but argue that he sets the standards for autonomy too low for them to be acceptable to common sense, and that the charge therefore still sticks.

(A) Autonomous Desire

Arrington argues that an autonomous desire is a first-order desire (a desire for some object, say, Pongo Peach cosmetics) accepted by the agent because it fulfils a second-order desire (a desire about a desire, say, a desire that my first-order desire for Pongo Peach be fulfilled), and that most of the first-order desires engendered in us by advertising are desires that we do accept. His example is an advertisement for Grecian Formula 16, which engenders in him a desire to be younger. He desires that both his desire to be younger and his desire for Grecian Formula 16 be fulfilled.

Unfortunately, this example is not obviously one of persuasive advertising. It may be the case that he just has this desire to look young again rather as I had certain sartorial tastes before I saw the ad about the clothes sale, and then decides to buy Grecian Formula 16 on the basis of these tastes. Imagine this form of advertisement: a person is depicted using Grecian Formula 16, and is then shown in a position of authority, surrounded by admiring members of the opposite sex. This would be a case of puffery. The advertisement implies that having hair coloured by the product will lead to positions of power, and to one's becoming more attractive to the opposite sex. It links, by suggestion, the product with my unconscious desires for power and sex. I may still claim that I am buying the product because I want to look young again. But the real reasons for my purchase are my unconscious desires for power and sex, and the link made between the product and the fulfilment of those desires by the advertisement. These reasons are not reasons I could avow to myself as good reasons for buying the product, and, again, the possibility of decision is absent.

Arrington's claim is that an autonomous desire is a first-order desire which we accept. Even if we allow that it is possible for the agent to consider whether to accept or to repudiate first-order desires induced by persuasive advertising, it seems that all first-order desires induced purely by persuasive advertising will be non-autonomous in Arrington's sense. Many of us have a strong second-order desire not to be manipulated by others without our knowledge, and for no good reason. Often, we are manipulated by others without our knowledge, but for a good reason, and one that we can accept. Take an accomplished actor: much of the skill of an actor is to be found in unconscious body-language. This manipulation we see as essential to our being entertained, and thus acquiesce in it. What is important about this case is that there seems to be no diminution of autonomy. We can still judge the quality of the acting, in that the manipulation is part of its quality. In other cases, however, manipulation ought not to be present, and these are cases where the ability to decide is importantly diminished by the manipulation. Decision is central to the theory of the market-process: I should be able to decide whether to buy product *A* or product *B*, by judging them on their merits. Any manipulation here I shall repudiate as being for no good reason. This is not to say, incidentally, that once the fact that my desires are being manipulated by others has been made transparent to me, my desire will lapse. The people in New Jersey would have been unlikely to cease their craving for ice cream, if we had told them that their desire had been subliminally induced. But they would no longer have voiced acceptance of this desire, and, one assumes, would have resented the manipulation of their desires by the management of the cinema.

Pace Arrington, it is no evidence for the claim that most of our desires are autonomous in this sense that we often return to purchase the same product over and over again. For this might well show that persuasive advertising has been supremely efficient in inducing non-autonomous desires in us, which we are unable even to attempt not to act on, being unaware of their origin. Nor is it an argument in Arrington's favour that certain members of our society will claim not to have the second-order desire we have postulated. For it may be that this is a desire which we can see is one that human beings *ought* to have, a desire which it would be in their interests to have, and the lack of which is itself evidence of profound manipulation.

(B) Rational Desire and Choice

One might argue that the desires induced by advertising are often irrational, in the sense that they are not present in an agent in full possession of the facts about the product. This argument fails, says Arrington, because if we require *all* the facts about a thing before we can desire that thing, then all our desires will be irrational; and if we require only the *relevant* information, then prior desires determine the relevance of information. Advertising may be said to enable us to fulfil these prior desires, through the transfer of information, and the supplying of means to ends is surely a paradigm example of rationality.

But, what about persuasive, as opposed to informative, advertising? Take puffery. Is it not true that a person may buy Pongo Peach cosmetics, hoping for an adventure in paradise, and that the product will not fulfil these hopes? Are they really in possession of even the relevant facts? Yes, says Arrington. We wish to purchase *subjective* effects, and these are genuine enough. When I use Pongo Peach, I will experience a genuine feeling of adventure.

Once again, however, our analysis can help us to see the strength of the objection. For a desire to be rational, in any plausible sense, that desire must at least not be induced by the interference of other persons with my system of tastes, against my will and without my knowledge. Can we imagine a person, asked for a reason justifying their purchase of Pongo Peach, replying: "I have an unconscious desire to experience adventure, and the product has been linked with this desire through advertising"? If a desire is to be rational, it is not necessary that all the facts about the object be known to the agent, but one of the facts about that desire must be that it has not been induced in the agent through techniques which the agent cannot accept. Thus, applying the schema of Arrington's earlier argument, such a desire will be repudiated by the agent as non-autonomous and irrational.

Arrington's claim concerning the subjective effects of the products we purchase fails to deflect the charge of overriding autonomy we have made against persuasive advertising. Of course, very often the subjective effects will be lacking. If I use Grecian Formula 16, I am unlikely to find myself being promoted at work, or surrounded by admiring members of the opposite sex. This is just straight deception. But even when the effects do manifest themselves, such advertisements have still overridden my autonomy. They have activated desires which lie beyond my awareness, and over behaviour flowing from which I therefore have no control. If these claims appear doubtful, consider whether this advertisement is likely to be successful: "Do you have a feeling of adventure? Then use this brand of cosmetics." Such an advertisement will fail, in that it appeals to a *conscious* desire, either which we do not have, or which we realise will not be fulfilled by purchasing a certain brand of cosmetics. If the advertisement were for a course in mountain-climbing, it might meet with more success. Our conscious self is not so easily duped by advertising, and this is why advertisers make such frequent use of the techniques of persuasive advertising.

(C) Free Choice

One might object to persuasive advertising that it creates desires so covert that an agent cannot resist them, and that acting on them is therefore neither free nor voluntary. Arrington claims that a person acts or chooses *freely* if they can adduce considerations which justify their act in their mind; and *voluntarily* if, had they been aware of a reason for acting otherwise, they could have done so. Only occasionally, he says, does advertising prevent us making free and voluntary choices.

Regarding free action, it is sufficient to note that, according to Arrington, if I were to be converted into a human robot, activated by an Evil Genius who has implanted electrodes in my brain, my actions would be free as long as I could cook up some justification for my behaviour. I want to dance this jig because I enjoy dancing. (Compare: I want to buy this ice cream because I like ice cream.) If my argument is right, we are placed in an analogous position by persuasive advertising. If we no longer mean by freedom of action the mere non-obstruction of behaviour, are we still ready to accept that we are engaged in free action? As for whether the actions of consumers subjected to persuasive advertising are voluntary in Arrington's sense, I am less optimistic than he is. It is likely, as we have suggested, that the purchasers of ice cream or Pongo Peach would have gone ahead with their purchase even if they had been made aware that their desires had been induced in them by persuasive advertising. But they would now claim that they themselves had not made the decision, that they were acting on a desire engendered in them which they did not accept, and that there was, therefore, a good reason for them not to make the purchase. The unconscious is not obedient to the commands of the conscious, although it may be forced to listen.

In fact, it is odd to suggest that persuasive advertising does give consumers a choice. A choice is usually taken to require the weighing-up of reasons. What persuasive advertising does is to remove the very conditions of choice.

(D) Control or Manipulation

Arrington offers the following criteria for control:

A person C controls the behaviour of another person P if
(1) C intends P to act in a certain way A
(2) C's intention is causally effective in bringing about A, and
(3) C intends to ensure that all of the necessary conditions of A are satisfied.

He argues that advertisements tend to induce a desire for X, given a more basic desire for Y. Given my desire for adventure, I desire Pongo Peach cosmetics. Thus, advertisers do not control consumers, since they do not intend to produce all of the necessary conditions for our purchases.

Arrington's analysis appears to lead to some highly counter-intuitive consequences. Consider, again, my position as human robot. Imagine that the Evil Genius relies on the fact that I have certain basic unconscious desires in order to effect his plan. Thus, when he wants me to dance a jig, it is necessary that I have a more basic desire, say, ironically, for power. What the electrodes do is to jumble up my practical reasoning processes, so that I believe that I am dancing the jig because I like dancing, while, in reality, the desire to dance stems from a link between the dance and the fulfilment of my desire for power, forged by the electrodes. Are we still happy to say that I am not controlled? And does not persuasive advertising bring about a similar jumbling-up of the practical reasoning processes of consumers? When I buy Pongo Peach, I may be unable to offer a reason for my purchase, or I may claim that I want to look good. In reality, I buy it owing to the link made by persuasive advertising between my unconscious desire for adventure and the cosmetic in question.

A more convincing account of behaviour control would be to claim that it occurs when a person causes another person to act for reasons which the other person could not accept as good or justifiable reasons for the action. This is how brain-washing is to be distinguished from liberal education, rather than on Arrington's ground that the brain-washer arranges all the necessary conditions for belief. The student can both accept that she has the beliefs she has because of her education and continue to hold those beliefs as true, whereas the victim of brain-washing could not accept the explanation of the origin of her beliefs, while continuing to hold those beliefs. It is worth recalling the two cases we mentioned at the beginning of this paper. I can accept my tastes in dress, and do not think that the fact that their origin is unknown to me detracts from my autonomy, when I choose to buy the jacket. The desire for ice cream, however, will be repudiated, in that it is the result of manipulation by others, without good reason.

• • •

It seems, then, that persuasive advertising does override the autonomy of consumers, and that, if the overriding of autonomy, other things being equal, is immoral, then persuasive advertising is immoral.

An argument has recently surfaced which suggests that, in fact, other things are not equal, and that persuasive advertising, although it overrides autonomy, is morally acceptable. This argument was first developed by Nelson (1978), and claims that persuasive advertising is a form of informative advertising, albeit an indirect form. The argument runs at two levels: first, the consumer can judge from the mere fact that a product is heavily advertised, regardless of the form or content of the advertisements, that that product is likely to be a market-winner. The reason for this is that it would not pay to advertise market-losers. Second, even if the consumer is taken in by the content of the advertisement, and buys the product for that reason, he is not being irrational. For he would have bought the product *anyway*, since the very fact that it is advertised means that it is a good product. As Nelson says:

> It does not pay consumers to make very thoughtful decisions about advertising. They can respond to advertising for the most ridiculous, explicit reasons and still do what they would have done if they had made the most careful judgements about their behaviour. "Irrationality" is rational if it is cost-free.

Our conclusions concerning the mode of operation of persuasive advertising, however, suggest that Nelson's argument cannot succeed. For the first level to work, it would have to be true that a purchaser of a product can evaluate that product on its own merits, and then decide whether to purchase it again. But, as we have seen, consumers induced to purchase products by persuasive advertising are not buying those products on the basis of a decision founded upon any merit the products happen to have. Thus, if the product turns out to be less good than less heavily advertised alternatives, they will not be disappointed, and will continue to purchase, if subjected to the heavy advertising which induced them to buy in the first place. For this reason, heavy persuasive advertising is not a sign of quality, and the fact that a product is advertised does not suggest that it is good. In fact, if the advertising has little or no informative content, it might suggest just the opposite. If the product has genuine merits, it should be possible to mention them. Persuasive advertising, as the executives on Madison Avenue know, can be used to sell anything, regardless of its nature or quality.

For the second level of Nelson's argument to succeed, and for it to be in the consumer's interest to react even unthinkingly to persuasive advertising, it must be true that the first level is valid. As the first level fails, there is not even a *prima facie* reason for the belief that it is in the interest of the consumer to be subjected to persuasive advertising. In fact, there are two weighty reasons for doubting this belief. The first has already been hinted at: products promoted through persuasive advertising may well not be being sold on their merits, and may, therefore, be bad products, or products that the consumer would not desire on being confronted with unembellished facts about the product. The second is that this form of "rational irrationality" is anything but cost-free. We consider it a great cost to lose our autonomy. If I were to demonstrate to you conclusively that if I were to take over your life, and make your decisions for you, you would have a life containing far more of whatever you think makes life worth living, apart from autonomy, than if you were to retain control, you would not surrender your autonomy to me even for these great gains in other values. As we mentioned above in our discussion of autonomous desire, we have a strong second-order desire not to act on first-order desires induced in us unawares by others, for no good reason, and now we can see that that desire applies even to cases in which we would *appear* to be better off in acting on such first-order desires.

Thus, we may conclude that Nelson's argument in favour of persuasive advertising is not convincing. I should note, perhaps, that my conclusion concerning persuasive advertising echoes that of Santilli (1983). My argument differs from his, however, in centering upon the notions of autonomy and causes of desires acceptable to the agent, rather than upon the distinction between needs and desires. Santilli claims that the arousal of a desire is not a rational process, unless it is preceded by a knowledge of actual needs. This, I believe, is too strong. I may well have no need of a new tennis-racket, but my desire for one, aroused by informative advertisements in the newspaper, seems rational enough. I would prefer to claim that a desire is autonomous and at least *prima facie* rational if it is not induced in the agent without his knowledge and for no good reason, and allows ordinary processes of decision-making to occur.

Finally, I should point out that, in arguing against all persuasive advertising, unlike Santilli, I am not to be interpreted as bestowing moral respectability upon all informative advertising. Advertisers of any variety ought to consider whether the ideological objections often made to their conduct have any weight. Are they, for instance, imposing a distorted system of values upon consumers, in which the goal of our lives is to consume, and in which success is measured by one's level of consumption? Or are they entrenching attitudes which prolong the position of certain groups subject to discrimination, such as women or homosexuals? Advertisers should also carefully consider whether their product will be of genuine value to any consumers, and, if so, attempt to restrict their campaigns to the groups in society which will benefit (see Durham, 1984). I would claim, for instance, that all advertising of tobacco-based products, even of the informative variety, is wrong, and that some advertisements for alcohol are wrong, in that they are directed at the wrong audience. Imagine, for instance, a liquor-store manager erecting an informative bill-board opposite an alcoholics' rehabilitation center. But these are secondary questions for prospective advertisers. The primary questions must be whether they are intending to employ the techniques of persuasive advertising, and, if so, how these techniques can be avoided.

References

Arrington, R.: 1982, "Advertising and Behaviour Control," *Journal of Business Ethics* I, 1.
Durham, T.: 1984, "Information, Persuasion, and Control in Moral Appraisal of Advertising Strategy," *Journal of Business Ethics* III, 3.

Nelson, P.: 1978, "Advertising and Ethics," in *Ethics, Free Enterprise, and Public Policy*, (eds.) R. De George and J. Pichler, New York: Oxford University Press.

Santilli, P.: 1983, "The Informative and Persuasive Functions of Advertising: A Moral Appraisal," *Journal of Business Ethics* II, I.

Seven Marketing Pitches

Consider the following seven marketing techniques:

1. An ad claiming that the Honda Accord has high satisfaction ratings among first-year owners.

2. A TV commercial in which James Garner exhibits the sporty, fun experience of driving the Mazda RX-7.

3. An ad for the Chevrolet Camaro presenting it as enhancing sex appeal by displaying the car among a group of attractive young men/women (your pick) in bathing suits.

4. An ad for Allstate life insurance that pictures two houses, one of which is fully involved in a fire, with a voice-over informing us that the real tragedy has just happened in the other house: The breadwinner died without sufficient life insurance to cover the mortgage.

5. An ad for a device which can summon medical assistance in an emergency; the ad shows an elderly woman falling down a flight of steps. Unfortunately, she is not wearing the device, and help arrives too late.

6. A Saturday morning TV ad for Smurf dolls; it is broadcast during a cartoon show starring the cute little creatures.

7. A subliminal message "Buy Coke" shown before intermission in a movie theater.

Which of these ads do you intuitively feel is a violation of the consumer's autonomy? If you feel as most people do, you will find the first ad unproblematic and the last ad to be a violation. If this is your response, you must identify the features of the subliminal technique that make it objectionable from the point of view of autonomy. You must also be consistent and willing to accept the consequences of your analysis. For instance, if the feature that makes the subliminal technique unacceptable is also present in the ad aimed at children, you must make the same judgment about both ads.

The most common explanation of the usual reaction to the seventh case relates the consumer's being unaware of the appeal. The subliminal technique is intended to manipulate consumers by making them less likely to resist the desire the ad may generate. (Note that this explanation makes the technique objectionable even if the consumer ultimately decides *not* to buy the product.)

Corporations in the Twenty-First Century

• *Case Study* •

Managing Without Managers

Ricardo Semler

In Brazil, where paternalism and the family business fiefdom still flourish, I am president of a manufacturing company that treats its 800 employees like responsible adults. Most of them—including factory workers—set their own working hours. All have access to the company books. The vast majority vote on many important corporate decisions. Everyone gets paid by the month, regardless of job description, and more than 150 of our management people set their own salaries and bonuses.

This may sound like an unconventional way to run a business, but it seems to work. Close to financial disaster in 1980, Semco is now one of Brazil's fastest growing companies, with a profit margin in 1988 of 10% on sales of $37 million. Our five factories produce a range of sophisticated products, including marine pumps, digital scanners, commercial dishwashers, truck filters, and mixing equipment for everything from bubble gum to rocket fuel. Our customers include Alcoa, Saab, and General Motors. We've built a number of cookie factories for Nabisco, Nestlé, and United Biscuits. Our multinational competitors include AMF, Worthington Industries, Mitsubishi Heavy Industries, and Carrier.

Management associations, labor unions, and the press have repeatedly named us the best company in Brazil to work for. In fact, we no longer advertise jobs. Word of mouth generates up to 300 applications for every available position. The top five managers—we call them counselors—include a former human resources director of Ford Brazil, a 15-year veteran Chrysler executive, and a man who left his job as president of a large company to come to Semco.

When I joined the company in 1980, 27 years after my father founded it, Semco had about 100 employees, manufactured hydraulic pumps for ships, generated about $4 million in revenues, and teetered on the brink of catastrophe. All through 1981 and 1982, we ran from bank to bank looking for loans, and we fought persistent, well-founded rumors that the company was in danger of going under. We often stayed through the night reading files and searching the desk drawers of venerable executives for clues about contracts long since privately made and privately forgotten.

Most managers and outside board members agreed on two immediate needs: to professionalize and to diversify. In fact, both of these measures had been discussed for years but had never progressed beyond wishful thinking.

For two years, holding on by our fingertips, we sought licenses to manufacture other companies' products in Brazil. We traveled constantly. I remember one day being in Oslo for breakfast, New York for lunch, Cincinnati for dinner, and San Francisco for the night. The obstacles were great. Our company lacked an international reputation—and so did our country. Brazil's political eccentricities and draconian business regulations scared many companies away.

Still, good luck and a relentless program of beating the corporate bushes on four continents finally paid off. By 1982, we had signed seven license agreements. Our marine division—once the entire company—was now down to 60% of total sales. Moreover, the managers and directors were all professionals with no connection to the family.

With Semco back on its feet, we entered an acquisitions phase that cost millions of dollars in expenditures and millions more in losses over the next two or three years. All this growth was financed by banks at interest rates that were generally 30% above the rate of inflation, which ranged from 40% to 900% annually. There was no long-term money in Brazil at that time, so all those loans had maximum terms of 90 days. We didn't get one cent in government financing or from incentive agencies either, and we never paid out a dime in graft or bribes.

How did we do it and survive? Hard work, of course. And good luck—fundamental to all business success. But most important, I think, were the drastic changes we made in our concept of management. Without those changes, not even hard work and good luck could have pulled us through.

Semco has three fundamental values on which we base some 30 management programs. These values—democracy, profit sharing, and information—work in a complicated circle, each dependent on the other two. If we eliminated one, the others would be meaningless. Our corporate structure, employee freedoms, union relations, factory size limitations—all are products of our commitment to these principles.

It's never easy to transplant management programs from one company to another. In South America, it's axiomatic that our structure and style cannot be duplicated. Semco is either two small, too big, too far away, too young, too old, or too obnoxious.

We may also be too specialized. We do cellular manufacturing of technologically sophisticated products, and we work at the high end on quality and price. So our critics may be right. Perhaps nothing we've done can be a blueprint for anyone else. Still, in an industrial world whose methods show obvious signs of exhaustion, the merit of sharing experience is to encourage experiment and to plant the seeds of conceptual change. So what the hell.

Participatory Hot Air

The first of Semco's three values is democracy, or employee involvement. Clearly, workers who control their working conditions are going to be happier than workers who don't. Just as clearly, there is no contest between the company that buys the grudging compliance of its work force and the company that enjoys the enterprising participation of its employees.

But about 90% of the time, participatory management is just hot air. Not that intentions aren't good. It's just that implementing employee involvement is so complex, so difficult, and, not uncommonly, so frustrating that it is easier to talk about than to do.

We found four big obstacles to effective participatory management: size, hierarchy, lack of motivation, and ignorance. In an immense production unit, people feel tiny, nameless, and incapable of exerting influence on the way work is done or on the final profit made. This sense of helplessness is underlined by managers who, jealous of their power and prerogatives, refuse to let subordinates make any decisions for themselves—sometimes even about going to the bathroom. But even if size and hierarchy can be overcome, why should workers *care* about productivity and company profits? Moreover, even if you can get them to care, how can they tell when they're doing the right thing?

As Antony Jay pointed out back in the 1950s in *Corporation Man*, human beings weren't designed to work in big groups. Until recently, our ancestors were hunters and gatherers. For more than five million years, they refined their ability to work in groups of no more than about a dozen people. Then along comes the industrial revolution, and suddenly workers are trying to function efficiently in factories that employ hundreds and even thousands. Organizing those hundreds into teams of about ten members each may help some, but there's still a limit to how many small teams can work well together. At Semco, we've found the most effective production unit to consist of about 150 people. The exact number is open to argument, but it's clear that several thousand people in one facility makes individual involvement an illusion.

When we made the decision to keep our units small, we immediately focused on one facility that had more than 300 people. The unit manufactured commercial food-service equipment—slicers, scales, meat grinders, mixers—and used an MRP II system hooked up to an IBM mainframe with dozens of terminals all over the plant. Paperwork often took two days to make its way from one end of the factory to the other. Excess inventories, late delivery, and quality problems were common. We had tried various worker participation programs, quality circles, kanban systems, and motivation schemes, all of which got off to great starts but lost their momentum within months. The whole thing was just too damn big and complex; there were too many managers in too many layers holding too many meetings. So we decided to break up the facility into three separate plants.

To begin with, we kept all three in the same building but separated everything we could—entrances, receiving docks, inventories, telephones, as well as certain auxiliary functions like personnel, management information systems, and internal controls. We also scrapped the mainframe in favor of three independent, PC-based systems.

The first effect of the breakup was a rise in costs due to duplication of effort and a loss in economies of scale. Unfortunately, balance sheets chalk up items like these as liabilities, all with dollar figures attached, and there's nothing at first to list on the asset side but airy stuff like "heightened involvement" and "a sense of belonging." Yet the longer term results exceeded our expectations.

Within a year, sales doubled; inventories fell from 136 days to 46; we unveiled eight new products that had been stalled in R&D for two years; and overall quality improved to the point that a one-third rejection rate on federally inspected scales dropped to less than 1%. Increased productivity let us reduce the work force by 32% through attrition and retirement incentives.

I don't claim that size reduction alone accomplished all this, just that size reduction is essential for putting employees in touch with one another so they can coordinate their work. The kind of distance we want to eliminate comes from having too many people in one place, but it also comes from having a pyramidal hierarchy.

Pyramids and Circles

The organizational pyramid is the cause of much corporate evil, because the tip is too far from the base. Pyramids emphasize power, promote insecurity, distort communications, hobble interaction, and make it very difficult for the people who plan and the people who execute to move in the same direction. So Semco designed an organizational *circle*. Its greatest advantage is to reduce management levels to three—one corporate level and two operating levels at the manufacturing units.

It consists of three concentric circles. One tiny, central circle contains the five people who integrate the company's movements. These are the counselors I mentioned before. I'm one of them, and except for a couple of legal documents that call me president, counselor is the only title I use. A second, larger circle contains the heads of the eight divisions—we call them partners. Finally, a third, huge circle holds all the other employees. Most of them are the people we call associates; they do the research, design, sales, and manufacturing work and have no one reporting to them on a regular basis. But some of them are the permanent and temporary team and task leaders we call coordinators. Counselors, partners, coordinators, and associates. Four titles. Three management layers.

The linchpins of the system are the coordinators, a group that includes everyone formerly called foreman, supervisor, manager, head, or chief. The only people who report to coordinators are associates. No coordinator reports to another coordinator—that feature of the system is what ensures the reduction in management layers.

Like anyone else, we value leadership, but it's not the only thing we value. In marine pumps, for example, we have an applications engineer who can look at the layout of a ship and then focus on one particular pump and say, "That pump will fail if you take this thing north of the Arctic Circle." He makes a lot more money than the person who manages his unit. We can change the manager, but this guy knows what kind of pump will work in the Arctic, and that's worth more. Associates often make higher salaries than coordinators and partners, and they can increase their status and compensation without entering the "management" line.

Managers and the status and money they enjoy—in a word, hierarchy—are the single biggest obstacle to participatory management. We had to get the managers out of the way of democratic decision making, and our circular system does that pretty well.

But we go further. We don't hire or promote people until they've been interviewed and accepted by all their future subordinates. Twice a year, subordinates evaluate managers. Also twice a year, everyone in the company anonymously fills out a questionnaire about company credibility and top management competence. Among other things, we ask our employees what it would take to make them quit or go on strike.

We insist on making important decisions collegially, and certain decisions are made by a companywide vote. Several years ago, for example, we needed a bigger plant for our marine division, which makes pumps, compressors, and ship propellers. Real estate agents looked for months and found nothing. So we asked the employees themselves to help, and over the first weekend they found three factories for sale, all of them nearby. We closed up shop for a day, piled everyone into buses, and drove out to inspect the three buildings. Then the workers voted—and they chose a plant the counselors didn't really want. It was an interesting situation—one that tested our commitment to participatory management.

The building stands across the street from a Caterpillar plant that's one of the most frequently struck factories in Brazil. With two tough unions of our own, we weren't looking forward to front-row seats for every labor dispute that came along. But we accepted the employees' decision, because we believe that in the long run, letting people participate in the decisions that affect their lives will have a positive effect on employee motivation and morale.

We bought the building and moved in. The workers designed the layout for a flexible manufacturing system, and they hired one of Brazil's foremost artists to paint the whole thing, inside and out, including the machinery. That plant really belongs to its employees. I feel like a guest every time I walk in.

I don't mind. The division's productivity, in dollars per year per employee, has jumped from $14,200 in 1984—the year we moved—to $37,500 in 1988, and for 1989 the goal is $50,000. Over the same period, market share went from 54% to 62%.

Employees also outvoted me on the acquisition of a company that I'm still sure we should have bought. But they felt we weren't ready to digest it, and I lost the vote. In a case like that, the credibility of our management system is at stake. Employee involvement must be real, even when it makes management uneasy. Anyway, what is the future of an acquisition if the people who have to operate it don't believe it's workable?

Hiring Adults

We have other ways of combating hierarchy too. Most of our programs are based on the notion of giving employees control over their own lives. In a word, we hire adults, and then we treat them like adults.

Think about that. Outside the factory, workers are men and women who elect governments, serve in the army, lead community projects, raise and educate families, and make decisions every day about the future. Friends solicit their advice. Salespeople court them. Children and grandchildren look up to them for their wisdom and experience. But the moment they walk into the factory, the company transforms them into adolescents. They have to wear badges and name tags, arrive at a certain time, stand in line to punch the clock or eat their lunch, get permission to go to the bathroom, give lengthy explanations every time they're five minutes late, and follow instructions without asking a lot of questions.

One of my first moves when I took control of Semco was to abolish norms, manuals, rules, and regulations. Everyone knows you can't run a large organization without regulations, but everyone also knows that most regulations are poppycock. They rarely solve problems. On the contrary, there is usually some obscure corner of the rule book that justifies the worst silliness people can think up. Common sense is a riskier tactic because it requires personal responsibility.

It's also true that common sense requires just a touch of civil disobedience every time someone calls attention to something that's not working. We had to free the Thoreaus and the Tom Paines in the factory and come to terms with that fact that civil disobedience was not an early sign of revolution but a clear indication of common sense at work.

So we replaced all the nitpicking regulations with the rule of common sense and put our employees in the demanding position of using their own judgment.

We have no dress code, for example. The idea that personal appearance is important in a job—any job—is baloney. We've all heard that salespeople, receptionists, and service reps are the company's calling cards, but in fact how utterly silly that is. A company that needs business suits to prove its seriousness probably lacks more meaningful proof. And what customer has ever canceled an order because the receptionist was wearing jeans instead of a dress? Women and men look best when they feel good. IBM is not a great company because its salespeople dress to the special standard that Thomas Watson set. It's a great company that also happens to have this quirk.

We also scrapped the complex company rules about travel expenses—what sorts of accommodations people were entitled to, whether we'd pay for a theater ticket, whether a free call home meant five minutes or ten. We used to spend a lot of time discussing stuff like that. Now we base everything on common sense. Some people stay in four-star hotels and some live like spartans. Some people spend $200 a day while others get by on $125. Or so I suppose. No one checks expenses, so there is no way of knowing. The point is, we don't care. If we can't trust people with our money and their judgment, we sure as hell shouldn't be sending them overseas to do business in our name.

We have done away with security searches, storeroom padlocks, and audits of the petty-cash accounts of veteran employees. Not that we wouldn't prosecute a genuinely criminal violation of our trust. We just refuse to humiliate 97% of the work force to get our hands on the occasional thief or two-bit embezzler.

We encourage—we practically insist on—job rotation every two to five years to prevent boredom. We try hard to provide job security, and for people over 50 or who've been with the company for more than three years, dismissal procedures are extra complicated.

On the more experimental side, we have a program for entry-level management trainees called "Lost in Space," whereby we hire a couple of people every year who have no job description at all. A "godfather" looks after them, and for one year they do anything they like, as long as they try at least 12 different areas or units.

By the same logic that governs our other employee programs, we have also eliminated time clocks. People come and go according to their own schedules—even on the factory floor. I admit this idea is hard to swallow; most manufacturers are not ready for factory-floor flextime. But our reasoning was simple.

First, we use cellular manufacturing systems. At our food-processing equipment plant, for example, one cell makes only slicers, another makes scales, another makes mixers, and so forth. Each cell is self-contained, so products—and their problems—are segregated from each other.

Second, we assumed that all our employees were trustworthy adults. We couldn't believe they would come to work day after day and sit on their hands because no one else was there. Pretty soon, we figured, they would start coordinating their work hours with their coworkers.

And that's exactly what happened, only more so. For example, one man wanted to start at 7 A.M., but because the forklift operator didn't come until 8, he couldn't get his parts. So a general discussion arose, and the upshot was that now everyone knows how to operate a forklift. In fact, most people can now do several jobs. The union has never objected because the initiative came from the workers themselves. It was their idea.

Moreover, the people on the factory floor set the schedule, and if they say that this month they will build 48 commercial dishwashers, then we can go play tennis, because 48 is what they'll build.

In one case, one group decided to make 220 meat slicers. By the end of the month, it had finished the slicers as scheduled—except that even after repeated phone calls, the supplier still hadn't produced the motors. So two employees drove over and talked to the supplier and managed to get delivery at the end of that day, the 31st. Then they stayed all night, the whole work force, and finished the lot at 4:45 the next morning.

When we introduced flexible hours, we decided to hold regular follow-up meetings to track problems and decide how to deal with abuses and production interruptions. That was years ago, and we haven't yet held the first meeting.

Hunting the Woolly Mammoth

What makes our people behave this way? As Antony Jay points out, corporate man is a very recent animal. At Semco, we try to respect the hunter that dominated the first 99.9% of the history of our species. If you had to kill a mammoth or do without supper, there was no time to draw up an organization chart, assign tasks, or delegate authority. Basically, the person who saw the mammoth from farthest away was the Official Sighter, the one who can run fastest was the Head Runner, whoever threw the most accurate spear was the

Grand Marksman, and the person all others respected most and listened to was the Chief. That's all there was to it. Distributing little charts to produce an appearance of order would have been a waste of time. It still is.

What I'm saying is, put ten people together, don't appoint a leader, and you can be sure that one will emerge. So will a sighter, a runner, and whatever else the group needs. We form the groups, but they find their own leaders. That's not a lack of structure, that's just a lack of structure imposed from above.

But getting back to that mammoth, why was it that all the members of the group were so eager to do their share of the work—sighting, running, spearing, chiefing—and to stand aside when someone else could do it better? Because they all got to eat the thing once it was killed and cooked. What mattered was results, not status.

Corporate profit is today's mammoth meat. And though there is a widespread view that profit sharing is some kind of socialist infection, it seems to me that few motivational tools are more capitalist. Everyone agrees that profits should belong to those who risk their capital, that entrepreneurial behavior deserves reward, that the creation of wealth should enrich the creator. Well, depending on how you define capital and risk, all these truisms can apply as much to workers as to shareholders.

Still, many profit-sharing programs are failures, and we think we know why. Profit sharing won't motivate employees if they see it as just another management gimmick, if the company makes it difficult for them to see how their own work is related to profits and to understand how those profits are divided.

In Semco's case, each division has a separate profit-sharing program. Twice a year, we calculate 23% of after-tax profit on each division income statement and give a check to three employees who've been elected by the workers on their division. These three invest the money until the unit can meet and decide—by simple majority vote—what they want to do with it. In most units, that's turned out to be an equal distribution. If a unit has 150 workers, the total is divided by 150 and handed out. It's that simple. The guy who sweeps the floor gets just as much as the division partner.

One division chose to use the money as a fund to lend out for housing construction. It was a pretty close vote, and the workers may change their minds next year. In the meantime, some of them have already received loans and have begun to build themselves houses. In any case, the employees do what they want with the money. The counselors stay out of it.

Semco's experience has convinced me that profit sharing has an excellent chance of working when it crowns a broad program of employee participation, when the profit-sharing criteria are so clear and simple that the least gifted employee can understand them, and, perhaps most important, when employees have monthly access to the company's vital statistics—costs, overhead, sales, payroll, taxes, profits.

Transparency

Lots of things contribute to a successful profit-sharing program: low employee turnover, competitive pay, absence of paternalism, refusal to give consolation prizes when profits are down, frequent (quarterly or semiannual) profit distribution, and plenty of opportunity for employees to question the management decisions that affect future profits. But nothing matters more than those vital statistics—short, frank, frequent reports on how the company is doing. Complete transparency. No hocus-pocus, no hanky-panky, no simplifications.

On the contrary, all Semco employees attend classes to learn how to read and understand the numbers, and it's one of their unions that teaches the course. Every month, each employee gets a balance sheet, a profit-and-loss analysis, and a cash-flow statement for his or her division. The reports contain about 70 line items (more, incidentally, than we use to run the company, but we don't want anyone to think we're withholding information).

Many of our executives were alarmed by the decision to share monthly financial results with all employees. They were afraid workers would want to know everything, like how much we pay executives. When we held the first large meeting to discuss these financial reports with the factory committees and the leaders of the metalworkers' union, the first question we got was, "How much do division managers make?" We told them. They gasped. Ever since, the factory workers have called them "maharaja."

But so what? If executives are embarrassed by their salaries, that probably means they aren't earning them. Confidential payrolls are for those who cannot look themselves in the mirror and say with conviction, "I live in a capitalist system that remunerates on a geometric scale. I spent years in school, I have years of experience, I am capable and dedicated and intelligent. I deserve what I get."

I believe that the courage to show the real numbers will always have positive consequences over the long term. On the other hand, we can show only the numbers we bother to put together, and there aren't as many as there used to be. In my view, only the big numbers matter. But Semco's accounting people keep telling me that since the only way to get the big numbers is to add up the small ones, producing a budget or report that includes every tiny detail would require no extra effort. This is an expensive fallacy, and a difficult one to eradicate.

A few years ago, the U.S. president of Allis-Chalmers paid Semco a visit. At the end of his factory tour, he leafed through our monthly reports and budgets. At that time, we had our numbers ready on the fifth working day of every month in super-organized folders, and were those numbers comprehensive! On page 67, chart 112.6, for example, you could see how much coffee the workers in Light Manufacturing III had consumed the month before. The man said he was surprised to find such efficiency in a Brazilian company. In fact, he was so impressed that he asked his Brazilian subsidiary, an organization many times our size, to install a similar system there.

For months, we strolled around like peacocks, telling anyone who cared to listen that our budget system was state-of-the-art and that the president of a Big American Company had ordered his people to copy it. But soon we began to realize two things. First, our expenses were always too high, and they never came down because the accounting department was full of overpaid clerks who did nothing but compile them. Second, there were so damn many numbers inside the folders that almost none of our managers read them. In fact, we knew less about the company then, with all that information, than we do now without it.

Today we have a simple accounting system providing limited but relevant information that we can grasp and act on quickly. We pared 400 cost centers down to 50. We beheaded hundreds of classifications and dozens of accounting lines. Finally, we can see the company through the haze.

(As for Allis-Chalmers, I don't know whether it ever adopted our old system in all its terrible completeness, but I hope not. A few years later, it began to suffer severe financial difficulties and eventually lost so much market share and money that it was broken up and sold. I'd hate to think it was our fault.)

In preparing budgets, we believe that the flexibility to change the budget continually is much more important than the detailed consistency of the initial numbers. We also believe in the importance of comparing expectations with results. Naturally, we compare monthly reports with the budget. But we go one step further. At month's end, the coordinators in each area make guesses about unit receipts, profit margins, and expenses. When the official numbers come out a few days later, top managers compare them with the guesses to judge how well the coordinators understand their areas.

What matters in budgets as well as in reports is that the numbers be few and important and that people treat them with something approaching passion. The three monthly reports, with their 70 line items, tell us how to run the company, tell our managers how well they know their units, and tell our employees if there's going to be a profit. Everyone works on the basis of the same information, and everyone looks forward to its appearance with what I'd call fervent curiosity.

And that's all there is to it. Participation gives people control of their work, profit sharing gives them a reason to do it better, information tells them what's working and what isn't.

Letting Them Do Whatever They Want

So we don't have systems or staff functions or analysts or anything like that. What we have are people who either sell or make, and there's nothing in between. Is there a marketing department? Not on your life. Marketing is everybody's problem. Everybody knows the price of the product. Everybody knows the cost. Everybody has the monthly statement that says exactly what each of them makes, how much bronze is costing us, how much overtime we paid, all of it. And the employees know that 23% of the after-tax profit is theirs.

We are very, very rigorous about the numbers. We want them in on the fourth day of the month so we can get them back out on the fifth. And because we're so strict with the financial controls, we can be extremely lax about everything else. Employees can paint the walls any color they like. They can come to work whenever they decide. They can wear whatever clothing makes them comfortable. They can do whatever the hell they want. It's up to them to see the connection between productivity and profit and to act on it.

Ricardo Semler's Guide to Compensation

Employers began hiring workers by the hour during the industrial revolution. Their reasons were simple and rapacious. Say you ran out of cotton thread at 11:30 in the morning. If you paid people by the hour, you could stop the looms, send everyone home, and pay only for hours actually worked.

You couldn't do such a thing today. The law probably wouldn't let you. The unions certainly wouldn't let you. Your own self-interest would argue strongly against it. Yet the system lives on. The distinction between wage-earning workers and salaried employees is alive but not well, nearly universal but perfectly silly. The new clerk who lives at home and doesn't know how to boil an egg starts on a monthly salary, but the chief lathe operator who's been with the company 38 years and is a master sergeant in the army reserve still gets paid by the hour.

At Semco, we eliminated Frederick Winslow Taylor's segmentation and specialization of work. We ended the wage analyst's hundred years of solitude. We did away with hourly pay and now give everyone a monthly salary. We set the salaries like this:

A lot of our people belong to unions, and they negotiate their salaries collectively. Everyone else's salary involves an element of self-determination.

Once or twice a year, we order salary market surveys and pass them out. We say to people, "Figure out where you stand on this thing. You know what you do; you know what everyone else in the company makes; you know what your friends in other companies make; you know what you need; you know what's fair. Come back on Monday and tell us what to pay you."

When people ask for too little, we give it to them. By and by, they figure it out and ask for more. When they ask for too much, we give that to them too— at least for the first year. Then, if you don't feel they're worth the money, we sit down with them and say, "Look, you make x amount of money, and we don't think you're making x amount of contribution. So either we find something else for you to do, or we don't have a job for you anymore." But with half a dozen exceptions, our people have always named salaries we could live with.

We do a similar thing with titles. Counselors are counselors, and partners are partners; these titles are always the same. But with coordinators, it's not quite so easy. Job titles still mean too much to many people. So we tell coordinators to make up their own titles. They know what signals they need to send inside and outside the company. If they want "Procurement Manager," that's fine. And if they want "Grand Panjandrum of Imperial Supplies," that's fine too.

Ricardo Semler's Guide to Stress Management

There are two things all managers have in common—the 24-hour day and the annoying need to sleep. Without the sleeping, 24 hours might be enough. With it, there is no way to get everything done. After years of trying to vanquish demon sleep and the temptation to relax, I tried an approach suggested by my doctor, who put it this way: "Slow down or kiss yourself good-bye."

Struck by this imagery, I learned to manage my time and cut my work load to less than 24 hours. The first step is to overcome five myths:

1. Results are proportional to efforts.   The Brazilian flag expresses this myth in a slightly different form. "Order and Progress," it says. Of course, it ought to say, "Order *or* Progress," since the two never go together.

2. Quantity of work is more important than quality.   Psychologically, this myth may hold water. The executive who puts in lots of hours can always say,

"Well, they didn't promote me, but you can see how unfair that is. Everyone knows I get here at 8 A.M. and that my own children can't see me without an appointment."

3. The present restructuring requires longer working hours temporarily. We think of ourselves as corks on a mountain stream headed for Lake Placid. But the lake ahead is Loch Ness. The present, temporary emergency is actually permanent. Stop being a cork.

4. No one else can do it right. The truth is, you *are* replaceable, as everyone will discover within a week of your funeral.

5. This problem is urgent. Come on. The real difference between "important" and "urgent" is the difference between thoughtfulness and panic.

Those are the myths. The second step is to master my eight cures:

1. Set an hour to leave the office and obey it blindly. If you normally go home at 7:00, start leaving at 6:00. If you take work home on weekends, give yourself a month or two to put a stop to this pernicious practice.

2. Take half a day, maybe even an entire Saturday, to rummage through that mountain of paper in your office and put it in three piles.

Pile A: Priority items that require your personal attention and represent matters of indisputable importance. If you put more than four or five documents in this category and are not currently the president of your country, start over.

Pile B: Items that need your personal attention, but not right away. This pile is very tempting; everything fits. But don't fall into the trap. Load this stuff on your subordinates, using the 70% test to help you do it. Ask yourself: Is there someone on my staff who can do this task at least 70% as well as I can? Yes? Then farm it out. Whether or not your subordinates are overworked should not weigh in your decision. Remember, control of your time is an exercise in selfishness.

Pile C: Items that fall under the dubious rubric "a good idea to look at." One of the most egregious executive fallacies is that you have to read a little of everything in order to stay well-informed. If you limit the number of newspapers, magazines, and internal communications that you read regularly, you'll have more time to do what's important—like think. And remember to keep your reading timely; information is a perishable commodity.

3. In dealing with Pile A, always start with the most difficult or the most time-consuming. It also helps to have a folder for the things that *must* be done before you go home that day and to make a list of the things that simply cannot go undone for more than a few days or a week. Everything else is just everything else.

4. Buy another wastepaper basket. I know you already have one. But if you invited me to go through that pile of papers on your desk, I could fill both in a trice. To help you decide what to toss and what to save, ask yourself the question asked by the legendary Alfred P. Sloan, Jr.: "What is the worst that can happen if I throw this out?" If you don't tremble, sweat, or grow faint when you think of the consequences, toss it.

This second wastebasket is a critical investment, even though you'll never be able to fill both on a regular basis. Keep it anyway. It has a symbolic value. It will babysit your in-basket and act like a governess every time you wonder why you bought it.

5. Ask yourself Sloan's question about every lunch and meeting invitation. Don't be timid. And practice these three RSVPs:

"Thanks, but I just can't fit it in."

"I can't go, but I think X can." (If you think someone should.)

"I'm sorry I can't make it, but do let me know what happened."

Transform meetings into telephone calls or quick conversations in the hall. When you hold a meeting in your office, sit on the edge of your desk, or when you want to end the discussion, stand up from behind your desk and say, "OK, then, that's settled." These tricks are rude but almost foolproof.

6. Give yourself time to think. Spend half a day every week away from your office. Take your work home, or try working somewhere else—a conference room in another office, a public library, an airport waiting room—any place you can concentrate, and the farther away from your office the better. The point is, a fresh environment can do wonders for productivity. Just make sure you bring along a healthy dose of discipline, especially if you're working at home.

7. About the telephone, my practical but subversive advice is: Don't return calls. Or rather, return calls only to people you want to talk to. The others will call back. Better yet, they'll write, and you can spend ten seconds with their letter and then give it to the governess.

Two ancillary bits of phone advice: Ask your assistants to take detailed messages. Ask them always to say you cannot take the call at the moment. (Depending on who it is, your assistants can always undertake to see if you can't be interrupted.)

8. Close your door. Oh, I know you have an open-door policy, but don't be so literal.

Managing for Organizational Integrity

LYNN SHARP PAINE

Many managers think of ethics as a question of personal scruples, a confidential matter between individuals and their consciences. These executives are quick to describe any wrongdoing as an isolated incident, the work of a rogue employee. The thought that the company could bear any responsibility for an individual's misdeeds never enters their minds. Ethics, after all, has nothing to do with management.

In fact, ethics has *everything* to do with management. Rarely do the character flaws of a lone actor fully explain corporate misconduct. More typically, unethical business practice involves the tacit, if not explicit, cooperation of others and reflects the values, attitudes, beliefs, language, and behavioral patterns that define an organization's operating culture. Ethics, then, is as much an organizational as a personal issue. Managers who fail to provide proper leadership and to institute systems that facilitate ethical conduct share responsibility with those who conceive, execute, and knowingly benefit from corporate misdeeds.

Managers must acknowledge their role in shaping organizational ethics and seize this opportunity to create a climate that can strengthen the relationships and reputations on which their companies' success depends. Executives who ignore ethics run the risk of personal and corporate liability in today's increasingly tough legal environment. In addition, they deprive their organizations of the benefits available under new federal guidelines for sentencing organizations convicted of wrongdoing. These sentencing guidelines recognize for the first time the organizational and managerial roots of unlawful conduct and base fines partly on the extent to which companies have taken steps to prevent that misconduct.

Prompted by the prospect of leniency, many companies are rushing to implement compliance-based ethics programs. Designed by corporate counsel, the goal of these programs is to prevent, detect, and punish legal violations. But organizational ethics means more than avoiding illegal practice; and providing employees with a rule book will do little to address the problems underlying unlawful conduct. To foster a climate that encourages exemplary behavior, corporations need a comprehensive approach that goes beyond the often punitive legal compliance stance.

An integrity-based approach to ethics management combines a concern for the law with an emphasis on managerial responsibility for ethical behavior. Though integrity strategies may vary in design and scope, all strive to define companies' guiding values, aspirations, and patterns of thought and conduct. When integrated into the day-to-day operations of an organization, such strategies can help prevent damaging ethical lapses while tapping into powerful human impulses for moral thought and action. Then an ethical framework becomes no longer a burdensome constraint within which companies must operate, but the governing ethos of an organization.

How Organizations Shape Individuals' Behavior

The once familiar picture of ethics as individualistic, unchanging, and impervious to organizational influences has not stood up to scrutiny in recent years. Sears Auto Centers' and Beech-Nut Nutrition Corporation's experiences illustrate the role organizations play in shaping individuals' behavior—and how even sound moral fiber can fray when stretched too thin.

In 1992, Sears, Roebuck & Company was inundated with complaints about its automotive service business. Consumers and attorneys general in more than 40 states had accused the company of misleading customers and selling them unnecessary parts and services, from brake jobs to front-end alignments. It would be a mistake, however, to see this situation exclusively in terms of any one individual's moral failings. Nor did management set out to defraud Sears customers. Instead, a number of organizational factors contributed to the problematic sales practices.

In the face of declining revenues, shrinking market share, and an increasingly competitive market for undercar services, Sears management attempted to spur the performance of its auto centers by introducing new goals and incentives for employees. The company increased minimum work quotas and introduced productivity incentives for mechanics. The automotive service advisers were given product-specific sales quotas—sell so many springs, shock absorbers, alignments, or brake jobs per shift—and paid a commission based on sales. According to advisers, failure to meet quotas could lead to a transfer or a reduction in work hours. Some employees spoke of the "pressure, pressure, pressure" to bring in sales.

Under this new set of organizational pressures and incentives, with few options for meeting their sales goals legitimately, some employees' judgment understandably suffered. Management's failure to clarify the line between unnecessary service and legitimate preventive maintenance, coupled with consumer ignorance, left employees to chart their own courses through a vast gray area, subject to a wide range of interpretations. Without active management support for ethical practice and mechanisms to detect and check questionable sales methods and poor work, it is not surprising that some employees may have reacted to contextual forces by resorting to exaggeration, carelessness, or even misrepresentation.

Shortly after the allegations against Sears became public, CEO Edward Brennan acknowledged management's responsibility for putting in place compensation and goal-setting systems that "created an environment in which mistakes did occur." Although the company denied any intent to deceive consumers, senior executives eliminated commissions for service advisers and discontinued sales quotas for specific parts. They also instituted a system of unannounced shopping audits and made plans to expand the internal monitoring of service. In settling the pending lawsuits, Sears offered coupons to customers who had bought certain auto services between 1990 and 1992. The total cost of the settlement, including potential customer refunds, was an estimated $60 million.

Contextual forces can also influence the behavior of top management, as a former CEO of Beech-Nut Nutrition Corporation discovered. In the early 1980s, only two years after joining the company, the CEO found evidence suggesting that the apple juice concentrate, supplied by the company's vendors for use in Beech-Nut's "100% pure" apple juice, contained nothing more than sugar water and chemicals. The CEO could have destroyed the bogus inventory and withdrawn the juice from grocers' shelves, but he was under extraordinary pressure to turn the ailing company around. Eliminating the inventory would have killed any hope of turning even the meager $700,000 profit promised to Beech-Nut's then parent, Nestlé.

A number of people in the corporation, it turned out, had doubted the purity of the juice for several years before the CEO arrived. But the 25% price advantage offered by the supplier of the bogus concentrate allowed the operations head to meet cost-control goals. Furthermore, the company lacked an effective quality control system, and a conclusive lab test for juice purity did not yet exist. When a member of the research department voiced concerns about the juice to operating management, he was accused of not being a team player and of acting like "Chicken Little." His judgment, his supervisor wrote in an annual performance review, was "colored by naïveté and impractical ideals." No one else seemed to have considered the company's obligations to its customers or to have thought about the potential harm of disclosure. No one considered the fact that the sale of adulterated or misbranded juice is a legal offense, putting the company and its top management at risk of criminal liability.

An FDA investigation taught Beech-Nut the hard way. In 1987, the company pleaded guilty to selling adulterated and misbranded juice. Two years and two criminal trials later, the CEO pleaded guilty to ten counts of mislabeling. The total cost to the company—including fines, legal expenses, and lost sales—was an estimated $25 million.

Such errors of judgment rarely reflect an organizational culture and management philosophy that sets out to harm or deceive. More often, they reveal a culture that is insensitive or indifferent to ethical considerations or one that lacks effective organizational systems. By the same token, exemplary conduct usually reflects an organizational culture and philosophy that is infused with a sense of responsibility.

For example, Johnson & Johnson's handling of the Tylenol crisis is sometimes attributed to the singular personality of then-CEO James Burke. However, the decision to do a nationwide recall of Tylenol capsules in order to avoid further loss of life from product tampering was in reality not one decision but thousands of decisions made by individuals at all levels of the organization. The "Tylenol decision," then, is best understood not as an isolated incident, the achievement of a lone individual, but as the reflection of an organization's culture. Without a shared set of values and guiding principles deeply ingrained throughout the organization, it is doubtful that Johnson & Johnson's response would have been as rapid, cohesive, and ethically sound.

Many people resist acknowledging the influence of organizational factors on individual behavior—especially on misconduct—for fear of diluting people's sense of personal moral responsibility. But this fear is based on a false dichotomy between holding individual transgressors accountable and holding "the system" accountable. Acknowledging the importance of organizational context need not imply exculpating individual wrongdoers. To understand all is not to forgive all.

The Limits of a Legal Compliance Program

The consequences of an ethical lapse can be serious and far-reaching. Organizations can quickly become entangled in an all-consuming web of legal proceedings. The risk of litigation and liability has increased in the past decade as lawmakers have legislated new civil and criminal offenses, stepped up penalties, and improved support for law enforcement. Equally—if not more—important is the damage an ethical lapse can do to an organization's reputation and relationships. Both Sears and Beech-Nut, for instance, struggled to regain consumer trust and market share long after legal proceedings had ended.

As more managers have become alerted to the importance of organizational ethics, many have asked their lawyers to develop corporate ethics programs to detect and prevent violations of the law. The 1991 Federal Sentencing Guidelines offer a compelling rationale. Sanctions such as fines and probation for organizations convicted of wrongdoing can vary dramatically depending both on the degree of management cooperation in reporting and investigating corporate misdeeds and on whether or not the company has implemented a legal compliance program.

Such programs tend to emphasize the prevention of unlawful conduct, primarily by increasing surveillance and control and by imposing penalties for wrongdoers. While plans vary, the basic framework is outlined in the sentencing guidelines. Managers must establish compliance standards and procedures; designate high-level personnel to oversee compliance; avoid delegating discretionary authority to those likely to act unlawfully; effectively communicate the company's standards and procedures through training or publications; take reasonable steps to achieve compliance through audits, monitoring processes, and a system for employees to report criminal misconduct without fear of retribution; consistently enforce standards through appropriate disciplinary measures; respond appropriately when offenses are detected; and, finally, take reasonable steps to prevent the occurrence of similar offenses in the future.

There is no question of the necessity of a sound, well-articulated strategy for legal compliance in an organization. After all, employees can be frustrated and frightened by the complexity of today's legal environment. And even managers who claim to use the law as a guide to ethical behavior often lack more than a rudimentary understanding of complex legal issues.

Managers would be mistaken, however, to regard legal compliance as an adequate means for addressing the full range of ethical issues that arise every day. "If it's legal, it's ethical," is a frequently heard slogan. But conduct that is lawful may be highly problematic from an ethical point of view. Consider the sale in some countries of hazardous products without appropriate warnings or the purchase of goods from suppliers who operate inhumane sweatshops in developing countries. Companies engaged in international business often discover that conduct that infringes on recognized standards of human rights and decency is legally permissible in some jurisdictions.

Legal clearance does not certify the absence of ethical problems in the United States either, as a 1991 case at Salomon Brothers illustrates. Four top-level executives failed to take appropriate action when learning of unlawful activities on the government trading desk. Company lawyers found no law obligating the executives to disclose the improprieties. Nevertheless, the executives' delay in disclosing and failure to reveal their prior knowledge prompted a serious crisis of confidence among employees, creditors, shareholders, and customers. The executives were forced to resign, having lost the moral authority to lead. Their ethical lapse compounded the trading desk's legal offenses, and the company ended up suffering losses—including legal costs, increased funding costs, and lost business—estimated at nearly $1 billion.

A compliance approach to ethics also overemphasizes the threat of detection and punishment in order to channel behavior in lawful directions. The underlying model for this approach is deterrence theory, which envisions people as rational maximizers of self-interest, responsive to the personal costs and benefits of their choices, yet indifferent to the moral legitimacy of those choices. But a recent study reported in *Why People Obey the Law* by Tom R. Tyler shows that obedience to the law is strongly influenced by a belief in its legitimacy and its moral correctness. People generally feel that they have a strong obligation to obey the law. Education about the legal standards and a supportive environment may be all that's required to insure compliance.

Discipline is, of course, a necessary part of any ethical system. Justified penalties for the infringement of legitimate norms are fair and appropriate. Some people do need the threat of sanctions. However, an overemphasis on potential sanctions can be superfluous and even counterproductive. Employees may rebel against programs that stress penalties, particularly if they are designed and imposed without employee involvement or if the standards are vague or unrealistic. Management may talk of mutual trust when unveiling a compliance plan, but employees often receive the message as a warning from on high. Indeed, the most skeptical among them may view compliance programs as nothing more than liability insurance for senior management. This is not an unreasonable conclusion, considering that compliance programs rarely address the root causes of misconduct.

Even in the best cases, legal compliance is unlikely to unleash much moral imagination or commitment. The law does not generally seek to inspire human excellence or distinction. It is no guide for exemplary behavior—or even good practice. Those managers who define ethics as legal compliance are implicitly endorsing a code of moral mediocrity for their organizations. As Richard Breeden, former chairman of the Securities and Exchange Commission, noted, "It is not an adequate ethical standard to aspire to get through the day without being indicted."

Integrity as a Governing Ethic

A strategy based on integrity holds organizations to a more robust standard. While compliance is rooted in avoiding legal sanctions, organizational integrity is based on the concept of self-governance in accordance with a set of guiding principles. From the perspective of integrity, the task of ethics management is to define and give life to an organization's guiding values, to create an environment that supports ethically sound behavior, and to instill a sense of shared accountability among employees. The need to obey the law is viewed as a positive aspect of organizational life, rather than an unwelcome constraint imposed by external authorities.

An integrity strategy is characterized by a conception of ethics as a driving force of an enterprise. Ethical values shape the search for opportunities, the design of organizational systems, and the decision-making process used by individuals and groups. They provide a common frame of reference and serve as a unifying force across different functions, lines of business, and employee groups. Organizational ethics helps define what a company is and what it stands for.

Many integrity initiatives have structural features common to compliance-based initiatives: a code of conduct, training in relevant areas of law, mechanisms for reporting and investigating potential misconduct, and audits and controls to insure that laws and company standards are being met. In addition, if suitably designed, an integrity-based initiative can establish a foundation for seeking the legal benefits that are available under the sentencing guidelines should criminal wrongdoing occur. (See the insert "The Hallmarks of an Effective Integrity Strategy.")

But an integrity strategy is broader, deeper, and more demanding than a legal compliance initiative. Broader in that is seeks to enable responsible conduct. Deeper in that it cuts to the ethos and operating systems of the organization and its members, their guiding values and patterns of thought and action. And more demanding in that it requires an active effort to define the responsibilities and aspirations that constitute an organization's ethical compass. Above all, organizational ethics is seen as the work of management. Corporate counsel may play a role in the design and implementation of integrity strategies, but managers at all levels and across all functions are involved in the process. (See the chart, "Strategies for Ethics Management.")

During the past decade, a number of companies have undertaken integrity initiatives. They vary according to the ethical values focused on and the implementation approaches used. Some companies focus on the core values of integrity that reflect basic social obligations, such as respect for the rights of others, honesty, fair dealing, and obedience to the law. Other companies emphasize aspirations—values that are ethically desirable but not necessarily morally obligatory—such as good service to customers, a commitment to diversity, and involvement in the community.

When it comes to implementation, some companies begin with behavior. Following Aristotle's view that one becomes courageous by acting as a courageous person, such companies develop codes of conduct specifying appropriate behavior, along with a system of incentives, audits, and controls. Other companies focus less on specific actions and more on developing attitudes, decision-making processes, and ways of thinking that reflect their values. The assumption is that personal commitment and appropriate decision processes will lead to right action.

Martin Marietta, NovaCare, and Wetherill Associates have implemented and lived with quite different integrity strategies. In each case, management has found that the initiative has made important and often unexpected contributions to competitiveness, work environment, and key relationships on which the company depends.

Martin Marietta: Emphasizing Core Values

Martin Marietta Corporation, the U.S. aerospace and defense contractor, opted for an integrity-based ethics program in 1985. At the time, the defense industry was under attack for fraud and mismanagement, and Martin Marietta was under investigation for improper travel billings. Managers knew they needed a better form of self-governance but were skeptical that an ethics program could influence behavior. "Back then people asked, 'Do you really need an ethics program to be ethical?'" recalls current President Thomas Young. "Ethics was something personal. Either you had it, or you didn't."

The corporate general counsel played a pivotal role in promoting the program, and legal compliance was a critical objective. But it was conceived of and implemented from the start as a companywide management initiative aimed at creating and maintaining a "do-it-right" climate. In its original conception, the program emphasized core values, such as honesty and fair play. Over time, it expanded to encompass quality and environmental responsibility as well.

Today the initiative consists of a code of conduct, an ethics training program, and procedures for reporting and investigating ethical concerns within the company. It also includes a system for disclosing violations of federal procurement law to the government. A corporate ethics office manages the program, and ethics representatives are stationed at major facilities. An ethics steering committee, made up of Martin Marietta's president, senior executives, and two rotating members selected from field operations, oversees the ethics office. The audit and ethics committee of the board of directors oversees the steering committee.

The ethics office is responsible for responding to questions and concerns from the company's employees. Its network of representatives serves as a sounding board, a source of guidance, and a channel for raising a range of issues, from allegations of wrongdoing to complaints about poor management, unfair supervision, and company policies and practices. Martin Marietta's ethics network, which accepts anonymous complaints, logged over 9,000 calls in 1991, when the company had about 60,000 employees. In 1992, it investigated 684 cases. The ethics office also works closely with the human resources, legal, audit, communications, and security functions to respond to employee concerns.

Shortly after establishing the program, the company began its first round of ethics training for the entire workforce, starting with the CEO and senior executives. Now in its third round, training for senior executives focuses on decision making, the challenges of balancing multiple responsibilities, and compliance with laws and regulations critical to the company. The incentive compensation plan for executives makes responsibility for promoting ethical conduct an explicit requirement for reward eligibility and requires that business and personal goals be achieved in accordance with the company's policy on ethics. Ethical conduct and support for the ethics program are also criteria in regular performance reviews.

Today top-level managers say the ethics program has helped the company avoid serious problems and become more responsive to its more than 90,000 employees. The ethics network, which tracks the number and types of cases and complaints, has served as an early warning system for poor management, quality and safety defects, racial and gender discrimination, environmental concerns, inaccurate and false records, and personnel grievances regarding salaries, promotions, and layoffs. By providing an alternative channel for raising such concerns, Martin Marietta is able to take corrective action more quickly and with a lot less pain. In many cases, potentially embarrassing problems have been identified and dealt with before becoming a management crisis, a lawsuit, or a criminal investigation. Among employees who brought complaints in 1993, 75% were satisifed with the results.

Company executives are also convinced that the program has helped reduce the incidence of misconduct. When allegations of misconduct do surface, the company says it deals with them more openly. On several occasions, for instance, Martin Marietta has voluntarily disclosed and made restitution to the government for misconduct involving potential violations of federal procurement laws. In addition, when an employee alleged that the company had retaliated against him for voicing safety concerns about his plant on CBS news, top management commissioned an investigation by an outside law firm. Although failing to support the allegations, the investigation found that employees at the plant feared retaliation when raising health, safety, or environmental complaints. The company redoubled its efforts to identify and discipline those employees taking retaliatory action and stressed the desirability of an open work environment in its ethics training and company communications.

Although the ethics program helps Martin Marietta avoid certain types of litigation, it has occasionally led to other kinds of legal action. In a few cases, employees dismissed for violating the code of ethics sued Martin Marietta, arguing that the company had violated its own code by imposing unfair and excessive discipline.

Still, the company believes that its attention to ethics has been worth it. The ethics program has led to better relationships with the government, as well as to new business opportunities. Along with prices and technology, Martin Marietta's record of integrity, quality, and reliability of estimates plays a role in the awarding of defense contracts, which account for some 75% of the company's revenues. Executives believe that the reputation they've earned through their ethics program has helped them build trust with government auditors, as well. By opening up communications, the company has reduced the time spent on redundant audits.

The program has also helped change employees' perceptions and priorities. Some managers compare their new ways of thinking about ethics to the way they understand quality. They consider more carefully how situations will be perceived by others, the possible long-term consequences of short-term thinking, and the need for continuous improvement. CEO Norman Augustine notes, "Ten years ago, people would have said that there were no ethical issues in business. Today employees think their number-one objective is to be thought of as decent people doing quality work."

NovaCare: Building Shared Aspirations

NovaCare Inc., one of the largest providers of rehabilitation services to nursing homes and hospitals in the United States, has oriented its ethics effort toward building a common core of shared aspirations. But in 1988, when the company was called InSpeech, the only sentiment shared was mutual mistrust.

Senior executives built the company from a series of aggressive acquisitions over a brief period of time to take advantage of the expanding market for therapeutic services. However, in 1988, the viability of the company was in question. Turnover among its frontline employees—the clinicians and therapists who care for patients in nursing homes and hospitals—escalated to 57% per year. The company's inability to retain therapists caused customers to defect and the stock price to languish in an extended slump.

After months of soul-searching, InSpeech executives realized that the turnover rate was a symptom of a more basic problem: the lack of a common set of values and aspirations. There was, as one executive put it, a "huge disconnect" between the values of the therapists and clinicians and those of the managers who ran the company. The therapists and clinicians evaluated the company's success in terms of its delivery and high-quality health care. In-Speech management, led by executives with financial services and venture capital backgrounds, measured the company's worth exclusively in terms of financial success. Management's single-minded emphasis on increasing hours of reimbursable care turned clinicians off. They took management's performance orientation for indifference to patient care and left the company in droves.

CEO John Foster recognized the need for a common frame of reference and a common language to unify the diverse groups. So he brought in consultants to conduct interviews and focus groups with the company's health care professionals, managers, and customers. Based on the results, an employee task force drafted a proposed vision statement for the company, and another 250 employees suggested revisions. Then Foster and several senior managers developed a succinct statement of the company's guiding purpose and fundamental beliefs that could be used as a framework for making decisions and setting goals, policies, and practices.

Unlike a code of conduct, which articulates specific behavioral standards, the statement of vision, purposes, and beliefs lays out in very simple terms the company's central purpose and core values. The purpose—meeting the rehabilitation needs of patients through clinical leadership—its supported by four key beliefs: respect for the individual, service to the customer, pursuit of excellence, and commitment to personal integrity. Each value is discussed with examples of how it is manifested in the day-to-day activities and policies of the company, such as how to measure the quality of care.

To support the newly defined values, the company changed its name to NovaCare and introduced a number of structural and operational changes. Field managers and clinicians were given greater decision-making authority; clinicians were provided with additional resources to assist in the delivery of effective therapy; and a new management structure integrated the various therapies offered by the company. The hiring of new corporate personnel with health care backgrounds reinforced the company's new clinical focus.

The introduction of the vision, purpose, and beliefs met with varied reactions from employees, ranging from cool skepticism to open enthusiasm. One employee remembered thinking the talk about values "much ado about nothing." Another recalled, "It was really wonderful. It gave us a goal that everyone aspired to, no matter what their place in the company." At first, some were baffled about how the vision, purpose, and beliefs were to be used. But, over time, managers became more adept at explaining and using them as a guide. When a customer tried to hire away a valued employee, for example, managers considered raiding the customer's company for employees. After reviewing the beliefs, the managers abandoned the idea.

NovaCare managers acknowledge and company surveys indicate that there is plenty of room for improvement. While the values are used as a firm reference point for decision making and evaluation in some areas of the company, they are still viewed with reservation in others. Some managers do not "walk the talk," employees complain. And recently acquired companies have yet to be fully integrated into the program. Nevertheless, many NovaCare employees say the values initiative played a critical role in the company's 1990 turnaround.

The values reorientation also helped the company deal with its most serious problem: turnover among health care providers. In 1990, the turnover rate stood at 32%, still above target but a significant improvement over the 1988 rate of 57%. By 1993, turnover had dropped to 27%. Moreover, recruiting new clinicians became easier. Barely able to hire 25 new clinicians each month in 1988, the company added 776 in 1990 and 2,546 in 1993. Indeed, one employee who left during the 1988 turmoil said that her decision to return in 1990 hinged on the company's adoption of the vision, purpose, and beliefs.

Wetherill Associates: Defining Right Action

Wetherill Associates, Inc.—a small, privately held supplier of electrical parts to the automotive market—has neither a conventional code of conduct nor a statement of values. Instead, WAI has *Quality Assurance Manual*—a combination of philosophy text, conduct guide, technical manual, and company profile—that describes the company's commitment to honesty and its guiding principle of right action.

WAI doesn't have a corporate ethics officer who reports to top management, because at WAI, the company's corporate ethics officer *is* top management. Marie Bothe, WAI's chief executive officer, sees her main function as keeping the 350-employee company on the path of right action and looking for opportunities to help the community. She delegates the "technical" aspects of the business—marketing, finance, personnel, operations—to other members of the organization.

Right action, the basis for all of WAI's decisions, is a well-developed approach that challenges most conventional management thinking. The company explicitly rejects the usual conceptual boundaries that separate morality and self-interest. Instead, they define right behavior as logically, expediently, and morally right. Managers teach employees to look at the needs of the customers, suppliers, and the community—in addition to those of the company and its employees—when making decisions.

WAI also has a unique approach to competition. One employee explains, "We are not 'in competition' with anybody. We just do what we have to do to serve the customer." Indeed, when occasionally unable to fill orders, WAI salespeople refer customers to competitors. Artificial incentives, such as sales contests, are never used to spur individual performance. Nor are sales results used in determining compensation. Instead, the focus is on teamwork and customer service. Managers tell all new recruits that absolute honesty, mutual courtesy, and respect are standard operating procedure.

Newcomers generally react positively to company philosophy, but not all are prepared for such a radical departure from the practices they have known elsewhere. Recalling her initial interview, one recruit described her response to being told that lying was not allowed, "What do you mean? No lying? I'm a buyer. I lie for a living!" Today she is persuaded that the policy makes sound business sense. WAI is known for informing suppliers of overshipments as well as undershipments and for scrupulous honesty in the sale of parts, even when deception cannot be readily detected.

Since its entry into the distribution business 13 years ago, WAI has seen its revenues climb steadily from just under $1 million to nearly $98 million in 1993, and this in an industry with little growth. Once seen as an upstart beset by naysayers and industry skeptics, WAI is now credited with entering and professionalizing an industry in which kickbacks, bribes, and "gratuities" were commonplace. Employees—equal numbers of men and women ranging in age from 17 to 92—praise the work environment as both productive and supportive.

WAI's approach could be difficult to introduce in a larger, more traditional organization. WAI is a small company founded by 34 people who shared a belief in right action; its ethical values were naturally built into the organization from the start. Those values are so deeply ingrained in the company's culture and operating systems that they have been largely self-sustaining. Still, the company has developed its own training program and takes special care to hire people willing to support right action. Ethics and job skills are considered equally important in determining an individual's competence and suitability for employment. For WAI, the challenge will be to sustain its vision as the company grows and taps into markets overseas.

At WAI, as at Martin Marietta and NovaCare, a management-led commitment to ethical values has contributed to competitiveness, positive workforce morale, as well as solid sustainable relationships with the company's key constituencies. In the end, creating a climate that encourages exemplary conduct may be the best way to discourage damaging misconduct. Only in such an environment do rogues really act alone.

The Hallmarks of an Effective Integrity Strategy

There is no one right integrity strategy. Factors such as management personality, company history, culture, lines of business, and industry regulations must be taken into account when shaping an appropriate set of values and designing an implementation program. Still, several features are common to efforts that have achieved some success:

- *The guiding values and commitments make sense and are clearly communicated.* They reflect important organizational obligations and widely shared aspirations that appeal to the organization's members. Employees at all levels take them seriously, feel comfortable discussing them, and have a concrete understanding of their practical importance. This does not signal the absence of ambiguity and conflict but a willingness to seek solutions compatible with the framework of values.

- *Company leaders are personally committed, credible, and willing to take action on the values they espouse.* They are not mere mouthpieces. They are willing to scrutinize their own decisions. Consistency on the part of leadership is key. Waffling on values will lead to employee cynicism and a rejection of the program. At the same time, managers must assume responsibility for making tough calls when ethical obligations conflict.

- *The espoused values are integrated into the normal channels of management decision making and are reflected in the organization's critical activities:* the development of plans, the setting of goals, the search for opportunities, the allocation of resources, the gathering and communication of information, the measurement of performance, and the promotion and advancement of personnel.

- *The company's systems and structures support and reinforce its values.* Information systems, for example, are designed to provide timely and accurate information. Reporting relationships are structured to build in checks and balances to promote objective judgment. Performance appraisal is sensitive to means as well as ends.
- *Managers throughout the company have the decision-making skills, knowledge, and competencies needed to make ethically sound decisions on a day-to-day basis.* Ethical thinking and awareness must be part of every managers' mental equipment. Ethics education is usually part of the process.

Success in creating a climate for responsible and ethically sound behavior requires continuing effort and a considerable investment of time and resources. A glossy code of conduct, a high-ranking ethics officer, a training program, an annual ethics audit—these trappings of an ethics program do not necessarily add up to a responsible, law-abiding organization whose espoused values match its actions. A formal ethics program can serve as a catalyst and a support system, but organizational integrity depends on the integration of the company's values into its driving systems.

Strategies for Ethics Management

Characteristics of Compliance Strategy

Ethos	conformity with externally imposed standards
Objective	prevent criminal misconduct
Leadership	lawyer driven
Methods	education, reduced discretion, auditing and controls, penalties
Behavioral Assumptions	autonomous beings guided by material self-interest

Characteristics of Integrity Strategy

Ethos	self-governance according to chosen standards
Objective	enable responsible conduct
Leadership	management driven with aid of lawyers, HR, others
Methods	education, leadership, accountability, organizational systems and decision processes, auditing and controls, penalties
Behavioral Assumptions	social beings guided by material self-interest, values, ideals, peers

Implementation of Compliance Strategy

Standards	criminal and regulatory law
Staffing	lawyers
Activities	develop compliance standards
	train and communicate
	handle reports of misconduct
	conduct investigations
	oversee compliance audits

| | enforce standards |
| Education | compliance standards and system |

Implementation of Integrity Strategy

Standards	company values and aspirations, social obligations, including law
Staffing	executives and managers with lawyers, others
Activities	lead development of company values and standards
	train and communicate
	integrate into company systems
	provide guidance and consultation
	assess values performance
	identify and resolve problems
	oversee compliance activities
Education	decision making and values
	compliance standards and system

Corporate Ethics Practices: An International Survey of Ethics Codes and Programs

THE CONFERENCE BOARD REPORT 986

EXECUTIVE SUMMARY

This study is designed to supplement the 1987 Conference Board study, *Corporate Ethics*. It seeks to answer many of the questions raised by the earlier report on efforts to formulate, disseminate and inculcate a company's ethical principles through the enactment of corporate ethics codes and the sponsorship of ethics training programs.

Corporate Ethics Practices reports on the prevalence of specific kinds of company ethics statements and the issues and policies they address. It discusses code revision and distribution procedures, examines board of directors ethics committees, and documents trends in company-sponsored ethics training programs. For possible use in ethics discussion groups, three new case studies and participant responses to these hypothetical examples are included. A further objective of this study, to improve the 1987 non-U.S. participation rate of 16 percent, was achieved—non-U.S. firms constitute 30 percent of this sample.

In contrast with the 1987 study's reliance on CEOs, this report also includes the views of senior human resource and finance executives, general counsels, and auditors. The greater involvement of functional department heads and the general counsel suggests that in many organizations, code formulation and ethics training programs have moved beyond the initial phase of

Reprinted by permission of *The Corporate Ethics Practices*.

CEO sponsorship and are now institutionalized responsibilities for certain senior executives.

The CEO remains the company's chief spokesperson on ethical issues. Nearly one-third of the responding companies (31 percent) said their CEO had issued a personal statement or formal discussion of ethics issues in 1991. The increase in CEO ethics pronouncements was particularly noteworthy in Europe (40 percent); according to some 1987 European study participants, company officials were said to be reluctant to engage in public discussion of business ethics.

Codes and Ethics Statements

Code drafting is an ongoing process—nearly half (45 percent) of the survey respondents that provided data on code adoption said they had enacted their statement since the last study was published in 1987. Codes continue to be less popular among European respondents (50 percent) and financial organizations (57 percent).

Those companies that do have ethics statements are now more willing to discuss them openly. In 1987, only a handful of respondents returned a copy of their code with a completed questionnaire. In 1991, more than one-third of the companies with ethics statements supplied them with their surveys.

These documents utilize one of three basic formats (most combine more than one of these approaches):

- Compliance codes—directive statements giving guidance and prohibiting certain kinds of conduct.
- Corporate credos—broad general statements of corporate commitments to constituencies, values and objectives.
- Management philosophy statements—formal enunciations of the company or CEO's way of doing business.

Compliance documents are the most common: 90 percent of the code companies say their statement enjoins particular kinds of employee or company behavior. Three-fourths said their code contained a credo and over half (57 percent) answered that their statement included declarations of management's business philosophy.

Content of Individual Codes

Most ethics codes (88 percent) include some statement of the company's fundamental principles. Of the nine most frequently cited specific issues in company codes, six relate in some degree to the employee's contract with the company. Purchasing guidelines (56 percent) and security of proprietary information (53 percent)—issues focused on employee honesty—were the only specific areas of concern cited by over half of the code companies.

Three subjects outside the employer-employee contract often included in ethics statements relate to corporate social accountability—environmental, marketing, and product safety responsibility. From 1987 to 1991, other than a new or revised formulation of guiding principles, environmental concern was the most popular subject of provisions added to company codes.

Consistent with the subject matter of these documents, senior human resource executives and the general counsel's office have played a major role in the drafting and preparation of the company's ethics statements. Survey participants of the 1991 study reported much higher involvement of boards of directors and general counsels than was noted by 1987 respondents. (The earlier questionnaire did not ask about human resource participation.)

A clear trend in favor of distributing the company's code to all employees emerged among 1991 survey participants—77 percent follow this practice, an increase over the nearly two-thirds who said they did so in 1987.

Ethics Training Programs

Almost one-fourth of the companies have sponsored new ethics training programs, ethics committees, or ombudsperson's offices since 1987. Among companies with codes, the percentage is nearly one-third because these undertakings are rare in companies without ethics statements. Such programs are less common in Europe and Canada than in the United States.

Study groups for middle managers was the most popular program initiative. Video productions and, in a few cases, board games were used in ethics discussion groups. Most training projects utilized materials developed in-house, and relied on company executives as facilitators.

Board of Directors Ethics Committees

About 10 percent of the boards of directors in the sample have an ethics committee. This practice is less common in Europe; only two European companies had ethics committees and they consisted solely of inside directors. In the United States and Canada there is a slight preference for a mix of inside and outside directors (13 companies) over limiting appointments to outside directors (nine companies). In the United States, the committee chairman is almost always an outside director (two exceptions), whereas the Canadian respondents with ethics committees were evenly divided (i.e., two have company board committees chaired by an inside director and two are headed by an outside director).

• • •

Biographical
Information

ROBERT L. ARRINGTON is Professor of Philosophy and Interim Dean of the College of Arts and Sciences at Georgia State University. He received his undergraduate degree from Vanderbilt University and did graduate work at Tulane University. He was an Honorary Woodrow Wilson Fellow, and he held an ACLS Fellowship in 1974–1975. His areas of specialization include ethics and the philosophy of Wittgenstein. He is author of *Rationalism, Realism and Relativism: Perspectives in Contemporary Moral Epistemology* (Cornell, 1989) and co-editor of Wittgenstein's *Philosophical Investigations* (Routledge, forthcoming).

KENNETH J. ARROW has held faculty positions at the University of Chicago, Harvard University, and Stanford University, the last from 1949 to 1968 and again from 1979 to 1981, when he retired. Among other current positions, he is also External Professor at the Santa Fe Institute. He has received a number of honors, the John Bates Clark Medal of the American Economic Association, the Nobel Memorial Prize in Economic Science, and the von Neumann Prize of The Institute of Management Sciences and the Operations Research Society of America. He has authored or co-authored seven books and about 170 papers.

FREDERICK B. BIRD is a Professor at Concordia University, Montreal, where he teaches Comparative Ethics. He recently co-authored a text on business ethics entitled *Good Management: Business Ethics in Action* and is in the process of completing a book on the comparative sociological study of moral systems. He has written numerous articles on business ethics, comparative ethics, and contemporary religious movements.

SISSELA BOK was born in Sweden and educated in Switzerland, France, and the United States. She received a Ph.D. in Philosophy from Harvard University in 1970. She has taught Philosophy at Brandeis University since 1985 and earlier taught courses in ethics and decision making at Harvard Medical School and the John F. Kennedy School of Government. She is the author of numerous articles on ethics, literature, and biography, and of *Lying: Moral Choice in Public and Private Life* (1978); *Secrets: On the Ethics of Concealment and Revelation* (1982); *A Strategy for Peace* (1989); as well as *Alva Myrdel: A Daughter's Memoir* (1991).

DAVID BOLLIER is an independent journalist and consultant with extensive expertise in electronic media, consumer advocacy, public policy and law. Since 1985 David has worked primarily with television writer/producer/Trust-founder Norman Lear on speeches, special events, and the founding of the Trust. David also consults with non-profit organizations, contributes to various magazines, and is the author of four books. He has previously worked as a congressional aide; as research director for People for the American Way; and as editor of *Public Citizen* magazine.

NORMAN E. BOWIE is the Elmer L. Andersen Chair of Corporate Responsibility and holds a joint appointment in the Departments of Strategic Management and Organization and Philosophy at the University of Minnesota. Professor Bowie is co-author of *Busi-*

ness Ethics (second edition) and the co-editor of *Ethical Theory and Business* (fourth edition). He is the author or co-editor of eleven other books on professional ethics and political philosophy and is a frequent contributor to scholarly journals and conferences.

ANDREW CARNEGIE was born in Scotland in 1835 and emigrated to the United States with his family in 1848. He worked in a cotton factory, was a telegraph operator, and introduced sleeping cars for the Pennsylvania Railroad. Foreseeing the future demand for iron and steel, he left the railroad and founded the Keystone Bridge Company and began to amass his fortune. The Carnegie companies were incorporated into U.S. Steel in 1901, when Carnegie retired and devoted himself to philanthropy.

ALBERT CARR was born in 1902 and educated at the University of Chicago, Columbia University, and the London School of Economics. He was active in business and politics, serving as economic advisor to President Truman. He wrote numerous books and articles, among them *Truman, Stalin, and Peace,* and *Business As a Game.* In addition, he authored several films and television plays. He died in 1971.

JOANNE B. CIULLA is the Boston Family Chair in Leadership and Ethics at the Jepson School of the University of Richmond. A Ph.D. in Philosophy, she has also held academic posts at LaSalle University, the Harvard Business School, the Wharton School, and Oxford University. Ciulla has published a number of articles on business ethics. She is currently working on a book called *Honest Work.*

PETER C. CRAMTON is an Associate Professor of Economics at the University of Maryland at College Park. Before joining the Maryland faculty in 1993, he was an Associate Professor at the Yale School of Management at Yale University, where he taught negotiation and economics. Most of his recent work has addressed incentive questions in bargaining. Cramton received his B.A. in Engineering from Cornell University and his Ph.D. in Business from Stanford University.

ROGER CRISP has recently received the degrees of B.A. and B.Phil. at Oxford University, and is presently working on a D.Phil. thesis in which an ideal utilitarian/perfectionist theory is developed. It is hoped that this theory will supply plausible solutions to a number of problems in practical ethics. His article, "The Argument from Marginal Cases," was published in the *Journal of Applied Philosophy* (II, 2, 1985).

DAN R. DALTON is the Dow Professor of Management, Graduate School of Business, Indiana University. Formerly with General Telephone and Electronics (GTE) for thirteen years, he received his Ph.D. from the University of California. He has published widely in business, ethics, and psychology.

J. GREGORY DEES is an Associate Professor at the Harvard Business School, where he teaches business ethics, entrepreneurship, and the management of social-purpose organizations. He previously taught at the Yale School of Management and worked as a consultant with McKinsey & Company. His research interests include social entrepreneurship, the moral fabric of business life, and the relationship between social values and economics.

RICHARD T. DE GEORGE is University Distinguished Professor of Philosophy and Courtesy Professor of Business Administration at the University of Kansas. A past president of the American Philosophical Association (Central Division) and the Society for Business Ethics, he is the author or editor of fifteen books, including *Business Ethics,* and is a frequent contributor to journals and anthologies on business ethics.

THOMAS J. DONALDSON is the John Connelly Professor in the School of Business at Georgetown University, where he also holds appointments in the Department of Philosophy and the Kennedy Institute of Ethics. His current research focuses on the intersection between social contract and stakeholder theories, especially in the context of international business.

THOMAS DUNFEE is the Kolodny Professor of Social Responsibility at the Wharton School, University of Pennsylvania. He has published articles on business law and business ethics in many journals, including the *Northwestern University Law Review, American Business Law Journal, Journal of Business Ethics, Business and Professional Ethics Journal,* and *Business Ethics Quarterly.* He was president of the American Business Law Association, 1989–1990, and is a former editor-in-chief of the *American Business Law Journal.*

WILLIAM M. EVAN is Professor of Management and Sociology at the Wharton School, University of Pennsylvania. He is best known for his contributions to organization theory and the sociology of law. Evan's work on "the organization set" laid the groundwork for much of interorganizational theory, especially stakeholder theory.

R. EDWARD FREEMAN joined the Darden Graduate School of Business Administration in 1987 as Elis and Signe Olsson Professor of Business Administration and Director of the Olsson Center for Applied Ethics. Prior to coming to the Darden School, Freeman taught at University of Minnesota and the Wharton School, University of Pennsylvania. His most recent books are *Ethics and Agency Theory* (with N. Bowie), *Business Ethics, The State of the Art, The Logic of Strategy* (with D. Gilbert, Jr., E. Hartman & J. Mauries), *Management,* 5th Edition (with J. Stoner), and *Corporate Strategy and the Search for Ethics* (with D. Gilbert, Jr.). He published *Strategic Management: A Stakeholder Approach* with Pitman Publishing in 1984.

MILTON FRIEDMAN, U.S. laissez-faire economist, Emeritus Professor at the University of Chicago, and Senior Research Fellow at the Hoover Institution, is one of the leading modern exponents of liberalism in the 19th-century European sense. He is the author of *Capitalism and Freedom* and co-author of *A Monetary History of the United States* and *Free to Choose.* He was awarded the Nobel Prize for Economics in 1976.

KENNETH GOODPASTER earned his A.B. in Mathematics from the University of Notre Dame and his A.M. and Ph.D. in Philosophy at the University of Michigan. He taught graduate and undergraduate philosophy at Notre Dame throughout the 1970's before joining the Harvard Business School faculty in 1980, where he taught MBAs and executives, and published numerous articles and case studies and authored several books. In the fall of 1989, Goodpaster accepted the David and Barbara Koch Chair in Business Ethics at the University of St. Thomas, St. Paul, MN.

EDMUND R. GRAY is Professor of Management at Loyola Marymount University and formerly Chair of the Department of Management at Loyola Marymount University and also Louisiana State University. He is the author and editor of five books and author of numerous articles in journals such as *Sloan Management Review, Academy of Management Journal,* and *Business Horizons.*

KIRK HANSON is a Senior Lecturer at the Stanford Graduate School of Business, specializing in business ethics and business responsibility. He was president of The Business Enterprise Trust from 1988 to 1993 and previously consulted with corporations on the design of corporate ethics and values programs. He is a graduate of Stanford and the Stanford Graduate School of Business and held fellowships for research and study at the Harvard Business School and Yale Divinity School.

JOHN HASNAS received his J.D. and Ph.D. in Philosophy from Duke University and his LL.M. in Legal Education from Temple University. He is currently an Assistant Professor of Business Ethics at Georgetown School of Business and a Senior Research Fellow at the Kennedy Institute of Ethics.

ROBERT D. HAY is University Professor of Management at the University of Arkansas. He retired in 1990 after 41 years of teaching, research, and service. He is author of 11 books and numerous articles and cases.

JOHN W. HILL is an Associate Professor of Accounting and Dow Teaching Fellow at the Graduate School of Business at Indiana University. He received his Ph.D. from the University of Iowa and holds A.B., B.S., M.B.A., and J.D. degrees. A former bank CFO, he has taught management and cost accounting at introductory through doctoral levels.

ROBERT JACKALL is Willmott Family Professor of Sociology and Social Thought at Williams College. He is the author of *Moral Mazes: The World of Corporate Managers* (New York: Oxford University Press, 1988), which elaborates fully the argument of the essay reprinted here. His most recent book is *Propaganda* (New York: New York University Press; London: Macmillan, 1995).

IMMANUEL KANT was born in 1724 in East Prussia where he took his master's degree at Konigsberg in 1755 and began teaching in the university as a Privatdozent, teaching a wide variety of subjects, including mathematics, physics, and geography, in addition to philosophy. Kant's publications during this period, primarily concerning the natural sciences, won him considerable acclaim in Germany, but he is most known today for his three critiques—the *Critique of Pure Reason*, the *Critique of Practical Reason*, and the *Critique of Judgement*—all of which were written and published after he obtained his professorship. Kant died in 1804.

ROSABETH MOSS KANTER holds the Class of 1960 Chair as Professor at the Harvard Business School, where she has taught since 1986. Her 12 influential books include *When Giants Fear to Dance, The Change Masters: The Challenge of Organizational Change,* and most recently, *World Class.*

ARTHUR L. KELLY is a graduate of Yale University and earned his M.B.A. from the University of Chicago. He was formerly a management consultant with A. T. Kearney, Inc., and later served as president and chief executive officer of LaSalle Steel Company. Currently Mr. Kelly is president of KEL Industries, a Chicago holding and investment company, and serves on a number of boards of directors.

STEVEN KELMAN is currently administrator of the Office of Federal Procurement Policy at the Office of Management and Budget.

STEFANIE ANN LENWAY is an Associate Professor in the Department of Strategic Management at the Carlson School of Management, University of Minnesota. Professor Lenway received her Ph.D. from the University of California at Berkeley in Business and Public Policy in 1982. Her past research has concentrated on the political role of business in U.S. international trade policy and the impact of trade protection on corporate competitive strategy. She has also written a book on business involvement in the Tokyo Round Table negotiations of the General Agreement on Tariffs and Trade.

JOHN LOCKE was born in 1632 and educated in classics, near-eastern languages, Scholastic philosophy and, later, in medicine. Active and influential in the political affairs of his time, Locke was forced to flee England and his position at Oxford after his close friend, the Earl of Shaftesbury, was tried for treason in 1681. After events turned to his advantage he returned to England from exile in Holland and subsequently published his two most famous works, the *Essay Concerning Human Understanding* and the *Second Treatise of Government*.

KARL MARX, the famous German political philosopher and revolutionary socialist, was born in 1818. His radical Hegelianism and militant atheism precluded an academic career in Prussia, and he subsequently lived the life of an exile in Paris and London. Financially supported by Friedrich Engels, he devoted himself to research and the development of his theory of socialism, and to agitation for social reforms. The *Communist Manifesto* was written in collaboration with Engels in 1847. His greatest work, *Das Kapital,* remained unfinished at the time of his death in 1883 and was carried to completion by Engels from posthumous papers.

BOWEN H. McCOY was a managing director of Morgan Stanley and President of Morgan Stanley Reality, Inc. He is also an elder of the United Presbyterian Church.

MICHAEL B. METZGER is a Professor of Business Law at Indiana University Graduate School of Business. Formerly Associate Dean for Academics and Chair of the Business Law Department, he received an A.B. from Indiana in 1966 and a J.D. from the Indiana University School of Law in 1969.

ROBERT NOZICK is Arthur Kingsley Porter Professor of Philosophy at Harvard University. In addition to *Anarchy, State and Utopia,* for which he won the National Book Award, he is the author of *Philosophical Explanations, The Normative Theory of Individual Choice, The Examined Life,* and *The Nature of Rationality.*

LYNN SHARP PAINE is Associate Professor at the Harvard Business School, specializing in management ethics.

JOHN A. QUELCH is Professor of Business Administration, Graduate School of Business Administration, Harvard University, where he heads the introductory Marketing course taken by all 900 MBA students each year. He has (co)authored ten books and is a frequent contributor to *Harvard Business Review* and *Sloan Management Review.* He serves as a director of Reebok International Ltd. and WPP Group plc.

TARA J. RADIN is a Ph.D. student in Business Ethics at the Darden School of Business Administration at the University of Virginia. She also completed her B.A. and J.D./M.B.A. at the University of Virginia. She has served as a consultant for British Petroleum and is currently serving as an ethics consultant with Citicorp. She was an editorial assistant for *Management,* 6th edition, by Stoner, Freeman, and Gilbert.

JOHN RAWLS is Professor of Philosophy at Harvard University and is among the leading moral and political theorists of this century. His book *A Theory of Justice* is a contemporary classic; it has prompted wide-ranging comment and discussion, not only by philosophers, but by economists, sociologists, political and legal theorists, and others. He is the author of numerous articles as well.

DIANA ROBERTSON is Senior Fellow in Business Ethics in the Legal Studies Department of the Wharton School, University of Pennsylvania. Robertson has been Visiting Lecturer at the London Business School, and she has received the University of Pennsylvania Provost's Award for Distinguished Teaching. Dr. Robertson received a B.A. degree from Northwestern University and an M.A. and Ph.D. in Sociology from U.C.L.A. In addition, she studied Sociology of Organizations at Harvard University.

MARK SAGOFF, Director of the Institute for Philosophy and Public Policy, holds an A.B. from Harvard and a Ph.D. in Philosophy from the University of Rochester. He has taught at Princeton, the University of Pennsylvania, the University of Wisconsin (Madison), and Cornell. Dr. Sagoff has published widely in journals of philosophy, law, and public policy. His book, *The Economy of the Earth: Philosophy, Law and the Environment,* was published by Cambridge University Press in 1988.

FELICE N. SCHWARTZ is president and founder of Catalyst, the national not-for-profit organization that works with business to effect change for women. Schwartz consults with corporate leaders about women and workplace issues. She is the author of the McKinsey-Award-winning *Harvard Business Review* article which sparked the heated "Mommy Track" debate. Extensively quoted in numerous publications, she has appeared on the *Today Show, Nightline,* and the *MacNeil/Lehrer Newshour.* Schwartz serves on the board of directors of the Business Council of New York State and the Advisory Board of the National Women's Political Caucus.

RICARDO SEMLER is president of Semco S/A, Brazil's largest marine and food processing machine manufacturer. His book, *Turning the Tables,* was on Brazil's best-seller list for 60 weeks.

AMARTYA SEN is Lamont University Professor and Professor of Economics and Philosophy at Harvard University. He has written on welfare economics, social choice theory, development economics, economic methodology, and ethics and political philosophy. He is Past President of the Econometrica Society, the International Economic Association, the Indian Economic Association, and the American Economic Association.

ADAM SMITH, first known as a moral philosopher, is now famous as a political economist. He was born in 1723 in Scotland and was later elected Professor of Logic at the University of Glasgow. He published *Theory of Moral Sentiments* in 1759 to great acclaim. He resigned his professorship at Glasgow and after ten years of work published *The Wealth of Nations,* for which his fame has endured. In 1778 he was appointed a commissioner of customs for Scotland. He died in 1790.

N. CRAIG SMITH is an Associate Professor at the School of Business Administration, Georgetown University. As a Visiting Professor at Harvard Business School, he developed with John Quelch the Ethics in Marketing Project, upon which *Ethics in Marketing* is based. He is the author of *Morality and the Market: Consumer Pressure for Corporate Accountability,* the co-author of a book on research, and has contributed journal articles on a variety of marketing, management, and business ethics topics. He consults with firms on problems of marketing ethics.

ROBERT C. SOLOMON is Quincy Lee Centennial Professor of Philosophy at the University of Texas at Austin. He is the author of three books about business ethics, including *Above the Bottom Line* (HBJ, 1983), *It's Good Business* (Atheneum, 1985) and *Ethics and Excellence* (Oxford, 1991). He is also the author of *The Passions* (Doubleday, 1976), *In the*

Spirit of Hegel (Oxford, 1983), *About Love* (Simon and Schuster, 1988), *A Passion for Justice* (Addison Wesley, 1990), and *Up the University* (Addison Wesley, 1993).

KERMIT VANDIVIER was formerly a data analyst and technical writer at the B.F. Goodrich plant in Troy, Ohio, where he blew the whistle in 1967. Since 1968 he has been a journalist at the *Troy Daily News*. He has served in several capacities at the newspaper, including a tour of duty as a correspondent in Vietnam in 1970, as Sunday Editor, and as Cable News Director. He is currently a columnist-staff writer and is writing a book, *Twentieth Century Troy*.

MANUEL G. VELASQUEZ is The Charles J. Dirken Professor of Business Ethics at Santa Clara University. He received his B.A. from Gonzaga University and his M.A. and Ph.D. from the University of California at Berkeley. He is a member of the American Philosophical Association and The Academy of Management. He is the author of *Business Ethics*, co-editor with Cynthia Rostankowski of *Ethical Theory*, and author of *Philosophy: A Text With Readings*.

MICHAEL WALZER is the UPS Foundation Professor of Social Science at the Institute for Advanced Study, Princeton University, Princeton, NJ. He is the author of a dozen books, including *The Company of Critics, Interpretation and Social Criticism*, and *Just and Unjust Wars*.

JAMES A. WATERS was Dean of the Graduate School of Management at Boston College. His research interests concerned the process of strategy formation in complex organizations, organizational change and development, and ethics in organizations. His work has been published in journals such as *Organizational Dynamics, Academy of Management Journal, Strategic Management Journal, California Management Review, Journal of Business Ethics*, and in numerous anthologies.

STEPHANIE WEISS is a recent graduate of the Stanford Graduate School of Business and is currently working as a Marketing Manager at Wells Fargo Bank in San Francisco. After receiving her undergraduate degree from Stanford, she worked as the Research Associate at The Business Enterprise Trust, performing in-depth research on nominees, writing case studies and monographs, and planning promotions. Stephanie has also worked with Hanna Andersson Corporation and the Nature Company.

PATRICIA H. WERHANE is the Ruffin Professor of Business Ethics in the Darden School at the University of Virginia, and former Henry J. Wirtenberger Professor of Business Ethics at Loyola University Chicago. She is the editor or author of several books and articles on business ethics, including *Adam Smith and His Legacy for Modern Capitalism; Persons, Rights and Corporations;* and *Profit and Responsibility*. She serves on the editorial board of a number of journals and is the editor-in-chief of *Business Ethics Quarterly*.

ALISTAIR D. WILLIAMSON is the director of Alyson Publications, the nation's largest publisher of gay and lesbian books. He is also a contributing editor to *The Harvard Gay & Lesbian Review*. He lives in Boston, where he was named Big Brother of the Year in 1993.

HANS WOLF was the former president of Semetech, a U.S. pharmaceutical company.